CHILD DEVELOPMENT

ABSTRACTS AND

BIBLIOGRAPHY

VOLUME 58 NUMBER 1 1984

PUBLISHED BY THE UNIVERSITY OF CHICAGO PRESS FOR THE

SOCIETY FOR RESEARCH IN CHILD DEVELOPMENT

Y-41

EDITOR

HOBEN THOMAS

The Pennsylvania State University

ASSOCIATE EDITOR

MARGARET L. SIGNORELLA
*The Pennsylvania State University
McKeesport*

ASSOCIATE EDITOR

ELEANOR W. WILLEMSEN
University of Santa Clara

MANAGING EDITOR

BETTY LOU KLINDIENST
University Park, Pennsylvania

COMPUTER CONSULTANT

WILLIAM H. VERITY
The Pennsylvania State University

Child Development Abstracts and Bibliography (ISSN 0009-3939) publishes abstracts from professional periodicals and reviews books related to the growth and development of children. When listed, author addresses are intended to be current mailing addresses. A list of journals regularly searched is included in numbers 5 & 6 of each volume. The Editor welcomes communication from readers. Especially encouraged are contributed abstracts from articles which appear in publications not normally searched. For this purpose, reprints are helpful. Please address all editorial correspondence to Editor, *Child Development Abstracts and Bibliography*, The Pennsylvania State University, 442 B. V. Moore Building University Park, Pennsylvania 16802. Postmaster: Send address changes to The University of Chicago Press, Journals Division, P.O. Box 37005, Chicago, Illinois 60637.

Child Development Abstracts and Bibliography, one of three publications of the Society for Research in Child Development, Inc., is published three times a year, two numbers in each issue, by The University of Chicago Press. Subscription rate, U.S.A.: 1 year $30.00. Other countries add $3.50 for each year's subscription to cover postage. Single copy rate: $10.50. Reprinted volumes 1–50 available from Kraus Reprint Co., Route 100, Millwood, New York 10546. Volumes 42 to date available in microfilm from University Microfilms International, 300 North Zeeb Road, Ann Arbor, Michigan 48106; in microfiche from KTO Microform, Route 100, Millwood, New York 10546.

Child Development is issued six times a year. Subscription rate, U.S.A.: 1 year $75.00. Other countries add $6.00 for each year's subscription to cover postage. Single copy rate: $13.00. Reprinted volumes 1–40 available from Kraus Reprint Co. Volumes 37 to date available in microfilm from University Microfilms International; in microfiche from KTO Microform.

Monographs of the Society for Research in Child Development is issued at irregular intervals during the year. Subscription rate, U.S.A.: 1 year $35.00. Other countries add $5.50 for each year's subscription to cover postage. Single copies $7.00; combined issues $10.00. Single copy bulk rate (10 or more copies of same issue): single issues $5.25; combined issues $7.50. Reprinted volumes 1–41 available from Kraus Reprint Co. Volumes 28 to date available in microfilm from University Microfilms International; in microfiche from KTO Microform. A list of available *Monographs* may be had on request.

Subscriptions (U.S.A.) to the three publications of the Society are available at the special rate of $125.00. Other countries add $15.00 for each year's combined subscription to cover postage.

A limited number of back issues of all publications is available.

© 1984 by the Society for Research in Child Development, Inc. All rights reserved.
PRINTED IN U.S.A.

R01179 95403

CHILD DEVELOPMENT

Abstracts and Bibliography

Volume 58   Numbers 1 & 2   February–April 1984

ABSTRACTS OF ARTICLES

BIOLOGY, HEALTH, MEDICINE

1.   ARMSTRONG, BARBARA B. (Jefferson County Public Schools, Louisville), & KNOPF, KAREN F. **Comparison of the Bender-Gestalt and revised Developmental Test of Visual-Motor Integration.** Perceptual and Motor Skills, 1982, **55**, 164–166.
Results for children ages 7–10 years suggest caution when using either of these tests to establish level of visuomotor functioning.—-Adapted from the Article.

2.   BAKER, LAURA A. (Univ. of Colorado); DeFRIES, J. C.; & FULKER, DAVID W. **Longitudinal stability of cognitive ability in the Colorado Adoption Project.** Child Development, 1983, **54**, 290–297.
Significant genetic influences were found at both 1 and 2 years of age, but no significant environmental influences shared by parents and children were observed at these ages. Short-term stability of mental ability between the 2 ages was relatively independent of both between-family genetic and environmental influences.—-From Authors' Abstract.

3.   BARNARD, KATHRYN E. (Univ. of Washington), & BEE, HELEN L. **The impact of temporally patterned stimulation on the development of preterm infants.** Child Development, 1983, **54**, 1156–1167.
Control subjects received regular hospital care; fixed-interval subjects received 15 min of rocking/heartbeat stimulation each hour; self-activating subjects received rocking stimulation for 15 min after every 90 sec, but only for 1 stimulation period per hour. All experimental infants showed decreased rates of activity while in the hospital, fewer abnormal reflexes, and better orienting responses. At 24 months, experimental infants scored significantly higher on the Mental Development Index of the Bayley Scales.—-From Authors' Abstract.

4.   BIRNHOLZ, JASON C. (Rush–Presbyterian–St. Luke's Medical Ctr., Chicago), & BENACERRAF, BERYL R. **The development of human fetal hearing.** Science, 1983, **222**, 516–518.
Blink-startle responses to vibroacoustic stimulation were monitored ultrasonically in human fetuses of known gestational age. Responses were first elicited between 24 and 25 weeks of gestational age and were present consistently after 28 weeks. Defining the developmental sequence for audition provides a foundation for diagnosing deafness and recognizing aberrant responses antenatally.—-From Authors' Abstract.

5.   BURNS, KAYREEN A. (Prentice Women's Hosp., 333 E. Superior, Chicago); DEDDISH, RUTH B.; BURNS, WILLIAM J.; & HATCHER, ROGER P. **Use of oscillating waterbeds and rhythmic sounds for premature infant stimulation.** Developmental Psychology, 1983, **19**, 746–751.
Experimental infants were placed in incubators equipped with oscillating waterbeds and rhythmic sound for 4 weeks. Control infants were placed in traditional incubators. No differences were obtained between the 2 groups on any physical measures. Motoric and state organization processes were superior for the experimental group.—-From Authors' Abstract.

6.   BUSBY, K. A., & PIVIK, R. T. (Ottawa General Hosp., 501 Smyth, Ottawa, Canada). **Sleep patterns in children of superior intelligence.** Journal of Child Psychology and Psychiatry, 1983, **24**, 587–600.

Y-41

Patterns and amounts of sleep stages in superior IQ children did not differ in any dramatic fashion from those of children with average IQ. Negative correlations between IQ measures and eye movement density during REM sleep are consonant with previous notions relating eye movement density to waking information processing strategies.—From Authors' Abstract.

7. CANDEE, DANIEL (Univ. of Connecticut Health Ctr., Farmington); SHEEHAN, T. JOSEPH; COOK, CHARLES D.; HUSTED, SUSAN D. R.; & BARGEN, MARK. **Moral reasoning and decisions in dilemmas of neonatal care.** Pediatric Research, 1982, **16,** 846–850.
The relationship between levels of moral reasoning and decisions in dilemmas of neonatal care was investigated in a sample of pediatricians.—Adapted from Authors' Abstract.

8. CHAMBERLAIN, R. N.; CHRISTIE, P. N.; HOLT, K. S. (Inst. of Child Health, The Wolfson Ctr., Mecklenburgh Square, London, England); HUNTLEY, R. M. C.; POLLARD, R.; & ROCHE, M. C. **A study of school children who had identified virus infections of the central nervous system during infancy.** Child: Care, Health and Development, 1983, **9,** 29–47.
Children who had a virus infection of the central nervous system when under 1 year of age were studied. After controlling for adverse birth and social histories, the index children still had a mean performance IQ 6 points lower than the control children, whereas there was less than 1 point difference between the verbal IQs.—From Authors' Abstract.

9. COLL, C. G. (Brown Univ.); SEPKOSKI, C.; & LESTER, B. M. **Effects of teenage childbearing on neonatal and infant behavior in Puerto Rico.** Infant Behavior and Development, 1982, **5,** 227–236.
Infants of adolescent and older mothers were assessed with the Brazelton Scale. Infants of adolescents were more variable. Follow up at 1 year showed no differences in mental or motor development or in temperament ratings.—From Authors' Abstract.

10. CUNNINGHAM, C. C. (Hester Adrian Research Ctr., The University, Manchester, England); AUMONIER, M.; & SLOPER, P. **Health visitor service for families with a Down's syndrome infant.** Child: Care, Health and Development, 1982, **8,** 311–326.
Parents' comments on the help received from the health visitors were recorded.—From Authors' Abstract.

11. CURZI-DASCALOVA, L. (Centres de Recherches de Biologie Foetale et Neonatale, Paris, France); LEBRUN, F.; & KORN, G. **Respiratory frequency according to sleep states and age in normal premature infants: a comparison with full term infants.** Pediatric Research, 1983, **17,** 152–156.
The frequency of respiration was higher in prematurely born infants reaching 37–40 weeks conceptional age, compared to that of newborns of the same gestational age. From 35 weeks gestational age onward, respiratory frequency was higher in active REM sleep than in quiet sleep.—Adapted from Authors' Abstract.

12. DANIEL, P. A. (Brown Univ.); ZAKRESKI, J. R.; & LIPSITT, L. P. **Effects of auditory and taste stimulation on sucking, heart rate, and movement in the newborn.** Infant Behavior and Development, 1982, **5,** 237–247.
Both low-intensity complex sound and sound and fluid together shortened latency to suck.—From Authors' Abstract.

13. DAR, HANNAH (Rothschild Univ. Hosp., Haifa, Israel), & JAFFE, MICHAEL. **Dermatoglyphic and palmar-crease alterations as indicators of early intra-uterine insult in mental retardation.** Developmental Medicine and Child Neurology, 1983, **25,** 53–59.
Ten percent of the children classified as idiopathically mentally retarded were shown to have been exposed to early intrauterine insult.—From Authors' Abstract.

14. DeFRIES, J. C. (Univ. of Colorado), & BAKER, LAURA A. **Parental contributions to longitudinal stability of cognitive measures in the Colorado Family Reading Study.** Child Development, 1983, **54,** 388–395.

With regard to reading data, it is suggested that parental influences contribute importantly to longitudinal stability for reading-disabled children but not for controls. Such a difference in covariance structure between the 2 types of families could be due to a gene (or genes) with major effect. In the case of coding and symbol processing speed, covariance structure is similar to the 2 types of families, and estimates indicate that parental contributions to longitudinal stability for this measure are relatively unimportant.—From Authors' Abstract.

15. DIAMOND, RHEA (Massachusetts Inst. of Technology); CAREY, SUSAN; & BACK, KAREN J. **Genetic influences on the development of spatial skills during early adolescence.** Cognition, 1983, **13,** 167–185.
The course of development of skill at face encoding is disrupted in early adolescence. Evidence is provided that the timing of this disruption is under genetic control. Regardless of their age, girls in the midst of pubertal change encode faces less efficiently than prepubescent or postpubescent controls. This maturational influence on face encoding is contrasted with a different effect of pubertal development on performance on the Embedded Figures Test.—From Authors' Abstract.

16. EATON, WARREN O. (Univ. of Manitoba, Winnipeg, Manitoba, Canada). **Measuring activity level with actometers: reliability, validity, and arm length.** Child Development, 1983, **54,** 720–726.
For 3–4-year-olds, gross motor scores from single actometers had low but meaningful levels of reliability; activity scores composited across multiple actometers had high reliability and correlated strongly with parent and teacher measures, even when age and sex effects were partialled. The possibility that limb length is a confounding factor of wrist-placed actometers does not appear serious.—From Author's Abstract.

17. GILLBERG, CHRISTOPHER (Göteborgs Univ., Box 7284, Göteborg, Sweden); RASMUSSEN, PEDER; & WAHLSTROM, JAN. **Minor neurodevelopmental disorders in children born to older mothers.** Developmental Medicine and Child Neurology, 1982, **24,** 437–447.
Fine-motor problems were 5 times more common among 5–6-year-olds born to mothers averaging 30 years than to mothers averaging 28 years.—Adapted from Authors' Abstract.

18. GOLDSMITH, H. H. (Univ. of Texas, Austin). **Genetic influences on personality from infancy to adulthood.** Child Development, 1983, **54,** 331–355.
This overview of the literature documents (1) the demonstration of genetic bases for stability of certain personality dimensions, (2) evidence suggesting that the most influential environmental sources of variation are those not jointly experienced by family members, and (3) continuing controversy regarding the convergence of genetic results for different assessment strategies and different development periods.—From Author's Abstract.

19. GOTTFRIED, ALLEN W. (California State Univ., Fullerton), & BATHURST, KAY. **Hand preference across time is related to intelligence in young girls, not boys.** Science, 1983, **221,** 1074–1075.
Consistency of hand preference was examined in a longitudinal study of children 18–42 months of age. Results showed a sex-specific relationship between hand consistency and intellectual development. Across a variety of intellectual abilities at all ages, females with consistency of handedness were precocious compared to females without such consistency. This relationship did not hold for males.—From Authors' Abstract.

20. GUTSTEIN, STEVEN E. (Houston Child Guidance Ctr., 3214 Austin, Houston), & TARNOW, JAY D. **Parental facilitation of children's preparatory play behavior in a stressful situation.** Journal of Abnormal Child Psychology, 1983, **11,** 181–192.
Parents were asked to prepare their 4–9-year-old children for elective surgery and were given stress-related hospital equipment to use with their child. Parent helping behaviors were significantly related to children's active preparatory play. With the exception of highly directive behav-

ior, however, the relationship of parent helping behavior to child play was dependent on the child's age.—From Authors' Abstract.

21. HARRIMAN, ARTHUR E. (Oklahoma State Univ.), & LUKOSIUS, PATRICIA A. **On why Wayne Dennis found Hopi infants retarded in age at onset of walking.** Perceptual and Motor Skills, 1982, **55,** 79–86.
Contemporary Hopi infants walk earlier than those tested by Dennis. This may reflect the enhanced quality of Hopi infant nutrition brought about by food supplement programs.—Adapted from Authors' Abstract.

22. HAY, DAVID A. (La Trobe Univ., Bundoora, Victoria, Australia), & O'BRIEN, PAULINE J. **The La Trobe Twin Study: a genetic approach to the structure and development of cognition in twin children.** Child Development, 1983, **54,** 317–330.
A mixed longitudinal analysis of twins, their siblings, and cousins, who are followed between the ages 3–15 years on a battery of physical and behavioral tests, is described. The criteria for choosing behavioral tests are discussed along with the questionnaires necessary to examine the children's development in the context of the stresses a multiple birth may impose on a family.—From Authors' Abstract.

23. HENDERSON, S. E. (Univ. of London Inst. of Education, London, England), & HALL, D. **Concomitants of clumsiness in young schoolchildren.** Developmental Medicine and Child Neurology, 1982, **24,** 448–460.
Teachers' assessments of clumsiness were consistent with those of a pediatric neurologist and a psychologist. As compared to controls, children identified as clumsy had lower scores on several measures of motor performance and a higher incidence of other educational and social problems.—Adapted from Authors' Abstract.

24. HEWITT, K. E. (Stoke Park Hosp., Stapleton, Bristol, England); NEWCOMBE, R. G.; & BIDDER, R. T. **Profiles of skill gain in delayed infants and young children.** Child: Care, Health and Development, 1983, **9,** 127–135.
Developmentally delayed preschool children were entered into a study to assess their developmental progress on skills checklists during a 3-month period. All children were receiving the South Glamorgan Home Advisory Service. Children made greater progress in inspection/tracking and perceptual problem-solving skills than in motor, self-help, and visuomotor areas.—From Authors' Abstract.

25. HORN, JOSEPH M. (Univ. of Texas, Austin). **The Texas Adoption Project: adopted children and their intellectual resemblance to biological and adoptive parents.** Child Development, 1983, **54,** 268–275.
Adopted children resemble their biological mothers more than they resemble the adoptive parents who reared them from birth. A small subset of the oldest adopted children did not resemble their biological mothers.—From Author's Abstract.

26. HUFNAGLE, JON (Illinois State Univ.). **Acoustic analysis of fundamental frequencies of voices of children with and without vocal nodules.** Perceptual and Motor Skills, 1982, **55,** 427–432.
Among children 6–8 years old, the group with vocal nodules had higher fundamental frequencies than the normal group.—Adapted from Author's Abstract.

27. JANICKI, MATTHEW P. (New York State Office of Mental Retardation and Developmental Disabilities, 44 Holland, Albany); LUBIN, ROBERT A.; & FRIEDMAN, ERWIN. **Variations in characteristics and service needs of persons with autism.** Journal of Autism and Developmental Disorders, 1983, **13,** 73–85.
Information concerning sociodemographics, disability characteristics, and services received and needed became available on approximately 900 autistic children and adults as a result of a statewide needs assessment and casefinding collection project conducted in New York.

Analyses of data on autistic children and adults showed a predominance of males and a high concomitant occurrence of mental retardation. The population had few problems with mobility, hearing, or vision, but they had moderate deficits in most skills related to activities of daily living and significant deficits in communication and basic independent functioning skills. Differences were observed between institutionalized and noninstitutionalized autistic persons.— From Authors' Abstract.

28. JONES, R. W. A. (Guy's Hosp., St. Thomas, London, England); RIGDEN, S. P.; BARRATT, T. M.; & CHANTLER, C. **The effects of chronic renal failure in infancy on growth, nutritional status and body composition.** Pediatric Research, 1982, **16,** 784–791. Similarities were found between children with early onset chronic renal failure and those with protein-calorie malnutrition. The results suggest the importance of nutritional deficiency and consequent body protein depletion in the early pathogenesis of the growth retardation of children with renal failure.—Adapted from Authors' Abstract.

29. JOOS, SANDRA K.; POLLITT, ERNESTO (Univ. of Texas Health Science Ctr., Houston); MUELLER, WILLIAM H.; & ALBRIGHT, DONNA L. **The Bacon Chow study: maternal nutritional supplementation and infant behavioral development.** Child Development, 1983, **54,** 669–676. The mental scale scores of infants of supplement mothers were not higher than infants of control mothers. However, the motor scores of supplement infants were higher than those of control infants.—From Authors' Abstract.

30. JUSCZYK, PETER W. (UNIV. OF OREGON); PISONI, DAVID B.; REED, MARJORIE A.; FERNALD, ANNE; & MYERS, MARY. **Infants' discrimination of the duration of a rapid spectrum change in nonspeech signals.** Science, 1983, **222,** 175–177. Two-month-olds discriminated complex sinusoidal patterns that varied in the duration of their initial frequency transitions. Discrimination of these nonspeech sinusoidal patterns was a function of both the duration of the transitions and the total duration of the stimulus pattern.—From Authors' Abstract.

31. KOPP, CLAIRE B. (483 W. Ave. 46, Los Angeles), & KRAKOW, JOANNE B. **The developmentalist and the study of biological risk: a view of the past with an eye toward the future.** Child Development, 1983, **54,** 1086–1108. From 1920 to World War II, research was primarily "catalog" and had diverse themes. During the postwar years, research often focused on the cognitive and emotional residuals of handicaps, particularly cerebral palsy and poliomyelitis. The 1960s marked the funding of major seminal longitudinal investigations of perinatal risk factors and studies of very young infants at risk. Technological advances of the 1970s were first applied to research with normally developing children and were then extended to at-risk groups and revolutionized with methods of studying risk.—From Authors' Abstract.

32. LANCIONI, G. E., & CARAMIA, G. (Inst. voor Orthopedagogiek, Nijmegen, Netherlands). **Valutazione comportamentale del neonato. Accorgimenti metodologici e prospettive diagnostiche** [Behavioral assessment of the neonate]. Età Evolutiva, 1983, **15,** 28–36. Infants tested with the Neonatal Behavioral Assessment Scale at 2 days through 1 month revealed substantial instability in early behaviors which became more stable in the third and fourth weeks.—Ed.

33. LASKY, ROBERT E. (Univ. of Texas Health Science Ctr., Dallas); TYSON, JON E.; ROSENFELD, CHARLES R.; PRIEST, MELODY; KRASINSKI, DEBRA; HEARTWELL, STEPHEN; & GANT, NORMAN F. **Differences on Bayley's Infant Behavior Record for a sample of high-risk infants and their controls.** Child Development, 1983, **54,** 1211–1216. High-risk infants were those who weighed 1,500 grams or less at birth and required no ventilator therapy, those weighing 1,500 grams or less at birth who required ventilator therapy, and newborns weighing more than 1,500 grams at birth who required ventilator therapy. All high-risk infants received less-desirable Bayley's Infant Behavioral Record (IBR) ratings on most items than their controls. Ventilated infants, regardless of birth weight, received the lowest ratings reflecting overall performance on the IBR; very low-birth-weight, ventilated newborns were more likely to receive ratings characterizing an overly active infant with a short attention span; and very low-birth-weight, never-ventilated infants were most likely to be rated as happy but passive and delayed.—From Authors' Abstract.

34. MATHENY, ADAM P., JR. (Univ. of Louisville). **A longitudinal twin study of stability of components from Bayley's Infant Behavior Record.** Child Development, 1983, **54,** 356–360.
There is reordering of individual differences for aspects of infant behavior from 1 age to the next, but the sequence of reordering is somewhat structured in accord with genotypic similarity.—From Author's Abstract.

35. MEDNICK, BIRGITTE R. (Univ. of Southern California); HOCEVAR, DENNIS; BAKER, ROBERT L.; & TEASDALE, THOMAS. **Effects of social, familial, and maternal state variables on neonatal and infant health.** Developmental Psychology, 1983, **19,** 752–765.
The medical protocols of a Danish cohort of 5,036 infants were summarized into 5 infant outcome measures: birth weight, neonatal physical health, neonatal neurological status, 1-year physical health, and 1-year motor development. Consistent negative environmental influences on neonatal outcomes were not found. Institutional daycare, mother's employment, family size, whether the child was planned, and socioeconomic status all contributed to 1-year physical health.—From Authors' Abstract.

36. MINFORD, A. M. B. (Leeds General Infirmary, Great George, Leeds, England); MINNS, R. A.; & BROWN, J. K. **Asymmetry of gait in normal children demonstrated by polarized light goniometry.** Child: Care, Health and Development, 1983, **9,** 97–108.
Asymmetry in terms of thigh and knee angle differences between right and left legs was common in children less than 10 years old but uncommon in children over 10. This asymmetry was predominantly in the direction of more flexion on the right side. It is suggested that angular asymmetry during gait which occurs in some children under 10 years of age may be related to unequal rates of maturation of the 2 hemispheres.—From Authors' Abstract.

37. MORANTE, ANA; DUBOWITZ, M. S. (Hammersmith Hosp., London, England); LEVENE, M.; & DUBOWITZ, V. **The development of visual function in normal and neurologically abnormal preterm and fullterm infants.** Developmental Medicine and Child Neurology, 1982, **24,** 771–784.
Among neurologically normal infants, pattern preference and visual acuity were comparable in preterm and newborn infants up to 36 weeks. At 40 weeks the preterm infants did slightly less well than the full-term newborn infants. Among neurologically abnormal infants, preterm infants with intraventricular hemorrhage had poorer visual acuity at 36 and 40 weeks than did preterm infants without such a hemorrhage.—Adapted from Authors' Abstract.

38. NELSON, C. A. (Univ. of Minnesota), & HOROWITZ, F. D. **The short-term behavioral sequelae of neonatal jaundice treated with phototherapy.** Infant Behavior and Development, 1982, **5,** 289–299.
The Brazelton Scale was administered to 1 group of infants after treatment and to an untreated comparison group before and after the treatment in the experimental group. Data indicated a trend toward more mature behaviors in the comparison group.—S. Thomas.

39. O'DOUGHERTY, MARGARET (Children's Hosp., 700 Children's, Columbus, OH); WRIGHT, FRANCIS S.; GARMEZY, NORMAN; LOEWENSON, RUTH B.; & TORRES, FERNANDO. **Later competence and adaptation in infants who survive severe heart defects.** Child Development, 1983, **54,** 1129–1142.
Adverse developmental outcome was significantly associated with the following medical risk variables: failure of palliative surgery to alleviate hypoxia, prolonged hypoxia, growth failure,

congestive heart failure, absence of ameliorating shunting heart defects, stroke, and CNS infection; and 2 psychosocial moderator variables: socioeconomic status and current life stress. The cumulative risk score highly correlated with composite neurologic outcome, achievement, and perceptual-motor function.—From Authors' Abstract.

40. PAINE, PATRICIA ANN, & PASQUALI, LUIZ (Univ. of Brasilia, Brazil). **Effects of intrauterine growth and gestational age upon infants' early psychomotor development in Brazil.** Perceptual and Motor Skills, 1982, **55**, 871–880.
Factors influencing psychomotor development, in order of importance, were gestational age, intrauterine growth, maternal parity, 5-min Apgar score, and SES.—Adapted from Authors' Abstract.

41. PAINE, PATRICIA ANN (Univ. of Brasilia, Brazil); PASQUALI, LUIZ; & SPEGIORIN, CLODOMIR. **Appearance of visually directed prehension related to gestational age and intrauterine growth.** Journal of Genetic Psychology, 1983, **142**, 53–60.
For infants, the age of the appearance of visually directed prehension was found to be largely a function of gestational age and intrauterine growth mediated in part by rate of postnatal growth. Sex was an irrelevant variable.—From Authors' Abstract.

42. PENNINGTON, BRUCE F. (Univ. of Colorado Health Sciences Ctr.), & SMITH, SHELLEY D. **Genetic influences on learning disabilities and speech and language disorders.** Child Development, 1983, **54**, 369–387.
The review covers 2 classes of studies: (1) those that begin with a learning disability (LD) or speech and language disorder (SLD) phenotype that appears to be familial and attempt to learn more about the specifics of genetic transmission, if any; and (2) those that begin with a group of individuals, all of whom share a given documented genetic risk factor, to see if it leads to a specific LD or SLD.—From Authors' Abstract.

43. PLOMIN, ROBERT (Univ. of Colorado). **Developmental behavioral genetics.** Child Development, 1983, **54**, 253–259.
The potentialities of developmental behavioral genetics are discussed.—Adapted from Author's Abstract.

44. PLOMIN, ROBERT (Univ. of Colorado), & DeFRIES, J. C. **The Colorado Adoption Project.** Child Development, 1983, **54**, 276–289.
Examples of the types of analyses that can be conducted using a prospective, multivariage design are presented. Illustrative analyses include examination of genetic and environmental sources of variance, identification of environmental influence devoid of genetic bias, assessment of genotype-environment interaction and correlation, and analyses of the etiology of change and continuity in development.—From Authors' Abstract.

45. POTHIER, PATRICIA C. (School of Nursing, Univ. of California, San Francisco); FRIEDLANDER, STEVEN; & MORRISON, DELMONT C. **Procedure for assessment of neurodevelopmental delay in young children: preliminary report.** Child: Care, Health and Development, 1983, **9**, 73–83.
The Primitive Reflex and Postural Adjustment Assessment (PRPAA) is designed to measure degrees of occurrence of remnants of primitive reflexes and immature postural adjustment. Preliminary findings show that the PRPAA procedure can successfully identify degrees of neurodevelopmental delay in young children, and that the procedure differentiates normal children from mentally retarded and emotionally disturbed children.—From Authors' Abstract.

46. ROBINSON, ARTHUR (National Jewish Hosp., and Research Ctr./National Asthma Ctr., 3800 E. Colfax, Denver); BENDER, BRUCE; BORELLI, JOYCE; PUCK, MARY; & SALBENBLATT, JAMES. **Sex chromosomal anomalies: prospective studies in children.** Behavior Genetics, 1983, **13**, 321–329.

This report represents a summary of the current status of a prospective study of 51 children with sex chromosomal aneuploidy. These children and adolescents have developmental patterns which, although within normal limits, in general are below the mean for their ages.—From Authors' Abstract.

47. ROSE, RICHARD J. (Indiana Univ.), & DITTO, W. BLAINE. **A developmental–genetic analysis of common fears from early adolescence to early adulthood.** Child Development, 1983, **54**, 361–368.
For all fear factors, co-twin's score and the interaction of co-twin's score with pair zygosity significantly contributed to the prediction of a twin's fearfulness. The findings suggest significant genetic modulation of developmental patterns in the acquisition and maintenance of some adaptive fears.—From Authors' Abstract.

48. ROVET, JOANNE (Hosp. for Sick Children, 555 Univ., Toronto, Ontario, Canada). **Cognitive and neuropsychological test performance of persons with abnormalities of adolescent development: a test of Waber's hypothesis.** Child Development, 1983, **54**, 941–950.
Children with idiopathic precocious puberty and adolescents with clinically delayed puberty were compared to controls. Results revealed poorer verbal and spatial abilities for precocious males and poorer verbal, but better spatial, abilities for precocious females. Delayed developing males demonstrated superior verbal skills compared with controls, whereas delayed developing females did more poorly than controls in both verbal and spatial areas. Delayed developing males demonstrated stronger lateral asymmetries in dichotic listening.—From Author's Abstract.

49. ROVET, JOANNE (Hosp. for Sick Children, 555 Univ., Toronto, Ontario, Canada), & NETLEY, CHARLES. **The triple X chromosome syndrome in childhood: recent empirical findings.** Child Development, 1983, **54**, 831–845.
Girls 8–11 years old who had been identified at birth as having an extra X chromosome were compared to controls. XXX girls had markedly lower verbal skills, greater verbal than spatial information processing deficits, and short-term memory deficits.—Adapted from Authors' Abstract.

50. ROWE, DAVID C. (Univ. of Oklahoma). **A biometrical analysis of perceptions of family environment: a study of twin and singleton sibling kinships.** Child Development, 1983, **54**, 416–423.
Correlations on 1 dimension of perceived home environment, Restrictiveness–Permissiveness, were equal and significant for all 4 kinships: MZ twins, DZ twins, same-sex siblings, and opposite-sex siblings. In contrast, the Acceptance–Rejection dimension fitted a model that makes the assumption that sibling similarity is the result of genetic factors and postulates an absence of shared environmental influences.—From Author's Abstract.

51. SCARR, SANDRA (Yale Univ.), & WEINBERG, RICHARD A. **The Minnesota Adoption Studies: genetic differences and malleability.** Child Development, 1983, **54**, 260–267.
Black and interracial children scored as well on IQ tests as adoptees in other studies. Individual differences among them, however, were more related to differences among their biological than adoptive parents, whether they lived together or not. Young siblings were found to be intellectually quite similar, whether genetically related or not. Adolescents' IQ test scores were similar to those of their parents and siblings only if they were biologically related.—From Authors' Abstract.

52. SIEGEL, LINDA S. (McMaster Univ. Health Sciences Ctr., Hamilton, Ontario, Canada). **Correction for prematurity and its consequences for the assessment of the very low birth weight infant.** Child Development, 1983, **54**, 1176–1188.
Uncorrected scores of preterms were significantly lower than those of the full-terms. Although the corrected scores were lower early in development, they were not lower at 5 years, with the

exception of a measure of perceptual-motor skills. In the first year, the corrected scores were typically more highly correlated with 3-year and 5-year test scores. From 12 months on, the uncorrected scores were usually more highly correlated.—From Author's Abstract.

53. STOCH, M. B.; SMYTHE, P. M. (Univ. of Natal, P.O. Box 17039, Congella, Durban 4000, South Africa); MOODIE, A. D.; & BRADSHAW, D. **Psychosocial outcome and CT findings after gross undernourishment during infancy: a 20-year developmental study.** Developmental Medicine and Child Neurology, 1982, **24,** 419–436.
This prospective 20-year follow-up study compares children who were grossly undernourished during infancy with controls. There were significant differences between the groups in head circumference, height, weight, IQ, and visuomotor perceptual function. The undernourished group members have integrated effectively into the community, and their children have not experienced nutritional deprivation.—From Authors' Abstract.

54. STREISSGUTH, ANN PYTKOWICZ (Univ. of Washington School of Medicine); BARR, HELEN M.; & MARTIN, DONALD C. **Maternal alcohol use and neonatal habituation assessed with the Brazelton Scale.** Child Development, 1983, **54,** 1109–1118.
Maternal alcohol use in midpregnancy was significantly related to poorer habituation and increased low arousal in newborn infants, even after adjusting for smoking and caffeine use by mothers, maternal age and nutrition during pregnancy, sex and age of infant, and obstetric medication.—From Authors' Abstract.

55. THELEN, ESTHER (Univ. of Missouri, Columbia). **Learning to walk is still an "old" problem: a reply to Zelazo (1983).** Journal of Motor Behavior, 1983, **15,** 139–161.
Zelazo proposes that 2 cognitive prerequisites are necessary for the development of locomotion: the conversion of neonatal reflexive stepping into instrumental behavior and a shift from stereotypical to relational play. This author argues that these cognitive assumptions are unnecessary.—From Author's Abstract.

56. TZOUMAKA-BAKOULA, C. G., & LOVEL, H. J. (Inst. of Child Health, 30 Guilford, London, England). **A household study of the pattern of utilization of mother and child health services in rural Greece and variation by socioeconomic status.** Child: Care, Health and Development, 1983, **9,** 85–95.
Particular causes for concern were the findings that 30% of the mothers said they had experienced at least 1 induced abortion, 5% had delivered without the help of any trained birth attendant, most of those who delivered in the district town (usually the better off) had received no postnatal care, and 37% of the children had not seen a doctor in their first year of life either for sickness or for a developmental assessment. Only 41% of the children were fully immunized for their age, and 23% of those who should have started their immunizations had not begun. It is suggested that the experienced rural community midwife is providing an excellent service to mothers from all social strata antenatally, in delivery and postnatal care for poorer mothers, and in informal child care for everyone.—From Authors' Abstract.

57. VON BARGEN, DONNA M. (Univ. of Manitoba, Winnipeg, Manitoba, Canada). **Infant heart rate: a review of research and methodology.** Merrill-Palmer Quarterly, 1983, **29,** 115–149.
This review is an attempt to alleviate uncertainties about evaluating cardiac data. Methodological issues such as reliability, stability, validity, factors which influence resting heart rate, and the Law of Initial Values are covered.—From Author's Abstract.

58. WACHS, THEODORE D. (Purdue Univ.). **The use and abuse of environment in behavior–genetic research.** Child Development, 1983, **54,** 396–407.
The measurements and conceptualizations of environment by environmentally oriented behavioral scientists and behavior geneticists are contrasted. Commonalities and joint research strategies are proposed for the areas of gene–environment correlation/transactional model and gene–environment interaction/organismic specificity.—From Author's Abstract.

59. WEATHERS, CAISLIN (Georgia Mental Health Inst., 1256 Briarcliff, Atlanta). **Effects of nutritional supplementation on IQ and certain other variables associated with Down syndrome.** American Journal of Mental Deficiency, 1983, **88**, 214–217.
In a double-blind study, 24 Down syndrome children, ages 6–17 years and living at home, were given a megadose multi-vitamin/mineral supplement for 4 months. No differences were found on any measures.—From Author's Abstract.

60. WILSON, RONALD S. (Univ. of Louisville). **The Louisville Twin Study: developmental synchronies in behavior.** Child Development, 1983, **54**, 298–316.
Monozygotic twins became increasingly concordant over ages. Dizygotic twins regressed to an intermediate level of concordance, comparable with that found for siblings and parent-offspring sets. The overall results pointed to a growth of intelligence principally guided by an intrinsic genetic ground plan. Qualitative features of home and family did, however, add significantly to prediction of offspring IQ.—From Author's Abstract.

61. ZELAZO, PHILIP R. (Tufts Univ. School of Medicine). **The development of walking: new findings and old assumptions.** Journal of Motor Behavior, 1983, **15**, 99–137.
Individual components of walking—stepping, standing, and placing, for example—are present at birth and can be maintained with practice. Moreover, consistent use can produce an earlier onset of unaided walking. Nonetheless, independent erect locomotion rarely occurs before about 9 months in most societies, implying that there is a maturational constraint.—From Author's Abstract.

COGNITION, LEARNING, PERCEPTION

62. ACKERMAN, BRIAN P. (Univ. of Delaware). **Children's judgements of the functional acceptability of referential communications in discourse contexts.** Journal of Child Language, 1983, **10**, 151–166.
Children 4 and 6 years old were read short stories containing terminal referential communications that were either ambiguous or informative relative to a perceptual display of candidate-referential objects and were required to say whether the listener in the story could identify 1 unique referent. Both groups of children were sensitive to the discourse context of the communications and discriminated between the functionally informative and ambiguous communications.—From Author's Abstract.

63. ACKERMAN, BRIAN P. (Univ. of Delaware). **Form and function in children's understanding of ironic utterances.** Journal of Experimental Child Psychology, 1983, **35**, 487–508.
First- and third-grade children and college adults were read short stories consisting of an utterance by a speaker and contextual information that was either neutral or that biased an ironic or literal interpretation of the utterance. The intonation of the utterance was either stressed or unstressed. The results suggest that evaluation of the literal form and inference to the speaker's intended use of an utterance are independent components of irony comprehension in children and that contextual discrepancy and intonation function differently in cueing these processes.—From Author's Abstract.

64. AKIYAMA, M. MICHAEL (Univ. of Oklahoma), & GUILLORY, ANDREA W. **The ontogeny of the verification system.** Journal of Verbal Learning and Verbal Behavior, 1983, **22**, 333–340.
Children ages 4–7 were asked to verify true affirmative statements (e.g., You are a child), false affirmative statements (e.g., You are a baby), false negative statements (e.g., You aren't a child) and true negative statements (e.g., You aren't a baby), and to answer corresponding yes-no questions. Children found negative statements difficult to verify, but found affirmative statements, affirmative questions, and negative questions equally easy.—From Authors' Abstract.

65. ALEXANDER, DEBORAH W. (Calgary Learning Ctr., 2315 First Ave., NW, Calgary, Alberta, Canada), & FROST, BARRY P. **Decelerated synthesized speech as a means of shaping speed of auditory processing of children with delayed language.** Perceptual and Motor Skills, 1982, **55,** 783–792.
Results indicated that among 7–11-year-olds stimuli with slowed down critical formant cues were easier to discriminate. Training with stimuli of extended duration generalized to stimuli of normal durations.—From Authors' Abstract.

66. ANGIOLILLO, CARL J. (Univ. of Chicago), & GOLDIN-MEADOW, SUSAN. **Experimental evidence for agent-patient categories in child language.** Journal of Child Language, 1982, **9,** 627–643.
Children 2–3 years described actions involving animate and inanimate entities playing both agent and patient roles. On every measure agents were treated differently from patients. For the most part, these agent-patient differences persisted when animate and inanimate entities were examined separately.—From Authors' Abstract.

67. ANTELL, SUE ELLEN, & KEATING, DANIEL P. (Univ. of Maryland, Baltimore County). **Perception of numerical invariance in neonates.** Child Development, 1983, **54,** 695–701.
Infants made a discrimination within a habituation/dishabituation paradigm for small number sets (2–3 and 3–2) but not for larger sets (4–6 and 6–4).—From Authors' Abstract.

68. ARBUTHNOT, JACK (Ohio Univ.); SPARLING, YVONNE; FAUST, DAVID; & KEE, WILLIAM. **Logical and moral development in pre-adolescent children.** Psychological Reports, 1983, **52,** 209–210.
Results showed that advanced concrete operations and beginning formal operations are necessary but not sufficient conditions for acquisition of Stage 2 and Stage 3 structures, respectively.—From Authors' Abstract.

69. ARLIN, MARSHALL (Univ. of British Columbia). **Children's comprehension of semantic constraints on temporal prepositions.** Journal of Psycholinguistic Research, 1983, **12,** 1–15.
Children in grades K, 2, and 4 judged the appropriateness of sentences containing temporal propositions and attempted to revise the ill-formed sentences. Kindergarten children could not discriminate between well- and ill-formed sentences. Second graders could discriminate but could not identify the reason for their discrimination, nor could they revise the ill-formed sentences. Fourth graders could discriminate and identify or revise the ill-formed sentences.—From Author's Abstract.

70. BAILYN, R. VICKI (Northwestern Univ.), & KRULEE, GILBERT K. **Organizing factors in remembering and comprehending: a developmental analysis.** Journal of Psycholinguistic Research, 1983, **12,** 171–198.
Adults perform more accurately with the paragraphs vs. the scrambled paragraphs and with the word lists as compared to the scrambled word lists. Accuracy with unrelated words is generally greater than with related words. The pattern of results for the fifth-grade subjects is quite different: they perform more accurately with the scrambled paragraphs than with the paragraphs and somewhat more accurately with scrambled word lists rather than with word lists.—From Authors' Abstract.

71. BALDWIN, R. SCOTT (Univ. of Miami); LUCE, TERRENCE S.; & READENCE, JOHN E. **The impact of subschemata on metaphorical processing.** Reading Research Quarterly, 1982, **17,** 528–543.
Results for fifth and sixth graders support the position that knowledge of the matching attribute is critical to the resolution of metaphors and similes.—Adapted from the Article.

72. BAMBER, J. H.; BILL, J. M.; BOYD, FLORENCE E.; & CORBETT, W. D. (Queen's Univ., Belfast, Ireland). **In two minds—arts and science differences at sixth-form level.** British Journal of Educational Psychology, 1983, **53,** 222–233.

A variety of cognitive, cultural, attitudinal, and personality tests were administered to sixth-form arts and science specialists. Scientists performed better on the cognitive and cultural variables, endorsed theoretical and economic values, and had lower Neuroticism and higher Psychoticism scores. Arts specialists endorsed aesthetic and social values marginally.—From Authors' Abstract.

73. BARCLAY, A. (Wright State Univ.); YATER, A.; & LAMP, R. **Heterogeneity of intellectual performance by disadvantaged children within a metropolitan area.** Perceptual and Motor Skills, 1982, **55**, 781–782.
IQs for Head Start children showed the group to be heterogeneous with respect to intelligence. There were no significant sex or race differences.—From Authors' Abstract.

74. BARNES, SALLY (Univ. of Bristol, England); GUTFREUND, MARY; SATTERLY, DAVID; & WELLS, GORDON. **Characteristics of adult speech which predict children's language development.** Journal of Child Language, 1983, **10**, 65–84.
Samples of the adult speech addressed to 2-year-olds were analyzed. The most highly loading variables on the first 6 components from 2 principal components analyses were correlated with children's language development. Polar interrogatives, directives, and extending utterances were all associated with at least 1 measure of development.—Adapted from Authors' Abstract.

75. BAROODY, ARTHUR J. (Univ. of Rochester), & WHITE, MARY S. **The development of counting skills and number conservation.** Child Study Journal, 1983, **13**, 95–105.
Kindergartners and first graders were tested on a variety of counting skills and 1 of 3 number conservation tasks. Counting skills develop before number conservation and may contribute to it.—From Authors' Abstract.

76. BELL, CHARLES R.; MUNDY, PETER; & QUAY, HERBERT C. (Univ. of Miami). **Modifying impulsive responding in conduct-disordered institutionalized boys.** Psychological Reports, 1983, **52**, 307–310.
Boys ages 10–16 years were trained in the use of rules for the solution of cognitive tasks. As compared to controls, the experimental group was less impulsive.—From Authors' Abstract.

77. BENNETT-KASTOR, TINA (Wichita State Univ.). **Noun phrases and coherence in child narratives.** Journal of Child Language, 1983, **10**, 135–149.
Stories from children ages 2–5 years were analyzed. In recognition of the agent-oriented nature of narrative and its sense of the succession of events, children introduced and reiterated primarily + animate NPs in their stories, expressing them predominantly as agents. With respect to discourse coherence in general, most reiterated NPs appeared in subject position both with introduction and subsequent mention, suggesting they were elements of focus.—From Author's Abstract.

78. BENTON, STEPHEN L.; GLOVER, JOHN A. (Univ. of Nebraska, Lincoln); MONKOWSKI, PAUL G.; & SHAUGHNESSY, MICHAEL. **Decision difficulty and recall of prose.** Journal of Educational Psychology, 1983, **75**, 727–742.
Both good and poor readers benefitted from making difficult decisions in much the same way. Results indicated that time was apparently not an important factor and that difficult decisions could affect recall in the absence of "directed attentional effects." Less difficult decisions were apparently not necessary in order for difficult decisions to be effective.—From Authors' Abstract.

79. BERG, KATHLEEN M. (Univ. of Florida), & SMITH, MELANIE C. **Behavioral thresholds for tones during infancy.** Journal of Experimental Child Psychology, 1983, **35**, 409–425.
Infants 6 and 10 months old were tested with headphone presentation of 500-, 2000-, and 8000-Hz tone bursts, while 10-, 14-, and 18-month-olds were tested in sound field. Infant threshold estimates for both headphone and sound field were within 15 dB of adult comparisons for all frequencies and age groups. Six-month-olds were significantly less sensitive to the

8000-Hz tone than to either of the lower frequency stimuli, but older infants demonstrated approximately equal sensitivity for all 3 frequencies tested.—From Authors' Abstract.

80. BERTENTHAL, BENNETT I. (Univ. of Virginia), & FISCHER, KURT W. **The development of representation in search: a social-cognitive analysis.** Child Development, 1983, **54**, 846–857.
With 12–24-month-olds, children did not recreate the path of the object, but by 24 months they did seem to treat the experimenter as an independent hider. When 24-month-olds saw the experimenter hide the object by moving his hand from end to end behind or under a row of screens, they consistently began their search in an end screen. The search of infants under 18 months was not affected in the same way by watching the experimenter. Infants between 18 and 24 months seemed to show the advanced search pattern only when they had extensive experience with the search situation.—From Authors' Abstract.

81. BEVERIDGE, M. (Univ. of Manchester, England), & DAVIES, M. **A picture-sorting approach to the study of child animism.** Genetic Psychology Monographs, 1983, **107**, 211–231.
A card-sort technique was used to examine animism thinking in children 5, 7, 9, and 11 years old. Attribution of life to inanimate objects was uncommon. With increasing age, the relationship between the different properties of life was seen. Apparently, animistic responses occur as a result of one or several determinants of which nonoperational thinking is just one.—From Authors' Abstract.

82. BISHOP, D. V. M. (Univ. of Newcastle-Upon-Tyne, England). **Comprehension of English syntax by profoundly deaf children.** Journal of Child Psychology and Psychiatry, 1983, **24**, 415–434.
Understanding of spoken language by 8–12-year-olds was below the 4-year-old level. On written and signed forms, many children responded to content words with little understanding of grammar. Others would interpret word order sequentially, producing characteristic errors.—From Author's Abstract.

83. BJORKLUND, DAVID F. (Florida Atlantic Univ.), & THOMPSON, BARBARA E. **Category typicality effects in children's memory performance: qualitative and quantitative differences in the processing of category information.** Journal of Experimental Child Psychology, 1983, **35**, 329–344.
Children in grades K, 3, and 6 received a cue-at-input/cue-at-output recall task, using category typical and atypical items that were based on either children's conceptions of item typicality or adults' conceptions of item typicality. At each grade level, recall was greater with the child-defined lists than with the adult-defined lists, and typical items were recalled to a greater extent than atypical items. The "typicality effect" in the adult-norm condition was due primarily to the children *not* realizing that many of the atypical items were appropriate category exemplars. In contrast, typicality effects in the child-norm condition were attributed to qualitative differences in the judged "goodness of example" of the typical and atypical items.—From Authors' Abstract.

84. BLATTER, PATRICIA (Univ. of Utah). **Sex differences in spatial ability: the X-linked gene theory.** Perceptual and Motor Skills, 1982, **55**, 455–462.
A review of the research done on X-linked recessive gene theory shows conflicting results.—From Author's Abstract.

85. BLEWITT, PAMELA (Villanova Univ.). ***Dog*** versus ***collie:*** **vocabulary in speech to young children.** Developmental Psychology, 1983, **19**, 602–609.
In speech to preschoolers, basic level nouns were the most frequently used. Adults produced significantly more basic level nouns than subordinate or superordinate nouns for child listeners only, suggesting the use of a simplification strategy.—From Author's Abstract.

86. BLEWITT, PAMELA (Villanova Univ.), & DURKIN, MARCIE. **Age, typicality, and task effects on categorization of objects.** Perceptual and Motor Skills, 1982, **55,** 435–445.
Three-year-olds manifested strong effects of typicality, suggesting that they matched items and judged category membership on the basis of a wholistic comparison process. Slightly older children and adults showed differential effects of typicality, suggesting the use of various processing strategies such as abstraction and logical classification skills.—Adapted from Authors' Abstract.

87. BOMBA, PAUL C., & SIQUELAND, EINAR R. (Brown Univ.). **The nature and structure of infant form categories.** Journal of Experimental Child Psychology, 1983, **35,** 294–328.
In a series of experiments employing 3 form categories composed of dot patterns, generalized habituation to new category members was used to assess categorization behavior in the recognition of visual forms. At 3–4 months of age, infants did not initially show any systematic preferences for "good" or symmetrical examples of a category relative to "distorted" examples. Infants showed generalized habituation to the previously unseen category prototypes following exposure to 6 exemplars within each of the 3 form categories. Infants could discriminate between the prototype and other category members. No evidence of a prototypicality structure was found for the form categories of infants when the number of exemplars during familiarization was limited to 6 and the test for form recognition followed immediately. However, a prototypicality structure for the remembered form categories was found when a 3-min delay was introduced between familiarization and tests for form recognition when 12 exemplars were presented during familiarization or when the prototype was included as 1 of the 6 exemplars during the familiarization period.—From Authors' Abstract.

88. BORKOWSKI, JOHN G. (Univ. of Notre Dame); PECK, VIRGINIA A.; REID, MOLLY K.; & KURTZ, BETH E. **Impulsivity and strategy transfer: metamemory as mediator.** Child Development, 1983, **54,** 459–473.
Strategy and metamemory scores were significantly higher for reflective than impulsive children. Strategy scores were higher for the reflective children during transfer but not training, suggesting a relationship between cognitive tempo and the ability to use strategies in new contexts. The correlation between metamemory and strategy use with cognitive tempo partialled out was significant, whereas the tempo-strategy use correlation was nonsignificant when metamemory was removed.—From Authors' Abstract.

89. BOWEY, JUDITH A. (Univ. of Melbourne, Australia). **The structural processing of the truncated passive in children and adults.** Journal of Psycholinguistic Research, 1982, **11,** 417–436.
Two types of truncated passive were distinguished, 1 predicted to be processed according to the standard transformational account and the other analogously to the predicate adjective construction. Both children and adults showed differential rates of agentive phrase recovery to the 2 types of truncated passive. The linguistic intuitions of adult subjects differed for the 2 types of truncated passive.—From Author's Abstract.

90. BRAINERD, CHARLES J. (Univ. of Alberta, Edmonton, Alberta, Canada). **Young children's mental arithmetic errors: a working-memory analysis.** Child Development, 1983, **54,** 812–830.
A stochastic model explaining mental arithmetic errors was tested on 4–5-year-olds and elementary school children. It appeared that improvements in short-term memory functioning were more important sources of developmental changes in arithmetic performance than were improvements in the accuracy of arithmetical processing.—From Author's Abstract.

91. BRAY, NORMAN W. (Univ. of Alabama); JUSTICE, ELAINE M.; & ZAHM, DAVID N. **Two developmental transitions in selective remembering strategies.** Journal of Experimental Child Psychology, 1983, **36,** 43–55.
A directed forgetting paradigm was used in which the person was presented 2 sets of pictures but only recalled 1 set on a trial. There were 2 developmental transitions, from ineffective to

effective selective remembering (between 7 and 11 years) and from the use of selective retrieval strategy to a more sophisticated rehearsal strategy (between 11 years and adulthood).—From Authors' Abstract.

92. BROWN, ANN L. (Univ. of Illinois, Champaign); DAY, JEANNE D.; & JONES, ROBERTA S. **The development of plans for summarizing texts.** Child Development, 1983, **54,** 968–979.
College and older high school students outperformed younger students in their propensity to plan ahead by making rough drafts, in their sensitivity to fine gradations of importance, and in their ability to condense more idea units into the same number of words. Planning, not age per se, was the best predictor of efficiency, although the propensity to plan and age were highly correlated.—From Authors' Abstract.

93. CHARLOP, MARJORIE H. (George Washington Univ.), & CARLSON, JERRY. **Reversal and nonreversal shifts in autistic children.** Journal of Experimental Child Psychology, 1983, **36,** 56–67.
Consistent with findings for normal children, older autistic children did better on reversal shifts, while younger children did better on nonreversal shifts.—From Authors' Abstract.

94. CHEYNE, J. ALLAN (Univ. of Waterloo, Ontario, Canada), & RUBIN, KENNETH H. **Playful precursors of problem solving in preschoolers.** Developmental Psychology, 1983, **19,** 577–584.
Preschoolers were permitted to play for 8 min with sticks of varying length as well as blocks. A problem-solving session ensued in which solution could be achieved by joining sticks to create a tool. Correlations were found between the discovery of the solution principle and the quality of combinatorial activity during play and problem-solving solution time.—From Authors' Abstract.

95. CHRISTIE, JAMES F. (Univ. of Kansas). **Play training strategies.** Canadian Journal of Early Childhood Education, 1982, **2,** 47–52.
The make-believe component of play has been found to foster children's creativity, problem solving, IQ scores, conservation attainment, language development, social knowledge, logical memory, and abstract thought. Four play training strategies are described that can be implemented at the preschool level. These strategies can be used most effectively if combined with systematic observations to see which children are in need of play training and which specific strategies to employ.—From Abstract by O. Weininger.

96. COHEN, SARALE E. (Univ. of California School of Medicine, Los Angeles), & PARMELEE, ARTHUR H. **Prediction of five-year Stanford-Binet scores in preterm infants.** Child Development, 1983, **54,** 1242–1253.
Preterm infants were followed from birth to age 5. The child's performance on the Stanford-Binet test at age 5 could not be predicted from early hazardous events in the obstetrical or neonatal period. Developmental outcome at age 5 could be predicted moderately from a single measure, infant visual attention, administered as early as term date. Social factors were more important than any other set of factors in relating to the child's mental performance at age 5.—From Authors' Abstract.

97. CORTE, MARIA DELLA (Michigan State Univ.); BENEDICT, HELEN; & KLEIN, DIANE. **The relationship of pragmatic dimensions of mothers' speech to the referential-expressive distinction.** Journal of Child Language, 1983, **10,** 35–43.
A 50-utterance corpus of maternal speech during caretaking situations was extracted from in-home tape recordings. The infants were classified according to Nelson's referential-expressive distinction. Mothers of referential children produced a greater number of utterances per caretaking incident, more description, and less prescriptives than did mothers of expressive children.—From Authors' Abstract.

98. COSTA PEREIRA, D. J. V., & MASKILL, R. (Univ. of East Anglia). **Structure and process in pupils' essays: a graphical analysis of the organisation of extended prose.** British Journal of Educational Psychology, 1983, **53,** 100–106.
A method for analyzing structure and process in prose was applied to 52 14-year-olds' essays. No distinction occurred between the reproductive/constructive paradigms of memory; pupils processed information in their essays in a manner closer to a parallel processing strategy.— From Authors' Abstract.

99. CRNIC, KEITH A. (Univ. of Washington); RAGOZIN, ARLENE S.; GREENBERG, MART T.; ROBINSON, NANCY M.; & BASHAM, ROBERT B. **Social interaction and developmental competence of preterm and full-term infants during the first year of life.** Child Development, 1983, **54,** 1199–1210.
Differences were found in both mothers' and preterm infants' interactive behavior across the first year of life. Preterms performed below full-terms on measures of cognitive and language development corrected for gestational age.—From Authors' Abstract.

100. CROCKENBERG, SUSAN (Univ. of California, Davis). **Early mother and infant antecedents of Bayley scale performance at 21 months.** Developmental Psychology, 1983, **19,** 727–730.
Questionnaires assessed maternal responsive attitude during the prenatal period. The Neonatal Behavioral Assessment Scale was administered at 5 and 10 days, and mothers and infants were observed together at 3 months. Babies were tested on the Bayley Scales of Infant Development (BSID) when they were 21 months of age. Mother's level of education, a responsive maternal attitude, and 3-month smiling and eye contact predicted infant performance on the Mental Scale of the BSID.—From Author's Abstract.

101. CUMMINGS, E. MARK, & BJORK, ELIZABETH LIGON (Univ. of California, Los Angeles). **Perseveration and search on a five-choice visible displacement hiding task.** Journal of Genetic Psychology, 1983, **142,** 283–291.
Infants 8–10 months old were presented with visible displacement hiding tasks at a first location (A), a second location (B), and, finally, a third location (C). Infants seldom searched perseveratively during either B or C hiding trials. These results challenge Piaget's notion that infants are incapable at this age of objectively representing the spatial location of hidden objects.—From Authors' Abstract.

102. CURRIE-JEDERMANN, JANICE L. (Scarborough Board of Education, 140 Borough, Scarborough, Ontario, Canada), & ANGLIN, JEREMY M. **The concrete to abstract progression revisited: evidence based on a release from proactive inhibition task.** Merrill-Palmer Quarterly, 1983, **29,** 209–225.
The present experiment has provided evidence for a developmental progression from concrete to abstract. Young children, who appear to appreciate relations only among words belonging to relatively concrete categories, eventually reach the adult endpoint where they understand relations among words belonging to categories of differing levels of abstractness. The concrete to abstract progression hypothesis appears to fit the data.—From the Article.

103. DANNEMILLER, JAMES L. (Univ. of Texas, Austin), & BANKS, MARTIN S. **Can selective adaptation account for early infant habituation?** Merrill-Palmer Quarterly, 1983, **29,** 151–158.
A model of early infant habituation based on selective adaptation of feature detectors is proposed as an alternative to Sokolovian models. The model is based on known neurophysiology and psychophysics.—From Authors' Abstract.

104. DAVIS, ALYSON M. (Univ. of Birmingham, P.O. Box 363, Birmingham, England). **Contextual sensitivity in young children's drawings.** Journal of Experimental Child Psychology, 1983, **35,** 478–486.

Children from 4 to 7 years were presented with contrasting models to copy. These included cups and sugar bowls in various combinations and orientations. In each experiment, the children's copies were scored for inclusion or omission of the occluded handle on the model. Nearly 1/3 of the children did not respond consistently by either copying accurately or by always including the occluded handle. Many children's responses were directed by the type of context presented within the arrays.—From Author's Abstract.

105. DeLISI, RICHARD (Rutgers Univ.). **Developmental and individual differences in children's representation of the horizontal coordinate.** Merrill-Palmer Quarterly, 1983, **29,** 179–196.
First, third, and fifth graders were observed on a portable-rod-and-frame test of field dependence-independence and on water bottle and crossbar measures of horizontality representation. Performance improved with increasing grade on each horizontality task, but children were more accurate on the crossbar than the water bottle task.—From Author's Abstract.

106. DeLOACHE, JUDY S. (Univ. of Illinois), & BROWN, ANN L. **Very young children's memory for the location of objects in a large-scale environment.** Child Development, 1983, **54,** 888–897.
Among 18–30-month olds, memory performance was better when a toy was hidden within the natural environment. No age differences were found when an object was hidden either in the natural environment or in 1 of a set of unmarked boxes. In the third condition the older subjects effectively used a landmark cue to help them remember in which plain box a toy had been hidden, but the younger subjects did not profit from such potential cues.—From Authors' Abstract.

107. DEMANY, L. (Centre Henri Piéron, Paris, France). **Auditory stream segregation in infancy.** Infant Behavior and Development, 1982, **5,** 261–276.
Infants were able to detect a change in the order of the component tones of certain repetitive melodic sequences.—S. Thomas.

108. DE VILLIERS, PETER A. (Smith Coll.). **Semantic and pragmatic factors in the acquisition of syntax.** Volta Review, 1983, **85,** 10–28.

109. DUNN, JUDY (Univ. of Cambridge), & KENDRICK, CAROL. **The speech of two- and three-year-olds to infant siblings: "baby talk" and the context of communication.** Journal of Child Language, 1982, **9,** 579–595.
Adjustments in speech made by 2–3-year-olds when talking to their 14-month-old siblings are described and compared with those made by mothers addressing their babies. "Clarification" adjustments were made by all the children, but there were marked individual differences in the frequency of questions and "affective-expressive" features–differences related to the quality of the relationship between the siblings. The pattern of speech adjustments reflected the social contexts in which the children addressed their siblings; within these contexts (prohibitory and playful) children as young as 2 make appropriate use of communicative devices.—From Authors' Abstract.

110. DURKIN, KEVIN (Univ. of Kent, Canterbury, England). **Children's comprehension of complex sentences containing the preposition between.** Child Study Journal, 1983, **13,** 133–147.
Children's comprehension of 3 different sentence structures containing *between* was tested. Children performed better than chance with the simplest structure but had difficulty with the most complex type.—From Author's Abstract.

111. DUSEK, JEROME B. (Syracuse Univ.), & JOSEPH, GAIL. **The bases of teacher expectancies: a meta-analysis.** Journal of Educational Psychology, 1983, **75,** 327–346.
A review of 77 pertinent studies using Stouffer's (1949) method of adding Zs led to the following conclusions. Student attractiveness, conduct, cumulative folder information, race, and social class were related to teacher expectancies. Student gender and the number of parents

at home were student characteristics not related to teacher expectancies; equivocal relations existed between teacher expectancies and student sex-role behavior, name stereotypes, and teachers having previously taught a sibling.—From Authors' Abstract.

112. ENDSLEY, RICHARD C. (Univ. of Georgia). **Tactual access and stimulus dimensionality as determinants of young children's identification and transformational questions.** Journal of Genetic Psychology, 1983, **142,** 97–105.
Preschool children were invited to look at 1 set of stimulus material. One third of the children were presented with 3-dimensional materials that they were free to touch, 1/3 with 3-dimensional materials that they could not touch, and 1/3 with life-size photographs of the objects. Children in each group asked a similar number of questions to identify the names of the objects. Children who could touch the objects asked the most "transformational" questions.—From Author's Abstract.

113. ENGEN, TRYGG (Brown Univ.); ENGEN, ELIZABETH A.; CLARKSON, RICHARD L.; & BLACKWELL, PETER M. **Discrimination of intonation by hearing-impaired children.** Applied Psycholinguistics, 1983, **4,** 149–160.
Most hearing-impaired children whose auditory input is limited to low frequencies do perceive differences in intonation.—From Authors' Abstract.

114. EVANS, ROSS A. (Univ. of Wisconsin). **Categorical list differentiation by mentally retarded adolescents as a function of transfer list composition and response mode.** American Journal of Mental Deficiency, 1983, **88,** 187–193.
Results suggest that the recognition task may be more vulnerable to interference than has been previously supposed.—From Author's Abstract.

115. FENNELL, EILEEN B. (Univ. of Florida); SATZ, PAUL; & MORRIS, ROBIN. **The development of handedness and dichotic ear listening asymmetries in relation to school achievement: a longitudinal study.** Journal of Experimental Child Psychology, 1983, **35,** 248–262.
Male schoolchildren were evaluated in grades K, 2, and 5 with a dichotic listening task and a hand-preference test. There was significant variability in handedness scores over time only for those subjects whose scores at initial testing identified them as non-right-handers. Both right and left handers had a significant increase in dichotic listening scores over time; however, only right handers had a significant right-ear advantage at each evaluation. Combined hand preference scores and ear recall scores accounted for almost 44% of the variance in achievement scores at grade 5. Ear asymmetry scores, however, were not predictive of school achievement.—From Authors' Abstract.

116. FLAVELL, JOHN (Stanford Univ.); FLAVELL, ELEANOR R.; & GREEN, FRANCES L. **Development of the appearance-reality distinction.** Cognitive Psychology, 1983, **15,** 95–120.
Three experiments investigated 3–5-year-old children's ability to distinguish between and correctly identify real vs. apparent object properties (color, size, and shape), object identities, object presence-absence, and action identities. Even the 3-year-olds appeared to have some ability to make correct appearance–reality discriminations, and this ability increased with age.—From Authors' Abstract.

117. FLEXER, B. K., & ROBERGE, J. J. (Temple Univ.). **A longitudinal investigation of field dependence–independence and the development of formal operational thought.** British Journal of Educational Psychology, 1983, **53,** 195–204.
The Group Embedded Figures Test and paper-and-pencil measures of formal operations were given to 120 pupils annually for 3 years. The impact of field dependence–independence on the development of formal operational thought was inconsequential.—From Authors' Abstract.

118. FORTIN, ANDREE (Univ. of Montreal, Quebec, Canada), & ROBERT, MICHELE. **Minimal modeling input and progress towards conservation mastery.** Journal of Genetic Psychology, 1983, **142,** 245–257.
Nonconservers 5 1/2–7 1/2 years observed a model adding to or not adding to conservation judgment acknowledgement of perceptual differences and judgment repetition. Subjects had to justify or not justify modeled judgments. Higher scores were associated with self-recognition.—From Authors' Abstract.

119. FOSTER, SUE (Univ. of Southern California). **Topic and the development of discourse structure.** Volta Review, 1983, **85,** 44–54.

120. FREED, NORMAN H. (Palo Alto). **Foreseeably equivalent math skills of men and women.** Psychological Reports, 1983, **52,** 334.
The author argues that in order to conclude that there are sex differences in mathematics, future controlled studies must show reliable differences across time, patterns of maturation, setting, and various populations.—Adapted from the Article.

121. GAINES, ROSSLYN (Univ. of California, Los Angeles). **Children's artistic abilities: fact or fancy?** Journal of Genetic Psychology, 1983, **143,** 57–68.
Theories are examined concerning the decline of involvement in art over the course of development.—Ed.

122. GARTON, ALISON F. (Murdoch Univ., Western Australia). **An approach to the study of determiners in early language development.** Journal of Psycholinguistic Research, 1983, **12,** 513–525.
Developmental research views the child as progressively attaining appropriate (adult) use of the 2 forms *a* or *the*. It is argued that instead of regarding the child's use of the articles as correct or incorrect, we should look at the form and function of those determiners used and omitted and consider why they are elicited.—From Author's Abstract.

123. GASH, HUGH (St. Patrick's Coll., Dublin, Ireland). **Associated structures: class inclusion and role-taking.** Journal of Genetic Psychology, 1982, **141,** 155–166.
Subjects were 5- and 7-year-old Irish children ($N = 72$) and 6- and 7-year-old French children ($N = 72$). Role-taking training, successful only with 7-year-olds, significantly increased class inclusion scores at this age level. Class inclusion training did not augment role-taking scores. Class inclusion structures apparently are embodied in this form of role taking.—From Author's Abstract.

124. GILMORE, PERRY (Univ. of Pennsylvania). **Ethnographic approaches to the study of child language: two illustrative studies.** Volta Review, 1983, **85,** 29–43.

125. GOBBO, CAMILLA (Univ. di Padova, Italy), & AGNOLI, FRANCA. **Children's comprehension of Italian comparative forms and the three-term problem solution.** Journal of Child Language, 1983, **10,** 203–222.
Children 7–10 years were required to solve 2- or 3-term relational problems. Early in development, children spatially represent the 2 terms of the positive comparatives in a contrastive-positional way, but later they represent the terms relationally. Comprehension of negative comparatives is characterized by 3 phases of development: a contrastive-positional phase, a presuppositional phase, and a relational representation.—From Authors' Abstract.

126. GOLBECK, SUSAN L. (Rutgers Univ.). **Reconstructing a large-scale spatial arrangement: effects of environmental organization and operativity.** Developmental Psychology, 1983, **19,** 644–653.
Children 5–9 years old were pretested and categorized as high, transitional, or low in operativity. Subsequently, they reconstructed 1 of 4 arrangements of 16 items of furniture. The 4 conditions varied in logical organization, clustering by similar physical attributes, and meaningful-

ness of spatial orientation. Clustering increased memory for spatial relations. Meaningful orientation interacted with clustering to improve memory. Operative knowledge increased memory for general location but did not show the expected interactions with environmental organization.—From Author's Abstract.

127. GOLD, RON (Univ. of Melbourne, Australia). **Inappropriate conservation judgments in the concrete operations period.** Genetic Psychology Monographs, 1983, **107**, 189–210.
This study of 5–11-year-olds employed an area- and a perimeter-conservation task. The study confirmed earlier findings that concrete-operational children give inappropriate as well as appropriate conservation judgments and demonstrated that the former do not occur simply as a result of order effects.—From Author's Abstract.

128. GOLDMAN, SUSAN R. (Univ. of California, Santa Barbara), & VARNHAGEN, CONNIE K. **Comprehension of stories with no-obstacle and obstacle endings.** Child Development, 1983, **54**, 980–992.
For children in grades 2–5, recall of actions taken to meet the goal was affected by both ending and whether they had read or listened to the stories. The inclusion of outcome information in free recall was affected by ending. Responses to causal inference questions provided evidence for differences in the causal links between the attempt and successful vs. unsuccessful goal attainment. These differences were attenuated in the adult data. There was a developmental trend toward increased preference for the obstacle stories.—From Authors' Abstract.

129. GREEN, LOGAN L. (Univ. of Kentucky). **Safety need resolution and cognitive ability as interwoven antecedents to moral development.** Social Behavior and Personality, 1981, **9**, 139–145.
Preservice teachers had a mean moral development score at about the national norm. For those whose academic success history was average, high levels of safety need satisfaction were an important antecedent of postconventional reasoning. Both the insecure and moderately secure among these average achievers received scores similar to those of senior high school students. These data suggest that constraints are placed on moral thought by prepotent conative level.—Adapted from Author's Abstract.

130. HARDY-BROWN, KAREN (Univ. of Colorado). **Universals and individual differences: disentangling two approaches to the study of language acquisition.** Developmental Psychology, 1983, **19**, 610–624.
A genetic contribution to individual differences in language development has not been widely considered because it is often confused with the idea of innate language universals or with single-gene Mendelian inheritance. An alternative research framework is outlined that provides a means to disentangle genetic and environmental influences.—From Author's Abstract.

131. HARGROVE, PATRICIA M. (Phillips Univ.), & PANAGOS, JOHN M. **Role saliency cues and children's sentence comprehension.** Journal of Psycholinguistic Research, 1982, **11**, 217–228.
Children 3–7 years old acted out active and passive sentences immediately after exposure to matching-information, mismatching-information, and no-information cues. The matching-information cues yielded the highest comprehensive scores, followed in order by the no-information and the mismatching-information cues. Active sentences were easier to comprehend than passive sentences, and comprehension scores improved with age.—From Authors' Abstract.

132. HARRIS, FRANCES N. (Univ. of Utah), & FLORA, JUNE A. **Children's use of get passives.** Journal of Psycholinguistic Research, 1982, **11**, 297–311.
Children performed significantly better on imitation and comprehension of passive sentences with *get* than with *be*. On the production task, children produced many more *get* passives than *be* passives and the frequency of *get* passives increased with age. Age-related changes in the pattern of linguistic strategies were examined.—Adapted from Authors' Abstract.

133. HARTLEY, J., & TRUEMAN, M. (Univ. of Keele). **The effects of headings in text on recall, search and retrieval.** British Journal of Educational Psychology, 1983, **53,** 205–214.
Headings aided recall, search, and retrieval, but position of the headings had no effect. The kind of headings (questions or statements) had no differential effect with readers of different ability, but low-ability participants appeared to do better with headings as questions.—From Authors' Abstract.

134. HASENSTAB, M. SUZANNE (Univ. of Virginia, Charlottesville). **Child language studies: impact on habilitation of hearing-impaired infants and preschool children.** Volta Review, 1983, **85,** 88–100.

135. HIRST, WILLIAM (Princeton Univ.), & WEIL, JOYCE. **Acquisition of epistemic and deontic meaning of modals.** Journal of Child Language, 1982, **9,** 659–666.
Children 3–6 years old heard 2 contradictory modal propositions concerning the location of a peanut (the epistemic condition), or they were commanded about what room a puppet should go to (the deontic condition). The child was to indicate which command should be followed. The greater the difference in the strength of the 2 modal propositions the earlier the difference was appreciated.—From Authors' Abstract.

136. HOFMANN, RICHARD (Miami Univ.), & TREPANIER, MARY L. **A cross-cultural influence on some basic graphic representations of young Chinese and African children.** Journal of Genetic Psychology, 1982, **141,** 167–175.
American and Chinese 4–6-year-olds' graphic representations were studied. Topological scores showed a primacy over Euclidean scores in both cultures at all age levels. The Chinese children performed better than the American children.—Adapted from Authors' Abstract.

137. HOLZMAN, THOMAS G. (Georgia State Univ.); PELLEGRINO, JAMES W.; & GLASER, ROBERT. **Cognitive variables in series completion.** Journal of Educational Psychology, 1983, **75,** 603–618.
The cognitive determinants of number series completion performance were studied in college adults and average- and high-IQ elementary-school children. Solution difficulty was most affected by the amount of information to be coordinated in working memory. Adults could coordinate more than children, but IQ levels did not differ.—From Authors' Abstract.

138. HORGAN, JAMES S. (Univ. of Illinois, Chicago), & HORGAN, JAMES. **Measurement bias in representing accuracy of movement on linear-positioning tasks.** Perceptual and Motor Skills, 1982, **55,** 971–981.
Results indicated that 7–9-year-olds were inferior to 10–12- and 14–16-year-olds in accuracy of recall. The 7–9-year-olds did not appear to rehearse spontaneously as did the older children.—Adapted from Authors' Abstract.

139. HOWES, M., & MORGAN, VICKY (Univ. of Leeds, England). **Intentionality and field dependence in children's moral judgments.** British Journal of Educational Psychology, 1983, **53,** 170–174.
Field dependence was related to moral judgmental ability in children 7–8 years old. An intermediate stage of production and mediational deficiency was identified in which the child had the concept of intention but failed to use it consistently.—From Authors' Abstract.

140. HUDSON, JUDITH, & FIVUSH, ROBYN (CUNY Graduate Ctr.). **Categorical and schematic organization and the development of retrieval strategies.** Journal of Experimental Child Psychology, 1983, **36,** 32–42.
Preschool and kindergarten children recalled either a taxonomic list or a story. Although preschool children's story recall was well organized, their list recall was poorly organized. Kindergarten children's recall of both the story and the list was well organized, and their recall was better organized on the second recall trial.—From Authors' Abstract.

141. HUDSON, JUDITH (CUNY Graduate School), & NELSON, KATHERINE. **Effects of script structure on children's story recall.** Developmental Psychology, 1983, **19**, 625–635.
Preschool and first-grade children's use of scripts in story recall was investigated. Both ages recalled more story units from the story about a more familiar event (birthday party), sequenced story units more accurately in the story about a more logically organized event (baking cookies), and tended to eliminate logically inconsistent information in order to preserve canonical event sequences. Preschoolers performed more poorly overall.—Adapted from Authors' Abstract.

142. HULME, CHARLES (Univ. of York, Heslington, York, England); BIGGERSTAFF, ANNE; MORAN, GEORGINA; & McKINLAY, IAN. **Visual, kinaesthetic and cross-model judgements of length by normal and clumsy children.** Developmental Medicine and Child Neurology, 1982, **24**, 461–471.
Clumsy children showed perceptual impairments, as indicated by their poor performance on visual, kinaesthetic, and cross-modal judgments of length and by their low scores on spatial subtests of the WISC.—From Authors' Abstract.

143. HUMMEL, DONNA DALTON (Cleveland State Univ.). **Syntactic and conversational characteristics of fathers' speech.** Journal of Psycholinguistic Research, 1982, **11**, 465–483.
The verbal interactions of fathers and mothers with their 2-year-olds were assessed during free play. No differences were found between fathers and mothers in the use of syntactic and conversational features. The results suggest that the amount of time fathers spend with their children does not dramatically affect the syntactic or conversational features of their speech.—From Author's Abstract.

144. IVES, S. W. (Spectrum Training Corp., Salem), & RAKOW, J. **Children's use of feature descriptions to solve spatial perspective and rotation problems.** British Journal of Educational Psychology, 1983, **53**, 143–151.
Children in grades K and 2 were asked to solve a spatial perspective task or a rotation task through either verbal description or picture selection. Verbalization aided performance on all conditions of the perspective task but only selectively in the rotation task. Language mapped onto feature descriptions which greatly facilitated perspective task performance.—From Authors' Abstract.

145. JACOBSON, JOSEPH L. (Wayne State Univ.); BOERSMA, DAVID C.; FIELDS, ROBERT B.; & OLSON, KAREN L. **Paralinguistic features of adult speech to infants and small children.** Child Development, 1983, **54**, 436–442.
Mean fundamental frequency and average variability both increased significantly over baseline when subjects were asked to imagine speaking to an infant or small child or when an infant or a small child was actually present. Nonparents who had little prior experience with infants modified their fundamental frequency as much as parents.—From Authors' Abstract.

146. JAMES, SHARON L. (Syracuse Univ.), & KHAN, LINDA M. L. **Grammatical morpheme acquisition: an approximately invariant order?** Journal of Psycholinguistic Research, 1982, **11**, 381–388.
Spontaneous language samples were recorded bimonthly in the children's homes for a period of 9 months. These samples were analyzed for correct use of the 14 morphemes. The correlation between the acquisition orders from the present study and the order from Brown's study was low, suggesting that the order of acquisition for these morphemes may not be invariant.—From Authors' Abstract.

147. JARDINE, ROSEMARY (Australian National Univ., Canberra, Australia), & MARTIN, N. G. **Spatial ability and throwing accuracy.** Behavior Genetics, 1983, **13**, 331–340.
Significant correlations have been found between several tests of throwing accuracy and spatial ability. This replicates an earlier finding and supports the hypothesis that past selection acting on hunting skills in males may partly account for the superior spatial ability observed in males today.—Authors' Abstract.

148. JORM, ANTHONY F. (Deakin Univ., Victoria, Australia), & SHARE, DAVID L. **Phonological recoding and reading acquisition.** Applied Psycholinguistics, 1983, **4,** 103–147.
Phonological recording plays a critical role in helping the child become a skilled reader. This article reviews the relevant evidence.—From Authors' Abstract.

149. JUNKALA, JOHN (Boston Coll.), & TALBOT, MICHAEL L. **Cognitive styles of students with cerebral palsy.** Perceptual and Motor Skills, 1982, **55,** 403–410.
Fourteen-year-old cerebral palsied students' cognitive styles were qualitatively similar to those of nonhandicapped students, although the extraocular movements of some students appeared to affect the classifications of cognitive style to which they were assigned by the data.—From Authors' Abstract.

150. KAHN, JAMES V. **Moral reasoning of Piagetian-matched retarded and nonretarded children and adolescents.** Journal of Genetic Psychology, 1983, **143,** 69–77.
Moral reasoning was assessed by an instrument based on Kohlberg's procedures. The Slosson Intelligence Test gave IQ measures. Piagetian stage was determined by conservation of number. There was no difference between the mildly retarded and the nonretarded, or between the mildly retarded and the moderately retarded subjects, but differences were found between the moderately retarded and the nonretarded subjects.—From Author's Abstract.

151. KALLIOPUSKA, MIRJA (Univ. of Helsinki, Finland). **Relationship between moral judgment and empathy.** Psychological Reports, 1983, **53,** 575–578.
Schoolchildren ages 9–12 years were tested with 2 Kohlberg dilemmas and the Mehrabian and Epstein scale of emotional empathy. The results confirm the positive relation found in earlier studies.—From Author's Abstract.

152. KANEKO, RYUTARO; TANAKA, AKIO; & MATSUI, MICHIKO (Hiroshima Univ., Japan). **Comparison of natural and model-trained conservers.** Psychological Reports, 1983, **53,** 623–630.
The results of Experiment 1 showed that the stability for conservation by trained conservers, especially low partial conservers, was less than that offered by natural conservers, although even low partial conservers maintained a high average score. The findings suggest that trained conservers can acquire stable conservation concepts through modeling, and that modeling is more effective when it is developmentally appropriate.—From Authors' Abstract.

153. KARNES, FRANCES A. (Univ. of Southern Mississippi); LEE, LETA A.; & MAY, BROOKES. **Correlations among scores on the 1966, 1973, and 1979 norms of Raven's Standard Progressive Matrices for economically disadvantaged students.** Perceptual and Motor Skills, 1982, **55,** 793–794.
Correlations among the scores on the 1966, 1973, and 1979 norms on Raven's Matrices for third to fifth graders were significantly high.—Adapted from Authors' Abstract.

154. KARR, SHARON K. (Emporia State Univ.). **Bender-Gestalt performance of Sierra Leone, West African children from four sub-cultures.** Perceptual and Motor Skills, 1982, **55,** 123–127.
The Bender performance of the most modernized subculture was higher than that of the 3 remaining subcultures. Boys' scores were higher than girls'.—Adapted from Author's Abstract.

155. KAVANAUGH, ROBERT D. (Williams Coll.); WHITTINGTON, SUE; & CERBONE, MARK J. **Mothers' use of fantasy in speech to young children.** Journal of Child Language, 1983, **10,** 45–55.
Observations were made of mothers in free-play interactions with their 12–27-month-old children. Fantasy speech to 1-year-olds was relatively infrequent and restricted to descriptions of the feelings, actions, and functions of objects. Mothers of 2-year-olds talked about nonexistent imaginary objects and often asked the child to extend a play episode by providing a new fantasy element.—From Authors' Abstract.

156. KAYE, DANIEL B.; POST, TIM A.; HOYER, WILLIAM J. (Syracuse Univ.); SAYNISCH, MICHAEL J.; & HAHN, MARSHA V. **Aging and visual search under consistent and varied mapping.** Developmental Psychology, 1983, **19**, 508–512.
Eight young and 8 elderly women participated in 6 sessions of hybrid memory-search/visual-search task. Half the subjects performed in a consistent-mapping condition in which memory sets were fixed. The other half performed in a varied-mapping condition. The amount of facilitation in controlled search associated with consistent mapping compared with varied mapping was greater for older subjects than for younger subjects.—From Authors' Abstract.

157. KINGMA, JOHANNES (State Univ. of Groningen, Netherlands). **The development of seriation, conservation, and multiple classification: a longitudinal study.** Genetic Psychology Monographs, 1983, **108**, 43–67.
Cognitive tasks were administered to kindergarten and primary graders on 3 occasions during a school year. Single seriation preceded multiple seriation. The majority showed gradual development of conservation.—From Author's Abstract.

158. KINGMA, JOHANNES (Twente Univ. of Technology, Enschede, Netherlands). **Seriation, correspondence, and transitivity.** Journal of Educational Psychology, 1983, **75**, 763–771.
Children from grades K-6 completed tasks similar to those used by Piaget. Correspondence, seriation, and transitivity reflected different underlying concepts.—From Author's Abstract.

159. KIRBY, JOHN R. (Univ. of Newcastle). **Cognitive processes, school achievement, and comprehension of ambiguous sentences.** Journal of Psycholinguistic Research, 1982, **11**, 485–499.
The results showed that comprehension of ambiguity was strongly related to level of English achievement, though deep structure ambiguities best discriminated the English achievement groups. Results also showed that perception of all types of ambiguity was related to both simultaneous and successive processing. Subjects with high successive processing scores had an additional advantage in perceiving deep structure ambiguities.—From Author's Abstract.

160. KNEPPER, WARREN; OBRZUT, JOHN E. (Univ. of Northern Colorado); & COPELAND, ELLIS P. **Emotional and social problem-solving thinking in gifted and average elementary school children.** Journal of Genetic Psychology, 1983, **142**, 25–30.
Matched populations of intellectually gifted and average elementary aged children were studied. The Means-Ends Problem-Solving scores of both groups support the notion that cognitive development does play a role in advanced interpersonal and intrapersonal cognitive problem-solving skill development.—From Authors' Abstract.

161. KOBASIGAWA, AKIRA (Univ. of Windsor, Canada). **Monitoring retrieval processes by children.** Journal of Genetic Psychology, 1983, **142**, 259–269.
Children ages 6 and 8 were shown a list of categorized items representing 3 different category sizes. Half of the children were asked to estimate the number of items assigned to each category prior to being tested for recall of the list, while the other half did not receive such instructions. Children's estimates of category sizes became progressively larger as the actual category sizes became larger, indicating that even 6-year-olds have the ability to acquire rather accurate knowledge about category size during the item presentation. They conducted an extended search when there were additional items unrecalled.—From Author's Abstract.

162. KOSE, GARY (Rutgers Univ.); BEILIN, HARRY; & O'CONNOR, JOSEPH M. **Children's comprehension of actions depicted in photographs.** Developmental Psychology, 1983, **19**, 636–643.
Children 3–6 years of age were asked to mimic the same poses of children depicted in black-and-white photographs, to mimic the same poses depicted by a live model, to describe the contents of the photographs, or to do these things with line drawings and a doll. Performance

was better with the live model than with the photographs, drawings, or doll.—From Authors' Abstract.

163. KUCZAJ, STAN A., III (Southern Methodist Univ.). **"I mell a kunk!"—evidence that children have more complex representations of word pronunciations which they simplify.** Journal of Psycholinguistic Research, 1983, **12,** 69–73.
A case study is reported in which a 3-year-old was asked to choose between his own forms and correct forms of pronunciation in a comprehension task. The results demonstrate that the child understood the correct forms to be the correct forms.—From Author's Abstract.

164. KUCZAJ, STAN A., III (Southern Methodist Univ.), & DONALDSON, SAM A., III. **If the boy loves the girl and the girl loves the dog, does the boy love the dog?: the overgeneralization of verbal transitive inference skills.** Journal of Psycholinguistic Research, 1982, **11,** 197–206.
Two studies investigated 4–10-year-olds' capacity to make verbal transitive inferences. The results of the 2 studies suggest that the development of transitive inference skills follows a specific to general developmental path, and that children overgeneralize their verbal transitive inference skills to inappropriate relational terms prior to determining the general principle that underlies the use of relational terms in transitive sentences.—Authors' Abstract.

165. LANE, DAVID M. (Rice Univ.), & PEARSON, DEBORAH A. **Can stimulus differentiation and salience explain developmental changes in attention? A reply to Hagen and Wilson, Jeffrey, and Odom.** Merrill-Palmer Quarterly, 1983, **29,** 227–233.
It is concluded that much of the data cannot be explained adequately in terms of stimulus differentiation and stimulus salience, and that there is as yet no framework capable of explaining all data on attention development.—From Authors' Abstract.

166. LANE, DAVID S. (Southwest Missouri State Univ.); FLETCHER, DONNA N.; & FLETCHER, HAROLD J. **Improving conditional syllogism performance of young normal and gifted students with discovery and rule instruction.** Journal of Educational Psychology, 1983, **75,** 441–449.
Ten-year-old gifted students and 12-year-old normal sixth graders were instructed in conditional syllogisms. Discovery instruction was generally more effective than rule instruction.—From Authors' Abstract.

167. LAWRY, JANICE A. (Univ. of California, Riverside); WELSH, MARILYN C.; & JEFFREY, WENDELL E. **Cognitive tempo and complex problem solving.** Child Development, 1983, **54,** 912–920.
As problem sets became more difficult, both reflective and impulsive children (ages 9–11 years) showed a pattern of increasing latencies and decreasing accuracy. Reflectives had reliably greater increases in latency across sets than impulsives. Change in latency from the first to the last set was a better predictor of overall accuracy in impulsives than reflectives.—From Authors' Abstract.

168. LEEDS, ALAN; DIRLAM, DAVID; & BRANNIGAN, GARY G. (SUNY, Plattsburgh). **The development of spatial representation in children from five to thirteen years of age.** Genetic Psychology Monographs, 1983, **108,** 137–165.
Three raters examined drawings from children 5–13 years old for 38 of Lowenfeld's and Piaget's structural features.—From Authors' Abstract.

169. LEMPERS, JACQUES D. (Iowa State Univ.), & ELROD, MIMI MILNER. **Children's appraisal of different sources of referential communicative inadequacies.** Child Development, 1983, **54,** 509–515.
Nursery school children and kindergartners served as listeners. Young children's appraisal skills as listener in referential communications depended on the specific source of the inadequacy in the message.—From Authors' Abstract.

170. LEONARD, LAURENCE B. (Purdue Univ.); CHAPMAN, KATHY; ROWAN, LYNNE E.; & WEISS, AMY L. **Three hypotheses concerning young children's imitations of lexical items.** Developmental Psychology, 1983, **19**, 591–601.
Evidence was found that imitation may facilitate children's ability to acquire words in production, and that imitation of such words may decline only after a period in which the words are used both imitatively and spontaneously.—From Authors' Abstract.

171. LEVINE, SUSAN COHEN (Univ. of Chicago), & CAREY, SUSAN. **Up front: the acquisition of a concept and a word.** Journal of Child Language, 1982, **9**, 645–657.
A complex disjunctive concept of front–back orientation was found to precede any knowledge of the words *front* and *back*. The word *back* is comprehended before *front*, and children at an intermediate state of lexical knowledge interpret *front* as if it means *back*.—From Authors' Abstract.

172. LEVY, YONATA (Hebrew Univ.). **The acquisition of Hebrew plurals: the case of the missing gender category.** Journal of Child Language, 1983, **10**, 107–121.
Longitudinal data showed that between the ages of 2 and 3, children determine their choice of the plural morpheme according to the nature of the final syllable, and they seem insensitive to the semantic notion and syntactic notion of gender that govern the choice of plurals for animate nouns and noun-adjective agreement.—Adapted from Author's Abstract.

173. LIGHT, PAUL (Univ. of Southampton, England), & NIX, CAROLYN. **"Own view" versus "good view" in a perspective-taking task.** Child Development, 1983, **54**, 480–483.
Children 4–6 years were tested on a spatial perspective-taking task from both good and poor viewing positions. Children did not show any bias toward their own view when it was a poor one. When they themselves had a good view of the objects, they chose their own rather than another equally good view.—From Authors' Abstract.

174. LIPSON, MARJORIE YOUMANS (Eastern Michigan Univ.). **The influence of religious affiliation on children's memory for test information.** Reading Research Quarterly, 1983, **18**, 448–457.
The findings indicate that Catholic and Jewish youngsters ages 10–12 years were much more likely to comprehend text when they had a culturally appropriate schema into which to incorporate the new information.—From Author's Abstract.

175. LLOYD, S. E., & FREEMAN, N. H. (Univ. of Bristol, 8–10 Berkeley Sq., Bristol, England). **Infant search strategies with containers that move but do not alter the location at which contents can be found.** Journal of Experimental Child Psychology, 1983, **35**, 449–456.
A number of hypotheses about infants' delayed search accuracy have been based upon the notion that a location associated with repeated retrieval of the object attains privileged status. A test is reported in which performance of 12- and 15-month-old infants was shown to be indifferent to the location.—From Authors' Abstract.

176. LODICO, MARGUERITE G.; GHATALA, ELIZABETH S. (Univ. of Houston); LEVIN, JOEL R.; PRESSLEY, MICHAEL; & BELL, JOHN A. **The effects of strategy-monitoring training on children's selection of effective memory strategies.** Journal of Experimental Child Psychology, 1983, **35**, 263–277.
Second-grade children were given training in general principles of strategy monitoring. Even though both experimental and placebo control groups could assess when they remembered better, more experimental than control children attributed performance differences to their strategic behavior and then selected the more effective strategy on a forced-choice trial.—From Authors' Abstract.

177. LORD, CATHERINE (Glenrose Hosp., 10230–11 Ave., Edmonton, Alberta, Canada), & LEIMBACH, MICHAEL P. **A longitudinal study of form-function relations in a mother's questions and her child's responses.** Developmental Psychology, 1983, **19**, 585–590.

A longitudinal study of a mother's questions to her daughter from infancy to early preschool age showed that the number of questions accounted for by statistically reliable form-function pairings was significantly greater in the early stages of the child's language acquisition than in later stages. During the 1-word stage and early Stage 1 the child was more likely to produce a correct verbal response to questions within semantic form-function pairings.—From Authors' Abstract.

178. LUND, ARNOLD M. (Bell Laboratories, Crawford Corner, Holmdel, NJ); HALL, JAMES W.; WILSON, KIM P.; & HUMPHREYS, MICHAEL S. **Frequency judgment accuracy as a function of age and school achievement (learning disabled versus non-learning-disabled) patterns.** Journal of Experimental Child Psychology, 1983, **35**, 236–247.
In Experiment 1, children with normal achievement in grades 2 and 3 were compared with such children in grades K and 5 as well as with 3 groups of low-achieving children in grades 2 and 3. Frequency judgment accuracy increased from kindergarten to grades 2 and 3. Experiment 2 confirmed both the above age difference and the absence of any frequency judgment deficiency on the part of the low-achieving groups.—From Authors' Abstract.

179. McCALL, ROBERT B. (Boys Town Ctr., Boys Town, NE). **Environmental effects on intelligence: the forgotten realm of discontinuous nonshared within-family factors.** Child Development, 1983, **54**, 408–415.
Environmental variation that occurs within families but is not shared by siblings—nonshared within-family environmental variation—is a major influence on general mental performance and has largely been ignored. Such factors may account for 15%-25% of all variability in IQ and 30%-50% of environmental variability in IQ.—From Author's Abstract.

180. McDONALD, GERALDINE (New Zealand Council for Educational Research). **Bierwisch's analysis as a test of the SFH.** Journal of Child Language, 1983, **10**, 167–186.
Four-year-olds were tested for word recognition of the spatial adjectives following Bierwisch's componential analysis. Results supported the view that word meaning is learned in bits, but they failed to support any other predictions based on the Semantic Feature Hypothesis.—From Author's Abstract.

181. McGHEE, PAUL E. (Texas Tech Univ.), & LLOYD, SALLY. **Behavioral characteristics associated with the development of humor in young children.** Journal of Genetic Psychology, 1982, **141**, 253–259.
The frequency of laughter and both behavioral and verbal attempts to initiate humor were observed during spontaneous free-play sessions at a preschool. Amount of time spent in social play accounted for the greatest amount of variance in the amount of laughter and humor initiation shown.—From Authors' Abstract.

182. McGINNIS, MARRY (Univ. of Southern California, Los Angeles). **Social language: toward fluency and flexibility.** Volta Review, 1983, **85**, 101–115.

183. MacKAIN, KRISTINE S. (Cornell Univ. Medical Coll.). **Assessing the role of experience on infants' speech discrimination.** Journal of Child Language, 1982, **9**, 527–542.
This paper argues that phonetic input cannot be specified and experience cannot be defined in this context without knowing how infants perceptually structure speech input. Consequently, the discrimination paradigm provides no test for the effect of experience on infants' speech discrimination. The conditions to be met in order to conclude an effect of experience are outlined.—From Author's Abstract.

184. McLESKEY, JAMES (Indiana Univ.). **Effects of verbal and written labeling on selective attention of mildly retarded children.** Perceptual and Motor Skills, 1982, **55**, 579–585.
Verbal and written labels were observed to influence retarded and normal children 9–13 years old to locate an object quicker, look at it longer, and recognize more of the treatment objects on a recognition-memory task.—Adapted from Author's Abstract.

185. MacWHINNEY, BRIAN (Carnegie–Mellon Univ.). **Miniature linguistic systems as tests of the use of universal operating principles in second-language learning by children and adults.** Journal of Psycholinguistic Research, 1983, **12**, 467–478.
This study examined 4 universal operating principles for first-language acquisition proposed by Slobin and MacWhinney. The results suggested that the principles played a major role in the learning of the system by 5–7-year-olds but not by adults. Modifications were made in the standard miniature linguistic system technique in order to maximize linguistic naturalness and referentiality. The result was a complex system that could still be taught even to 5-year-olds in the space of a few hours.—From Author's Abstract.

186. MADDEN, DAVID J. (Duke Univ. Medical Ctr.). **Aging and distraction by highly familiar stimuli during visual search.** Developmental Psychology, 1983, **19**, 499–507.
On days 1–4, 10 younger and 10 older adults performed a search task. Performance on a search task 5 days later was disrupted when these familiar stimuli appeared as noise items in the displays, as compared with trials on which only new, unpracticed stimuli were used. The magnitude of the distraction was equivalent for the 2 age groups. Age differences in day-5 search performance did increase as more items in the stimulus display required inspection.—From Author's Abstract.

187. MALONE, MARY JO (Memphis State Univ.), & GUY, REBECCA F. **A comparison of mothers' and fathers' speech to their 3-year-old sons.** Journal of Psycholinguistic Research, 1982, **11**, 599–608.
Ten-minute mother-son and father-son conversations were recorded in the home during a free-play session. Mothers and fathers used a similar number of utterances in conversing with their sons. Fathers' communication was viewed as more controlling and involving the child less, while mothers' communication was viewed as more child-centered and involving the child more.—From Authors' Abstract.

188. MARCON, REBECCA A., & COON, ROBERT C. (Louisiana State Univ.). **Communication styles of bilingual preschoolers in preferred and nonpreferred languages.** Journal of Genetic Psychology, 1983, **142**, 189–202.
Language samples of 31 bilingual preschoolers were transcribed from conversations with a puppet. When young children were able to speak in the language in which they are spoken to, they usually did.—From Authors' Abstract.

189. MASUR, ELISE FRANK (Northern Illinois Univ.). **Gestural development, dual-directional signaling, and the transition to words.** Journal of Psycholinguistic Research, 1983, **12**, 93–109.
This paper describes the emergence and development of pointing, extending objects, and open-handed reaching from 9 to 18 months and the accompanying acquisition of conventional words. Dual-directional signaling sending simultaneously 2 coordinated but divergently directed nonverbal signals of gesture and gaze appeared concurrently across gestures. Verbal accompaniments appeared with gestures only when the children had mastered dual-directional signaling.—From Author's Abstract.

190. MAURER, DAPHNE (McMaster Univ., Hamilton, Ontario, Canada). **The scanning of compound figures by young infants.** Journal of Experimental Child Psychology, 1983, **35**, 437–448.
Compound stimuli (either squares or a schematic face) were presented with features inside a frame, the frame alone, and the features alone. Newborns and 1-month-olds looked at the small square when it was presented alone, but rarely looked at it when it was framed by the larger square. In contrast, 2-month-olds looked at the small square for long periods whether or not it was framed. However, when newborns and 1-month-olds were shown a schematic face, they looked at its internal features at least half the time.—From Author's Abstract.

191. MEACHAM, JOHN A. (SUNY, Buffalo), & KELLER, ANN. **The role of remembering in planning dependent sequences of action.** Journal of Genetic Psychology, 1983, **143,** 39–44.
A task calling for sequencing of choices was administered to 4-, 7-, and 10-year-olds. Performance was better in a facilitation-of-remembering condition than in a remembering (control) condition, but only for 4-year-olds, indicating that the failure to remember alternatives, rather than a lack of other cognitive abilities, may be a major obstacle in preschoolers' development of planning abilities.—From Authors' Abstract.

192. MELTZOFF, ANDREW N. (Univ. of Washington), & MOORE, M. KEITH. **Newborn infants imitate adult facial gestures.** Child Development, 1983, **54,** 702–709.
Infants up to 71 hours old imitated adult mouth opening and tongue protrusion.—From Authors' Abstract.

193. MENDELSON, MORTON J. (McGill Univ., Montreal, Quebec, Canada). **Attentional inertia at four and seven months.** Child Development, 1983, **54,** 677–685.
No evidence of attentional inertia (the conceptual obverse of habituation) was found in these infants.—Adapted from Author's Abstract.

194. MICHAELS, SARAH (Harvard Graduate School.). **The role of adult assistance in children's acquisition of literate discourse strategies.** Volta Review, 1983, **85,** 72–86.

195. MILLER, C. L. (Univ. of Western Ontario, Canada); YOUNGER, B. A.; & MORSE, P. A. **The categorization of male and female voices in infancy.** Infant Behavior and Development, 1982, **5,** 143–159.
At 7 months, infants were able to discriminate male and female voices. Pitch of voice partially explained the voice classification.—From Abstract by S. Thomas.

196. MILLER, JOANNE L. (Northeastern Univ.), & EIMAS, PETER D. **Studies on the categorization of speech by infants.** Cognition, 1983, **13,** 135–165.
Complexities exist in the mapping between the acoustic information in the speech signal and the phonetic categories of adult language users. We investigated whether the same complexities exist in the mapping between the speech signal and the forerunners of these categories in infants. For 2 classes of complexity, the manner in which the categorization of information for speech occurs was identical in infant and adult listeners.—From Authors' Abstract.

197. MOERK, ERNST L. (California State Univ.). **A behavioral analysis of controversial topics in first language acquisition: reinforcements, corrections, modeling, input frequencies, and the three-term contingency pattern.** Journal of Psycholinguistic Research, 1983, **12,** 129–155.
Brown's transcripts of the interactions of Adam and Eve with their mothers were analyzed. Thirty-nine teaching techniques of the mothers and 37 learning strategies of the children were differentiated. The teaching techniques included conditioned positive reinforcement, obvious linguistic corrections, conditioned punishment, several forms of less obvious corrections, and various forms of modeling.—From Author's Abstract.

198. MOORE, DeWAYNE (Clemson Univ.), & RIEMER, BARBARA S. **Relationship between achievement judgments and cognitive maturity.** Journal of Genetic Psychology, 1982, **141,** 197–201.
First and third graders evaluated the achievement behavior or hypothetical others and completed 4 cognitive tasks. Effort, ability, and outcome were influential determinants for both age groups, and even preoperational children used effort and outcome to evaluate the performance of others.—From Authors' Abstract.

199. MORAN, JAMES D., III (Virginia Polytechnic Inst. and State Univ.); MILGRAM, ROBERTA M.; SAWYERS, JANET K.; & FU, VICTORIA R. **Original thinking in preschool children.** Child Development, 1983, **54,** 921–926.

Original thinking in preschoolers was shown to be distinct from intelligence. Quantity of ideational output was related to its originality. A stronger order effect (popular responses occurring earlier and original responses later in the response sequence) was evidenced for high than for low original subjects.—From Authors' Abstract.

200. MORRISON, FREDERICK J. (Univ. of Minnesota), & LORD, CATHERINE. **Age differences in recall of categorized material: organization or retrieval?** Journal of Genetic Psychology, 1982, **141**, 233–241.
Adults and 5- and 8-year-olds were tested for recall of 15 pictures from 3 categories under 4 different conditions. The pattern of findings suggested that retrieval operations were relatively more important in accounting for age differences in recall of categorical material than organization at presentation.—From Authors' Abstract.

201. MORRISON, HELEN, & KUHN, DEANNA (Teachers Coll., Columbia Univ.). **Cognitive aspects of preschoolers' peer imitation in a play situation.** Child Development, 1983, **54**, 1054–1063.
Preschool children were observed playing in small groups with a construction set. Attention to others' activity increased with age. Subjects who showed stable gains in performance level across sessions engaged in more observation of others' activity than did subjects who showed only temporary gains, who in turn engaged in more observation of others' activity than did subjects who showed no gains.—From Authors' Abstract.

202. MORRONGIELLO, B. A.; CLIFTON, R. K. (Univ. of Massachusetts); & KULIG, J. W. **Newborn cardiac and behavioral orienting responses to sound under varying precedence-effect conditions.** Infant Behavior and Development, 1982, **5**, 249–259.
Infants correctly turned to sound from a single loudspeaker but did not turn to any of the precedence-effect stimuli.—S. Thomas.

203. MORSS, J. R. (Ulster Polytechnic, England). **Cognitive development in the Down's syndrome infant: slow or different?** British Journal of Educational Psychology, 1983, **53**, 40–47.
A longitudinal investigation of object permanence development in 8 Down's syndrome (DS) infants and 26 normals was performed. DS infants manifested delayed achievement of all steps in the sequence. DS infants were less likely than normals to repeat an achieved success. DS development is different as well as slow.—Adapted from Author's Abstract.

204. MOSS, S. C. (Hester Adrian Research Ctr., Univ. of Manchester, England), & HOGG, J. **The development and integration of fine motor sequences in 12- to 18-month-old children: a test of the modular theory of motor skill acquisition.** Genetic Psychology Monographs, 1983, **107**, 145–187.
Experiment 1 was a longitudinal study of 6 children from 12 to 20 months old using manipulative tasks. Experiment 2 was a cross-sectional study of performance consistence in rod placement ($N=30$). Consistence decreased as proficiency increased. These results did not fit well with the idea that skills are acquired with modules organized into "subroutines."—Adapted from Authors' Abstract.

205. MURRAY, FRANK B. (Univ. of Delaware), & HOLM, JANET. **The absence of lag in conservation of discontinuous and continuous materials.** Journal of Genetic Psychology, 1982, **141**, 213–217.
Children in grades K-2 were given conservation of length, substance, and weight tasks with continuous and discontinuous quantities. No differences were found in conservation between continuous or discontinuous materials. The usual horizontal décalage appeared.—From Authors' Abstract.

206. NELSON, CHARLES A. (Purdue Univ.), & HOROWITZ, FRANCES DEGEN. **The perception of facial expressions and stimulus motion by two- and five-month-old infants using holographic stimuli.** Child Development, 1983, **54**, 868–877.

Five-month-olds were asked to discriminate a change in facial expression and pose in a holographic stereogram that either moved or remained stationary. The experimental group did not show evidence of discrimination. Two-month-olds succeeded in discriminating the change in expression/pose. When the contributions of motion to face were explored in 5-month-old infants, there was strong evidence that motion contrasts facilitate face recognition.—From Authors' Abstract.

207. NEWCOMBE, NORA (Temple Univ.), & BANDURA, MARY M. **Effect of age at puberty on spatial ability in girls: a question of mechanism.** Developmental Psychology, 1983, **19**, 215–224.
Eighty-five 11-year-old girls' data showed (a) spatial ability positively correlated with later maturation; (b) spatial ability positively correlated with masculine personality traits, masculine intellectual interests in the ideal self, and wanting to be a boy; (c) earlier maturation positively correlated with femininity and negatively correlated with participation in 22 spatial activities; and (d) performance on the dichaptic task was not correlated with either timing of puberty or spatial ability. Psychosocial factors may account for the interaction rate's relation to spatial skills.—From Authors' Abstract.

208. NICHOLLS, JOHN G. (Purdue Univ.), & MILLER, ARDEN T. **The differentiation of the concepts of difficulty and ability.** Child Development, 1983, **54**, 951–959.
At the least differentiated level, "hard" is equivalent to "hard for me." At the second level, children recognize continua of objective difficulty and recognize that more objectively difficult tasks demand more ability. Only at the normative difficulty level is difficulty judged independently of the subjective experience of difficulty and the concepts of difficulty and ability clearly differentiated.—From Authors' Abstract.

209. OLLER, D. K. (Univ. of Miami), & EILERS, R. E. **Similarity of babbling in Spanish- and English-learning babies.** Journal of Child Language, 1982, **9**, 565–577.
The babbling of Spanish- and English-learning 12-month-olds was recorded. Babies from both groups produced predominantly CV syllables with voiceless, unaspirated plosive consonants. Vowel production was also perceived as notably alike. Possible differences in babbling of the 2 groups may be hard for even sophisticated listeners to notice.—From Authors' Abstract.

210. OLSEN-FULERO, LYNDA (Antioch Coll.). **Style and stability in mother conversational behaviour: a study of individual differences.** Journal of Child Language, 1982, **9**, 543–564.
An analysis of the functionally coded speech of mothers showed statistically significant variability among mothers, especially in those behaviors most closely associated with intention. Further, mothers showed stability in these behavior patterns across 2 sessions. A typology of mother style, based on the intentions of mothers to direct or converse with their children, is suggested and illustrated by individual cases.—From Author's Abstract.

211. OLSON, MYRNA R. (Univ. of North Dakota). **A study of the exploratory behavior of legally blind and sighted preschoolers.** Exceptional Children, 1983, **50**, 130–137.
Each child was videotaped interacting with a novel toy and a commercial toy for the purpose of looking for initiative-aggressiveness, interest, mode of examination, sensory utilization, assistance needed to solve each toy, and verbalizations during exploration and about the "solution" of each toy.—From Author's Abstract.

212. OWENS, HENRY M., & HOGAN, JOHN D. (St. John's Univ.). **Development of humor in children: roles of incongruity, resolution, and operational thinking.** Psychological Reports, 1983, **53**, 477–478.
The responses of children in grades 1–3 to various jokes and cartoons revealed that the comprehension of humorous material was related to grade and conservation ability, but neither of these variables related to the appreciation of humor.—From Authors' Abstract.

213. PAULSEN, KAREN (Univ. of Arizona), & ARIZMENDI, THOMAS. **Matching Familiar Figures Test norms based on IQ.** Perceptual and Motor Skills, 1982, **55**, 1022.
Results for 8-year-olds showed IQ to be significantly correlated with both latency and errors.—Adapted from the Article.

214. PAYNE, M. CARR, JR. (Georgia Inst. of Technology), & HOLZMAN, THOMAS G. **Auditory short-term memory and digit span: normal versus poor readers.** Journal of Educational Psychology, 1983, **75**, 424–430.
College students performed better when the first pattern was auditory than when it was visual or tactual, but no relationship was found for either college or fifth-grade students between digit span and comparing patterns of tones. Both tasks discriminated between normal and poor comprehension scores on a standardized test.—From Authors' Abstract.

215. PAYNE, V. GREGORY (California State Polytechnic Univ.). **Current status of research on object reception as a function of ball size.** Perceptual and Motor Skills, 1982 **55**, 953–954.
Possible bases for discrepancies in studies of catching a ball are outlined.—Adapted from Author's Abstract.

216. PEA, ROY D. (Clark Univ.). **Origins of verbal logic: spontaneous denials by two- and three-year-olds.** Journal of Child Language, 1982, **9**, 597–626.
Children 2–3 years of age spontaneously correct false statements and affirm true ones in a modified sentence verification paradigm. Such performances imply that very young children display knowledge of the rules of correspondence between language and reality (truth conditions) which are central to propositional logic.—From Author's Abstract.

217. PEISACH, ESTELLE, & HARDEMAN, MILDRED (CUNY, Queens Coll.). **Moral reasoning in early childhood: lying and stealing.** Journal of Genetic Psychology, 1983, **142** 107–120.
First graders' responses to questions designed to elicit their reasons for not lying and stealing were analyzed in terms of Kohlberg's stage theory. Only about 20% of the responses fell into Stage 1. Very few of the responses were in Stage 2. Approximately 3/4 of the responses were in Stage 3. A distinction was made between stereotypic and nonstereotypic Stage 3 responses. Approximately 40% of Stage 3 responses were nonstereotypic.—From Authors' Abstract.

218. PELLEGRINI, ANTHONY D. (Univ. of Georgia). **Facilitating class-inclusion skills in school-age children.** Journal of Genetic Psychology, 1983, **143**, 29–37.
Children in grades 1, 2, 4, and 5 were asked to describe and note similarities and/or differences between subordinate classes. On previously examined classes, boys performed better than girls, older better than younger, and children exposed to descriptive, similarities, and difference questions better than children exposed to either descriptive and similarities or descriptive and difference questions. For unexamined classes, the young children transferred paradigm variants best, whereas older children transferred the total paradigm best.—From Author's Abstract.

219. PENMAN, ROBYN (Univ. of Melbourne, Australia); CROSS, TONI MILGROM-FRIEDMAN, JEANNETTE; & MEARES, RUSSELL. **Mothers' speech to prelingual infants: a pragmatic analysis.** Journal of Child Language, 1983, **10**, 17–34.
Mother-infant dyads were recorded during free play at 3 and 6 months. Regardless of infant age, mothers were found to modify their speech style as a function of infant behavior. Speech style also was found to change from 3 to 6 months. Affect-oriented speech was more sensitive to infant behavior than informative speech.—Adapted from Authors' Abstract.

220. PERNER, JOSEF (Univ. of Sussex, Brighton, England), & MANSBRIDGE, DAVID G. **Developmental differences in encoding length series.** Child Development, 1983, **54** 710–719.

For 6–7-year-olds, interlinked pairs were much more difficult to retain than unrelated pairs, whereas the opposite held true for college students. The linguistic form of questions and the number of different lengths of sticks were varied, but the same results were obtained.—From Authors' Abstract.

221. PETERSON, LIZETTE (Univ. of Missouri, Columbia). **Understanding of ratioproportionality rules and equality vs equity in children's sharing.** Journal of Genetic Psychology, 1983, **142**, 239–244.
Preschoolers and children in first and sixth grades played a game that assessed the use of ratioproportionality rules, thought to be a precursor to equity allocations. Although both ratioproportionality ability and the tendency to allocate in response to equity rather than equality or selfishness increased with age, these abilities were not correlated within age groups.—From Author's Abstract.

222. PEZDEK, KATHY (Claremont Graduate School, Calaremont, CA), & HARTMAN, EILEEN F. **Children's television viewing: attention and comprehension of auditory versus visual information.** Child Development, 1983, **54**, 1015–1023.
Children 5 years old effectively distributed their attention such that they could process auditory and visual information from television while performing other activities. The children were sensitive to which segments required visual attention and which did not, and they were able to spontaneously adjust their pattern of visual attention appropriately.—From Authors' Abstract.

223. PIERSEL, WAYNE C. (Univ. of Nebraska), & SANTOS, LANDE. **Comparison of McCarthy and Goodenough-Harris scoring systems for kindergarten children's human figure drawings.** Perceptual and Motor Skills, 1982, **55**, 633–634.
Substantial agreement between the 2 scoring systems was observed. The McCarthy scoring system should be used when large numbers of children are being evaluated within short time periods.—Adapted from Authors' Abstract.

224. PIOTROWSKI, CHRIS (Univ. of West Florida). **Factor structure on the semantic differential as a function of method of analysis.** Educational and Psychological Measurement, 1983, **43**, 283–288.
Fifth-grade pupils were administered a test packet which contained a locus of control measure, the HURRICANE, MY CITY, and MYSELF semantic differentials rated on the same 19 scales. The method of analysis revealed the relative unimportance of the Evaluation dimension, but the other dimensions were viewed as important.—Adapted from the Article.

225. PONZO, E., & ERCOLANI, A. P. (Univ. of Rome, Italy). **Lo stereotipo di sottovalutazione delle capacità infantili. Un modo per diminuirlo** [A way to reduce the stereotyped underestimation of abilities in two-five years old children]. Età Evolutiva, 1983, **15**, 56–64.
When noninformed persons were asked by means of a standard questionnaire at which age children are able to perform items of a developmental test, most persons showed a tendency to overestimate the age at which 2–5-year-olds are able to perform.—Adapted from Authors' Abstract.

226. PRATT, MICHAEL W. (Children's Health Council, 700 Willow, Palo Alto), & WICKENS, GARTH. **Checking it out: cognitive style, context, and problem type in children's monitoring of text comprehension.** Journal of Educational Psychology, 1983, **75**, 716–726.
In Experiment 1, reflective kindergarten and second-grade listeners were generally more effective detectors of referentially ambiguous terms in brief texts than were their impulsive agemates. Perceptual context facilitated ambiguity detection as well. Subsequent replication attempts gave mixed results. A manipulation of motivation to comprehend was not effective.—Adapted from Authors' Abstract.

227. PRESSLEY, MICHAEL (Univ. of Western Ontario, London, Ontario, Canada), & MacFADYEN, JANET. **Mnemonic mediator retrieval at testing by preschool and kindergarten children.** Child Development, 1983, **54**, 474–479.

Mnemonic + retrieval subjects were provided interactive pictures of paired items and were instructed at testing to retrieve the mediators. At the preschool level, mnemonic + retrieval subjects remembered more paired associations than subjects in the other 2 conditions. The recall of kindergarten mnemonic + retrieval and mnemonic subjects did not differ significantly.—From Authors' Abstract.

228. RABINOWITZ, F. MICHAEL (Memorial Univ. of Newfoundland, St. John's, Newfoundland, Canada). **Cross-modal transfer and intermediate-size transposition.** Journal of Experimental Child Psychology, 1983, **35**, 223–235.
Kindergarten and third-grade boys learned an intermediate-size problem either visually or tactually. They were then tested either visually or tactually. The test sets were separated from the training set by either 1, 2, or 4 steps. There were markedly different transposition gradients exhibited by the boys in the visual–visual and visual–tactual groups.—From Author's Abstract.

229. REGARD, MARIANNE (Univ. Hosp., Zurich, Switzerland); STRAUSS, ESTHER; & KNAPP, PAUL. **Children's production on verbal and non-verbal fluency tasks.** Perceptual and Motor Skills, 1982, **55**, 839–844.
Children 6–13 years old were given verbal and and nonverbal fluency tasks and the Vocabulary and Block Design subtests of the WISC-R. The fluency tasks were age but not sex dependent and were only modestly correlated to each another and to standard measures of intelligence.—From Authors' Abstract.

230. RESNICK, DAVID A. (Columbia Univ.). **A developmental study of proverb comprehension.** Journal of Psycholinguistic Research, 1982, **11**, 521–538.
Proverbs of 2 structural types were administered to students in grades 3–7. ANOVA yielded main effects for grade, tasks, and proverbs. Proverb structure had no measurable impact on difficulty. The sequential order of abilities received only weak confirmation, though tasks did correlate among themselves with medium strength.—From Author's Abstract.

231. ROBERTS, KENNETH (Univ. of Kansas). **Comprehension and production of word order in Stage I.** Child Development, 1983, **54**, 443–449.
Early Stage I children comprehended the sentences in these verb contexts. Late Stage I children comprehended word order in the context of all test verbs.—From Author's Abstract.

232. ROBERTS, RALPH J., JR. (Univ. of Denver), & PATTERSON, CHARLOTTE J. **Perspective taking and referential communication: the question of correspondence reconsidered.** Child Development, 1983, **54**, 1005–1014.
Children 4–6 years old were tested on separate measures of perspective-taking and communication skill. The ability to appreciate a listener's informational needs was strongly related to referential communication performance.—From Authors' Abstract.

233. ROBINSON, E. J., & ROBINSON, W. P. (Univ. of Bristol, 35 Berkeley Sq., Bristol, England). **Children's uncertainty about the interpretation of ambiguous messages.** Journal of Experimental Child Psychology, 1983, **36**, 81–96.
Awareness of uncertainty when making an interpretation may not be necessary for the development of understanding ambiguity.—From Authors' Abstract.

234. ROBINSON, E. J. (Univ. of Bristol, England), & ROBINSON, W. P. **Knowing when you don't know enough: children's judgments about ambiguous information.** Cognition, 1982, **12**, 267–280.
In Experiment 1, children judged whether they had been told/shown enough to identify which 1 of a set of cards the experimenter had chosen. In 1 game, the experimenter gave verbal messages about her chosen cards, and in a second game, she gave visual messages. No difference was found between verbal and visual conditions. In Experiment 2, children judged in 1 game whether they had been told enough about the experimenter's chosen card. In a second game, the child judged whether a window showed enough to tell which card a pointer indi-

cated. Again, correct judgments about ambiguity occurred with the same frequency in both games.—From Authors' Abstract.

235. ROCISSANO, LORRAINE (New York Univ.), & YATCHMINK, YVETTE. **Language skill and interactive patterns in prematurely born toddlers.** Child Development, 1983, **54,** 1229–1241.
Interactions between prematurely born toddlers and their mothers were described. The children could be divided into 2 linguistic groups. Children in the Hi group used word combinations productively and talked about relations between objects and events. Children in the Lo language group produced few word combinations and were limited in the relations they talked about. The Lo language pairs did not share common topics as frequently as the Hi pairs. No single style was used by Lo language dyads in breaking joint attention.—From Authors' Abstract.

236. ROEMER, DANIELLE (Purdue Univ.). **Children's verbal folklore.** Volta Review, 1983, **85,** 55–71.

237. ROSE, SUSAN A. (Albert Einstein Coll. of Medicine). **Differential rates of visual information processing in full-term and preterm infants.** Child Development, 1983, **54,** 1189–1198.

238. ROSE, SUSAN A. (Albert Einstein Coll. of Medicine); GOTTFRIED, ALLEN W.; & BRIDGER, WAGNER H. **Infants' cross-modal transfer from solid objects to their graphic representations.** Child Development, 1983, **54,** 686–694.
Twelve-month-olds showed recognition memory on 3 visual intramodal problems but showed cross-modal transfer only when objects were used as test stimuli. With increased familiarization times, transfer from tactually presented samples to both pictorial displays was achieved. With reduced familiarization times, there was no evidence for transfer from visually presented samples to the 2 pictorial displays.—From Authors' Abstract.

239. ROSENBLUM, TAMAR, & PINKER, STEVEN A. (Massachusetts Inst. of Technology). **Word magic revisited: monolingual and bilingual children's understanding of the word–object relationship.** Child Development, 1983, **54,** 773–780.
Preschool children were asked whether various objects could be renamed and then were asked to identify objects by nonsense names and names for other objects. Neither bilingual nor monolingual children was necessarily subject to "word magic." Rather, monolinguals had learned that an object can have more than 1 name by virtue of its various attributes, whereas bilingual children had learned, in addition, that an object can have more than 1 name by virtue of the different social contexts in which its name is used.—From Authors' Abstract.

240. ROSSER, ROSEMARY A. (Univ. of Arizona). **The emergence of spatial perspective taking: an information-processing alternative to egocentrism.** Child Development, 1983, **54,** 660–668.
Children ages 4–18 were administered 4 visual perspective-taking tasks. Of the 4 task types, type A tasks necessitated awareness of possible variations in external relations, types B and C tasks required both awareness and computation of changes in those external relationships, and type D tasks required simultaneous coordination of internal and external spatial relationships. As predicted, the order of task difficulty was A<B, B=C, and C<D.—From Author's Abstract.

241. ROTH, CHRISTOPHER (Univ. of Pittsburgh). **Factors affecting developmental changes in the speed of processing.** Journal of Experimental Child Psychology, 1983, **35,** 509–528.
Strategies used by subjects and their domain knowledge were independently assessed by a number of tasks. Processing rate measures were obtained for a task in which domain knowledge was manipulated independently of age while controlling for strategy usage. The usual

adult superiority in speed of processing could be markedly reduced if children possessed equivalent amounts of domain knowledge and this effect was domain specific. Differences in knowledge affected processing rates in both knowledgeable adults and children and to about the same extent.—From Author's Abstract.

242. RUMAIN, BARBARA (New York Univ.); CONNELL, JEFFREY; & BRAINE, MARTIN D. S. **Conversational comprehension processes are responsible for reasoning fallacies in children as well as adults: if is not the biconditional.** Developmental Psychology, 1983, **19,** 471–481.
Ten-year-olds and adults were given conditional reasoning problems. Some of these had a major premise consisting of a single *if-then* sentence. Some had a more elaborate major premise in which invited inferences were countermanded. In another study, subjects were adults and 7- and 10-year-olds who saw premises varying in complexity. All age groups committed the fallacies in the simple condition but not in the more complex condition.—From Authors' Abstract.

243. RUSSAC, R. J. (Univ. of North Florida). **Early discrimination among small object collections.** Journal of Experimental Child Psychology, 1983, **36,** 124–138.
Children 2–4 years old were reinforced for choosing either a 2- or 3-item array when length–density cues were manipulated across 2 training phases. Most 2-year-olds were able to learn the discrimination while at the same time displaying little quantitative ability. Their transfer responses were transpositional in nature.—From Author's Abstract.

244. RUSSELL, JAMES (Univ. of Liverpool, England). **Facilitation of children's allocentric placement by reducing task complexity and providing a verbal rule.** Journal of Genetic Psychology, 1982, **141,** 203–212.
Children 5–6 years old were given an allocentric placement task, similar to Piaget's but with reduced stimulus complexity and with instructions cleared of ambiguities. Only 25% of the total sample was successful without training, but verbal rule provision resulted in 55% posttest gain in 5-year-olds and 25% in 6-year-olds.—From Author's Abstract.

245. SALING, MICHAEL (Univ. of Witwatersrand, South Africa), & BONERT, RENEE. **Lateral cradling preferences in female preschoolers.** Journal of Genetic Psychology, 1983, **142,** 149–150.

246. SCHAIE, K. WARNER (Pennsylvania State Univ.), & HERTZOG, CHRISTOPHER. **Fourteen-year cohort-sequential analyses of adult intellectual development.** Developmental Psychology, 1983, **19,** 531–543.
This report provides a comprehensive analysis of data on 5 primary mental abilities for 2 14-year longitudinal sequences. Comparable data are also reported on cross-sectional sequences. Decline in adult intelligence becomes clearly evident after age 60, with from a 1/3 to a 1/2 standard deviation decrement over a 14-year-period.—From Authors' Abstract.

247. SCHER, ANAT (Univ. of Calgary, Canada). **The axis feature: illusionary effects on children's judgments of length.** Perceptual and Motor Skills, 1982, **55,** 720–722.
Five-year-olds described the on-axis line as longer than the off-axis line. The presence of this illusion supports the context model of visual anomalies.—From Author's Abstract.

248. SCHMIDT, CONSTANCE R. (Virginia Polytechnic Inst. and State Univ.), & PARIS, SCOTT G. **Children's use of successive clues to generate and monitor inferences.** Child Development, 1983, **54,** 742–759.
Children 5–10 years of age listened to short stories and answered questions about presented and implied information. Performance on inference questions improved with age and with the number of clues provided. Older children generated a greater variety of inferences and monitored those inferences more effectively than younger children. Older children apparently integrated clue information to derive inferences, but young children tended to treat clues as isolated sources of information.—From Authors' Abstract.

249. SCHUEPFER, THERESE (State Univ. Coll., Oswego), & GHOLSON, BARRY. **From response-set to prediction hypotheses: rule acquisition among preschoolers and second graders.** Journal of Experimental Child Psychology, 1983, **36**, 18–31.
Preschool and second-grade children exhibited response patterns that corresponded to hypotheses in most of their probes. Children who did not achieve criterion failed because they exhibited mostly position hypotheses and/or because the strength of win–stay object remained weak throughout all sessions.—From Authors' Abstract.

250. SCHWARTZ, RICHARD G. (Purdue Univ.), & TERRELL, BRENDA Y. **The role of input frequency in lexical acquisition.** Journal of Child Language, 1983, **10**, 57–64.
Children were presented with contrived lexical concepts involving a nonsense word and 4 referents. The children named more frequently presented exemplars than infrequently presented exemplars. With number of presentations held constant, distributed presentation led to greater acquisition than massed presentation.—From Authors' Abstract.

251. SHIPLEY, ELIZABETH F. (Univ. of Pennsylvania), & KUHN, IVY F. **A constraint on comparisons: equally detailed alternatives.** Journal of Experimental Child Psychology, 1983, **35**, 195–222.
It is hypothesized that alternative classes are erroneously formed subject to the constraint that the same kinds of properties are criterial for each alternative. This hypothesis is tested in 3 experiments with hierarchically organized stimuli and requests to compare a superordinate class and a nonincluded subclass. In all 3 experiments, 4-year-olds' comparisons were found to be in accord with the hypothesis. In the first experiment, both perceptual and linguistic factors determined which classes were compared. In the second experiment, erroneous subclass comparisons were more common when all subclasses were distinguished by the same kinds of properties. In the third experiment, when the children were asked to partition the stimulus objects into the classes to be compared, the vast majority of partitions were erroneous.—From Authors' Abstract.

252. SHWALB, DAVID W. (Univ. of Michigan), & IMAIZUMI, NOBUTO. **College-educated fathers' view of their impact on school-age children: Japan and the United States.** Hiroshima Forum for Psychology, 1981, **8**, 59–67.
American fathers claimed to share responsibility with their spouses for most of the children's activities, while Japanese fathers' role was largely limited to that of authority figures and weekend leisure-time companions. The American fathers spent more time with and felt they had more impact on their children than did the Japanese fathers.—From Authors' Abstract.

253. SIMPSON, GREG B. (Univ. of Nebraska, Omaha), & LORSBACH, THOMAS C. **The development of automatic and conscious components of contextual facilitation.** Child Development, 1983, **54**, 760–772.
The patterns of response latencies indicated that, for the youngest children, the facilitation for stimuli presented in a related context was attributable to an automatic activation process. The use of a second component, the conscious allocation of attention, increased with age.—From Authors' Abstract.

254. SLOATE, PHYLLIS L. (CUNY), & VOYAT, GILBERT. **Language and imitation in development.** Journal of Psycholinguistic Research, 1983, **12**, 199–222.
The authors reviewed the problem of imitation from both cognitive developmental and psychoanalytic perspectives. They have specifically delineated Piagetian views regarding the origins of imitation and traced its relationship to the emergence of language, while attempting to clarify various psychoanalytic formulations on this topic. This dual theoretical perspective is then reconsidered within the framework of the current empirical infancy literature.—From Authors' Abstract.

255. SLOBIN, DAN I. (Univ. of California, Davis), & BEVER, THOMAS G. **Children use canonical sentence schemas: a crosslinguistic study of word order and inflections.** Cognition, 1982, **12**, 229–265.
The results show that children fail to respond systematically to sequences that violate the canonical sentence form of their particular language. They develop distinct word-order and inflectional strategies appropriate to the regularities of their language. The early behavioral emergence of linguistically appropriate canonical sentences and processing strategies suggests a behavioral foundation for linguistic constraints on the surface form of sentences.—From Authors' Abstract.

256. SMITH, LINDA B. (Indiana Univ.). **Development of classification: the use of similarity and dimensional relations.** Journal of Experimental Child Psychology, 1983, **36**, 150–178.
Preschoolers and kindergartners classified sets of multidimensional stimuli that could be organized into categories by overall similarity or by dimensional attributes. Preschoolers in particular showed marked difficulty in using similarity to form categories of more than 2 objects. The developmental changes appeared to be in the ability to execute a classification.—From Author's Abstract.

257. SOMERVILLE, SUSAN C.; WELLMAN, HENRY M. (Ctr. for Human Growth and Development, 300 N. Ingalls Bldg., Ann Arbor); & CULTICE, JOAN C. **Young children's deliberate reminding.** Journal of Genetic Psychology, 1983, **143**, 87–96.
Mothers were instructed to present deliberate reminding tasks to their 2–4-year-olds. Unprompted deliberate reminding of high-interest tasks was frequent, both for 5-min and 4–8-hour delays. Two-year-olds remembered such tasks 80% of the time.—From Authors' Abstract.

258. SOMMER, ROBERT (Univ. of California, Davis), & SOMMER, BARBARA A. **Mystery in Milwaukee: early intervention, IQ, and psychology textbooks.** American Psychologist, 1983, **38**, 982–985.
Textbooks in developmental psychology and abnormal psychology were examined for references to the Milwaukee study of the effects of early intervention on intelligence. The study is a cautionary example of how research data can appear in textbooks in 2 major areas of psychology and seep into the research literature without ever having gone through the journal review process.—From Authors' Abstract.

259. SONNENSCHEIN, SUSAN (Univ. of Maryland, Baltimore County), & WHITEHURST, GROVER J. **Training referential communication skills: the limits of success.** Journal of Experimental Child Psychology, 1983, **35**, 426–436.
Five-year-olds received either speaker training, listener training, or both speaker and listener training. Children were tested for transfer on speaking and listening tasks after a 1-week-delay. The results suggest that although speaking and listening tasks appear to require, at least in part, certain of the same skills, preschoolers do not exhibit spontaneous intermodality transfer.—From Authors' Abstract.

260. SOPHIAN, CATHERINE (Carnegie–Mellon Univ.), & WELLMAN, HENRY M. **Selective information use and perseveration behavior of infants and young children.** Journal of Experimental Child Psychology, 1983, **35**, 369–390.
The first experiment tested 9- and 6-month-olds' use of information from previous experiences with an object (prior information) and from the most recent hiding (current information) to locate a hidden object. In the second experiment, 2-, 2 1/2-, and 4-year-olds received these same sources of information along with new forms of prior and current information: information about the typical locations of objects (location specificity) and verbal information. No systematic perseveration was observed at 9 months.—From Authors' Abstract.

261. STANKOV, LAZAR (Univ. of Sydney, New South Wales, Australia). **Attention and Intelligence.** Journal of Educational Psychology, 1983, **75**, 471–490.

This article reviews empirical evidence that attention and intelligence are related at the empirical level.—From Author's Abstract.

262. STARKEY, PRENTICE (Univ. of Pennsylvania); SPELKE, ELIZABETH S.; & GELMAN, ROCHEL. **Detection of intermodal numerical correspondences by human infants.** Science, 1983, **222,** 179–181.
Infants prefer to look at an array of objects that corresponds in number to a sequence of sounds, indicating that infants possess a mechanism that enables them to obtain information about number.—From Authors' Abstract.

263. STERN, D. N. (Cornell Univ. Medical Ctr.); SPIEKER, S.; BARNETT, R. K.; & MacKAIN, K. **The prosody of maternal speech: infant age and context related changes.** Journal of Child Language, 1983, **10,** 1–15.
Mothers' speech to neonates was characterized by elongated pauses. At 4 months, the extent of pitch contouring and repetitiveness was greater than at earlier or later ages. By 24 months, the vocalizations and MLU became longer.—Adapted from Authors' Abstract.

264. STERNBERG, LES (Florida Atlantic Univ.); WALDRON, PAMELA; & MILLER, TED L. **Cognitive tempo and cognitive level relationships among mentally retarded children.** Perceptual and Motor Skills, 1982, **55,** 463–470.
Among moderately retarded junior high children, elements of cognitive level predicted elements of cognitive tempo, but not the reverse.—Ed.

265. SUGARMAN, SUSAN (Princeton Univ.). **Developmental change in early representational intelligence: evidence from spatial classification strategies and related verbal expressions.** Cognitive Psychology, 1982, **14,** 419–449.
Children spontaneously manipulated 2-class arrays and participated in 2 experimental probes of object groupings. Children 1–2 years of age grouped classes by looking for 1 kind of thing at a time, and they verbally marked single classes. Children 2 1/2–3 years old employed spatial grouping procedures that required simultaneous consideration of 2 classes, and they referred to relations between classes.—From Author's Abstract.

266. SUNSERI, ANITA B. (314 Valley View, San Jose). **Intellectual deficiencies in left-handers: a review of the research.** Perceptual and Motor Skills, 1982, **55,** 235–238.
Deficits in left-handers have not been demonstrated.—Ed.

267. SURBER, JOHN R. (Univ. of Wisconsin, Milwaukee), & SURBER, COLLEEN F. **Effects of inference on memory for prose.** Merrill-Palmer Quarterly, 1983, **29,** 197–207.
In Experiment 1, adjunct questions were used to manipulate the probability that children in grades K and 2 would make inferences during comprehension. The results showed that adjunct inference questions did not facilitate later memory for explicit information. Experiment 2 was an investigation of the relative influence of memory for details, memory for explicit information, and age on memory for inferences. The results showed that memory for explicit information was the best predictor of memory for inferences, and when memory for explicit information was partialled out, neither age nor memory for details contributed significantly to memory for inferences.—From Authors' Abstract.

268. SVENSON, OLA (Univ. of Stockholm, Sweden), & SJÖBERG, KIT. **Speeds of subitizing and counting processes in different age groups.** Journal of Genetic Psychology, 1983, **142,** 203–211.
Subitizing and counting were studied in 88 subjects ages 7–15 and adults. The subjects were asked in individual sessions to report the number of dots exposed on a screen as fast as possible. The speeds of the 2 processes of subitizing (immediate apprehension of the number of stimuli) and counting increased with age.—From Authors' Abstract.

269. SWANSON, H. L. (Univ. of Northern Colorado). **Relations among metamemory, rehearsal activity and word recall of learning disabled and non-disabled readers.** British Journal of Educational Psychology, 1983, **53**, 186–194.
Readers 8–10 years free-recalled unrelated word lists of 3 different levels of rehearsal activity. Prior to recall they estimated their ability, while retrieval knowledge was assessed after recall. Older children free-recalled more words than younger, and nondisabled more than disabled. Learning-disabled and nondisabled readers were comparable in their initial estimates of recall; however, skill of memory appraisal was unrelated to learning-disabled readers' recall accuracy.—From Author's Abstract.

270. TAN, LESLEY E. (Inst. of Early Child Development, Victoria, Australia). **Laterality and directional preferences in preschool children.** Perceptual and Motor Skills, 1982, **55**, 863–870.
For simple line drawings, both right and left handers preferred outward movements. For the tracing task, both groups exhibited directional preference for the right hand only.—Adapted from Author's Abstract.

271. TANZ, CHRISTINE (Univ. of Arizona). **Asking children to ask: an experimental investigation of the pragmatics of relayed questions.** Journal of Child Language, 1983, **10**, 187–194.
The results confirm the hypothesis that if children do not know the information, they relay the question, i.e., *ask*. If they do know the answer, they supply it, i.e., *tell*. By literally asking, the children in the "don't know" condition demonstrate that they are capable of decoding *ask* constructions semantically and syntactically. The tendency of the children in the "know" condition to *tell* is then interpreted as revealing not semantic confusion but pragmatic skill.—From Author's Abstract.

272. TFOUNI, LEDA VERDIANI (Univ. of California, Santa Barbara), & KLATZKY, ROBERTA L. **A discourse analysis of deixis: pragmatic, cognitive and semantic factors in the comprehension of "this," "that," "here" and "there."** Journal of Child Language, 1983, **10**, 123–133.
Children were asked as to the comprehension of the deictic words. Comprehension was better when the child was the addressee rather than just a spectator. Comprehension with a pointing gesture accompanying the utterance was better than when the gesture was absent. *This* and *here* were more difficult to comprehend than *that* and *there*.—Adapted from Authors' Abstract.

273. TIZARD, B. (Thomas Coran Research Unit, London, England); HUGHES, M.; CARMICHAEL, H.; & PINKERTON, G. **Language and social class: is verbal deprivation a myth?** Journal of Child Psychology and Psychiatry, 1983, **24**, 533–542.
There were social class differences in frequency of complex usages of language, but almost all the usages appeared in the talk of almost all the mothers and children at least once.—From Authors' Abstract.

274. TOWNSEND, MICHAEL A. R. (Univ. of Auckland, New Zealand). **Schema shifting: children's cognitive monitoring of the prose-schema interaction in comprehension.** Journal of Experimental Child Psychology, 1983, **36**, 139–149.
Facility in shifting between familiar schemata in a listening comprehension task was examined in children in grades 3 and 6 (ages 8 and 11 years, respectively). Younger children had more difficulty than the older children, although children at both grade levels demonstrated deficiencies in cognitive monitoring of the prose–schema interaction.—From Author's Abstract.

275. TOYOTA, HIROSHI (Osaka Univ. of Education, Japan). **Effects of sentence context on memory attributes in children.** Psychological Reports, 1983, **52**, 243–246.
Second and sixth graders learned a word list in either word or sentence presentation. For second graders, the semantic attribute was dominant in the sentence presentation only, while for sixth graders the semantic attribute was dominant in both presentations.—From Author's Abstract.

276. TREIMAN, REBECCA (Indiana Univ.), & BREAUX, ANNA MARIE. **Common phoneme and overall similarity relations among spoken syllables: their use by children and adults.** Journal of Psycholinguistic Research, 1982, **11,** 569–598.
The classification of syllables and the memory confusions among syllables by preliterate children and college students. Results suggest that overall similarity relations are primary for preliterate children, while common phoneme relations are primary for adults. Children's limited use of common phoneme relations is not confined to tasks that require explicit judgments about language.—From Authors' Abstract.

277. TRUHON, STEPHEN A. (Valparaiso Univ.). **Playfulness, play, and creativity: a path analytic model.** Journal of Genetic Psychology, 1983, **143,** 19–28.
Thirty kindergartners played for 10 min and were then given creativity tests. Observers rated their play on the Playfulness Scale. Cluster analysis resulted in 6 clusters: playfulness-intelligence, playfulness-fun, shifts, complexity, verbal creativity, and nonverbal creativity. Results suggest that there are 2 parts to the Playfulness Scale: the cognitive and affect aspects.—From Author's Abstract.

278. TUNMER, WILLIAM E. (Univ. of Western Australia, Nedlands, Western Australia); NESDALE, ANDREW R.; & PRATT, CHRIS. **The development of young children's awareness of logical inconsistencies.** Journal of Experimental Child Psychology, 1983, **36,** 97–108.
Children were asked to judge the acceptability of stories and were asked to justify their responses. By age 7, most children were quite capable of evaluating sentences for their logical consistency. However, 5-year-olds did not perform as well on the task, especially when the information upon which the logical cohesiveness of the stories rested was implicitly, rather than explicitly, stated.—From Authors' Abstract.

279. UDWIN, ORLEE (Univ. of London, Inst. of Psychiatry, De Crespigny Park, Denmark Hill, London, England), & YULE, WILLIAM. **A comparison of performance on the Reynell Developmental Language Scales with the results of syntactical analysis of speech samples.** Child: Care, Health and Development, 1982, **8,** 337–343.
The Reynell Expressive Language Scale was found to be a valid and meaningful measure of executive syntactical competence in language-disordered and normal children. The Reynell Comprehension Scale correlated significantly with the syntactical measures in the group of normal speakers but not in the group of language-disordered children.—From Authors' Abstract.

280. UDWIN, ORLEE (Univ. of London, Inst. of Psychiatry, De Crespigny Park, Denmark Hill, London, England), & YULE, WILLIAM. **Validation data on Lowe and Costello's Symbolic Play Test.** Child: Care, Health and Development, 1982, **8,** 361–366.
The Symbolic Play Test was assessed by comparing the performance of preschoolers on this test with the levels of imaginative play manifested during periods of free play, and by comparing the test scores of normal speakers and children diagnosed as exhibiting developmental language disorder. Correlations emerged between the test scores and ratings of imaginativeness in free play.—From Authors' Abstract.

281. UNGERER, JUDY A. (Univ. of California School of Medicine, Los Angeles), & SIGMAN, MARIAN. **Developmental lags in preterm infants from one to three years of age.** Child Development, 1983, **54,** 1217–1228.
Clear effects of biological maturity on play and sensorimotor skills were demonstrated at 13 1/2 months, and less pervasive effects remained at 22 months. The preterm infants were significantly delayed in sensorimotor, personal-social, and gross motor abilities at 13 1/2 months and in language abilities at 22 months beyond that predicted by biological maturity alone. While these deficits were mostly overcome by 3 years, the preterm infants performed somewhat more poorly on visual information-processing tasks.—From Authors' Abstract.

282. VAN DER MOLEN, H. H.; VAN DEN HERIK, J.; & VAN DER KLAAUW, C. (Univ. of Groningen, Netherlands). **Pedestrian behaviour of children and accompanying parents during school journeys: an evaluation of a training programme.** British Journal of Educational Psychology, 1983, **53**, 152–168.
Video observations of the road-crossing behavior of 63 preschool children and their parents before and after training showed that: (1) parents gave better examples and more verbal instruction after training, and (2) the children displayed trained behaviors more frequently.—From Authors' Abstract.

283. VAN KLEECK, ANNE (Univ. of Texas, Austin), & STREET, RICHARD. **Does reticence mean just talking less? Qualitative differences in the language of talkative and reticent preschoolers.** Journal of Psycholinguistic Research, 1982, **11**, 609–629.
The spontaneous language produced by children who varied in degree of talkativeness was studied. Analysis of structural complexity and discourse features showed differences between talkative and reticent children. While the structural complexity of the adults' language was not influenced by child talkativeness, several discourse parameters did reveal significant adjustments.—Adapted from Authors' Abstract.

284. VON HOFSTEN, C. (Univ. of Uppsala, Sweden), & LINDHAGEN, K. **Perception of visual occlusion in 4 1/2-month-old infants.** Infant Behavior and Development, 1982, **5**, 215–226.
A habituation-dishabituation paradigm was used to assess infant reactions to changed and unchanged objects after occlusion. Results indicated that infants were able to predict reappearance of an object.—From Authors' Abstract.

285. WALES, ROGER (Univ. of Melbourne, Parkville, Victoria, Australia); COLMAN, MICHELLE; & PATTISON, PHILIPPA. **How a thing is called—a study of mothers' and children's naming.** Journal of Experimental Child Psychology, 1983, **36**, 1–17.
Mothers named objects for their 2-year-olds, their 4-year-olds, and the experimenter. Contextual factors were found to have a primary role in determining mothers' selections of category names.—From Authors' Abstract.

286. WARREN-LEUBECKER, AMYE, & BOHANNON, JOHN NEIL, III (Georgia Inst. of Technology). **The effects of verbal feedback and listener type on the speech of preschool children.** Journal of Experimental Child Psychology, 1983, **35**, 540–548.
The present study simultaneously assessed the relative contributions of feedback indicative of comprehension and the apparent age of the listener, either an adult or a doll which resembled a toddler. The doll was constructed with an internal speaker such that it could actually carry on a conversation with the children. All children appropriately modified the length of their utterances in the doll condition but not in the adult condition. Older children were more likely than younger children, and girls more likely than boys, to adjust the length of their utterances appropriately to each type of feedback, slightly increasing the length of the subsequent utterance to a comprehension signal and decreasing the length to a noncomprehension signal. The younger children were also more likely to respond with a simple repetition to noncomprehension cues from the adult.—From Authors' Abstract.

287. WATERS, HARRIET SALATAS (SUNY, Stony Brook), & LOMENICK, TERRI. **Levels of organization in descriptive passages: production, comprehension, and recall.** Journal of Experimental Child Psychology, 1983, **35**, 391–408.
Thirty descriptive passages generated by adults from prompt word outlines that defined familiar topics were used to develop a 7-point scale of increasing organization in descriptive passages. Developmental data were collected on the relationships between levels of organization and recall in subjects who generated their own passages and in subjects who listened to passages generated by others. Recall was correlated with organization in both generate and listen conditions in adults. Recall was only correlated with organization in the generate condition in sixth graders and was not correlated with recall in either condition in third graders.—From Authors' Abstract.

288. WATSON, MALCOLM W. (Brandeis Univ.), & AMGOTT-KWAN, TERRY. **Transitions in children's understanding of parental roles.** Developmental Psychology, 1983, **19,** 659–666.
Children 3–7 1/2 years were tested with structured doll play for a predicted sequence of parental role concepts. The sequence was scalable. By 7 years, most children could explain how 2 family role relationships could occur simultaneously for the same person.—From Authors' Abstract.

289. WEIST, RICHARD M. (SUNY). **Prefix versus suffix information processing in the comprehension of tense and aspect.** Journal of Child Language, 1983, **10,** 85–96.
Children 2–4 years old were given a picture-sentence matching task. Aspect picture sets contrasted completed with incompleted situations, and sentences contrasted perfective with imperfective verbs differing by a prefix or a suffix. Tense picture sets portrayed ongoing vs. anticipated action or results of action vs. anticipated action contrasts. Again, sentences differed in verb forms either by prefixes or suffixes. The children paid attention to the beginnings of words as easily as to the ends of words and understood a wide range of aspect and tense distinctions.—From Author's Abstract.

290. WEIST, RICHARD M. (SUNY). **The word order myth.** Journal of Child Language, 1983, **10,** 97–106.
Children 2–4 years acted out sentences with toys. Context sentences established given information that was in initial or final position in the target sentences. When inflectional information was available, all the children used it effectively with very little interference from OVS and new-given arrangements. Children also used word order to recover semantic functions with uninflected sentence problems.—From Author's Abstract.

291. WENTWORTH, NAOMI, & WITRYOL, SAM L. (Univ. of Connecticut). **Is variety the better part of novelty?** Journal of Genetic Psychology, 1983, **142,** 3–15.
Ten fifth graders were given 2-choice preference tests designed to separate the effects of variety from those of novelty in determining children's material reward choices. Variety and novelty contributed independent variance.—From Authors' Abstract.

292. WHITE, HEDY (Univ. of California, Los Angeles). **Comprehending surface and deep structure subjects: children's understanding of implied vs. explicitly stated nouns.** Journal of Child Language, 1983, **10,** 195–202.
Two experiments compared kindergartners' interpretations of 1- and 2-noun sentences. With 2-noun sentences (i.e., *John is easy for Jim to please*), which explicitly stated the surface object, consistency in choosing the surface subject decreased.—From Author's Abstract.

293. WHITNEY, PAUL, & KUNEN, SETH (Univ. of New Orleans). **Development of hierarchical conceptual relationships in children's semantic memories.** Journal of Experimental Child Psychology, 1983, **35,** 278–293.
Children ages 5–9 answered either semantic or sensory questions about a list of words composed of either superordinate terms, prototypical category instances, or moderately typical instances. In a later unanticipated cued recall task the children were given taxonomically related cues composed of the 2 remaining word types not used in the orienting phase. The range of information contained in the 5-year-olds' conceptual hierarchies was considerably narrower than that of the 9-year-olds'. It was found that the object-sorting task overestimated, while the class-inclusion task underestimated, the extent to which conceptual information is hierarchically organized in 5-year-olds.—From Authors' Abstract.

294. WILKINSON, ALEX CHERRY (Univ. of Wisconsin); DeMARINIS, MARGARET; & RILEY, SUSAN J. **Developmental and individual differences in rapid remembering.** Child Development, 1983, **54,** 898–911.

Children 10–14 years old tried to identify and remember words presented visually with a backward mask. They also recalled freely or serially, recognized by making a rapid forced-choice response, or named words as they were presented. The same children had participated in a similar study 1 year earlier. Two sources of developmental and individual variation were naming and associative storage.—From Authors' Abstract.

295. WIMMER, HEINZ (Univ. of Salzburg, Germany), & PERNER, JOSEF. **Beliefs about beliefs: representation and constraining function of wrong beliefs in young children's understanding of deception.** Cognition, 1983, **13**, 103–128.
Subjects observed how a protagonist put an object into a location X and then witnessed that in the absence of the protagonist the object was transferred from X to location Y. Subjects had to indicate where the protagonist would look for the object upon his return. None of the 3–4-year-olds, 57% of the 4–6-year-olds, and 86% of the 6–9-year-olds pointed correctly to location X in both sketches. Subjects were also told about the protagonist's intention to either deceive an antagonist or truthfully inform a friend about the object's location. Independent of age, children who had correctly thought that the protagonist would search in X also correctly thought that he would direct his antagonist to location Y and his friend to location X. In a more story-like situation, another group of children had to infer a deceptive play from the depiction of a goal conflict between 2 story characters and 1 character's expedient utterance. Very few 4–5-year-olds correctly judged this utterance, while most 5–6-year-olds did so.—Adapted from the Article.

296. WITRYOL, SAM L. (Univ. of Connecticut), & WANICH, GLENN A. **Developmental invariance of novelty functions contrasted to age differences in the Moss-Harlow effect.** Journal of Genetic Psychology, 1983, **143**, 3–8.
When preschoolers' performance was compared to that of first and fifth graders, it was found that, for all grade levels, mean percent choice of the incentive object increased as a function of increasing novelty. This conclusion is at variance with results from discrimination-learning studies.—From Authors' Abstract.

297. WITRYOL, SAM L., & WENTWORTH, NAOMI (Univ. of Connecticut). **A paired comparisons scale of children's preferences for monetary and material rewards used in investigations of incentive effects.** Journal of Genetic Psychology, 1983, **142**, 17–23.
First-, third-, and fifth-grade children's preferences for 12 objects frequently employed as rewards were studied. Increases in both intraindividual consistency and interindividual agreement were obtained as a function of developmental level.—From Authors' Abstract.

298. WORDEN, PATRICIA (California State Univ., Fullerton), & SHERMAN-BROWN, SUSAN. **A word-frequency cohort effect in young versus elderly adults' memory for words.** Developmental Psychology, 1983, **19**, 521–530.
For old subjects, the feature of early high frequency promoted better recall (in the popular and dated lists) than did present-day high frequency. The results suggest the existence of a word-frequency cohort effect and that high-frequency words from one's youth are particularly memorable.—From Authors' Abstract.

299. YARROW, L. J. (NICHHD, Bethesda); MORGAN, G. A.; JENNINGS, K. D.; HARMON, R. J.; & GAITER, J. L. **Infants' persistence at tasks: relationships to cognitive functioning and early experience.** Infant Behavior and Development, 1982, **5**, 131–146.
A technique for measuring infants' persistence at tasks is described. Significant relationships were found between persistence at the mastery tasks and the Bayley MDI.—From Authors' Abstract.

300. YEATES, KEITH OWEN; MacPHEE, DAVID; CAMPBELL, FRANCES A.; & RAMEY, CRAIG T. (Frank Porter Graham Child Development Ctr., Chapel Hill). **Maternal IQ and home environment as determinants of early childhood intellectual competence: a developmental analysis.** Developmental Psychology, 1983, **19**, 731–739.

Children at risk for sociocultural mental retardation were studied longitudinally from birth to 4 years of age. Children's IQs and home environments were assessed at regular intervals during the first 4 years of life. The overall pattern suggested a monotonic increase in the predictability of child IQ within the context of a shift in the relative importance of maternal IQ and home environment as predictors.—From Authors' Abstract.

301. YOUNGER, BARBARA A., & COHEN, LESLIE B. (Univ. of Texas, Austin). **Infant perception of correlations among attributes.** Child Development, 1983, **54,** 858–867.
In a habituation-dishabituation paradigm, 10-month-old infants clearly responded on the basis of the correlation among attributes. In contrast, 4- and 7-month-olds responded primarily on the basis of specific featural information, but did not respond reliably to the correlation.—From Authors' Abstract.

302. ZIVIAN, MARILYN T. (Atkinson Coll., York Univ., Downsview, Ontario, Canada), & DARJES, RICHARD W. **Free recall by in-school and out-of-school adults: performance and metamemory.** Developmental Psychology, 1983, **19,** 513–520.
Forty women were asked to study and recall a randomly presented categorized word list and then to indicate the mnemonic strategies they had used. On almost all measures of recall, the 2 in-school groups were more similar to each other, and the 2 out-of-school groups were more similar to each other than were the 2 middle-aged groups.—From Authors' Abstract.

SOCIAL PSYCHOLOGICAL, CULTURAL, AND PERSONALITY STUDIES

303. AFFLECK, GLENN (Univ. of Connecticut School of Medicine); ALLEN, DEBORAH; McGRADE, BETTY JO; & McQUENNEY, MARIA. **Maternal and child characteristics associated with mothers' perceptions of their high risk/developmentally delayed infants.** Journal of Genetic Psychology, 1983, **142,** 171–180.
Mothers of 46 high-risk infants were visited at home at 9 months post expected date of delivery and took the Perception of Baby Temperament (PBT) scales, the Profile of Mood States, and an observation of infant, parent, and parent-infant behavior was made. Infants were most likely to receive higher PBT scores if their mothers were educated and reported lesser degrees of depression and anxiety. Mothers were more responsive to babies they saw as active.—From Authors' Abstract.

304. AINSLIE, RICARDO C. (Univ. of Texas, Austin); SOLYOM, ANTAL E.; & McMANUS, MICHAEL E. **On the infant's meaning for the parent: a study of four mother-daughter pairs.** Child Psychiatry and Human Development, 1982, **13,** 97–110.
Mother-daughter pairs were systematically followed from the third trimester of pregnancy through the first 8 months postpartum by semistructured interviews and by naturalistic observations in the hospital, home, and office. The psychological meaning of the pregnancy and fetus/infant appeared to have shaped the neonatal perceptions and early mother-infant relationships, and seemed to correlate with specific mothering behaviors.—From Authors' Abstract.

305. ALBERT, ALEXA A. (Univ. of Rhode Island), & PORTER, JUDITH R. **Age patterns in the development of children's gender-role stereotypes.** Sex Roles, 1983, **9,** 59–67.
In doll-play interviews, 4-year-olds were more reluctant than 5–6-year-olds to associate positive gender-role stereotypes with opposite-sex figures and to accept negative stereotypes as characteristic of their own sex.—Adapted from Authors' Abstract.

306. ASHTON, ELEANOR (Worcester State Coll.). **Measures of play behavior: the influence of sex-role stereotyped children's books.** Sex Roles, 1983, **9,** 43–47.
Preschool children played with sex-stereotyped and neutral toys. Each child was then read a sex-role stereotypic or nonstereotypic picture book. Another play session followed. Children chose toys that matched the stereotyping of the story they had heard.—Adapted from Author's Abstract.

307. AVERY, ARTHUR W. (Univ. of Arizona). **Escaping loneliness in adolescence: the case for androgyny.** Journal of Youth and Adolescence, 1982, **11,** 451–459.
Junior and senior high school students completed the Bem Sex Role Inventory Short Form and the UCLA Loneliness Scale. Androgynous individuals were significantly less lonely than masculine, feminine, and undifferentiated individuals. Both masculinity and femininity significantly predicted loneliness.—From Author's Abstract.

308. BELLINGER, DAVID C. (Children's Hosp. Medical Ctr., 300 Longwood, Boston), & GLEASON, JEAN BERKO. **Sex differences in parental directives to young children.** Sex Roles, 1982, **8,** 1123–1139.
In a construction task with preschoolers, fathers provided more directives and phrased them as imperatives or as highly indirect hints more often than mothers, who relied more on relatively transparent indirect forms. There were no differences in the form of the directives addressed to girls and boys, nor were there any cross-sex effects.—From Authors' Abstract.

309. BERNSTEIN, ROBERT M. (Worcester Youth Guidance Ctr.). **The relationship between developments in self- and peer perception during adolescence.** Journal of Genetic Psychology, 1983, **142,** 75–83.
The sample consisted of 80 15–18-year-old males. A structured interview was employed to obtain descriptions of self and a best friend. The study's hypothesis was supported: self-perception is more mature than peer perceptions.—Adapted from Author's Abstract.

310. BETTON, JENNIE PLOTT, & KOESTER, LYNNE SANFORD (Univ. of North Carolina, Greensboro). **The impact of twinship: observed and perceived differences in mothers and twins.** Child Study Journal, 1983, **13,** 85–93.
Thirty mothers of twins 3 months to 12 years participated. It was hypothesized that mothers would intervene less with 1 twin alone than with both twins. Support for this hypothesis as measured by a puzzle task was found. Mothers gave more positive feedback to the 1 twin alone.—Adapted from Authors' Abstract.

311. BLYTH, DALE A. (Ohio State Univ.); HILL, JOHN P.; & THIEL, KAREN SMITH. **Early adolescents' significant others: grade and gender differences in perceived relationships with familial and nonfamiliar adults and young people.** Journal of Youth and Adolescence, 1982, **11,** 425–450.
The Social Relations Questionnaire was administered to 3,000 seventh through tenth graders. Parents and siblings were almost always listed as significant others. The majority listed at least 1 extended family adult and 1 nonrelated adult as important in their lives. The nonrelated adults lived closer and were seen more frequently in more contexts than extended family members. Females listed more significant others than males.—From Authors' Abstract.

312. BOND, LYNNE A. (Univ. of Vermont), & DEMING, SARA. **Children's causal attributions for performance on sex-stereotypic tasks.** Sex Roles, 1982, **8,** 1197–1208.
Children in grades 3, 5, and 11 attributed males' and females' successes and failures on sex-stereotypic tasks to task difficulty, effort, luck, or skill. There were no age or sex differences. Effort was emphasized for sex-inconsistent tasks. Failures were treated as anticipated outcomes for females.—From Authors' Abstract.

313. BOTVIN, ELIZABETH M. (Teachers Coll., Columbia Univ.). **Developmental changes in attitudes toward cigarette smokers during early adolescence.** Psychological Reports, 1983, **53,** 547–553.
The findings suggest that there is a shift toward a more positive social image of cigarette smoking that is unrelated to the smoking status of friends.—From Author's Abstract.

314. BRADBARD, MARILYN R. (Auburn Univ.), & ENDSLEY, RICHARD C. **The effects of sex-typed labeling on preschool children's information-seeking and retention.** Sex Roles, 1983, **9,** 247–260.

Preschool children explored less frequently, asked fewer questions, and recalled the names of objects less frequently when the objects were labeled for the opposite sex than when they were labeled either for their own sex or for both sexes.—From Authors' Abstract.

315. BRITAIN, SUSAN D. (Union Coll.), & COKER, MARCIA. **Recall of sex-role appropriate and inappropriate models in children's songs.** Sex Roles, 1982, **8**, 931–934.
Children 6 years old listened to songs with male dominant/female subordinate, female dominant/male subordinate, or neutral lyrics. Children recalled more when the same-sex character was dominant. Boys liked males more than females. Both boys and girls wanted to be more like the subordinate than the dominant characters.—From Authors' Abstract.

316. BRODY, GENE H. (Univ. of Georgia); GRAZIANO, WILLIAM G.; & MUSSER, LYNN MATHER. **Familiarity and children's behavior in same-age and mixed-age peer groups.** Developmental Psychology, 1983, **19**, 568–576.
Previously unacquainted first- and third-grade children were assigned to same- and mixed-age triads, and their performance at a tower-building task was assessed. They then were assigned randomly to familiarization conditions. Some of the differences found between same-age and mixed-age interaction were decreased when older children became familiar with their younger teammates.—From Authors' Abstract.

317. BROOK, JUDITH S. (Mt. Sinai School of Medicine); WHITEMAN, MARTIN; GORDON, ANN SCOVELL; & BROOK, DAVID W. **Fathers and sons: their relationship and personality characteristics associated with the son's smoking behavior.** Journal of Genetic Psychology, 1983, **142**, 271–281.
A sample of 246 male adolescents and their fathers from intact homes was administered questionnaires. Each of the 3 domains was significantly associated with the son's tobacco use, and the effectiveness of the father may interact synergistically with or be mitigated by the son's personality attributes in its association with the son's tobacco use.—From Authors' Abstract.

318. BROWN, K. ELIOT, & KARNES, FRANCES A. (Univ. of Southern Mississippi). **Representative and non-representative items for gifted students on the Piers-Harris Children's Self-Concept Scale.** Psychological Reports, 1982, **51**, 787–790.
Gifted students had positive self-concepts while being relatively immune to external influences.—From Author's Abstract.

319. BULDAIN, ROGER W. (Michigan State Univ.); CRANO, WILLIAM D.; & WEGNER, DANIEL M. **Effects of age of actor and observer on the moral judgments of children.** Journal of Genetic Psychology, 1982, **141**, 261–270.
Three stories, which experimentally varied the age, intentions, and outcomes of 3 hypothetical children, were read to children in grades K, 3, and 6. The relationship between observer age and reliance on outcome information was inverse. Regardless of the age of observor, same-aged actors were judged more leniently than younger or older actors when destructive outcomes were produced with good intentions. There was leniency in judgments of younger actors who produced destructive acts with bad intentions.—Adapted from Authors' Abstract.

320. CALLAGHAN, CAROL (Univ. of Manchester, England), & MANSTEAD, A. S. R. **Causal attributions for task performance: the effects of performance outcome and sex of subject.** British Journal of Educational Psychology, 1983, **53**, 14–23.
Sixth-form grammar school students were allocated to 1 of 4 treatments produced by the factorial combination of manipulations of their performance (success or failure) on 2 successive anagram tasks. Self-reports of anxiety and performance expectations were obtained, and after each task subjects were asked to make attributions about the outcome. The results tended to support the predictions derived from the self-serving analysis.—From Authors' Abstract.

321. CANN, ARNIE (Univ. of North Carolina), & HAIGHT, JEANNE M. **Children's perceptions of relative competence in sex-typed occupations.** Sex Roles, 1983, **9**, 767–773.

Children have clear sex-typed expectations concerning occupational competence.—From Authors' Abstract.

322. CHRISTENSEN, ANDREW (Univ. of California, Los Angeles); PHILLIPS, SUSAN; GLASGOW, RUSSELL E.; & JOHNSON, STEVEN M. **Parental characteristics and interactional dysfunction in families with child behavior problems: a preliminary investigation.** Journal of Abnormal Child Psychology, 1983, **11**, 153–166.
Correlational analyses across problem and nonproblem families revealed a strong association between marital discord and the parental index of child behavior problems. Observational data indicated a significant relationship between parental perception of child behavior problems and parental negative behavior toward the child, but no significant relationship between parent perception of child behavior problems and child behavior, even when child behavior was weighted by parents' reactions to that behavior.—From Authors' Abstract.

323. COBB, NANCY J. (California State Univ., Los Angeles); STEVENS-LONG, JUDITH; & GOLDSTEIN, STEVEN. **The influence of televised models on toy preference in children.** Sex Roles, 1982, **8**, 1075–1080.
Preschoolers viewed videotapes in which characters labeled toys as masculine, feminine, or neutral. Afterward, children of both sexes spent more time playing with the same-sex toys than with control toys, but more time playing with control toys than other-sex toys.—Adapted from Authors' Abstract.

324. CÔTÉ, JAMES E., & LEVINE, CHARLES (Univ. of Western Ontario, London, Ontario, Canada). **Marcia and Erikson: the relationships among ego identity status, neuroticism, dogmatism, and purpose in life.** Journal of Youth and Adolescence, 1983, **12**, 43–53.
Implicit in Marcia's writings and derived studies is the assumption that 4 ego identity statuses are developmentally ordered. If one assumes that Erikson's perspective is valid, then the results of a construct-validity study fail to support Marcia's continuum assumption. Marcia's instrument may not assess Erikson's concept.—From Authors' Abstract.

325. COTTERELL, JOHN L. (Univ. of Queensland, Australia). **Student experiences following entry into secondary school.** Educational Research, 1982, **24**, 296–302.
Students displayed anxiety about the organizational aspects of school and the presence of older students. Anxiety about school work increased, while reports of interesting learning experiences declined.—From Author's Abstract.

326. COVELL, KATHERINE (Simon Fraser Univ., Canada), & TURNBULL, WILLIAM. **The long-term effects of father absence in childhood on male university students' sex-role identity ad personal adjustment.** Journal of Genetic Psychology, 1982, **141**, 271–276.
A questionnaire comprising biographic items, subsections of the California Personality Inventory, and Bem's Sex Role Inventory were completed by 89 father-absent and 84 father-present male university students. Differences were found only between father-absent males who had experienced the onset of father absence either before or after age 5 on self-esteem and self-confidence.—From Authors' Abstract.

327. CRAIN, WILLIAM C. (CUNY); E'ALESSIO, ESTERINA; McINTYRE, BRENDA; & SMOKE, LESLEE. **The impact of hearing a fairy tale on children's immediate behavior.** Journal of Genetic Psychology, 1983, **143**, 9–17.
As anticipated from Bettelheim's writing and informal observations, those who had heard the fairy tale subsequently played in the most subdued and self-absorbed manner.—From Authors' Abstract.

328. CRAWLEY, SUSAN B. (Univ. of Illinois, Chicago), & SPIKER, DONNA. **Mother-child interactions involving two-year-olds with Down syndrome: a look at individual differences.** Child Development, 1983, **54**, 1312–1323.

Ratings of maternal, child, and dyadic qualities in semistructured free-play interactions, as well as Bayley Mental Development Index (MDI) scores, were obtained. Social initiative, social responsivity, and play maturity of the children were correlated with MDI. Maternal stimulation value was the major maternal quality found to be positively correlated with child MDI. A dyadic rating of mutuality was also positively correlated with child MDI.—From Authors' Abstract.

329. CROCKENBERG, S. B. (Univ. of California, Davis), & SMITH, P. **Antecedents of mother-infant interaction and infant irritability in the first three months of life.** Infant Behavior and Development, 1982, **5,** 105–119.

Mothers and their newborn infants were observed at 1 and 3 months. Prenatal maternal questionnaires and neonatal behavioral assessments were administered. Observed irritability was associated with unresponsive maternal attitudes and behavior. Mothers were more responsive to female infants.—From Authors' Abstract.

330. DAY, DAN E., & ROBERTS, MARK W. (Idaho State Univ.). **An analysis of the physical punishment component of a parent training program.** Journal of Abnormal Child Psychology, 1983, **11,** 141–152.

The contribution of spanking to compliance in a clinic analog setting was evaluated. Time-out duration and child disruption at time-out release were balanced across spank and no-spank ("barrier") conditions. The data indicated that both spank and barrier procedures were equally effective at increasing compliance ratios.—From Authors' Abstract.

331. DE ANDA, DIANE (Univ. of California, Los Angeles). **Pregnancy in early and late adolescence.** Journal of Youth and Adolescence, 1983, **12,** 33–42.

The younger group had begun dating and particularly steady dating at a significantly earlier age than the older group, and they used birth control less often. Pregnancy created more dependence upon their mothers for younger adolescents.—From Author's Abstract.

332. DeMARSH, JOSEPH P., & ADAMS, GERALD R. (Utah State Univ.). **Development of social competencies: preschool influences upon perspective taking and listening skill development.** Child Study Journal, 1983, **13,** 75–84.

A highly structured, adult-directed preschool program was hypothesized to have positive influences upon affective/perceptual perspective-taking and listening skills. Only listening skill development was influenced.—From Authors' Abstract.

333. DeSTEFANO, C. T. (Syracuse Univ.), & MUELLER, E. **Environmental determinants of peer social activity in 18-month-old males.** Infant Behavior and Development, 1982, **5,** 175–183.

The effects of play materials on the social activity of 18-month-old male infants were examined. More desirable and undesirable social activities were observed when play equipment was absent. More positive interactions were present with large toys, while small toys fostered conflict.—Adapted from Authors' Abstract.

334. D'HONDT, WALTER, & VANDEWIELE, MICHEL (Univ. de Dakar, Senegal). **How Senegalese adolescents perceive traveling and adventure.** Perceptual and Motor Skills, 1982, **55,** 1019–1021.

Senegalese adolescents have a keen interest in traveling and adventure. They regard it as a means of initiation into a better, fuller social life within their society at large.—Adapted from Authors' Abstract.

335. DIAZ, RAFAEL M. (Univ. of New Mexico), & BERNDT, THOMAS J. **Children's knowledge of a best friend: fact or fancy?** Developmental Psychology, 1982, **18,** 787–794.

Fourth and eighth graders were questioned about a best friend. Eighth graders knew more than fourth graders about a friend's personality and preferences. Cognitive level, frequency of contact, and the duration of a friendship, but not age, predicted external knowledge.—From Authors' Abstract.

336. DIX, THEODORE (New York Univ.), & GRUSEC, JOAN E. **Parental influence techniques: an attributional analysis.** Child Development, 1983, **54**, 645–652.
Subjects 5 years old to adults made casual attributions for the helping of story characters and rated the extent to which these characters possessed an altruistic trait. Conditions of parental influence in the stories included power assertion, modeling, and reasoning. Power assertion produced external attributions and discounting of altruistic traits. Modeled and spontaneous helping produced internal attributions and stronger inferences about the presence of altruistic traits.—From Authors' Abstract.

337. DIX, THEODORE (SUNY, Stony Brook), & HERZBERGER, SHARON. **The role of logic and salience in the development of causal attribution.** Child Development, 1983, **54**, 960–967.
Children 6–10 years and adults made attributions for the behavior of story characters that either contrasted with or was congruent with the behavior of other characters. Children made logically complex person attributions earlier in development than simpler stimulus attributions.—From Authors' Abstract.

338. DOLLINGER, STEPHEN J. (Southern Illinois Univ., Carbondale), & McGUIRE, BETH **The development of psychological-mindedness: children's understanding of defense mechanisms.** Journal of Clinical Child Psychology, 1981, **10**, 117–121.
Children were presented with 7 stories illustrating defense mechanisms in make-believe peers. Children were asked to explain each story character's behavior and evaluate defensive characters for goodness, smartness, happiness, and likableness. Age trends reflected increasing defense understanding with age.—From Authors' Abstract.

339. DOWNS, A. CHRIS (Univ. of Houston, Clear Lake City). **Letters to Santa Claus: elementary school-age children's sex-typed toy preferences.** Sex Roles, 1983, **9**, 159–163.
Girls requested more toys than boys and were especially likely to request neutral toys, while boys were equally likely to request neutral or masculine-typed toys. Children preferred sex-appropriate to inappropriate toys.—From Author's Abstract.

340. DUBANOSKI, RICHARD A. (Univ. of Hawaii), & TOKIOKA, ABE B. **The effects of verbal pain stimuli on the behavior of children.** Social Behavior and Personality, 1981, **9**, 159–162.
Verbal pain or nonpain stimuli, contingent or noncontingent on a target response, within an aggressive or nonaggressive setting, and delayed with or without affect were presented to third and fourth graders. The pain stimuli had both a reinforcing and an instigating effect on the behavior of boys. For girls, the pain stimuli served a reinforcing function but had a tendency to inhibit overall responding. When the stimuli were delivered in an affective manner, it facilitated the responding more than did a nonaffective presentation.—From Authors' Abstract.

341. DUNN, JUDY (Univ. of Cambridge, Madingley, Cambridge, England). **Sibling relationships in early childhood.** Child Development, 1983, **54**, 787–811.
This review considers recent evidence on the nature of sibling interaction from observational studies of preschool children and the developmental implications of this evidence. Sibling influence is most plausibly associated with the reciprocal features of the relationship and with sociocognitive development. "Sibling status" variables, the focus of previous research, are not consistently related to the reciprocal but to the complementary features, which are probably of less developmental significance.—From Author's Abstract.

342. EISEN, MARVIN (Univ. of Texas); ZELLMAN, GAIL L.; LEIBOWITZ, ARLEEN; CHOW, WINSTON K.; & EVANS, JEROME R. **Factors discriminating pregnancy resolution decisions of unmarried adolescents.** Genetic Psychology Monographs, 1983, **108**, 69–95.
Discriminant function analysis of the decision to have an abortion or to deliver the child indicated that psychological, background, and economic variables each made significant contributions. A 4-item Abortion Approval Index, the women's perception of the prospective father

abortion opinion, personal knowledge of other unmarried teenagers who delivered, self-reported grade average, and receipt of state financial aid in the form of AFDC or Medicaid payments were the most powerful discriminators.—From Authors' Abstract.

343. EISENBERG, NANCY (Arizona State Univ.). **Children's differentiations among potential recipients of aid.** Child Development, 1983, **54,** 594–602.
The most important discriminations for both older and younger children were between family and friends vs. others and disliked individuals vs. others. The tendency to make differentiations based on the recipient's identity decreased with age, especially for distinctions involving disliked others and criminals. Children who verbalized higher level prosocial moral reasoning were somewhat less likely to differentiate among potential recipients of aid.—From Author's Abstract.

344. EISENBERG, NANCY (Arizona State Univ.); BARTLETT, KIM; & HAAKE, ROBERT. **The effects of nonverbal cues concerning possession of a toy on children's proprietary and sharing behaviors.** Journal of Genetic Psychology, 1983, **143,** 79–85.
Subjects in triads with a toy that (1) previously had been in no one's possession or (2) 1 of the 3 had possessed it. The children's sharing, defensive, and impinging behaviors were observed, and the subjects were interviewed. They did not view possession as ownership; they were incapable or unwilling to modify their behavior consistent with nonverbal cues regarding possession. Girls shared spontaneously or when asked more than boys.—From Authors' Abstract.

345. ERDWINS, CAROL J. (George Mason Univ.); TYER, ZITA E.; & MELLINGER, JEANNE C. **Achievement and affiliation needs of young adult and middle-aged women.** Journal of Genetic Psychology, 1982, **141,** 219–224.
Women in their forties and fifties expressed greater achievement motivation than women in their twenties with mature homemakers' achievement needs characterized by conformity and cooperation, while mature students expressed greater independence and self-reliance in their achievement strivings. Midlife students achieved higher grade point averages than did younger students. Affiliation needs were greater for mature women who remain in the traditional homemaker role in comparison to younger women.—From Authors' Abstract.

346. ESCHER-GRÄUB, D. (Univ. Regensburg, West Germany); MORATH, M.; & TODT, D. **Timing of visual interaction between infants and an approaching stranger.** Infant Behavior and Development, 1982, **5,** 203–207.
Videotapes of 10 stranger-infant interactions showed that infants changed duration of eye contact with strangers in a predictable manner. When the stranger crouched next to the infant, the infant gazed at the stranger at regular intervals.—S. Thomas.

347. FEINMAN, SAUL (Univ. of Wyoming), & LEWIS, MICHAEL. **Social referencing at ten months: a second-order effect on infants' responses to strangers.** Child Development, 1983, **54,** 878–887.
Ten-month-olds received positive or neutral nonverbal messages, or no message, about a stranger either directly from the mother when she spoke to the infant, or indirectly when the infant observed her speaking to the stranger. Infants were friendlier to the stranger when the mothers had spoken positively rather than neutrally, but only when the message had been provided directly to the infants.—From Authors' Abstract.

348. FINCH, A. J., JR. (Medical Univ. of South Carolina), & EASTMAN, EDWARD S. **A multimethod approach to measuring anger in children.** Journal of Psychology, 1983, **115,** 55–60.
Children in a psychiatric hospital served as subjects. Results indicated that there was a relationship between a child's self-report score obtained on the Children's Inventory of Anger and their behavior as perceived by peers at the time of admission to the hospital.—From Authors' Abstract.

349. FINE, MARK A.; MORELAND, JOHN R.; & SCHWEBEL, ANDREW I. (Ohio State Univ.). **Long-term effects of divorce on parent-child relationships.** Developmental Psychology, 1983, **19**, 703–713.
College psychology students with parents who divorced 7 or more years ago and students from continuously intact families completed self-report questionnaires. Subjects from divorced families perceived their relationships with their parents, especially their fathers, less positively. These potentially negative consequences were attenuated by healthy predivorce family life, a successful childhood adjustment before the divorce, and a higher quality relationship between the ex-spouses after divorce.—From Authors' Abstract.

350. FINKELSTEIN, NEAL W., & HASKINS, RON (Frank Porter Graham Child Development Ctr., Univ. of North Carolina, Chapel Hill). **Kindergarten children prefer same-color peers.** Child Development, 1983, **54**, 502–508.
As compared with a random model of selecting same-color peers for social interaction, both black and white children showed same-color preferences in their social behavior. This tendency was greater during recess than during classroom instruction and was greater in the spring than in the fall.—From Authors' Abstract.

351. FOX, CYNTHIA, & POPPLETON, PAM (Univ. of Sheffield, England). **Verbal and nonverbal communication in teaching: a study of trainee P.E. teachers in the gymnasium.** British Journal of Educational Psychology, 1983, **53**, 107–120.
Seventy-seven female student teachers at a specialist physical education college were observed during practice. Cluster analysis identified 4 stable lesson "styles" that could be ordered along a dimension of pupil involvement.—From Authors' Abstract.

352. FOX, JUDITH E., & HOUSTON, B. KENT (Univ. of Kansas). **Distinguishing between cognitive and somatic trait and state anxiety in children.** Journal of Personality and Social Psychology, 1983, **45**, 862–870.
The results indicated that reliable trait and state measures of cognitive and somatic anxiety were successfully developed. The trait measures of cognitive and somatic anxiety were found to be relatively impervious to induced anxiety states. Cognitive trait anxiety but not somatic trait or state anxiety was found to be related to task performance.—From Authors' Abstract.

353. FRANK, SUSAN (Illinois Inst. of Technology, Chicago); ATHEY, JANET; COULSTON, SUSAN; & PARSONS, MARY. **The relation of ego development to sex-stereotyping in caretakers' expectations for adolescents.** Journal of Youth and Adolescence, 1982, **11**, 461–477.
In comparison to their conformist counterparts, the postconformist counselors were expected to make more sex-stereotyped goals for disturbed adolescents; postconformist parents were expected to make less sex-stereotyped goals for undergraduates. Hypotheses were confirmed for counselors, but not parents.—From Authors' Abstract.

354. FRANKEL, MARC T., & ROLLINS, HOWARD A., JR. (Emory Univ.). **Does mother know best? Mothers and fathers interacting with preschool sons and daughters.** Developmental Psychology, 1983, **19**, 694–702.
Parents played with their child using a puzzle and taught the child to remember 24 picture cards in categories. Parents attempted to teach their sons more general strategies and were both more directive and more evaluative of sons than of daughters. Parents interacted with daughters in a more cooperative, concrete, and specific fashion.—From Authors' Abstract.

355. FRASER, B. J. (Western Australian Inst. of Technology), & FISHER, D. L. **Student achievement as a function of person-environment fit: a regression surface analysis.** British Journal of Educational Psychology, 1983, **53**, 89–99.
Achievement of junior high pupils on 9 affective and cognitive outcomes was related to interactions between actual and preferred classroom individualization. Actual–preferred interactions accounted for a significant increment in outcome variance beyond that attributable to corresponding pretest, general ability, and actual individualization.—From Authors' Abstract.

356. FREUD, ANNA (1895–1982). **Obituary.** Journal of Child Psychology and Psychiatry, 1983, **24**, 333–338.

357. FRIEDMAN, S. L. (National Inst. of Education, Washington); ZAHN-WAXLER, C.; & RADKE-YARROW, MARIAN. **Perceptions of cries of full-term and preterm infants.** Infant Behavior and Development, 1982, **5**, 161–173.
Mothers rated cries of healthy full-term, low-risk preterm, and medium-risk preterm neonates. Cries of medium-risk neonates were rated more negatively, but there was no consistent pattern of differences in rating between full-term and low-risk neonates.—S. Thomas.

358. FROMING, WILLIAM J. (Univ. of Florida); ALLEN, LETICIA; & UNDERWOOD, BILL. **Age and generosity reconsidered: cross-sectional and longitudinal evidence.** Child Development, 1983, **54**, 585–593.
Generosity has been assumed to increase in a simple linear fashion between the ages of 5 and 10. With data gathered both cross-sectionally and longitudinally, the existence of a nonlinear trend in addition to the linear trend is demonstrated.—From Authors' Abstract.

359. FU, VICTORIA R., & FOGEL, SUSAN W. (Virginia Polytechnic Inst. and State Univ.). **Prowhite/antiblack bias among southern preschool children.** Psychological Reports, 1982, **51**, 1003–1006.
Both black and white children demonstrated a white-positive/black-negative bias. The black children showed a preference for black but identified with it less intensely than did the white children with white.—From Authors' Abstract.

360. FU, VICTORIA R. (Virginia Polytechnic Inst. & State Univ.); HINKLE, DENNIS E.; & KORSLUND, MARY K. **A developmental study of ethnic self-concept among preadolescent girls.** Journal of Genetic Psychology, 1983, **142**, 67–73.
The present study explored the developmental changes in the self-concepts of 9–11-year-old girls from Euro-, Afro-, and Mexican-American backgrounds. The Euros had a higher self-concept than the Afros, and both of these groups had higher self-concepts than the Mexican-Americans. Also, 11-year-olds had a higher mean than both the 9- and 10-year-olds.—From Authors' Abstract.

361. FUNDER, DAVID C. (Harvard Univ.); BLOCK, JEANNE H.; & BLOCK, JACK. **Delay of gratification: some longitudinal personality correlates.** Journal of Personality and Social Psychology, 1983, **44**, 1198–1213.
Two brief laboratory tasks measuring delay of gratification in different ways were administered to 116 4-year-olds. Boys who delayed gratification tended to be independently and consistently described as deliberative, attentive and able to concentrate, reasonable, reserved, cooperative, and generally manifesting an ability to modulate motivational and emotional impulse. Boys who did not delay gratification, by contrast, were irritable, restless and fidgety, aggressive, and generally not self-controlled. Girls who delayed gratification were independently and consistently described as intelligent, resourceful, and competent. Girls who did not delay tended to go to pieces under stress, to be victimized by other children, and to be easily offended, sulky, and whiny.—From Authors' Abstract.

362. FURMAN, WYNDOL (Univ. of Denver), & BIERMAN, KAREN L. **Developmental changes in young children's conceptions of friendship.** Child Development, 1983, **54**, 549–556.
Common activities, affection, support, and propinquity were all found to be salient aspects of most children's conceptions. Friendship expectations concerning affection and support increased in frequency with age, while references to physical characteristics decreased.—From Authors' Abstract.

363. GABRAYS, JOHN B. (Mental Health Ctr., Chilliwack, British Columbia, Canada). **Contrasts in social behavior and personality of children.** Psychological Reports, 1983, **52,** 171–178.
Children from 9 to 16 years were given the Eysenck Personality Questionnaire-Junior. Prosocial children were low on Psychoticism, low on Neuroticism, and high on the Lie scale, while antisocial children scored high on Psychoticism, high on Neuroticism, and low on the Lie scale.—From Author's Abstract.

364. GALEJS, IRMA (Iowa State Univ.); DHAWAN, GITA; & KING, ALBERT. **Popularity and communication skills of preschool children.** Journal of Psychology, 1983, **115,** 89–95.
Ranked popularity was correlated with listening skills but not with ability to describe or with sex of the children; teachers perceived older children to be more popular than younger children.—From Authors' Abstract.

365. GALEJS, IRMA (Iowa State Univ.), & STOCKDALE, DAHLIA F. **Social competence, school behaviors, and cooperative–competitive preferences: assessments by parents, teachers, and school-age children.** Journal of Genetic Psychology, 1982, **141,** 243–252.
Children from grades 4–6 indicated their cooperative and competitive preferences. Parents and teachers completed standardized ratings of social behavior. Parents and teachers agreed in their ratings of children's behaviors at home and school. No relationships were found between children's social behaviors and cooperative–competitive preferences. Girls were rated as more achievement oriented, and boys as having significantly more negative school behaviors.—Adapted from Authors' Abstract.

366. GARRISON, STUART R., & STOLBERT, ARNOLD L. (Virginia Commonwealth Univ.). **Modification of anger in children by affective imagery training.** Journal of Abnormal Child Psychology, 1983, **11,** 115–130.
From a school population of normal third through fifth graders, 30 children initially identified as "angry" were randomly assigned to either an affective imagery training groups, an attention group, or a control group. Results suggested that, as a result of affective imagery training, angry children's perceptions and cognitions shifted from "angry" toward "sad," and there was a concomitant decrease in observed aggressive classroom behavior.—From Authors' Abstract.

367. GEIGER, KATHLEEN M., & TURIEL, ELLIOT (Univ. of California, Berkeley). **Disruptive school behavior and concepts of social convention in early adolescence.** Journal of Educational Psychology, 1983, **75,** 677–685.
Disruptive students ($N = 22$) and nondisruptive students ($N = 20$) were interviewed for concepts of social conventions. Disruptive subjects were reinterviewed 1 year later, and behavioral records were reassessed. Disruptive behavior was partially related to thinking characterized by rejection of conventional regulations. All subjects disruptive at Time 2 had not changed to the next level, whereas the majority of those no longer disruptive had shifted.—From Authors' Abstract.

368. GENTA, M. L.; COSTABILE, A.; & BERTACCHINI, P. A. **Aggressione, gioco e agonismo. Lo status sociale nei bambini della scuola materna** [Aggression, competition and play]. Età Evolutiva, 1983, **15,** 5–14.
Aggression and competition tend to result in a convergent index of dominance behaviors. Subjects were 5–6-year-olds.—Adapted from Authors' Abstract.

369. GERSHMAN, ELAINE S., & HAYES, DONALD S. (Univ. of Maine). **Differential stability of reciprocal friendships and unilateral relationships among preschool children.** Merrill-Palmer Quarterly, 1983, **29,** 169–177.
Preschoolers named and cited reasons for liking their 2 closest friends in an initial testing session and again in a 4–6-month follow-up. Mutual friendships were also verified through observation of free play in the classroom. One unilateral relationship remained constant across the 2 testing sessions; 2/3 of the reciprocal relationships remained stable.—From Authors' Abstract.

370.   GIBLIN, PAUL T. (Wayne State Univ.); BEZAIRE, MARY M.; & AGRONOW, SAMUEL J. **Affective investments of preschool children: positive responsivity.** Journal of Genetic Psychology, 1982, **141,** 183–195.
An observational checklist assessed in 30-sec segments the presence or absence of 55 behaviors in 11 dimensions of positive affective tone. With increasing age, affective expression was found to increase in incidence, duration, and appropriateness to task demands.—From Authors' Abstract.

371.   GJESME, TORGRIM (Univ. of Oslo, Norway). **Worry and emotionality components of test anxiety in relation to situational and personality determinants.** Psychological Reports, 1983, **52,** 267–280.
The influence of both cognitive and motivational factors on amount of worry and emotionality increased significantly as the perceived importance of the school activity increased.—From Author's Abstract.

372.   GLADSTEIN, GERALD A. (Univ. of Rochester). **Understanding empathy: integrating counseling, developmental, and social psychology perspectives.** Journal of Counseling Psychology, 1983, **30,** 467–482.
Reviews of the empathy and counseling/psychotherapy outcome literature have drawn different conclusions. Probably the primary reason for the confusion is that various theoretical models have been used in defining and measuring empathy. In an effort to gain additional insights regarding this confusion, an analysis of the social and developmental psychology literatures was made.—From Author's Abstract.

373.   GOLDMAN, JULIETTE D. G. (La Trobe Univ., Bundoora, Australia), & GOLDMAN, RONALD J. **Children's perceptions of parents and their roles: a cross-national study in Australia, England, North America, and Sweden.** Sex Roles, 1983, **9,** 791–812.
Within a broader project on children's sexual thinking, children ages 5–15 years were interviewed. Mother was seen by all children as predominantly concerned with domestic duties, care of children, and low-status occupations, while father was seen overwhelmingly in a leisure role, as occupier of high-status occupations, and playing authority-leadership roles within the family.—From Authors' Abstract.

374.   GOLDSTEIN, HARRIS S. (Rutgers Medical School). **Fathers' absence and cognitive development of 12- to 17-year-olds.** Psychological Reports, 1982, **51,** 843–848.
Significant differences between father-present and father-absent groups on the WISC and WRAT were almost entirely due to parental education and income and not the fathers' absence.—Adapted from Author's Abstract.

375.   GOLOMBOK, S. (Univ. of London, England); SPENCER, A.; & RUTTER, M. **Children in lesbian and single-parent households: psychosexual and psychiatric appraisal.** Journal of Child Psychology and Psychiatry, 1983, **24,** 551–572.
The 2 groups did not differ in terms of their gender identity, sex-role behavior, or sexual orientation, or on most measures of emotions, behavior, and relationships.—From Authors' Abstract.

376.   GORDON, BETTY NYE (Univ. of North Carolina, Chapel Hill). **Maternal perception of child temperament and observed mother-child interaction.** Child Psychiatry and Human Development, 1983, **13,** 153–167.
The results indicated that difficult and easy children did not behave differently with their mothers. Mothers did show behavioral differences as a function of their child's temperament classification. In addition, the children's behavior varied as a function of sex and temperament when level of maternal control was considered as a variable.—From Author's Abstract.

377.   GORDON, MICHAEL (SUNY Upstate Medical Ctr.), & TEGTMEYER, PAUL F. **The Egocentricity Index and self-esteem in children.** Perceptual and Motor Skills, 1982, **55,** 335–337.

Among nonpatient children 6–14 years old, the Egocentricity Index may be more related to an unconscious process of self-focus than to conscious feelings of self-worth.—Adapted from Authors' Abstract.

378. GRANTHAM-McGREGOR, SALLY (Univ. of the West Indies, MONA, Kingston 7, Jamaica); LANDMAN, JACQUELINE; & DESAI, PATRICIA. **Child rearing in poor urban Jamaica.** Child: Care, Health and Development, 1983, **9,** 57–71.
A pattern emerged of many social contacts, outdoor activities, and authoritarian discipline. While teaching and preparation for school were highly regarded, there was little conscious effort to foster cognitive and language development through play. Developmental assessments correlated positively with an index of stimulation.—From Authors' Abstract.

379. GREENBERG, ROGER P., & GORDON, MICHAEL (SUNY). **Examiner's sex and children's Rorschach productivity.** Psychological Reports, 1983, **53,** 355–357.
It was hypothesized that 6–12-year-olds would produce the most Rorschach responses when tested by an adult of the same sex. Protocols obtained from 83 children supported the hypothesis.—From Authors' Abstract.

380. GREENE, JAMIE G.; FOX, NATHAN A. (Univ. of Maryland); & LEWIS, MICHAEL. **The relationship between neonatal characteristics and three-month mother-infant interaction in high-risk infants.** Child Development, 1983, **54,** 1286–1296.
The behavior of healthy term, healthy preterm, sick preterm, and sick full-term infants was assessed in the neonatal period. At 3 months postterm, infants and their mothers were observed and videotaped in a free-play session. Illness of the infant affected both infant performance and maternal behavior during the interaction at 3 months. Infants who were ill performed poorly on an orientation dimension; this dimension was found to be associated with maternal and infant behaviors at 3 months.—From Authors' Abstract.

381. GRIFFING, PENELOPE (Ohio State Univ.); STEWART, LUAN W.; McKENDRY, MARY ANN; & ANDERSON, RUTH M. **Sociodramatic play: a follow-up study of imagination, self-concept, and school achievement among black school-age children representing two social-class groups.** Genetic Psychology Monographs, 1983, **107,** 249–301.
A follow-up study of imagination, self-concept, and school achievement was conducted among 56 low- and high-SES black 10–11-year-old children whose sociodramatic play had been studied when they were in kindergarten. There were no SES differences in self-concept, fluency in storytelling, or imaginative ideas. High-SES children scored higher for story organization, quality of imagination, and school achievement.—From Authors' Abstract.

382. GUNN, P.; BERRY, P. (Univ. of Queensland, St. Lucia, Australia); & ANDREWS, R. J. **The temperament of Down's syndrome toddlers: a research note.** Journal of Child Psychology and Psychiatry, 1983, **24,** 601–603.
Infants who had been scored as showing signs of difficult temperament moved toward the easier signs on the toddler scale.—From Authors' Abstract.

383. HALPIN, BRUCE M., & OTTINGER, DONALD R. **Children's locus-of-control scales: a reappraisal of reliability characteristics.** Child Development, 1983, **54,** 484–487.
The relationship between reliability of locus-of-control scales and verbal ability may be both grade and scale specific.—From Authors' Abstract.

384. HARGREAVES, DAVID J. (Leicester Univ.); COLMAN, ANDREW M.; & SLUCKIN, WLADYSLAW. **The attractiveness of names.** Human Relations, 1983, **36,** 393–402.
Name selections for newborns were studied from 2 perspectives. Zajonc's "mere exposure" hypothesis suggests a positive, monotonic relationship. Often-used names were judged more attractive and were used more frequently. Wundt's inverted-U hypothesis proposed a trend toward increased use and increased attractiveness of names to a peak after which both attractiveness and frequency declined. The latter would account for the cyclical popularity of some

first names. Using a preference feedback technique, it was shown that Zajonc's hypothesis was correct for short periods of time or where choice was severely restricted, as with surnames. Over longer periods of time and with more latitude of choice, the inverted-U provided a better descriptor.—From Abstract by G. T. Kowitz.

385.   HARRIS, MARY B., & SMITH, SARA DAWN (Univ. of New Mexico). **Beliefs about obesity: effects of age, ethnicity, sex and weight.** Psychological Reports, 1982, **51**, 1047–1055.
Older subjects and female subjects were more likely to know people who were fat and to give complex causal explanations for obesity. Adults were less likely than children to see the fat individuals as responsible for their obesity. There were no ethnic or weight-of-subject differences.—Adapted from Authors' Abstract.

386.   HAY, D. F. (SUNY, Stony Brook), & MURRAY, P. **Giving and requesting: social facilitation of infants' offers to adults.** Infant Behavior and Development, 1982, **5**, 301–310.
The study examined the effect of different interactive experiences on the tendency of 12-month-old infants to offer objects to their companions. Modeling alone was less effective than modeling with prompts or interaction.—From Authors' Abstract.

387.   HAY, DALE F. (SUNY, Stony Brook); NASH, ALISON; & PEDERSEN, JAN. **Interaction between six-month-old peers.** Child Development, 1983, **54**, 557–562.
It appears that the increase in peer contact that occurs in the absence of toys is mediated by corresponding increases in individual infants' gestural activity, which increases the likelihood of contact; however, gestural activity does not predict the initiation of contact when toys are present and does not predict an infant's tendency to reciprocate the peer's overture in either trial.—From Authors' Abstract.

388.   HAZZARD, ANN (Emory Medical School, Grady Memorial Hosp., Atlanta); CHRISTENSEN, ANDREW; & MARGOLIA, GAYLA. **Children's perceptions of parental behaviors.** Journal of Abnormal Child Psychology, 1983, **11**, 49–60.
On the Parent Perception Inventory (PPI), boys reported more positive parental behaviors, particularly for fathers, and children reported more negative (disciplinary) behaviors by mothers. PPI scores were predictably related to child's self-concept and behavior problems and generally unrelated to measures of child's achievement. Children from nondistressed families viewed their parents as behaving more similarly on the PPI than did children from distressed families.—From Authors' Abstract.

389.   HOLMAN, J., & BRAITHWAITE, V. A. (Australian National Univ., P.O. Box 4, Canberra, Australia). **Parental lifestyles and children's television.** Australian Journal of Psychology, 1982, **34**, 375–382.
This study established that the importance placed by parents on TV as a leisure activity was related to both the type and quantity of TV viewed by preschoolers, as were parental attitudes to the medium and socioeconomic status.—From Authors' Abstract.

390.   HOUSE, WILLIAM C. (Case Western Reserve Univ. School of Medicine). **Variables affecting the relationship between depression and attribution of outcomes.** Journal of Genetic Psychology, 1983, **142**, 293–300.
Male and female subjects ($N = 229$) passed or failed an identity-relevant or non-identity-relevant task. Half were told their attributions would be observed by a peer, and half believed their attributions would only be seen anonymously by the experimenter (nonobservation group). The hypothesis that the relationship between depression and ability attributions was stronger under observation conditions than under nonobservation conditions was supported.—From Author's Abstract.

391.   HOWES, CAROLLEE (Univ. of California, Los Angeles). **Patterns of friendship.** Child Development, 1983, **54**, 1041–1053.

Subjects were children in a child-care center or in programs for the emotionally disturbed Younger children had fewer and more stable friendships. Emotionally disturbed children limited their friendships to single partners and returned to these partners following disruptions in the friendship. Over a school year, the greatest increases in complexity of social interaction were observed within stable friendship pairs.—From Author's Abstract.

392. HUBBLE, L. M. (Purdue Univ.), & GROFF, M. G. **WISC-R Verbal Performance IQ discrepancies among Quay-classified adolescent male delinquents.** Journal of Youth and Adolescence, 1982, **11**, 503–508.
Within-subject differences on intellectual measures were obtained for both the psychopathic and subcultural, but not the neurotic, delinquent adjustment classification. There is consistence of intellectual asymmetry across behaviorally diverse delinquent subgroups.—From Authors Abstract.

393. HUGHES, STELLA P. (Oklahoma State Univ.), & DODDER, RICHARD A. **Alcohol-related problems and collegiate drinking patterns.** Journal of Youth and Adolescence, 1983 **12**, 65–76.
A path analysis of 534 participants' questionnaire responses explained 47% of the variation in certain kinds of problem drinking. The strongest single predictor was quantity and frequency of consumption, but precollege drinking was also important.—From Authors' Abstract.

394. JOHNSON, FERN L. (Univ. of Massachusetts), & ARIES, ELIZABETH J. **Conversational patterns among same-sex pairs of late-adolescent close friends.** Journal of Genetic Psychology, 1983, **142**, 225–238.
Do female friendship pairs and male friendship pairs differ in conversational patterns? A group of 176 college students completed the Close Friendship Questionnaire. Females were found to converse more frequently and in greater depth about topics involving themselves and their close relationships, while males were found to converse more frequently and in greater depth about activity-oriented topics.—From Authors' Abstract.

395. KAFFMAN, M. (Kibbutz Child and Family Clinic, Tel Aviv, Israel), & ELIZUR, E. **Bereavement responses of kibbutz and nonkibbutz children following the death of the father.** Journal of Child Psychology and Psychiatry, 1983, **24**, 435–442.
In both kibbutz and urban settings the loss of a father becomes a serious traumatic situation for a large proportion of the children, influencing multiple areas of functioning and causing manifold behavioral symptoms.—From Authors' Abstract.

396. KAISER, SUSAN B. (Univ. of California, Davis), & PHINNEY, JEAN S. **Sex typing of play activities by girls' clothing style: pants versus skirts.** Child Study Journal, 1983, **13**, 115–132.
Preschool children were asked to match line drawings of a girl in pants or one in a skirt with each of 15 drawings of play activities. The masculine/active activities were more frequently matched with the pants, while the feminine/quiet activities were more frequently associated with the skirt.—From Authors' Abstract.

397. KEYES, SUSAN (Univ. of California, Berkeley). **Sex differences in cognitive abilities and sex-role stereotypes in Hong Kong Chinese Adolescents.** Sex Roles, 1983, **9**, 853–870.
Sex differences were discovered in patterns of performance on a battery of cognitive tests, with males performing better on spatial ability and females performing better on fluent production. There were no relationships between sex-role identification and patterns of ability.—From Author's Abstract.

398. KLINGE, VALERIE (Lafayette Clinic, Detroit); CULBERT, JAMES; & PIGGOTT, LEONARD R. **Efficacy of psychiatric inpatient hospitalization for adolescents as measured by pre- and post-MMPI profiles.** Journal of Youth and Adolescence, 1982, **11**, 493–502.

The efficacy of inpatient hospitalization on emotionally impaired adolescents was investigated using the MMPI. There was a flattening of the profile toward normalcy from time of admission to discharge.—From Authors' Abstract.

399. KLONSKY, BRUCE G. (SUNY, Coll. at Fredonia). **The socialization and development of leadership ability.** Genetic Psychology Monographs, 1983, **108**, 97–135.
The present study investigated the familial antecedents of leadership. Subjects were members of baseball and softball teams. Parental warmth, achievement demands, principled discipline, authority discipline, the adolescent's share of family responsibilities, and ordinal position all predicted adolescent behavior.—Adapted from Author's Abstract.

400. KOPP, CLAIRE B. (483 W. Ave. 46, Los Angeles); KRAKOW, JOANNE B.; & JOHNSON, KIM L. **Strategy production by young Down syndrome children.** American Journal of Mental Deficiency, 1983, **88**, 164–169.
Results indicated that Down syndrome children were less able to delay touching than were nonretarded children of similar developmental or language level. In addition, several kinds of within-task strategy behavior were identified that facilitated performance of the nonretarded children.—From Authors' Abstract.

401. KROPP, JERRI JAUDON (Wayne State Univ.), & HALVERSON, CHARLES F. **Preschool children's preferences and recall for stereotyped versus nonstereotyped stories.** Sex Roles, 1983, **9**, 261–272.
Children preferred stories with same-sex characters in traditional activities. One day later, children remembered the most about the stories they had liked the least immediately.—Adapted from Authors' Abstract.

402. KURTZ, CLAIRE ANN, & EISENBERG, NANCY (Arizona State Univ.). **Role-taking, empathy, and resistance to deviation in children.** Journal of Genetic Psychology, 1983, **142**, 85–95.
Eighty-one third graders who previously had been tested with 2 role-taking tasks and an empathy questionnaire were administered a standard resistance-to-temptation task after exposure to 1 of 4 prohibitions: simple, explicit person-oriented, inexplicit person-oriented, and object-oriented. The explicit person-oriented and simple prohibitions were more effective at reducing deviation than was the object-oriented rationale.—From Authors' Abstract.

403. LACHMAN, MARGIE E. (Brandeis Univ.). **Perceptions of intellectual aging: antecedent or consequence of intellectual functioning?** Developmental Psychology, 1983, **19**, 482–498.
A battery of personality and intelligence tests was administered 2 years apart to 76 community-residing elderly persons. Two dimensions, Memory and Efficacy, exhibited marked change in interindividual rankings. The impact of personality and intelligence on these changes was examined with causal modeling. Changes in perceived Intellectual Self-Efficacy were predicted by Fluid Intelligence and Internal Locus of Control.—From Author's Abstract.

404. LADD, GARY W. (Purdue Univ.); LANGE, GARRETT; & STREMMEL, ANDREW. **Personal and situational influences on children's helping behavior: factors that mediate compliant helping.** Child Development, 1983, **54**, 488–501.
Older children were more likely than younger children to decide to help with tasks that were familiar and indicative of a peer's need for help. Peer need and knowledge about how to help produced greater helping persistence. Older children's persistence exceeded that of younger children, and persistence was enhanced by exhoration. Helping decisions of older children were influenced less by constraint information than those of younger children.—From Authors' Abstract.

405. LAMB, MICHAEL E. (Univ. of Utah); FRODI, MAJT; HWANG, CARL-PHILIP; & FRODI, ANN M. **Effects of paternal involvement on infant preferences for mothers and fathers.** Child Development, 1983, **54**, 450–458.

Among Swedish infants, degree of paternal involvement had no effect on preferences displayed on measures of attachment and affiliative behaviors. Infants showed clear preferences for their mothers over their fathers, which contrasts with the lack of preference evident in previous studies of American infants. Swedish fathers are not distinguished by an involvement in play and so may be less affectively salient to their infants.—From Authors' Abstract.

406. LAZARUS, PHILIP J. (Florida International Univ.). **Correlation of shyness and self-esteem for elementary school children.** Perceptual and Motor Skills, 1982, **55**, 8–10.
Shyness was related to low self-esteem.—From Author's Abstract.

407. LEATHER, PAUL (Univ. of Lancaster). **Desire: a structural model of motivation.** Human Relations, 1983, **36**, 109–122.
It is argued that motivation arises from the breaking of the mother-infant relation and the emergence of a new person. Through the use of language, the demands of the young child for need satisfaction develop into desires. Thus, motivation is properly regarded as an interpersonal relationship.—From Abstract by G. T. Kowitz.

408. LEMPERS, JACQUES D. (Iowa State Univ.), & MILETIC, GORDANA. **The immediate and delayed effects of different modeling strategies on children's question-asking behavior with different kinds of messages.** Journal of Genetic Psychology, 1983, **142**, 121–133.
Children in nursery school, kindergarten, and first grade were exposed to 2 different models. In the general modeling condition the subjects heard the model react to inappropriate messages with a question; in a specific modeling condition the model was heard to react with a question that specified the exact kind of information needed. Two kinds of inappropriate messages were used: a functionally ambiguous message and a semantically too complex message. Type of message but not mode of modeling affected recall.—From Authors' Abstract.

409. LeRESCHE, LINDA; STROBINO, DONNA; PARKS, PEGGY; FISCHER, PAMELA; & SMERIGLIO, VINCENT (Johns Hopkins School of Hygiene & Public Health). **The relationship of observed maternal behavior to questionnaire measures of parenting knowledge, attitudes, and emotional state in adolescent mothers.** Journal of Youth and Adolescence, 1983, **12**, 19–31.
Adolescent mothers completed questionnaires measuring perception of the newborn, knowledge of influences on child development, and emotional state. Mothers with nonpositive attitudes interacted less adequately with their babies in an observation session than those with positive attitudes.—From Authors' Abstract.

410. LEVINE, LAURA E. (1131 Mixtwood, Ann Arbor). **Mine: self-definition in 2-year-old boys.** Developmental Psychology, 1983, **19**, 544–549.
Seventy-eight 2-year-old boys were administered 4 measures of self-definition, and 40 were then paired with like-scoring peers in 2 peer-interaction sessions. Boys scoring high in self-definition claimed toys and commented on peers more than did low-scoring boys, and they more often defined their territory in play to a peer by claiming toys prior to positive verbal interaction.—From Author's Abstract.

411. LEY, R. G., & KOEPKE, J. E. (Simon Fraser Univ.). **Attachment behavior outdoors: naturalistic observations of sex and age differences in the separation behavior of young children.** Infant Behavior and Development, 1982, **5**, 195–201.
Children from 12 to 36 months were observed in a city park. Boys separated more often than girls, and younger children separated more often than older children.—From Abstract by S. Thomas.

412. LIBERMAN, DOV (Univ. of Houston); GAA, JOHN P.; & FRANKIEWICZ, RONALD G. **Ego and moral development in an adult population.** Journal of Genetic Psychology, 1983, **142**, 61–65.

The present study employed only adult subjects in which a nonlinear, nonparametric measure of correlation was developed to examine the relationship between ego and moral development scores.—From Authors' Abstract.

413. LONGO, JOSEPHINE; HARVEY, ANN; WILSON, SUSAN; & DENI, RICHARD (Rider Coll.). **Toy play, play tempo, and reaction to frustration in infants.** Perceptual and Motor Skills, 1982, **55**, 239–242.
A relationship was found between response persistence during toy play and attempts to escape from a frustrating situation.—From Authors' Abstract.

414. McBRIDE, ANGELA BARRON (Indiana Univ. School of Nursing). **Differences in parents' and their grown children's perceptions of parenting.** Developmental Psychology, 1983, **19**, 686–693.
Undergraduates and their same-sex parents made attributions to explain parenting success/failure and judge personality traits for a stimulus family. Males of both generations made greater use of the factor Child's Fault in explaining parenting failure than did the females.—Adapted from Author's Abstract.

415. McCARTHY, E. DOYLE (Fordham Univ.); GERSTEN, JOANNE C.; & LANGNER, THOMAS S. **The behavioral effects of father absence on children and their mothers.** Social Behavior and Personality, 1982, **10**, 11–23.
AFDC families and lower middle income families were surveyed. Children of surrogate fathers had more behavioral difficulties than those reported for children living with natural fathers and for children with no father in the home. Lower middle income children and mothers were more adversely affected by father absence than AFDC children.—Adapted from Authors' Abstract.

416. McCORNACK, BARBARA L. (Colorado State Univ.). **Effects of peer familiarity on play behavior in preschool children.** Journal of Genetic Psychology, 1982, **141**, 225–232.
Preschool children played both with a familiar same-sex peer and an unfamiliar same-sex peer. Younger girls and older boys interacted more with familiar peers. Younger boys seemed little influenced by familiarity, while older girls showed more social interactions with unfamiliar peers.—Adapted from Author's Abstract.

417. McLAUGHLIN, BARRY (Univ. of California, Santa Cruz). **Child compliance to parental control techniques.** Developmental Psychology, 1983, **19**, 667–673.
Mothers and fathers of children 1 1/2, 2 1/2, and 3 1/2 years were videotaped in a free-play situation at home. There were few differences between mothers and fathers in control directives. Children complied equally to fathers and mothers but more to attention than to action controls. Direct controls were more effective with 1 1/2-year-olds but less effective with 3 1/2-year-olds.—From Author's Abstract.

418. McLOYD, VONNIE C. (Univ. of Michigan). **The effects of the structure of play objects on the pretend play of low-income preschool children.** Child Development, 1983, **54**, 626–635.
High-structure objects increased noninteractive pretend play in 3 1/2-year-old triads but not in 5-year-old triads. High-structure objects also elicited more associative pretend play and overall pretend play. However, the structure of the play objects did not significantly affect cooperative pretend play. Substitution was more frequent with low-structure objects, while high-structure objects were associated with more pretend themes and onomatopoeia.—From Author's Abstract.

419. McLOYD, VONNIE C. (Univ. of Michigan), & RATNER, HILARY HORN. **The effects of sex and toy characteristics on exploration in preschool children.** Journal of Genetic Psychology, 1983, **142**, 213–224.
An independent assessment of panel preference with 35 boys and girls indicated that girls preferred the house panel, while boys preferred the car panel. Children in both a car and a house

condition spent significantly more time manipulating the novel toy and less time manipulating the familiar toys during a 15-min free-play session than children in a control group.—From Authors' Abstract.

420. MAQSUD, M. (Bayero Univ., Kano, Nigeria). **Relationships of locus of control to self-esteem, academic achievement, and prediction of performance among Nigerian secondary school pupils.** British Journal of Educational Psychology, 1983, **53**, 215–221.
Eighty secondary school boys completed the Socioeconomic Background Questionnaire, the Raven's Standard Progressive Matrices, and the Brookover Scale of Self-Concept of Academic Ability and provided estimates of prediction of their own academic performance. The analyses of data revealed that: (1) socioeconomic background, locus of control, intelligence, and self-esteem had positive effects on academic achievement; (2) internality positively correlated with intelligence, self-esteem, and academic achievement; and (3) the internals were significantly more accurate predictors of their own academic performance than the externals.—From Author's Abstract.

421. MARSH, H. W. (Univ. of Sydney, Australia); PARKER, J. W.; & SMITH, I. D. **Preadolescent self-concept: its relation to self-concept as inferred by teachers and to academic ability.** British Journal of Educational Psychology, 1983, **53**, 60–78.
Student–teacher agreement on student self-concept varied from modest to good for 7 self-concept dimensions (mean $r = 0.40$), was higher in academic areas than nonacademic areas, and was particularly good for academic self-concept in the high SES sample ($r = 0.74$). The idea that self-concept is multifactored is supported.—From Authors' Abstract.

422. MARSH, HERBERT W. (Univ. of Sydney, New South Wales, Australia); SMITH, IAN D.; BARNES, JENNIFER; & BUTLER, SUSAN. **Self-concept: reliability, stability, dimensionality, validity, and the measurement of change.** Journal of Educational Psychology, 1983, **75**, 772–790.
Six-month test-retest data were collected for preadolescent self-concepts in 7 areas, teachers' ratings of student self-concepts in these same areas, and academic ability. Student self-concept ratings were internally consistent, reasonably stable over time, and measured distinct components of self-concept consistent with the design of the instrument used to collect the ratings. Student–teacher agreement was good and specific to particular dimensions. Academic ability measures were uncorrelated with self-concept in 4 nonacademic areas and most highly correlated with the particular area of academic self-concept most logically related to the particular ability measure.—From Authors' Abstract.

423. MARTIN, CAROL LYNN (Univ. of British Columbia, Vancouver, British Columbia, Canada), & HALVERSON, CHARLES F., JR. **The effects of sex-typing schemas on young children's memory.** Child Development, 1983, **54**, 563–574.
Children 5–6 years old tended to distort information in memory by changing the sex of the actor in sex-inconsistent pictures and not by changing the sex of actor on sex-consistent pictures. Children were also more confident of memory for pictures remembered as sex consistent (whether distorted or not) than for inconsistent pictures.—From Authors' Abstract.

424. MARTIN, CAROL LYNN, & HALVERSON, CHARLES F., JR. (Univ. of Georgia). **Gender constancy: a methodological and theoretical analysis.** Sex Roles, 1983, **9**, 775–790.
Two widely used tests of gender constancy, 1 verbal and 1 perceptual, were given to 26 4–6-year-olds. Children were classified at different levels of gender constancy, depending on which test was used. The majority of children answered gender constancy questions as though they were referring to a "pretend," as opposed to a "real," situation; such responses decreased scores of gender constancy on both tests.—From Authors' Abstract.

425. MILLER, SHIRLEY M. (Southwest Texas State Univ.); GINSBURG, HARVEY J.; & ROGOW, SHARON G. **Self-esteem and sharing in fourth-grade children.** Social Behavior and Personality, 1981, **9**, 211–212.

Children who had earned tokens were then given the opportunity to donate tokens to others and/or exchange them for various prizes. Sharing with needy children was positively correlated with self-esteem, and retaining tokens for prizes was negatively correlated with self-esteem.— Adapted from Authors' Abstract.

426. MINNETT, ANN M.; VANDELL, DEBORAH LOWE (Univ. of Texas, Dallas); & SANTROCK, JOHN W. **The effects of sibling status on sibling interaction: influence of birth order, age spacing, sex of child, and sex of sibling.** Child Development, 1983, **54,** 1064–1072.
Firstborn 7–8-year-olds were more likely to praise and teach their siblings, while their second-born counterparts showed more joyful behavior and self-deprecation. The children were more aggressive with a closely spaced sibling and showed more positive behaviors and affection with a widely spaced sibling. Girls were more likely to praise and teach their sibling, while boys were more likely to engage in neutral behaviors. Cheating, aggression, and dominance were more characteristic of the children's behaviors with a same-sex sibling than with an opposite-sex sibling.—From Authors' Abstract.

427. MISCHEL, HARRIET NERLOVE (Stanford Univ.), & MISCHEL, WALTER. **The development of children's knowledge of self-control strategies.** Child Development, 1983, **54,** 603–619.
Children begin to understand 2 basic rules for effective delay of gratification by about the end of their fifth year: cover rather than expose the rewards, and engage in task-oriented rather than in consummatory ideation while waiting. By grade 6, children indicated that abstract ideation would help delay more than consummatory ideation. Preference for the delay-defeating strategy (exposing the rewards) waned toward the end of the fourth year and was replaced by a growing preference for the delay-facilitating strategy (covering the rewards).—From Authors' Abstract.

428. MITCHELL, D. R. (Univ. of Waikato, New Zealand); HAY, J.; & McMANUS, P. J. T. **Aspirations of fourth form students in relation to ethnicity, cultural factors, SES and sex.** New Zealand Journal of Educational Studies, 1982, **17,** 47–56.
Fourth-form pupils aged 14 years completed a questionnaire concerning educational and vocational aspirations. The lower educational aspirations of Maori children as opposed to white children were a function of socioeconomic status (SES), while the lower vocational aspirations were affected by both SES and cultural factors.—M. A. R. Townsend.

429. MÖNKS, FRANZ J. (Catholic Univ. of Nijmegen, Holland), & FERGUSON, TAMARA J. **Gifted adolescents: an analysis of their psychosocial development.** Journal of Youth and Adolescence, 1983, **12,** 1–18.
A model for viewing adolescent psychosocial development is outlined and used as a framework for reviewing literature regarding gifted adolescents' psychosocial adjustment. The literature provides a positive view of the psychosocial adjustment of gifted adolescents.—From Authors' Abstract.

430. MONTEMAYOR, RAYMOND (Univ. of Utah), & CLAYTON, MARK D. **Maternal employment and adolescent development.** Theory into Practice, 1983, **22,** 112–118.
The relationship between maternal employment and adolescent development is enormously complex, and no simple generalizations are possible.—From the Article.

431. MOORE, DENNIS R. (Moore/Arthur Associates, 191 Crest Dr., Eugene), & MUKAI, LEONA H. **Aggressive behavior in the home as a function of the age and sex of control-problem and normal children.** Journal of Abnormal Child Psychology, 1983, **11,** 257–272.
Aggressive behaviors, except for verbal aggression, decreased with age. Sex differences were small or nonexistent.—Ed.

432. MOORE, DeWAYNE (Clemson Univ.), & SCHULTZ, NORMAN R., JR. **Loneliness at adolescence: correlates, attributions, and coping.** Journal of Youth and Adolescence, 1983, **12**, 95–100.

Loneliness was positively related to state and trait anxiety, an external locus of control, depression, self-consciousness, and social anxiety and negatively related to self-reported attractiveness, likability, happiness, life satisfaction, and social risk taking. Adolescents most often attributed loneliness to boredom and most often coped by watching TV or listening to music.—From Authors' Abstract.

433. MORGAN, MARK (St. Patrick's Coll. of Education, Dublin, Ireland). **Decrements in intrinsic motivation among rewarded and observer subjects.** Child Development, 1983, **54**, 636–644.

When subjects merely observed another child perform an activity for a promised reward, such observer subjects manifested a short-term decrement that was not significantly different from the involved reward group. In the long term, the decrement did not persist. The recovery of the observed group was due to their trying out the activity.—From Author's Abstract.

434. NEWCOMB, MICHAEL D.; HUBA, G. J. (Univ. of California, Los Angeles); & BENTLER, PETER M. **Mothers' influence on the drug use of their children: confirmatory tests of direct modeling and mediational theories.** Developmental Psychology, 1983, **19**, 714–726.

Mothers completed questionnaires assessing their personality and drug use, and their daughters and sons independently responded to self-report questionnaires. The data supported a cognitive mediational linkage between mother and child for alcohol and pill use.—From Authors' Abstract.

435. NEY, PHILIP G. (Univ. of Otago, Christchurch, New Zealand). **A consideration of abortion survivors.** Child Psychiatry and Human Development, 1983, **13**, 168–179.

It is hypothesized that children who have siblings terminated by abortion have similar psychological conflicts to those children who survive disasters or siblings who die of accident or illness.—From Author's Abstract.

436. NIHIRA, KAZUO (MRRC, 760 Westwood Plaza, Los Angeles); MEYERS, C. EDWARD & MINK, IRIS T. **Reciprocal relationship between home environment and development of TMR adolescents.** American Journal of Mental Deficiency, 1983, **88**, 139–149.

Partial correlation and multiple regression analysis revealed bidirectional effects between home environment and psychosocial adjustment of TMR adolescents. The environmental effects on the adolescents appear to be broad and dynamic, whereas the adolescents' effects on the home environment appear to be direct and specific.—From Authors' Abstract.

437. NORCINI, JOHN J. (American Board of Internal Medicine, 3624 Market, Philadelphia), & SNYDER, SAMUEL S. **The effects of modeling and cognitive induction on the moral reasoning of adolescents.** Journal of Youth and Adolescence, 1983, **12**, 101–115.

Junior high students were exposed to moral reasoning either 1 stage above or 1 stage below their dominant stage. It was attributed to a model of either high, neutral, or low status. A multiple-choice adaptation of the Kohlberg interview was used. Results indicated significant and stable change in moral reasoning associated with the developmental stage of the message and significant temporary change associated with the characteristics of the model.—From Authors' Abstract.

438. NOWICKI, STEPHEN, JR. (Emory Univ.), & SCHNEEWIND, KLAUS. **Relation of family climate variables to locus of control in German and American students.** Journal of Genetic Psychology, 1982, **141**, 277–286.

Family Environment and locus-of-control scales were completed by 12- and 18-year-old Germans and Americans. There were stable ecological family variables related to locus-of-control orientation across sex, culture, and age.—From Authors' Abstract.

439. NUNN, GERALD D. (Special Education Services, County Office Bldg., Eldora, IA); PARISH, THOMAS S.; & WORTHING, RALPH J. **Perceptions of personal and familial adjustment by children from intact, single-parent, and reconstituted families.** Psychology in the Schools, 1983, **20,** 166–174.
The results revealed: (a) less positive adjustment among children from divorced families (whether the remaining parent remarried or not) as opposed to children from intact families, (b) mixed findings regarding comparisons of psychosocial adjustment between single-parent and remarried groups, and (c) a pattern of effects in which males appeared to be favorably affected within the single-parent configuration, while females were more favorably adjusted within the reconstituted family.—From Authors' Abstract.

440. PELA, O. A., & REYNOLDS, CECIL R. (Texas A&M Univ.). **Cross-cultural application of the Revised-Children's Manifest Anxiety Scale: normative and reliability data for Nigerian primary school children.** Psychological Reports, 1982, **51,** 1135–1138.

441. PETERSON, GARY W.; SOUTHWORTH, LOIS E.; & PETERS, DAVID F. (Univ. of Tennessee). **Children's self-esteem and maternal behavior in three low-income samples.** Psychological Reports, 1983, **52,** 79–86.
For fifth and sixth graders, maternal loving and demanding were positively correlated and maternal punishment was negatively correlated with children's self-esteem.—From Authors' Abstract.

442. PIOTROWSKI, CHRIS (Univ. of West Florida), & DUNHAM, FRANCES Y. **Stability of factor structure in fifth graders on the children's Nowicki-Strickland Internal-External Control Scale.** Journal of Psychology, 1983, **115,** 13–16.
There was much similarity for Factor I items on the CNS-IE between the present sample and Nowicki's sample. Also, there was a high degree of similarity for Factor I items for the present sample on both testings. Factors II and III showed little similarity.—From Authors' Abstract.

443. PRAGER, KAREN J. (Univ. of Texas, Dallas). **Identity development and self-esteem in young women.** Journal of Genetic Psychology, 1982, **141,** 177–182.
Identity status, measured with and without sexual values questions, and self-esteem were determined for 88 undergraduate college women. Differences in self-esteem as measured by the Texas Social Behavior Inventory were found for women in the 4 identity statuses. Achievement women scored higher than Moratorium and Diffusion women, but not Foreclosure women. Moratorium women had the lowest self-esteem.—Adapted from Author's Abstract.

444. PUSHKIN, ISIDORE (West London Inst. of Higher Education, London, England), & NORBURN, VERONICA. **Ethnic preferences in young children and in their adolescence in three London districts.** Human Relations, 1983, **36,** 309–344.
White children ages 3–7 were tested for ethnic (race) preference. Two groups lived with considerable white/black contact, 1 harmonious and 1 intense. The third group had little white/black contact. Doll choice and house distance tests were used. Own-race preference rose to a peak around age 6. Neither sex, father's status, nor mother's child-control attitudes were related to preference. Hostility in mother's ethnic attitude was related to preference.—From Abstract by G. T. Kowitz.

445. RAVIV, A. (Tel Aviv Univ., Israel); BAR-TAL, D.; RAVIA, ALONA; & LEVIT, RUTH. **Research symposium: attribution theory students' reactions to attributions of ability and effort.** British Journal of Educational Psychology, 1983, **53,** 1–13.
Students in grades 5 and 10 and college received 8 different hypothetical stories for which classmate's ability (high or low), exerted effort (high or low), and outcome (success or failure) were varied. Following each story the students were asked to rate the predicted grade given by a teacher, teacher's appreciation, own appreciation, projected classmate's satisfaction, and own willingness to resemble the classmate. The results showed that while students believe that teachers and they themselves show more appreciation of effort exertion than ability, they

project feelings of satisfaction and would like to be perceived more as having ability than exerting effort.—From Authors' Abstract.

446. REAVES, JUANITA Y. (Roy Littlejohn Associates, 1331 H St., N.W., Suite 400, Washington, DC), & ROBERTS, ALBERT. **The effect of type of information on children's attraction to peers.** Child Development, 1983, **54**, 1024–1031.
Each level of information—physique, preferences, and character—significantly influenced attraction ratings by second graders. Character had the strongest effect.—From Authors' Abstract.

447. REES, CONSTANCE D. (1704 Oak Meadows, Irving, TX), & WILBORN, BOBBIE L. **Correlates of drug abuse in adolescents: a comparison of families of drug abusers with families of nondrug abusers.** Journal of Youth and Adolescence, 1983, **12**, 55–63.
Drug-abusing adolescents and their families were compared with non-drug-abusing adolescents and their families. The adolescent's self-esteem and perception of parental behavior, the ability of the parents to predict the child's parental perceptions, and the professed parental attitudes toward confidence and responsibility in child rearing differentiate the drug-abusing adolescent from the non-drug-abusing adolescent.—From Authors' Abstract.

448. REICHENBACH, LISA, & MASTERS, JOHN C. (Vanderbilt Inst. for Public Policy Studies, 1208 18th Ave. S., Nashville). **Children's use of expressive and contextual cues in judgments of emotion.** Child Development, 1983, **54**, 993–1004.
Preschool and third-grade children judged the emotional states of other children on the basis of expressive cues alone, contextual cues alone, or both. Older children were more accurate than younger only when given multiple cues. Contextual cues led to greater accuracy in the recognition of emotional states than did expressive cues. When multiple cues were inconsistent with 1 another, younger children relied more on expressive cues, while older children preferred contextual ones.—From Authors' Abstract.

449. REKERS, GEORGE A. (Kansas State Univ.); MEAD, SHASTA L.; ROSEN, ALEXANDER C.; & BRIGHAM, STEVEN L. **Family correlates of male childhood gender disturbance.** Journal of Genetic Psychology, 1983, **142**, 31–42.
Significantly fewer male role models were found in the family backgrounds of the severely gender-disturbed boys as compared to the mild-to-moderately gender-disturbed boys. Male childhood gender disturbance was also found to be correlated with a high incidence of psychiatric problems in both the mothers and fathers.—From Authors' Abstract.

450. RENNINGER, K. ANN (Swarthmore Coll.), & SNYDER, SAMUEL S. **Effects of cognitive style on perceived satisfaction and performance among students and teachers.** Journal of Educational Psychology, 1983, **75**, 668–676.
The influence of matched or mismatched cognitive styles on perceived satisfaction and performance among students and teachers was examined in 8 secondary school classrooms. Matched styles went with higher student perceptions of satisfaction and perceptions of teacher effectiveness. Grades were unrelated to cognitive style.—From Authors' Abstract.

451. RICHMAN, CHARLES L. (Wake Forest Univ.); NOVACK, TOM; PRICE, CLAIRE; ADAMS, KATHRYNN A.; MITCHELL, DAVID; REZNICK, J. STEVEN; & KAGAN, JEROME. **The consequences of failing to imitate.** Motivation and Emotion, 1983, **7**, 157–167.
Infants were shown 3 modeled acts presented in sequence. Imitation of 1, 2, or 3 of the modeled acts or failure to imitate was then observed. Distress was assessed prior to and following modeling. Infants who failed to imitate at least 1 act displayed a high level of distress.—From Authors' Abstract.

452. RICKEL, ANNETTE U. (Wayne State Univ.); ESHELMAN, ANNE K.; & LOIGMAN, GAIL A. **Social problem solving training: a follow-up study of cognitive and behavioral effects.** Journal of Abnormal Child Psychology, 1983, **11**, 15–28.

Preschool-age children received 46 sessions of intervention by specially trained assistants. Support was found for the cognitive effectiveness of social problem-solving training with aberrant children at posttest in that they gained significantly in their ability to generate alternative solutions to interpersonal problems. This effect was not sustained at follow-up. Blind teacher ratings of behavioral adjustment and independent observers' ratings of behavior revealed no significant behavioral training effects at posttest or at follow-up.—From Authors' Abstract.

453. ROBINSON, ELIZABETH A. (Univ. of Washington), & ANDERSON, LINDA L. **Family adjustment, parental attitudes, and social desirability.** Journal of Abnormal Child Psychology, 1983, **11**, 247–256.
The more positive the report of marital adjustment, the fewer the number of child problem behaviors endorsed by parents. When social desirability is controlled, however, the marital-child adjustment relationship is nonsignificant.—From Authors' Abstract.

454. RÖDHOLM, M. (Univ. of Götenborg, Sweden), & LARSSON, K. **The behavior of human male adults at their first contact with a newborn.** Infant Behavior and Development, 1982, **5**, 121–130.
Male medical students and fathers of newborns showed similar behavior patterns: touching extremities, then trunk, and finally the face, using fingertips and proceeding to palm.—S. Thomas.

455. ROLLINS, JUDY (Kansas State Univ.), & WHITE, PRISCILLA N. **The relationship between mothers' and daughters' sex-role attitudes and self-concepts in three types of family environment.** Sex Roles, 1982, **8**, 1141–1155.
Mothers' and daughters' attitudes toward marriage, children, and careers were related, but not their self-concepts. Mothers who were involved in careers that were personally salient differed from mothers who were employed because of economic necessity and from mothers who were full-time homemakers.—Adapted from Authors' Abstract.

456. ROSENTHAL, DOREEN A. (Univ. of Melbourne, Australia), & CHAPMAN, DIANE C. **The lady spaceman: children's perceptions of sex-stereotyped occupations.** Sex Roles, 1982, **8**, 959–965.
Children from grades 1, 4, and 6 were asked to name male and female occupants of traditionally male and traditionally female roles. Use of linguistic markers (e.g., lady doctor) or stereotypically inappropriate responses (e.g., naming a female doctor "nurse," while correctly naming the male occupants of this role "doctor") occurred with the nontraditional roles.—From Authors' Abstract.

457. ROSENTHAL, DOREEN A. (Univ. of Melbourne, Parkville, Victoria, Australia); MOORE, SUSAN M.; & TAYLOR, MEREDITH J. **Ethnicity and adjustment: a study of the self-image of Anglo-, Greek-, and Italian-Australian working class adolescents.** Journal of Youth and Adolescence, 1983, **12**, 117–135.
The Erikson Psychosocial Stage Inventory and the Offer Self-Image Questionnaire were administered to 450 working-class Anglo-, Greek-, and Italian-Australian ninth and eleventh graders. Anglo- and Greek-Australian adolescents scored similarly and significantly higher than Italian-Australians on a number of subscales. Culture conflict may be more influential in the adjustment of Italian-Australians than Greek-Australians.—From Authors' Abstract.

458. ROSENTHAL, MIRIAM K. (Hebrew Univ., Jerusalem, Israel). **State variations in the newborn and mother-infant interaction during breast feeding: some sex differences.** Developmental Psychology, 1983, **19**, 740–745.
Thirty male and 33 female newborns were observed being breast-fed in the maternity ward. Although male dyads showed more interactive activity on the asleep end of the scale, female dyads showed more interactive activity on the awake end of the scale. Although males spent less time than females in the fussy state, when they were fussy they seemed to be more agitated than the females.—From Author's Abstract.

459. ROTH, KARLSSON, & EISENBERG, NANCY (Arizona State Univ.). **The effects of children's height on teachers' attributions of competence.** Journal of Genetic Psychology, 1983, **143,** 45–50.
Female elementary teachers rated photographs of children varying in relative height. They assigned punishment for hypothetical transgressions. Teachers rated tall boys as less competent but older. There were no effects of height on teachers' attributions of competency or assignment of punishment for girls. Height did not affect punishments assigned.—Adapted from Authors' Abstract.

460. ROTHBART, MARY K. (Univ. of Oregon), & HANSON, MARCI J. **A caregiver report comparison of temperamental characteristics of Down syndrome and normal infants.** Developmental Psychology, 1983, **19,** 766–769.
The temperamental characteristics of Down syndrome and nonhandicapped infants were compared using the Infant Behavior Questionnaire at 3-month intervals during the first year of life. Differences were found for smiling and laughter, duration of orienting, fear, vocal activity, startle, and motor development.—From Authors' Abstract.

461. RUBENSTEIN, J. L. (Tufts Medical Ctr., Boston); HOWES, C.; & PEDERSEN, F. A. **Second order effects of peers on mother-toddler interaction.** Infant Behavior and Development, 1982, **5,** 185–194.
The influence of adult and toddler peers on toddler-mother interaction was studied in the home environment. With toddler peers present, children made fewer bids toward mothers and mothers showed less affect expression.—S. Thomas.

462. RUBIN, KENNETH H. (Univ. of Waterloo, Ontario, Canada), & CLARK, M. LOUISE. **Preschool teachers' ratings of behavioral problems: observational, sociometric, and social-cognitive correlates.** Journal of Abnormal Child Psychology, 1983, **11,** 273–286.
Children rated highly on the Preschool Behavior Questionnaire's Anxious–Fearful, Hostile–Aggressive, and Hyperactive–Distractible factors (a) displayed less mature and more aggressive in-class behaviors, (b) were less popular among their peers, and (c) were more likely to suggest negative affect strategies on the social problem-solving measure.—From Authors' Abstract.

463. SAGAR, H. ANDREW (Elizabethtown Coll.); SCHOFIELD, JANET WARD; & SNYDER, HOWARD N. **Race and gender barriers: preadolescent peer behavior in academic classrooms.** Child Development, 1983, **54,** 1032–1040.
Sixth graders interacted primarily with others of their own race and sex, although gender aggregation was less pronounced for blacks than for whites. Boys interacted more across racial lines than girls. Blacks were almost twice as likely as whites to be the source of cross-race interactions. Peer behaviors were more likely to be task-related when directed toward white rather than black interactants.—From Authors' Abstract.

464. SAKLOFSKE, D. H. (Univ. of Saskatchewan, Canada), & EYSENCK, S. B. G. **Impulsiveness and venturesomeness in Canadian children.** Psychological Reports, 1983, **52,** 147–152.
Factor analyses yielded results similar to those obtained for British children. Reliabilities were satisfactory. Boys scored higher than girls on impulsiveness and venturesomeness but lower on empathy.—From Authors' Abstract.

465. SAKLOFSKE, D. H. (Univ. of Saskatchewan, Canada), & McKERRACHER, D. W. **Preliminary New Zealand norms for the Junior Eysenck Personality Questionnaire.** New Zealand Journal of Educational Studies, 1982, **17,** 81–83.

466. SAKLOFSKE, D. H. (Univ. of Saskatchewan, Canada); McKERRACHER, D. W.; & CAMERON, P. E. **A New Zealand version of an anxiety questionnaire for school age children.** New Zealand Journal of Educational Studies, 1982, **17,** 78–80.

Local norms for the Frost Self-Description Questionnaire revealed that girls aged 8–14 years tended to score higher than boys on the 7 anxiety scales.—From Abstract by M. A. R. Townsend.

467. SCHALLER, J. (Univ. of Göteborg, Sweden); CARLSSON, S. G.; & LARSSON, K. **Early proximo-distal development in the mother's contact behavior during nursing.** Infant Behavior and Development, 1982, **5**, 209–213.
Observations of primiparous mothers on days 2, 4, and 42 postpartum showed that mothers decreased proximal contact during the first 6 weeks.—From Abstract by S. Thomas.

468. SCHLUDERMANN, SHIRIN (Univ. of Manitoba, Winnipeg, Canada), & SCHLUDERMANN, EDUARD. **Sociocultural change and adolescents' perceptions of parent behavior.** Developmental Psychology, 1983, **19**, 674–685.
The Children's Report of Parent Behavior Inventory (CRPBI) was given to adolescents from 2 cities in India and 1 city in Canada. Factor analyses of CRPBI scales revealed 3 replicable factors: Acceptance, Firm Control (FC), and Psychological Control (PC). Younger adolescents consistently reported more PC and FC than did older adolescents. Modern adolescents reported most FC, and traditional adolescents reported most PC.—From Authors' Abstract.

469. SCHUNK, DALE H. (Univ. of Houston). **Reward contingencies and the development of children's skills and self-efficacy.** Journal of Educational Psychology, 1983, **75**, 511–518.
Children received didactic instruction in division operations and were offered rewards contingent on their actual performance, rewards for simply participating, or no rewards. Performance-contingent rewards led to the highest levels of division skill and self-efficacy, as well as the most rapid problem solving. Rewards for participation resulted in no benefits.—From Author's Abstract.

470. SCHWARTZ, PAMELA (Univ. of Michigan). **Length of day-care attendance and attachment behavior in eighteen-month-old infants.** Child Development, 1983, **54**, 1073–1078.
Eighteen-month-old full-time, part-time, and non-daycare infants from intact middle-class homes were compared. Home-observation and rating scale scores of maternal behaviors directed at the child yielded few group differences. More full-time daycare children (but not part-time children) were found to display avoidance of the mother during the final reunion episode of the strange-situation procedure than did non-daycare children.—From Author's Abstract.

471. SCHWARZ, J. CONRAD (Univ. of Connecticut); SCHRAGER, JANET B.; & LYONS, ANDREA E. **Delay of gratification by preschoolers: evidence for the validity of the choice paradigm.** Child Development, 1983, **54**, 620–625.
With a long delay, children were less likely to choose the delayed reward; the effect was the same for 3–5-year-olds. Choice of the delayed reward was unrelated to age or vocabulary IQ.—From Authors' Abstract.

472. SILVERMAN, WENDY K., & DRABMAN, RONALD S. (Univ. of Mississippi Medical Ctr.). **Affective matching in nine-year-old girls.** Journal of Psychology, 1983, **115**, 123–129.
Girls were asked to judge how happy, sad, angry, and fearful their peers would feel in 4 situations. The girls agreed among themselves on how their peers would feel. Their judgments concerning their peers' feelings did not differ from their own self-report.—From Authors' Abstract.

473. SIMPSON, MADELINE L. (Longwood Coll.). **Time-of-day effects in performance by seventh grade students on two measures of impulse control.** Perceptual and Motor Skills, 1982, **55**, 115–121.
There were no differences between morning and afternoon groups. Girls showed more circadian effects, made fewer delayed reward choices, and made less accurate time estimations than boys.—From Author's Abstract.

474. SMEETS, PAUL M. (Univ. of Leiden, Netherlands), & KAUFFMAN, JAMES M. **On children being imitated: predictability of vs. reinforcement by the observer's imitations.** Journal of Genetic Psychology, 1983, **142**, 135–142.
Sixty Dutch school-age children participated in an experiment consisting of a modeling-only condition and 3 imitation conditions (contingent, concontingent, and consistent). The results revealed that the contingent imitation of the children's target response did not cause them to demonstrate that response more often and that it did not lead to increased imitations on subsequent modeling trials.—From Authors' Abstract.

475. SMEETS, PAUL M., & KAUFFMAN, JAMES M. (Univ. of Virginia). **Effects of being imitated and being not imitated in children: predictability vs. topography of the observer's responses.** Journal of Genetic Psychology, 1983, **142**, 43–52.
Children of 4 grade levels participated. The experiment used 4 conditions: modeling only, nonimitation, imitation, and contraimitation. Children of all grade levels copied the adults' imitative behavior, and the older children showed an increased tendency to copy his contraimitative behavior.—From Authors' Abstract.

476. SMERIGLIO, VINCENT L. (Johns Hopkins School of Hygiene and Public Health), & PARKS, PEGGY. **Measuring mothers' perceptions about the influences of infant caregiving practices.** Child Psychiatry and Human Development, 1983, **13**, 189–200.
The Infant Caregiving Inventory, which measures mothers' perceptions of the influences of infant caregiving practices on infants' present and future well-being, is described.—Adapted from Authors' Abstract.

477. SOBESKY, WILLIAM E. (Univ. of Colorado). **The effects of situational factors on moral judgments.** Child Development, 1983, **54**, 575–584.
When the negative consequences for the actor were severe, high school and college students were less certain that they should and would act to help another person; they also displayed less principled thinking. When the consequences for another were severe, individuals who had displayed a greater predisposition to make use of principled thinking were more certain of acting to help.—From Author's Abstract.

478. ST. GEORGE, ALISON (Massey Univ., New Zealand). **Teacher expectations and perceptions of Polynesian and Pakeha pupils and the relationship to classroom behaviour and school achievement.** British Journal of Educational Psychology, 1983, **53**, 48–59.
A study of 90 9-year-olds in 5 ethnically mixed New Zealand classrooms was undertaken. The Polynesian minority group pupils were perceived less favorably than the Pakeha majority on dimensions reflecting parent–home factors and academic work skills. Teachers held lower expectations for the ability of Polynesian pupils than their Pakeha classmates.—From Author's Abstract.

479. STERICKER, ANNE B. (Wright State Univ.), & KURDEK, LAWRENCE A. **Dimensions and correlates of third through eighth graders' sex-role self-concepts.** Sex Roles, 1982, **8**, 915–929.
Most children's sex-role self-concepts were congruent with their biological sex, although about 1/3 of both males and females had androgynous self-concepts. Cross-sex-role self-concepts were rare. There were no age changes in the frequencies of children in each self-concept category.—Adapted from Authors' Abstract.

480. SUOMI, STEPHEN J. (Univ. of Wisconsin); MINEKA, SUSAN; & DeLIZIO, ROBERTA D. **Short- and long-term effects of repetitive mother-infant separations on social development in rhesus monkeys.** Developmental Psychology, 1983, **19**, 770–786.
Monkey mother-infant dyads were subjected to 16 4-day physical separations between the infants' third and ninth months of life. The infants displayed protest following each separation but only minimal despair. Protest diminished over repeated separations. Mothers' separation reactions were considerably milder. Separated infants displayed excessive levels of infantile

behaviors, although their mothers did not differ from controls. After final separation, differences emerged between previously separated and control subjects, but separated monkeys avoided their mothers when they were exposed to them.—Adapted from Authors' Abstract.

481. SUSSMAN, STEVE (Univ. of Illinois, Chicago); MUESER, KIM T.; GRAU, BARRY W.; & YARNOLD, PAUL R. **Stability of females' facial attractiveness during childhood.** Journal of Personality and Social Psychology, 1983, **44,** 1231–1233.
Facial attractiveness of the same 13 girls was rated at 4 equally spaced times between grades 1 and 10 by 4 independent groups of male college students. Results indicated that the girls differed from one another in attractiveness averaged over time but that substantial intraindividual changes occurred as well.—From Authors' Abstract.

482. TABOR, CAROLE (Univ. of Georgia), & SHAFFER, DAVID R. **Effects of age of bene-factor, attractiveness of the recipient, and the recipient's need for assistance on proso-cial behavior in children's dyads.** Social Behavior and Personality, 1981, **9,** 163–169.
Children aged 5–6, 7–8, and 9–10 years were first given an opportunity to share with either an attractive or an unattractive peer, then to help the peer who appeared to have either high or low need for assistance. Older children shared more of their resources than did their younger counterparts, while helpful responses were affected only by the peer's apparent need for assistance. Children's sharing and their responses to the emergency were positively correlated with empathy.—From Authors' Abstract.

483. THELEN, MARK H. (Univ. of Missouri, Columbia); MILLER, DAVID J.; FEHRENBACH, PETER A.; & FRAUTSCHI, NANETTE M. **Reactions to being imitated: effects of perceived motivation.** Merrill-Palmer Quarterly, 1983, **29,** 159–167.

484. THOMAN, EVELYN B. (Univ. of Connecticut); ACEBO, CHRISTINE; & BECKER, PATRICIA T. **Infant crying and stability in the mother-infant relationship: a systems analysis.** Child Development, 1983, **54,** 653–659.
For each pair, consistence in allocation of time to 4 interactional contexts (feeding, changing or bathing, social attention, and baby alone) was assessed. High interactional stability was strongly linked to low levels of crying during social attention.—From Authors' Abstract.

485. THOMAS, JAMES H. (Northern Kentucky Univ.). **The influence of sex, birth order, and sex of sibling on parent–adolescent interaction.** Child Study Journal, 1983, **13,** 107–114.
Relationships between parents and their adolescent children were investigated using tape-recorded interactions. Parental involvement and support were high for firstborn girls with sisters and low for those with brothers. Among second-born girls, support was high for those with brothers and low for those with sisters. Interaction with sons was not affected by birth order.—Adapted from Author's Abstract.

486. THOMPSON, R. A. (Univ. of Nebraska), & LAMB, M. E. **Stranger sociability and its relationships to temperament and social experience during the second year.** Infant Behavior and Development, 1982, **5,** 277–287.
At 20 months, fearfulness, distress due to limitations, smiling and laughter, and activity level were related to stranger sociability. There were fewer significant correlations at 12 months. Sociability and temperament were stable from 12 to 20 months.—From Authors' Abstract.

487. THOMPSON, ROSS A. (Univ. of Nebraska); LAMB, MICHAEL E.; & ESTES, DAVID. **Harmonizing discordant notes: a reply to Waters.** Child Development, 1983, **54,** 521–524.

488. THORBECKE, WILLIAM, & GROTEVANT, HAROLD D. (Univ. of Texas, Austin). **Gender differences in adolescent interpersonal identity formation.** Journal of Youth and Adolescence, 1982, **11,** 479–492.

High school subjects were interviewed and assessed on progress toward interpersonal identity achievement in friendship and dating relationships. Young women were more identity achieved than men in the friendship domain; no differences emerged in the dating domain. The processes of interpersonal and vocational identity formation appeared to be more interrelated for females than males. Different gender achievement orientations were revealed by positive correlations between several interpersonal identity ratings and mastery for males and lack of correlation between interpersonal identity and mastery for females. Commitment to a conception regarding friendships was positively correlated with competitiveness for males and negatively correlated with competitiveness for females.—From Authors' Abstract.

489. UDWIN, ORLEE (Univ. of London, England). **Imaginative play training as an intervention method with institutionalised preschool children.** British Journal of Educational Psychology, 1983, **53**, 32–39.
Children removed from deleterious family backgrounds and placed in institutional care were exposed to 10 30-min sessions of imaginative play training. Subjects showed significant post-training increments in levels of imaginative play, positive emotionality, prosocial behaviors, and in measures of divergent thinking and storytelling skills; subjects showed decreased levels of overt aggression. Age, nonverbal intelligence, and fantasy predisposition influenced subjects' responsiveness to the training program.—From Author's Abstract.

490. VACC, NICHOLAS A. (Univ. of North Carolina). **Development of a nonsexist-language form of the Adapted Modified Role Repertory Test for children.** Perceptual and Motor Skills, 1982, **55**, 338.
Results suggest that the original and nonsexist forms are comparable.—Adapted from the Article.

491. VAUGHN, BRIAN E. (Univ. of Illinois, Chicago), & LANGLOIS, JUDITH H. **Physical attractiveness as a correlate of peer status and social competence in preschool children.** Developmental Psychology, 1983, **19**, 561–567.
Ratings of physical attractiveness and 2 competence scores were obtained for preschool children. Physical attractiveness was a significant correlate of 1 competence rank but not the other. Sociometric data may be influenced by variables such as physical attractiveness that are not related to social competence.—From Authors' Abstract.

492. WALDEN, TEDRA A. (Vanderbilt Univ.), & RAMEY, CRAIG T. **Locus of control and academic achievement: results from a preschool intervention program.** Journal of Educational Psychology, 1983, **75**, 347–358.
Children who had been judged to be at risk for academic difficulties and who had participated in a 5-year, efficacy-oriented intervention program were compared to a group of high-risk non-intervention children and a low-risk comparison group. The high-risk intervention and low-risk children had stronger beliefs in personal control over academic success, and these beliefs were good predictors of achievement and task-related classroom behaviors.—From Authors' Abstract.

493. WATERS, EVERETT (SUNY, Stony Brook). **The stability of individual differences in infant attachment: comments on the Thompson, Lamb, and Estes contribution.** Child Development, 1983, **54**, 516–520.

494. WATERS, EVERETT (SUNY, Stony Brook); GORNAL, MORAG; GARBER, JEANNE; & VAUGHN, BRIAN E. **Q-sort correlates of visual regard among preschool peers: validation of a behavioral index of social competence.** Developmental Psychology, 1983, **19**, 550–560.
Visual regard received from peers was assessed by time sampling in 3 preschool classes, and the behavior of each child was described using Q sorts. Visual regard and a global social competence score were correlated ($r = .60$). Correlates of the visual regard measure were also correlates of the global social competence scores, but the latter measure had additional correlates.—From Authors' Abstract.

495. WEINRAUB, MARSHA (Temple Univ.), & WOLF, BARBARA M. **Effects of stress and social supports on mother-child interactions in single- and two-parent families.** Child Development, 1983, **54**, 1297–1311.
Single parents tended to be more socially isolated than married parents, worked longer hours, and received less emotional and parental support. They tended to have less stable social networks and experienced more potentially stressful life changes. Predicting optimal mother-child interaction in single-parent families were fewer stressful life events, reduced social contact, increased parenting support, and hours maternal employment. Predicting optimal interaction in 2-parent families were fewer stressful life events, satisfaction with emotional support, and the availability of household help.—From Authors' Abstract.

496. WEISS, MICHAEL G., & MILLER, PATRICIA H. (Univ. of Florida). **Young children's understanding of displaced aggression.** Journal of Experimental Child Psychology, 1983, **35**, 529–539.
Young children do not understand displaced aggression. The present study examines the early phases of the understanding of the causes of moderately and extremely displaced aggression. Preschool and kindergarten children viewed videotaped episodes of displaced aggression. By age 5, most children had some understanding of displaced aggression, but this understanding was not complete. The early understanding revealed in the present study may be due to the use of short, simple, realistic videotaped episodes.—From Authors' Abstract.

497. WILKINSON, J. E., & MURPHY, H. F. (Child Guidance Service, Strathclyde Regional Council, Renfrew Division, Carbrook, Paisley, Scotland). **'Flitting' in nursery school children.** Child: Care, Health and Development, 1983, **9**, 19–28.
This study is concerned with the social and cognitive behavior of 4-year-olds in nursery school who exhibit frequent change of activity. The high flitters (a majority of whom were boys) received less adult attention, preferred the company of 1 other child, and performed less well intellectually.—From Authors' Abstract.

498. WINEFIELD, ANTHONY H. (Univ. of Adelaide, South Australia). **Cognitive performance deficits induced by exposure to response-independent positive outcomes.** Motivation and Emotion, 1983, **7**, 145–155.
Private secondary school students differing in achievement motivation took part in a learned helplessness experiment using a triadic design and noncontingent rewards. A learned helplessness effect was observed in both high and low achievement motivation groups.—From Author's Abstract.

499. ZAKIN, DAVID F. (Univ. of Michigan). **Physical attractiveness, sociability, athletic ability, and children's preference for their peers.** Journal of Psychology, 1983, **115**, 117–122.
Physical attractiveness was more important than sociability or athletic ability in determining friendship choices for all children.—From Author's Abstract.

500. ZERN, DAVID S. (Clark Univ.). **The relationship of certain group-oriented and individualistically oriented child-rearing dimensions to cultural complexity in a cross-cultural sample.** Genetic Psychology Monographs, 1983, **108**, 3–20.
The relationship of 6 basic childrearing dimensions to the development of cultural complexity is explored in a sample of 38 societies. There was a strong relationship between pressure to conform to norms and measures of cultural complexity.—From Author's Abstract.

501. ZERN, DAVID S. (Clark Univ.). **The role of schooling in socializing and skill-building: a cross-cultural study.** Genetic Psychology Monographs, 1983, **107**, 233–248.
A systematic cross-cultural study involving 186 societies showed strong relationships are established between the amount of schooling and the degree of pressure to conform to social norms, especially for children 4–8 years old. There are much stronger connections between

pressure to conform and complexity in those societies where there is extensive schooling than in those societies where there is minimal schooling.—From Author's Abstract.

502. ZESKIND, PHILIP SANFORD (Virginia Polytechnic Inst. & State Univ.). **Cross-cultural differences in maternal perceptions of cries of low- and high-risk infants.** Child Development, 1983, **54,** 1119–1128.
The tape-recorded cries of low- and high-risk newborn infants were rated by inner-city Anglo-American, black-American, and Cuban-American mothers during the hospital lying-in period following childbirth. Differences were found between low- and high-risk infant cries on all perceptual responses with the effects of culture and parental experience affecting the degree of differences.—From Author's Abstract.

503. ZUCKERMAN, DIANA M. (Radcliffe Coll.), & SAYRE, DONALD H. **Cultural sex-role expectations and children's sex-role concepts.** Sex Roles, 1982, **8,** 853–862.
Children 4–8 years old expressed nonstereotyped attitudes toward occupations and activities, but chose very traditional careers for themselves.—From Authors' Abstract.

EDUCATIONAL PROCESSES

504. ALEGRIA, JESUS (Universite Libre des Bruxelles, Belgium); PIGNOT, ELISABETH; & MORAIS, JOSE. **Phonetic analysis of speech and memory codes in beginning readers.** Memory and Cognition, 1982, **10,** 451–456.
Children who began to learn to read following the phonic method did better than those who began with the whole-word method in the "phonic reversal" task, but not on the "syllable reversal" task. The difference in performance on the rhyming and nonrhyming series of memory items was significant in both groups.—Adapted from Authors' Abstract.

505. AYERS, DOUGLAS (Univ. of Victoria, Canada), & DOWNING, JOHN. **Testing children's concepts of reading.** Educational Research, 1982, **24,** 277–283.
Data are reported on the reliability and validity of the LARR Test, a test of children's concepts of literacy.—Adapted from the Article.

506. BACKMAN, JOAN (McGill Univ., Montreal, Quebec, Canada). **The role of psycholinguistic skills in reading acquisition: a look at early readers.** Reading Research Quarterly, 1983, **18,** 466–479.
The role of speech-sound segmentation, blending, and discrimination in reading acquisition was examined in children who learned to read prior to formal instruction in school, in comparison with age-matched nonreaders, and older children reading at the same level. None of the skills assessed appeared to be true prerequisites to beginning reading.—Adapted from Author's Abstract.

507. BADGER, M. E. (NFER, The Mere, Upton Park, Slough Berks, England). **Why aren't girls better at maths? A review of research.** Educational Research, 1981, **24,** 11–23.
It is concluded that, although spatial ability may affect performance, girls' diminishing achievement can largely be accounted for in social terms. Attitudes, rooted in the cultural milieu and reinforced by society, are probably the determining factor in whether or not girls succeed in mathematics.—From Author's Abstract.

508. BARCLAY, ALLAN (Wright State Univ.), & ALLEN, JOHN. **Effect of Headstart programs on the factor structure of mental ability.** Psychological Reports, 1982, **51,** 512–514.
Third graders of lower socioeconomic status were compared to a matched sample of children who had been involved 5 years earlier in a Headstart program. Previous Headstart experience was not related to any factor structure changes on the Iowa Tests of Basic Skills.—Adapted from Authors' Abstract.

509. BECK, ISABEL L. (Univ. of Pittsburgh); OMANSON, RICHARD C.; & McKEOWN, MARGARET G. **An instructional redesign of reading lessons: effects on comprehension.** Reading Research Quarterly, 1982, **17**, 462–481.
Reading lessons were redesigned based on the role of prior knowledge in comprehension and the establishment of important story content. Third graders who received such lessons recalled more than the controls.—Adapted from Authors' Abstract.

510. BECKER, CURTIS A. (Bell Telephone Laboratories, Lincroft, NJ). **The development of semantic context effects: two processes or two strategies?** Reading Research Quarterly, 1982, **17**, 482–502.
The results from a lexical-decision (word vs. nonword) task given to third and fifth graders strongly supported the strategy assumption while disconfirming the 2-process theory.—Adapted from Author's Abstract.

511. BIEMILLER, ANDREW (Univ. of Toronto, Canada). **Research on early childhood education: some observations on the problems and possibilities in Canada.** Canadian Journal of Early Childhood Education, 1982, **2**, 73–79.

512. BLACKWELL, SCOTT L.; McINTYRE, CURTIS W. (Southern Methodist Univ.); & MURRAY, MICHAEL E. **Information processed from brief visual displays by learning-disabled boys.** Child Development, 1983, **54**, 927–940.
The spans of apprehension of learning-disabled and normal boys were compared by means of a forced-choice letter-recognition task involving tachistoscopic exposures of letter displays. This task provides an estimate of the span that is relatively insensitive to memory or motivational influences. Results of the experiments indicated that the decreased spans of apprehension resulted either from greater distractiveness, from the slower pick-up of information, or both.—From Authors' Abstract.

513. BRADY, SUSAN (Haskins Laboratories, 270 Crown, New Haven); SHANKWEILER, DONALD; & MANN, VIRGINIA. **Speech perception and memory coding in relation to reading ability.** Journal of Experimental Child Psychology, 1983, **35**, 345–367.
The aim of the present study was to explore whether poor readers' memory deficit may have its origin in the encoding of stimuli. Among third graders, the poor readers were found to perform less well on recall of random word strings and to be less affected by the phonetic characteristics (rhyming or not rhyming) of the items. In addition, the poor readers produced more errors of transposition (in the nonrhyming strings) than did the good readers. The poor readers made significantly more errors than the good readers when listening to speech in noise but did not differ in perception of speech without noise or in perception of nonspeech environmental sounds, whether noise-masked or not.—From Authors' Abstract.

514. BROPHY, JERE E. (Michigan State Univ.). **Research on the self-fulfilling prophecy and teacher expectations.** Journal of Educational Psychology, 1983, **75**, 631–661.
The literature on self-fulfilling prophecy effects is reviewed, with emphasis on application.—From Author's Abstract.

515. BROPHY, JERE (Michigan State Univ.); RASHID, HAKIM; ROHRKEMPER, MARY; & GOLDBERGER, MICHAEL. **Relationships between teachers' presentations of classroom tasks and students' engagement in those tasks.** Journal of Educational Psychology, 1983, **75**, 544–552.
Student engagement was generally higher when teachers moved directly into tasks than when they began with some presentation statement.—From Authors' Abstract.

516. CARVER, RONALD P. (Univ. of Missouri, Kansas City). **Is reading rate constant or flexible?** Reading Research Quarterly, 1983, **18**, 190–215.
Students from grade 4 through college read at a constant rate rather than adjusting their rate to the difficulty level of the material.—Adapted from Author's Abstract.

517. CLEAVE, SHIRLEY (National Foundation for Educational Research, England). **Continuity from pre-school to infant school.** Educational Research, 1982, **24**, 163–173.
The report identifies some of the critical features of continuity and suggests ways of easing transition from preschool to school.—From Author's Abstract.

518. COHEN, RONALD L. (Glendon Coll., 2275 Bayview, Toronto, Ontario, Canada). **Reading disabled children are aware of their cognitive deficits.** Journal of Learning Disabilities, 1983, **16**, 286–289.
Reading-disabled children were compared with a control group on a battery of cognitive tests. Following each test, children were asked to rate their own performance relative to how they thought other children of their own age would perform. The ratings showed that the reading-disabled children had a surprisingly accurate awareness of their own deficits.—From Author's Abstract.

519. COPELAND, ANNE P. (Boston Univ.), & WEISSBROD, CAROL S. **Cognitive strategies used by learning disabled children: does hyperactivity always make things worse?** Journal of Learning Disabilities, 1983, **16**, 473–477.
Results indicated that learning-disabled (LD) children performed less well than the non-LD children on tasks requiring internal strategies or plans. Generally, hyperactive and nonhyperactive LD children performed similarly.—From Authors' Abstract.

520. DELAMATER, ALAN M. (Washington Univ., St. Louis), & LAHEY, BENJAMIN B. **Physiological correlates of conduct problems and anxiety in hyperactive and learning-disabled children.** Journal of Abnormal Child Psychology, 1983, **11**, 85–100.
Thirty-six learning-disabled children (21 of whom were also classified as hyperactive) were subgrouped according to teacher ratings of tension-anxiety and conduct problems. Children rated high on the conduct problem dimension evidenced smaller amplitude-specific skin conductance responses. Anxiety appeared to exert a moderating effect on physiological responses. When the hyperactive sample was considered separately, lower skin conductance levels were observed in children rated high on conduct problems than in hyperactive children rated low on conduct problems.—From Authors' Abstract.

521. DiBENEDETTO, BARBARA; RICHARDSON, ELLIS (Rockland Research Inst., Orangeburg, NY); & KOCHNOWER, JEFF. **Vowel generalization in normal and learning disabled readers.** Journal of Educational Psychology, 1983, **75**, 576–582.
Vowel-sound associations were studied in 20 learning-disabled (LD) children and normal readers matched with the LD children on vocabulary or on age. The LD children applied regular vowel associations less frequently and ungeneralized vowel associations more frequently than the vocabulary-matched group.—From Authors' Abstract.

522. DILLON, RONNA F. (Southern Illinois Univ., Carbondale), & STEVENSON-HICKS, RANDY. **Competence vs. performance and recent approaches to cognitive assessment.** Psychology in the Schools, 1983, **20**, 142–145.
Traditional methods of test administration are less than optimally sensitive to the cognitive abilities and processes under investigation. Recent approaches aimed at lessening the gap between competence and performance are discussed, along with their strengths and weaknesses.—From Authors' Abstract.

523. DONALD, D. R. (Univ. of Cape Town, South Africa). **The use and value of illustrations as contextual information for readers at different progress and developmental levels.** British Journal of Educational Psychology, 1983, **53**, 175–185.
Good and poor readers at reading ages 7 and 9 read with or without illustrations. Illustrations were adaptively used by good readers at reading age 7. Poor readers showed illustration effects but in a nonadaptive way. Good readers at reading age 9 were independent of illustrative information.—From Author's Abstract.

524. FELL, LARRY, & FELL, SUSAN SCHMIDT (Cooperative Education Services, Agency No. 18, Burlington, WI). **Effectiveness of WISC-R short forms in screening gifted children.** Psychological Reports, 1982, **51,** 1017–1018.
Short-form combinations of Similarities-Vocabulary and Similarities-Object Assembly were the best predictors of Full Scale IQ greater than or equal to 130.—From Authors' Abstract.

525. FONTENELLE, SCUDDY, & ALARCON, MOLLIE (Ochsner Clinic, New Orleans). **Hyperlexia: precocious word recognition in developmentally delayed children.** Perceptual and Motor Skills, 1982, **55,** 247–252.

526. FOSTER, RENEE N., & GAVELEK, JAMES R. (Michigan State Univ.). **Development of intentional forgetting in normal and reading-delayed children.** Journal of Educational Psychology, 1983, **75,** 431–440.
First-, third-, and fifth-grade boys were presented with picture slides of common objects derived from 6 conceptual categories. Remember and forget cue slides followed each picture. Boys from all grades in both reading groups differentiated between remember and forget items. This differentiation increased as a function of developmental level and reading ability.—From Authors' Abstract.

527. FOX, ROBERT; ROTATORI, ANTHONY F. (Univ. of New Orleans); GREEN, HERMAN; MACKLIN, FAYE; & ZEVON, MICHAEL. **Gaining research access to retarded children in public schools.** Journal of Psychology, 1983, **115,** 61–64.
Preliminary steps completed prior to conducting a research investigation in the school settings are described within the framework of 2 independent studies. The important role of the special education teacher in conducting research in the natural environment is delineated.—From Authors' Abstract.

528. FRY, P. S. (Univ. of Calgary, Canada). **Process measures of problem and non-problem children's classroom behaviour: the influence of teacher behaviour variables.** British Journal of Educational Psychology, 1983, **53,** 79–88.
Analyses of 15 teacher and pupil process measure variables were conducted to explore teachers' interactions with problem and nonproblem children. Deterioration was noticeable in teachers' interactions with problem children receiving more negative affect and less sustaining feedback over the course of 4 months. Problem children's behavioral interactions showed an increase in serious misdemeanors and a decline in sustained attention.—From Author's Abstract.

529. FUCHS, LYNN S. (Univ. of Minnesota); FUCHS, DOUGLAS; & DENO, STANLEY L. **Reliability and validity of curriculum-based Informal Reading Inventories.** Reading Research Quarterly, 1982, **18,** 6–26.
The external validity of using a 95% accuracy criterion for word recognition to determine instructional level was supported. The reliability and validity of arbitrarily selecting a passage to represent basal reader difficulty level was questioned.—Adapted from Authors' Abstract.

530. GADOW, KENNETH D. (SUNY, Stony Brook). **Effects of stimulant drugs on academic performance in hyperactive and learning disabled children.** Journal of Learning Disabilities, 1983, **16,** 290–299.
It is concluded that while stimulants may increase academic productivity, the effect on standardized achievement test scores is not particularly robust, and individual reaction is quite variable.—From Author's Abstract.

531. GARGIULO, RICHARD M., & YONKER, ROBERT J. (Bowling Green State Univ.). **Assessing teachers' attitude toward the handicapped: a methodological investigation.** Psychology in the Schools, 1983, **20,** 229–233.
The attitudes of regular and special educators toward teaching the special needs pupil were assessed physiologically via changes in pulse and skin temperature and with self-report. Sta-

tistically significant differences were not observed among the groups on the self-report measure; however, the physiological index of change in mean pulse rate indicated that preservice educators, in comparison to experienced teachers, perceived teaching the handicapped child to be significantly more stressful.—From Authors' Abstract.

532. GENESEE, FRED (McGill Univ., Montreal, Quebec, Canada). **An invited article. Bilingual education of majority-language children: the immersion experiments in review.** Applied Psycholinguistics, 1983, **4,** 1–46.
Second-language immersion school programs developed in Canada and the United States during the last 2 decades are described, and the results of evaluative research are reviewed.—From Author's Abstract.

533. GERBER, MICHAEL M. (Univ. of California, Santa Barbara). **Learning disabilities and cognitive strategies: a case for training or constraining problem solving?** Journal of Learning Disabilities, 1983, **16,** 255–260.
An adequate conceptual analysis of the notion of "strategy" is necessary to avoid inevitable confusion resulting from its use in interpreting empirical data.—From Author's Abstract.

534. GETTINGER, MARIBETH (Educational Psychology Dept., 1025 W. Johnson, Madison), & LYON, MARK A. **Predictors of the discrepancy between time needed and time spent in learning among boys exhibiting behavior problems.** Journal of Educational Psychology, 1983, **75,** 491–499.
Ninety-six boys with behavior problems were studied. Reading achievement, attention deficits, low self-concept, locus of control, interest level, and IQ accounted for 63% of the variability in the discrepancy between time spent learning and the time needed for mastery.—Adapted from Authors' Abstract.

535. GOLDWASSER, EVELYN; MEYERS, JOEL (Temple Univ.); CHRISTENSON, SANDRA; & GRADEN, JANET. **The impact of PL 94–142 on the practice of school psychology: a national survey.** Psychology in the Schools, 1983, **20,** 153–165.
This legislation has had little impact on the evaluation procedures used or on the school psychologist's role. The 2 changes that have occurred were an increased focus on handicapped children and increased paperwork.—From Authors' Abstract.

536. GULLO, DOMINIC F. (Kent State Univ.), & McLOUGHLIN, CAVEN S. **Comparison of scores for normal preschool children on Peabody Picture Vocabulary Test-Revised and McCarthy Scales of Children's Abilities.** Psychological Reports, 1982, **51,** 623–626.
Scores on the PPVT-R correlated significantly with the General Cognitive Index, Verbal, and Perceptual scales of the McCarthy tests for 3-year-olds and with the Index, Verbal, Perceptual, and Motor scales for 4-year-olds. Three-year-olds had a lower Peabody than McCarthy score.—From Authors' Abstract.

537. HEGARTY, SEAMUS (National Foundation for Educational Research, England). **Meeting special educational needs in the ordinary school.** Educational Research, 1982, **24,** 174–181.

538. HIEBERT, ELFRIEDA H. (Univ. of Kentucky). **An examination of ability grouping for reading instruction.** Reading Research Quarterly, 1983, **18,** 231–255.
This paper reviews differences in the reading process for groups of different ability.—Adapted from Author's Abstract.

539. HILL, CAROL L. (Mt. St. Vincent Univ.), & HILL, KENNETH A. **Achievement attributions of learning-disabled boys.** Psychological Reports, 1982, **51,** 979–982.
Learning-disabled boys in grades 3 and 6 had an external locus of control for their successes but did not differ in control orientation from nondisabled boys regarding failures. The internal attributions learning-disabled boys made for successes were likely to involve ability rather than

effort. However, these boys did not differ from non-learning-disabled boys in the perception of effort or ability in failure. Results do not support learned helplessness as a model for learning disabilities.—From Authors' Abstract.

540. HISHIYAMA, YOKO (Tokyo Metropolitan Mental Health Ctr., 1–1–3 Shitaya, Taito-ku, Tokyo, Japan), & FURUKAWA, HACHIRO. **A statistical study of the refusal to attend school—social factors and the change in incidence rate in Japan.** Japanese Journal of Child and Adolescent Psychiatry, 1983, **23**, 223–234.
There appear to be certain factors that affect the incidence rate in geographical areas which show social, cultural, and economic changes in social structure.—From Authors' Abstract.

541. HOHN, WILLIAM E., & EHRI, LINNEA C. (Univ. of California, Davis). **Do alphabet letters help prereaders acquire phonemic segmentation skill?** Journal of Educational Psychology, 1983, **75**, 752–762.
Three treatment groups of prereaders were formed: (1) segment blends using letter tokens, (2) segment blends with tokens lacking letters, and (3) no training. Experimental groups took about the same time and number of trials to reach criterion. Letters helped subjects learn to distinguish phoneme-size units and to remember the correct sounds during the task. Letter and nonletter subjects segmented unpracticed blends better than controls. Letter subjects were superior to nonletter subjects in segmenting practiced sounds.—From Authors' Abstract.

542. HOWELL, KENNETH W. (Arizona State Univ.); RUEDA, ROBERT; & RUTHERFORD, ROBERT B., JR. **A procedure for teaching self-recording to moderately retarded students.** Psychology in the Schools, 1983, **20**, 202–209.

543. KAMEENUI, EDWARD J. (Univ. of Montana), & CARNINE, DOUGLAS W. **An investigation of fourth-graders' comprehension of pronoun constructions in ecologically valid texts.** Reading Research Quarterly, 1982, **17**, 556–580.
Expository passages involving social studies content were more difficult than narrative passages for both pronoun-specific and general comprehension questions. In expository passages, replacing pronoun constructions resulted in greater comprehension for pronoun-specific questions. Expository passages were more comprehensible when questions were asked during passage reading instead of after.—Adapted from Authors' Abstract.

544. KARNES, FRANCES (Univ. of Southern Mississippi); McCALLUM, R. STEVE; & BRACKEN, BRUCE A. **Comparison of the PPVT and PPVT-R as possible instruments for screening gifted children.** Psychological Reports, 1982, **51**, 591–594.
Among gifted children, PPVT IQ was significantly higher than PPVT-R, Form L, standard score.—From Authors' Abstract.

545. KINGMA, JOHANNES (Twente Univ. of Technology, Enschede, Netherlands). **Piagetian tasks and traditional intelligence as predictors of performance on addition and subtraction tasks in primary school grades one and two.** Journal of Psychology, 1983, **115**, 39–53.
Conservation, seriation, multiple classification, and subtests from the PMA were administered to children from primary school grades 1 and 2. Nine months after the first test administration, the children completed addition and subtraction tasks and reversal arithmetic tasks. Conservation and seriation were better predictors of the achievement on the addition and subtraction tasks than 2 intelligence subtests.—From Author's Abstract.

546. KLICPERA, C. (Max-Planck-Institut für Psychiatrie, Kraepelinstrasse 10, München, Germany). **Poor planning as a characteristic of problem-solving behavior in dyslexic children: a study with the Rey-Osterrieth complex figure test.** Acta Paedopsychiatrica, 1983, **49**, 73–82.
There were no clear differences in coding strategies between normal and poor readers or between subgroups of poor readers with different levels of verbal and nonverbal ability. The

dyslexic children were clearly poorer than the controls in reproducing the structure of the complex figure.—From Author's Abstract.

547. KOLZAK, JENNIFER (CREC Hearing Impaired Program, Wethersfield, CT). **The impact of child language studies on mainstreaming decisions.** Volta Review, 1983, **85,** 129–137.

548. KRAMER, JACK J. (Univ. of Oklahoma); MARKLEY, ROBERT P.; SHANKS, KAY; & RYABIK, JAMES E. **The seductive nature of WISC-R short forms: an analysis with gifted referrals.** Psychology in the Schools, 1983, **20,** 137–141.
The results indicated that the short form could be effective in the prediction of Full Scale IQ. Practitioners are cautioned against indiscriminate use of shortened IQ tests.—From Authors' Abstract.

549. LEIGH, CHERYL J. (Univ. of Nebraska), & REYNOLDS, CECIL R. **Morning versus afternoon testing and children's intelligence test performance.** Perceptual and Motor Skills, 1982, **55,** 93–94.
There were no significant differences in mean IQs as a function of time of day of testing.—Adapted from Authors' Abstract.

550. LIPA, SALLY E. (State Univ. Coll., Geneseo). **Reading disability: a new look at an old issue.** Journal of Learning Disabilities, 1983, **16,** 453–457.
One case of severe reading disability appears related to dysfunction or "difference" in functioning of the language area in the left hemisphere. Research suggests lateralization differences, temporal sequencing difficulties, and undifferentiated left-hemisphere processing as characteristic of children with reading problems.—From Author's Abstract.

551. LOMAN, NANCY LOCKITCH (Univ. of California, Santa Barbara), & MAYER, RICHARD E. **Signaling techniques that increase the understandability of expository prose.** Journal of Educational Psychology, 1983, **75,** 402–412.
High school students read and listened to either a signaled or nonsignaled expository passage. The signals consisted of preview sentences, underlined headings, and logical connective phrases. The signaled groups performed better on recall of conceptual information and on generating high-quality problem solutions, whereas the nonsignaled groups excelled on recall of information from the beginning and end of the passage and on generating low-quality problem solutions.—From Authors' Abstract.

552. LORANGER, MICHEL; LaCROIX, ODETTE; & KALEY, RICHARD (Universite Laval). **Validity of teachers' evaluations of students' social behavior.** Psychological Reports, 1982, **51,** 915–920.
Thirteen-year-old boys with learning difficulties were observed. Teachers' judgments of the students' behaviors correlated with results from systematic observations.—Ed.

553. McGEE, LEA M. (Louisiana State Univ.). **Awareness of text structure: effects on children's recall of expository text.** Reading Research Quarterly, 1982, **17,** 581–590.
Fifth-grade good readers were more aware of text structure and recalled proportionately more total and superordinate ideas than fifth-grade poor or third-grade good readers. Fifth-grade poor readers had developed some sensitivity to text structure, while third-grade good readers displayed little awareness of text structure.—Adapted from the Article.

554. MARR, MARY BETH (SUNY, Albany), & GROMLEY, KATHLEEN. **Children's recall of familiar and unfamiliar text.** Reading Research Quarterly, 1982, **18,** 89–104.
Retelling elicited text-based responses, whereas probing encouraged more responses based on prior knowledge. Prior knowledge was the strongest predictor of ability to draw inferences and elaborate. Students also exhibited the use of analogical knowledge to comprehend related passages.—Adapted from Authors' Abstract.

555. MEYER, LINDA A. (Univ. of Illinois). **The relative effects of word-analysis and word-supply correction procedures with poor readers during word-attack training.** Reading Research Quarterly, 1982, **17,** 544–555.
There were no differences in oral reading accuracy between special education students taught using either word-analysis or word-supply correction procedures, although both groups showed improvement.—Adapted from Author's Abstract.

556. MILLER, LOUISE B. (Univ. of Louisville), & BIZZELL, RONDEALL P. **Long-term effects of four preschool programs: sixth, seventh, and eighth grades.** Child Development, 1983, **54,** 727–741.
IQs did not differ significantly among the program groups. Males from nondidactic programs were significantly higher in achievement than males from didactic programs. Montessori males were consistently the highest group.—From Authors' Abstract.

557. MISHRA, SHITALA P. (Univ. of Arizona). **Effects of examiners' prior knowledge of subjects' ethnicity and intelligence on the scoring of responses to the Stanford-Binet scale.** Psychology in the Schools, 1983, **20,** 133–136.
Thirty-six real Stanford-Binet protocols were assigned to examiners for the purposes of scoring. The protocols varied in the amount of information revealed about the subjects' ethnicity and IQ. No bias in the scoring was found.—From Author's Abstract.

558. MOXLEY-HAEGERT, LINDA (Concordia Univ., Montreal, Quebec, Canada), & SERBIN, LISA A. **Developmental education for parents of delayed infants: effects on parental motivation and children's development.** Child Development, 1983, **54,** 1324–1331.
This study compared the effectiveness of developmental education for parents with parent education in child management and with a no-education control condition in motivating parents to participate in home treatment programs for developmentally delayed infants. The children in the developmental education group gained a greater number of skills, and their parents participated more in the assigned home-treatment programs than did parents in the other 2 groups.—From Authors' Abstract.

559. NIDIFFER, F. DON (Univ. of Virginia Medical Ctr.); CIULLA, ROBERT P.; RUSSO, DENNIS C.; & CATALDO, MICHAEL F. **Behavioral variability as a function of noncontingent adult attention, peer availability, and situational demands in three hyperactive boys.** Journal of Experimental Child Psychology, 1983, **36,** 109–123.
The most disruptions and least efficient task performance occurred in the group-teaching situation with 1 adult. The most efficient task performance and fewest disruptions in a teaching situation occurred in the individual-teaching setting with high-density noncontingent adult attention.—From Authors' Abstract.

560. ONG, JIN (724 Bush, San Francisco), & JONES, LOWELL, JR. **Memory-for-Designs, intelligence, and achievement of educable mentally retarded children.** Perceptual and Motor Skills, 1982, **55,** 379–382.
High correlations of Memory-for-Designs with WISC Verbal, Performance, and Full Scale IQs and with WRAT Reading and Arithmetic suggest that Memory-for-Designs may supplement the other tests in placement of children into EMR classes.—Adapted from Authors' Abstract.

561. PARAMESH, C. R. (Larned State Hosp., Kansas). **Relationship between Quick Test and WISC-R and reading ability as used in a juvenile setting.** Perceptual and Motor Skills, 1982, **55,** 881–882.
Significant correlations were obtained between adolescents' Quick Test and WISC-R IQs and between Quick Test and WRAT Reading scores.—Adapted from Author's Abstract.

562. PERRY, BETTY M. L. (97 Beeches, Chelmsford, England). **The four-year-old in school.** Educational Research, 1982, **24,** 303–304.

Students in primary schools can spend up to 1/4 of their time accommodating to routines, and they can have much less opportunity to develop and use their language than nursery pupils.—Adapted from the Article.

563. REICHMAN, JULIE, & HEALEY, WILLIAM C. (Univ. of Arizona). **Learning disabilities and conductive hearing loss involving otitis media.** Journal of Learning Disabilities, 1983, **16,** 272–278.

564. ROE, KIKI V. (Univ. of California School of Medicine, Los Angeles); McCLURE, ANNE; & ROE, ARNOLD. **Infant Gesell scores vs. cognitive skills at age 12 years.** Journal of Genetic Psychology, 1983, **142,** 143–147.
It was found in an earlier study that infant performance on the Gesell correlated better with performance on nonverbal than verbal cognitive skills up to the age of 5 years. The same male middle-class subjects were retested with the WISC-R, WRAT, and PPVT when they were 12 years old. Performance on the Gesell was found to relate to WISC-R Performance IQ and to a lesser extent to PPVT IQ, but it did not relate to WISC-R Verbal IQ nor to performance on the WRAT. The results suggest that the Gesell has a better predictive validity for nonverbal than verbal skills.—From Authors' Abstract.

565. SAMETZ, LYNN (Cleveland State Univ.); McLOUGHLIN, CAVEN S.; & STREIB, VICTOR L. **Children's constitutional rights: interpretations and implications.** Psychology in the Schools, 1983, **20,** 175–183.
This paper discusses children's constitutional rights as delineated in the First, Fourth, Fifth, Sixth, Eighth, and Fourteenth Amendments and implications for the role of the school psychologist.—From Authors' Abstract.

566. SCHIFF, MICHEL (INSERM, France); DUYME, MICHEL; DUMARET, ANNICK; & TOMKIEWICZ, STANISLAW. **How much could we boost scholastic achievement and IQ scores? A direct answer from a French adoption study.** Cognition, 1982, **12,** 165–196.
Infants whose biological parents were both unskilled workers were placed into families from the top of the socioprofessional scale. Comparisons were made with children of unskilled workers and the subjects' half siblings who had been reared in their "natural" environment. The subjects showed an increase in mean IQ score and a reduction in the probability of repeating a grade.—From Authors' Abstract.

567. SCHMID, W. (Institut für Medizinische Genetik der Universitäat Zürich, Switzerland); BÄCHLER, A.; FREY, D.; GERTH, J. H.; PRIM, J.; HÄNSLER, A.; & AUGSBURGER, TH. **Genetische, medizinische und psychosoziale Faktoren bei der Lernbehinderung eines Jahrganges von Elfjährigen ("Winterthurer Studie")** [Genetical, medical and psychosocial factors as cause of learning difficulties in a cohort of 11-year-old pupils ("Winterthur Study")]. Acta Paedopsychiatrica, 1983, **49,** 9–45.
The greatest differences between probands and controls were found in the incidence of psychosocial risk factors: marital discord with or without divorce, early mother-child separation, rearing of the child outside the family, parental alcoholism, difficult youth of the parents, illegitimate birth, unwanted pregnancy, financial difficulties, school and behavioral problems in siblings, physical or mental disability of a family member.—From Authors' Abstract.

568. SCHMIDT, H. P. J., & SAKLOFSKE, D. H. (Brandon School Division, Canada). **Comparison of the WISC-R patterns of children of average and exceptional ability.** Psychological Reports, 1983, **53,** 539–544.
No differences in discrepancies in Verbal-Performance IQs occurred among the 4 groups, although learning-disabled children more often showed Performance-Verbal discrepancies.—From Authors' Abstract.

569. SILVERMAN, RITA (Rutgers Univ.), & ZIGMOND, NAOMI. **Self-concept in learning disabled adolescents.** Journal of Learning Disabilities, 1983, **16,** 478–482.

The Piers-Harris Children's Self-Concept Scale was administered to learning-disabled (LD) adolescents in a large urban school system and in urban, suburban, and rural junior high schools. Results indicated that mean self-concept scores of LD adolescents were comparable to those of the age-appropriate norm population.—From Authors' Abstract.

570. SOBOL, MICHAEL P. (Univ. of Guelph, Ontario, Canada); EARN, BRIAN M.; BENNETT, DARLENE; & HUMPHRIES, TOM. **A categorical analysis of the social attributions of learning-disabled children.** Journal of Abnormal Child Psychology, 1983, **11,** 217–228.
The learning-disabled (LD) group used luck more frequently and personality interaction less frequently as explanations for social outcomes than did the controls. LD children also had the lowest expectation of social success and a poorer self-image.—From Authors' Abstract.

571. STEHBENS, JAMES A. (Univ. of Iowa Hosp.); KISKER, C. THOMAS; & WILSON, BERRY K. **School behavior and attendance during the first year of treatment for childhood cancer.** Psychology in the Schools, 1983, **20,** 223–228.
The school behavior and achievement of children with cancer and hemophilia were rated by their teachers before and after first being seen in a large pediatric center. No pre-vs.-post diagnosis differences were noted with either the cancer or hemophilia children. School absenteeism for the children with cancer was 4 times greater than that of healthy children, and absenteeism of children with hemophilia was twice normal.—From Authors' Abstract.

572. SUPRAMANIAM, SARADHA (Open Univ., P.O. Box 188, Milton Keynes, England). **Proofreading errors in good and poor readers.** Journal of Experimental Child Psychology, 1983, **36, 68–80.**
Seven-year-old children classified as good and poor readers carried out a proofreading task on 2 passages varying in level of difficulty. While both groups of readers were able to identify the correct spelling of misspelled words on a spelling test, poor readers made significantly more proofreading errors.—From Author's Abstract.

573. SVENDSEN, D. **Factors related to changes in IQ: a follow-up study of former slow learners.** Journal of Child Psychology and Psychiatry, 1983, **24,** 405–413.
Former slow learners were tested as children and at the age of 30 years. The subjects with the greater number of personal problems and further education improved their IQ scores by 18.1 points, as compared to 5.0 points in the group with 1 or no problems and without further education.—From Author's Abstract.

574. SWANSON, H. LEE (Univ. of Northern Colorado). **A developmental study of vigilance in learning-disabled and nondisabled children.** Journal of Abnormal Child Psychology, 1983, **11,** 415–429.
Learning-disabled children made fewer correct detections and more false responses and were less sensitive to critical stimuli than were nondisabled children at all ages. Learning-disabled children applied different response criteria across age when compared to nondisabled children.—From Author's Abstract.

575. SWANSON, H. LEE (Univ. of Northern Colorado), & MULLEN, ROBERT C. **Hemispheric specialization in learning disabled readers' recall as a function of age and level of processing.** Journal of Experimental Child Psychology, 1983, **35,** 457–477.
Two age groups of learning-disabled and nondisabled readers were compared on diotic and dichotic listening recall tasks for semantically organized, phonemically organized, and categorically unrelated word lists presented in either the left, right, or both ears. Recall increases were a function of age, group, and level of word processing. However, the results clearly demonstrated that age and group recall differences were an interaction of both mode of presentation and level of processing. The recall differences between reading groups were attributed to word knowledge (superordinate categorization) rather than recall organization within cerebral hemispheres or differences in hemispheric capacity, per se.—From Authors' Abstract.

576. TAYLOR, JANET B. (Auburn Univ.). **Influence of speech variety on teachers' evaluation of reading comprehension.** Journal of Educational Psychology, 1983, **75,** 662–667.
Contrasts between the evaluations of 2 readers, 1 a black English speaker and 1 a standard English speaker, were found with teachers who held negative attitudes toward black English, but not with teachers who held positive attitudes.—From Author's Abstract.

577. TAYLOR, MARAVENE BETH, & WILLIAMS, JOANNA P. (Teachers Coll., Columbia Univ.). **Comprehension of learning-disabled readers: task and text variations.** Journal of Educational Psychology, 1983, **75,** 743–751.
Learning disabled (LD) and normal readers had similar skill in title selection and summary sentence writing. LD readers in a reading-with-listening condition detected deviant sentences more accurately than both LD readers in a reading-only condition and normal readers.—From Authors' Abstract.

578. TEW, BRIAN J. (Univ. Coll. Cardiff, Llantrisant, Cardiff, Wales), & LAURENCE, K. M. **The relationship between spina bifida children's intelligence test scores on school entry and at school leaving: a preliminary report.** Child: Care, Health and Development, 1983, **9,** 13–17.
Correlations are reported for Wechsler scores taken at 5, 10, and 16 years, indicating that, for the majority of spina bifida children, reliable predictions regarding intellectual status at 16 years of age can be made upon entry to school.—From Authors' Abstract.

579. TOBIAS, SIGMUND (CUNY); ZIBRIN, MARA; & MENELL, CINDY. **Special education referrals: failure to replicate student–teacher ethnicity interaction.** Journal of Educational Psychology, 1983, **75,** 705–707.
Responses of 320 teachers to a systematically varied protocol showed that recommendations were influenced by teacher ethnicity and teaching level but not by student sex or race. Black and white teachers recommended more males, whereas Hispanics recommended more females for special education.—From Authors' Abstract.

580. TYLER, SHERMAN W. (Univ. of Pittsburgh); DELANEY, HAROLD; & KINNUCAN, MARK. **Specifying the nature of reading ability differences and advance organizer effects.** Journal of Educational Psychology, 1983, **75,** 359–373.
Subjects read short passages, in some cases preceded by a given type of advance organizer, then recalled the information therein, and finally sorted ideas from the passage into groups of similar ideas. Good readers were better at recalling propositions and organizing ideas than poorer readers. Good readers usually showed greater recall of detail when given either type of advance organizer, whereas poorer readers displayed enhanced recall of detail only for a particular type of advance organizer.—From Authors' Abstract.

581. VOGLER, GEORGE P. (Univ. of Colorado), & FULKER, DAVID W. **Familial resemblance for educational attainment.** Behavior Genetics, 1983, **13,** 341–354.
Correlations for years of education completed by spouses, by parents and their offspring, by siblings, by dizygotic twins, and by monozygotic twins are analyzed using path analysis. Two models are employed. One allows environmental transmission from parental phenotype to child's environment, and the other allows direct transmission from parental environment to child's environment.—From Authors' Abstract.

582. WALKER, WILLIAM J. (Alfred Univ.). **Potentially creative adolescents view their school experience.** Psychological Reports, 1982, **51,** 1271–1274.
Adolescents identified as potentially creative wrote essays describing their educational experiences. The adolescents had generally positive attitudes toward their school experiences whether in open or traditional settings.—Adapted from Author's Abstract.

583. WILSON, LONNY R. (800 23rd, Bettendorf, IA); CONE, THOMAS E.; BUSCH, ROBERT; & ALLEE, TERRY. **A critique of the expectancy formula approach: beating a dead horse?** Psychology in the Schools, 1983, **20,** 241–249.

The expectancy and severe discrepancy formulas provide methods of quantifying academic discrepancy. All variations of this approach have several major weaknesses. First, the expectancy formulas themselves are predicated upon the assumption that achievement follows a straight-line growth pattern. Second, when discrepancy values are obtained by multiplying the expected values by a factional constant, the approach is necessarily biased in the direction of applying a more stringent underachievement criterion for older and brighter children. Third, the formulas employ a grade equivalent scale that results in inconsistencies. Finally, the expectancy approach does not consider errors in measurement or regression effects.—From Authors' Abstract.

584. WIXSON, KAREN K. (Univ. of Michigan). **Postreading question–answer interactions and children's learning from text.** Journal of Educational Psychology, 1983, **75,** 413–423.
Fifth-grade students read 1 of 7 short, nonnarrative passages and wrote answers to a set of either textually explicit (TE), textually implicit (TI), schema-based (SB), or text-irrelevant (CONTROL) questions. TI question–answer interactions resulted in the generation of larger proportions of text-based inferences than the other types of interactions. TE question–answer interactions resulted in the production of equal amounts of explicit information, text-based inferences, and schema-based inferences. Finally, SB question–answer interactions and interactions with text-irrelevant questions both resulted in larger proportions of schema-based inferences than either TE or TI interactions.—From Author's Abstract.

585. YSSELDYKE, JAMES E. (Univ. of Minnesota); PIANTA, BOB; CHRISTENSON, SANDRA; WANG, JING-JEN; & ALGOZZINE, BOB. **An analysis of prereferral interventions.** Psychology in the Schools, 1983, **20,** 184–190.
An analysis of the interventions used by elementary classroom teachers before referring students for psychoeducational evaluation showed that most interventions were teacher-directed actions that were implemented for an unspecified time period with few measures of observed success or failure. Few types of interventions were related to the reasons for referal cited by the teachers.—From Authors' Abstract.

PSYCHIATRY, CLINICAL PSYCHOLOGY

586. ARNOLD, GAIL, & SCHWARTZ, STEVEN (Univ. of Queensland, St. Lucia, Brisbane, Queensland, Australia). **Hemispheric lateralization of language in autistic and aphasic children.** Journal of Autism and Developmental Disorders, 1983, **13,** 129–139.
Autistic, language-impaired, and non-language-impaired children were compared on a dichotic listening task. Language-impaired children were found to exhibit a left-ear bias for language material, whereas the autistic and non-language-impaired children showed the opposite, right-ear bias.—From Authors' Abstract.

587. BALK, DAVID (La Frontera Ctr., Tucson). **Adolescents' grief reactions and self-concept perceptions following sibling death: a study of 33 teenagers.** Journal of Youth and Adolescence, 1983, **12,** 137–161.
Thirty-three teenagers were interviewed regarding their grief reactions and self-concept perceptions following sibling death. The participants were as adjusted as same-age same-sex norm groups. Sex and age differences are discussed.—From Author's Abstract.

588. BARGLOW, P. (Univ. of Chicago); EDIDIN, D. V.; BUDLONG-SPRINGER, A. S.; BERNDT, D.; PHILLIPS, R.; & DUBOW, E. **Diabetic control in children and adolescents: psychosocial factors and therapeutic efficacy.** Journal of Youth and Adolescence, 1983, **12,** 77–94.
Forty-two insulin-dependent diabetics were studied over 4 months. Half received a multicomponent intervention designed to enhance diabetic regulation. Life event changes predicted initial status, while ego development predicted improved control.—From Authors' Abstract.

589. BERG, I.; FORSYTHE, I.; HOLT, P.; & WATTS, J. (Airedale General Hosp., Keighley, West Yorkshire, England). **A controlled trial of "Senokot" in faecal soiling treated by behavioural methods.** Journal of Child Psychology and Psychiatry, 1983, **24,** 543–549.
Improvement occurred following 3 months of outpatient treatment using a behavioral approach and either Senokot (a laxative), placebo, or no medication. There was no evidence that the laxative contributed to relieving the problem.—From Authors' Abstract.

590. BERLIN, IRVING N. (Univ. of New Mexico School of Medicine), & CRITCHLEY, DEANE L. **The work of play for parents of schizophrenic children.** Child Psychiatry and Human Development, 1982, **13,** 111–119.
During treatment, the schizophrenic child begins to emerge from his constructed, self-centered world and to enjoy interaction, play, and playfulness. Many of the parents are as constricted and unable to play as their children. The use of a play corner, dress-up clothes, and a staff member who can model roles to play helps reduce the "work" of play for parents and child.—From Authors' Abstract.

591. BOAKE, CORWIN (St. Anthony Ctr., 6301 Almeda, P.O. Box 14708, Houston); SALMON, PAUL G.; & CARBONE, GREGORY. **Torque, lateral preference, and cognitive ability in primary-grade children.** Journal of Abnormal Child Psychology, 1983, **11,** 77–84.
Among kindergartners and first graders, rate of torque decreased with age and was greater among males. Children with complete clockwise or counterclockwise circling at both assessments differed in pattern but not in overall level of cognitive ability. Results of this and other studies are seen as inconsistent with proposals that torque is symptomatic of psychopathology.—From Authors' Abstract.

592. BOWERS, A. J. (Cambridge Inst. of Education, Shaftesbury, Cambridge, England), & SAGE, L. R. **Solvent abuse in adolescents: the Who? What? and Why?** Child: Care, Health and Development, 1983, **9,** 169–178.

593. BRESLAU, NAOMI (Case Western Reserve Univ.). **The psychological study of chronically ill and disabled children: are healthy siblings appropriate controls?** Journal of Abnormal Child Psychology, 1983, **11,** 379–391.
Comparisons with both siblings and randomly selected controls indicated that children with cystic fibrosis are not an increased risk for psychopathology, whereas children with cerebral palsy, myelodisplasia, and multiple handicaps show a substantial excess in Mentation Problems and Isolation. Comparisons with matched siblings underestimated Regressive–Anxiety and aggressive behavior in the disabled children.—Adapted from Author's Abstract.

594. BRIMER, ELAINE, & LEVINE, FREDRIC M. (SUNY, Stony Brook). **Stimulus-seeking behavior in hyperactive and nonhyperactive children.** Journal of Abnormal Child Psychology, 1983, **11,** 131–140.
The results indicate that after controlling for motor activity level, hyperactive children preferred auditory stimulation more than the control children. There were no differences in stimulus-seeking preferences in the visual modality.—From Authors' Abstract.

595. BUSBY, KEITH A., & BROUGHTON, ROGER J. (Ottawa General Hosp., 501 Smyth, Ottawa, Ontario, Canada). **Waking ultradian rhythms of performance and motility in hyperkinetic and normal children.** Journal of Abnormal Child Psychology, 1983, **11,** 431–442.
Testing was conducted for 5 min every 15 min over a 6-hour period on 2 consecutive days. Hyperkinetic subjects made fewer detections and were more active during off-task periods on both days. False positives and global body movements failed to differentiate the groups. Some subjects in both groups showed evidence of ultradian peaks.—From Authors' Abstract.

596. CANTWELL, DENNIS P. (Univ. of California, Los Angeles), & BAKER, LORIAN. **Depression in children with speech, language, and learning disorders.** Journal of Children in Contemporary Society, 1983, **15,** 51–59.

Among 600 children studied, it was found that 4% had some type of affective disorder, according to DSM-III diagnostic criteria.—From Authors' Abstract.

597. CHANDLER, LOUIS A. (Univ. of Pittsburgh). **Brief therapy: Ronny G.** Psychology in the Schools, 1983, **20**, 215–218.
Brief therapy is an active, focused, incisive intervention especially useful with children typically seen by the school psychologist because of emotional adjustment problems. This paper illustrates the process.—From Author's Abstract.

598. CHARLOP, MARJORIE H. (George Washington Univ.); SCHREIBMAN, LAURA; & TRYON, ADELINE S. **Learning through observations: the effects of peer modeling on acquisition and generalization in autistic children.** Journal of Abnormal Child Psychology, 1983, **11**, 355–366.
Autistic children learned through observation of their peer model. Generalization and maintenance of correct responding were superior when the children learned through observation rather than by trial and error.—From Authors' Abstract.

599. COHEN, N. J. (Hosp. for Sick Children, Toronto, Ontario, Canada), & MINDE, K. **The "hyperactive syndrome" in kindergarten children: comparison of children with pervasive and situational symptoms.** Journal of Child Psychology and Psychiatry, 1983, **24**, 443–455.
Biological and psychological test data did not differentiate the various groups of children. The clearest differentiation between groups emerged when children were observed directly.—From Authors' Abstract.

600. COLLETTA, NANCY DONOHUE (Univ. of Maryland). **At risk for depression: a study of young mothers.** Journal of Genetic Psychology, 1983, **142**, 301–310.
Mothers 15–19 years of age were used to investigate the relationship between depression and the maternal behavior of young mothers. Depression, as measured by the Center for Epidemiologic Studies of Depression Scale, varied with marital status, education, and maternal age and was related to hostile, indifferent, and rejecting patterns of mother-child interaction.—From Author's Abstract.

601. DISCHE, SYLVIA (King's Coll. Hosp., Denmark Hill, London, England); YULE, WILLIAM; CORBETT, JOHN; & HAND, DAVID. **Childhood nocturnal enuresis: factors associated with outcome of treatment with an enuresis alarm.** Developmental Medicine and Child Neurology, 1983, **25**, 67–80.
Family difficulties were the most important predictor of treatment outcome.—Adapted from Authors' Abstract.

602. DOLLINGER, STEPHEN J. (Southern Illinois Univ., Carbondale). **On the varieties of childhood sleep disturbance.** Journal of Clinical Child Psychology, 1982, **11**, 107–115.
Cluster analysis was applied to the sleep problem checklist data of 81 children seen in a clinical setting. In a series of analyses, 4 groups of children were identified: those with moderate, immature, severe, and few or no sleep problems. The moderate sleep problem group appeared to involve children who were afraid to sleep. The immature problem group involved children who "magically" attempted to protect themselves at bedtime and/or manipulate parents regarding bedtime issues. The severe sleep problem group included children with severe distress and anxiety which "breaks through" during sleep.—From Author's Abstract.

603. DOUGLAS, VIRGINIA I., & PARRY, PENNY A. (Univ. of Victoria, British Columbia, Canada). **Effects of reward on delayed reaction time task performance of hyperactive children.** Journal of Abnormal Child Psychology, 1983, **11**, 313–326.
Although noncontingent reward resulted in faster reaction times for control subjects, performance of hyperactives deteriorated under noncontingent reward and improved when it was withdrawn. Reaction times of controls during extinction remained superior to baseline, whereas performance of hyperactives returned to baseline level.—From Authors' Abstract.

604. DUBEY, DENNIS R. (Sagamore Children's Ctr., Box 755, Melville, NY); O'LEARY, SUSAN G.; & KAUFMAN, KENNETH F. **Training parents of hyperactive children in child management: a comparative outcome study.** Journal of Abnormal Child Psychology, 1983, **11,** 229–246.
Parents of hyperactive children were assigned to a behavior modification group, a communications group (PET), or a control group. Both treatment methods were more effective than the control condition in reducing hyperactivity ratings, problem severity ratings, and daily problem occurrence. Parents receiving behavior modification training rated their children as more improved than did PET parents, were more willing to recommend the program to a friend, felt the program was more applicable to them, and were less likely to drop out of the program.—From Authors' Abstract.

605. EDELSON, STEPHEN M. (Univ. of Illinois, Champaign); TAUBMAN, MITCHELL T.; & LOVAAS, O. IVAR. **Some social contexts of self-destructive behavior.** Journal of Abnormal Child Psychology, 1983, **11,** 299–312.
Social interactions between autistic, schizophrenic, and mentally retarded children and hospital staff were recorded along with subjects' self-destructive behavior. The results showed a substantial increase in self-destructive behavior following the staff's presentation of demands, denials, and punishments in 19 of the 20 subjects.—From Authors' Abstract.

606. FELDMAN, WENDY S. (Orthopaedic Hosp., 2400 S. Flower, Los Angeles); MANELLA, KATHLEEN J.; & VARNI, JAMES W. **A behavioural parent training programme for single mothers of physically handicapped children.** Child: Care, Health and Development, 1983, **9,** 157–168.
A 9-week training program was developed to instruct parents in the systematic utilization of behavioral techniques for teaching their children self-help skills and reducing behavior problems. The mothers successfully taught their children 7 self-help skills, with average self-help skill performance increasing from 18% correct during baseline to 99% correct during a 5-month follow-up period.—From Authors' Abstract.

607. FIALKOV, M. JEROME (Western Psychiatric Inst. and Clinic, 3811 O'Hara, Pittsburgh); SONIS, WILLIAM A.; RAPPORT, MARK D.; & KAZDIN, ALAN E. **An interdisciplinary approach to the diagnosis and management of a complex case of postencephalitic behavioral disorder.** Journal of Autism and Developmental Disorders, 1983, **13,** 107–115.
The present paper describes the clinical state of a 13-year-old pubertal female who presented 9 years after the original acute febrile illness. A behavioral approach to treatment of intractable seizures and aggressive behavior is described.—From Authors' Abstract.

608. FIEDLER, NANCY L., & ULLMAN, DOUGLAS G. (Bowling Green State Univ.). **The effects of stimulant drugs on curiosity behaviors of hyperactive boys.** Journal of Abnormal Child Psychology, 1983, **11,** 193–206.
Comparisons on object, manipulative, conceptual, perceptual, and reactive curiosity tasks indicated that stimulants reduced only the object curiosity task performance of hyperactive boys, although the level tended to remain above that of nonhyperactive boys.—From Authors' Abstract.

609. FINE, PAUL (Creighton Univ. School of Medicine). **Play and family therapy as core skills for child psychiatry: some implications of Piaget's theory for integrations in training and practice.** Child Psychiatry and Human Development, 1982, **13,** 79–96.
Core experiences with play therapy and family therapy enable child psychiatrists to apply the entire spectrum of modern treatment modalities in ways that are developmentally and socially appropriate. Piaget's genetic system of psychology provides guidelines for integrating disparate skills toward meaningful practice.—From Author's Abstract.

610. FIRESTONE, PHILIP (Univ. of Ottawa, Ontario, Canada), & PRABHU, ANAND N. **Minor physical anomalies and obstetrical complications: their relationship to hyperactive, psychoneurotic, and normal children and their families.** Journal of Abnormal Child Psychology, 1983, **11**, 207–216.
Hyperactive boys and their families had more minor physical anomalies (MPA) than the combined group of psychoneurotic and normal control children and their families. The combination of numerous obstetrical complications and a high number of MPA significantly increased the probability of a child being diagnosed as hyperactive.—From Authors' Abstract.

611. GALLOWAY, D. (Victoria Univ. of Wellington). **Research note: truants and other absentees.** Journal of Child Psychology and Psychiatry, 1983, **24**, 607–611.
There were few differences in the social and financial circumstances of the 2 groups but considerable differences in the children's behavior and in family relationships.—From Author's Abstract.

612. GARRISON, WILLIAM; EARLS, FELTON (Washington Univ. School of Medicine, St. Louis); & KINDLON, DANIEL. **An application of the pictorial scale of perceived competence and acceptance within an epidemiological survey.** Journal of Abnormal Child Psychology, 1983, **11**, 367–377.
Children 6–7 years old were administered the WISC-R, the WRAT, the Lie Scale for Children, and the Perceived Competence and Acceptance Scale (PCS). Children tended to more accurately report about cognitive competence. Children who reported atypically high or low PCS levels were not found to differ from the remainder of the sample on 2 clinical indices. Children who tended to exaggerate PCS levels, as compared to teacher ratings, had more behavior problems in school and were rated as currently maladjusted.—From Authors' Abstract.

613. GENTILE, PHILIP S. (Fordham Univ.); TRENTALANGE, MARK J.; ZAMICHEK, WALTER; & COLEMAN, MARY. **Brief report: trace elements in the hair of autistic and control children.** Journal of Autism and Developmental Disorders, 1983, **13**, 205–206.
Autistic children had elevated hair magnesium and potassium levels as compared to controls.—Ed.

614. GERSTEN, RUSSELL (Univ. of Oregon). **Stimulus overselectivity in autistic, trainable mentally retarded, and non-handicapped children: comparative research controlling chronological (rather than mental) age.** Journal of Abnormal Child Psychology, 1983, **11**, 61–76.
Results indicated no significant differences between the autistic and trainable mentally retarded samples, but significant differences between the handicapped samples and the non-handicapped group. Some, but not all, of the handicapped children displayed overselectivity.—From Author's Abstract.

615. GILLBERG, C. (Univ. of Uppsala, Sweden). **Perceptual, motor and attentional deficits in Swedish primary school children. Some child psychiatric aspects.** Journal of Child Psychology and Psychiatry, 1983, **24**, 377–403.
Prevalence figures for marked psychiatric abnormality in MBD were shown to be higher than for psychiatric abnormality in children with "neuroepileptic" disorders. Psychotic behavior was found to be specifically associated with MBD. Nonoptimal psychosocial factors appear to interact with the MBD syndrome in the molding of psychiatric disorders.—From Author's Abstract.

616. GILLBERG, CHRISTOPHER (Göteborgs Univ., Box 7284, Göteborg, Sweden), & GILLBERG, I. CARINA. **Infantile autism: a total population study of reduced optimality in the pre-, peri-, and neonatal period.** Journal of Autism and Developmental Disorders, 1983, **13**, 153–166.
Autistic children, as compared to controls, showed greatly increased scores for reduced optimality, especially with regard to prenatal factors.—From Authors' Abstract.

617. GILLBERG, CHRISTOPHER (Göteborgs Univ., Box 7284, Göteborg, Sweden); ROSENHALL, ULF; & JOHANSSON, ELISABETH. **Auditory brainstem responses in childhood psychosis.** Journal of Autism and Developmental Disorders, 1983, **13**, 181–195.
Auditory brainstem responses (ABR) were compared in autistic children, children with other childhood psychoses, and normal children. One-third of the autistic children showed abnormal ABR indicative of brainstem dysfunction and correlating with muscular hypotonia and sever language impairment. The children with other psychoses and the normal children showed normal results.—From Authors' Abstract.

618. GILLBERG, CHRISTOPHER (Göteborgs Univ., Box 7284, Göteborg, Sweden), & SVENDSEN, PÅL. **Childhood psychosis and computed tomographic brain scan findings.** Journal of Autism and Developmental Disorders, 1983, **13**, 19–32.
Autistic, psychotic, mentally retarded, and normal children were examined. Gross abnormalities were seen in 26% of the autism cases. Abnormalities in the region of the frontal horns of the ventricular system tended to be more common in the psychosis groups than in the normal group. Right occipital protuberation was common in the psychoses cases but was only marginally more common in the autism than in the normal group.—From Authors' Abstract.

619. GROB, MOLLIE C. (McLean Hosp., 115 Mill, Belmont, MA); KLEIN, ARTHUR A.; & EISEN, SUSAN V. **The role of the high school professional in identifying and managing adolescent suicidal behavior.** Journal of Youth and Adolescence, 1983, **12**, 163–173.
Eighty high school professionals were interviewed in a semistructured format. Respondents identified more than 30 signs of potential vulnerability to suicide. Among predisposing factors, those related to alienation within the family were most prominent. Other risk factors were low self-esteem, difficulty in peer relationships, and economic or ethnic differences.—From Authors' Abstract.

620. HIRSHOREN, ALFRED (St. John's Univ.), & SCHNITTJER, CARL J. **Behavior problems in blind children and youth: a prevalence study.** Psychology in the Schools, 1983, **20**, 197–201.
The Behavior Problem Checklist was completed by classroom teachers at a state residential school for the blind. The blind children had a similar frequency of problems to hearing-impaired children in a residential setting, both of which were higher than the frequencies for nonhandicapped and hearing-impaired children living at home.—Ed.

621. HOLMES, CLARISSA S. (Univ. of Iowa); HAYFORD, JOHN T.; & THOMPSON, ROBERT G. **Parents' and teachers' differing views of short children's behaviour.** Child: Care, Health and Development, 1982, **8**, 327–336.
Children over 2 standard deviations below height expectation with constitutional delay (CD), growth hormone deficiency (GHD), or Turner's syndrome (TS) were studied. Adolescent females were rated by teachers and parents as showing greatest behavioral immaturity and emotional inhibition of the groups studied. Parent ratings appeared more influenced by children's diagnoses. Significant school problems were noted on parent ratings for all groups of children except the young CD group. Peer teasing was frequently reported, and a relatively large proportion (25%) of the studied short children were retained in kindergarten through second grade, apparently because of small size and immaturity.—From Authors' Abstract.

622. JACOBSEN, REBECCA H.; LAHEY, BENJAMIN B. (Univ. of Georgia); & STRAUSS, CYD C. **Correlates of depressed mood in normal children.** Journal of Abnormal Child Psychology, 1983, **11**, 29–40.
The Children's Depression Inventory (CDI), the Peer Nomination Inventory for Depression (PNID), and a teacher rating of depression were given along with the Conners Teacher Rating Scale (TRS); teacher ratings of somatic complaints, peer popularity, and absenteeism; and peer ratings of popularity. While few sex differences were found on mean depression scores, different patterns of correlations were found for the 2 sexes. For males, there were no significant correlations among the 3 depression measures, but all 3 depression measures were cor-

elated with unpopularity and conduct problem ratings on the TRS. For females, the 3 epression measures were adequately intercorrelated. The teacher rating of depression was orrelated with general deviance as measured by the TRS, but the CDI and PNID were corre- ated with TRS ratings of conduct problems, with peer ratings of unpopularity, and with teacher atings of somatic complaints.—From Authors' Abstract.

23. JAMES, ANGELA L., & BARRY, ROBERT J. (Univ. of New South Wales, Kensington, Australia). **Developmental effects in the cerebral lateralization of autistic, retarded, and normal children.** Journal of Autism and Developmental Disorders, 1983, **13,** 43–56. Unwarned simple reaction time (RT) to monaural presentation of tones was investigated. Anal- sis of RTs and relative ear advantage indicated that the autistic children showed significant evelopmental delay in both RT and the establishment of cerebral dominance compared to the ontrol groups.—From Authors' Abstract.

24. KASHANI, JAVAD H. (Univ. of Missouri, Columbia). **Depression in the preschool child.** Journal of Children in Contemporary Society, 1983, **15,** 11–17. here are no systematic studies that deal primarily with the investigation of depression among reschool age children. This paper discusses contributory factors, symptomatology, epidemiol- gy, assessment, and intervention.—From Author's Abstract.

25. KAZDIN, ALAN E. (Univ. of Pittsburgh School of Medicine); ESVELDT-DAWSON, KAREN; UNIS, ALAN S.; & RANCURELLO, MICHAEL D. **Child and parent evaluations of depression and aggression in psychiatric inpatient children.** Journal of Abnormal Child Psychology, 1983, **11,** 401–413. Children provided less severe ratings than their parents. Children who met DSM III criteria for major depression or conduct disorder were significantly higher in their ratings of depression and aggression than children without these diagnoses. Child and parent ratings were low to moderately correlated, whereas mother and father ratings were moderately to highly corre- ated.—Adapted from Authors' Abstract.

26. KAZDIN, ALAN E. (Univ. of Pittsburgh School of Medicine); FRENCH, NANCY H.; & UNIS, ALAN S. **Child, mother, and father evaluations of depression in psychiatric inpa- ient children.** Journal of Abnormal Child Psychology, 1983, **11,** 167–180. Children ages 6–13 years independently diagnosed as depressed rated themselves and were ated by their parents as more depressed than nondepressed children. Even so, children con- istently rated themselves as less depressed across the measures than did their parents. Rat- ngs varied as a function of child IQ, gender, race, and family welfare status.—From Authors' Abstract.

27. KETTLEWELL, PAUL W. (Geisinger Medical Ctr., Danville, PA), & KAUSCH, DONALD F. **The generalization of the effects of a cognitive–behavioral treatment program for aggressive children.** Journal of Abnormal Child Psychology, 1983, **11,** 101–114. Treatment consisted of 4 weeks of coping-skills training using behavioral rehearsal and self-in- struction training. There was an improvement in interpersonal problem-solving skills and a decrease in being disciplined for fighting. No changes were found, however, in physical or ver- al aggression or in peer rating of aggression.—From Authors' Abstract.

28. KIERNAN, C. (41 Brunswick, London, England). **The use of nonvocal communica- ion techniques with autistic individuals.** Journal of Child Psychology and Psychiatry, 1983, 24, 339–375. Studies suggest that sign language and symbol systems can be used in communication by ndividuals who are mute and mentally handicapped.—From Author's Abstract.

29. KOBAYASHI, RYUJI (Fukuoka Univ., 7–45–1 Nanakuma, Jonan-ku, Fukuoka-shi, Japan). **The psychopathological characteristics of adolescent autistics based on the fea- ures of their language disturbances.** Japanese Journal of Child and Adolescent Psychiatry, 1983, **23,** 235–260.

The results suggest that the basic disability in adolescent autistics is in the cognitive awareness of other people, not in language cognition. Thus, even cases showing favorable clinical course have a cognitive disability in the differentiation of the self from objects and show weakness in ego integration.—From Author's Abstract.

630. KOSKY, R. (Mental Health Services of Western Australia, Leederville, Western Australia). **Childhood suicidal behaviour.** Journal of Child Psychology and Psychiatry, 1983, 24, 457–468.
Suicidal behavior was associated with the male sex, personal experiences of significant losses, academic underachievement, marital disintegration among the parents, and past intrafamilial violence, including physical abuse of the index child.—From Author's Abstract.

631. KRAKOW, JOANNE B. (Univ. of California, Los Angeles), & KOPP, CLAIRE B. **The effects of developmental delay on sustained attention in young children.** Child Development, 1983, 54, 1143–1155.
Attention deployment behaviors of normally developing (ND), Down's syndrome (DS), and developmentally delayed with uncertain etiology (UE) groups were examined. Among infants with developmental ages of 12–24 months, UE subjects spent less time engaged with toys than ND or DS subjects, and both delayed groups had less simultaneous appraisal of the environment, more time unoccupied in any way, and more throwing behavior than the ND group. At the 22–30-month developmental age range, DS and UE subjects had patterns of play that included many primitive activities such as banging and mouthing.—From Authors' Abstract.

632. LANCIONI, GIULIO E. (Univ. of Nijmegen, Irasmusplein 1, Nijmegen, Holland). **Using pictorial representations as communication means with low-functioning children.** Journal of Autism and Developmental Disorders, 1983, 13, 87–105.
The subjects were first trained to associate cards representing objects with the corresponding objects. Then they were trained to respond to: (a) cards depicting body positions, (b) cards depicting body positions related to objects, and (c) cards representing simple activities as well as activities involving 2 children. Next they were trained to complete cards representing activities involving 2 activities. High generalization learning was observed.—From Author's Abstract.

633. LeBOW, HADASSAH (Hadassah Univ. Hosp., Jerusalem, Israel); SCHILLER, MEDAD; CAPLAN, GERALD; & SELINGER, DRORA. **The integration of the emotional and surgical treatment of children hospitalized on a pediatric-surgical ward.** Child Psychiatry and Human Development, 1983, 13, 180–188.
The use of executive meetings between the heads of both departments and the psychiatrist allowed for immediate clarification of misunderstandings and the formalization of decisions into administrative procedures. The special technique whereby the surgeon, on the basis of psychiatric information, acts as the spokesman for the joint psychiatric-surgical decision is discussed.—From Authors' Abstract.

634. LIM, M. H., & BOTTOMLEY, V. (Lister Health Ctr., London, England). **A combined approach to the treatment of effeminate behaviour in a boy: a case study.** Journal of Child Psychology and Psychiatry, 1983, 24, 469–479.
A 5 1/2-year-old boy with persistent effeminate behavior had individual therapy sessions which combined psychodynamic and behavioral elements. There were positive changes in the child, his parents, and his grandmother which were maintained at follow up.—From Authors' Abstract.

635. LINKS, PAUL S. (McMaster Univ., St. Joseph's Hosp., 301 S. James South, Hamilton, Ontario, Canada). **Community surveys of the prevalence of childhood psychiatric disorders: a review.** Child Development, 1983, 54, 531–548.
Sixteen major community surveys designed to measure the prevalence of emotional and behavioral conditions of childhood are reviewed.—From Author's Abstract.

36. LOEBER, ROLF (Oregon Social Learning Ctr., 207 E. 5th Ave., Eugene); WEISSMAN, WENDY; & REID, JOHN B. **Family interactions of assaultive adolescents, stealers, and nondelinquents.** Journal of Abnormal Child Psychology, 1983, **11**, 1–14.
Assaultive adolescents, unlike their controls, ranked significantly higher among their own family members in terms of their total aversive behavior in the family home. Assaultive adolescents had more female siblings than male siblings, whereas nondelinquent adolescents had more male than female siblings.—From Authors' Abstract.

37. LORD, CATHERINE (Glenrose Hosp., 10230–111 Ave., Edmonton, Alberta, Canada); MERRIN, DAVID J.; VEST, LINDA O.; & KELLY, KIM M. **Communicative behavior of adults with an autistic four-year-old boy and his nonhandicapped twin brother.** Journal of Autism and Developmental Disorders, 1983, **13**, 1–17.
Preschool teachers were videotaped playing in dyads with a nonverbal, socially unresponsive autistic boy and his nonhandicapped fraternal twin brother. One-half were informed that the autistic child had a language disability and did not talk or understand much language; one-half were not informed about any differences between the children. Language to the autistic child was simpler, more concrete, and more often accompanied by gestures than language to his brother for both groups of subjects. Informed teachers made greater speech modifications to the autistic child and were more successful at keeping him on-task than uninformed adults.—From Authors' Abstract.

38. McCONVILLE, BRIAN J. (Queen's Univ., Kingston, Ontario, Canada). **The causes and treatment of depression in young children.** Journal of Children in Contemporary Society, 1983, **15**, 61–68.
Symptoms of sadness and misery occur frequently in children, but do not always cause frank depressive symptoms or minor or major childhood affective disorders. This paper indicates some studies suggesting that although most children adapt quickly, sustained depression and cumulative losses cause more severe conditions.—From Author's Abstract.

39. McGIBONEY, GARRY WADE (Dekalb School System, Georgia), & CARTER, CLIFFORD. **Test-retest reliability of the Hand Test with acting-out adolescent subjects.** Perceptual and Motor Skills, 1982, **55**, 723–726.
Results support the reliability of the Hand Test variables related to acting-out behavioral tendencies and adjustment problems—From Authors' Abstract.

40. MASTERTON, B. A. (Peel Board of Education, 30 Kennedy N., Brampton, Ontario, Canada), & BIEDERMAN, G. B. **Proprioceptive versus visual control in autistic children.** Journal of Autism and Developmental Disorders, 1983, **13**, 141–152.
Autistic, retarded, and normal subjects were required to adapt to a prism-induced lateral displacement of the visual field. Only autistic subjects demonstrated transfer of adaptation to the nonhandicapped hand, indicative of a reliance on proprioception rather than vision to accomplish adaptation.—From Authors' Abstract.

41. MOTTI, FROSSO; CICCHETTI, DANTE; & SROUFE, L. ALAN (Univ. of Minnesota). **From infant affect expression to symbolic play: the coherence of development in Down syndrome children.** Child Development, 1983, **54**, 1168–1175.
With corrections for mental age, the play of these children was similar to that of nonhandicapped children. Moreover, individual differences in the level and quality of play were strongly predicted from Bayley DQ scores obtained at age 2 and by several indexes of affective expressiveness, including 1 obtained in the first year of life.—From Authors' Abstract.

42. NIWA, SHIN-ICHI (Univ. of Tokyo, Japan); OHTA, MASATAKA; & YAMAZAKI, KIYOYUKI. **P300 and stimulus evaluation process in autistic subjects.** Journal of Autism and Developmental Disorders, 1983, **13**, 33–42.
Autistic subjects demonstrated a lower amplitude of the P300 component than normal subjects and subjects with Down's syndrome.—Adapted from Authors' Abstract.

643. ORVASCHEL, HELEN (Yale Univ. School of Medicine). **The epidemiology of depres** **sion in young children.** Journal of Children in Contemporary Society, 1983, **15**, 79–86.
There is currently very little direct information available on the epidemiology of depression young children.—From Author's Abstract.

644. OWNBY, RAYMOND L. (1315 Anita Ct., #204, Kent). **A cognitive behavioral inter** **vention for compulsive handwashing with a thirteen-year-old boy.** Psychology in th Schools, 1983, **20**, 219–222.
The principal cognitive intervention used was thought-stopping. Handwashing was reduce during treatment to fewer than 6 occurrences per day, and behavior change was maintained 6- and 18-month follow-ups.—From Author's Abstract.

645. PARRY, PENNY A. (Univ. of Victoria, British Columbia, Canada), & DOUGLAS VIRGINIA I. **Effects of reinforcement on concept identification in hyperactive childrer** Journal of Abnormal Child Psychology, 1983, **11**, 327–340.
Previous findings of a performance deficit in hyperactives under partial reward were rep cated.—From Authors' Abstract.

646. PETER, DENNIS; ALLAN, JOHN (Univ. of British Columbia, Vancouver, British Colum bia, Canada); & HORVATH, ADAM. **Hyperactive children's perceptions of teachers' class** **room behavior.** Psychology in the Schools, 1983, **20**, 234–240.
Hyperactive behavior in boys was found to be significantly related to less perceived accep tance and more perceived demand. Hyperactive boys perceived significantly less acceptanc and more demand than did their nonhyperactive peers.—From Authors' Abstract.

647. PETTI, THEODORE A. (Univ. of Pittsburgh School of Medicine). **The assessment** **depression in young children.** Journal of Children in Contemporary Society, 1983, **15** 19–28.
A variety of scales and interviews that are of potential use to the caretakers of young childre are reviewed.—From Author's Abstract.

648. PFEFFER, CYNTHIA R. (Cornell Univ. Medical Coll.). **Clinical observations of suic** **dal behavior in a neurotic, a borderline, and a psychotic child: common processes o** **symptom formation.** Child Psychiatry and Human Development, 1982, **13**, 120–134.
This paper illustrates the characteristics of suicidal behavior in 3 psychiatrically hospitalize children with neurotic, borderline, and psychotic disorders. The author proposes that the natur of suicidal fantasies and the mode of ego functioning associated with suicidal behavior in thes disorders are similar. However, it is emphasized that other differences in the fantasies and eg functioning exist for these distinct disorders. The paper presents a hypothetical model of ho suicidal behavior of children develops.—From Author's Abstract.

649. PIROZZOLO, FRANCIS J. (Baylor Coll. of Medicine); OBRZUT, JOHN E.; & HESS, D WILSON. **Construct validity of the Illinois Test of Psycholinguistic Abilities for clini** **population.** Psychology in the Schools, 1983, **20**, 146–152.
Results generally support the independence of the channel dimension (visual vs. auditory) While the process dimension (receptive, expressive, and associative) was not found to be a independent measure, the dimension of levels (representational vs. automatic) was substanti ated for this clinical population.—From Authors' Abstract.

650. PORTNER, ELAINE S. (Univ. of Pittsburgh School of Medicine). **Depressive theme** **in children's fantasies.** Journal of Children in Contemporary Society, 1983, **15**, 29–39.
Puppet stories were elicited spontaneously from 65 8–9-year-olds in a recent study designe to collect normative data. Findings provided an opportunity to study more closely a subgrou within the population.—From Author's Abstract.

651. POZNANSKI, ELVA ORLOW (Univ. of Illinois). **Controversy and conflicts in child** **hood depression.** Journal of Children in Contemporary Society, 1983, **15**, 3–10.

Clinically, the group who is the most honest and the most accurate in recognizing depressive behavior in themselves and others has been children. Children, rather than their parents, give the best description of their feelings, especially in the affective disorders.—From Author's Abstract.

652. PRINZ, RONALD J. (Univ. of South Carolina); DEROSSET, MYERS; HOLDEN, E. WAYNE; TARNOWSKI, KENNETH J.; & ROBERTS, WILLIAM A. **Marital disturbance and child problems: a cautionary note regarding hyperactive children.** Journal of Abnormal Child Psychology, 1983, **11**, 393–399.
Marital discord in families with a hyperactive boy did not explain differential rates of aggressive behavior despite definite variability in both the marital and child behavioral measures. Marital discord was marginally related to severity of attentional deficit on the Continuous Performance Test.—From Authors' Abstract.

653. RICHMOND, GLENN (Murdoch Ctr., Butner, North Carolina). **Shaping bladder and bowel continence in developmentally retarded preschool children.** Journal of Autism and Developmental Disorders, 1983, **13**, 197–204.
During baseline, the children were taken to the toilet on a regular schedule, once an hour. The training program increased this frequency to once every 15 min for the first week, every 30 min for the second week, every hour the third week, and every 2 hours in the fourth week. Using the toilet appropriately was reinforced with social praise and liquids. Accidents resulted in a brief verbal reprimand and simple correction. All 4 children showed improvement in their bladder and bowel continence.—From Author's Abstract.

654. RIDER, ROBERT A. (Florida State Univ.), & CANDELETTI, GLENN. **Influence of motor therapy on children with multisensory disabilities: a preliminary study.** Perceptual and Motor Skills, 1982, **55**, 809–810.
Subjects 7–11 years old improved performance after therapy.—Adapted from Authors' Abstract.

655. RIMLAND, BERNARD, & LARSON, GERALD E. **Hair mineral analysis and behavior: an analysis of 51 studies.** Journal of Learning Disabilities, 1983, **16**, 279–285.
An attempt was made to compile and summarize all available studies on the relationship between hair mineral levels and various aspects of human behavior. The 51 studies located covered a wide range of behaviors. High levels of certain minerals, especially lead and cadmium, and low levels of other minerals, especially potassium and sodium, tended to be associated with undesirable behavior.—From Authors' Abstract.

656. RUTTER, MICHAEL (Univ. of London, England). **Cognitive deficits in the pathogenesis of autism.** Journal of Child Psychology and Psychiatry, 1983, **24**, 513–531.
Autistic children suffer from crucial cognitive deficits that are not secondary to other autistic features and that underlie many of the important handicaps of autistic children. We remain ignorant of connections among abnormalities of cognition, conation, and affect.—From the Article.

657. SAMEROFF, ARNOLD J. (Univ. of Illinois, Chicago), & SEIFER, RONALD. **Familial risk and child competence.** Child Development, 1983, **54**, 1254–1268.
Components of familial risk (parental mental health, social status, parental perspectives, and family stress) are examined in the context of a 4-year longitudinal study of children with mentally ill mothers. Parental beliefs, attitudes, and coping abilities are hypothesized to be important mediators between environmental stress and child competencies.—From Authors' Abstract.

658. SHAH, A. (Univ. of London, England), & FRITH, U. **An islet of ability in autistic children: a research note.** Journal of Child Psychology and Psychiatry, 1983, **24**, 613–620.

An aspect of cognitive functioning in autistic children was investigated by comparing their per formance on the Children's Embedded Figures Test with that of MA-matched normal and MA and CA-matched mentally retarded nonautistic children. The autistic children were significantl more competent at this task than either group of control children and also showed qualitativel different strategies.—From Authors' Abstract.

659. ST. LOUIS, KENNETH O. (West Virginia Univ.); CLAUSELL, PAUL L.; THOMPSON JEAN NAMET; & RIFE, CONSTANCE C. **Preliminary investigation of EMG biofeedbac induced relaxation with a preschool aged stutterer.** Perceptual and Motor Skills, 1982, 55 195–199.
The child was able to reduce the level of tension in the laryngeal area by using EMG biofeec back. There was a small reduction in stuttering.—Adapted from Authors' Abstract.

660. STEIN, STEVEN J. (Thistletown Regional Ctr., 51 Panorama Court, Rexdale, Ontaric Canada), & McNAIRN, CYNTHIA. **The changing nature of diagnosis in an inpatient ser vice over 20 years.** Journal of Abnormal Child Psychology, 1983, **11**, 443–461.
Files of child and adolescent patients from 1961 to 1978 revealed that the proportion of case diagnosed as schizophrenic decreased by 1/3, those diagnosed as neurotic increased over 1 times, and significant increases occurred in the proportion of children diagnosed as autistic personality disorder, and behavior disorder of childhood and adolescence. There was decrease in cases between 6 and 12 years of age and a significant increase 13–18-year-olds.—From Authors' Abstract.

661. STEINER, HANS (Stanford Univ., Children's Hosp.). **The socio-therapeutic enviro ment of a child psychosomatic ward (or, Is pediatrics bad for your mental health?).** Chil Psychiatry and Human Development, 1982, **13**, 71–78.
The results support the notion that conjoint, intensive psychiatric and pediatric treatment psychosomatic patients does not impede the formation of a very active psychiatric treatmen milieu.—From Author's Abstract.

662. STRICKLIN, ANN BURNS, & AUSTAD, CAROL SHAW (Connecticut Valley Hosp. **Perceptions of neglected children and negligent parents about causes for removal fro parental homes.** Psychological Reports, 1982, **51**, 1103–1108.
Neglected children and their parents from South Africa were interviewed. Both parents ar children perceived the removal of the child to be a function of some action or personality cha acteristic of the child. Parents described their children in a negative, disapproving manner ar appeared to be immature and irresponsible in their attitudes toward their offspring.—Fro Authors' Abstract.

663. SVERD, JEFFREY (Long Island Research Inst., Stony Brook); COHEN, SHELLY; CAMP, JANET A. **Brief report: effects of propranolol in Tourette syndrome.** Journal Autism and Developmental Disorders, 1983, **13**, 207–213.
Propranolol, a beta-adrenergic blocking agent, was administered to 5 patients with Touret syndrome in a placebo-controlled study and was found ineffective in ameliorating symptoms Tourette syndrome.—From Authors' Abstract.

664. TANOUE, YOKO (Univ. of Tsukuba, Japan). **Systematic observation of the beha iour of infantile autism patients using the computerized behaviour analysis system—wi classification according to patient's interactions with the mothers and toys.** Japanes Journal of Child and Adolescent Psychiatry, 1983, **23**, 205–222.

665. TRITES, R. L. (Royal Ottawa Hosp., Canada), & LAPRADE, K. **Evidence for an ind pendent syndrome of hyperactivity.** Journal of Child Psychology and Psychiatry, 1983, 2 573–586.
Factor analysis suggested that hyperactivity and an aggressive conduct disorder can exi independently in children.—From Authors' Abstract.

666. TSAI, LUKE Y. (Univ. of Iowa Coll. of Medicine), & STEWART, MARK A. **Etiological implication of maternal age and birth order in infantile autism.** Journal of Autism and Developmental Disorders, 1983, **13**, 57–65.
An excess of mothers aged 35 or older was observed in the autistic group, though the mean maternal age for the whole group was very similar to those of the general population. More autistics were products of at-risk pregnancies (defined as either first, fourth, or later born or born to mothers aged 30 or older) than the base population. The results suggest that at least some environmental factors are involved in the causation of autism.—From Authors' Abstract.

667. WALKER, ELAINE (Cornell Univ.), & EMORY, EUGENE. **Infants at risk for psychopathology: offspring of schizophrenic parents.** Child Development, 1983, **54**, 1269–1285.
High-risk infants are not exposed to greater exogenous stress during the prenatal and perinatal periods, although subsequent caregiving provided by disturbed mothers may be nonoptimal. Several findings point to the existence of a constitutionally vulnerable subgroup of high-risk infants. Fetal and neonatal deaths, unrelated to obstetrical complications, may be more common among high-risk offspring, and neuromotor abnormalities are apparent in a subgroup of high-risk subjects across the life span. There is evidence to suggest that offspring of schizophrenics are uniquely susceptible to obstetrical complications when they occur.—From Authors' Abstract.

668. WEIR, KIRK (Guy's Hosp., London, England). **Night and day wetting among a population of three-year-olds.** Developmental Medicine and Child Neurology, 1982, **24**, 479–484.
Mothers of 3-year-olds were interviewed. Fifty-six percent of boys and 40% of girls were reported to be wet at night; 22% of boys and 12% of girls were wet by day.-Adapted from Author's Abstract.

669. WERRY, JOHN S. (Univ. of Auckland, New Zealand); METHVEN, R. JAMES; FITZPATRICK, JOANNE; & DIXON, HAMISH. **The interrater reliability of DSM III in children.** Journal of Abnormal Child Psychology, 1983, **11**, 341–354.
The DSM III as a whole and the major categories were of high or acceptable reliability. The subcategories were found to vary widely in reliability both as a whole across the system and within parent major categories.—From Authors' Abstract.

670. WOLCHIK, SHARLENE A. (Arizona State Univ., Tempe). **Language patterns of parents of young autistic and normal children.** Journal of Autism and Developmental Disorders, 1983, **13**, 167–180.
Syntactic and functional aspects of parental language were assessed during a 20-min interaction. Parents of autistic children used more non-language-oriented language but did not differ from parents of normal children in the percentage scores for any language category. Although parents of autistic children spoke more often, complexity of language was comparable across the groups. Several differences emerged between mothers' and fathers' language patterns.—From Author's Abstract.

671. ZUCKER, KENNETH J. (Clarke Inst. of Psychiatry, 250 College, Toronto, Ontario, Canada); FINEGAN, JO-ANNE K.; DOERING, ROBERT W.; & BRADLEY, SUSAN J. **Human figure drawings of gender-problem children: a comparison to sibling, psychiatric, and normal controls.** Journal of Abnormal Child Psychology, 1983, **11**, 287–298.
Gender-problem children were more likely to draw an opposite-sex person when requested to "draw a person" than were controls. Gender-problem children who drew an opposite-sex person were more likely to play with opposite-sex toys and dress-up apparel than were the gender-problem children who drew a same-sex person. Normal children had a smaller proportion of emotional disturbance indicators in their same-sex drawings than did the others.—From Authors' Abstract.

HISTORY, THEORY, AND METHODOLOGY

672. BURROWS, KATHERINE ROGERS (Mott Children's Health Ctr., 806 W. 6th Ave., Flint, MI), & KELLEY, CRYSTAL K. **Parental interrater reliability as a function of situational specificity and familiarity of target child.** Journal of Abnormal Child Psychology, 1983, **11,** 41–48.
Child behavior ratings were made by 17 mothers and fathers of their children. Parents achieved higher rates of agreement than have previously been reported. Increasing the specificity of the behavior being rated did not significantly affect agreement. Those parent pairs who agreed the most did not necessarily spend a large amount of time in the same kind of situations with their child. Agreement was significantly greater when parents rated their own children's videotaped behavior sample as opposed to that of an unknown child.—From Authors' Abstract.

673. CADWELL, JOEL (Rutgers Univ.), & PULLIS, MICHAEL. **Assessing changes in the meaning of children's behavior: factorial invariance of teachers' temperament ratings.** Journal of Educational Psychology, 1983, **75,** 553–560.
The present study tested the assumption that temperament ratings measure the same thing across age with 24 teachers of 564 kindergarten through fourth-grade children. A LISREL analysis supported the hypothesized 3-factor model and established factorial invariance.—From Authors' Abstract.

674. HOFMANN, RICHARD J. (Miami Univ.). **Assessing developmental stages with a contingency table: a triangular hypothesis.** Genetic Psychology Monographs, 1983, **108,** 21–42.
A statistical procedure is described for analyzing a square contingency table. The pattern of cell entries for a contingency table of stages will be triangular if the developmental stages are related and the pattern is properly referred to as a divergent décalage or triangular hypothesis. A statistical index, delta, is developed to describe the extent to which a developmental contingency table conforms to a divergent décalage.—From Author's Abstract.

675. MILGRAM, ROBERTA M. (Tel Aviv Univ., Ramat Aviv, Israel). **Validation of ideational fluency measures of original thinking in children.** Journal of Educational Psychology, 1983, **75,** 619–624.
Original thinking was examined in 142 children across a wide range of age, IQ, and SES. There were consistently high relationships between corresponding scores on lenient and stringent criterion measures, and of quantity and quality scores. Lower class children scored lower on original thinking than middle-class children when a stringent standard was invoked.—Adapted from Author's Abstract.

676. PETTI, THEODORE A. (Univ. of Pittsburgh School of Medicine). **Future trends in the study and treatment of depression in young children.** Journal of Children in Contemporary Society, 1983, **15,** 87–95.

677. SCARR, SANDRA (Yale Univ.), & McCARTNEY, KATHLEEN. **How people make their own environments: a theory of genotype —> environment effects.** Child Development, 1983, **54,** 424–435.
Genotypic differences are proposed to affect phenotypic differences, both directly and through experience, via 3 kinds of genotype —> environment effects: a passive kind, through environments provided by biologically related parents; an evocative kind, through responses elicited by individuals from others; and an active kind, through the selection of different environments by different people.—From Authors' Abstract.

678. SNYDERMAN, MARK (Harvard Univ.), & HERRNSTEIN, R. J. **Intelligence tests and the Immigration Act of 1924.** American Psychologist, 1983, **38,** 986–995.

The testing community did not generally view its findings as favoring restrictive immigration policies like those in the 1924 Act, and Congress took virtually no notice of intelligence testing, as far as can be ascertained from the records and publications of the time.—From Authors' Abstract.

679. WEINER, BERNARD (Univ. of California, Los Angeles). **Some methodological pitfalls in attributional research.** Journal of Educational Psychology, 1983, **75**, 530–543.
A number of methodological errors in attributional research are pointed out.—From Author's Abstract.

BOOK NOTICES

680. BERLINSKY, ELLEN B., & BILLER, HENRY B. **Parental Death and Psychological Development.** D. C. Heath, 1982. xi + 160 p. $21.95.
This book presents an exhaustive review of research studies that have examined the impact of parental death during childhood. The primary material included in the review are some 100 empirical studies on the topic. This material is augmented by an equal number of theoretical and review papers. The authors have developed a 5-level rating scale on which to assess the methodological adequacy of empirical studies. While studies at all levels of adequacy are considered in the review, the authors are careful to identify the methodology rating of the findings under consideration. Findings are organized under 3 major headings, each the subject of a chapter. First, the book considers behaviors that have been identified as consequences of parental death. These behaviors include emotional disturbance, personality changes, sex-role, sexual and personality behaviors, moral development, antisocial behavior, and cognitive and achievement-related behaviors. Second, the book reviews studies that identify family and situational variables that may affect the impact of parental death, such as the sex of the parent and the reason for the parent's absence. Third, the book reviews findings that concern the characteristics of the child at the time of the parent's death, notably the child's age and sex and the child's development of a concept of death. The review is thorough, and the authors make clear, concise summary statements throughout, always citing the methodological constraints on their conclusions. The review of findings supports the conclusion that there are both long-term and short-term differences between groups who have experienced parental death and those who have not. The review also points out the dearth of studies that have considered contextual variables in assessing the impact of parental death on children. Thus, the authors' frequent pleas for more complex, multivaried, and longitudinal studies are more than adequately justified. The book's major contributions are the identification of studies on parental death, the clear organization of findings, and, most importantly, the evaluation of each study's methodological adequacy. The book will be of greatest interest to other researchers.—C. Longfellow.

681. BORMAN, KATHRYN M. (Ed.). **The Social Life of Children in a Changing Society.** Lawrence Erlbaum/Ablex, 1982. xviii + 294 p. $29.95.
This book presents papers from a 1979 symposium on the social development of preschool and young elementary school-age children. Contributions are from anthropologists, psychologists, and sociologists and are grouped into 3 sections: agents of socialization (parents and others), language as a primary socializer for normal and developmentally delayed children, and a cross-cultural perspective on socialization. This organization appears arbitrary: frequently, papers are only tangentially related to the section in which they are placed, and chapter titles are often misleading. The introductory chapter presents a superficial review of sociobiology. Concepts associated with this rubric (e.g., canalization, critical periods) are introduced but are not further developed. Subsequent chapters present general reviews of the influence of teachers' expectations on children's classroom performance (Leacock), socialization in the context of play (Sutton-Smith), parent influences on the language acquisition of their children (Snow), sociolinguistic and ethnographic analyses of socialization (Wallat and Green), and a cultural ecological approach to the linkage of personality and behavioral patterns with adaptations due to biological pressures (Ogbu). A few of these reviews are interesting (Ogbu, Wallat & Green,

Sutton-Smith); all are brief. Other chapters include descriptions of teacher strategies to facilitate children's communicative skills (Ramey, et al.) and a coding scheme for representing children's mental states and perceptual experiences (Gearhart & Hall). A few of these chapters might serve as useful outside readings for undergraduate courses. Disappointingly little is learned from this book about the social lives of children and what constitutes a changing society.—P. T. Giblin.

682. BRAINERD, CHARLES J. (Ed.). **Recent Advances in Cognitive-Developmental Theory: Progress in Cognitive Development Research.** Springer-Verlag, 1983. xiii + 270 p. $29.95.

This book consists of 5 chapters, each outlining a different theoretical perspective on some aspect of cognitive development. This is the third in a continuing series to be published examining issues in cognitive development. Brainerd (the series editor) selected theories as a topic because of "the extreme theoretical pluralism, coupled with much uncertainty about where we are going" (p. vii). Theoretical pluralism probably is a good description of work of developmental psychologists today. This collection contributes further to that pluralism with 5 chapters: a contextual view of cognitive development by Barry J. Zimmerman, a descriptive theory of 2 concepts by Robert S. Siegler and D. D. Richards, a sociobiological view of cognitive development prepared by C. J. Lumsden, a contribution by Brainerd detailing a mechanistic view of the role of memory processes as cognitive processes, and an ethological analysis of problem-solving by W. R. Charlesworth. Zimmerman first outlines the contextualist view of the interplay between behavior events and the social-environmental context within which these events occur. Next, he uses social learning theory (à la Bandura & Walters) as an important basis for explaining several cognitive phenomena (rule learning, rule interdependence and learning, language acquisition). As a statement of the principles and tenets of contextual points of view, Zimmerman's chapter can serve as an excellent introduction and starting point for further study. Siegler and Richards describe the development of the concept of numbers and the concept of life (with data from several new experiments) in their chapter. Their approach, more descriptive than theoretical (in that the how and why of cognitive changes or reorganizations are not discussed), includes several very detailed models of different levels of number and life concepts. As always, Siegler's descriptions of children's rule usage is provocative and carefully defined. Lumsden's treatment of cognitive development will be the most unfamiliar to most developmental psychologists, and the author does not do enough to reduce that unfamiliarity. Brainerd's chapter on working memory challenges Piaget's account of cognitive development by proposing that memory underlies gradual (incremental) changes in cognitive abilities (rather than the cognitive reorganizations that characterize Piaget's stages). Charlesworth's chapter is a fitting finale to this collection. He argues persuasively for an ethological view, and in the process combines some of the better features of contextualism, sociobiology, and Siegler's various analyses of the rules that describe children's concepts. The point seems to be that we should more carefully examine the behaviors and/or functions we propose to understand and analyze. While I agree completely with that point of view, I also believe that understanding development ultimately entails explaining, anticipating, and, perhaps, controlling development. These are issues the chapters in this collection do not seem ready to challenge.—S. I. Offenbach.

683. BRAINERD, CHARLES J., & PRESSLEY, MICHAEL (Eds.). **Verbal Processes in Children: Progress in Cognitive Development Research.** Springer-Verlag, 1982. xiv + 289 p. $24.50.

This work, the second in a new series, includes discussions of current theory and research in 5 areas of cognitive development, which, as the editors say, "have historically been islands unto themselves," but which can be loosely subsumed under the rubric "verbal processes." The 5 areas include main-line language development, bilingualism and second-language acquisition, reading and reading disabilities, the teaching of memory strategies, and story-grammar oriented work on children's extemporaneous verbal protocols. The language-development entries include 3 contributions. Dixon provides an extremely comprehensive review and analysis of referential communication research in which he concludes, among other things, that the constructs "egocentrism" and "role-taking" have virtually nothing to do with referential communication; Kuczaj offers a fascinating theoretical discussion of semantic development in which he departs somewhat from the current craze for fuzzy sets to focus primarily on semantic relations; Hood, Fliess, and Aron adopt a Vygotskian perspective on the acquisition of causal language and argue that, both ontogenetically and historically, ideas about causality are determined culturally, not logically. Vihman and McLaughlin provide the 1 chapter on bilingualism and second-language acquisition; they argue cogently that simultaneous and successive acquisition of 2 languages have very different cognitive effects, and so must be carefully distinguished. Opposing approaches to the understanding of "specific" reading disabilities are provided by Morrison and Manis, and Vellutino and Scanlon, respectively. The former argue that these difficulties arise from deficits of 1 or more elementary cognitive processes, whereas the latter contend that the problems stem specifically from linguistic deficits. From an outsider's perspective, the theoretical clash is illuminating. Pressley, Heisel, McCormick, and Nakamura offer the 1 chapter on memory strategy instruction. Their extensive review leads them to conclude that progress in memory training has been sufficient to have already laid the groundwork for revolutionizing instructional practice in the schools. Finally, Stein and Trabasso, in the sole original research report, present data that they believe demonstrate that children must and can infer and use goal information in making moral judgments, and that developmental differences in this domain index quantitative differences in inference-making and using abilities, not qualitative, structural differences. Critics may argue that the organization of this volume fails because it falls between 2 stools. It is neither a collection of clearly independent and self-sufficient discussions, like the typical "advances" volume, nor does it focus on a single, narrowly defined, unifying theme. I think such critics would be wrong. Workers in any of the research areas represented will find the contributions from the other areas thought-provoking and illuminating, and the volume may well have the synergistic effect of encouraging cross-fertilization among areas that have previously been too isolated. Indeed, one could wish for an even more heterogeneous collection. For example, discussions of semantic development from a Roschian perspective, of the current thrust in metacognition research, and of the new work in Genevan developmental psycholinguistics would have added to the possibilities for across-area inspiration. As it is, though, the book serves an important purpose by reminding us all that no research area is an island.—J. R. Speer.

684. BROCKINGTON, I. F., & KUMAR, R. (Eds.). **Motherhood and Mental Illness.** Academic Press (London), 1982. xi + 265 p. $31.00.
This book is a collection of papers on postpartum psychosis, epidemiological aspects of mental illness associated with childbearing, neurotic disorders in childbearing women, the maternity blues, and pathological mother-child relationships. It also includes chapters on early maternal attachment, baby units for women who are psychiatric patients, and drug addiction during pregnancy and lactation. The book is very effective in illustrating, by omission, the lack of women's voice in the consideration of motherhood and mental illness and the consequence of that deficit. In the preface, Brockington and Kumar state that "the ways in which childbearing may be linked with psychiatric disorder remain uncertain and controversial" (p. vii). This statement is amply confirmed by the book as a whole. For example, Brockington, Winokur, and Dean note in the conclusion of their chapter on "Puerperal Psychosis" that very little new information has been added on this topic in the last 120 years. We are told that the difficulties of motherhood deserve our best efforts "because of the pervasive effects on the family and on the psychological development of young children" (p. viii) and "most importantly, they may exert undesirable effects on the psychological development of the newborn child" (p. 71). While family and children are undeniably important, the implicit assumption that mothers are less so undoubtedly has an effect on the incidence and treatment of difficulties associated with motherhood. The slow progress evidenced in the area might be changed by the addition of women's perspective, provided by the voices of pregnant women, mothers, women doctors and nurses, and women researchers. Except for the chapter on "Early Maternal Attachment," by Kay Mordecai Robson and Elizabeth Powell, such perspectives are absent in this anthology. Women might, for example, consider such variables as the attitude of the father toward the mother's role, the participation of the father in child care, societal attitudes toward maternal

responsibility regarding children, the way children affect a woman's life, and the development of the attachment between the father and the child, to mention but a few possibilities. Most important would be a consideration of the normal difficulties of motherhood encountered in our culture. Whatever the contribution of biological factors to illness associated with motherhood, neglect of sociocultural factors, and lack of attention to the perspectives of women can only impede progress in an area that, as J. A. Hamilton points out in the chapter on "The Identity of Postpartum Psychosis," affects millions of women.—C. A. Adamsky. .

685. CAFAGNA, A. C.; PETERSON, R. T.; & STAUDENBAUR, C. A. (Eds.). **Philosophy, Children and the Family. Child Nurturance,** Vol. **1.** Plenum, 1982. xiv + 377 p. $35.00.
KOSTELNIK, M. J.; RABIN, A. I.; PHENICE, L. A.; & SODERMAN, A. K. (Eds.). **Patterns of Supplemental Parenting. Child Nurturance,** Vol. **2.** Plenum, 1982. vii + 323 p. $32.50.
FITZGERALD, H. E.; MULLINS, J. A.; & GAGE, P. (Eds.). **Studies of Development in Non-human Primates. Child Nurturance** Vol. **3.** Plenum, 1982. xiii + 274 p. $29.50.
It took a long time to read through the first 3 volumes of this series, Child Nurturance, not because the material was uninteresting but because there was so much of it. Peterson's introduction to Volume 1 is a useful perspective on the essays or reviews, which are organized in sections on conceptualizing the family, women and family life, children's rights, moral education, and medical decisions affecting children. Santilli's essay on the family and the social contract begins the section on Conceptualizing the Family. Santilli warns against extending notions of self-interested rationality appropriate to the competitive marketplace to the family as an institution. He argues that we need to conceive of broader community values in order to understand families. Struckmeyer turns to systems theory as a way of conceiving the organic unity of family life. Hoaglund examines issues concerning voluntary 1-parent families, especially the issue of artificial insemination and homosexual parents. He suggests that misguided individualism leads to fragmentation, which results in families where children lack the relationships with both parents that are essential for the development of coherent personalities. Ames questions Hoaglund's citation of higher incidence of delinquency for children from single-parent families and points out that this delinquency is also affected by poverty, divorce, and other external factors. Grandstaff reflects upon some relationships between family, schools, and social class differences. He suggests that there are as many different kinds of relationships between families and schools as there are kinds of families. Flay criticizes Grandstaff's argument that schools work in ways that serve the purposes of the dominant class and reminds us that social thought cannot become so abstract as to ignore the experience of the individual. Wilder's essay, the first of 2 in a section on Women and Family Life, presents a critical analysis of arguments for the uniqueness of maternal parenting. Ruddick describes "maternal thinking" as a distinctive type of thought arising out of maternal practices organized in the interests of offspring preservation, growth, and acceptability. Frye, responding to Wilder, points out that "just because the patriarchal family is man-made and not natural does not mean that it is easier to change than the weather." In her response to Ruddick, Frye suggests that images of "mothers of both sexes," presented as progressive and utopian, are perplexing and problematic and should not be embraced hastily. Cafagna's introduction to the section on Children's Rights presents a number of important distinctions (e.g., positive/negative, legal/moral rights), and then discusses in general terms 3 representative topics: whether we should ascribe equal rights to children; whether, or how, parents' and children's rights actually or potentially conflict with one another; and what are the outstanding or unmet rights of children. With respect to equal rights, Cohen observes that our understanding of obligation to children has shifted from protecting them to protecting their rights. Ruddick sharply objects to extending adult rights to children and claims that children are not mistreated when they are treated as immature. As Cafagna points out, although Cohen and Ruddick reach opposite conclusions about children's rights, they agree that unless society can provide some way for children to exercise rights, we cannot ascribe them rights. Perkins writes that children may gain a chance to enjoy freedom only in cases where parents decide to limit their own. The notion of irreconcilable rights, Perkins says, is deeply rooted in traditional liberalism. Schoeman argues that conflict over unequal rights reflects an imbalance between values of intimacy invested by society in families, and values of family autonomy which must be protected from encroachment by the state. Evans says that

because we hold so tightly to misconceived ideals for the identity development and socialization of children, we overlook children's rights to integrate themselves. Finally, Black claims that since children's toys are the essence of play, children have the implicit right to have their toys taken seriously by adults. Staudenbaur provides a summary of Kohlberg's ideas about moral development in his introduction to the section on Moral Education, and Friquegnon begins the section with a critical analysis of Kohlberg's theory. Friquegnon warns that the belief that moral education can be attained leads to moral authoritarianism in moral education. Levande, also addressing Kohlberg's theory, suggests that the distinction between form and content in moral reasoning is not as clearcut as Kohlberg may believe. Ferree and Vaughn provide relief from this scrutiny of Kohlberg's ideas by reminding us that Bertrand Russell held that moral education was obtained not through stages of reasoning but through from optimum environments for the development of sound habits of character. Hoffman concludes this section by recommending that moral educators should promote virtues like justice even though such virtues do not necessarily fit the individual harmoniously into society. Staudenbaur begins the final section of this volume by distinguishing between 2 approaches to medical decisions affecting children: the child-centered approach, which concerns itself with the interests and rights of the affected child; and the social-policy approach, which concerns itself with the effects or costs of decisions to society. Donchin presents the case for defective infants and, from a child-centered viewpoint, offers 5 arguments for parental consent for infant treatment. She contends that consent to treatment for infants cannot be informed consent, even by extension of the concept, since what is essential to informed consent is that it is voluntary. Bartholome, also from a child-centered viewpoint, also has reservations about the applicability of accepted notions of proxy consent with respect to medical decisions about affected children. He insists that if an infant is to develop as a person, it must be treated as a person. He concludes the section and the volume by presenting a series of "claims" which can form the basis of policy guidelines for provision of medical services to infants. The range of these philosophically oriented essays is considerable, and the number of issues discussed is overwhelming. While the volume is impressive in its own right, it is a pity that nonphilosophers were not asked to respond to some of these essays. On the other hand, the editors are to be commended for their introductions to sections which provide readers with necessary "advanced organizers" to the content of essays. *Patterns of Supplemental Parenting*, Volume 2 of this series, contains 10 essays. Soderman, Kostelnik, Ames, and Phenice begin by considering various definitions of family, describing its legitimately dynamic attributes as a social system and the more intimate tasks performed by family systems. Campbill and Bubolz discuss parenting by related adults and conclude that with difficult economic times the extended family may become more significant in child care and nurturance. Furman and Buhrmester undertake to describe the ways in which siblings and peers participate in the parenting process. They argue that parenting no longer need be viewed as the unique function of biological parents but as sets of processes and inputs which any member of the social environment can contribute. Peters and Belsky present an excellent summary of the status of the daycare movement. They conclude that, in 100 years, daycare has grown in the number of children it serves, has diversified in the types of programs offered, and has changed in the characteristics of clientele and professionalism of staff. Guerney examines the effectiveness of foster care and notes that foster care has been used extensively in the past decade as a less restrictive and less expensive alternative to residential home settings. Grossbard writes about residential home settings and observes that the traditional institution for children of problem homes has been replaced by residential treatment centers for problem children. Notwithstanding the benefits of such a shift in emphasis, Grossbard warns of the danger of fragmentation and dilution of basic child-adult relationships, the relative neglect of parents, and the serious gaps of service during children's re-entry into society. Werner points out that in other cultures, exclusive nurturance of the young by their parents, especially their mothers, is the exception rather than the rule. She presents some conceptual models which have guided cross-cultural research of childrearing and concludes with a review of effects of rapid social change on caretakers and children. Hildebrand claims that we must be concerned with all families around the globe, that we must outgrow the meism that typifies most of the current research on childrearing. Rabin reviews issues involved in multiple parenting and describes childrearing in kibbutz. Lastly, Kaplan examines alternatives and continuities running through the preceeding essays and emphasizes the point that each essay supports the notion that something basic has shifted in traditional roles assumed by members of the nuclear family. The uneven quality of essays of this second volume is unfortunately emphasized by the lack of an overview of topics and issues. Although Kaplan's summary is useful, it would help readers understand the organization of essays and the relationship of issues better if such a roadguide had been included. As the volume now stands, you have to read each essay in order to know whether the effort was worthwhile. The theme of Volume 3, *Studies of Development in Nonhuman Primates,* is the quest for further understanding of human behavior through the examination of similarities between human and other primate behaviors. Riopelle begins the volume with a comparison of the effects of protein deprivation and malnutrition upon offspring behavior. No longer is it possible to believe that the fetus is a perfect parasite—able to extract whatever nutrients it requires from its mother. Nash and Wheeler examine the way in which behavioral variability resulting from adaptation to different environments affects the mother-infant relationships both within and between primate species. Snowdon and Suomi consider some of the varieties of paternal care found in human societies and relate these to the varieties found in the nonhuman primates. This comparison is especially interesting when read in conjunction with Wilder's essay on maternal parenting in Volume 1. Vogt and Hennessy discuss the literature on infant separation in monkeys and concentrate particularly upon situations where the infant has access to another adult female during the separation period, to situations where the infant is separated from the artificial maternal substitute upon which it has been reared, and to situations where the responses of other animals to the infant-mother separation have been assessed. Savage-Rumbaugh next responds to the question "How do we know what primates are saying?" in chimpanzee language studies. She describes a series of experiments designed to provide information about the cognitive levels of awareness and the complex inferential processes that permit primates to use the same set of words to mean different things. Fouts, Hirsch, and Fouts present evidence that chimpanzee mothers can teach their offspring language in the form of American Sign Language. Mineka reviews the literature on depression in primates and focuses upon the learned-helplessness model for understanding such depression. Finally, Moyer examines studies of brain stimulation, pathology, and lesions as they affect aggressive behavior and proposes a physiological model based upon the premise that there are neural systems in the brains of animals and humans that, when fired in the presence of a relevant target, will result in aggressive or destructive behavior toward that target. Volume 3 contains some very stimulating contributions, particularly Snowdon and Suomi and Savage-Rumbaugh, but as with the second volume, the lack of a preface to provide some justification for inclusion of these essays and not others handicaps the reader. Although the quality of essays varies across the 3 volumes of this series, the range of argument and the amount of information more than make up for this weakness. The content of these volumes should serve a wide audience for some years to come.—J. Eliot.

686. DE GELDER, BEATRICE (Ed.). **Knowledge and Representation.** Routledge & Kegan Paul (London), 1982. xii + 218 p. $30.00.
The 13 essays in this book were originally presented in 1979 at a conference at the Netherlands Institute for Advanced Studies in Wassenaar by an international group of researchers. By design, the essays are not in any particular order, nor is there any other structural development to the book. An attempt is made by the editor to contrast 3 approaches to the study of representation: the computational model, which describes the rules by which the organism computes information (Fodor); biological and competence models (Chomsky); and a constructivist model (Piaget). Like most collections based upon conference proceedings, there is little thematic consistency across the chapters. These range from straightforward research reports and methodological critiques to full-blown theoretical analyses. The salient topics covered are: imitation (a comprehensive examination of the Genevan thesis), imagery, picture recognition, drawing, shape perception, causality, spatial development, scripts and plans, gestures, and Turing's test for human thinking. On the whole, each author advances a domain-specific thesis about representation and supports it with selected research results. For most, representation is taken as the means by which sense is made out of things, by which meaning emerges from the interaction of the organism with that about it. The relationship among a particular mental repre-

sentation, the thing represented, and the behavioral representation or meaningful act is continually examined. The degree to which the competence to represent is present innately is treated along with the case for the development of that competence. Arguments are advanced throughout for the parallel functioning of several modes or representational codes that develop, become modified, and become more consistent and integrated—beyond the level needed for the organism's need to respond to particular environmental demands. Not much is said about knowledge, except to say that representational theories are about it.—F. B. Murray.

687. DIELMAN, T., & BARTON, K. **Child Personality Structure and Development: Multi-variate Theory and Research.** Praeger, 1983. xiv + 204 p. $29.95.
This book, written by 2 of R. B. Cattell's colleagues and with a foreword by Cattell himself, presents essentially 1 viewpoint on child personality structure and development—R. B. Cattell's. The usefulness of the book therefore depends on your predilection for Cattell's ideas. The book is not entirely parochial; Cattell's work is discussed within the context of other child research from Baldwin, Cooley, and Mead to Sears, Whiting, and Bandura. Unfortunately, the authors' preoccupation with social learning theory makes even their "broader context" 1-sided. The book is intended for students with little exposure to research methods and statistics and therefore begins with an introduction to these topics. Chapters 1 and 2 instruct the reader in the conceptual and computational details of bivariate correlation, analysis of variance, and factor analysis. In my judgment, this introduction is too difficult for a student without a good background in multivariate statistics and is therefore useful only as a review for persons already familiar with the concepts. Chapter 3 selectively reviews research on imitation, aggression, and identification, concentrating on reinforcement/modeling theories (particularly Bandura's). This review emphasizes the inadequacies of bivariate research and sets the stage for a discussion of Cattell's multivariate research, presented in Chapter 4. Roughly a quarter of Chapter 4 is text, and the remainder contains tables showing the results of factor analyses. Chapter 5, which discusses the relationship between childrearing variables and personality, is also heavy on tables. Fifteen of the 33 pages in Chapter 5 are devoted to a single table. The next 2 chapters address specific topics—personality and school achievement and the personality of exceptional children. Although Chapter 6 ignores an enormous amount of research on personality, cognitive patterns, and school achievement (notably absent are studies using the California Psychological Inventory), it nonetheless presents some valuable information on the subject. Teachers would be particularly interested in the instructional implications in this chapter. Chapter 7 discusses personality traits and coping styles of children with physical, intellectual, and emotional handicaps. The authors suggest that 5 Cattellian second-order personality factors may help us conceptualize and organize research findings in this area. Empirically, however, only 3 factors appear to be relevant. The book concludes with a chapter on suggestions for future research, which, not surprisingly, amount to a continuation of Cattell's research program. Due in part to the single-mindedness of the book, 3 important subjects are not covered in this book. First, the authors say nothing about the influence of nonparental role models, except to note that these influences become increasingly important as a child grows older. Second, the authors fail to discuss temperament and behavior genetics. Cattell, in his foreword, attributes this omission to the dearth of information in these areas. That explanation will not do—behavior genetics, which relies heavily on the type of multivariate techniques discussed in the book, is a substantial and rapidly growing field. Finally, the authors fail to confront a fundamental paradox in the field of personality development: How can one talk about personality *development* (which implies changes over time) using the language of personality *traits* (which implies consistent, persistent, stable characteristics)? Dielman and Barton's only relevant comment, in their last chapter, is that time relationships between variables are actually rather unimportant. One can conclude from this comment that the authors are far more concerned with personality structure than development; the content of their book confirms this conclusion.—J. A. Johnson.

688. ENTWISLE, DORIS R., & HAYDUK, LESLIE A. **Early Schooling: Cognitive and Affective Outcomes.** Johns Hopkins Univ. Press, 1982. xv + 215 p. $30.00.
In *Early Schooling,* the authors basically present the results of their investigation concerning achievement and affective outcomes of schooling. The variables of interest in this investigation

were: race, sex, IQ, parents' general ability estimate, parents' expectations, children's expectations, classroom marks, peer-popularity ratings, and school absence. Pilot work was begun on this project in 1969, and data were systematically collected from 1971–1977. In the first few chapters of the book, general terminology is discussed along with a scholarly review of previous research on the psychological and sociological effects of early schooling. The authors contrast results from what they term "macro" studies like that of the Coleman Report (1966), which typically have shown little if any effect of schooling, with "mid-range" studies, which typically reveal that schools have substantial differential effects on students. Later, Entwisle and Hayduk present their research model and the results of their investigation. This section of the book and the rest which follows are technically quite complicated. Readers should be advised that unless they are well grounded in advanced statistical procedures they will probably be overwhelmed by the reading. As an example of the technical difficulty, the following sentence was excerpted from a discussion concerning the research model: "The clustering of triplicate expectation variables and the clustering of reading and arithmetic, both with correlated disturbances, makes the models almost block recursive within cycles" (p. 51). The remainder of the text discusses the estimation of the research model used, alternate models of the schooling process, and the results of the investigation. The conclusions are characterized by words like *might, may,* and *if.* As the authors point out, 3 schools do not provide a sufficient basis for generalizing their results to other situations. The results of this investigation are therefore generally restricted to the 3 institutions studied. Major conclusions include the following: (1) The process of schooling can differ from 1 school to another, even though the outcomes of the schools are the same. (2) Early affective growth may be quite sensitive to school climate. (3) The parents' expectations in all 3 schools were able to predict the first grades their children received, but only the middle-class parents were able to retain their predictive influence past the beginning of first grade. (4) Children have little expectation about themselves as academic learners when they first begin school; however, through the influences of being evaluated by others and themselves, they construct impressions of themselves as academic learners. (5) Peer popularity was found to be unrelated to children's expectations in all grades. (6) Teacher's expectations for children had no influence on children's expectations above that accounted for by the teacher's grades for the children. (7) The comparisons between the schools suggested that socioeconomic status rather than race accounted for achievement differences across the schools. (8) Gender influences on early schooling were mainly effected through conduct differences noted between boys and girls. (9) The study reported results that were contrary to the typical self-fulfilling prophesy literature. Lower-class children did not have low expectations for themselves. In fact, their expectations were so unrealistically high that they could not process the feedback from their significantly lower marks. According to the authors: "The unrealistic expectations of the lower-class children may interfere with the causal efficacy of expectations via at least two mechanisms. First, shielding oneself by ignoring feedback may be self-protective, but it also eliminates the information necessary for learning....Another way high expectations may undercut the effectiveness of expectations is that, if one truly believes one is doing well, there is no reason to try to improve" (p. 152–153). (10) Finally, the results refute the pygmalion studies which argue that one could improve a student's performance by increasing the teacher's expectations. The authors state that the alternative that student achievement causes teachers' expectations is more appealing and is supported by their study. Four appendices, which include discussions of the limitations and measurement issues involved in the design, follow.. A final appendix includes the data matrices that were used in the project.—R. L. Hale.

689. ERNST, CÉCILE, & ANGST, JULES. **Birth Order: Its Influence on Personality.** Springer–Verlag, 1983. xvii + 343 p. $29.80.
Over 1,300 studies from 1946 to 1980 are reported on and discussed in this book. There are chapters on birth order in relation to biological difference, twins, IQ, school achievement, occupational status, socialization and personality, and mental illness. Succinctly given, their conclusions are these: (1) "There is evidence that birth order differences in IQ are artifacts, due to inadequate methodology"; and (2) "Birth order and sibship size do not have a strong impact on personality." They found most studies involving birth order do not take into account social ori-

gins, family income, education of parents, religion, the urban-rural dichotomy, and birth rate as it varies owing to economic depressions and cataclysms such as major wars. Worst of all, very few studies match their experimental group with adequate controls. They further report that, "The hypothesis that psychiatric illness is unrelated to birth order has yet to be refuted." Their recipe for future research includes adequate methodology; theory that permits well-conceived, specific hypotheses; and complete statistical treatment. In their essay of theorists relating to birth order (Adler, Schachter, Toman, Zajonc), they are less than kind, finding little in the research studies to support the theorists' contentions. They publish as a sort of addendum some empirical research from their home base in German-speaking Switzerland on the epidemiology of tobacco, alcohol, and drug consumption. They found more smoking among the youngest children and somewhat more drinking among the youngest male sibs in large families. The study of Belmont, involving nearly 400,000 Dutch draftees in the 1940s and addressing the question of birth order and intelligence is rather skittishly handled. This is the study with the largest sample size, and it offers a number of controls: chronological age, sex, language and nationality, and 3 categories of occupational derivation. For the total group (family occupation not considered), intelligence as determined by the Raven test was hierarchical to a highly significant degree with respect to both birth order and family size. In only 1 of these groups, the farmers, was the intelligence hierarchy somewhat inconsistent. If the data on these recruits are still available, Ernst and Angst might consider trying out their methodology and statistical sophistication on a large representative sample of Belmont's study to determine whether Raven scores are truly related to birth order. The accuracy of the authors in reporting their 1,300 or so references is occasionally suspect. A 1967 study by Altus is twice adverted to: in 1 instance it is reported to deal with a topic it did not touch, and in other, a significant finding is given in a manner diametrically in opposition to the facts. The gist of the book is that birth order adds little, if anything, to personality differentials. Many researchers in the are would disagree with their conclusion, even when using the tabular evidence they so copiously present. Eminence in relation to birth order is not sufficiently touched on, nor is it adequately explained. Galton's pioneer study of the 1870s is faulted for lack of control groups involving his eminent men of science, though how controls for these men extending over a span of several generations could be obtained is difficult, if not impossible, to imagine. There are amusing errors in the book. At least twice, "is" is printed as "ist," apparently a carryover from the German language. Pidgin English sometimes obtrudes: on page 58 "college goers" refers, presumptively, to "college students"; and the locution "oldest of two" may be noted. On the positive side, however, the Teutonic assiduity of the authors gives us over 40 printed pages of references, which should prove invaluable to anyone who may be interested in the topic of birth order.—W. D. Altus.

690. EXNER, JOHN E., JR., & WEINER, IRVING B. **The Rorschach: A Comprehensive System.** Vol. **3. Assessment of Children and Adolescents.** Wiley-Interscience, 1982. xvi + 449 p. $42.50.

This excellent volume on the assessment of children's personality demonstrates clearly that contrary to widespread rumors the Rorschach is alive and well—thanks considerably to the efforts of author John Exner and a cohort of energetic colleagues. Exner and his group are responsible for the Comprehensive System of Rorschach scoring which is rapidly becoming dominant in the field. The scores in this system have a solid empirical base, which is ever expanding as the research efforts continue—obviously an area of serious deficiency in some of the earlier, pioneering Rorschach systems. Beginning in 1974, 4 years were devoted to testing a stratified sample of children, patients and nonpatients, that finally numbered some 2,500 cases. This sample was refined and broadened in a subsequent 3-year study that added 1,000 records, increased the number of nonpatient children, and included a series of retest studies to establish the extent of temporal consistency among the various scores. This approach carefully distinguishes between using the Rorschach as a perceptual-cognitive task, reflected in the various scores, and using it as a stimulus to fantasy and interpreting personality dynamics from the content. As the authors point out and as is documented in Volumes 1 and 2 and other sources, there is now extensive validating evidence for the significance of the formal scores, whereas symbolic interpretations of content remain much more speculative. The norms for the various scores included in the book cover the age range of 5–16 years and are used extensively in the sample cases presented. After a preliminary discussion of basic principles of interpretation, using the Rorschach with the young client, application of normative data, and new research bearing on interpretation, 19 cases are presented, including case history, protocols and scoring, interpretation, and follow-up clinical notes. Structural interpretation, scoring sequence, and content are thoroughly discussed and integrated in a summary interpretation. The types of cases covered include normal children, depression, schizophrenia, school learning problems, problems in behavior, and forensic issues. The volume concludes with recommendations for report writing. The chapter on schizophrenia is particularly strong. There are useful clinical discussions of each type of problem, summarizing recent research literature and theoretical stances, in general and as these problems are reflected in Rorschach protocols. The major drawback of the volume is that it assumes knowledge of the Comprehensive System of scoring as presented in Volumes 1 and 2. Even though a clinician familiar with other approaches to the Rorschach will be able to follow most of the interpretation, a summary of the scoring system would have been very useful. On balance, the book remains a most significant 1 for the clinician involved in the assessment of personality in the child and the adolescent.—L. J. Hedstrom.

691. FELDMAN, ROBERT S. (Ed.). **Development of Nonverbal Behavior in Children.** Springer-Verlag, 1982. xii + 315 p. $27.50.
This book is an outgrowth of a symposium on the development of nonverbal behavior. It is an informative and readable volume; however, the actual topic would be more accurately identified if the title read, *Development of Facial Expressions in Children and Primates.* What the editor describes as a very "rich" topic is also a very diverse 1, particularly in its use of methodologies. The first 3 chapters (Camras, Buck, Zivin) use ethological and psychobiological methods. These chapters could be improved by an increase in the number of photographs. The authors admit that several terms exist for the investigated facial expressions, and so even experienced readers may be unsure as to whether they are correctly visualizing "oblique brows." Shennum and Bugental, and Saarni, in a section entitled Social Developmental Approaches, present a review article and a gamelike methodology investigating the growth of control over facial expressions. The third section (De Paulo & Jordan, Morency & Krauss) describes the processes of encoding and decoding. Blanck and Rosenthal and Volkmar and Siegel investigate children's responses to discrepant verbal-nonverbal messages. An entertaining sidelight—females' observed inferiority in identifying deceit is entitled "politeness." The concluding chapters (Feldman, White & Lobato, Field) represent contemporary thoughts on individual differences; particularly fascinating is the literature on newborns and young infants. The interested reader will find much impetus to thought and future research, as many sections conclude with, "The underlying mechanisms are unknown." Perhaps 1 of these interested readers will investigate the development of facial expressions or politeness in non-Western societies for the next edition of this book.—J. A. Rysberg.

692. FIELD, TIFFANY M., & FOGEL, ALAN (Eds.). **Emotion and Early Interaction.** Lawrence Erlbaum, 1982. ix + 299 p. $29.95.
This book is a collection of papers on the development in infancy of emotional expression and social interaction. The papers were originally presented at a symposium. The 12 papers are grouped in 3 parts: 5 papers about face-to-face interactions in early infancy, 3 papers on play interactions in later infancy, and 4 papers on methodology of observational data collection and analysis. The studies in Part 1 are linked by their use of a common procedure, face-to-face interaction of mothers and infants. Malatesta focuses on facial expression of emotions, showing that 3-month-old infants display a variety of differentiated facial expressions, and that already they are subject to maternal influence. Fogel's interest centers on sequences of emotion and their time course. He constructs a model based on 2 dimensions—arousal and ability to self-regulate—illustrating it with data from 2 infants. The next 2 papers introduce experimental manipulations to face-to-face interaction. Stoller and Field instruct the mother to keep a "still face" and monitor heart rate as an indicator of physiological arousal. Tronick, Ricks, and Cohn instruct mothers to simulate depression during the interaction and find that it produces wari-

ness and protest in infants. Field, comparing the facial expressions of preterm, postterm, and term infants, finds that term infants do more smiling, vocalizing, and happy face and less crying, sad face, and heart-rate acceleration than the others. She interprets these results in terms of an arousal model with some similarity to Fogel's model. The studies making up Part 2 report on older infants and use more varied procedures. Demos describes facial expressions as they occur spontaneously in the home using Ekman's method of microanalysis of facial movements. Brooks-Gunn and Lewis report on social interactions between handicapped children and their mothers observed in a standard playroom and find them to differ from those of normal children. Lewis and Michalson examine the socialization of young children's emotions with particular attention to acquisition of labels for specific emotions. Observational methodology, used in all the studies in the book, becomes the focus of attention in Part 3. Adamson and Bakeman consider the problems inherent in designing a behavior code capable of capturing context and emotional tone as well as events. Kaye contributes a "hitchhiker's guide to microanalysis" (in the editors' phrase) a thoughtful discussion of research design, analysis, and interpretation of findings much of which has relevance beyond microanalysis. Hannon deals with problems of categorization of units of behavior in applying Ekman's type of analysis to the hands and fingers of young infants. Gottman, Rose, and Mettetal present clearly the applicability of time series analysis to timed sequences of mother-infant interaction. The book is organized around a clearly defined area of research. All the papers deal with studies of human infants in interaction with their mothers, and all use observational methods. The similarities in subject matter serve to highlight a tension throughout the book between 2 approaches to the problems under study. The 2 approaches are best described by Malatesta in Chapter 1. She distinguishes between a typological model exemplified by the work of Tomkins, Izard, and Ekman, which "stresses the differential signal value and phenomenology of discrete classes of emotional events," and a dimensional model used by Lindsley, Magoun, and Spencer et al., which postulates "a continuum of activation, arousal, intensity, hedonic tone, or other general polar scale." Among the papers in the book, those by Malatesta, Demos, and Hannon elegantly exemplify the typological model; those by Fogel, Field, Gottman, and co-workers exemplify the dimensional model. This reviewer agrees with Malatesta that the newer typological approach "appears to be an especially promising way to proceed in the investigation of emotional/personality dynamics." Inclusion of studies providing good examples of both approaches makes this book an important contribution to the literature on emotional and social development in infancy.—M. F. Elias.

693. GUALTIERI, C. THOMAS (North Carolina Memorial Hosp., Chapel Hill); KORIATH, URSULA; & VAN BOURGONDIEN, MARY E. **"Borderline" children.** Journal of Autism and Developmental Disorders, 1983, **13**, 67–72.
Sixteen children said to be "borderline" were referred for comprehensive evaluation. None met DSM III criteria for borderline personality disorder. Referring psychiatrists and psychologists seemed to base their impressions on the child's disorganized thinking and irrational, erratic behavior. The borderline label had a negative impact on some children and was not helpful for treatment planning or disposition.—From Authors' Abstract.

694. HALE, JANICE E. **Black Children: Their Roots, Culture, and Learning Styles.** Brigham Young Univ. Press, 1982. xv + 191 p. $9.95.
It appears as though psychologists and educators have not been sufficiently concerned with the psychosocial and cognitive development of black children in America. Evidence of this can be found in the limited amount of empirical research devoted to this area and the lack of attention given to this subject in developmental psychology texts. As yet, we do not have a firm base of knowledge of ethnic and racial differences in growth, development, and cognition; nor do we completely understand how the distinctive features of the Afro-American culture influence black children's learning styles. This volume by Hale is designed to fill a portion of that gap in our knowledge. The 7 chapters of this text are organized around a central theme of encouraging the reader to become more sensitive to the unique features of the Afro-American child's culture and how these cultural patterns influence the way they think and learn. In Chapter 1, Hale briefly traces the heritage of black Americans, beginning with their ancestors in West Africa. Hale demonstrates that through overt and covert mechanisms, black Americans

have retained many aspects of their West African culture. She concludes that ethnic group membership transcends social class influences and affects a wide range of behaviors. The author, in Chapter 2, asks and attempts to answer fair questions, especially for those psychologists and educators who question the efficacy of a cross-cultural approach to the understanding of the cognitive and social development of black children. For example, she asks, "How much of the variance among people is attributable to culture? What is the predominant cognitive style that characterizes black children? Is there 1 particular cognitive style that results in superior school performance?" In the remaining 2/3 of the book, Hale begins with reviewing the literature on the childrearing practices of Afro-Americans. She argues that it is the cultural mismatch between child and teacher that often leads to the poor academic performance of black children. In part, this could be avoided, Hale insists, if educators become more aware of how black children are socialized. Of interest is the belief presented that black children are socialized in ways to insure their survival in America. The dilemma, however, is that these practices often are misunderstood and even punished by the educational system. Chapter 4 gives the rationale for examining children's play as a vehicle for obtaining valuable information about the ways in which young children process information. Hale points out that research on the play behavior of black children has been fragmented and unsystematic. In Chapter 5 of this text, literary precedents for the meaning of black culture are explored. The author provides an intriguing argument for social scientists to pay more attention to the humanities as a rich source for understanding cultural beliefs and experiences that account for behaviors of black children. Chapter 6 describes the development of an instrument that can be used to assess the coping styles, skills, and childrearing practices of black Americans. The final chapter presents a general framework of education that Hale believes to be compatible with the culturally influenced learning styles of black children. Additionally, Hale examines current educational practices and astutely brings to the reader's attention the challenges that black parents and educators are currently faced with. She concludes with a set of recommendations for future research directions.—L. P. Anderson.

695. KRESS, GUNTHER. **Learning to Write.** Routledge & Kegan Paul, 1982. xii + 205 p. $25.00.
The author's focus in this book is on 2 related questions: What is it that children learn when they learn to write? and What can be learned about children, society, and ourselves by examining the process? The book opens with a consideration of the major differences between speech and writing and then goes on to develop the thesis that learning to write involves the learning of new forms of syntactic and textual structures, new genres, and new ways of relating to unknown audiences. Detailed analyses of texts produced by children ages 6–14 serve to illustrate various aspects of the child's developing mastery of written language. Particularly interesting is a chapter on the development of the child's conception of the sentence, in which the author argues that children's early written sentences correspond to textual rather than syntactic units. Since the child's conception of the sentence differs from the adult's conception, a teacher's "corrections" are unlikely to be meaningful to the child. This failure to recognize that children may be using different rule systems is a recurring theme in subsequent chapters as well, which examine the development of different genres of writing, the development of conjoined sentence structures, and the child's expression of causality. The book admirably reflects current perspectives in text linguistics and sociolinguistics, but its treatment of the cognitive aspects of learning to write is weakened by its failure to acknowledge the contributions of the many North American psychologists who have been active in this field. The author intends the book to be helpful to teachers in examining the writing of their pupils, to parents interested in the language of their children, and to linguists as a suggestion for future research. It would be a rare book that could satisfy the needs of such a diverse audience, and this 1 does not quite succeed; its scholarly treatment of the subject matter would probably prove difficult for readers without some grounding in linguistics. Nevertheless, it is a well-written and thought-provoking volume in its concern not only with the processes of learning to write but with the associated social and ideological implications.—L. Baker.

696. LAMB, MICHAEL E. (Ed.). **Non-Traditional Families: Parenting and Child Development.** Lawrence Erlbaum, 1982. xii + 364 p. $29.95.

Michael Lamb begins this collection of essays and studies with a discussion of 4 assumptions about the traditional family which became commonplace around the turn of the century: namely, that children need 2 parents, 1 of each sex; that family responsibilities should be divided between parents, with fathers as economic providers and mothers as homemakers and caretakers; that mothers are better suited for child rearing and caretaking; and that family members should provide primary caretaking for young children. Each of these assumptions serves as a topical focus by different authors in the remainder of the book. Phyllis Moen examines the 2-provider family and considers problems and payoffs with respect to family roles and resources. Michael Lamb reviews the effects of maternal employment on family dynamics. Jay Belsky, Laurence Steinberg, and Ann Walker describe the status of daycare today and argue that daycare has never been viewed in this country as an acceptable alternative to full-time childrearing in the traditional home environment. Michael Lamb, Ann Frodi, Carl-Philip Hwang, and Majt Frodi report the results of a study conducted in Sweden that examined attitudinal and behavioral correlates to varying degrees of paternal involvement in infant care. Graeme Russell reports results from an Australian study on the effects of shared-caregiving lifestyles on families. Norma Radin reports the results from a study of perceptions of parental roles by children in families where fathers are the primary caregivers. Abraham Sagi reports results from a study of nontraditional fathers in different Israeli populations, including kibbutz families. E. Mavis Hetherington, Martha Cox, and Roger Cox examine some effects of divorce on parents and children and urge the development of support systems to assist families in their adjustment to the stresses and changes associated with divorce. John Santrock, Richard Warshak, and Gary Elliot present results from a study of child-custody relationships, especially those involving step-mother and father-custody families. They report that sex of child in combination with sex of custodial parent and step-parent have rather strong influences on the child's social behavior. Lastly, Bernice Eiduson, Madeleine Kornfein, Irla Zimmerman, and Thomas Weisner describe results from the Family Styles Project and comment upon differing socialization practices in traditional and alternative families. Overall, this is a tightly edited, extremely well-organized book which should appeal to a diverse audience. It should be of particular interest to all those responsible for the development of social policy concerning families and children.—J. Eliot.

697. LEE, BENJAMIN, & NOAM, GIL G. (Eds.). **Developmental Approaches to the Self.** Plenum, 1983. vii + 400 p. $42.50.

This collection of 8 papers represents an attempt to integrate psychoanalytic, cognitive-developmental, and Vygotskian views of the self. Stemming from a Conference on the Self, the discussions are primarily theoretical, presenting little research data. A general theme running through most of the papers is that interactions between the child and the social environment play a critical role in the development of the self. In the first 6 papers, the focus in on integrating cognitive-developmental and psychoanalytic views. In the initial paper, Basch rejects Freud's emphasis on a biological impetus for personality development and suggests that the modes of representation described by Piaget may be useful in determining how affective experiences are interpreted at different stages of development. In a paper by Noam, Kohlberg, and Snarey, a distinction is made between structural (Kegan, Loevinger) and functional (A. Freud, Erikson) views of self, and suggestions for research strategies integrating them are given. In van de Voort's paper, development of the self/other distinction is described as based on interaction with other people, in contrast to the Piagetian focus on interaction with inanimate objects. In his paper, Blasi makes a distinction between self as one's self-concept and self as a primary (innate?) ability to direct and evaluate cognitive activity. Blasi argues that self in the second sense is a prerequisite for knowledge acquisition, while self-concept is effected by cognitive processing. Papers by Broughton and Kegan extend the discussion of self-development beyond childhood. Broughton notes that structural theories used to explain development through adolescence cannot encompass changes resulting in transition to adulthood. He argues for the need for reevaluate cognitive-developmental theory to minimize biological, structural explanations and form a "new" theory of adolescence based on historical and political functions. In sharp contrast to Broughton, Kegan presents a neo-Piagetian, structural model of personality development across the life span. He argues that the self/other distinction, described by Piaget as occurring during the Sensorimotor Stage, actually represents a recurring process of differentiation and integration of self and other. Six stages of subject-object relations are described and discussed as the basis for cognitive and affective development. The final 2 chapters in the book present views of the development of self based on Vygotsky's general theory of psychology. Lee, Wertsch, and Stone summarize the theory with its emphasis on sociohistorical experience as the basis for development. Vygotsky's research on the origin and role of social, egocentric, and inner speech is described and contrasted with the views of Piaget. In the final paper, Lee and Hickmann discuss Vygotsky's description of the relationships among inner speech, play, and motivation and their implications for a theory of the development of the self. They conclude that Vygotsky's theory suggests that the self emerges as a product of language use in interpersonal situations. Although concrete suggestions for research are relatively scarce, this book provides provocative food for thought for those interested in the development of the self across the life span.—E. M. Justice.

698. LIPSITT, LEWIS P. (Ed.). **Advances in Infancy Research**, Vol. **2**. Ablex, 1983. xxix + 314 p. $30.00.
Lipsitt's intent in this series is to provide a forum for new directions in infant research; this is largely accomplished in this collection. Butterworth critiques Piaget's concepts of adualism and intramodal specificity in perceptual development. He focuses on his own research suggesting that infants are considerably less egocentric than Piaget proposed. Fagan and Singer present provocative evidence that recognition memory may serve as the long-sought measure of infant intelligence (with predictive ability!). Reznick and Kagan, emphasizing methodological issues, review the literature on category detection during the first year. Lockman and Ashmead examine the development of manual behaviors, especially visuomotor coordination. Schubert, in what is probably the best written article in this book, critiques various theories of object concept. This chapter could well become standard reading in seminars on infancy or Piaget. Sullivan and Horowitz attempt to integrate the intermodal perception literature and the maternal speech literature. They intentionally avoid building a theory of model, however. Von Hofsten pleas more for ecologically valid research in the area of perception. In reviewing the infant perception literature (including object, event, and social perception), he frequently points out how artificial conditions have yielded erroneous information concerning infant abilities. Finally, Maltzoff and Moore examine infant imitation. They review available theories, examine the existing data, consider methodological issues, and offer their own model (admittedly incomplete) of imitation in early infancy. Although there is no stated theme in this volume, most of the articles deal with Piagetian concepts as well as intermodal perception. It would have been interesting to see connections among these topics drawn by either the authors or the editor.—L. M. Smolak.

699. McANARNEY, E. R. (Ed.). **Premature Adolescent Pregnancy and Parenthood.** Grune & Stratton, 1983. xx + 418 p. $39.50.
In this edited volume, 32 contributors, most of whom are physicians, write about a variety of issues concerning adolescent pregnancy. The 21 papers written especially for this book are divided into 5 parts plus a summary. In Part One, historical trends in birth rates to teenagers, adolescent abortion rates, and patterns of contraception use are examined. In addition, Melvin Zelnik discusses some aspects of his work on the sexual activity of adolescents during the 1970s. The 2 papers in Part Two focus on contraception use by adolescents. Donald Greydanus provides a very thorough review of the physical side effects of contraceptive methods, information which would be of value to a health-care provider who is attempting to help an adolescent decide which method would be most suitable for his or her circumstances. In the third part, the biological effects of pregnancy on adolescent mothers and their infants are examined. Two papers examine the relationship between maternal age and obstetrical risk and the nutritional needs of pregnant teenagers. A third paper reviews the literature on the risks of infection to pregnant teenagers. In another paper the authors conclude that from a biological perspective the ideal time to give birth appears to be between the ages of 16 and 19 years, provided the mothers are given adequate prenatal care, while the data on the psychological and social development of infants born to teenage mothers, which are less rigorous, uniformly

show negative effects. The last paper in this section describes a study that examines the biological effects of teenage pregnancy on infants and the psychological and social effects on the mothers. Part Four is entitled Psychosocial Aspects of Adolescent Pregnancy and Parenthood. The research described in this part shows that the infants at greatest risk for poor outcome are those born and raised by the very youngest mothers and those with the least adequate family support system. In regard to teenage fathers, Elster and Panzarine report that the majority of them cope reasonably well with the pregnancy of their girlfriends or wives. Kinard and Klerman describe their own work on the intellectual development of children born to teenage mothers and report that these children consistently score lower than those born to mothers over 20 years of age, although the magnitude of this difference is small (less than 1 standard deviation). In a final paper on psychosocial risk to teenage mothers, it is shown that young mothers are more likely now than in the past to stay in school while pregnant and to return to school immediately after giving birth. In Part Five, a variety of service programs for pregnant and parenting adolescents are described. The papers in this section focus mainly on those programs that are hospital based and provided by health-care professionals. Notably lacking are descriptions and evaluations of school-based sex education programs. The last article in this section is a description of the variety of abortion methods that are currently in use. Finally, in the summary part, McAnarney and Thiede pose several questions about adolescent pregnancy that need to be answered. As is true of most edited volumes, this 1 contains some articles that are superficial and inadequate. In general, however, the contributions are worthwhile additions to our understanding of adolescent pregnancy. The articles have a decidedly medical and applied orientation to them, which should be helpful for nurses and physicians and of interest to social scientists who are not well acquainted with the medical data in this area.—R. Montemayor.

700. MANGAY-MAGLACAS, A., & PIZURKI, H. (Eds.). **The Traditional Birth Attendant in Seven Countries: Case Studies in Utilization and Training.** World Health Organization, Public Health Papers, No. 75. 1981. 211 p. $7.00.
Two members of the Division of Health Manpower Development of the World Health Organization (WHO) have edited papers on traditional birth attendants (TBA) in Ecuador, Honduras, Philippines, Sierra Leone, Sri Lanka, Sudan, and Thailand. TBAs deliver as many as 80% of the babies in the developing world, or well over 50% of the babies worldwide. WHO has determined that TBAs need to be trained to deliver primary health care to mothers and babies because the TBA often sees the mother in the last trimester, at delivery, and in the weeks that follow. The chapters on each country have been written by health officials of the country or by international consultants. For the most part, each chapter is based on data available to the central government on the activity and training of TBAs. Most countries have set a goal of giving a few weeks of training to TBAs so that they will avoid spreading infection to the newborn and, in some countries, give up the practice of abdominal massage of the pregnant woman and of turning of the fetus in utero. In some instances, they are also trained to promote family planning and to make contraceptive methods and materials available. The report is primarily from the perspective of an administrator in that it presents data on the organization of training and administration of trained TBAs and does not deal with the day-to-day activities of TBAs nor their belief systems about pregnancy and child care. The work of the TBA is important because it influences the child's care and diet during its most vulnerable days.—G. M. Guthrie.

701. MELTON, GARY B.; KOOCHER, GERALD P.; & SAKS, MICHAEL J. (Eds.). **Children's Competence to Consent.** Plenum, 1983. xv + 270 p. $29.50.
This anthology focuses on a problem most researchers, clinicians, educators, and other human service professionals encounter daily but confront rarely: children's competence to consent in decisions affecting their own welfare. Since 1967, when the landmark case In re Gault was brought before the Supreme Court, children's rights to due process and to other constitutional safeguards have been guaranteed. Nevertheless, as Donald Bersoff remarks, legally, children remain like the hero of Ralph Ellison's novel, "invisible persons whose views are infrequently evoked and whose wishes are rarely controlling" (p. 158). The chapters in this book explore legal, psychological, sociological, and ethical perspectives concerning children's competence

to consent. The first section confronts general psychological issues that are related to increasing children's self-determination. Melton reviews the conditions under which some children become better decision makers than others; Saks presents a social-psychological perspective demonstrating how education in self-determination that can be considered advocacy by some may be thought of as manipulation by others. The second section of the volume presents specific legal, medical, and psychological perspectives on consent. Lewis reports data from several training studies designed to teach children decision making; Grodin and Alpert recommend the primary care setting as the best model for medical consent. Koocher discusses the problem of the "doubly incompetent": those who legally are minors and who psychologically or intellectually have diminished abilities. The third section explores consent in delinquency proceedings (Grisso), psychoeducational assessment (Bersoff), and research studies (Keith-Spiegel). Finally, Tapp and Melton discuss the implications of legal socialization research, and Weithorn presents guidelines for professionals concerned with increasing children's self-determination. All of the chapters are clearly written, and all suggest a range of research possibilities. As a whole, the anthology serves 2 further purposes: it demonstrates how uninformed judicial decisions regarding children's rights are about children's development, and it sensitizes us as researchers to the multitude of complex issues that lies behind our human subject approval forms.—S. J. Meisels.

702. MILLER, PEGGY J. **Amy, Wendy, and Beth: Learning Language in South Baltimore.** Univ. of Texas Press, 1982. xii + 196 p. $18.95.
Amy, Wendy, and Beth is a sensitive and compelling study of 3 young children's language socialization into an urban, working-class community. Miller focuses on the early language development of 2-year-olds in a desire to learn how individual children from poor families learn to use language in their homes and beyond. In Chapter 1, Miller reviews the research literature on the relationship between language development and social class and then critiques the bias inherent in the tasks and settings used in the normative studies. For her purposes she chooses an ethnographic case study as the method to best describe the specific contexts of children's language use during a 10-month period and the values and beliefs of the people who shape their development. Chapter 2 describes the community of South Baltimore, her search for 2-year-old subjects, data collection methods, and the qualitative and quantitative techniques used in discussing her findings. In Chapter 3, Miller paints detailed portraits of the children and their families: the mothers tell us about what is significant to them, their beliefs about the language-learning process, and their hopes and expectations for their daughters' lives. In Chapter 4, Miller follows a mother's suggestion that she study the ways families teach language to children. Here she describes the 7 categories of instruction found in the transcripts and presents a detailed analysis of naming sequences. This chapter includes the study's most exciting and powerful findings. Miller examines the contexts and content of the mothers' instruction as they teach their daughters how to care for babies, to talk back, assert, challenge, and to comply; these descriptions reveal much about the culture into which the children are being socialized and how their intentional use of language is shaped in the instructional contexts. In Chapter 5, she pursues a question adopted from Bloom's research, asking whether children of the urban poor express the same kinds of meanings, in the same developmental sequence, as do middle-class children in their 2- and 3-word utterances. Finally, Miller summarizes her findings, describes the research process as she and the families she studied experienced it, and poses questions for both linguistic researchers and teachers of poor children. This study moves far beyond the characteristic and predictable in language research because Miller makes a commitment to be fair to her subjects and to write for the families as well as for scholars, to "use language to include, not exclude." Her method demands far more commitment and entails more risks than most researchers are willing to undertake: spending months before the onset of the study developing relationships with the children, their families, and their communities; giving the mothers a voice and following their suggestions in deciding which research questions are meaningful to study; sharing with the families the responsibility for and power in transcribing data; showing her final descriptions to her subjects for their comments and approval; and confronting the ethical questions involved in videotaping and describing human lives. An important transformation occurs in this study as dichotomous roles of investigator and subject

become that of collaborators. Through facing these challenges, Miller gives us ethnographic research at its finest: she discovers the story of how 3 children in South Baltimore learn language and their world skillfully and perceptively as she learns with them. This book would be of great interest to all language researchers, psychologists, and educators involved with young children and their families.—R. M. Stoddart.

703. MITCHELL, DAN C. **The Process of Reading. A Cognitive Analysis of Fluent Reading and Learning to Read.** John Wiley, 1982. xiii + 244 p. $39.95.
This book presents an analysis of those components of cognitive processing that research has identified as related to word recognition and reading. The first 5 chapters of the book analyze cognitive processes that are involved in reading, utilizing such categories as extracting information during fixation, iconic memory, visual memory, word recognition, sentence comprehension, and the construction of meaning. The sixth chapter describes some cognitive models of the reading process and provides the author's own model based on the evidence presented in the first 5 chapters. Chapter 7 analyzes processing difficulties in patients who have lost the ability to read fluently following head injuries or cerebrovascular accidents, poor readers in school, inexperienced readers, and slow (but effective) adult readers. Chapter 8 considers a few issues in learning to read. This book emphasizes general models of cognitive processing, paying little attention to individual differences. The predominant focus is on the cognitive components of the process of fluent reading, while the discussion of learning to read is limited.—W. L. Faust.

704. MODGIL, SOHAN, & MODGIL, CELIA (Eds.). **Jean Piaget: Consensus and Controversy.** Praeger, 1982. 446 p. $35.00.
The timeliness, imaginative format, and breadth of this volume are bound to make it a valuable resource for researchers in a wide variety of developmental domains. Piaget has touched us all in 1 way or another, and now that his theory is increasingly being criticized with what appears to some to be an unseemly degree of enthusiasm, it sometimes seems as if the very foundation of our discipline is being threatened. In Piagetian terms, what many of us are experiencing is a bad case of disequilibrium, the resolution of which can only come through grappling with the issues. Such an analogy makes the format of this book particularly appropriate. The 10 sections that comprise the meat of the book are each devoted to a different dimension of Piagetian theory, and each contains 2 chapters, the first primarily critical of Piaget's contribution to the issue, the second primarily positive. The chapters are then immediately followed by a brief direct exchange between the authors. The result of this unique format is to provide the reader with the kind of conflicting information Piaget argued was essential for intellectual growth. And it works. Reading each section is like being present at a stimulating debate. All the chapters are comparatively short, well written, and to the point; the final exchanges are inevitably direct—and sometimes fiery. It is a format that arouses the reader's interest in topics he or she might otherwise have ignored. What's more, the editors have brought together in 1 place a wide range of issues upon which Piaget has been criticized. The validity of "stages" of development, for example, is addressed in section after section, with the result that the reader gets not just 1, but close to a dozen different perspectives on the problem. Although some issues, like that of "stages," cut across topics, the main purpose of the book is to focus on 10 specific dimensions of the theory or its application and to present positive and negative views of Piaget's contribution: (1) philosophical underpinnings (Denis Phillips, negative; Wolfe Mays, positive), (2) the psychology of cognitive development (Linda Siegel & Barbara Hodkin, negative; Jacques Vonèche & Magali Bovet, positive), (3) the development of logic (Robert Ennis, negative; Carol Tomlinson-Keasey, positive), (4) the role of language (Alison Elliot & Margaret Donaldson, negative; Hermina Sinclair, positive), (5) moral development (Helen Weinreich-Haste, negative; Derek Wright, positive), (6) psychometric applications (Richard Hofmann, negative; Colin Elliott, positive), (7) cross-cultural perspectives (Susan Buck-Morss, negative; Paul Ghuman, positive), (8) education (Derek Boyle, negative; Joan Tamburrini, positive), (9) science education (Joseph Novak, negative; Rosalind Driver, positive), and (10) special education (Frank Fincham, negative; Thomas McFarland & Frederick Grant, positive). As if all this were not enough, the editors have added a very instructive final chapter by Bärbel Inhelder in

which she reviews alterations in the theory made by Piaget during the last decade of his life. This chapter is followed by an extensive outline of the pro and con arguments raised in each of the 10 sections. The editors wisely, however, refrain from providing any neat and tidy final decision about the merits of the theory. As Piaget would have wished, it is up to each reader to grapple with the information and forge a new equilibrium—a task I am confident this book will stimulate many of us to try.—L. P. Acredolo.

705. PATTERSON, GERALD. **Coercive Family Process. Social Learning Approach Series,** Vol. **3.** Castalia, 1982. xiii + 368 p. $24.95.
This book is a personal statement of the development of an important research career. It is an important research career because it is an exemplar of programmatic research. Chapter 1 is historical. It presents an intellectual history of ideas that influenced Patterson's work. This book should be read if only for the methodological contributions of this line of work. The methodological contributions of the Oregon Social Learning Group include the discovery of observer drift and decay, as well as solutions to these problems, the systematic study of observer presence effects, the use of the inability to fake good (particularly nonverbal behavior) as an index of distress, and a model for psychometry of observational data (including issues of test-retest reliability, time and event sampling, validation of codes, and the application of generalizability theory). What is probably more important, this research program is a model for the application of a richly descriptive observational coding system that has served both purposes of hypothesis generating and theory building. It is a model because it has been useful and because it led to the search for temporal pattern. Patterson wrote, "it seemed that *some* events were patterned, and that these patterns were repeated again and again. We began to notice that each interaction sequence was not unique" (p. 3). In his current thinking, Patterson noted that "we can place behavioral events in the sequence like beads on a string" (p. 5). All this effort took place within what Patterson calls "an applied mission." The focus was on understanding the dramatic phenomenon of antisocial children. Chapter 2 is an eclectic review of the literature. We learn about the stability of aggression over time, its stability across settings, and the fact that these children are indeed at psychological risk. We learn of the growing body of evidence that points repeatedly to these children. The recent work of John Coie at Duke and Ken Dodge at Indiana also points us in this direction. Patterson's review of the literature concluded that an understanding of this dramatic phenomenon lies in "innocuous, garden-variety aversive events, such as teasing and scolding [which] can, under certain conditions escalate to high intensity aggression" (p. 13). The coersive family must be understood by taking note of low-key aversive events that are trivial taken individually, "a process that is comprised of events that are inherently banal" (p. 68). These are part of a pattern of emotional arousal, attribution, and anger, a process John Reid calls "nattering." Parental involvement extends these low-intensity interchanges. Chapters 5–9 detail the anatomy of these microsocial coercive events. In Chapter 5, Patterson discusses the new concepts implied by sequential analysis. Contrary to Skinnerian notions, he argues that the connection between the antecedent, A_i, and the response, R_j, should be described by the conditional probability of $p(R_jA_i)$. Patterson believes that 2 reinforcement forcement mechanisms operate: (1) negative reinforcement in which the termination of an aversive event strengthens the connection between the aversive antecedent (A_i and the counterattack terattack (e.g., in the sequence Mother scold—>Child whine—>Mother talk, the connection is strengthened between mother scold and child whine) and (2) positive reinforcement for aversive behavior. Chapter 8 details extended irritable interactions in mother-child dyads with 4 sequential variables, the probabilities of crossover, counterattack, punishment acceleration, hapter 8 Patterson shares with us his thinking about family process and structure. The chapter is methodologically as well as substantively useful. Chapters 10–12 place the microsocial processes in a larger social context and select "macrosocial" variables that impinge on and interact with microsocial processes. This extension e is critical, and once again it presents both a model for observational researchers for thinking on a larger social scale and a model for sociologists who currently primarily ignore observational methods.—J. M. Gottman.

706. PERLMUTTER, MARION (Ed.). **Development and Policy Concerning Children with Special Needs. The Minnesota Symposium on Child Psychology,** Vol. **16.** Lawrence Erlbaum, 1983. viii + 263 p. $24.95.
This book contains the 6 papers presented at the 1981 sixteenth Minnesota Symposium in Child Psychology, with each paper followed by a reaction written by a scholar from the University of Minnesota. All of the chapters are concerned with children with special needs. The content areas covered include: interactions of high-risk infants and parents (Field), maladaptation in preschoolers (Sroufe), self-control in young handicapped children (Kapp, Krakow, Vaughn), attention deficit disorder (Kinsbourne), preschool intervention for the poor (Weikart), and abused and neglected children (Wald, Carlsmith, Leiderman, & Smith). Many of the chapters are directly concerned with the effects of particular kinds of intervention, while all have implications for intervention. The scope of the chapters is varied. Wald et al., for example, report on an elaborate "real life" research design recently begun, while Weikart discusses 20 years of longitudinal research. The rest of the chapters typically summarize and integrate a number of articles that have been published elsewhere. The comments following each chapter are critical in the best sense of the word. Overall, the content of this book is of high quality. Probably the major complaint one could make about this book is the surprising number of printing errors.—K. N. Black.

707. POTEGAL, MICHAEL (Ed.). **Spatial Abilities: Developmental and Physiological Foundations.** Academic Press, 1982. xv + 409 p. $36.00.
This collection contains 15 chapters dealing with "the ability of organisms to organize the space around them and the nature of the brain mechanisms underlying this organization." Many of the chapters were presented earlier at a Teachers College conference on The Neural and Developmental Bases of Spatial Orientation. The editor's hope was that certain "parallels and convergences" between human and animal research and between experimental or physiological and field research would emerge from the collection of papers. However worthy the difficult goal of integrating these diverse perspectives on spatial ability, it was not achieved in this volume. One of the problems and sources of disappointment is the fact that only 7 of the 15 chapters are primarily about children or developmental issues. This is surprising for a book that is part of Academic Press's Developmental Psychology Series. In general, the nondevelopmental chapters are the most difficult in the collection, a fact that contributes heavily to the failure to achieve the editor's goal. The topics covered by the chapters are as follows: perceptual cues related to spatial orientation, impaired and nonimpaired children's coding of spatial information in different modalities, spatial orientation and mobility in blind pedestrians, object localization in infancy, children's cognitive mapping, children's perception of obliques, mental rotation, heredity and spatial ability, sex-related differences in spatial ability, history of brain-related disorders in spatial thinking, cerebral lesions and spatial orientation disorders, single-cell mechanisms and spatial skill in the monkey, spatially organized behaviors in animals, and vestibular and neostriatal contributions to spatial orientation. The chapters that stand out as interesting and well-written reviews with clear developmental messages are those by Bremner (object constancy in infants), Pick and Rieser (cognitive mapping), Hart and Berzok (cognitive mapping in natural environments), and Newcombe (sex-related differences in spatial ability).—M. L. Signorella and W. Jamison.

708. SERAFICA, FELICISIMA C. (Ed.). **Social-Cognitive Development in Context.** Guilford, 1982. xi + 283 p. $22.50.
Serafica describes this volume as a collection of contemporary attempts to advance scientific understanding of the interface between cognitive and social functioning. The book grew out of an SRCD Study Group on Social Cognition, and the principal authors are all prominent scholars in that field. Their contributions are diverse, but they share a belief that the field needs to move beyond what Chandler calls a "1-sided constructivism," which overlooks or at best underestimates the social structures outside the self with which the self must interact. In addition to the role of contextual factors in ontogenesis, the more widely researched issues of the relation between structural levels of cognitive and social development and the relation between cognition and social behavior are considered. Several contributors are clinicians, and the

research problems they address have their roots in therapy with children. Susan Harter describes the developmental course of children's understanding of conflicting feelings and traits in themselves and others. Her work provides insight into the dimensions underlying children's self-esteem and their understanding of their own and others' emotions. Robert Selman describes the efforts of his research group to relate his levels of reflective social conceptions to behavior in real-life social interactions involving normal and disturbed children. David Bearison, too, advocates the systematic observation of how children interact when solving cognitive problems and illustrates this paradigm with some of his own work. Michael Chandler demonstrates through a series of cleverly designed studies that children's understanding of psychological defenses and the behavioral outcomes of their moral deliberations are a joint function of the structural complexity of both the person and the situation. Carolyn Shantz, too, asserts that the construction of social reality is a bidirectional process involving both the child and the social environment. She supports her claim with evidence that environmental responses to violations of social-conventional and moral rules vary both in terms of who responds and what is said. Thus, she provides an environmental explanation (isomorphism) for the distinction between social-conventional and moral rules made by her subjects, as well as those of Turiel, Damon, and others. Myrna Shure describes the effects on behavioral adjustment of training inner-city preschoolers and their mothers on interpersonal problem solving. Felicisima Serafica reviews structural and content-oriented approaches to studying friendship in children and young adults. She suggests an intriguing application of ethological constructs to investigate the correspondence between children's friendship concepts and their interaction. The volume concludes with a sociological perspective from Dale Blyth, who describes 3 different techniques for mapping the social world of the adolescent. This book provides an up-dated review of a variety of social cognitive research programs, new and interesting data generated as a result of those programs, and thought-provoking suggestions for future research.—L. M. Hudson.

709. STRAUSS, SIDNEY, & STAVY, RUTH (Eds.). **U-shaped Behavioral Growth.** Academic Press, 1982. xiv + 299 p. $29.00.
In spite of its arresting title—how often do we come across a volume that has as its subject a characteristic of developmental functions?—the contents of this volume are less unified than one might have expected. Based on a workshop held at the University of Tel Aviv (Israel), the editors' avowed purpose was to provide some answers to the puzzle afforded by instances in which some behavioral measure shows a pattern of decline and subsequent recovery during the course of development to maturity and to compare the interpretations of this phenomenon from differing perspectives on development. Predictably, the highly diverse contributions to this volume further that aim to varying degrees. An initial set of 4 chapters considers the question in the context of information-processing views of cognitive development: Stavy et al. and Richards and Siegler present relevant data from ratio judgments and balance problems, where the suggestion of U-shaped changes with age in certain cases is readily interpretable on the basis of changes in information-processing strategies. Klahr and Wallace follow with 2 contrasting chapters. The former dismisses the significance of U-shaped trends as essentially trivial and concentrates on an account of his production-system approach to the analysis of cognitive-task performance, while the latter, though more sanguine about the interest of U-shaped trends, provides an extensive discussion of long-term memory storage, without very direct reference to that phenomenon. The concluding chapter, by Mehler, might be considered to fit the same information-processing mold, but the interest in the U-shaped phenomenon is more evident and more effectively integrated into the author's conception of the transition from an initial to a stable state. In between, we have a set of disparate chapters that contain some of the most interesting material. They include 1 by Carey on facial recognition, where some puzzling temporary reversals in the progress of development are to be found. To the author's credit, she recognizes that what might pass for U-shaped age changes are in fact more limited departures from monotonicity, when viewed in the context of longer term developmental function. Emmerich's chapter on children's conceptions of gender constancy, although dealing with a briefer time span (4–8 years), likewise takes the developmental-function concept seriously; like Carey, he argues from quantitative measures that provide rather more convincing evidence on the reality of U-shaped trends than do the percentage-of-response data reported in the first 2 chap-

ters. Finally, we find 3 nonempirically oriented chapters that are rather speculative and nonformal in tone. Bamberger presents a reinterpretation of earlier work on children's drawings of auditory rhythms; however fascinating, its relevance to the theme of the workshop is unclear. Gardner and Winner discuss the development of artistic production and sensitivity, finding a U-shaped trend of a sort in the general waning of creative activity in the arts following early childhood, and its revival in selected cases in adolescence and adulthood, but we are clearly faced with a dimension of individual differences here, complicating the issue of U-shaped development. Finally, Schön muses in refreshingly free-wheeling fashion on the general topic of intuitive thinking, which he considers as underlying many of the phenomena of U-shaped trends. If there is 1 unifying theme to this collage of essays, it might be phrased as a problem to which Heinz Werner called attention over 40 years ago: that of the uncertain relationship between process and achievement.—J. F. Wohlwill.

710. SUGARMAN, S. **Children's Early Thought.** Cambridge Univ. Press, 1983. xii + 234 p. $29.95.

This book summarized an extensive systematic study of classification by 1–3-year-old children. The major orientation of the research was the attempt to observe within the context of classification the process whereby "children not only represent their experience but reflect on and regulate the way in which they do so"; in other words, how they "structure the way they structure things." The research strategy entailed the detailed analysis of videotaped records of the performance of 40 children on 9 different classification tasks to determine not so much what was produced as how the children produced the forms. The underlying assumption was that the emphasis on how would permit inferences to cognitive organization that could not be drawn by looking only at final products. Sugarman makes a reasonable case for this, and the strategy appears to have paid off. By studying object grouping and related behaviors, the author finds several phases in the cognitive organization of children from 1 to 3 years of age such that by the third year children not only appear to be using different cognitive relations to classify but are also coordinating these relations into relations of relations. "Children move quickly beyond the ability simply to symbolize something, or conceptually relate that thing to another particular thing, to an ability to reflect on and interrelate such representations or conceptualizations." Following a brief introduction, Chapter 2 presents the overall research design and procedure. Chapters 3–10 present the main results on spontaneous and elicited organization of subjects into 2 groups, Chapter 11 extends the inquiry to coordination of convergent criteria in spontaneous and provoked organization, Chapter 12 indicates that the main trends occur in seriation as well, and Chapter 13 shows that children's verbal references to classes and between-class relations also follow the main sequence of development. Chapter 14 provides some concluding remarks on cognitive development in the light of the results of the investigation. An appendix presents some classification data from 6 deaf preschoolers also showing the increasing ability to coordinate conceptual comparisons of objects. I found the book to be rich in interesting data, including may detailed descriptions of children's behavior sequences with the various tasks. The book was less elaborate so far as theory is concerned, and I particularly missed some careful attempt at formulating the process involved in the transitions from phase to phase. I consider the book to be an extremely useful source of empirical information on early classification behavior and cognitive development.—R. S. Bogartz.

711. TIGHE, THOMAS J., & SHEPP, BRYAN E. (Eds.). **Perception, Cognition, and Development: Interactional Analyses.** Lawrence Erlbaum, 1983. xiv + 363 p. $39.95.

This book is based on a conference held in 1981. The first chapter, by Garner, provides definitions and a framework for some of the following chapters. The first half of the book is devoted to the empirical and theoretical advances by investigators in the tradition of children's discrimination learning. The major theme of the book is the developmental change in learning that occurs between the preschool years and the school years. The change is characterized as an increasing ability to attend to dimensions as opposed to particular object or stimulus characteristics, an increasing tendency toward more analytic as opposed to holistic perception, and an increasing use of efficient strategies. The chapters by Shepp, Kemler, Zeaman and Hanley, Kendler, and Spiker and Cantor discuss these changes in some detail and are rather complete reviews of the work and theory of those investigators. The chapters by Medin, Anderson, and Wolford and Fowler discuss work from different traditions. Medin's chapter on categorization ends with the intriguing notion that the lack of strategy may be adaptive for the young child. Wolford and Fowler suggest that the difficulties in reading are due to the poor perception and use of partial stimulus information, a failure that may reflect immaturity in analytic perception. Anderson's chapter stands out in that he proposes a view of learning and development that is fundamentally different from those presented in the other chapters, particularly those on discrimination learning. The book ends with 3 chapters by Pick, E. J. Gibson, and Estes, who discuss and criticize ideas presented in the earlier chapters. As with most edited volumes, the book is not tightly organized, but the juxtaposition of the ideas of the different investigators suggests some interesting points of convergence.—H. A. Ruff.

712. WAGNER, D. A. (Ed.). **Child Development and International Development: Research-Policy Interfaces. New Directions for Child Development. No. 20.** Jossey-Bass, 1983. 123 p. $7.95.

This book is number 20 in Jossey-Bass Publishing Company's quarterly series, New Directions for Child Development, under the editorship of William Damon. The audience for the series is professionals and graduate students. The series is particularly appropriate for college professors for several reasons: the articles give overviews of newer research ideas and findings without being so comprehensive that one drowns, there is usually a helpful example of the methodology common to a topic, and reference lists to direct the teacher to additional useful general sources are provided. This volume, edited by Daniel Wagner, is a 1982 AAS symposium. The topic is innovative and interdisciplinary: child development in relation to economic development in third-world countries. The papers are unique in several ways: (1) the methodology brings together for comparison the macrolevel data of economic development—infant mortality, per-capita income, health care availability—with the microlevel data of individual psychology—child-bearing choices, maternal attitudes toward infants, and the needs of the individual child; (2) they illustrate the application of multivariate statistical methods such as structural modeling, step-wise regression, and microanalyses to the problems and questions of individual child development; (3) the emphasis on third-world cultures forces us to notice how culture bound the emphasis on individual mother-child relationships within the field of child development research is; and (4) the authors make a plea for researchers to be more explicitly concerned with the well being of the world's children, and that this concern be expressed both by our choice of research questions with direct application to improving the quality of children's lives around the world and by writing papers that call for social change. The first paper, by Hollnsteiner and Tacon, reports on statistics about the movement of population into the cities as countries undergo economic development. The authors show that this trend often exposes the children to multiple adversities: father absence, premature parenting responsibility for preadolescents, lack of schooling, poor nutrition and health care, and homelessness. The plight of street children in Latin America is cited as an illustration. Chapter 2, by Cochrane and Mebra, uses multiple regression techniques to analyze the determinants of infant mortality. The major predictor of survival for children is the mother's educational level. This in turn is associated with improved sanitation in the home, improved nutrition, and the use of medical care for family illness. Several studies on various countries from the African and Asian continents are included. The third chapter, by anthropologist LeVine, presents a path-analytic model to explain the associations between mother's education and fertility and child survival rates. He postulates that there are 4 stages of fertility-rate development paralleling economic development and that each has a unique parental investment strategy. These begin with Stage 1, in which birth and infant mortality rates are both very high and survival of the child is the chief concern; little concern with individual parent-child relationship is possible. By Stage 4, such concern is dominant and can be sustained because families have small numbers of children whose survival they can assume. LeVine's interesting model assumes that women's decisions about fertility are both a direct consequence of cultural norms shifting with development and as a consequence of what happens when children demand more individual attention, which itself is a result evolving out of cultural change. The fourth chapter, by Engle, presents data from Guatemala to illustrate an unexpected consequence of mothers' going to work away from home. In 4 villages where nutritional intervention was being carried on, a longitudinal study of the child-bearing life cycle of 462 women was done. A multiple regression model for the prediction of child survival past the first year showed such survival to be positively related to the mother's work away from home. The fifth chapter, by editor Wagner, illustrates the problems that can occur when professional development bureaucrats take over a social institution in order to improve it. In this case, it is education in Islamic schools in North Africa, the Middle East, and in Indonesia. The indigenous schools use what Western educators might call an individualized approach. They do, in fact, focus on literacy and achieve it in many cases. The new reform schools of the international developers have a large improvement in literacy as a stated goal, but provide a rigid standardized curriculum to achieve it. Wagner's plea is for those of us who are "helping" to first look at what is already going on in the culture. The sixth chapter, by Moore, is actually an annotated bibliography on child labor in the third world. There are 51 entries covering many different societies in Africa, Asia, Latin America, and Oceania and 150 years of change. This is sure to be a useful resource for interested scholars. Chapter 7, by Sutton, is an eloquent plea for policy-aimed research, and the final chapter, by Wagner, points the reader to relevant journals and reference handbooks for further research. This little volume is not only innovative and interesting, but it also provides the interested novice scholar with more help in 1 place than is common in the field.—E. W. Willemsen.

13. WAGNER, DANIEL A., & STEVENSON, HAROLD W. (Eds.). **Cultural Perspectives on Child Development.** W. H. Freeman, 1982. xiv + 315 p. $19.95 (cloth); $10.95 (paper). This volume was designed to provide students with a cross-cultural perspective on child development research that would be less encyclopedic than that conveyed by recent handbooks, yet more detailed than that provided by textbook summaries. Recognized researchers (e.g., Patricia Greenfield, Wayne Holtzman, Gustav Jahoda) were invited to describe selected aspects of their work and to summarize the results of a single study or a short series of studies in a straightforward, nontechnical manner. The substance of the book consists of 12 original chapters dealing with varied aspects of development (i.e., affective, physical, linguistic, perceptual, personality, mental, moral) as well as with the impact of formal schooling and informal training. Cognitive developmental concerns, the interactive nature of culture and development, and the complex methodological problems involved in conducting valid cross-cultural research are stressed throughout. The studies summarized were conducted primarily at sites in North America, South America, and Africa, with subjects in varied stages of childhood and adolescence. Full reports of these studies have appeared previously in the professional literature. Selected chapters from this volume can be used to good advantage to supplement the treatment of standard topics in human development, child development, and child psychology texts. For examples, chapters such as those by Greenfield and Love ("Cognitive Aspects of Informal Education") and by Townsend et al. ("Nutrition and Preschool Mental Development," the NCAP study) provide excellent descriptions of well-designed, carefully executed field research that can be easily understood by students with little previous training in theory, methodology, or statistics. Lester and Brazelton's chapter moves beyond standard discussions of nature-nurture interaction, drawing on data for neonates in 8 cultures to illustrate how cross-cultural comparisons can extend our understanding of the range and variability of adaptive behavior as well as our understanding of the blend of cultural practice and biological predisposition underlying development. Other chapters clearly document the importance of questioning generalizations about human behavior based on limited cultural samples (e.g., chapters by Williams, Jahoda & McGurk, and Blount concerning moral development, picture perception, and parental speech, respectively). They also clarify major conceptual and methodological problems inherent in generalizations about behavior across cultures (e.g., chapters by Nyiti and by Ciborowski & Price-Williams concerning rate of Piagetian cognitive development and animistic cognition, respectively). Surprisingly, since the book is intended for student use, the editors did not include either an introductory or a concluding chapter to assist the reader in integrating the content or to provide an overview of the current status of cross-cultural developmental research. The volume suffers as a teaching resource on this account. Most individual chapters include a brief overview of research trends relevant to their specific topics, so orientation to the disciplines involved in current cross-cultural developmental research is not entirely lacking. For

example, Super and Harkness's chapter on the development of affect includes a brief discussion of factors underlying the demise of the "culture-and-personality era" and the emergence of the new "interdiscipline" of psychological anthropology and comparative child development. References cited throughout the text are listed by chapter at the end of Chapter 12. A comprehensive index and brief biographical sketch of all contributors enhance the usefulness of the volume.—S. M. Bennett.

714. WALKER, STEPHEN. **Animal Thought.** Routledge & Kegan Paul, 1983. xiv + 437 p. $35.00.
Walker presents 2 major arguments for the proposition that vertebrate animals think. He postulates that thoughts are brain states and that animals with brains like humans are likely to have brain states and thoughts like those of humans. Accordingly, he extensively reviews the recent work in comparative neurology which indicates the basic functional organization of the brain remains constant throughout vertebrate phylogeny (e.g., the forebrain mediates perception and cognition in both fish and monkeys, although the larger forebrain of monkeys mediates more sophisticated information processing than the forebrain of fish). Walker's second thesis is that animals often behave in ways that are difficult to explain by simple conditioning theories; for example, infant gorillas succeed on most of the tasks Piaget devised to test sensory motor intelligence in preverbal children. Other phenomena demonstrated in animals that are cited to support the notion of animal thought include object constancy, serial reversal learning, learning sets, abstraction of principles like oddity, conditional discrimination, delayed response, and delayed matching to sample. Walker may be correct in construing the material he reviews as evidence for thought in animals, but one need not be a radical behaviorist to have reservations about the value of an impalpable entity inaccessible to objective measurement.—J. M. Warren.

715. ZIGLER, EDWARD F., & GORDON, EDMUND W. (Eds.). **Day Care: Scientific and Social Policy Issues.** Auburn House, 1982. ix + 515 p. $24.95 (cloth); $12.95 (paper).
This volume is a collection of chapters illustrating the range and complexity of issues facing daycare policy makers. It is published under the auspices of the American Orthopsychiatric Association and includes contributions from experimental psychology, psychoanalytic training, early childhood education, public health, pediatrics, economics, and public office holders. Several of the authors are students or colleagues of the editors at Yale. The 24 chapters are organized into 3 sections. The first focuses on some of the theoretical perspectives and recent daycare research, with particular emphasis on the group care of infants and toddlers. It begins with a reprint of M. Rutter's review of the social-emotional consequences of daycare originally published in the *American Journal of Orthopsychiatry*. S. Provence follows with an articulate rationale for providing for the range of developmental needs (beyond cognitive stimulation) of infants and their parents. A. L. Siegler describes a psychoanalytic approach to early intervention. R. R. Ruopp and J. Travers summarize the National Day Care Study conducted by Abt Associates and the policy implications of the findings. E. A. Farber and B. Egeland report on the effects of out-of-home care for a low-income population participating in a longitudinal study of mother-child interactions. K. McCartney, S. Scarr, D. Phillips, S. Grajek, and J. C. Schwarz present preliminary results of their Bermuda study examining the effects of center characteristics and caregiver behavior on cognitive, language, and social development. A. Robertson reports a retrospective comparison of school-age children who attended "average quality" daycare as preschoolers with a group who did not. E. F. Zigler and P. Turner look at relations between parents and daycare workers. Early results from the Yale Child Welfare Research Program are presented by L. A. Rescorla, S. Provence, and A. Naylor, with 5-year follow-up data reported by P. K. Trickett, N. H. Apfel, L. K. Rosenbaum, and E. F. Zigler. The final 2 chapters in this section (D. Frye and V. Seitz) address methodological issues in daycare research. The views of Senators Orrin Hatch and Edward Kennedy comprise the second section of the book. The final section identifies policy questions and alternatives related to the delivery and funding of daycare services. J. R. Nelson, Jr., describes the politics of federal daycare regulation. R. Beck identifies options for child-care policy for the 1980s and suggests some principles for their evaluation. E. F. Zigler and J. Goodman offer some observations on federal involvement with child care in the United States. W. G. Winget presents and evaluates

3 options for making affordable child care available to the working poor. J. A. Levine examines some assumptions and potential problems in providing child-care information and referral services. S. L. Kagan and T. Glennon discuss proprietary child care. E. Moore, Director of the National Black Child Development Institute, shows how daycare problems are exacerbated for the working poor and black families. J. B. Richmond and J. M. Janis point out the need for the inclusion of health-care services in daycare. Issues related to school-age child care are described by members of the School-Age Child Care Project. In the final chapter, M. Almy discusses the relation between early childhood education and daycare, and her concerns related to the promotion of child development and the professionalization of the field. This is a very readable volume which should be useful to anyone interested in daycare policy. It would be particularly appropriate for a graduate seminar to introduce students from various social science backgrounds to the issues, constituencies, and intricacies of social policy making.—S. J. Kilmer.

ARCHIVES

716. History of Child Development: Primary Source Materials: First Compilation of Abstracts.

In 1976, Alice Smuts, a historian writing on the early history of child development, told our Society that primary source materials in this field were very difficult to locate, and that many valuable materials were being lost at an alarming rate. In 1977, the Society's Governing Council established the Committee on Preservation of Historical Materials to try to remedy this situation by locating and arranging the personal papers of scientists and certain scientific administrators and the records of research institutes, child guidance clinics, philanthropic organizations, associations of developmentalists, etc. Primary source materials, in the Committee's definition, have come to mean any kind of useful unpublished materials. The initial efforts of the Committee have been directed toward the clinical and research areas of child development, including disciplines that have specialities in that area, such as pediatrics, psychology, orthodontics, nutrition, psychiatry, physical growth, sociology, etc. We have included parent education and early childhood education only in their linkage with child development research institutes, since these fields are too broad for our present scale of effort. Excellent programs to preserve historical materials in the field of social and child welfare already exist, and therefore we have excluded these fields. The Committee's 2-year planning period and pilot work were supported by the William T. Grant Foundation. Under the Committee Chair, Robert R. Sears, the Committee conducted a survey to assess the probable results of preservation in the field without its efforts; sobered by the dismaying results of its preliminary investigations, the Committee decided to embark upon a full-fledged program of identification and preservation. It identified 193 individuals and 43 organizations whose papers should be preserved. Following further surveys and after consultation with historians and archivists, the Committee obtained grants from the National Historical Records and Publications Commission and from the National Science Foundation. To begin systematic work in September 1980, it retained a professional archivist, Lynn A. Bonfield, of San Francisco, to begin the work of locating the papers of those individuals and organizations active at any time in child development from the later nineteenth century to World War II. In June 1982, Hamilton Cravens became Committee Chair. At his request, he was relieved of his responsibilities in April 1983. Appointed as his successor was Sheldon H. White. Since September 1982, L. H. Curry has served as project archivist. Special note should be taken of the pioneering work of Milton J. E. Senn. He conducted a large number of interviews of child developmentalists and of workers in child guidance and psychiatry (approximately 200 individuals). The transcripts of these interviews have been deposited at the National Library of Medicine.[1] Senn also published 2 books which will be found very useful.[2] Indeed, Senn's contributions inspired the Committee to continue its efforts. To this point, the Committee has had 4 main goals. The first has been to locate the primary source materials. A second function has been to alert archivists and historians of the importance of these materials and to encourage them to help preserve these materials. A third activity has been to alert the present generation of senior but active members of the field to the importance of planning for the preservation of their own papers. Many universities, states and other politic॥ subdivisions, as well as the Library of Congress have final archival repositories and are willin॥ and eager to collaborate with individuals and institutions for the preservation of material॥ Arrangements should be made well in advance of the submission of such documents. All fin॥ arrangements are made between the owners of the papers and the archives. Developmenta॥ ists who are looking forward to the ultimate placement of their papers are encouraged to cor᛫ sult with the Committee or our archivist. The fourth goal of the Committee has been to publis in *Child Development Abstracts and Bibliography* periodic compilations of our findings. Th᛫ first of these is printed here. It represents a listing of all collections of individuals whose mater᛫ als we have been able to find which are currently accessioned in a reputable repository an᛫ available for scholarly use. We have not included materials that were identified but remain i private hands or that are on deposit in a repository but not yet catalogued and arranged f᛫ scholarly use. As such materials are transferred and made available for scholarly use, th Committee will hope to include this information in subsequent published compilations. Furtt᛫ ermore, we have not included in our compilation the many oral histories that Senn conducte᛫ as these are listed elsewhere.[3] We have included materials that we have found and material᛫ listed in standard listings, including the *National Union Catalog of Manuscript Collection॥ Michael M. Sokal and Patrice A. Rafail, Comps., *A Guide to Manuscripts Collections in th᛫ History of Psychology and Related Areas* (Krause International Publications, 1982); Elizabet᛫ B. Mason and Louis M. Starr, Eds., *The Oral History Collection of Columbia Universit* (Columbia University Oral History Office, 1979); and in *Women's History Sources: A Guide t᛫ Archives and Manuscripts Collections in the United States* (Bowker, 1979). We have n᛫ attempted to duplicate in complete detail these entries here. The materials listed have bee᛫ arranged alphabetically, by individual.[4] In its next compilation, the Committee will publis᛫ further listings of individuals and of organizations. The members of the Committee during all c᛫ part of its existence since 1977 have been: Hamilton Cravens, Dale B. Harris, Marjorie Honzi᛫ Arthur Parmelee, Philip Sapir, Robert R. Sears, Alice Smuts, Hoben Thomas, and Sheldon ᛫ White. The Committee has been well served by a Board of Archival Consultants, whose men᛫ bers have included Herbert Finch, Robert M. Warner, Joan N. Warnow, and Manfred Wase᛫ man. The Committee appreciates the assistance it has received from these individuals an᛫ from many archivists, historians, and developmentalists. The Committee is now embarke᛫ upon the second phase of its archival preservation program, that of working with current men᛫ bers of the Society to assist in the orderly preservation of their papers. Individuals are encoun᛫ aged to contact Committee members, the new Committee Chair, or the project archivist.[5]

Committee on Preservation of Historical Source Materials
Society for Research in Child Development

Sheldon H. White, Chair, 1983-
Department of Psychology and Social Relations
Harvard Univ.
Cambridge, MA 02138

Linda Heath Curry, Project Archivist
1125 14th Street
Santa Rosa, CA 95404

NOTES

1. Contact Manfred Waserman, Curator of Modern Manuscripts, Historical Division, National L᛫ brary of Medicine, Bethesda, MD, 20014, to order microfilms.

2. Milton J. E. Senn, Insights on the Child Development Movement in the United States. *Mono graphs of the Society for Research in Child Development,* Vol. 40, Nos. 3–4, Serial No. 16᛫ 1975; Milton J. E. Senn, *Speaking Out for America's Children* (New Haven: Yale Univ. Press 1977).

3. See Michael M. Sokal and Patrice Rafail, Comps., *A Guide to Manuscript Collections in the History of Psychology and Related Areas* (Millwood, NY: Krause International Publications, 1982), pp. 177–180.

4. The abstracts for this compilation were prepared by L. H. Curry. The text was written by the outgoing Chair, H. Cravens, and revised after consultation with Committee members.

5. At the Society's 1983 biennial convention, the Governing Council changed the name of the Committee to the Committee on the History of Child Development. Subsequent contributions will reflect this change of title and function.

ABBOTT, EDITH (1876–1957), & ABBOTT, GRACE (1878–1939).
Papers, 1903–1954. 45 ft. In Univ. of Chicago, Regenstein Library, Dept. of Special Collections. Correspondence, notes, documents, pamphlets, bibliography, and other papers, mostly since 1910. Relates to the professional and academic careers of Edith Abbott as Dean of the Univ. of Chicago School of Social Service Administration, and her sister, Grace Abbott, as Chief of the U.S. Children's Bureau.
Papers, 1897–1954. 6 cu. ft. In Univ. of Nebraska-Lincoln Archives. General and family correspondence; lecture notes and material relating to such topics as child labor, juvenile delinquency, housing, immigration, poor laws, social welfare, and the status of women; biographical material; and scrapbooks and photographs concerning the Abbott sisters' family life.

ACKERLY, SAMUEL SPAFFORD (1895–1981).
Oral history, 1977. 2 hours. In Univ. of Louisville Archives. Interview covers Ackerly's experiences in World War I and how this influenced his subsequent decisions; Ackerly's medical education at Yale Univ., M.D. 1925; his coming to the Dept. of Psychiatry at the Univ. of Louisville in the 1930s; the formation of the Louisville Child Guidance Clinic; and his efforts to improve treatment for mental illness in city and state hospitals.

ADLER, ALFRED (1870–1937).
Papers, ca. 1921–1936. Ca. 650 items. In Library of Congress, Manuscript Division. Correspondence, clinical and postgraduate lectures, patient case studies, unpublished writings, reports of medical meetings, and biographical materials. Also, photographs and an interview with Adler by Helena Smith. Patient notebook restricted until 2003.

ALLEN, FREDERICK H. (1890–1964).
Papers, n.d. 1 folder. In Univ. of Pennsylvania Archives. Biographical material and photographs.

ALSCHULER, ROSE HAAS (1887-).
Papers, 1916–1973. 11 ft. plus oversize material. In Univ. of Illinois at Chicago Circle Library, Manuscript Collection. Personal and professional correspondence, minutes of meetings, legal and financial records, photographs, newspaper clippings, newsletters, books, catalogs, artwork, bulletins, and personal momentos.

AMES, LOUISE BATES (1908-).
Papers, 1939–1964. 10 ft. In Library of Congress, Manuscript Division. Correspondence; bibliography of Ames (articles, monographs, reviews, films, and TV series) 1933–1965; statement of Ames' work, 1939–1949; correspondence, clippings, printed matter, and memorabilia relating to the work of Ames and her collaborator, Frances Lillian Ilg, as columnists and doctors, and to the Gesell Inst. of Child Development.

BALDWIN, BIRD THOMAS (1875–1928).
Papers, 1917–1928. n.v. In Univ. of Iowa Archives. Extensive correspondence arranged chronologically in President's Office correspondence, 1887–1969.

CHILD DEVELOPMENT ABSTRACTS AND BIBLIOGRAPHY

Papers, 1917–1928. 1 file folder. In Univ. of Iowa Archives. Correspondence in Vertical File or Faculty and Staff, 1855–.

BALDWIN, J. MARK (1861–1934).
Papers, 1903–1911. n.v. In Johns Hopkins Univ., Ferdinand Hamburger, Jr., Archives. Material in the papers of the Office of the President. Entries under "Appointments in Philosophy, Teachers' Lectures," "Appointment 1903," and "Papers referring to the resignation of J. M Baldwin, Feb. 20, 1911."
Papers, n.d. 10 inches. In Princeton Univ. Library. Correspondence to Mrs. Baldwin at time o husband's death, press clippings, offprints of articles, and photographs.

BANHAM, KATHERINE (1897-).
Papers, 1948–1977. 14 record storage boxes. In Duke Univ. Archives. Professional papers including course notes, research notes, and studies on the aged and young children. Includes many original tests and validation studies of articles subsequently published. Materials relating to testing include the "Quick Screening Scale of Mental Development"; the "Ring and Peg Tests of Mental Development," used to measure the intelligence of infants; correspondence articles about tests; test responses; and statistical analysis. Course materials include syllabi course notes, examinations, student papers, grade books (restricted), bibliographies, and notes on courses by others dating from graduate student days to her retirement in 1967. Also papers relating to the activities of and her participation in professional organizations such as the International Council of Women Psychologists and the AAUW. Taped interview and transcript included.

BAUMGARTNER, LEONA (1902-).
Papers, ca. 1930–1960. 7 boxes. In Yale Univ. Library. Research material on early bacteriology; correspondence relating to the Florida Medical School Survey, 1948–1949; correspondence with Dr. Arnold Carl Klebs, 1932–1942; material from the American Public Health Association when Baumgartner was President in 1959; correspondence and reports on public health in industrialized countries, particularly the USSR and Japan; 3 volumes of notes from labs and lectures at Cornell, 1930s.
Papers, 1937–. Ca. 100 ft. In Harvard Univ., Countway Library of Medicine. Correspondence memoranda, diaries, research notes, drafts of speeches, administrative reports, clippings. The collection documents Baumgartner's career from her medical education and training in public health at Yale Univ., through her association from 1937 with the Health Dept. of New York City where she served as Commissioner of Health from 1954 to 1961, to her work as an advisor to the Agency for International Development. Her files also contain family correspondence and information about child welfare, pediatrics, social work, women's groups, medical research institutes, and economic development.

BEERS, CLIFFORD WHITTINGHAM (1876–1943).
Papers, 1905–1918, 1966. 4 ft. In Yale Univ. Library. Drafts and notes for Beers' book, A Mind That Found Itself (1908), and printed material, pamphlets, and clippings relating to Beers' work in the field of mental hygiene.

BENEDICT, RUTH FULTON (1887–1948).
Papers, ca. 1909–1959. Ca. 12 ft. In Vassar Coll. Library. Correspondence, journals, diaries photography, and manuscripts of Benedict's writings. Includes the long draft of Margaret Mead's "An Anthropologist at Work."

BLANTON, MARGARET GRAY (1887–1973), & BLANTON, SMILEY (1882–1972).
Papers, 1897–1972. 12 ft. (6,300 items). In Univ. of Tennessee Library. Includes personal correspondence, research material, unpublished manuscripts, article columns, publications, photographs.

LATZ, W. E. (1919–1966).
apers, 1919–1970. 48 boxes and 10 filing cabinets. In Univ. of Toronto, Thomas Fisher Rare
ook Library. Personal and professional papers, 1919–1966; historical materials relating to the
st. of Child Study and its associated schools, 1926-ca. 1970; research material (restricted)
onnected with projects carried out at the Institute, 1926–64.

OAS, FRANZ (1858–1942).
apers, 1862–1942. Ca. 50,000 items. In American Philosophical Society Library. Family cor-
spondence, including letters to and from his parents, wife, and children; professional corres-
ondence (with abstracts of many letters in non-English languages) on anthropology, teaching
d research at Columbia Univ., scientific societies, publications, etc.; correspondence relating
the Germanistic Society and to German National Socialism, the expulsion of European scho-
rs, and efforts to establish them in British and American institutions; diary of his first field trip
the Northwest, 1886; diplomas and certificates of membership. Also a dictionary, texts,
otes, and papers on the ethnology and language of the Kwatiutl Indians.
apers, ca. 1894–1937. 4 file folders. In Columbia Univ. Libraries, Central Files. Extensive
orrespondence, chiefly between Boas and the University Presidents Seth Low and Nicholas
urray Butler concerning the development of anthropology as a curriculum at the University,
d various proposals for personnel appointments and research projects.
ral history, 1972. 76 pp. In Columbia Univ., Oral History Research Office. Reminiscences by
anziska Boas of her father, Franz Boas. (Permission required to cite or to quote.)

OTT, EDWARD ALEXANDER (1887-).
apers, ca. 1920s-1950s. n.v. In Univ. of Toronto Archives. Some correspondence relating to
ott in various official University records, particularly in those of the Office of the President;
tensive newspaper clipping file.

OWDITCH, HENRY PICKERING (1840–1911).
apers, n.d. Ca. 12 boxes. In Harvard Univ., Countway Library of Medicine. Research materi-
s (3 boxes), administrative correspondence as professor of physiology and dean of medical
hool, and family papers (6 boxes). Correspondents include Edith Boyd (3 letters, 1961) and
, Stanley Hall (2 letters, 1921).
apers, n.d. 1 folder and 1 vol. In Harvard Univ. Archives. Notes on growth of children and 1
lume of publications and reference material.

RONNER, AUGUSTA FOX (1881-).
ee entry for William Healy.

ARMICHAEL, LEONARD (1898–1973).
apers, n.d. Ca. 400,000 items. In American Philosophical Society Library. Correspondence,
mmittee reports and records, articles and speeches, drafts of papers and books, and note-
oks spanning Carmichael's career. About 10 folders relate to the Society for Research in
hild Development including correspondence with Robert S. Woodworth, Carroll E. Palmer, W.
Krogman, Dale B. Harris, Nancy Bayley, Roger G. Barker, John E. Anderson, and Arnold
esell. Also material from the Division of Anthropology and Psychology of the National
esearch Council and the Yerkes Laboratories of Primate Biology.

ANIELS, AMY L.
apers, 1918–1962. 1 folder. In Univ. of Iowa Archives. Correspondence in Vertical File on
aculty and Staff, 1855–.

EARBORN, WALTER F. (1878–1955).
apers, 1917–1930, 1935–1945. 1 box and 1 vol. In Harvard Univ. Archives. Papers relating
Dearborn's teaching in the Graduate School of Education, ca. 1935–1945, including lecture
tes, course syllabi, examination questions, and reports. Also a grade book, 1917–1930.

DENNIS, WAYNE (1905–1976).
Papers, 1929–1976. 31 boxes and 9 vol. In National Library of Medicine, History of Medicin
Division. Includes correspondence, drawings, notes, diaries, and reprints. A sizable portion
the collection consists of children's drawings collected by Dennis in his cross-cultural studies
behavior and intelligence. Includes a large number of notes and printed matter on the subje
of intelligence testing of children. Contains material on which Dennis was working at the time
his death.

DOLL, EDGAR ARNOLD (1889–1969).
Papers, 1915–1958. 23 ft. In Univ. of Akron, Archives of the History of American Psycholog
Correspondence, tests, raw and normative data, calculation sheets, and prepublication man
scripts, chiefly relating to the Vineland Social Maturity Scale, of which Doll was the autho
Includes correspondence pertaining to personnel, patients, and research, and permission
translate the scale and plans for its foreign adaptations. Correspondents include Henry I
Goddard, William Healy, Stanley D. Porteus, and Lewis M. Terman.

DUMMER, ETHEL STURGES (1866–1954).
Papers, 1766–1954. 8 file drawers. In Radcliffe Coll., Schlesinger Library on the History
Women in America. Correspondence, reports, minutes of meetings, photos, speeches ar
articles by and about Dummer. Documents her efforts in behalf of the juvenile delinquent, th
prostitute, and the illegitimate child; her interest in progressive education and public schools
Chicago; and her work with leaders in the mental hygiene movement.

ELIOT, ABIGAIL ADAMS (1892-).
Papers, ca. 1960–1974. 4.5 archival boxes, 2 folders, and other items. In Radcliffe Col
Schlesinger Library on the History of Women in America. Correspondence, diaries from trip
lecture notes, photos, articles, clippings, and memorabilia.
Papers, 1922–1967. Ca. 2 folders. In Tufts Univ. Wessell Library. Correspondence, typ
scripts of articles and book chapters, offprints of articles, articles about Eliot, honorary citatic
(LHD, Tufts, 1967), and photographs mostly from the 1930s and 1940s.

ELIOT, MARTHA MAY (1891–1978).
Papers, 1898–1975. 76 archival boxes, 1 oversize folder, and 1 oversize volume. In Radclif
Coll., Schlesinger Library on the History of Women in America. Correspondence, speeche
articles, photos, clippings, posters, and other papers. Documents Eliot's career as founder
the World Health Organization and the fourth head of the Children's Bureau, as well as h
work in international, national, state, and local organizations that promoted maternal and chi
health.
Oral history, 1966. 115 pp. In Columbia Univ., Oral History Research Office. Includes discu
sion of the origins of the Public Health Service, Children's Bureau, and Social Security Admi
istration; AMA's role in medical care and insurance programs; public health legislation; Cor
mittee on Costs of Medical Care, 1920s; Committee on Economic Security, 1930s; Soci
Security Act; Wagner-Murray Dingell health insurance bills; Hill-Burton Bill; first National Heal
Conference, 1938. (Permission required to cite or to quote.)

FRANK, LAWRENCE K. (1890–1968).
Papers, 1919–1969. 26 boxes. In National Library of Medicine. Correspondence; memorand
1919–1960s; minutes and notes of meetings, 1921–1964; speeches; radio scripts; and man
scripts for book chapters, 1914–1968.

GARDNER, GEORGE (1904–1982).
Papers, ca. 1950–1970. 11 boxes. In Harvard Univ., Countway Library of Medicine. Materi
from Judge Baker and Harvard's Social Relations Dept. including letters from William Heal
Augusta Bronner, Sheldon and Eleanor Glueck, Douglas Thom, David Levy, Eveoleen Re
ford, and Marion Kenworthy. Papers show Gardner's involvement with the American Academ
of Child Psychiatry, the American Child Guidance Foundation, and the American Psychia
Association's Committee on Child Psychiatry.

GESELL, ARNOLD LUCIUS (1880–1961).
Papers, 1870–1961. 100 ft. (90,000 items). In Library of Congress, Manuscript Division. Correspondence, abstracts, addresses, announcements appointment books, biographical material, books and articles and galleys of the same, Gesell's reviews of others' books, broadcasts, bulletins, certificates, charts, clinical records, clippings, contracts, diplomas, film scripts, financial papers, genealogical records, illustrations, lectures, legal papers, personnel records, photos, press releases, reports, scrapbooks, and other papers concerning Gesell's professional life.
Papers, n.d. n.v. In Columbia Univ., Teachers Coll. Library, Dept. of Special Collections. Material in files of President William Russell.
Films, n.d. 2,164 items. In Univ. of Akron, Child Development Film Archives. Research films by Gesell.

GLUECK, BERNARD C. (1884–1972).
Papers, 1904–1965. 13 boxes. In Western History Research Center, Univ. of Wyoming, Laramie. Addresses, speeches, unpublished materials (chiefly drafts of articles and books), reports, documents, and reprints.

GLUECK, SHELDON (1896–1980), & GLUECK, ELEANOR TOUROFF (1898–1972).
Papers, 1911–1972. 50 ft. In Harvard Law School Library. Correspondence; diaries; drafts of unpublished and published books, articles, and speeches; notes; bibliographies; tables; reports; minutes of meetings; press releases; clippings; and other items. From 1925 until 1974, Sheldon Glueck was director of a law school project on the causes, treatment, and prevention of juvenile delinquency. Serving as his research assistant from 1930–1953, Eleanor Glueck became research associate and then in 1966 co-director of the project. Collection also pertains to professional associations and meetings the Gluecks participated in concerning mental illness and mental health, social welfare, child psychiatry, delinquency, crime, and penal law.
Papers, n.d. 4 vols. In Harvard Univ. Archives. Publications and reference material gathered for their work in juvenile delinquency where they were joint researchers in criminology.

GODDARD, HENRY HERBERT (1866–1957).
Papers, 1833–1952. Ca. 8 ft. In Univ. of Akron, Archives of the History of American Psychology. Correspondence (1906–1952); diary-ledger-scrapbook (1833–1864) used by Goddard's mother, Sarah Goddard; records of unpublished laboratory data; pamphlets; clippings; scrapbooks; professional and avocational photos; glass slides; films; and personal ephemera. Includes material relating to Goddard's professional activities.

GOODENOUGH, FLORENCE LAURA (1886–1959).
Papers, 1936–1978. 8 folders. In Univ. of Minnesota Archives. Personal and professional correspondence, mainly 1936–1947, arranged chronologically, relating to her career at the Inst. of Child Welfare. Correspondence chiefly discusses publications and developments in the field of child welfare, with many letters soliciting her opinion. Professional correspondents include Dale Harris, Leta Hollingworth, Helen Koch, Dorothea McCarthy, Mary Shirley, Lewis Terman. Also biographical material collected by Theta Wolf.

GRUENBERG, SIDONIE M. (1881–1974).
Papers, 1878–1974. 55.6 ft. In Library of Congress, Manuscript Division. Joint collection with husband, Benjamin C. Gruenberg (1875–1965), arranged mainly in chronological order. Includes journals and diaries, family and general correspondence, book manuscripts, notes, drafts of speeches and writings, scrapbooks, and printed material.

HALL, GRANVILLE STANLEY (1844–1924).
Papers, 1844–1924. 46 boxes. In Clark Univ. Archives. Personal and family papers and some professional material, 1844–1924 (2 boxes); correspondence and other materials relating to Clark Univ. during Hall's presidency, 1888–1920 (21 boxes); professional correspondence, 1876–1924 (4 boxes); correspondence with graduate students (13 boxes); and miscellaneous

speeches, notes, articles, and biographical material (5 boxes). Also 71 items in the Sigmund Freud papers, 1908–1923.
Papers, 1889–1921. 3 ft. In Univ. of Akron, Archives of the History of American Psychology. Principally notes from Hall's readings of the professional literature, some correspondence, numerous manuscripts and drafts of publications, and minutes of a few meetings of the Committee on the Examination of Recruits, 1917.
Papers, n.d. n.v. In Columbia Univ., Teachers Coll. Library, Dept. of Special Collections. Material in files of President William Russell.

HARLOW, HARRY (1905–1981).
Papers, 1965–1981. 2 ft. In Univ. of Wisconsin-Madison Archives. Includes correspondence, drafts of reports, publications, and speeches primarily from Harlow's Arizona years and some from his work at the Univ. of Wisconsin. Additions anticipated.

HARTSHORNE, HUGH (1885–1967).
Papers, 1910–1966. 3 boxes. In Yale Divinity School Library. Correspondence primarily with Raymond P. Morris, Librarian at Yale Divinity School, 1934–1964; notes taken as a Yale student; writings, primarily articles, 1910–1966; a list of publications and reviews of his books; diplomas; photographs; and programs.
Papers, n.d. n.v. In Columbia Univ., Teachers Coll. Library, Dept. of Special Collections. Material in the files of President William Russell.

HAVINGHURST, ROBERT (1900-).
Papers, n.d. n.v. In Univ. of Chicago, Regenstein Library, Dept. of Special Collections. Files relating to the General Education Board, 1932–1941, the Experimental Collect Program, and the Quincy-River City Project.

HEALY, WILLIAM (1869–1962), & BRONNER, AUGUSTA FOX (1881-).
Oral history, 1960, 1961. 276 pp. In Harvard Univ., Houghton Library. Transcript of interview by John C. Burnham, January 1960 and June 1961. No tape.

HELMHOLZ, HENRY FREDERIC (1882–1958).
Papers, 1902–1958. Ca. 9 items. In Johns Hopkins Univ., Chesney Medical Archives. 1 biographical file containing 3 letters, 3 newspaper clippings, 1 photograph, 1 student record file.

HILDRETH, GERTRUDE H. (1898-).
Papers, 1935–1946. 1 folder. In Columbia Univ., Teachers Coll. Library, Dept. of Special Collections. Materials in President William Russell's files.

HILL, PATTY SMITH (1868–1946).
Papers, 1878–1942. 1,245 items. The Filson Club (Louisville, KY). Correspondence; transcripts of speeches, articles, and lectures; papers on kindergarten, nursery schools, teacher education, and other topics; an autobiographical sketch; and material about her professional trip to Russia in 1929, her honorary degree from Columbia Univ. in 1929, the Patty Smith Hill Fund, the Utopia Children's House, Hilltop, the Patty Smith Hill Farm, and other plans to aid needy children during the depression.
Papers, 1925–1928. 3 in. In Columbia Univ., Teachers Coll. Library, Dept. of Special Collections. Typescripts of speeches, interviews, and biographical accounts of Patty Smith Hill. Included are transcripts of interviews given in 1925 (7 typed pages) and in 1927 (both original typescript and revised version which appeared in the Survey Graphic). Biographical essay written ca. 1925 by one of her students.
Papers, n.d. In Columbia Univ., Teachers Coll. Library, Dept. of Special Collections. Correspondence in President James E. Russell's papers, 1904–1927.

HOLLINGWORTH, LETA STETTER (1886–1939).
Papers, 1913–1939. Ca. 4 ft. In Univ. of Akron, Archives of the History of American Psychology. Chiefly material relating to the class for gifted children in Speyer School, P.S. 500, New York City. Includes records of students with high IQs, school reports, transcripts of staff meetings and projections for the future of the class. Other papers include early publications, photos, and memorabilia dealing with Hollingworth's life and career.
Papers, 1914–1939. Ca. 600 items. In Nebraska State Historical Society. Includes printed matter, 1914–1939; manuscripts, 1914–1939; and biographical material. The bulk of the collection consists of printed materials and manuscripts relating to Hollingworth's work in the field of educational psychology, especially to the subject of the gifted child. Most of the materials are reprints of articles and other publications by Hollingworth which appeared in scholarly journals.

HOLT, LUTHER EMMETT, JR. (1895–1974).
Papers, 1916–1974. 1 file folder. In Johns Hopkins Univ., Chesney Medical Archives. Biographical file includes newspaper clippings, 1 photo, 10 letters, and 1 student record file.

HOOBLER, ICIE MACY (1892-).
Papers, 1921–1974. 35 ft. In Univ. of Michigan, Bentley Historical Library, Michigan Historical Collections. Correspondence, scientific reports, publications, and other papers. Pertain to her interest in the problems of nutrition and aging; her work with the Merrill-Palmer School in Detroit, the Detroit Inst. of Cancer Research, the Children's Fund of Michigan, and Grand Valley State Coll. in Allendale, Michigan; and her membership in the White House Conference on Food, Nutrition, and Health, and in various White House conferences on children and youth since 1930.

HUNT, J. McVICKER (1906-).
Papers, 1931–1977. 27.3 ft. In Univ. of Illinois at Urbana-Champaign Archives. Correspondence, manuscripts, reports, studies, publications, course materials, and examinations relating to clinical, child, and developmental psychology; American Psychological Association (1946–1975); New York Community Service Study-Institute on Welfare Research (1944–1969); National Inst. of Mental Health (1962–1977) and Subcommittee on Psychology of its Training Committee (1960–1972); Tehran Research Unit infant development research (1961–1972) list and copies of publications (1931–1977); research material and manuscripts for *Intelligence and Experience* (1961), *Toward Ordinal Scales of Psychological Development in Infancy* (1968–1972), and *Assessment in Infancy* (1975); therapeutic counseling (1953–1961); stimulus-response inventory of traits (1964–1968); recommendations (1950–1972) and job openings (1961–1972); speaking, writing, and consulting (1946–1972); and course materials from Brown Univ. (1936–1945), Columbia Univ. (1948–1950), New York Univ. (1950–1951), and Illinois Univ. at Urbana-Champaign (1951–1973).

IRWIN, ORVIS CARL (1891–1979).
Papers, 1928–1952. 1 file folder. In Univ. of Iowa Archives. Correspondence in Vertical File on Faculty and Staff, 1855–.
Papers, ca. 1958–1968. Ca. 12 items. In Inst. of Logopedics. Memorandum dated October 5, 1964; 3 photographs; and 2–3 films from Irwin's work at the Inst. of Logopedics; bibliographies of publications by Irwin, 1930–1965; some reprints. (Requests for access to the collection should be made through the Institute Director, Dr. Frank R. Kleffner.)

JACKSON, EDITH BANFIELD (1895–1977).
Papers, 1907–1977. 8 boxes and 10 photograph folders. In Radcliffe Coll., Schlesinger Library on the History of Women in America. Personal papers and correspondence with colleagues, including Lawrence Frank and Benjamin Spock; correspondence with refugees from Europe, 1938–1941; 7 folders of family correspondence, 1907–1974; some papers from her work with the U.S. Public Health Service and other hospitals; photographs, mainly from Rooming-In Unit at Yale; materials from conferences attended by Jackson; copies of remarks made at her memorial service, 1977; and copies of articles by Jackson.

CHILD DEVELOPMENT ABSTRACTS AND BIBLIOGRAPHY

Papers, 1947–1959. 2 boxes including 4 vol. In Yale Univ. Library. Material relating to rooming-in including the Grace–New Haven Community Hosp. Rooming-In Unit blueprint and model; guest book, 1947–1952; and 4 scrapbooks of letters, newspaper clippings, programs, and magazine articles.

JEANS, PHILIP CHARLES (1883–1952).
Papers, 1926–1940. 1 file folder. In Univ. of Iowa Archives. Correspondence in Vertical File on Faculty and Staff, 1855–.

JERSILD, ARTHUR THOMAS (1902-).
Oral history, 1967. 255 pp. In Columbia Univ., Oral History Research Office. Includes discussion of education in South Dakota and Nebraska; Columbia Univ. Teachers Coll., 1929; his work as consulting psychologist to CBS, 1935–1948; Inst. for Educational Leadership in Japan, 1948–1949; work as school consultant; impressions of educators James Russell and William Russell, William H. Kilpatrick, and Edward G. Thorndike. (Permission required to cite or quote.)

JOHNSON, BUFORD JEANNETTE (1880-).
Papers, 1929–1933, 1937–1938. Ca. 25 items. In Johns Hopkins Univ., Ferdinand Hamburger, Jr. Archives. Papers in Records of the Office of the President, 1903–1963, and Executive Committee of the Board of Trustees. Includes correspondence and memos.

KANNER, LEO (1894–1981).
Papers, 1930–1976. 4 ft. In American Psychiatric Assoc. Archives. Personal and professional correspondence, arranged alphabetically by correspondent; a geographical file of professional correspondence, 1932–1976; autobiography; and reprints. Also an oral history interview, 31 pages of transcription.

KROGMAN, WILTON MARION (1903-).
Papers, n.d. 2 folders. In Univ. of Chicago, Regenstein Library, Dept. of Special Collections. Correspondence in Dept. of Anthropology records.

LENROOT, KATHARINE FREDRICA (1891–1982).
Papers, 1919–1971. 30 archive boxes, 1 oversize item. In Columbia Univ., Rare Book and Manuscript Library. Correspondence; reports; manuscripts of speeches and articles (1919–1958); files on individuals, subjects, and organizations; Children's Bureau files; clippings; personal documents and memoranda; and printed material. Concerns Lenroot's work with the Children's Bureau of the U.S. Dept. of Labor from 1915 to 1951, with UNICEF, and with other social welfare organizations.
Oral history, 1965. 173 pp. In Columbia Univ., Oral History Research Office. Includes discussion of Lenroot's family background; childhood in Wisconsin; and education at the Univ. of Wisconsin, 1912; Wisconsin Industrial Commission, 1913–1914; U.S. Children's Bureau from 1915; studies on infant mortality and child labor, early Mothers' Aid laws, development of the Social Security Act, and the Bureau's relations with states and Congress; Reorganization Act, 1945; Bureau under the Social Security Administration; impressions of Emma Lundberg, Edwin White, Frances Perkins, Harry Hopkins, Eleanor Roosevelt, and others. (Permission required to cite or quote.)

LEVY, DAVID M. (1892–1977).
Papers, 1921–1968. 55 ft. In New York Hosp.–Cornell Medical Center, Dept. of Psychiatry, History of Psychiatry Section. In addition to correspondence with individuals and organizations and material related to Levy's many publications, the major portion of the collection deals with the research Levy engaged in over the years. The first part of the collection comprises Levy's personal material, followed by professional correspondence alphabetically arranged in broad chronological sections. Following this are his general research notes of the 1920s through the 1950s. The third section deals with large individual research projects, such as maternal feelings, maternal overprotection and rejection, sibling rivalry; his Attitude Study Project, which

ARCHIVES

covered several years; and studies with the Rorschach Test and the Levy Movement Blots. Following the major research projects are sections on Levy's U.S. Army experiences after World War II, work done at Smith Coll. and Tulane Univ., as well as the Society for Research in Child Development. The collection closes with sections devoted to miscellaneous research and test materials as well as his files of case studies from the Inst. for Child Guidance (case records are restricted).

LEWIN, KURT (1890–1947).
Papers, 1929–1943. 6 boxes. In Univ. of Akron, Archives of the History of American Psychology. Correspondence (1928–1935), some lecture notes, unpublished manuscripts, typed interview by Robert R. Sears, a photograph, and material collected by his biographer, Alfred Morrow.
Papers, 1944–1946. 4 folders. In Massachusetts Inst. of Technology, Inst. Archives and Special Collections. Papers on the Research Center for Group Dynamics among the records of the School of Humanities, Office of the Dean. Scattered material on Lewin's appointment and the founding of the Research Center among the records of the President, 1930–1959.
Papers, 1935–1947. 1 file folder. In Univ. of Iowa Archives. Correspondence in Vertical File on Faculty and Staff, 1855–.
Films, n.d. 44 items. In Univ. of Akron, Child Development Film Archives. 44 research films by Lewin.
Films, n.d. 4 items. In Univ. of Kansas, Dept. of Psychology. Entails 4 reels of 16 mm safety film copied from motion pictures made by Lewin while he was in Berlin. They are: "Field Forces as Impediments to a Performance," "The Child and the Field Forces," "Level of Aspiration in Young Children," and "Walking Upstairs for the First Time." (Contact Sharon S. Brehm, Associate Chairperson of the Psychology Dept., to make arrangements to view the films. Copies may be obtained through the Calvin Company, Kansas City, MO).

LITTLEDALE, CLARA SAVAGE (1891–1956).
Papers, 1913–1955. 3 file boxes. In Radcliffe Coll., Schlesinger Library on the History of Women in America. Primarily Littledale's articles, radio talks, and speeches on childrearing problems written during the years she was the first editor of Parent's Magazine.

McCOLLUM, ELMER VERNER (1879–1967).
Papers, 1919–1965. 8 archive boxes. In Univ. of Kansas Archives. Correspondence; scientific notebooks; notes from professional society involvements; scrapbook; tape recordings and film of McCollum at events honoring his work; photographs of McCollum in a variety of situations; slides of his birthplace; offset plates of textbook; citations and awards; reprints of articles by McCollum and others; typed manuscript of The Chemistry of Living Matter; clippings; pamphlets; artifacts; paperback book entitled Elmer Verner McCollum by Harry G. Day, 1974; and biographical sketches of McCollum and materials from commemorative activities held in 1979.
Papers, 1919–1959. 9 items. In Johns Hopkins Univ., Eisenhower Library. Correspondence between McCollum and Isaiah Bowman (1942, 1949), and to Josephine Cole (1959), Hermann Collitz (1925), Louis Kuethe (1950), and Ch. Wm. Emil Miller (1919).

MAHLER, MARGARET.
Oral history, 1974. 116 pp. In Columbia Univ., Oral History Research Office. Includes discussion of youth and education in Hungary and Germany; work with Von Pirquet and Moll Clinics, Vienna; undergoing analysis; association with second generation psychoanalysts; acceptance in Vienna Psychoanalytic Inst., 1933; Rorschach studies; establishment of first psychoanalytic child guidance clinic, 1933; Nazi oppression and escape to New York City; work with the New York Psychiatric Inst.; and child development, analysis, and psychosis studies. (Permission required to cite or quote. Certain pages closed.)
Films, n.d. 264 items. In Univ. of Akron, Child Development Film Archives. Research films by Mahler.

MALINOWSKI, BRONISLAW (1884–1942).
Papers, ca. 1917–1942. Ca. 150 boxes. In British Library of Political and Economic Science. Research, personal, and University papers, including records of fieldwork in the Trobriand Isles, Paua, New Guinea. (Researchers are requested to write for an appointment: Archivist, British Library of Political and Economic Science, 10 Portugal St., London WC2A 2HD.) Papers, 1860–1946. Ca. 13 ft. In Yale Univ. Library. Correspondence, manuscripts of writings and lectures, fieldwork notebooks, memorabilia, photos, and other papers. Relates to Malinowski's work in cultural anthropology and ethnology among the natives of New Guinea and the Trobriand Islands and his professional and personal associations with anthropologists, psychologists, and sociologists in Europe, Asia, Africa, and the U.S. Also, papers of the Malinowski family.

MARSTON, LESLIE RAY (1894–1979).
Papers, ca. 1915–1930. Ca. 4 file drawers. In Free Methodist Church Headquarters, Marston Memorial Historical Center (Winona Lake, IN). 1 file drawer of child development materials, including correspondence; notes from classes relating to child development from Marston's undergraduate and graduate work at the Univ. of Illinois and Univ. of Iowa; his master's degree thesis; course outline in psychology taught by Marston at the Univ. of Michigan in the 1920s; clinical syllabus for doctoral dissertation, entitled *The Emotions of Young Children*, ca. 1923; psychological tests and scales developed by him; some reprints of articles; correspondence from his work on the National Research Council 3–4 NRC yearbooks edited by him, ca. 1925–1928; all of his notes from the White House Conference on Child Health and Protection, 1930. Also, 3 file drawers, 1930–1979, from Marston's churchwork as bishop of the Free Methodist Church.

MEAD, MARGARET (1901–1978).
Papers, n.d. 1 vol. In the American Philosophical Society Library. Working draft of a book Ruth Benedict wrote about Mead which was published in 1959. Also includes correspondence of Benedict with Mead and Franz Boas.
Papers, 1838–1980. Over 500,000 manuscript items, 50,000 photographic images, many reels of motion picture films, and ca. 1,000 recordings. In Manuscripts Division, Library of Congress. Contains extensive family, personal, professional, and organizational correspondence; field notes and other data; publications; and materials on her career as a teacher, public appearances, etc. Correspondents include Ruth Benedict, Franz Boas, Lawrence K. Frank, Frank Fremont-Smith, Frances Ilg, Gardner and Lois B. Murphy, John W. M. Whiting, and many organizations. Also included are the papers of colleagues, including Ruth Benedict (3 containers). (Access partly restricted.)

MEREDITH, HOWARD V. (1903-).
Papers, 1949–1955. 1 file folder. In Univ. of Iowa Archives. Correspondence in Vertical File on Faculty and Staff, 1855–.

MEYER, ADOLF (1866–1950).
Papers, ca. 1885–1948. Ca. 400 ft. In Johns Hopkins Univ., Chesney Medical Archives. Correspondence, diaries, notebooks, manuscripts of writings, lecture notes, documents, and pictures. Extensive personal and professional correspondence with many of the leading figures in early twentieth century American psychiatry. Child development correspondents include Buford Johnson (10 letters); L. E. Holt., Jr. (7 letters); Carroll Palmer (14 letters); and Henry Helmholz (5 letters). In addition, there is an extensive collection of family correspondence and other biographical materials. The collection has a complete inventory and name index.

MITCHELL, LUCY SPRAGUE (1878–1967).
Papers, 1878–1967. 6,700 items. In Columbia Univ., Rare Book and Manuscript Library. Correspondence, manuscripts, and notes pertaining to Mitchell's books; personal correspondence with friends and family; diaries; and speeches.

Oral history, 1960. 1 tape, 167 pp. In Univ. of California at Berkeley, The Bancroft Library, Manuscript Division. Includes discussion of work as Dean of Women at the Univ. of California, 1906; marriage to Dr. Wesley Clair Mitchell and their move to New York in 1912; her interest in experimental education and the founding of the Bank Street School; and teaching and writing for children. (Permission required to cite or quote. Copy also available at the Columbia Univ. Oral History Research Office.)

MURPHY, GARDNER (1895–1979).
Papers, ca. 1916–1979. n.v. In Concord Free Public Library. The King–Murphy collection includes correspondence to and from Murphy; theses written by him while at Yale; papers on his early life, parapsychology, organism and quantity, psychology of music; experimental studies on normal children; Murphy's *Novum Organum; Human Nature and Enduring Peace: Third Yearbook of the Society for Psychological Study of Social Issues,* edited by Murphy in 1945; original typescript of the *Childhood of Joan of Arc*; draft typescript of *A Story of Dydactic Thought and Work with Gardner and Lois Murphy,* as written by Murphy, 1968; Fetschrift for Murphy edited by John G. Peatman and Eugene L. Hartley; 9 photographs of Murphy; and gold medal award, 1972. Many other items relate to Murphy's family.
Papers, n.d. 8 vertical file drawers. In Menninger Foundation Archives. Correspondence and research data, particularly from his years on the Menninger Foundation staff.

MURPHY, LOIS BARCLAY (1902–).
Papers, n.d. Ca. 150 cabinets. In Menninger Foundation Archives. Correspondence and research data.
Papers, 1935–1971. 25 boxes. In National Library of Medicine. Personal and professional correspondence, speeches, and reprints.
Papers, n.d. n.v. In Sarah Lawrence Coll. Archives. Includes materials relating to a study done with Eugene Lerner, entitled "Information on Children in Warfare," 1943; course materials, class notes, assignments, and discriptions of interdisciplinary courses taught with Dr. Madeline Grant; and reprints of articles, reviews, books, monographs, and bibliographies. Also a transcript of an oral history interview of Murphy by Helen McMasters, 1964.

OLSON, WILLARD CLIFFORD (1899–1978).
Papers, 1924–1973. 4 boxes. In Univ. of Michigan, Bentley Historical Library, Michigan Historical Collections. Professional correspondence and topical files concerning Olson's interest in the Univ. of Michigan's elementary school, the Inter-American Society of Psychology, and UNESCO. Also reprints and manuscripts of writings and speeches relating to education, child development, and child psychology.

PINTNER, RUDOLF (1884–1942).
Papers, 1921–1943. 1 folder. In Columbia Univ., Teachers Coll. Library, Dept. of Special Collections. Correspondence in the files of President William Russell.

POWERS, GROVER F. (1887–1968).
Papers, 1920–1966. 3 boxes. In Yale Univ. Library. Correspondence concerning Henry Ford Hosp., 1926–1927, including a report on "Ford Hospital Nurses Ousted for Smoking," 1926; Long Island offer, 1935; and 20th Anniversary Celebration at Yale. Office files on American Pediatrics Society, 1961–1964; Committee on Education of the American Academy of Pediatrics, 1952–1954; budgets at Yale, 1926–1949; and his letter concerning retirement to President Griswold. Some papers relating to Southbury Training School, and the National Association for Retarded Children's Scientific Research Advisory Board, 1954–1964.

RANK, OTTO (1884–1939).
Papers, ca. 1903–1930. Ca. 25 boxes. In Columbia Univ., Rare Books Manuscript Library. Correspondence, manuscripts of Rank's writings, daybooks, notebook of dreams, poems, and other papers by and about Rank. Includes the manuscript of Der Künstler, and Rank's own listing and comments on his writings and publications. The correspondence includes letters

(1906–1924) between Sigmund Freud and Rank, some on the controversy over Rank's book *The Trauma of Birth*; a few letters to and from Sandor Ferenczi; and copies or originals of the circular letters (1920–1924) by members of the inner circle, Abraham Eitingon, Sandor Ferenczi, Sigmund Freud, Ernest Jones, and Rank.

RIDENOUR, NINA (1904-).
Papers, 1921–1948. 7 boxes. In Menninger Foundation Archives. Correspondence and manuscripts relate chiefly to Ridenour's work in New York City, her publications, and plays depicting mental health problems staged by the American Community Theatre Wing.

ROBERTS, LYDIA J. (1879–1964).
Papers, n.d. n.v. In Univ. of Chicago, Regenstein Library, Dept. of Special Collections. Material in the files of the University Presidents' Papers.
Papers, 1943–1965. 4 folders. In Vanderbilt Univ., Medical Center Library. Correspondence between Roberts and Mrs. Ethel Austin Martin, who revised Robert's book, *Nutrition Work with Children.*

ROBINSON, VIRGINIA POLLARD (1883–1977).
Papers, n.d. 1 folder. In Univ. of Pennsylvania Archives. Includes 7-page biographical sketch, 1959; critique of Robinson's doctoral dissertation; material relating to a special retirement dinner in her honor; 2 cards of records of her alumni contributions; 3 pages of obituaries.

ROGERS, CARL RANSOM (1902-).
Papers, ca. 1944–1974. 15.6 ft. In Library of Congress, Manuscript Division. Correspondence, 1967–1974; case files, 1957–1971; research files, 1944–1969; dissertations; and sound recordings. (Additions anticipated)

RUML, BEARDSLEY (1894–1960).
Papers, 1917–1950. 7 ft. In Univ. of Chicago, Regenstein Library, Dept. of Special Collections. Includes correspondence; biographical material and sketches; speeches and articles concerned with national economic conditions and policy; miscellaneous correspondence of a mixed personal and professional nature; clippings and reprints of articles on Ruml, including interviews and autobiographical material. The speech files contain drafts of numerous articles and correspondence related to the Laura Spelman Rockefeller Memorial.

SALMON, THOMAS (1876–1934).
Papers, 1897–1934. 5 boxes. In The New York Hosp.–Cornell Medical Center, Dept. of Psychiatry, History of Psychiatry Section. Material in the American Foundation of Mental Hygiene Collection, including personal and professional correspondence; biographical material; and papers relating to World War I, Salmon's public health and Marine Hospital service, and immigration. (Researchers are requested to write in advance to Dr. Eric T. Carlson, The New York Hosp.–Cornell Medical Center.)

SCAMMON, RICHARD (1883–1952).
Papers, n.d. n.v. In Univ. of Chicago, Regenstein Library, Dept. of Special Collections. Material in the files of the University Presidents' Papers.
Papers, n.d. 60 inches. In Univ. of Minnesota Archives. Research material compiled by Harry A. Wilmer, M.D., for his proposed biography of Scammon, including a transcription of Wilmer's interviews with Scammon.

SEARS, ROBERT RICHARDSON (1908-).
Papers, 1941–1949. 1 file folder. In Univ. of Iowa Archives. Correspondence in Vertical File on Faculty and Staff, 1855–.

SENN, MILTON J. E. (1902-).
Papers, 1947–1968. 10 boxes. In National Library of Medicine. Correspondence; speeches; and reports. Includes adoption research conducted under a Russell Sage Grant, 1950–1952; Institute of Child Development, New York Hosp.–Cornell Medical Center; Child Study Center, Yale Univ., 1949–1962.

SHINN, MILICENT WASHBURN (1858–1940).
Papers, ca. 1882–1906. 1 box and 1 portfolio. In Univ. of California at Berkeley, The Bancroft Library, Manuscripts Division. Papers include a continuation of Shinn's Ph.D. dissertation on child development, parts of which were published in the University of California Publications in Education; and school compositions by her and her sister.

SKEELS, HAROLD MANVILLE (1901–1970).
Papers, 1938–1946. 1 file folder. In Univ. of Iowa Archives. Correspondence in Vertical File on Faculty and Staff, 1855–.

SONTAG, LESTER W. (1901-).
Papers, 1937–1942. 1 box. In National Library of Medicine. Correspondence.

SOUTHARD, ELMER ERNEST (1876–1920).
Papers, ca. 1900–1919. 5 ft. In Harvard Univ., Countway Library of Medicine. Professional papers; cases for the study of the anatomy of mental disease; drafts of articles; lectures in psychiatry, 1916; criminology notes and letters; and autopsy reports.

SPITZ, RENE (1887–1974).
Papers, ca. 1947–1953. n.v. In Univ. of Colorado Medical School, Denver Inst. for Psychoanalysis, Dept. of Psychiatry, Rene Spitz Film Archives. Includes catalogued original films of Spitz's institutionalized infants; Spitz's documentary of his other developmental studies; story films he used to illustrate his lectures in the 1950s–1960s. Most of the lectures he conducted with the films are on file with designations as to where the illustrative films were used. Also, 10 16mm published films: *Grief, A Peril in Infancy,* 1947; *Birth and the First 15 Minutes of Life,* 1947; *Somatic Consequences of Emotional Starvation in Infants,* 1948; *The Smiling Response (An Experimental Investigation into the Ontogenesis of Social Relations),* 1948; *Genesis of Emotions,* 1948; *Grasping,* 1949; *Psychological Diseases in Infancy,* 1952; *Motherlove,* 1952; *Shaping the Personality—The Role of Mother–Child Relations in Infancy,* 1952; *Anxiety: Its Phenomenology in the First Year of Life,* 1953. (The 10 published films are available for circulation through the New York University Film Library.)
Oral history, 1965. 104 pp. In Columbia Univ., Oral History Research Office. Includes discussion of Spitz's introduction to psychoanalysis; his early career; Vienna, Paris, and the U.S.; theories; research in the nature of thought process; cross-cultural studies; psychoanalytic groups in the U.S. (Permission required.)

SPOCK, BENJAMIN McLAND (1903-).
Papers, 1937–1967. 44 ft. In Syracuse Univ. Library. Correspondence, manuscripts of writings, minutes and proceedings, documents, appointment books, awards, financial records, newspaper clippings, memorabilia, and printed material. Relates to pediatric medicine, child care, war and peace, and various political, social, medical, and child-care organizations.

STANLEY, LOUISE (1883–1954).
Records, 1923–1941. 253 cu. ft. In the National Archives and Records Service. Records of the Bureau of Human Nutrition and Home Economics (Record Group 176) include Stanley's correspondence as chief of the Bureau.

STODDARD, GEORGE DINSMORE (1897–1981).
Papers, 1933–1955. 88.6 ft. In Univ. of Illinois at Urbana-Champaign Archives. 79.3 ft. of material primarily relating to Stoddard's presidency of the Univ. of Illinois, including general correspondence, reports, memoranda, publications, and files. Also 3.3 ft. of manuscript copies

of his public addresses and statements concerning child psychology, mental health, public education, education in wartime, educational trends, higher education, democracy, postwar planning, UNESCO, Univ. of Illinois taxation and budgets, alumni, children, and youth; subject file (6 ft.) including correspondence, reports and working papers relating to his presidency and to his participation on the Mid-Century White House Conference on Children and Youth National Committee; and 3 ft. of reprinted addresses by Stoddard on higher education and public policy, science, Krebiozen, educational issues, child psychology, freedom, national issues, UNESCO, and his presidency.
Papers, ca. 1928–1949. n.v. In Univ. of Iowa Archives. Scattered correspondence in Papers of the Presidents of the Univ. of Iowa.
Papers, 1887–1972. 2 ft. In Univ. of Iowa Archives. Newspaper clippings and photographs concerning Stoddard's residence near Iowa City, Iowa, and Grant Wood, artist. Publications of Stoddard and others. Also newspaper clippings, publications, and typescripts of Norman Foerster-Sinclair Lewis correspondence. (Collection may be dispersed when processed.)
Papers, 1927–1981. 1 file folder. In Univ. of Iowa Archives. Correspondence in Vertical File on Faculty and Staff, 1855–.

STOLZ, LOIS HAYDEN MEEK (1891-).
Papers, n.d. n.v. In Columbia Univ., Teachers Coll. Library, Dept. of Special Collections. Correspondence and reports from Stolz included in the files of the Child Development Inst. (Inst. for Child Welfare Research) within the files of Dean James Earl Russell.
Oral history, 1977. 283 pp. In National Library of Medicine. Includes discussion of Stolz's professional career; the progress of the movement from the 1920s, particularly early childhood education programs and parent education; her research in the field, including her project for the Inst. of Child Welfare, Univ. of California at Berkeley; teaching at Stanford Univ. Interview conducted by Professor Ruby Takanishi. (Copy available at the Univ. of California at Berkeley, The Bancroft Library, Manuscripts Division.)

STONE, LAWRENCE JOSEPH (1912–1975).
Papers, 1934–1975. Ca. 20 ft. In Univ. of Akron, Archives of the History of American Psychology. Includes correspondence and other materials on films and on the Vassar Nursery School; lecture notes; research notes; collaborative work and correspondence with Benjamin Spock, L. K. Frank, Milton Senn, Margaret Mead, Lois Murphy, and Nancy Bayley; and reports of research in Greece, Israel, and India.
Films, n.d. 1,048 items. In Univ. of Akron, Child Development Film Archives. Research films by Stone.

STUART, HAROLD COE (1891–1976).
Papers, n.d. 2 boxes. In Harvard Univ., Countway Library of Medicine. Documents and letters on the Children's Hosp. Medical Center, 1945–1956; the Department of Maternal and Child Health of the School of Public Health; and other materials relating to the institutes and teaching programs held for nurses, social workers, and physicians sponsored by the School of Public Health.

TAFT, JESSIE (1882–1960).
Papers, n.d. 1 folder. In Univ. of Pennsylvania Archives. Biographical material, mainly newspaper clippings.

TEMPLIN, MILDRED (1913-).
Papers, ca. 1947–1970. 90 inches. In Univ. of Minnesota Archives. Professional correspondence, thesis material, and scientific publications. Material from her work at the Inst. of Child Development.

TERMAN, LEWIS MADISON (1877–1956).
Papers, n.d. n.v. In Columbia Univ., Teachers Coll. Library, Dept. of Special Collections. Material in President William Russell's files.

Papers, 1910–1959. 21 ft. In Stanford Univ. Archives. Correspondence, tables, calculations, charts, notebooks, clippings, reprints, and other papers. Relates to Terman's marriage study of gifted subjects, his investigation of the gifted and of child prodigies, tests, and testing.

THOMAS, WILLIAM ISAAC (1863–1947).
Papers, 1894–1915. 35 items. In Univ. of Chicago, Regenstein Library, Dept. of Special Collections. Correspondence relating to Thomas' dismissal from the University, in Presidents' Papers, 1889–1925. (Additional scattered papers in other archival collections.)
Papers, 1895–1905. 47 items. In Univ. of Chicago, Regenstein Library, Dept. of Special Collections. Correspondence and other materials in Library Records, Series I, relating to Thomas' position as Superintendent of Departmental Libraries, a post which he held concurrently with his appointment in the Dept. of Sociology and Anthropology.

THOMPSON, HELEN (1897–).
Papers, 1926–1936. 1 box. In National Library of Medicine. Correspondence, 1926–1938.

THORNDIKE, EDWARD LEE (1874–1949).
Papers, 1899–1922. 3 folders. In Columbia Univ., Teachers Coll., Dept. of Special Collections. Correspondence in President James E. Russell's files; Thorndike's 25th Anniversary Committee; education in Washington, D.C., 1912–1913, Carnegie Foundation for the Advancement of Teaching.
Papers, ca. 1900–1938. Ca. 100 items. In Library of Congress, Manuscript Division. Articles, lectures, speeches, and research notes associated with Thorndike's pioneer studies in educational psychology. Includes 3 items of correspondence.

UPDEGRAFF, RUTH (1902–).
Papers, 1930–1951. 1 file folder. In Univ. of Iowa Archives. Correspondence in Vertical File on Faculty and Staff, 1855–.
Oral history, 1977. 66 pp. (transcript only). In Univ. of Iowa Archives, Iowa City. Includes discussion of entire professional career at Iowa Child Research Welfare Research Station since 1925; work as research assistant, director of nursery school, etc.; leadership abilities and styles of various Station directors, including Bird T. Baldwin, Boyd McCandless, Robert R. Sears, George D. Stoddard, and others; research programs and personnel in physical growth, nutrition, social psychology, orphanage studies; work of various colleagues, notably Amy Daniels and Kurt Lewin; influence of Carl Seashore; and relations between Station and parent groups. Unrestricted.

VAN WATERS, MIRIAM (1887–1974).
Papers, n.d. n.v. In Framingham Public Library (Massachusetts). Papers include pamphlet about the State Reformatory for Women at Framingham (later named the Massachusetts Correctional Institution); clippings; a copy of her book, Youth in Conflict, 1925; and a biography of her.
Papers, 1924–1931. 11 ft. In Harvard Law School Library. Correspondence, memoranda, notes, transcripts of interviews, case histories, statistical summaries, reports, and printed matter of Van Waters. The papers concern her participation in the Harvard Survey of Crime and Criminal Justice in Greater Boston and her work as a consultant to the National Commission of Law Observance and Enforcement. These files contain information on investigations made in individual institutions, social agencies, and court systems that aided juvenile delinquents.
Papers, 1894–1971. Ca. 52 archival boxes, 10 cartons, 6 recording discs, and 1 microfilm reel. In Radcliffe Coll., Schlesinger Library on the History of Women in America. Correspondence, diaries, notes, lectures, speeches, articles, reports, scrapbooks, photos, clippings, and printed and other material of Van Waters. Professional correspondence includes letters from prisoners and from prominent individuals who were concerned with penology and juvenile delinquency.

WARING, ETHEL BUSHNELL (1887–1972).
Papers, ca. 1925–1956. 86 ft. In Cornell Univ., Dept. of Manuscripts and University Archives. Correspondence, research reports, motion pictures, nursery school records, and other papers. The papers document the history of the department of child development and family relationships from its origin as a group of courses in child guidance in the 1924 summer school to its present status. Also research notes on violet ray study, sleep study, and 3-year analysis of Beham, Tashi Study. Unpublished manuscript, "Preprimary Education: Its Values and Standards." Also see transcript of tape-recorded interviews of the New York State Coll. of Home Economics staff.

WATSON, JOHN BROADUS (1878–1958).
Papers, n.d. 1 archive box. In Furman Univ. Library, Dept. of Special Collections. Miscellaneous assortment of information on Watson's family and his time at Furman. Includes a copy of his transcript; some information about Furman, its requirements, and some of the faculty; notes on conversations with people who knew Watson; and some reprints of articles about Watson. Also 3 taped interviews with Watson's relatives and acquaintances.
Papers, 1908–1920. 59 items. In Johns Hopkins Univ., Ferdinand Hamburger, Jr., Archives. Correspondence and other materials relating to Watson's work at Johns Hopkins in Records of the Office of the President, 1903–1963.
Papers, 1910–1958. Ca. 100 items. In Library of Congress, Manuscript Division. Chiefly printed speeches and articles by Watson, relating to his work in behavioral psychology. Includes biographical information, correspondence (7 items), and 2 articles by Watson's wife, Rosalie Alberta Rayner Watson.
Papers, 1903–1909. 20 items. In Univ. of Chicago, Regenstein Library, Dept. of Special Collections. Correspondence in Presidents' Papers, 1889–1925.

WELLMAN, BETH L. (1895–1952).
Papers, 1924–1978. 1 file folder. In Univ. of Iowa Archives. Correspondence in Vertical File on Faculty and Staff, 1855–.

WILE, IRA SOLOMON (1877–1943).
Papers, ca. 1894–1943. 21 boxes. In Univ. of Rochester Library. Correspondence, articles, speeches, and other papers reflecting Wile's many interests, particularly public health and social medicine. Includes much material on the early birth control movement in the U.S., many letters from Margaret Sanger, founder of the American Birth Control League. Also papers relating to Wile's extensive study of left and right handedness and to other aspects of psychology, social and mental hygiene, and pediatrics.

WILLIAMS, FRANKWOOD (1883–1936).
Papers, 1906–1936. 2 boxes. In Menninger Foundation Archives. Correspondence and other material relating primarily to the National Association of Mental Hygiene.
Papers, n.d. n.v. In New York Hosp.—Cornell Medical Ctr., Dept. of Psychiatry, History of Psychiatry Section. Material in the American Foundation of Mental Hygiene Collection.

WITMER, LIGHTNER (1867–1956).
Papers, n.d. 1 box. In Univ. of Pennsylvania Archives. Biographical material including newspaper clippings and photographs. Letters from biographers of Witmer.

WOODWORTH, ROBERT SESSIONS (1869–1962).
Papers, 1935–1964. Ca. 500 items. In Library of Congress, Manuscript Division. Professional correspondence; typescript of Woodworth's *Dynamics of Behavior,* 1964; notes for class lectures; obituaries and tributes to Woodworth; articles; and photos, chiefly 1948–1962, the years of Woodworth's retirement.

WOOLLEY, HELEN THOMPSON (1874–1947).
Papers, 1925–1936. 1 in. In Columbia Univ., Teachers Coll. Library, Dept. of Special Collections. Papers in the files of President William F. Russell relating to Woolley's work at Teachers Coll., and especially to the conflicts regarding her resignation from the college around 1931.

WYLIE, MARGARET (1889–1964).
Papers, 1926–1963. 69 ft. In Cornell Univ., Dept. of Manuscripts and Univ. Archives. Papers pertaining to the establishment of the extension program in family life. Includes correspondence; reports; printed materials concerning conferences, workshops, and committees; course outlines (1931–1939); record cards (1933–1963) giving dates of meetings, attendance, and topics discussed at Cornell Child Study Clubs throughout New York State. Also 7 recording discs of the 1950 White House Conference on Children and Youth.

YERKES, ROBERT MEARNS (1876–1956).
Papers, 1898–1956. 1,275 folders. In Yale Univ. Library. Correspondence from professional colleagues and incidental writers totaling 1,787 correspondents. Files cover Yerkes's career at 3 universities: Harvard (1901–1917), Minnesota (1917–1919), and Yale (1924–1958). Papers cover service in 2 World Wars, including the organization of Army Mental Testing, service to the American Psychological Association, and his work with the National Research Council. Correspondence includes matters of editing the *Journal of Comparative Neurology and Psychology* and the *Journal of Animal Behavior,* and the founding and development of the Yale Laboratory of Primate Biology. Major correspondents include Edward Boring, Leonard Carmichael, C. B. Davenport, E. A. Doll, L. K. Frank, Arnold Gesell, H. H. Goddard, G. Stanley Hall, G. V. T. Hamilton, H. F. Harlow, William Healy, D. G. Marquis, M. A. May, Adolf Meyer, Beardsley Ruml, E. E. Southard, Lewis M. Terman, E. L. Thorndike, John B. Watson, R. S. Woodworth, and H. T. Woolley.
Papers, 1930–1941. 1 item. In Emory Univ., Yerkes Regional Primate Research Center. Log.

JOURNALS ABSTRACTED IN CURRENT ISSUE

Acta Paedopsychiatrica
American Journal of Mental Deficiency
American Psychologist
Applied Psycholinguistics
Australian Journal of Psychology
Behavior Genetics
British Journal of Educational Psychology
Canadian Journal of Early Childhood Education
Child: Care, Health and Development
Child Development
Child Psychiatry and Human Development
Child Study Journal
Cognition
Cognitive Psychology
Developmental Medicine and Child Neurology
Developmental Psychology
Educational and Psychological Measurement
Educational Research
Età Evolutiva
Exceptional Children
Genetic Psychology Monographs
Hiroshima Forum for Psychology
Human Relations
Infant Behavior and Development
Japanese Journal of Child and Adolescent Psychiatry
Journal of Abnormal Child Psychology
Journal of Autism and Developmental Disorders
Journal of Child Language
Journal of Child Psychology and Psychiatry
Journal of Children in Contemporary Society
Journal of Clinical Child Psychology
Journal of Counseling Psychology
Journal of Educational Psychology
Journal of Experimental Child Psychology
Journal of Genetic Psychology
Journal of Learning Disabilities
Journal of Motor Behavior
Journal of Personality and Social Psychology
Journal of Psycholinguistic Research
Journal of Psychology
Journal of Verbal Learning and Verbal Behavior
Journal of Youth and Adolescence
Memory and Cognition
Merrill-Palmer Quarterly
Motivation and Emotion
New Zealand Journal of Educational Studies
Pediatric Research
Perceptual and Motor Skills
Psychological Reports
Psychology in the Schools
Reading Research Quarterly
Science
Sex Roles
Social Behavior and Personality
Theory into Practice
Volta Review

Subscriptions are accepted on a calendar-year basis only.

Subscriptions, address changes, and business communications regarding publication should be sent to THE UNIVERSITY OF CHICAGO PRESS, Journals Division, P.O. Box 37005, Chicago, Illinois 60637. Please give four weeks' notice when changing your address, giving both old and new addresses. Undelivered copies resulting from address changes will not be replaced; subscribers should notify the post office that they will guarantee forwarding postage. Other claims for undelivered copies must be made within four months of publication.

Membership communications and requests for permission to reprint should be addressed to DOROTHY H. EICHORN, Executive Officer, Society for Research in Child Development, 5801 Ellis Avenue, Chicago, Illinois 60637.

MONOGRAPHS

OF THE SOCIETY FOR RESEARCH IN CHILD DEVELOPMENT

CURRENT:

The Concept of Dimension in Research on Children's Learning—STUART I. OFFENBACH (*Serial No. 204*, 1983, $7.00)

Returning the Smile of the Stranger: Developmental Patterns and Socialization Factors—YAEL E. BABAD, IRVING E. ALEXANDER, AND ELISHA Y. BABAD (*Serial No. 203*, 1983, $7.00)

Early Intervention and Its Effects on Maternal Behavior and Child Development—DIANA T. SLAUGHTER (*Serial No. 202*, 1983, $7.00)

How Children Become Friends—JOHN M. GOTTMAN (*Serial No. 201*, 1983, $7.00)

A Longitudinal Study of Moral Development—ANNE COLBY, LAWRENCE KOHLBERG, JOHN GIBBS, AND MARCUS LIEBERMAN (*Serial No. 200*, 1983, $10.00)

Early Development of Children at Risk for Emotional Disorder—ARNOLD J. SAMEROFF, RONALD SEIFER, AND MELVIN ZAX (*Serial No. 199*, 1982, $7.00)

The Skills of Mothering: A Study of Parent Child Development Centers—SUSAN RING ANDREWS ET AL. (*Serial No. 198*, 1982, $7.00)

Parent Pathology, Family Interaction, and the Competence of the Child in School—ALFRED L. BALDWIN, ROBERT E. COLE, AND CLARA T. BALDWIN (Eds.) (*Serial No. 197*, 1982, $7.00)

Traditional and Modern Contributions to Changing Infant-rearing Ideologies of Two Ethnic Communities—DANIEL G. FRANKEL AND DORIT ROER-BORNSTEIN (*Serial No. 196*, 1982, $7.00)

Lasting Effects of Early Education—IRVING LAZAR, RICHARD B. DARLINGTON, HARRY MURRAY, JACQUELINE ROYCE, AND ANN SNIPPER (*Serial No. 195*, 1982, $10.00)

Rules of Causal Attribution—THOMAS R. SHULTZ (*Serial No. 194*, 1982, $7.00)

Social Class and Racial Influences on Early Mathematical Thinking—HERBERT P. GINSBURG AND ROBERT L. RUSSELL (*Serial No. 193*, 1981, $7.00)

The Development of Comprehension Monitoring and Knowledge about Communication—JOHN H. FLAVELL, JAMES RAMSEY SPEER, FRANCES L. GREEN, AND DIANE L. AUGUST (*Serial No. 192*, 1981, $7.00)

The Development of the Self-Concept during the Adolescent Years—JEROME B. DUSEK AND JOHN F. FLAHERTY (*Serial No. 191*, 1981, $7.00)

A Longitudinal Study of the Consequences of Early Mother-Infant Interaction: A Microanalytic Approach—JOHN A. MARTIN (*Serial No. 190*, 1981, $7.00)

FORTHCOMING:

Difficult Children as Elicitors and Targets of Adult Communication Patterns: An Attributional-Behavioral Transactional Analysis—DAPHNE B. BUGENTAL AND WILLIAM A. SHENNUM (*Serial No. 205*, 1984, $7.00)

Order From

CHILD DEVELOPMENT PUBLICATIONS
THE UNIVERSITY OF CHICAGO PRESS

CHILD DEVELOPMENT

ABSTRACTS AND BIBLIOGRAPHY

VOLUME 58 NUMBER 2   1984

CHICAGO PUBLIC LIBRARY

SEP - - 1984

SOCIAL SCIENCES

PUBLISHED BY THE UNIVERSITY OF CHICAGO PRESS FOR THE

SOCIETY FOR RESEARCH IN CHILD DEVELOPMENT

EDITOR

HOBEN THOMAS

The Pennsylvania State University

ASSOCIATE EDITOR
MARGARET L. SIGNORELLA
The Pennsylvania State University
McKeesport

ASSOCIATE EDITOR
ELEANOR W. WILLEMSEN
University of Santa Clara

MANAGING EDITOR
BETTY LOU KLINDIENST
University Park, Pennsylvania

COMPUTER CONSULTANT
WILLIAM H. VERITY
The Pennsylvania State University

Child Development Abstracts and Bibliography (ISSN 0009-3939) publishes abstracts from professional periodicals and reviews books related to the growth and development of children. When listed, author addresses are intended to be current mailing addresses. A list of journals regularly searched is included in numbers 5 & 6 of each volume. The Editor welcomes communication from readers. Especially encouraged are contributed abstracts from articles which appear in publications not normally searched. For this purpose, reprints are helpful. Please address all editorial correspondence to Editor, *Child Development Abstracts and Bibliography*, The Pennsylvania State University, 442 B. V. Moore Building University Park, Pennsylvania 16802. Postmaster: Send address changes to The University of Chicago Press, Journals Division, P.O. Box 37005, Chicago, Illinois 60637.

Child Development Abstracts and Bibliography, one of three publications of the Society for Research in Child Development, Inc., is published three times a year, two numbers in each issue, by The University of Chicago Press. Subscription rate, U.S.A.: 1 year $35.00. Other countries add $3.50 for each year's subscription to cover postage. Single copy rate: $11.50. Reprinted volumes 1-50 available from Kraus Reprint Co., Route 100, Millwood, New York 10546. Volumes 42 to date available in microfilm from University Microfilms International, 300 North Zeeb Road, Ann Arbor, Michigan 48106; in microfiche from KTO Microform, Route 100, Millwood, New York 10546.

Child Development is issued six times a year. Subscription rate, U.S.A.: 1 year $80.00. Other countries add $6.00 for each year's subscription to cover postage. Single copy rate: $14.00. Reprinted volumes 1-40 available from Kraus Reprint Co. Volumes 37 to date available in microfilm from University Microfilms International; in microfiche from KTO Microform.

Monographs of the Society for Research in Child Development is issued at irregular intervals during the year. Subscription rate, U.S.A.: 1 year $40.00. Other countries add $5.50 for each year's subscription to cover postage. Single copies $9.00; combined issues $13.00. Single copy bulk rate (10 or more copies of same issue): single issues $7.00; combined issues $11.00. Reprinted volumes 1-41 available from Kraus Reprint Co. Volumes 28 to date available in microfilm from University Microfilms International; in microfiche from KTO Microform. A list of available *Monographs* may be had on request.

Subscriptions (U.S.A.) to the three publications of the Society are available at the special rate of $140.00. Other countries add $15.00 for each year's combined subscription to cover postage.

A limited number of back issues of all publications is available.

© 1984 by the Society for Research in Child Development, Inc. All rights reserved.

PRINTED IN U.S.A.

CHILD DEVELOPMENT
Abstracts and Bibliography

Volume 58   Number 2   1984

ABSTRACTS OF ARTICLES

BIOLOGY, HEALTH, MEDICINE

717.   ANDERSON, GENE CRANSTON (Univ. of Florida, Coll. of Nursing); McBRIDE, MELEN R.; DAHM, JANET; ELLIS, MARLA K.; & VIDYASAGAR, DHARMAPURI. **Development of sucking in term infants from birth to four hours postbirth.** Research in Nursing and Health, 1982, **5**, 21–27.
The sucking response was investigated in 30 normal infants from 1 to 5 min postbirth until their first feeding 4 hours later. Maximum sucking pressures were measured with a research nipple attached to a portable electronic suckometer. Mean suction (negative pressure) began at 5 Torr at birth, peaked at 103 Torr at 90 min, and decreased thereafter to 65 Torr at 4 hours. – From Authors' Abstract.

718.   AUMONIER, M. E. (The University, Manchester, England), & CUNNINGHAM, C. C. **Breast feeding in infants with Down's syndrome.** Child: Care, Health and Development, 1983, **9**, 247–255.
Infants with Down's syndrome do not inevitably have initial feeding problems and can be breast-fed successfully, but their mothers need to persevere and to be given hospital support and encouragement. – From Authors' Abstract.

719.   BACON, ELLEN H., & RUBIN, DAVID C. (Duke Univ. Medical Ctr.). **Story recall by mentally retarded children.** Psychological Reports, 1983, **53**, 791–796.
Mildly retarded young adolescents and nonretarded children of comparable mental age did not differ in the amount or structure of recalled story parts. – Adapted from Authors' Abstract.

720.   BIRRELL, J.; FROST, G. J.; & PARKIN, J. M. (Royal Victoria Infirmary, Newcastle upon Tyne, England). **The development of children with congenital hypothyroidism.** Developmental Medicine and Child Neurology, 1983, **25**, 512–519.
The mean IQ of the hypothyroid group was 1–2 standard deviations below the population mean. – From Authors' Abstract.

721.   BRUMBACK, ROGER A. (Univ. of Rochester Medical Ctr.), & STATON, R. DENNIS. **An hypothesis regarding the commonality of right-hemisphere involvement in learning disability, attentional disorder, and childhood major depressive disorder.** Perceptual and Motor Skills, 1982, **55**, 1091–1097.
Anatomical disturbance of right-hemisphere function by a major depressive episode may produce exacerbate learning disability or attentional disorder. – From Authors' Abstract.

722.   BRUNSWICK, ANN F. (Columbia Univ.), & MESSERI, PETER. **Causal factors in onset of adolescents' cigarette smoking: a prospective study of urban black youth.** Advances in Alcohol and Substance Abuse, 1983/1984, **3**, 35–52.
Variables from 5 domains influenced subsequent smoking, but different predictors were implicated for adolescent males vs. females. The salient experiences that governed the decision to start smoking were different for black males and females. – From Authors' Abstract.

723.   BUTLER, CHARLEME (2143 N. Northlake, Seattle); OKAMOTO, GARY A.; & McKAY, TAMMY M. **Powered mobility for very young disabled children.** Developmental Medicine and Child Neurology, 1983, **25**, 472–474.

Motor-disabled children with normal intelligence attained control of a motorized wheelchair between 20 and 39 months of age. – Adapted from Authors' Abstract.

724. DEGENHARDT, ANNETTE (Univ. Frankfurt, Germany), & KELLER, HEIDI. **Reaktionen Neugeborenen auf taktile, olfaktorische und akustische Reize: Reife- und Geschlechtsunterschiede.** Zeitschrift für Entwicklungspsychologie und Pädagogische Psychologie, 1983, **15,** 183–195.
The analysis of motor behavioral patterns and autonomous responses to acoustic, olfactoric, and tactile stimuli indicate that newborns with a lower maturation level exhibit more reflexive behavior, such as startle and rhythmical mouthing, as compared to newborns with a higher maturation level. – From Authors' Abstract.

725. EICKELBERG, WARREN (Human Resource Ctr., I.U. Willets, Albertson, NY); KAYLOR, PATRICIA; LESS, MEL; BARUCH, INGRID; & MEGARR, JACK. **Effects of passive physical exercise on peripheral vision in muscular dystrophic children.** Perceptual and Motor Skills, 1983, **56,** 167–170.
Analysis indicated that 6 min of passive exercise of the arms increased the peripheral vision of muscular dystrophic children ages 9–13 years. – From the Article.

726. EISER, CHRISTINE, & PATTERSON, DAVID (Univ. of Exeter, Washington Singer Laboratories, Exeter, England). **Slugs and snails and puppy-dog tails'—children's ideas about the inside of their bodies.** Child: Care, Health and Development, 1983, **9,** 233–240.
Although knowledge of the inside of the body increased with age, it was consistently below that reported in earlier American studies. – From Authors' Abstract.

727. EISER, CHRISTINE (Univ. of Exeter, Washington Singer Laboratories, Exeter, England); PATTERSON, DAVID; & EISER, J. RICHARD. **Children's knowledge of health and illness: implications for health education.** Child: Care, Health and Development, 1983, **9,** 285–292.
Children's knowledge of diseases and their prevention was poor. Children assigned a central role to diet in maintaining good health. – From Authors' Abstract.

728. FEIN, EDITH (Child & Family Services, Hartford); MALUCCIO, ANTHONY N.; HAMILTON, V. JANE; & WARD, DARRYL E. **After foster care: outcomes of permanency planning for children.** Child Welfare, 1983, **62,** 483–567.
The entire issue, in 11 chapters, is devoted to a research report of permanency planning. Chapters included are concerned with methodology and disruptive placements. – Ed.

729. FEIN, GRETA G. (Univ. of Maryland); SCHWARTZ, PAMELA M.; JACOBSON, SANDRA W.; & JACOBSON, JOSEPH L. **Environmental toxins and behavioral development.** American Psychologist, 1983, **38,** 1188–1197.
Childhood exposure to chemicals routinely encountered in the environment has become an issue of scientific and public concern. Recent research has revealed the inadequacy of traditional notions in which chemically induced illness was likened to overt biological disease. The implications of behavioral teratology for the study of human development are discussed. – From Authors' Abstract.

730. FERRARI, FABRIZIO (1st Clinica Pediatrica, Cattedra Patologia Neonatale, Policlinico Universitario, 41100 Modena, Italy); GROSOLI, MARIA V.; FONTANA, GIORGIO; & CAVAZZUTI, GIOVANNI B. **Neurobehavioral comparison of low-risk preterm and fullterm infants at term conceptual age.** Developmental Medicine and Child Neurology, 1983, **25,** 450–458.
Low gestational age is associated with behavior that is different, more heterogeneous, and poorer than that of full-term infants. – From Authors' Abstract.

731. FIRTH, MELINDA (St. George's Hosp., Morpeth, Northumberland, England); GARDNER-MEDWIN, DAVID; HOSKING, GWILYM; & WILKINSON, ELIZABETH. **Interviews with parents of boys suffering from Duchenne muscular dystrophy.** Developmental Medicine and Child Neurology, 1983, **25,** 466–471.
Three major categories of problems were identified in Duchenne muscular dystrophy families: services problems, practical problems, and emotional problems. – From Abstract by B. B. Keller.

732. FLETCHER, JACK M. (Texas Research Inst. of Mental Sciences, 1300 Moursund, Houston), & TAYLOR, H. GERRY. **Neuropsychological approaches to children: towards a developmental neuropsychology.** Journal of Clinical Neuropsychology, 1984, **6,** 39–56.
Developmental neuropsychology is not just the application of a general body of neuropsychological knowledge to children. The neuropsychologist's role extends beyond simplistic inferences about brain status based on behavioral test results or observations. The developmental neuropsychologist focuses on relationships among the manifest disabilities and the basic competencies as well as on relationships between these behavioral variables and CNS factors. – From Authors' Abstract.

733. FULLER, PETER W.; GUTHRIE, ROBERT D.; & ALVORD, ELLSWORTH C., JR. (Univ. of Washington School of Medicine). **A proposed neuropathological basis for learning disabilities in children born prematurely.** Developmental Medicine and Child Neurology, 1983, **25,** 214–231.
The brains of 16 premature infants who died within the first month of life were studied in microscopic examination. Significant neuropathological findings in gray-matter and white-matter were found in many areas, including both superficial cortical and deep basal brain structures. – From Authors' Abstract.

734. FUNDERBURK, STEVE J. (Neuropsychiatric Inst., 760 Westwood Plaza, Los Angeles); CARTER, JANICE; TANGUAY, PETER; FREEMAN, BETTY JO; & WESTLAKE, JOAN R. **Parental reproductive problems and gestational hormonal exposure in autistic and schizophrenic children.** Journal of Autism and Developmental Disorders, 1983, **13,** 325–332.
The incidence of infertility and 2 or more spontaneous abortions was increased in the parents of patients evaluated for major childhood psychoses. In addition, 18% of the patients had a history of early gestational exposure to progesterone/estrogen compounds and to cortisone. – From Authors' Abstract.

735. GACHOUD, J. P. (Univ. of Geneva, Switzerland); MOUNOUD, P.; HAUERT, C. A.; & VIVIANI, P. **Motor strategies in lifting movements: a comparison of adult and child performance.** Journal of Motor Behavior, 1983, **15,** 202–216.
The patterns of motor commands, as expressed by the electromyographic recordings, are different. Adults plan the movement with a careful balance between agonist muscle activity and passive, viscoelastic forces, whereas children use both agonist and antagonist active forces. – From Authors' Abstract.

736. GALLAHUE, DAVID L. (Indiana Univ.). **Assessing motor development in young children.** Studies in Educational Evaluation, 1983, **8,** 247–252.
The validity of many tests is suspect because of the lack of sound rationale or because of inadequate correlational studies with other tests. – From the Article.

737. GANCHROW, J. R. (Hebrew Univ., Jerusalem); STEINER, J. E.; & DAHER, M. **Neonatal facial expressions in response to different qualities and intensities of gustatory stimuli.** Infant Behavior and Development, 1983, **6,** 198–200.
Neonates reacted differentially to increased concentrations of oral stimuli. – From Abstract by S. Thomas.

738. GILLBERG, I. CARINA (Univ. of Uppsala, Göteborg, Sweden), & GILLBERG, CHRISTOPHER. **Three-year follow-up at age 10 of children with minor neurodevelopmental disorders. 1: Behavioral problems.** Developmental Medicine and Child Neurology, 1983, **25**, 438–449.
Children having both attentional deficit and motor perception dysfunction were rated by teachers and parents as showing high rates of behavioral problems. – B. B. Keller.

739. GUNN, TANIA R. (St. Helens Hosp., Linwood, Auckland, New Zealand); LEPORE, ELIZABETH; & OUTERBRIDGE, EUGENE W. **Outcome at school-age after neonatal mechanical ventilation.** Developmental Medicine and Child Neurology, 1983, **25**, 305–314.
Neurological sequelae were significantly associated with perinatal asphyxia and with low birthweights. Neurological sequelae and socioeconomic factors were the major determinants of ability. – Adapted from Authors' Abstract.

740. HARDING, CHRISTINA M. (Univ. of Exeter, Washington Singer Laboratories, Exeter, England). **Whopping cough vaccination: a review of the controversy since the 1981 DHSS report.** Child: Care, Health and Development, 1983, **9**, 257–272.

741. HEINZ, JOHN (U.S. Senate, Washington). **National leadership for children's television.** American Psychologist, 1983, **38**, 817–819.
Clearly it is time for us to begin to offer our children a wider menu of TV choices. We cannot legislate limited consumption of TV, but we can make the diet more nutritious. – From the Article.

742. HINES, MELISSA (Univ. of California School of Medicine, Los Angeles), & SHIPLEY, CARL. **Prenatal exposure to diethylstilbestrol (DES) and the development of sexually dimorphic cognitive abilities and cerebral lateralization.** Developmental Psychology, 1984, **20**, 81–94.
Women who had been exposed prenatally to diethylstilbestrol (DES), a synthetic estrogen, were compared to their unexposed sisters. The DES-exposed women showed a more masculine pattern of lateralization than did their sisters on a verbal dichotic task. However, no differences were seen in verbal or visuospatial ability. – From Authors' Abstract.

743. HUNT, ANN (Park Hosp. for Children, Old Road, Headington, Oxford, England). **Tuberous sclerosis: a survey of 97 cases. III: Family aspects.** Developmental Medicine and Child Neurology, 1983, **25**, 353–357.
The majority of the children were mentally retarded, and speech was more affected than gross motor development. – From Author's Abstract.

744. KHRIZMAN, T. P.; YEREMEYEVA, V. D.; BELOV, I. M.; BANNOVA, M. M.; & OUTIANOVA, T. A. **Brian's functional asymmetry and development of speech in children.** Questions of Psychology (translation of Russian title), 1983, **5**, 110–115.
Functional asymmetry of the brain as measured by indices of the leading arm, leg, and eye were studied among healthy 2–7-year-olds and 5–6-year-olds with speech disturbances. It was found that functional asymmetry is already present by the age of 2. – From Authors' Abstract.

745. KRAEMER, DIANE (SUNY, Plattsburgh); CANAVAN, PATRICK; BRANNIGAN, GARY G.; & HIJIKATA, SUSAN. **The Torque Test as a measure of lateral dominance.** Journal of Genetic Psychology, 1983, **143**, 251–258.
A low but statistically significant correlation was found between torque and total lateral dominance. – From Authors' Abstract.

746. LANGLEY, JOHN (Univ. of Otago Medical School, P.O. Box 913, Dunedin, New Zealand); McGEE, ROB; SILVA, PHIL; & WILLIAMS, SHEILA. **Child behavior and accidents.** Journal of Pediatric Psychology, 1983, **8**, 181–189.

The results indicated strong linear relationships between number of accidents and both antisocial behavior and parental discipline. – From Authors' Abstract.

747. LaVECK, BEVERLY; HAMMOND, MARY A. (Univ. of Washington); TELZROW, ROBERT; & LaVECK, GERALD D. **Further observations on minor anomalies and behavior in different home environments.** Journal of Pediatric Psychology, 1983, **8,** 171–179.
No reliable associations between anomalies and developmental measures were seen among children in relatively organized and stimulating environments. Correlations between anomalies scores and measures of behavior, language, and motor development differed between groups living in different home environments. – From Authors' Abstract.

748. LIECHTY, EDWARD A. (Indiana Univ. School of Medicine); GILMOR, R. L.; BRYSON, CAROLYN Q.; & BULL, MARILYN J. **Outcome of high-risk neonates with ventriculomegaly.** Developmental Medicine and Child Neurology, 1983, **25,** 162–168.
There was a trend toward lower developmental scores as ventricular size increased. – Adapted from Authors' Abstract.

749. LOEHLIN, JOHN C. (Univ. of Texas, Austin). **Familial correlations and X-linked genes: a comment.** Psychological Bulletin, 1984, **95,** 332–333.

750. McCRACKEN, HUGH D. (Northeastern Univ.). **Movement control in a reciprocal tapping task: a developmental study.** Journal of Motor Behavior, 1983, **15,** 262–279.
The data showed eye movement flexibility increased with age, and that faster tapping was afforded by less direct visual monitoring of the hand. – From Author's Abstract.

751. McDONOUGH, S. C. (Univ. of Illinois, Chicago). **Attention and memory in cerebral palsied infants.** Infant Behavior and Development, 1982, **5,** 347–353.
Cerebral palsied infants' latencies were longer than normal infants' on all attention-getting measures but the same on attention-holding measures. Both groups habituated at the same rate. – Adapted from Author's Abstract.

752. MACE, SHARON E. (Mt. Sinai Medical Ctr., 1800 E. 105th St., Cleveland), & LEVY, MATTHEW N. **Neural control of heart rate: a comparison between puppies and adult animals.** Pediatric Research, 1983, **17,** 491–495.
At any given stimulation frequency, the heart-rate responses were significantly greater in adult dogs than in puppies. – Adapted from Authors' Abstract.

753. MARKOWITZ, PHILIP I. (Medical Coll. of Virginia). **Autism in a child with congenital cytomegalovirus infection.** Journal of Autism and Developmental Disorders, 1983, **13,** 249–253.
Congenital cytomegalovirus infection in an autistic child was suggested by the presence of an antibody response to the virus, culture of the virus in the urine, sensorineural hearing loss, and inflammatory damage to the retina of the eye. An ability of the agent to establish chronic infection may predispose to behavioral aberration. – From Author's Abstract.

754. MOLINA, GILBERTO (Unidad de Investigación Biomédica del Noreste, Apartado Postal 020-E, Monterrey, Nuevo León, Mexico); ZÚÑIGA, MIGUEL A.; CÁRDENAS, ADOLFO; ALVAREZ, ROLANDO MEDINA; SOLÍS-CÁMARA, PEDRO, JR.; & SOLÍS-CÁMARA, PEDRO. **Psychological alterations in children exposed to a lead-rich home environment.** Bulletin of the Pan American Health Organization, 1983, **17,** 186–192.
Children with high blood-lead concentrations belonging to pottery-making families in a Mexican village were tested for psychological abnormalities. The results suggest that lead intoxication contributed to these children's delayed mental development. – Authors' Abstract.

755. MOORE, GARY T. (Univ. of Wisconsin, Milwaukee). **An empirical test of design patterns for children's environments.** In D. Joiner (Ed.), *People and the Physical Environment Research.* Ministry of Works & Development (Wellington, New Zealand), 1983, 290–301.

Results are reported showing that spatially well-defined behavior settings in child-care centers have measurable impacts on children's engagement, initiation of activities, exploratory behavior, and type and degree of social interaction. – Author's Abstract.

756. MOORE, GARY T. (Univ. of Wisconsin, Milwaukee); COHEN, URIEL; & McGINTY, TIM. **Designed environments for early childhood development.** Day Care Journal, 1982, **1,** 29–38.
Results from the 2-year Children's Environments Project are summarized and implications are drawn for selecting appropriate locations and the spatial organization of early childhood development centers. Topics covered include the provision of open space, zoning, and circulation. – Authors' Abstract.

757. O'LEARY, DANIEL S. (Univ. of Health Sciences/Chicago Medical School); LOVELL, MARK R.; SACKELLARES, J. CHRIS; BERENT, STANLEY; GIORDANI, BRUNO; SEIDENBERG, MICHAEL; & BOLL, THOMAS J. **Effects of age of onset of partial and generalized seizures on neuropsychological performance in children.** Journal of Nervous and Mental Disease, 1983, **171,** 624–629.
Neuropsychological performance data from children with epilepsy were evaluated to determine the effects of seizure type and age of onset. Results indicate that variables associated with an early onset of seizures, regardless of type, place a child at risk for cognitive dysfunction. – From Authors' Abstract.

758. PETERSEN, ANNE C. (Pennsylvania State Univ.); ROBIN-RICHARDS, MARYSE; & BOXER, ANDREW. **Puberty: its measurement and its meaning.** Journal of Early Adolescence, 1983, **3,** 47–62.
The results showed only minimal effects of pubertal change and only with the variables (such as body image and feelings of attractiveness) most proximal to that change. We might expect to see much stronger effects of pubertal status in societies where adult status is based upon one's pubertal status. – From Authors' Abstract.

759. PRIOR, MARGOT (La Trobe Univ., Bundoora, Victoria, Australia); LEONARD, ANNE; & WOOD, GLENICE. **A comparison study of preschool children diagnosed as hyperactive.** Journal of Pediatric Psychology, 1983, **8,** 191–207.
Although the hyperactive and controls were different, the interpretation of the sources of these differences supported the desirability of focusing on the mother-child interaction in treatment rather than following the medical model of seeing the hyperactive child as "ill."—From Authors' Abstract.

760. PRZETACZNIKOWA, MARIA, & KACZANOWSKA, ANIELA (Jagiellonian Univ., Cracow, Poland). **Environmental determination of accelerated physical, motor, and mental development in children and youth.** Psychologia Wychowawcza (Educational Psychology: Bimonthly of the Polish Teachers Union), 1983, **26,** 1–17.
An analysis of data from longitudinal studies conducted over the years 1975–1980 in the Institute of Developmental and Educational Psychology of the Jagiellonian University revealed that for mental development, environmental differentiation was found in favor of the city children. Body height and weight showed no clear intensification of developmental processes. – From Authors' Abstract.

761. RAMSAY, DOUGLAS S. (Rutgers State Univ.). **Onset of duplicated syllable babbling and unimanual handedness in infancy: evidence for developmental change in hemispheric specialization?** Developmental Psychology, 1984, **20,** 64–71.
Thirty infants were tested for unimanual hand preference at weekly intervals from 5 months of age through 8 weeks after the onset of duplicated syllable babbling. Infants began to demonstrate unimanual right handedness on the week of babbling onset, whereas they did not show any significant hand preference on the preceding weeks. A temporary loss of handedness occurred 3–4 weeks after babbling onset. Results suggest developmental change in hemispheric specialization. – From Author's Abstract.

762. RIDER, ROBERT A. (Florida State Univ.); MAHLER, TIMOTHY J.; & ISHEE, JIMMY. **Comparison of static balance in trainable mentally handicapped and nonhandicapped children.** Perceptual and Motor Skills, 1983, **56,** 311–314.
Total balance time was different in the 2 groups. – Adapted from Authors' Abstract.

763. RIESE, M. L. (Univ. of Louisville). **Assessment of behavioral patterns in neonates.** Infant Behavior and Development, 1983, **6,** 241–246.
Assessment procedures for 5 categories of behavior—irritability, resistance to soothing, reactivity, reinforcement value, and activity level—were evaluated with 120 infants. – S. Thomas.

764. ROCHAT, PHILIPPE (Univ. of Geneva, Switzerland). **Oral touch in young infants: response to variations of nipple characteristics in the first months of life.** International Journal of Behavioral Development, 1983, **6,** 123–133.
Newborns and 1- and 4-month-olds were presented with nipples varying in shape and in shape plus material. Results suggest that a developmental trend exists, showing an increase in oral exploration and a decrease in sucking. – From Author's Abstract.

765. ROWE, DAVID C. (Univ. of Oklahoma). **Biometrical genetic models of self-reported delinquent behavior: a twin study.** Behavior Genetics, 1983, **13,** 473–489.
Monozygotic twins were more alike in their rates of antisocial behavior than dizygotic twins, and this result held for both sexes. – From Author's Abstract.

766. SHARPE, THOMAS R. (Univ. of Mississippi), & SMITH, MICKEY C. **Patterns of medication use among children in households enrolled in the aid to families with dependent children program.** Pediatric Research, 1983, **17,** 617–619.
Households ($N = 540$) participated in a poll concerning medication use over a 2-week period. Thirteen percent of the children had received prescription medication, and 21% had received over-the-counter medicine. – Adapted from Authors' Abstract.

767. SHIELDS, STEPHANIE A. (Univ. of California, Davis). **Development of autonomic nervous system responsivity in children: a review of the literature.** International Journal of Behavioral Development, 1983, **6,** 291–319.
Normative developmental changes in cardiovascular activity (heart rate and blood pressure), electrodermal activity, and the dynamic balance between branches of the autonomic nervous system are summarized. Several issues that appear to have potential for further developmental study are identified. – From Author's Abstract.

768. SINGER, JEROME L. (Yale Univ.), & SINGER, DOROTHY G. **Psychologists look at television: cognitive, developmental, personality, and social policy implications.** American Psychologist, 1983, **38,** 826–834.
Evidence accumulates suggesting that heavy viewing of currently available television fare by children may be harmful. Research suggesting potential benefits of the medium for education and constructive development has not generally been translated into regular age-specific programming for children by the television industry. – From Authors' Abstract.

769. STELLERN, JOHN (Univ. of Wyoming); MARLOWE, MIKE; COSSAIRT, ACE; & ERRERA, JOHN. **Low lead and cadmium levels and childhood visual-perception development.** Perceptual and Motor Skills, 1983, **56,** 539–544.
Lead and cadmium levels of 6–12-year-olds correlated negatively with age-deviations of Bender Visual-Motor Gestalt Test errors. – Adapted from Authors' Abstract.

770. TEETER, PHYLLIS ANNE (Univ. of Wisconsin, Milwaukee). **The relationship between measures of cognitive-intellectual and neuropsychological abilities for young children.** Clinical Neuropsychology, 1983, **5,** 151–158.

The McCarthy Scales of Children's Abilities and subtests of the Reitan-Indiana Neuropsychological Test Battery were administered to kindergarten children. The data suggest that while cognitive-intellectual abilities in young children are related to performance on some subtests that are sensitive to brain functioning, cognitive and neuropsychological measures are not necessarily interchangeable. – From Author's Abstract.

771. THATCHER, R. W. (Univ. of Maryland Eastern Shore); LESTER, M. L.; McALASTER, R.; HORST, R.; & IGNATIUS, S. W. **Intelligence and lead toxins in rural children.** Journal of Learning Disabilities, 1983, **16**, 355–359.
These results demonstrate a continuous inverse relationship between intelligence and relatively low levels of body lead in which the higher levels of cognitive function are affected before any signs of gross motor impairment are seen. – From Authors' Abstract.

772. THELEN, ESTHER (Univ. of Missouri, Columbia), & FISHER, DONNA M. **The organization of spontaneous leg movements in newborn infants.** Journal of Motor Behavior, 1983, **15**, 353–377.
Spontaneous, supine kicking in newborn infants is described in terms of its temporal structure, interjoint coordination, and muscle activation characteristics as measured by surface electromyography. – From Authors' Abstract.

773. TRAMONTANA, MICHAEL G. (Bradley Hosp., 1011 Veterans Memorial Parkway, East Providence, RI); SHERRETS, STEVEN D.; & WOLF, BRIAN A. **Comparability of the Luria–Nebraska and Halstead–Reitan neuropsychological batteries for older children.** Clinical Neuropsychology, 1983, **5**, 186–190.
Each of the 11 Luria scales showed correspondence with total Halstead–Reitan results, and inspection of the pattern of correlations between the batteries tended to support the construct validity of the individual Luria scales. – From Authors' Abstract.

774. TRAUSE, MARY ANNE (Fairfax Hosp., 3300 Gallows, Falls Church, VA), & KRAMER, LLOYD I. **The effects of premature birth on parents and their relationship.** Developmental Medicine and Child Neurology, 1983, **25**, 459–465.
Parents of both preterm and full-term infants described their feelings in similar ways except at 1 month postpartum. – From Abstract by B. B. Keller.

775. TURKEWITZ, GERALD (CUNY, Hunter Coll.), & ROSS-KOSSAK, PHYLLIS. **Multiple modes of right-hemisphere information processing: age and sex differences in facial recognition.** Developmental Psychology, 1984, **20**, 95–103.
Hemispheric differences in processing tachistoscopically presented faces were examined in 8-, 11-, and 13-year-olds. The data were interpreted as indicating that younger children and males at all ages use a diffuse right-hemisphere processing strategy in recognizing faces, whereas some older females use a more integrated right-hemisphere strategy. – From Authors' Abstract.

776. UNGERER, JUDY A. (Univ. of California, Los Angeles School of Medicine); SIGMAN, MARIAN; BECKWITH, LEILA; COHEN, SARALE E.; & PARMELEE, ARTHUR H. **Sleep behavior of preterm children at three years of age.** Developmental Medicine and Child Neurology, 1983, **25**, 297–304.
At 3 years, sleep disturbances were frequent but similar to full-term children in previous studies. By 5 years, the number of children having sleeping problems had decreased, and they were not the same children with sleep problems at 3 years. – Adapted from Authors' Abstract.

777. WING, E., & ROUSSOUNIS, S. H. (St. James's Univ. Hosp., Beckett, Leeds, England). **A changing pattern of cerebral palsy and its implications for the early detection of motor disorders in children.** Child: Care, Health and Development, 1983, **9**, 227–232.
Hemiplegic cerebral palsy is appearing as the commonest cerebral palsy syndrome, and in the majority of cases does not follow a definable perinatal injury. A large proportion of these children will now be detected at well-baby clinics rather than at hospital neonatal at-risk clinics. – From Authors' Abstract.

778. WOLFF, P. H. (Children's Hosp. Medical Ctr., Boston); GUNNOE, C. E.; & COHEN, C. **Associated movements as a measure of developmental age.** Developmental Medicine and Child Neurology, 1983, **25,** 417–429.
Children 5–6 years old were examined for synkineses and mirror movements. The frequency of associated movements changed in the expected direction over a 12-month period. – From Authors' Abstract.

779. WRIGHT, JOHN C. (Univ. of Kansas), & HUSTON, ALETHA C. **A matter of form: potentials of television for young viewers.** American Psychologist, 1983, **38,** 835–843.
The authors conclude that television has a rich and as yet largely untapped potential to educate and enhance the development of young children. Public funding of educational television for children is a cost-effective investment in their intellectual and social development. – From Authors' Abstract.

780. YOGMAN, M. W. (Children's Hosp. Medical Ctr., Boston); COLE, P.; ALS, H.; & LESTER, B. M. **Behavior of newborns of diabetic mothers.** Infant Behavior and Development, 1982, **5,** 331–340.
Healthy newborns of diabetic mothers earned lower scores on the Neonatal Behavioral Assessment Scale. – Adapted from Authors' Abstract.

781. YOUNG, I. D. (Univ. of Leicester, England), & HARPER, P. S. **The natural history of the severe form of Hunter's syndrome: a study based on 52 cases.** Developmental Medicine and Child Neurology, 1983, **25,** 481–489.
Hunter's syndrome manifested with initial developmental delay and behavioral disturbance, followed by regression, convulsions, and pyramidal tract signs. – From Authors' Abstract.

COGNITION, LEARNING, PERCEPTION

782. ABKARIAN, G. G. (Colorado State Univ.). **More negative findings for positive prepositions.** Journal of Child Language, 1983, **10,** 415–429.
Children 3–4 years were tested on their comprehension of the locative prepositions *in front of, in back of, ahead of,* and *behind.* Those prepositions characterized as positive were comprehended more poorly than their negative counterparts. – From Author's Abstract.

783. ACKERMAN, BRIAN P. (Univ. of Delaware). **Encoding distinctiveness and the encoding shift penalty in children and adults.** Journal of Experimental Child Psychology, 1983, **36,** 257–283.
The critical manipulation involved the use of semantic orienting questions at both acquisition and retrieval for elementary school children. The results suggest that (1) the acquisition encoding of adults is more distinctive than is that of children, and (2) encoding distinctiveness affects the probability of sampling and resampling compatible cue information and the identification of target event information once cue compatability is ensured at retrieval. – From Author's Abstract.

784. AKIYAMA, M. MICHAEL (Univ. of Oklahoma); BISCOE, BELINDA; & O'SULLIVAN, CHRIS. **Children's representation of knowledge in verification.** Journal of Psycholinguistic Research, 1983, **12,** 297–309.
Children ages 8–9 and 10–11 were asked to perform 2 statement verification tasks. Task 1 consisted of statements that were likely to elicit an affirmative knowledge representation. Task 2 consisted of statements that were likely to elicit a negative knowledge of representation. Negative statements in Task 1 were found to be more difficult for children to verify than those in Task 2. – From Authors' Abstract.

785. AKOPOV, A. Yu. **Comparative study of predictive activity in preschool children, adults, and schizophrenic patients.** Questions of Psychology (translation of Russian title), 1983, **3**, 97–100.
Preschool children tested by a method of play at guesses were compared with healthy adults and adult subjects with schizophrenia and oligophrenia. Subjects of all groups noticed sequences of signals in the experimental cyclic environments. Stochastic environments were found to provoke the effect of leveling off the rates of predictions. It was assumed that man relies in all his milieus not on the rate but on the sequence of signals. This capacity, connected with the ability to store behavioral information, starts developing from 6 years of age. Behavior of children aged 4–7 and of oligophrens in all milieus was typically alternating. – From Author's Abstract.

786. ALLEN, RHIANON (CUNY), & SHATZ, MARILYN. **"What says meow?" The role of context and linguistic experience in very young children's responses to what-questions.** Journal of Child Language, 1983, **10**, 321–335.
Children ages 1–4 to 1–6 were asked common *what*-questions. The presence of a feature was found to have a significant effect on the nonverbal components of children's responses, while linguistic sophistication and type of question asked affected vocal responses but did not produce any consistent effects on nonverbal responses. – From Authors' Abstract.

787. ANDERSON, ARIEL L. H., & PRAWAT, RICHARD S. (Michigan State Univ.). **When is a cup not a cup? A further examination of form and function in children's labeling responses.** Merrill-Palmer Quarterly, 1983, **29**, 375–385.
The results revealed that in the verbal-presentation condition the intermediate-aged and older subjects were more influenced by manipulations in functional context than were the younger subjects. The Age Level X Context interaction was not significant in the pictorial presentation condition. The data were not supportive of a function-to-form developmental sequence. – From Authors' Abstract.

788. ANDERSON, DEAN F. (Iowa State Univ.); GEBHART, JAMES A.; PEASE, DALE G.; & LUDWIG, DAVID A. **Effects of age and temporal placement of a modeled skill on children's performance on a balance task.** Perceptual and Motor Skills, 1982, **55**, 1263–1266.
Analysis of the results for boys aged 7 and 9 years indicated effects of age, temporal appearance of the model, and an interaction of model by age for time on balance. Model affected younger subjects but not older ones. – From Authors' Abstract.

789. ARDONE, RITAGRAZIA (Univ. of Rome, Italy), & D'ATENA, PAOLA. **Riflessività-Impulsività e articolazione dello schema corporeo** [Reflectivity–Impulsivity and articulation of body concept]. Età Evolutiva, 1983, **16**, 13–20.
The results suggest that reflectivity-impulsivity is correlated with sophistication of body concept. Impulsive 6–7-year-olds have a less sophisticated body concept than reflective children. – From Authors' Abstract.

790. ASHCRAFT, MARK H. (Cleveland State Univ.). **Procedural knowledge versus fact retrieval in mental arithmetic: a reply to Baroody.** Developmental Review, 1983, **3**, 231–235.

791. BALL, WILLIAM A. (Swarthmore Coll.); BALLOT, RICHARD; & DIBBLE, ANN. **Stimulus dimensionality and infants' perceived movement in depth.** Journal of Genetic Psychology, 1983, **143**, 193–200.
Infants 34–70 days observed expanding shadows or filmed stimuli that simulated an approaching object on a collision course. Expansion of shadows in both horizontal and vertical dimensions produced head withdrawal more frequently than expansion in the horizontal dimension alone. Expansion of a stimulus undergoing continuous changes in form produced more head withdrawal than the same changes without expansion. – From Authors' Abstract.

792. BARD, ELLEN GURMAN (Univ. of Edinburgh, England), & ANDERSON, ANNE H. **The unintelligibility of speech to children.** Journal of Child Language, 1983, **10**, 265–292.
Words artificially isolated from 12 parents' speech to their children were less intelligible to adult listeners than words originally spoken to an adult. Parents adjusted intelligibility inversely to the observed predictability of the sampled words in their sentence contexts. – From Authors' Abstract.

793. BAROODY, ARTHUR J. (Univ. of Rochester). **The development of procedural knowledge: an alternative explanation for chronometric trends of mental arithmetic.** Developmental Review, 1983, **3**, 225–230.
Ashcraft concluded that the development of number fact efficiency is due to a shift from relying on procedural knowledge such as counting to relying on declarative knowledge. This model assumes that all procedural processes are slow or remain slow, which is probably not the case. An alternative account posits that the key change in number fact efficiency involves a shift from slow counting procedures to principled procedural knowledge. – From Author's Abstract.

794. BEARISON, DANIEL J.; BAIN, JEAN M.; & DANIELE, RICHARD (CUNY). **Developmental changes in how children understand television.** Social Behavior and Personality, 1982, **10**, 133–144.
Younger and less cognitively mature viewers were more likely to structure televised social content in terms of overt descriptive features, action, and literal repetition of dialogue. Older children and adolescents were more likely to consider the inferential aspects of social interaction and to offer interpretations based on psychological qualities. – From Authors' Abstract.

795. BELMONT, JOHN M. (Univ. of Kansas Medical Ctr.); KARCHMER, MICHAEL A.; & BOURG, JAMES W. **Structural influences on deaf and hearing children's recall of temporal/spatial incongruent letter strings.** Educational Psychology, 1983, **3**, 259–274.
It was concluded that individual differences in deaf children's initial orientations bear upon differences in performance because of these children's relatively weak adaptive responses under challenging conditions. – From Authors' Abstract.

796. BENBOW, CAMILLA PERSSON (Johns Hopkins Univ.), & STANLEY, JULIAN C. **Sex differences in mathematical reasoning ability: more facts.** Science, 1983, **222**, 1029–1031.
By age 13, a large sex difference in mathematical reasoning ability exists, and it is especially pronounced at the high end of the distribution. Among students who scored 700 or above, boys outnumbered girls 13 to 1. – From Authors' Abstract.

797. BERKOWITZ, MARVIN W. (Marquette Univ.), & GIBBS, JOHN C. **Measuring the developmental features of moral discussion.** Merrill-Palmer Quarterly, 1983, **29**, 399–410.
Developmentally effective discussion is termed transactive discussion and consists of an interpenetration of reasoning by discussants. This study offers evidence of the validity of the relationship of such discussion in college-age same-sex dyads to significant pretest to posttest moral stage development as measured by Kohlberg's stage scheme. – From Authors' Abstract.

798. BERNARD, ROBERT M. (Concordia Univ., Montreal, Quebec, Canada). **Young children's perception of implied motion portrayal in still photographs.** Perceptual and Motor Skills, 1982, **55**, 1267–1276.
Cognitive-developmental differences in young children as well as difference in age may explain how children come correctly to perceive dynamic elements in static photographs. – From Author's Abstract.

799. BERNSTEIN, MARK E. (Univ. of Texas, Austin). **Formation of internal structure in a lexical category.** Journal of Child Language, 1983, **10**, 381–399.

Adults consistently judged some objects to be better examples than others, and the provision of function information affected the judgments in a characteristic way. A different, less stable typicality structure was found in the children's category. Function cues caused the children's rank order judgments to change greatly. – From Author's Abstract.

800. BERNSTEIN, MARK E. (Univ. of Texas, Austin), & FINNEGAN, MARGARET H. **Internal speech and deaf children.** American Annals of the Deaf, 1983, **128**, 483–489.
The position is supported that the use of forms of manual communication in the education of deaf students is highly effective and desirable, but a reinterpretation of Canrad's position believed to be on more solid theoretical ground is offered. – Adapted from Authors' Abstract.

801. BIBER, DOUGLAS (Univ. of Southern California). **Differential competence in Somali: evidence from the acquisition of noun definitization.** Journal of Psycholinguistic Research, 1983, **12**, 275–295.
A large percentage of the population never acquired parts of the rule of noun definitization at all. The major factor influencing this acquisition process was an urban vs. nomadic childhood home. – From Author's Abstract.

802. BJORKLUND, DAVID F. (Florida Atlantic Univ.), & ZEMAN, BARBARA R. **The development of organizational strategies in children's recall of familiar information: using social organization to recall the names of classmates.** International Journal of Behavioral Development, 1983, **6**, 341–353.
Children in grades 1, 3, and 5 were asked to recall the names of their classmates. Although levels of recall and clustering were high, the majority of subjects at each grade level was unable to describe accurately a strategy they had used in recalling their classmates' names. – From Authors' Abstract.

803. BONVILLIAN, JOHN D. (Univ. of Virginia). **Effects of signability and imagery on word recall of deaf and hearing students.** Perceptual and Motor Skills, 1983, **56**, 775–791.

804. BONVILLIAN, JOHN D. (Univ. of Virginia); ORLANSKY, MICHAEL D.; & NOVACK, LESLEY LAZIN. **Developmental milestones: sign language acquisition and motor development.** Child Development, 1983, **54**, 1435–1445.
Children of deaf parents showed accelerated early language development. The structure and content of the subjects' 50-sign vocabularies closely resembled those for children at the same stage of spoken language acquisition. The pattern of synchrony between motor and language development reported for children learning to speak was not found in the present study. – From Authors' Abstract.

805. BOTUCK, SHELLY, & TURKEWITZ, GERALD (Albert Einstein Coll. of Medicine). **Auditory–Visual integration by mentally retarded adolescents.** American Journal of Mental Deficiency, 1984, **88**, 446–448.
The findings suggest that for retarded individuals intersensory integration is not fully developed. – From the Article.

806. BOZINOU, EFFIE (Teachers Coll., Columbia Univ.). **Effects of context, transformational complexity, and verbal cue on young children's performance on the present progressive and past tenses.** Journal of General Psychology, 1983, **109**, 133–147.
These findings demonstrate that language performance is the result of a complex interrelationship between transformational complexity and the perceptual properties of linguistic structures. – From Author's Abstract.

807. BRABECK, MARY (Boston Coll.). **Moral judgment: theory and research on differences between males and females.** Developmental Review, 1983, **3**, 274–291.
The theory of an ethic of care is described and contrasted with Kohlberg's morality of justice. The empirical support for Gilligan's claim that men and women differ in their moral orientations is examined and an integrated theory of morality is offered. – From Author's Abstract.

808. BRENER, ROSEMARY (Univ. of Hull, England). **Learning the deictic meaning of third person pronouns.** Journal of Psycholinguistic Research, 1983, **12,** 235–262.
Errors made by children ages 3–6 showed that initially gender was the variable used to identify referents and that person was used only later. – From Author's Abstract.

809. BRETHERTON, INGE (Colorado State Univ.); McNEW, SANDRA; SNYDER, LYNN; & BATES, ELIZABETH. **Individual differences at 20 months: analytic and holistic strategies in language acquisition.** Journal of Child Language, 1983, **10,** 292–320.
The language abilities of 20-month-old children were assessed by observation and maternal interviews. All interview and observation clusters predicted 28-month MLU, but the grammatical morpheme clusters did not predict later performance on a grammatical morpheme test. – From Authors' Abstract.

810. BRODY, LESLIE R. (Boston Univ.); ZELAZO, PHILIP R.; & CHAIKA, HELENE. **Habituation–Dishabituation to speech in the neonate.** Developmental Psychology, 1984, **20,** 114–119.
Twenty-four full-term newborns performed in a head-turning sound-localization task. The results clearly showed spatial orientation to sounds and response decrement to repeated speech sounds followed by response increment to novel speech sounds. – From Authors' Abstract.

811. BROWN, RONALD T. (Univ. of Illinois, Chicago), & WYNNE, MARTHA ELLEN. **An analysis of attentional components in hyperactive and normal boys.** Journal of Learning Disabilities, 1984, **17,** 162–166.
Normal children were superior to hyperactive children in attentional performance, while hyperactive adolescents demonstrated improvement with age only in the area of coming to attention. – From Authors' Abstract.

812. BRUNT, DENIS (Univ. of Texas, Austin); HOUSNER, LYNN D.; & McELROY, JOE. **Manipulation of dominant/non-dominant hand and ipsilateral/contralateral movement as a function of response organization in fourth grade children.** Perceptual and Motor Skills, 1983, **56,** 331–334.
Analysis indicated that knowing which hand to use played a major role in response organization. When the subject was unsure of which hand to use but the other variables were precued, reaction time increased. – From Authors' Abstract.

813. BURRIS, VAL (Univ. of Oregon). **Stages in the development of economic concepts.** Human Relations, 1983, **36,** 791–812.
Using a Piagetian perspective, children 4–12 were interviewed about economic concepts (commodity, value, exchange, property, work, and income). They showed the requirements for developments stages in economic reasoning. – From Author's Abstract.

814. BURTCHEN, IRENE (Univ. München, Germany). **Analyse von Spielverhalten im Vor- und Grundschulalter unter dem Aspekt des gemeinsamen Objektbezugs.** Zeitschrift für Entwicklungspsychologie und Pädagogische Psychologie, 1983, **15,** 139–148.
An action-theoretical approach is proposed as an integrative perspective for the research in play activities. The central category of this concept, the object relation, was used to analyze 46 spontaneous play interactions of children 3–10 years old. – From Author's Abstract.

815. BUSHNELL, I. W. R. (Univ. of Glasgow, Scotland); GERRY, G.; & BURT, K. **The externality effect in neonates.** Infant Behavior and Development, 1983, **6,** 151–156.
A visual-following paradigm with 1-week-olds found no evidence of visual discrimination for bounded stimuli. – From Abstract by S. Thomas.

816. CARTER, PHILIP; PAZAK, BARBARA; & KAIL, ROBERT (Purdue Univ.). **Algorithms for processing spatial information.** Journal of Experimental Child Psychology, 1983, **36,** 284–304.
In a mental rotation task in which the stimuli were letter-like characters, at ages 9, 13, and adult most persons solved the problems using the same algorithm. When the stimuli were multielement flags, the modal algorithm for both 9- and 13-year-olds differed from that of adults, whose modal algorithm was the same as for letter stimuli. – From Authors' Abstract.

817. CASELLI, MARIA CRISTINA (Istituto di Psicologia del CNR, Rome, Italy). **Gesti comunicativi e prime parole** [Communicative gestures and first words]. Età Evolutiva, 1983, **16,** 36–51.
Data refer to a child followed longitudinally from 10 to 20 months of age and were collected through diary accounts and periodical videotaped sessions. Results show that it is possible to distinguish 2 types of gestures. – From Author's Abstract.

818. CASEY, PAUL J. (Riverina Coll. of Advanced Education), & HEATH, RICHARD A. **Categorization reaction time, category structure, and category size in semantic memory using artificial categories.** Memory and Cognition, 1983, **11,** 228–236.
Significantly longer categorization reaction times were required for instances from the hierarchical categories, but no set size effect was found. Subjects' free-recall data revealed that subjects had acquired the hierarchical structures but imposed their own structures on the other categories. – From Authors' Abstract.

819. CHIAT, SHULAMUTH (City Univ., London, England). **Why Mikey's right and my key's wrong: the significance of stress and word boundaries in a child's output system.** Cognition, 1983, **14,** 275–300.
A study of the environments in which a phonologically delayed child fronts velar stops revealed that fronting is dependent on word stress and boundaries, shows lexical exceptions, and occurs in output only. This distribution suggests that input and output lexical representations are independent. – From Author's Abstract.

820. CLARK, JULIA V. (Howard Univ.). **Development of seriation and its relation to the achievement of inferential transitivity.** Journal of Research in Science Teaching, 1983, **20,** 781–794.
The study ascertained the influence of intervention in the development of operational seriation and transitivity in kindergarten and first-grade children who initially failed to demonstrate the ability to do seriation and transitivity problems. The subjects showed advancement toward concrete operation on the seriation problems but not on transitivity problems. – From Author's Abstract.

821. CLARKSON, MARSHA G.; MORRONGIELLO, BARBARA A.; & CLIFTON, RACHEL K. (Univ. of Massachusetts). **Stimulus-presentation probability influences newborns' head orientation to sound.** Perceptual and Motor Skills, 1982, **55,** 1239–1246.
The likelihood of correct head turning increased linearly as the lateral-stimulus-presentation probability increased. – From Authors' Abstract.

822. COCKERILL, IAN M. (Univ. of Birmingham, England), & MILLER, BRIAN P. **Children's colour preferences and motor skill performance with variation in environmental colour.** Perceptual and Motor Skills, 1983, **56,** 845–846.
Subjects 6–11 years old made fewer errors and took less time while working under their preferred colors. – From Authors' Abstract.

823. COHEN, HERBERT (Arizona State Univ.). **A comparison of the affect of two types of student behavior with manipulatives on the development of projective spatial structures.** Journal of Research in Science Teaching, 1983, **20,** 875–883.

The results clearly indicate that directed study, directed in the sense of having subjects view objects from a variety of points of view, does enhance the development of the projective spatial conceptual ability in elementary-age children. – From the Article.

824. CORMIER, PIERRE, & DAGENAIS, YVON (Univ. of Montreal, Quebec, Canada). **Class-inclusion developmental levels and logical necessity.** International Journal of Behavioral Development, 1983, **6**, 1–14.
Among the results, subjects using logical reasons differ from those using counting in only 1 specific situation, the ability to reject the impossible case, while subjects who fail class-inclusion problems also fail all necessity tasks. – From Authors' Abstract.

825. CORNELL, EDWARD H. (Univ. of Alberta, Canada), & BERGSTROM, LINDA I. **Serial-position effects in infants' recognition memory.** Memory and Cognition, 1983, **11**, 494–499.
Infants 7 months old were repeatedly shown photographs of adult female faces in a probe-recognition test. The bowed serial-position and recency effects found match the performance of older subjects in verbal learning tasks and suggest an underlying automatic process. – From Authors' Abstract.

826. CRAMER, PHEBE (Williams Coll.). **Homonym understanding and conservation.** Journal of Experimental Child Psychology, 1983, **36**, 179–195.
In a longitudinal study of kindergarten and first-grade children, conservation status was related to homonym understanding over and above the age or general vocabulary level of the child. – From Author's Abstract.

827. CRUM, RUTH ANN (Univ. of Kentucky); THORNBURG, KATHY; BENNINGA, JACQUES; & BRIDGE, CONNIE. **Preschool children's object substitutions during symbolic play.** Perceptual and Motor Skills, 1983, **56**, 947–955.
Children were better able to substitute symbolic for actual objects using objects similar in physical attributes than using objects similar in function. – Adapted from Authors' Abstract.

828. CULTICE, JOAN C. (Arizona State Univ.); SOMERVILLE, SUSAN C.; & WELLMAN, HENRY M. **Preschoolers' memory monitoring: feeling-of-knowing judgments.** Child Development, 1983, **54**, 1480–1486.
Children were shown color photographs of other children and adults, varying in familiarity, and were asked initially to recall their names. Feeling-of-knowing judgments and judgments about whether the child had seen the person were obtained in all cases where naming failed. Both types of judgment were found to predict subsequent recognition performance, indicating accurate memory monitoring. – From Authors' Abstract.

829. CUMMINGS, E. MARK (National Inst. of Mental Health, Bldg. 15K, Bethesda), & BJORK, ELIZABETH L. **Search behavior on multi-choice hiding tasks: evidence for an objective conception of space in infancy.** International Journal of Behavioral Development, 1983, **6**, 71–87.
The findings suggest that infants do not err on visible displacement tasks because they (a) link objects with previous action locations, (b) rely upon egocentric spatial reference systems, or (c) confuse different hiding locations as a result of a specific form of retrieval competition from the previous hiding location. – From Authors' Abstract.

830. CURLEY, JAMES F. (St. John's Univ.), & HOGAN, MAUREEN A. **Reversed memory coding and symbol reversal in children.** Perceptual and Motor Skills, 1983, **56**, 431–437.
Boys 7 years old were chosen on the basis of tendency to confuse mirror and aligned written symbols. Evidence was insufficient to conclude that mirror-same bilateral presentation facilitated responses of either group over aligned-same or peripheral conditions. – Adapted from Authors' Abstract.

831. CZERNIAWSKA, EWA (Univ. of Warsaw, Poland). **Introducing the problem of meta-memory.** Psychologia Wychowawcza (Educational Psychology: Bimonthly of the Polish Teachers Union), 1982, **25**, 27–38.
The article presents views of investigators in the structure of metamemory and methods of studying metamemory and considers the question of the regulative function of metamemory in the memorial process. – From Author's Abstract.

832. CZERNIAWSKA, EWA (Univ. of Warsaw, Poland). **Metamemory, a literature review.** Psychologia Wychowawcza (Educational Psychology: Bimonthly of the Polish Teachers Union), 1983, **26**, 143–158.
The article presents selected investigations on metamemory. They concern metamemory sensitivity, knowledge of the role of variables in memory processes, and knowledge of the interaction of variables in memory processes. The discussion includes information about the relations between memory and metamemory, although the data in this area are limited and equivocal. – From Author's Abstract.

833. DAS, J. P. (Univ. of Alberta, Edmonton, Alberta, Canada). **Memory for spatial and temporal order in deaf children.** American Annals of the Deaf, 1983, **128**, 894–899.
Results showed that the deaf pupils did not recall spatial order better than temporal. Compared to the hearing pupils, the deaf pupils were not less competent in probed recognition. – From Author's Abstract.

834. DEAN, ANNE L. (Univ. of New Orleans); DUHE, DEBRA A.; & GREEN, DOUGLAS A. **The development of children's mental tracking strategies on a rotation task.** Journal of Experimental Child Psychology, 1983, **36**, 226–240.
Children 5–13 years old were required to mentally track the rotation of a pointer around a circular backdrop and to indicate the pointer's imagined position on the backdrop at the sound of a signal. Children older than 8 years of age generated Linear Distance X Time functions, indicating mental tracking, but younger children did not. The proportions of children at each grade level using holistic or part-to-part strategies to mentally track the pointer were comparable, as were mental tracking rates. – From Authors' Abstract.

835. DeLOACHE, JUDY S. (Univ. of Illinois, Urbana-Champaign), & BROWN, ANN L. **Where do I go next? Intelligent searching by very young children.** Developmental Psychology, 1984, **20**, 37–44.
The task required the child to remember in what natural location in his or her own home a toy had been hidden. Older (27 months) and younger (21 months) subjects achieved a high level of errorless retrievals. When the hidden toy was moved surreptitiously, the children's search behavior was compared to their error trials. Both age groups showed greater persistence in their initial search on surprise than on error trials, indicating that their retrieval effort was based on their level of subject certainty. The older, but not the younger, subjects searched differently on surprise and error trials. On surprise trials they searched selectively and intelligently, confining their search primarily to locations that were nearby or in some way related to the place where the toy had actually been hidden. The related searching of older children suggested that they had made intelligent guesses about plausible alternative locations for the missing toy. – From Authors' Abstract.

836. DEL REY, PATRICIA (Univ. of Georgia); WHITEHURST, MICHAEL; & WOOD, JUDITH M. **Effects of experience and contextual interference on learning and transfer by boys and girls.** Perceptual and Motor Skills, 1983, **56**, 581–582.

837. DODDS, ALLAN G. (Univ. of Nottingham, University Park, Nottingham, England), & CARTER, DAVID D. **Memory for movement in blind children: the role of previous visual experience.** Journal of Motor Behavior, 1983, **15**, 343–352.
Results showed that the congenitally blind reproduce movements at a low level of accuracy compared with the other 2 groups. Analysis showed that although the congenitally blind could

reproduce the extent of the movement accurately, the movement was poorly reproduced in terms of its orientation to the criterion movement. – From Authors' Abstract.

838. DOLITSKY, MARLENE (Univ. of Paris, France). **The birth of grammatical morphemes.** Journal of Psycholinguistic Research, 1983, **12**, 353–360.
A longitudinal study was carried out on a bilingual French/English child from ages 2 to 3. – From Author's Abstract.

839. DOLLINGER, STEPHEN J. (Southern Illinois Univ., Carbondale), & READER, MARK J. **Attributions, deadlines, and children's intrinsic motivations.** Journal of General Psychology, 1983, **109**, 157–166.
The 2 findings run counter to attribution theory. Given the presence of deadlines, relevant attributions resulted in less subsequent intrinsic interest as compared to irrelevant attributions. In the presence of irrelevant attributions, deadlines resulted in greater task interest when compared with no deadlines. – From Authors' Abstract.

840. DOLMAN, DAVID (William Rainey Harper Coll.). **A study of the relationship between syntactic development and concrete operations in deaf children.** American Annals of the Deaf, 1983, **128**, 813–819.
The linguistic and cognitive skills of deaf children ages 7–15 were examined. Students were administered a test of syntactic comprehension and 4 Piagetian operational tasks in the areas of conservation, classification, seriation, and numeration. Operational deaf children performed better than nonoperational deaf children on the test of syntactic comprehension. – From Author's Abstract.

841. DUNHAM, PAUL, JR. (Univ. of Wyoming), & DUNHAM, SANDRA L. **Resemblance in motor skill performance of sixth graders and their parents.** Journal of Psychology, 1983, **115**, 193–197.
The results revealed a lack of familial resemblance in performance on all tasks as indicated by the low interfamily correlations. – From Authors' Abstract.

842. EDWARDS, DOROTHY, & CURTIS, SCOTT (Univ. of Georgia). **The child's conceptualization of speech and language.** First Language, 1983, **4**, 41–50.
Children 5–14 years old were interviewed to determine their views on such matters as how people talk, why babies can't talk, etc. The children's responses were categorized and are discussed as they changed across age levels. – From Authors' Abstract.

843. ELROD, MIMI MILNER (Iowa State Univ.). **Young children's responses to direct and indirect directives.** Journal of Genetic Psychology, 1983, **143**, 217–227.
Children 3–6 years were tested on 2 types of directives: (1) nonconventional indirect directives (NID) and (2) conventional directives (CD). The children responded as appropriately to NID as they did to CD. – From Author's Abstract.

844. ENGLE, RANDALL W. (Univ. of South Carolina), & MARSHALL, KATHY. **Do developmental changes in digit span result from acquisition strategies?** Journal of Experimental Child Psychology, 1983, **36**, 429–436.
With slow presentation, experimenter-provided grouping eliminated the span differences between sixth graders and adults, but, while grouping helped first graders more than adults, a sizable difference in digit span remained. With fast presentation, grouping increased the adults' performance more than the childrens'. – From Authors' Abstract.

845. ENRIGHT, MARY K.; ROVEE-COLLIER, CAROLYN K. (Rutgers Univ.); FAGEN, JEFFREY W.; & CANIGLIA, KAREN. **The effects of distributed training on retention of operant conditioning in human infants.** Journal of Experimental Child Psychology, 1983, **36**, 209–225.

Three-month-olds were trained in footkicking for either 1 18-min session or for 2 9-min or 3 6-min sessions separated by 24-hr intervals. All infants exhibited retention during a test administered immediately after training, but only those trained in a single session continued to perform the conditioned response during cued-recall tests 7 or 14 days later. – From Authors' Abstract.

846. EVANS, MARY ANN (Univ. of Guelph, Ontario, Canada), & RUBIN, KENNETH H. **Developmental differences in explanations of childhood games.** Child Development, 1983, **54**, 1559–1567.
Children in grades K, 1, 4, and 8 were asked to explain common childhood games and then were explicitly questioned about information omitted from or ambiguously expressed in their spontaneous explanations. All age groups volunteered the game rules in the order of the game sequence and knew the game rules equally well. However, the younger children volunteered less information, focusing on the actions of the games and omitting rules outlining how the games were set up or drew to a conclusion. – From Authors' Abstract.

847. EWERT, OTTO M. (Univ. Mainz, Germany), & SCHUMANN, RUTH. **Entwicklungspsychologische Voraussetzungen von Benennungsflexibilität.** Zeitschrift für Entwicklungspsychologie und Pädagogische Psychologie, 1983, **15**, 121–138.
Definitive descriptions is the accentuation of those features of an object by which it is distinguished from others in a given situation. Some authors assume Piaget's stage of concrete operations as a prerequisite for such a performance. In this study, a continuous quantitative variable, the M-operator, is substituted for the discontinuous qualitative description of cognitive structures. – From Authors' Abstract.

848. FAGEN, JEFFREY W., & ROVEE-COLLIER, CAROLYN (Rutgers Univ.). **Memory retrieval: a time-locked process in infancy.** Science, 1983, **222**, 1349–1351.
Infants 3 months old learned to activate an overhead crib mobile by operant footkicking and received a visual reminder of the event (a "reactivation treatment") 2 weeks later, after forgetting had occurred. Subsequent manifestation of the association was a monotonic increasing function of time since the reactivation treatment. – From Authors' Abstract.

849. FANTINO, EDMUND (Univ. of California, San Diego); CASE, DAVID A.; & ALTUS, DEBORAH. **Observing reward-informative and -uninformative stimuli by normal children of different ages.** Journal of Experimental Child Psychology, 1983, **36**, 437–452.
Normal children ages 4–5, 9–10, and 13–14 years received points independent of responding according to a variable-time 30-sec schedule which alternated randomly with an extinction component. Presses on each of 2 levels produced stimuli. Stimuli positively correlated with points and stimuli uncorrelated with points were each chosen over stimuli correlated with extinction in every age group. – From Authors' Abstract.

850. FELDMAN, DAVID HENRY (Tufts Univ.). **Piaget on giftedness—a very short essay.** The Genetic Epistemologist, 1983, **12**, 1–10.

851. FINLAY, DAVID (Univ. of Newcastle, New South Wales, Australia), & IVINSKIS, ALGIS. **Cardiac and visual responses to moving stimuli presented either succesively or simultaneously to the central and peripheral visual fields in 4-month-old infants.** Developmental Psychology, 1984, **20**, 29–36.
Cardiac and visual orienting responses were measured as indexes of attention in 4-month-old infants. In the first situation, the presentation of a peripheral stimulus followed the offset of a central fixation stimulus. In the second situation, the peripheral stimulus came on while the central fixation stimulus was on. With simultaneous presentation, the probability of orienting to the peripheral stimulus was decreased. – From Authors' Abstract.

852. FLAVELL, JOHN H. (Stanford Univ.); ZHANG, XIAO-DONG; ZOU, HONG; DONG, QI; & QI, SEN. **A comparison between the development of the appearance–reality distinction in the People's Republic of China and the United States.** Cognitive Psychology, 1983, **15**, 459–466.
A study of the appearance–reality distinction in American 3–5-year-olds was replicated with Chinese 3–5-year-olds. The error patterns, age changes, and absolute levels of performance were similar in the 2 samples. It was speculated that the acquisition of this distinction may be a universal, possibly age-linked, development that is probably fueled by experiences with appearance–reality discrepancies that are available in all cultures. – Authors' Abstract.

853. FLOOD, JAMES (San Diego State Univ.), & MENYUK, PAULA. **The development of metalinguistic awareness and its relation to reading achievement.** Journal of Applied Developmental Psychology, 1983, **4**, 65–80.
Subjects, fourth grade to adult, were asked to judge and produce corrections of nongrammatical, anomalous, and ambiguous stimulus items presented orally or written. Reading achievement and age were positively related to metalinguistic ability. Good readers' performance on oral tasks equalled their performance on written tasks by adulthood. – From Authors' Abstract.

854. FOLARIN, BAMIDELE ADEPEJU (Univ. of Lagos, Nigeria). **The effect of spacing category members on children's memory.** Journal of Psychology, 1983, **114**, 167–177.
Long-term memory was studied in Yoruba-speaking Nigerian boys and girls in grades 1, 3, and 6 by spacing category members with 0, 3, or 7 unrelated words, each presented at 1-, 4-, and 6-sec rate. Spacing decreased recall of words, categories, words within categories, and clustering. There was a Rate X Grade interaction for word recall, category recall, and clustering. – From Author's Abstract.

855. FORD, H. THOMAS, JR. (Auburn Univ.), & PUCKETT, JOHN R. **Comparative effects of prescribed weight-training and basketball programs on basketball skill test scores of ninth grade boys.** Perceptual and Motor Skills, 1983, **56**, 23–26.
No differences were found among groups. – From Authors' Abstract.

856. FRANKEL, MARC T. (Missouri Inst. of Psychiatry). **Children's recall and organization of noncategorical associated pictures.** Psychological Reports, 1983, **52**, 787–790.
Subjects in grades K, 4, and 10 were tested for their memory of 24 noncategorical pictures partially composed of highly associated items. Only the tenth graders grouped associated material together at recall. Younger subjects did not improve recall or organization across 3 trials with the same stimuli. – From Author's Abstract.

857. FREEMAN, MARK (Univ. of Chicago). **History, narrative, and life-span developmental knowledge.** Human Development, 1984, **27**, 1–19.
The problem of finding continuity across the life course can be tied in part to a theoretical perspective that looks essentially forward in time. It can, however, be minimized within a framework that is more genuinely historical, one that looks back over the flow of events in an attempt to understand and explain their possible connections. – From Author's Abstract.

858. FRIEDENSBERG, EWA (SGGW-AR, Warsaw, Poland). **Some indicators of individual work style from the developmental point of view.** Psychologia Wychowawcza (Educational Psychology: Bimonthly of the Polish Teachers Union), 1983, **26**, 257–267.
Research is presented concerning the relationship between the functional structure of simple constructional action and the level of reactivity and intelligence. Five age levels were studied: 6, 8, 10, 13, and 16 years. Reactivity was measured by an observational rating scale used by teachers. Intelligence was measured by the Raven test. Individual work style acquired shape with age. Intelligence level was found to affect work style formation in persons of low reactivity to a greater degree than in persons of high reactivity. – From Author's Abstract.

859. FRUCHTER, ARLENE; WILBUR, RONNIE B. (Purdue Univ.); & FRASER, J. BRUCE. **Comprehension of idioms by hearing-impaired students.** Volta Review, 1984, **86**, 7–19.

The results indicate that when offered a picture that depicts a literal interpretation of the idiom as 1 of 4 response choices, hearing-impaired students correctly chose the literal picture 92.8% of the time. Subjects were 14 years old. – From Authors' Abstract.

860. GABBARD, CARL (Texas A&M Univ.). **Muscular endurance and experience with playground apparatus.** Perceptual and Motor Skills, 1983, **56**, 538.

It was concluded that young children in a free-play condition would produce sufficient activity to increase significantly their level of upper body muscular endurance. – From the Article.

861. GARDNER, J. M. (Albert Einstein Coll. of Medicine), & TURKEWITZ, G. **The effect of arousal level on visual preference in preterm infants.** Infant Behavior and Development, 1982, **5**, 369–385.

Infants viewed cubes varying in size and number or viewed light panels varying in frequency of illumination. Preferences were for the most stimulation when least aroused. – Adapted from Authors' Abstract.

862. GASIOROWSKA-NOZKA, JOLANTA (Jagiellonian Univ., Cracow, Poland). **Accelerating the development of creative drawing in children. The usefulness of the Goodenough Draw-a-Man technique in testing mental level.** Psychologia Wychowawcza (Educational Psychology: Bimonthly of the Polish Teachers Union), 1982, **25**, 272–279.

An analysis of the relation of the quantitative results to the existing norms points to the need of establishing a new upper age bound for the application of the draw-a-man technique. – From Author's Abstract.

863. GELMAN, ROCHEL (Univ. of Pennsylvania), & MECK, ELIZABETH. **Preschoolers' counting: principles before skill.** Cognition, 1983, **13**, 343–359.

Children's ability to detect errors in a puppet's application of the 1–1, stable-order, and cardinal count principles were assessed. Since they did well in these experiments, there is support for the view that errors in counting—at least for set sizes up to 20 – reflect performance demands and not the absence of implicit knowledge of the counting principles. – From Authors' Abstract.

864. GEPPERT, ULRICH (Ruhr-Univ. Bochum, P.O. Box 10 21 48, Bochum, West Germany), & KÜSTER, URSULA. **The emergence of "wanting to do it oneself": a precursor of achievement motivation.** International Journal of Behavioral Development, 1983, **6**, 355–369.

Classifying the children's various reactions to the experimental manipulations revealed different behavioral patterns that supported the hypothesis of developmental stages of wanting to do things oneself; these stages corresponded to the degree of development of self-concept. – From Authors' Abstract.

865. GIACALONE, WILLIAM R. (Univ. of California, Berkeley). **An examiner-induced visual vigilance apparatus.** Perceptual and Motor Skills, 1983, **56**, 744–746.

A film/record instrument is described that measures attention, distractibility, hyperkinetic movement, and selected aspects of visual perception. – From Author's Abstract.

866. GIGERENZER, GERD (Univ. Bielefeld, Germany). **Informationsintegration bei Kindern: Eine Erwiderung auf Wilkening.** Zeitschrift für Entwicklungspsychologie und Pädagogische Psychologie, 1983, **15**, 216–221.

Wilkening's attempt to solve the theoretical contradiction between the assumptions of decomposability and nondecomposability is not convincing. – From Author's Abstract.

867. GIGERENZER, GERD (Univ. Bielefeld, Germany). **Über die Anwendung der Informations-Integrations-Theorie auf entwicklungspsychologische Problemstellungen: Eine Kritik.** Zeitschrift für Entwicklungspsychologie und Pädagogische Psychologie, 1983, **15**, 101–120.

The application of N. H. Anderson's information integration theory to developmental psychology is criticized using the perception of rectangle area as an example. – From Author's Abstract.

868. GLIDDEN, LARAINE MASTERS (St. Mary's Coll. of Maryland); BILSKY, LINDA HICKSON; MAR, HARVEY H.; JUDD, THOMAS P.; & WARNER, DARCEY A. **Semantic processing can facilitate free recall in mildly retarded adolescents.** Journal of Experimental Child Psychology, 1983, **36**, 510–532.
Compared with controls, neither of 2 semantic strategies for memorizing a 15-word list helped recall either in original learning or in transfer. Subjects were then provided with experimenter-composed stories. They showed better immediate recall and retention after 2 months than did no-strategy controls, but not after 1 year. – From Authors' Abstract.

869. GLIDDEN, LARAINE MASTERS (St. Mary's Coll. of Maryland), & WARNER, DARCEY A. **Semantic processing and recall improvement of EMR adolescents.** American Journal of Mental Deficiency, 1983, **88**, 96–105.
Semantic processing, in the form of stories linking to-be-remembered words, was compared with cumulative rehearsal in a free-recall task. Educable mentally retarded adolescents were either taught to generate a story, provided with a story, taught to rehearse cumulatively, or assigned to no-strategy control groups. Semantic-processing subjects showed better recall at original learning. – From Authors' Abstract.

870. GLOBERSON, TAMAR (Tel-Aviv Univ., Ramat Aviv, Israel). **Mental capacity, mental effort, and cognitive style.** Developmental Review, 1983, **3**, 292–302.
This study tests the relationship between Pascual-Leone's mental capacity and Kahneman's mental effort. Positive correlations exist between empirical measures of the constructs. – From Author's Abstract.

871. GOLD, RON (Univ. of Melbourne, Parkville, Victoria, Australia). **Reasons for the décalage between identity conservation and equivalence conservation.** International Journal of Behavioral Development, 1983, **6**, 321–339.
The results suggested that "perceptual seduction" accounts for at least the greater portion of the identity–equivalence décalage; as such, the décalage is in good accord with Piaget's theory. Implications of the results for performance in "informal conservation situations" are discussed. – From Author's Abstract.

872. GOLDFIELD, EUGENE C. (Children's Hosp. Medical Ctr., 300 Longwood, Boston). **The ecological approach to perceiving as a foundation for understanding the development of knowing in infancy.** Developmental Review, 1983, **3**, 371–404.
Changes with development in infant sensorimotor functioning may be explained by a process of increasing economy in noticing potentially available affordances, rather than a process of constructing a representational system for making present something not present. Studies of 3 infant skills widely attributed to the onset of representation are examined with regard to this ecological thesis. – From Author's Abstract.

873. GREENBERG, JEFF (Univ. of Arizona); KUCZAJ, STAN A., II; & SUPPIGER, ANN E. **An examination of adapted communication in young children.** First Language, 1983, **4**, 31–40.
In Study 1, children ages 2–6 years were asked to describe 1- and 2-object referent sets to 1 listener who could see the objects and 1 listener who could not see the objects. The results indicated that all the children gave more information when describing 2-object referent sets, and that the 5–6-year-olds provided more information to the listener who could not see the objects than to the listener who could see the objects. – From Authors' Abstract.

874. GREESON, LARRY E. (Miami Univ.). **Effects of observational learning, overt activity, and class placement on children's mediated associative learning.** Journal of General Psychology, 1984, **110**, 61–68.

Verbal-mediation responding resulted in more effective mediator use and recall performance than did imagery or control responding; this effect interacted with class placement. – From Author's Abstract.

875. GROBE, RÜDIGER (Univ. Mannheim, Germany), & HOFER, MANFRED. **Kognitiv-motivationale Korrelate von Schulnoten: Typen motivierter Schüler.** Zeitschrift für Entwicklungspsychologie und Pädagogische Psychologie, 1983, **15**, 292–316.
Pupils from grades 7–9, after having received feedback from a written examination in mathematics, were asked about their views concerning their own future efforts and also about 4 hypothetical cognitive conditional variables. Configural frequency analyses of these 4 variables showed configural types of motivational conditions. These results were largely corroborated by a second set of cognitive variables. – From Authors' Abstract.

876. GULLO, DOMINIC F. (Kent State Univ.), & BERSANI, CAROL. **Effects of three experimental conditions on preschool children's ability to coordinate visual perspectives.** Perceptual and Motor Skills, 1983, **56**, 675–678.
Differences were observed among the (1) "Three Mountain Task," (2) identification of objects a doll could see against the side of 2 intersecting walls, and (3) choosing a picture that represented which object the doll could see. More children responded correctly to the latter 2 tasks. – Adapted from the Article.

877. GUTTENTAG, ROBERT E. (Univ. of Winnipeg, Manitoba, Canada). **Semantic memory organization in second graders and adults.** Journal of General Psychology, 1984, **110**, 81–86.
Adult and second-grade subjects experienced more interference from within-category than cross-category printed words. The pattern of associative and categorical interference effects was similar for both groups. – From Author's Abstract.

878. HALPERN, ESTHER (Tel-Aviv Univ., Ramat Aviv, Israel); CORRIGAN, ROBERTA; & AVIEZER, ORA. **In, on, and under: examining the relationship between cognitive and language skills.** International Journal of Behavioral Development, 1983, **6**, 153–166.
Scalogram analyses of the construction, comprehension, and production tasks indicated that *in* space developed earlier than *on* space, which developed before *under* space. Subjects were Israeli children 14–30 months old. – Adapted from Authors' Abstract.

879. HANSEN, JANE (Univ. of New Hampshire), & PEARSON, P. DAVID. **An instructional study: improving the inferential comprehension of good and poor fourth-grade readers.** Journal of Educational Psychology, 1983, **75**, 821–829.
Treatment consisted of 3 parts: (*a*) making students aware of the importance of drawing inferences, (*b*) getting students to discuss something similar to the text and to hypothesize what would happen, and (*c*) providing inferential questions to discuss after reading the selection. Poor readers benefited from the instruction, but good readers did not. – From Authors' Abstract.

880. HARDWICK, DOUGLAS A. (Illinois State Univ.). **Cognitive development and the utilization of memorization strategies in middle childhood.** Journal of Psychology, 1983, **114**, 207–218.
The relationship between cognitive development and the use of memorization strategies in a free-recall task was assessed in first, third, and fifth graders. The results indicated a prerequisite relationship in which changes in underlying cognitions proceed in advance of the spontaneous and deliberate use of memorization strategies. – From Author's Abstract.

881. HARRINGTON, DAVID M. (Univ. of California, Santa Cruz); BLOCK, JACK; & BLOCK, JEANNE H. **Predicting creativity in preadolescence from divergent thinking in early childhood.** Journal of Personality and Social Psychology, 1983, **45**, 609–623.
Among the major results of this study, it was found that sixth-grade teachers were able to provide construct-validating creativity evaluations of their students, scores based on divergent

thinking (DT) tests administered in early childhood correlated with teacher-evaluated creativity in preadolescence, and DT responses in early childhood clearly measured characteristics related to preadolescent creativity. – From the Article.

882. HARRIS, MARGARET (Birkbeck Coll., Malet, London, England); JONES, DAVID; & GRANT, JULIA. **The nonverbal context of mothers' speech to infants.** First Language, 1983, **4**, 21–30.
Infants were videotaped twice between 6 and 10 months of age while engaged in a free play session with their mothers. Division of the mothers' utterances into verbal episodes revealed that for all mothers, the majority of episodes began in response to something done by the child: from session 1 to session 2, the number of episodes initiated by a shift in the child's gaze decreased and the number initiated by a child action increased. – From Authors' Abstract.

883. HEMMER, KARIN (Technische Univ. Braunschweig, Germany); KRÄMER, DAGMAR; & WILKENING, FRIEDRICH. **Zur Entwicklung der analytischen Wahrnehmung: Eine Test der Separabilitätshypothese.** Zeitschrift für Entwicklungspsychologie und Pädagogische Psychologie, 1983, **15**, 89–100.
The separability hypothesis of perceptual development was tested by functional measurement. Children 5 and 10 years old and adults judged both integral and separable stimuli. Integral stimuli were the nose of a teddy bear, varying in color and brightness. Separable stimuli were manikin figures. Five-year-olds perceived the separable stimuli in an analytic mode; they extracted the dimensional structure as well as the adults. – From Authors' Abstract.

884. HERMAN, JAMES F. (Washington Univ.); NORTON, LAURA M.; & ROTH, STEPHEN F. **Children and adults' distance estimations in a large-scale environment: effects of time and clutter.** Journal of Experimental Child Psychology, 1983, **36**, 453–470.
Subjects ages 8, 10, 12, and 19 walked a straight line distance through a large-scale environment and were then asked to estimate the time taken to traverse each half of the walk and to estimate the distance between objects along the walk. Time and distance estimates were related, and there was no clutter effect. There were no consistent developmental differences. – From Authors' Abstract.

885. HORAN, PATRICIA F., & ROSSER, ROSEMARY A. (Univ. of Arizona). **The function of response mode in the coordination of perspectives.** Contemporary Educational Psychology, 1983, **8**, 347–354.
It was concluded that while both 3- and 4-year-olds were able to demonstrate perspective-taking competence, the 3-year-olds performed better with the turning task; 4-year-olds were equally successful in either mode. – From Authors' Abstract.

886. HORGAN, JAMES S. (Univ. of Illinois, Chicago). **Measurement bias in memory for movement by mentally retarded and nonretarded children.** Perceptual and Motor Skills, 1983, **56**, 663–670.
An angular dependent measure is the most direct representation of arm movement, regardless of differences in arm length. – From the Article.

887. HOROWITZ, FRANCES DEGEN (Univ. of Kansas). **A behavioral alternative to an ecological approach to understanding the development of knowing in infancy: a commentary.** Developmental Review, 1983, **3**, 405–409.
While the use of affordances is regarded as an improvement over the concept of representation, an argument is put forth that a more parsimonious and scientifically useful approach to the development of knowing in infancy is to be found in a behavioral analysis of a learned association of stimulus cues with behavior patterns. – From Author's Abstract.

888. JENKINS, JOSEPH R. (Univ. of Washington), & DIXON, ROBERT. **Vocabulary learning.** Contemporary Educational Psychology, 1983, **8**, 237–260.

Neither direct instruction of meanings nor learning word meanings from context seems to account for the growth in vocabulary that is thought to occur during the elementary school years. – From Authors' Abstract.

889. JOHNSON, D. B. (Harvard Univ.). **Self-recognition in infants.** Infant Behavior and Development, 1983, **6**, 211–222.
Infants 12–26 months old viewed a TV image of self or other infant before and after application of a mark to the nose. Older infants displayed mark-directed behavior, which may be an indication of self-recognition. – S. Thomas.

890. JOHNSON, JAMES E. (Pennsylvania State Univ.). **Context effects on preschool children's symbolic behavior.** Journal of Genetic Psychology, 1983, **143**, 259–268.
Preschoolers were tested individually for symbolic use of objects when realistic props or no props were present. Three-year-olds but not 4-year-olds performed less well when realistic props were within sight. Older preschoolers were rated as more imaginative than younger preschoolers, while children were rated more physically active with realistic props present. – From Author's Abstract.

891. KATO, TADAAKI (Univ. Hosp., Univ. of Tokyo, Japan); TAKAHASHI, ETSUJIRO; SAWADA, KEIJI; KOBAYASHI, NOBORU; WATANABE, TOMIO; & ISHII, TAKEMOCHI. **A computer analysis of infant movements synchronized with adult speech.** Pediatric Research, 1983, **17**, 625–628.
Results suggest not only the ability of a neonate to move his body synchronously with his mother's speech, but also that a mother talks to her infant by reacting to his movements. – Adapted from Authors' Abstract.

892. KAUSLER, DONALD H. (Univ. of Missouri, Columbia), & HAKAMI, MALEKEH K. **Memory for activities: adult age differences and intentionality.** Developmental Psychology, 1983, **19**, 889–894.
Young and elderly adults were given varied memory tests that varied along the rote–cognitive dimension. Half of the participants were forewarned of the subsequent memory test (intentional learning); half were not (incidental learning). Overall, younger adults remembered better, but the magnitude of the age difference was small for cognitively demanding tasks and pronounced for less demanding activities. Memory was unaffected by the forewarning variable for both age groups. – From Authors' Abstract.

893. KEE, DANIEL W. (California State Univ., Fullerton); NAKAYAMA, SUSAN Y.; CERVANTES, MARIA; & OSAZE, JANA D. **Automatic conceptual encoding of printed verbal material: assessment of population differences.** Contemporary Educational Psychology, 1984, **9**, 74–83.
Population differences in buildup and release from proactive interference were not detected between low-SES black and middle-SES white fourth-grade children. – From the Article.

894. KEIL, FRANK C. (Cornell Univ.). **On the emergence of semantic and conceptual distinctions.** Journal of Experimental Psychology: General, 1983, **112**, 357–385.
Three studies investigated how children's knowledge of certain conceptual distinctions emerges and how this knowledge becomes mapped onto the natural language terms and predicates relevant to those distinctions. The distinctions were between the ontological categories of events and all physical objects and between the ontological categories of animals, plants, and other physical objects. Two patterns of knowledge development were seen that depended on the nature of the distinction learned. In the events/physical-objects case, a totally new distinction was discovered and was first learned by means of the predicates relevant to that distinction. – From Author's Abstract.

895. KELLMAN, PHILIP J. (Swarthmore Coll.), & SPELKE, ELIZABETH S. **Perception of partly occluded objects in infancy.** Cognitive Psychology, 1983, **15**, 483–524.

Infants 4 months old sometimes could perceive the unity of a partly hidden object. In each of a series of experiments, infants were habituated to 1 object whose top and bottom were visible but whose center was occluded by a nearer object. They were then tested with a fully visible continuous object and with 2 fully visible object pieces with a gap where the occluder had been. Patterns of dishabituation suggested that infants perceived the boundaries of a partly hidden object by analyzing the movements of its surfaces; infants perceived a connected object when its ends moved in a common translation behind the occluder. Infants did not appear to perceive a connected object when its visible parts were stationary, its color was homogeneous, its edges were aligned, and its shape was simple and regular. These findings do not support the thesis, from gestalt psychology, that object perception first arises as a consequence of a tendency to perceive the simplest, most regular configuration, or the Piagetian thesis that object perception depends on the prior coordination of action. Perception of objects may depend on an inherent conception of what an object is. – Authors' Abstract.

896. KEMLER, DEBORAH G. (Swarthmore Coll.). **Exploring and reexploring issues of integrality, perceptual sensitivity, and dimensional salience.** Journal of Experimental Child Psychology, 1983, **36**, 365–379.
A variety of findings and lines of inference converge on the conclusion that, in young children, the use of overall similarity relations to organize perception and cognition predominates over the use of dimensional relations (and that the relative balance between these stimulus relations changes in development). – From Author's Abstract.

897. KIELAR, MARIA (Jagiellonian Univ., Cracow, Poland). **Developmental and environmental differentiation of concepts of type.** Psychologia Wychowawcza (Educational Psychology: Bimonthly of the Polish Teachers Union), 1982, **25**, 488–500.
Research is reported on the internal structure of type concepts and their structural differentiation as related to age and social-educational environment. The data analyzed were results of the Rey test on measurement of lexical accessibility in the area of superordinate names, and of the Rosch test on exemplars of superordinate categories. Pupils from grades 2, 4, 6, and 8 were examined, 100 from rural environments and 400 from urban. The results support the Rosch hypothesis on the existence of a relatively stable core of meaning as indicated by best examples of a category. The findings speak for a hierarchical, multilevel structure of type concepts. – From Author's Abstract.

898. KINGMA, JOHANNES (Twente Univ. of Technology, Netherlands). **A comparison of four methods of scaling for the acquisition of early number concept.** Journal of General Psychology, 1984, **110**, 23–45.
The stochastic Mokken scale analysis was the most suitable for constructing a developmental scale of number comparison tasks. – From Author's Abstract.

899. KINGMA, JOHANNES (Twente Univ. of Technology, Netherlands). **A criterion problem: the use of different operationalizations in seriation research.** Perceptual and Motor Skills, 1982, **55**, 1303–1316.
Children in grades K-6 were given 8 seriation tasks. With the use of the new-Genevan criteria, no clear distinction could be made between partial and operational seriators. – From Author's Abstract.

900. KINGMA, JOHANNES (Twente Univ. of Technology, Netherlands). **Length seriation and serial correspondence.** Perceptual and Motor Skills, 1983, **56**, 603–610.
Most kindergartners solved serial-correspondence tasks by means of direct correspondence, whereas children in grades 1–6 frequently used double seriation as a solution strategy. – Adapted from Author's Abstract.

901. KITCHENER, KAREN STROHM (Univ. of Denver). **Cognition, metacognition, and epistemic cognition: a three-level model of cognitive processing.** Human Development, 1983, **26**, 222–232.

At the first level, individuals compute, memorize, read, etc. At the second level, individuals monitor their own progress when they are engaged in first-order tasks. At the third level, individuals reflect on the limits of knowing, the certainty of knowing, and criteria of knowing. – From Author's Abstract.

902. KONOVALOV, V. F., & BOURKOVETSKAYA, ZH. I. **Peculiarities of functioning of the "biological clock" in schoolchildren.** Questions of Psychology (translation of Russian title), 1983, **3,** 106–111.
A procedure involving mono- and binaural listening to tones presented with 15-sec intervals has been performed on schoolchildren with the view to compare the degree of participation of the left and right brain hemispheres in functioning of the "biological clock." In 7–8-year-old boys, reproduction of the interstimulus pause has been accompanied by the binaural effect and by the effect of the left ear. In girls of the same age, the monaural effect is present. A monaural effect independent of age is characteristic of 16–17-year-old subjects. – From Authors' Abstract.

903. KORTHASE, KATHLEEN M. (Elmhurst Coll.), & TRENHOLME, IRENE. **Children's perceptions of age and physical attractiveness.** Perceptual and Motor Skills, 1983, **56,** 895–900.
Perceived physical attractiveness decreased as perceived age increased. – Ed.

904. KREITLER, SHULAMITH; ZIGLER, EDWARD (Yale Univ.); & KREITLER, HANS. **The effect of memory and abstractive integration on children's probability learning.** Child Development, 1983, **54,** 1487–1496.
Assessments were made of the memory and abstractive integration skills of boys and girls 6–7 years old, from both low- and middle-SES classes. Levels of these skills were related to correct responding (maximizing), systematic alternation, and perseveration on a 3-choice, partially reinforced discrimination-learning task. Memory was found to be related negatively to systematic alternation, and abstractive integration level was positively related to maximizing scores. – From Authors' Abstract.

905. LAMB, MICHAEL E. (Univ. of Utah); FRODI, ANN M.; HWANG, CARL-PHILIP; & FRODI, MAJT E. **Interobserver and test-retest reliability of Rothbart's Infant Behavior Questionnaire.** Scandinavian Journal of Psychology, 1983, **24,** 153–156.
Results suggest that the IBQ in a Swedish translation may be a reliable and valid instrument. – From Authors' Abstract.

906. LANE, DAVID S. (Oklahoma State Univ.). **Using observation and action instruction to facilitate conditional reasoning performance in early adolescents.** Journal of Early Adolescence, 1983, **3,** 335–347.
Early adolescent students received 2 50-min periods of instruction designed to increase their conditional syllogistic performance. Results confirmed that the basic instructional method is a viable way to positively affect early adolescents' reasoning performance. – From Author's Abstract.

907. LAWSON, ANTON E. (Arizona State Univ.); LAWSON, DAVID I.; & LAWSON, CHESTER A. **Proportional reasoning and the linguistic abilities required for hypothetico-deductive reasoning.** Journal of Research in Science Teaching, 1984, **21,** 119–131.
This result supports the hypothesis that the internalization of linguistic elements of argumentation is a prerequisite for proportional reasoning and by inference other advanced reasoning schemata as well. – From Authors' Abstract.

908. LAWSON, KATHERINE R. (Albert Einstein Coll. of Medicine); RUFF, HOLLY A.; McCARTON-DAUM, CECELIA; KURTZBERG, DIANE; & VAUGHAN, HERBERT G., JR. **Auditory–Visual responsiveness in full-term and preterm infants.** Developmental Psychology, 1984, **20,** 120–127.

After familiarization with a silent moving object, 3-month-old full-term infants recognized the object when it was stationary. When sound accompanied the moving object during familiarization, infants showed increased attention to the object but no subsequent recognition of that object. Neither high- nor low-risk preterms, at a comparable conceptional age, recognized the objects under any condition, but the low-risk preterms did show greater attention to the moving objects with sound. At 6 months only the high-risk preterms were different from the full-term infants. – From Authors' Abstract.

909. LEE, YEONG K., & LEE; SEONG-SOO (Univ. of British Columbia, Vancouver, British Columbia, Canada). **Multidimensional unfolding of children's causal beliefs: one aspect of construct validation.** Applied Psychological Measurement, 1983, **3**, 323–332.
A 2-dimensional assessment device of children's causal beliefs was constructed on the basis of 4 perceived causes of success and failure consequences, given 12 situations, each describing circumstances for a consequence. The internal analysis recovered the 2 causal dimensions perceived by children as hypothesized by the model. – From Authors' Abstract.

910. LEFEBVRE-PINARD, MONIQUE (Univ. of Quebec, Montreal, Quebec, Canada). **Understanding and auto-control of cognitive functions: implications for the relationship between cognition and behavior.** International Journal of Behavioral Development, 1983, **6**, 15–35.
The paper reviews cognitive psychology, particularly with respect to problems of consciousness. It notes the poorly understood relationship between cognition and behavior. – Adapted from Author's Abstract.

911. LEIFER, J. S., & LEWIS, M. (Rutgers Medical School). **Maternal speech to normal and handicapped children: a look at question-asking behavior.** Infant Behavior and Development, 1983, **6**, 175–187.
Mothers of handicapped children gauge their speech to the child's language level, a process viewed as having a facilitative effect on language learning. – From Authors' Abstract.

912. LEŚNIAK, TERESA, & LEGIEN, MAREK (Wroclaw Univ., Poland). **Application of a graphological method in assessment of children's reading and writing readiness.** Psychologia Wychowawcza (Educational Psychology: Bimonthly of the Polish Teachers Union), 1983, **26**, 287–302.
Children attending kindergarten groups were studied. The psychological tests used were the Bender-Koppitz, KSI, and Draw-a-Man tests, as well as phonematic tests. A graphological test was specially constructed. Criminalistic interpretation principles were used in assessment of the latter test. A correlation was found between the psychological and the graphological assessments. – From Authors' Abstract.

913. LIGEZA, MARIA (Jagiellonian Univ., Cracow, Poland). **The cognitive function of questions in the early years.** Psychologia Wychowawcza (Educational Psychology: Bimonthly of the Polish Teachers Union), 1982, **25**, 501–519.
The article reports analyses of the cognitive function of questions in young children. The study was a continuation of Szuman's research on the significance of questions in the child's development. The data consisted of 5,085 single questions and 1,775 question series produced by 4 children from 18 months to 6 years of age, as noted in speech diaries. – From Author's Abstract.

914. LIGHT, LEAH L., & ZELINSKI, ELIZABETH M. (Univ. of Southern California, Los Angeles). **Memory for spatial information in young and old adults.** Developmental Psychology, 1983, **19**, 901–906.
Young and older adults studied a map containing 12 structures. Half of the subjects in each age group were asked to remember both the structures and their locations (intentional learning), and the remaining half was told to learn structures (incidental learning). Both age and test expectations affected memory for locations, with older people and people in the incidental groups performing more poorly. – From Authors' Abstract.

915. LIGHT, PAUL (Univ. of Southampton, England), & GILMOUR, AMANDA. **Conservation or conversation? Contextual facilitation of inappropriate conservation judgments.** Journal of Experimental Child Psychology, 1983, **36**, 356–363.
Six-year-olds made a judgment as to the equality in area of 2 square fields, each made up from 8 interlinked fence sections. Then the child saw 1 of the fields transformed into a rectangle, without the fences being disconnected, and was asked for a second judgment as to the equality of the fields. In the modified condition, the transformation made sense in terms of creating a space for the farmhouse. Higher levels of conserving judgments were obtained in the modified than in the standard condition. – From Authors' Abstract.

916. LINN, MARCIA C. (Univ. of California, Berkeley). **Content, context, and process in reasoning during adolescence: selecting a model.** Journal of Early Adolescence, 1983, **3**, 63–82.
Content, context, and process influences on reasoning need to be incorporated into models of adolescent reasoning performance. Both models from cognitive science and models from philosophy of science offer promise. – From the Article.

917. LINN, MARCIA C. (Univ. of California, Berkeley); CLEMENT, CATHY; & PULOS, STEVEN. **Is it formal if it's not physics? (The influence of content on formal reasoning).** Journal of Research in Science Teaching, 1983, **20**, 755–770.
Subjects 13, 15, and 17 years old received both laboratory and naturalistic content tasks that required ability to control variables. Expectations about the variables in each task were measured. Results revealed that 8%-20% of the variance in performance was associated with task content. – From Authors' Abstract.

918. LUFTIG, RICHARD L. (Miami Univ., Oxford). **Variables influencing the learnability of individual signs and sign lexicons: a review of the literature.** Journal of Psycholinguistic Research, 1983, **12**, 361–376.
This paper reviews existing literature in the area of sign learning and identifies psycholinguistic, psychological, and production features that may influence learning and recall of individual signs as well as sign lexicons. – From Author's Abstract.

919. McFARLAND, CARL E., JR. (Univ. of Alabama, Birmingham); DUNCAN, EDWARD; & BRUNO, JAN MARIE. **Developmental aspects of the generation effect.** Journal of Experimental Child Psychology, 1983, **36**, 413–428.
The developmental emergence of the "generation effect" was dependent on both encoding orientation and the type of retention task employed. A substantial generation effect first emerged (7-year-olds) for standard recognition in the semantic condition. A similar effect for recall was evident for 9-year-olds. – From Authors' Abstract.

920. McLOUGHLIN, CAVEN S. (Kent State Univ.), & GULLO, DOMINIC F. **Perceptual, motor, memory, and quantitative elements of language behavior: differences between 3- and 4-year-old performance.** Perceptual and Motor Skills, 1982, **55**, 1038.
Verbal performance was significantly related to quantitative and memory scales at the 3-year-old level and perceptual, quantitative, and motor scales for the 4-year-old age group. – From the Article.

921. MAHLIOS, MARC C. (SUNY, Binghamton), & D'ANGELO, KAREN. **Group Embedded Figures Test: psychometric data on children.** Perceptual and Motor Skills, 1983, **56**, 423–426.

922. MARTIN, SUE (Univ. of Arkansas, Fayetteville), & COWLES, MILLY. **Locus of control among children in various educational environments.** Perceptual and Motor Skills, 1983, **56**, 831–834.

The Stephens–Delys Reinforcement Contingency Interview showed significant sex, family income, and educational program interactions for locus of control in 6–7-year-olds. – Ed.

923. MATCZAK, ANNA (Univ. of Warsaw, Poland). **Individual properties of cognitive functioning as indicators of creativity.** Psychologia Wychowawcza (Educational Psychology: Bimonthly of the Polish Teachers Union), 1982, **25,** 1–14.
The article discusses the connection between individual differences in terms of creativity and properties of cognitive style, in particular, field independence, tolerance of cognitive instability, and reflectivity vs. impulsivity. A survey of the relevant empirical findings is presented with reference to the author's own research conducted mainly on secondary school students. – From Author's Abstract.

924. MAY, JO WHITTEN (Winston-Salem State Univ.), & MAY, J. GAYLORD. **Effects of age on color preference for black and white by infants and young children.** Perceptual and Motor Skills, 1983, **56,** 323–330.
As age increased, young Afro-Americans but not Euro-Americans showed an increase in their preference for the color white. – From Authors' Abstract.

925. MERVIS, CAROLYN B. (Univ. of Massachusetts). **Acquisition of a lexicon.** Contemporary Educational Psychology, 1983, **8,** 210–236.
The paper considers the early acquisition of a concrete object lexicon. Children are able to make an initial mapping between object words and their referents relatively easily when a transparent relationship between the 2 is present. – From the Article.

926. MEYERS, LAWRENCE S. (California State Univ., Sacramento); ANDERSEN, COLLEEN; & LIDDICOAT, CATHARINE M. **Perceived communication needs of developmentally delayed nonspeaking children.** The Psychological Record, 1984, **34,** 55–68.
The study described the communication needs of a group of school-aged nonspeaking children and young adults from the perspective of those who knew the students best. These needs were found to span 4 dimensions. – From the Article.

927. MILLER, KEVIN (Michigan State Univ.), & GELMAN, ROCHEL. **The child's representation of number: a multidimensional scaling analysis.** Child Development, 1983, **54,** 1470–1479.
Judgments of similarities between numbers were solicited from children in grades K, 3, and 6 as well as from adults. Children become sensitive to an expanding set of numerical relations during this period, although even kindergartners appear to understand the importance of magnitude as a basis for judging similarity between numbers. Results implicate the acquisition of numerical skills and operations such as counting, addition, and multiplication in this broadening of the concept of number. – From Authors' Abstract.

928. MIMS, MICHAEL (Southeastern Louisiana Univ.); CANTOR, JOAN H.; & RILEY, CHRISTINE A. **The development of representation skills in transitive reasoning based on relations of equality and inequality.** Child Development, 1983, **54,** 1457–1469.
Subjects were trained to remember premise relations concerning the heights of colored sticks. Kindergarten, third-grade, and adult subjects were successful on all inferences involving only equalities or only inequalities across the various conditions and procedures. A dramatic developmental increase in performance was found on inferences based on the combination of equality and inequality relations. In most cases, accuracy on inferences was highly correlated with the ability to remember premises. – From Authors' Abstract.

929. MINAMI, HIROFUMI (Hiroshima Univ., Japan). **Developmental differences in distortion of visual pattern representation: explanation and prediction by M-space model.** Hiroshima Forum for Psychology, 1981, **8,** 91–103.
The discrepancy between the predicted and the obtained results suggested that the stimulus presentation condition might have interacted with the general effects of M-space and the task demand. Two commentaries follow the article. – From Author's Abstract.

930.   MOE, GLENN L. (Washington School District, 8610 N. 19th Ave., Phoenix), & HARRIS, JERRY D. **Effects of encoding and retrieval strategies on the recall of learning disabled and normal children.** Journal of General Psychology, 1983, **109**, 233–246.
LD children recalled fewer pictures than normal children except under the cued recall condition. Clustering scores for LD and normal children did not differ. – From Authors' Abstract.

931.   MONTARE, ALBERTO (William Paterson Coll.). **Temporal correlates of children's discrimination learning.** Journal of Psychology, 1983, **115**, 137–144.
The results indicate that (a) temporal performance tends to be less variable than learning performance, and (b) a significant, negative correlation exists between mean time-estimation scores and mean learning scores. – From Author's Abstract.

932.   MYERS, FLORENCE L. (Adelphi Univ.), & MYERS, RUSSELL W. **Perception of stress contrasts in semantic and nonsemantic contexts by children.** Journal of Psycholinguistic Research, 1983, **12**, 327–338.
Task I consisted of discriminating whether 2 syllables in bisyllabic nonsense words had the same or different stress patterns. Task II consisted of sentence pairs, for half of which the first sentence in each pair provided appropriate lexical as well as stress patterns for the second sentence. The first sentence in the remaining sentence pairs provided the appropriate lexical context but an inappropriate stress context for the second sentence. Results yielded lawfulness in the developmental trends of children in grades K-6 for both tasks. – From Authors' Abstract.

933.   NACHSHON, ISRAEL (Bar-Ilan Univ., Ramat-Gan, Israel). **Directional preferences of bilingual children.** Perceptual and Motor Skills, 1983, **56**, 747–750.
Children in grades 1–6 showed increasing left-right directional preference to all stimuli but Hebrew letters. Data suggest the effects of reading and writing habits on directional preferences. – From Author's Abstract.

934.   NELSON, KATHERINE (CUNY Graduate Ctr.). **Concepts, words, and experiments: comment on "When is a cup not a cup?" by Anderson and Prawat.** Merrill-Palmer Quarterly, 1983, **29**, 387–394.
Anderson and Prawat's conclusion that they have disconfirmed Nelson's theory is challenged on the grounds that they have mischaracterized Nelson's theory and that their data are not relevant to concept formation. – From Author's Abstract.

935.   NELSON-SCHNEIDER, AUDREY (Univ. of Colorado). **Inductive acuity and the acquisition of language.** Journal of Psycholinguistic Research, 1983, **12**, 263–273.
Children who are superior inductors scored higher on semantic tests but not on syntactic tests. – From Author's Abstract.

936.   O'CONNOR, MARY J. (Univ. of California, Los Angeles); COHEN, SARALE; & PARMELEE, ARTHUR H. **Infant auditory discrimination in preterm and full-term infants as a predictor of 5-year intelligence.** Developmental Psychology, 1984, **20**, 159–165.
At 4 months, cardiac response to repetitive and novel auditory stimulation was assessed. Children were followed until the age of 5 years, and intellectual performance was measured using the Stanford–Binet Intelligence Scale. A correlation of .60 was found between infant novelty response scores and 5-year intelligence scores. – From Authors' Abstract.

937.   OFFENBACH, STUART I. (Purdue Univ.). **The concept of dimension in research on children's learning.** Monographs of the Society for Research in Child Development, 1983, **48**(6), 1–71.
The first goal was to show that the stimuli in discrimination learning tasks could and should be specified more precisely and completely. To that end, I conducted 2 experiments applying multidimensional scaling analyses to children's and adults' judgments of color (Experiment 1) and

form (Experiment 2) similarities. The results of Experiment 1 showed a trend toward better differentiation of the color attribute from age 4 through the college adult level. The identical developmental pattern was observed in Experiment 2 with the form attribute. The second major goal of this research was to show that more precisely defined stimulus attributes would add to the developmental literature concerned with learning. Experiment 3 tested Kendler's proposition that "dimensional dominance" is a function of stimulus similarity. The data did not support Kendler's position. – From Author's Abstract.

938. O'HARE, DAVID (Univ. of Otago, Box 56, Dunedin, New Zealand), & WESTWOOD, HELEN. **Features of style classification: a multivariate experimental analysis of children's responses to drawings.** Developmental Psychology, 1984, **20**, 150–158.
Subjects were asked to judge the similarity of 12 line drawings which were specially prepared to vary along 3 dimensions salient in adults' discriminations. Analyses confirmed that the youngest children were able to make systematic stylistic comparisons utilizing the 3 dimensions. – From Authors' Abstract.

939. OLOFSSON, AKE (Univ. of Umea, Sweden), & LUNDBERG, INGVAR. **Can phonemic awareness be trained in kindergarten?** Scandinavian Journal of Psychology, 1983, **24**, 35–44.
A clear improvement in the ability to segment and blend 3-phoneme words was observed in the highly structured training condition, especially among the children with poor pretest performance, while no clear changes from pre- to posttest were found in the other groups. – From Authors' Abstract.

940. OLOWU, AKINSOLA A. (Univ. of Ife, Ile-Ife, Nigeria). **Age trend of cognitive style among Nigerian preschool children.** Journal of Psychology, 1984, **116**, 7–10.
An Embedded Figure Test was administered to 3–5-year-old children. Field independence increased with age for both sexes. – From Author's Abstract.

941. OLSON, SHERYL L. (Univ. of Maine); BATES, JOHN E.; & BAYLES, KATHRYN. **Mother–Infant interaction and the development of individual differences in children's cognitive competence.** Developmental Psychology, 1984, **20**, 166–179.
The antecedents of individual differences in children's cognitive/language competence at 24 months were assessed using multivariate methods at ages 6, 13, and 24 months. Mother–child warm, verbal interactions at each age were associated with a composite index of child competence at 24 months. A path analysis showed that 40% of the variance in competence was explained by interaction at 3 ages and SES. – From Authors' Abstract.

942. OSBORNE, ROGER J. (Univ. of Waikato, Hamilton, New Zealand), & COSGROVE, MARK M. **Children's conceptions of the changes of state of water.** Journal of Research in Science Teaching, 1983, **20**, 825–838.
The results indicate that children do have ideas about the changes of state of water which are quite different from the views of scientists. It would also appear that these ideas can sometimes be influenced in unintended ways by science teaching. – From Authors' Abstract.

943. OZIOKO, JULIUS O. C. (Univ. of Nigeria, Nsukka, Nigeria). **A comparison of reversal and extra dimensional shifts in Igbo (Nigerian) children.** International Journal of Behavioral Development, 1983, **6**, 197–203.
Reversal shift was more difficult for the younger subjects, but performance improved as age increased. The extradimensional shift did not follow a developmental trend; the 7-year-olds found it more difficult than either the 4-year- or 10-year-olds. – From Author's Abstract.

944. PÊCHEUX, MARIE-GERMAINE (Laboratoire de Psychologie Expérimentale, 28, rue Serpente, Paris, France), & LÉCUYER, ROGER. **Habituation rate and free exploration tempo in 4-month-old infants.** International Journal of Behavioral Development, 1983, **6**, 37–50.

Four-month-old infants were habituated to 4 stimuli (2 geometric patterns and 2 faces) successively, in 2 sessions, and were observed in a free-exploration situation. The number of trials required to reach criterion in the habituation situations were not correlated, but total looking times to criterion were. – From Authors' Abstract.

945. PERONE, MICHAEL (Univ. of North Carolina, Wilmington), & BARON, ALAN. **Reduced age differences in omission errors after prolonged exposure to response pacing contingencies.** Developmental Psychology, 1983, **19**, 915–923.
Operant methods were used to study older and younger men under schedules in which monetary reinforcement depended on emission of complex response sequences. In 1 component, a new sequence was required for each session, but in the other component the sequence never changed. Disruption was greater in acquisition of novel sequences than in performance of the established 1 and was evidenced more in failures to respond (omission errors) than in commission of errors. After extended exposure to each of several time limits, age differences were substantially reduced. – From Authors' Abstract.

946. PETROS, TOM (Univ. of North Dakota); TABOR, LILA; COONEY, TERESA; & CHABOT, ROBERT J. **Adult age differences in sensitivity to semantic structure of prose.** Developmental Psychology, 1983, **19**, 907–914.
Young and older adults from low- and high-education populations heard narrative passages and immediately recalled them. Younger adults remembered more than older adults, but all subjects favored main ideas. Also, all could identify the important information. – From Authors' Abstract.

947. PEZDEK, KATHY (Claremont Graduate School). **Memory for items and their spatial locations by young and elderly adults.** Developmental Psychology, 1983, **19**, 895–900.
Young (M age = 17 years) and elderly (M age = 68 years) adults studied a display of 16 items in specific locations. Items were either small objects or the 1-word verbal label for each. The young adults were more accurate on both items recalled and locations recalled. The age differences in memory are explained in terms of age differences in encoding and rehearsal strategies. – From Author's Abstract.

948. PISSANOS, BECKY W. (Auburn Univ.); MOORE, JANE B.; & REEVE, T. GILMOUR. **Age, sex, and body composition as predictors of children's performance on basic motor abilities and health-related fitness items.** Perceptual and Motor Skills, 1983, **56**, 71–77.
Results for students in grades 1–3 indicated that age was a significant factor in predicting performance on most variables. Sex and body composition predicted few variables. – Adapted from Authors' Abstract.

949. PITT, RUTH B. (Univ. of Minnesota). **Development of a general problem-solving schema in adolescence and early adulthood.** Journal of Experimental Psychology: General, 1983, **112**, 547–584.
A model of problem solving incorporating both information-processing and Piagetian paradigms was used to analyze verbal protocols from tenth graders and college juniors. Twenty-four subroutines measured overall, heuristic, and strategic processing. Although all groups used the same general heuristic and basic strategies, tenth graders defined problems inadequately and generated ill-formed, inaccurate hypotheses. – From Author's Abstract.

950. PLATT, CAROLE BUTLER (Univ. of Denver), & MACWHINNEY, BRIAN. **Error assimilation as a mechanism in language learning.** Journal of Child Language, 1983, 1 401–414.
Children were asked to judge their own or other children's sentences as correct or incorrect. Significantly fewer corrections were made in the sentences with subject-generated errors than in the sentences with similar errors or "baby errors."—From Authors' Abstract.

951. PLICHTOVÁ, JANA (Slovak Academy of Sciences, Kocelova 821 08, Bratislava, Czechoslovakia). **Training of memory strategy and its effect on recall.** Studia Psychologica, 1983, **25,** 271–286.
Does categorization strategy improve retrieval or recall, and can categorization strategy be successfully rehearsed? Training of categorization strategy proved effective only in adults and in eighth-form students of above-average intelligence, while more complex degrees of training yielded better results in the initial stages of learning and in subjects of a relatively lower intellectual level. – From Author's Abstract.

952. POULSON, CLAIRE L. (Vanderbilt Univ., Peabody Coll.). **Differential reinforcement of other-than-vocalization as a control procedure in the conditioning of infant vocalization rate.** Journal of Experimental Child Psychology, 1983, **36,** 471–489.
Mothers of 2 1/2–3-month-old infants provided social reinforcement for their infants' vocalization under 2 schedules: continuous reinforcement (CRF) and differential reinforcement of other-than-vocalization. In a repeated-reversal single-subject experimental design, all infants produced systematically higher vocalization rates during CRF. – From Author's Abstract.

953. PRAWAT, Richard S. (Michigan State Univ.), & ANDERSON, ARIEL L. H. **A reply to Nelson's comments on "When is a cup not a cup?"** Merrill-Palmer Quarterly, 1983, **29,** 395–397.

954. PRZETACZNIKOWA, MARIA (Jagiellonian Univ., Cracow, Poland). **Studies of Professor Stefan Szuman on child language development and their continuations in the Crawcow Centre.** Psychologia Wychowawcza (Educational Psychology: Bimonthly of the Polish Teachers Union), 1982, **25,** 474–487.
The article reviews the research on child speech development conducted at the Jagiellonian University by Professor Stefan Szuman and sketches the trends in which the research is being continued in the Cracow Centre. – From Author's Abstract.

955. PSTRUŽINOVÁ, JAROSLAVA (Pedagogický ústav J. A. Komenského ČSAV, Praha, Czechoslovakia). **K otázkám rozboru verbálních asociací** [On the analysis of verbal associations]. Československá Psychologie, 1983, **27,** 59–65.
The paper presents and interprets some of the results of an empirical study of the verbal ability of third graders. It concentrates especially on verbal associations that were observed by 2 subtests—free paired associations and completion of sentences—as part of a series of subtests used in the study. – From Author's Abstract.

956. RAKOWSKA, ALICJA (Higher School of Pedagogy, Cracow, Poland). **Characteristic features of syntactic structures in children with mild mental retardation.** Psychologia Wychowawcza (Educational Psychology: Bimonthly of the Polish Teachers Union), 1983, **26,** 327–338.
Spoken linguistic material (over 30,000 words), obtained from mildly retarded children ages 7–12 years, was used to study abilities of these children to generate sentences. Comparisons were made among environments (urban, small town, village) and among school grades. – From Author's Abstract.

957. RAUSTE-VON WRIGHT, MAIJALIISA (Univ. of Turku, Finland). **"Maturity of thinking" of 15-year-old girls and boys as assessed from the reasons given for answers to questions about their beliefs.** Scandinavian Journal of Psychology, 1983, **24,** 67–74.
The reliability of the maturity of thinking (MOT) sum scale was high; MOT was unrelated to most of the ability tests included and to parents' standard of living, but was related to school achievement (including achievement 3 years later), teachers' ratings, and subjects' reading and TV-watching habits. – From Author's Abstract.

958. RESENDIZ, PEDRO SOLIS CAMARA, & FOX, ROBERT (Marquette Univ.). **Impulsive versus inefficient problem solving in retarded and nonretarded Mexican children.** Journal of Psychology, 1983, **114,** 187–191.

The results indicated that the MFFT was appropriate for use with Mexican retarded and nonretarded subjects. Comparisons between groups showed retarded performers to be less efficient information processors than nonretarded subjects. – From Authors' Abstract.

959. RICE, MABEL (Univ. of Kansas). **The role of television in language acquisition.** Developmental Review, 1983, **3**, 211–224.
The conventional view among developmental psychologists is that television viewing does not contribute to a young viewer's language acquisition. That assumption is challenged. Evidence is presented that suggests that children can learn about language as they view television: for example, from age 2, children attend to television and view in an active, purposeful manner. Some programs present dialogue in an attention-getting, content-redundant context. – From Author's Abstract.

960. RIDENOUR, MARCELLA V. (Temple Univ.). **Infant walkers: developmental tool or inherent danger.** Perceptual and Motor Skills, 1982, **55**, 1201–1202.
The infant walker does not accelerate the onset of walking and can be dangerous unless the infant is constantly supervised. – Adapted from the Article.

961. RIDENOUR, MARCELLA V. (Temple Univ.). **Influence of inter-rung distance on self-prediction and success.** Perceptual and Motor Skills, 1983, **56**, 751–754.
Rung distance did not affect the accuracy of 6-year-old boys' self-prediction of jumping success, but it did influence task success. – From Author's Abstract.

962. RINDEL, ROLF (Univ. Kaiserslautern, Germany). **Der lateralitätseffekt im Wahrscheinlichkeitslernen fünfjähriger rechts- und linkshändiger kinder** [Effect of laterality in probabilistic learning in 5-year-old right- and left-handed children]. Studia Psychologica, 1983, **25**, 133–139.
Righthanders show stronger initial and persistent preferences for their right hand than the lefthanders for their left hand. Lefthanders are more sensitive to the variation of the probability parameters. – From Author's Abstract.

963. ROBINSON, E. J., & ROBINSON, W. P. (Univ. of Bristol, 35 Berkeley Sq., Bristol, England). **Communication and metacognition: quality of children's instructions in relation to judgments about the adequacy of instructions and the locus of responsibility for communication failure.** Journal of Experimental Child Psychology, 1983, **36**, 305–320.
Communicative performance of 5–7-year-olds was assessed in terms of quality of instructions given for constructing a Lego model or a picture from felt pieces. Children with more advanced understanding about communication gave more detailed descriptions of pieces needed and supplied more information about positioning pieces. – From Authors' Abstract.

964. ROGERS, K. W. (Univ. of Sydney, New South Wales, Australia). **The development of children's concepts of time: the contributions of Piaget and other authors (part 3).** The Genetic Epistemologist, 1983, **12**, 11–23.

965. ROHWER, WILLIAM D., JR. (Univ. of California, Berkeley), & LITROWNIK, JAMES. **Age and individual differences in the learning of a memorization procedure.** Journal of Educational Psychology, 1983, **75**, 799–810.
A study of maintenance of an elaborative procedure following instruction given to 11- and 17-year-olds showed maintenance was equivalent across age on a task of low processing demand and was more complete among older students on a more demanding task. – From Authors' Abstract.

966. ROSS, SUSAN M. (Univ. of Wisconsin, Madison), & ROSS, LEONARD E. **The effects of onset and offset warning and post-target stimuli on the saccade latency of children and adults.** Journal of Experimental Child Psychology, 1983, **36**, 340–355.

Saccade latency was reduced when foveal stimulus onsets or offsets preceded the target. When stimulus onset occurred 100 msec after target onset, the stimulus interfered with responding, with this interference effect significantly greater for children than for adults. When stimuli were presented in the peripheral visual field, facilitation and interference effects were similar for children and adults. – From Authors' Abstract.

967. RUFF, HOLLY A. (Albert Einstein Coll. of Medicine). **Infants' manipulative exploration of objects: effects of age and object characteristics.** Developmental Psychology, 1984, **20,** 9–20.
Mouthing decreased with age, whereas more precise forms of manipulation increased. Infants adjusted their behavior to the particular characteristics of the objects. Decrements with increasing familiarization were also seen in most behaviors. Different kinds of manipulation were used to explore different changes in objects. – From Author's Abstract.

968. RUISEL, IMRICH (Slovak Academy Sciences SAS, 821 08 Bratislava, Kocelova, Czechoslovakia). **Referring of adjectives and memory.** Studia Psychologica, 1983, **25,** 311–314.
It was found that the items with positive emotional charge had prevailed in the recalled lists. Referring influences only the recall of positively oriented adjectives. – From Author's Abstract.

969. RUSSELL, JAMES (Univ. of Liverpool, England). **Nonverbal and verbal performance on a number conservation problem and a proposal about the determinants of nonconservation.** Educational Psychology, 1983, **3,** 107–113.
This study compared the ease of verbal and nonverbal versions of a number-conservation problem for 4–5-year-olds. The nonverbal task was the easier. Children's justifications showed that verbal processes may have been responsible for both correct and incorrect performance in many cases. – From Author's Abstract.

970. SARACHO, OLIVIA N. (Univ. of Maryland). **Assessing individual differences in young children.** Studies in Educational Evaluation, 1983, **8,** 229–236.
An assessment of cognitive styles provides an appraisal that extends the assessment of mental performance beyond the levels of achievement to patterns of cognitive functioning. – From the Article.

971. SAXBY, L. (Univ. of Waterloo, Ontario, Canada), & BRYDEN, M. P. **Left-ear superiority in children for processing auditory emotional material.** Developmental Psychology, 1984, **20,** 72–80.
Children in grades K, 4, and 8 reported on the emotional content and on the verbal content of dichotically presented sentences. A left-ear advantage for reporting on the emotional material and a right-ear advantage for reporting on the verbal material were shown. – From Authors' Abstract.

972. SCHAFFER, H. R. (Univ. of Strathclyde, Glasgow, Scotland); HEPBURN, ANNE; & COLLIS, G. M. **Verbal and nonverbal aspects of mothers' directives.** Journal of Child Language, 1983, **10,** 337–355.
Maternal directives to children ages 10 and 18 months were analyzed. No indication was found for this age range that verbal devices come to replace nonverbal ones. At both ages, most utterances were accompanied by some form of nonverbal behavior. – From Authors' Abstract.

973. SCHER, ANAT (Univ. of Calgary, Canada). **Position and axis features in young children's oblique judgments: partial replication.** Perceptual and Motor Skills, 1982, **55,** 1317–1318.
The representation assigned to obliques within a square display is characterized by the coding of position and axis information. Orientation comparisons are based on matching the coded information. As mental operations are limited, young children often do not respond correctly. – From Author's Abstract.

974. SCHIFF, WILLIAM (New York Univ.). **Conservation of length redux: a perceptual-linguistic phenomenon.** Child Development, 1983, **54,** 1497–1506.
Children 3 1/2–5 1/2 years old who were unable to conserve length with Piaget's classical task did conserve length with parallel nonverbal tasks. Preoperational children apparently fail verbal response tasks because they use an end-alignment criterion for applying the words "same length" to pairs of sticks or lines, and apply an end-protrusion criterion for the words "longer than" in similar situations. – From Author's Abstract.

975. SCHNEIDERMAN, MAITA H. (Univ. of Pennsylvania). **"Do what I mean, not what I say!" Changes in mothers' action-directives to young children.** Journal of Child Language, 1983, **10,** 357–367.
Children perceived as most limited in inferential skills elicited the most restricted input. External supports were removed gradually in response to the mother's perception of her child's increasing ability to draw extralinguistic inferences. – From Author's Abstract.

976. SCHULTZ, E. EUGENE, JR. (Univ. of North Carolina, Asheville). **Depth of processing by mentally retarded and MA-matched nonretarded individuals.** American Journal of Mental Deficiency, 1984, **88,** 307–313.
Retarded individuals required progressively more encoding time relative to nonretarded individuals as processing depth increased. Both encoding and recognition accuracy were equivalent for both groups. – From Author's Abstract.

977. SCHWARTZ, RICHARD G. (Purdue Univ.). **The role of action in early lexical acquisition.** First Language, 1983, **4,** 5–20.
These findings indicate that the relationship between action performance and lexical acquisition is not straightforward. In some respects (i.e., temporally) action performance appears to impede production, in some cases it appears to have no effect, and finally in others it appears to aid acquisition. Generally, the performance of referent actions appears to have little effect upon the acquisition of action words. – From the Article.

978. SCRUGGS, THOMAS E. (Utah State Univ.), & COHN, SANFORD J. **Learning characteristics of verbally gifted students.** Gifted Child Quarterly, 1983, **27,** 169–172.
There is no evidence that verbally gifted students learn in a manner that differs qualitatively from more typical individuals. – From the Article.

979. SEXTON, M. E. (Univ. of Massachusetts). **The development of the understanding of causality in infancy.** Infant Behavior and Development, 1983, **6,** 201–210.
Infants ages 11, 17, and 23 months viewed events caused by the mother, experimenter, or seemingly neither. Results were consistent with Piaget's theory of causality. – From Abstract by S. Thomas.

980. SHATZ, MARILYN (Univ. of Michigan); WELLMAN, HENRY M.; & SILBER, SHARON. **The acquisition of mental verbs: a systematic investigation of the first reference to mental state.** Cognition, 1983, **14,** 301–321.
Studies of 2-year-olds suggest that the earliest uses of mental verbs such as "think" and "know" are for conversational functions rather than for mental reference. The absence of mental state reference despite the linguistic knowledge necessary for reference suggests that young children lack awareness of mental states. – Adapted from Authors' Abstract.

981. SHERMAN, JULIA A. (WRI of Wisconsin, 3917 Plymouth, Madison). **Continuing in mathematics: a longitudinal study of the attitudes of high school girls.** Psychology of Women Quarterly, 1982, **7,** 132–140.
The mathematics attitudes of ninth-grade girls of similar intellect who subsequently took 1–4 years of college preparatory math were compared. Math-enrollment groups differed significantly on the following scales: Usefulness of Mathematics, Confidence in Learning Mathematics, Teacher (perceived attitude toward the student as a learner of mathematics), and Effec-

tance Motivation in Mathematics as assessed in grades 9 and 12 and on the Math as a Male Domain Scale as assessed in grade 12. From grade 9 to 12, scores on the Attitude toward Success in Math Scale became significantly more positive. – From Author's Abstract.

982. SHUGAR, GRACE WALES (Warsaw Univ., Warsaw, Poland). **Speech variation and the realization of social roles by preschoolers.** Psychologia Wychowawcza (Educational Psychology: Bimonthly of the Polish Teachers Union), 1981, **23**, 549–559.
By age 4, the child has already attained important communicative skills enabling him to adapt his speech to different partner types. Adaptation to listeners implies underlying abilities to take into account the perspective of others, an implication that is contrary to the prevailing view about the cognitive egocentrism of the preschool child. – From Author's Abstract.

983. SIEGEL, PAUL S. (Univ. of Alabama), & CRAWFORD, KATHERYN A. **Two-year follow-up study of discrimination learning by mentally retarded children.** American Journal of Mental Deficiency, 1983, **88**, 76–78.
Subjects were taught to discriminate the dimensions of a visual display using a matching-to-sample procedure that provided full verbal feedback of the reasons for successes and failures. A control group attempted the matching procedure but received no feedback. The trained subjects exhibited marked superiority in intradimensional transfer. Two years later, the trained subjects continued their advantage. – From Authors' Abstract.

984. SIMNER, MARVIN L. (Univ. of Western Ontario, London, Ontario, Canada). **The grammar of action and reversal errors in children's printing.** Developmental Psychology, 1984, **20**, 136–142.
Thirty-six left-handed and 36 right-handed kindergarten children were asked to print after seeing a series of reversible letters and numbers presented individually on slides or flash cards. The results showed that, independent of handedness, both groups of children found the left–right orientation cues of the same letters and numbers difficult to recall. This challenges a proposal expressed in the "grammar of action" that claims that certain reversal errors in children's printing result from the inappropriate application of the horizontal motor rule. – From Author's Abstract.

985. SMITH, GUDMUND J. W. (Univ. of Lund, Sweden), & CARLSSON, INGEGERD. **Creativity in early and middle school years.** International Journal of Behavioral Development, 1983, **6**, 167–195.
The study followed the development of creativity in children ages 7–11 years. The low creativity tide in 7-year-olds could perhaps be associated with the beginning of regular school in Sweden, but the high tide at the age of 10–11 years would perhaps point to an autonomous developmental rhythm. – From Authors' Abstract.

986. SMOLAK, LINDA (Kenyon Coll.), & WEINRAUB, MARSHA. **Maternal speech: strategy or response?** Journal of Child Language, 1983, **10**, 369–380.
Mothers of high- and low-level language children were compared when talking to their daughters and to another girl the same age as their daughter. Analysis indicated a striking amount of similarity and consistency in high vs. low mothers' speech to both their daughters and the other child. – From Authors' Abstract.

987. SONG, AGNES (Central Wisconsin Ctr., 317 Knutson, Madison); JONES, STEPHEN; LIPPERT, JANET; METZGEN, KARIN; MILLER, JACKIE; & BORRECA, CHRIS. **Wisconsin Behavior Rating Scale: measure of adaptive behavior for the developmental levels of 0 to 3 years.** American Journal of Mental Deficiency, 1984, **88**, 401–410.
The scale was standardized on institutionalized mentally retarded persons and nonretarded infants and young children. Reliability and validity were established. Cognitive and psychomotor abilities accounted for approximately 83% of the explained variance. – From Authors' Abstract.

988. SOPHIAN, CATHERINE (Carnegie–Mellon Univ.). **Spatial transpositions and the early development of search.** Developmental Psychology, 1984, **20**, 21–28.
Children received 2 kinds of transpositions: (1) relevant (switching a cup containing an object with 1 of 2 other, empty cups); and (2) irrelevant (switching 2 empty cups, while leaving in place a third cup containing the object). Children performed well on irrelevant transpositions but had more trouble with relevant transpositions. They did not select the correct cup until 42 months. Twenty-month-olds searched primarily at the initial hiding location. – From Author's Abstract.

989. SOUVOROV, A. V. **The problem of forming imagination in blind-deaf-and-dumb children.** Questions of Psychology (translation of Russian title), 1983, **3**, 62–72. In Russian, abstract in English. – Ed.

990. STOKLOSA, BOGUMILA (Higher School of Pedagogy, Rzeszow, Poland) **Speech comprehension of preschoolers depending on verbal and pictorial context.** Psychologia Wychowawcza (Educational Psychology: Bimonthly of the Polish Teachers Union), 1981, **23**, 595–607.
Two experiments are reported dealing with speech comprehension in children of preschool age, 1 using artificial words and the other using verbal-pictorial material. The experiments were aimed at establishing the role of the linguistic and the visual context in the process of speech comprehension in children. – From Author's Abstract.

991. SPUNGEN, LINDA B. (Albert Einstein Coll. of Medicine), & GOODMAN, JOAN F. **Sequencing strategies in children 18–24 months: limitations imposed by task complexity.** Journal of Applied Developmental Psychology, 1983, **4**, 109–124.
Three tasks were presented in 2 forms, varying only in number of elements. Subjects were 38 children 18–24 months of age. When number of elements increased, there was a dramatic decrease in orderliness of approach. Children used a consistent pattern of organization. Sequencing skills correlated with Denver scores. – From Authors' Abstract.

992. STAVER, JOHN R. (Univ. of Illinois, Chicago), & PASCARELLA, ERNEST T. **The effect of method and formation on the responses of subjects to a Piagetian reasoning problem.** Journal of Research in Science Teaching, 1984, **21**, 305–314.
Neither method nor format of task administration influenced subjects' scores. – From the Article.

993. STRAUSS, SIDNEY (Tel-Aviv Univ., Ramat Aviv, Israel); GLOBERSON, TAMAR; & MINTZ, RACHEL. **The influence of training for the atomistic schema on the development of the density concept among gifted and nongifted children.** Journal of Applied Developmental Psychology, 1983, **4**, 125–147.
Training was given for the schema of atomism to children at different stages and with varying M-capacities. Training and IQ were significant even when stage and M-capacity were partialed out, while the age variable was not. – Adapted from Authors' Abstract.

994. STRAWITZ, BARBARA M. (Louisiana State Univ.). **Cognitive style and the acquisition and transfer of the ability to control variables.** Journal of Research in Science Teaching, 1984, **21**, 131–141.
This study examined the effects of an instructional procedure designed to teach both field-dependent and field-independent sixth graders to control variables and to transfer this ability to novel tasks. Results indicated that students receiving the special instructional treatment correctly tested more variables on the posttest tasks than did students in the other group. – From Author's Abstract.

995. SUGIMURA, TAKESHI (Nara Univ. of Education, Japan). **Oddity and discrimination learning after pretraining on a nonrepeated oddity task.** Perceptual and Motor Skills, 1983, **56**, 27–30.

With increasing numbers of pretraining trials, the repeated oddity learning became easier, but ease of the discrimination learning did not change. – From the Article.

996. SVENSON, OLA (Univ. of Stockholm, Sweden), & SJÖBERG, KIT. **Evolution of cognitive processes for solving simple additions during the first three school years.** Scandinavian Journal of Psychology, 1983, **24**, 117–124.
This study has described the gradual development of children's strategies for solving simple additions during their first 3 school years. First, a child may not know how to solve a problem at all. Then they may start counting both addends on their fingers. Later, only the smaller number is counted with the aid of that external memory. – Adapted from the Article.

997. SZMIGIELSKA, BARBARA (Jagiellonian Univ., Cracow, Poland). **Perception of the relation between action and subsequent events in children of middle school age.** Psychologia Wychowawcza (Educational Psychology: Bimonthly of the Polish Teachers Union), 1981, **24**, 469–480.
Are there differences in sense of control between girls and boys? Is sense of control age related? What relationship is there between sense of control and type of activity? The Tel Aviv Locus of Control Scale was used. Both girls and boys gave evidence of a sense of internal control, the strongest in fifth-grade pupils. All groups showed a greater intensity of sense of internal control in relation to statements describing situations in which the individual experienced success as compared with statements describing situations of failure. – From Author's Abstract.

998. TAYLOR, DEBORAH A., & HARRIS, PAUL L. (Univ. of Oxford, South Parks, Oxford, England). **Knowledge of the link between emotion and memory among normal and maladjusted boys.** Developmental Psychology, 1983, **19**, 832–838.
Normal and emotionally maladjusted boys 7–8 years and 10–11 years old all knew that (1) emotion gradually declines in intensity, (2) variation between people in their emotion will persist despite any decline in intensity over time, and (3) an episode will be more or less memorable depending on whether it arouses emotion or not. Subjects were generally not knowledgeable about the control of emotion. – Adapted from Authors' Abstract.

999. TEGANO, DEBORAH (Virginia Polytechnic Inst.); FU, VICTORIA R.; & MORAN, JAMES D., III. **Divergent thinking and hemispheric dominance for language function among preschool children.** Perceptual and Motor Skills, 1983, **56**, 691–698.
Divergent thinking is associated with right hemispheric dominance at age 4. – From Authors' Abstract.

1000. THAL, JAMES S.; HARRIS, JERRY D. (Arizona State Univ.); & STOCK, WILLIAM. **Locus of control and depth of processing in children.** Journal of General Psychology, 1983, **109**, 31–42.
Support was provided for the contention that externals tend to encode stimuli in more superficial ways than do internals, although the amount of variance in recognition memory accounted for by the locus-of-control measure was small. – From Authors' Abstract.

1001. TOLMAN, CHARLES (Univ. of Victoria, British Columbia, Canada). **Categories, logic, and the problem of necessity in theories of mental development.** Studia Psychologica, 1983, **25**, 179–190.
The theoretical positions of Piaget, Riegel, and Lerner are briefly reviewed to see the extent to which they contain genuine and consistent dialectic. They reveal varying degrees of deficiency and promise. The developmental psychology of Leontyev is presented as exemplifying a consequent application of dialectical principles. – From Author's Abstract.

1002. TRICKETT, PENELOPE K. (National Inst. of Mental Health, Bldg. 15K, 9000 Rockville, Bethesda). **The interaction of cognitive styles and classroom environment in determining first-graders' behavior.** Journal of Applied Developmental Psychology, 1983, **4**, 43–64.

Three types of classrooms differing in classroom climate were selected: open, intermediate, and traditional. Subjects were 109 children in these classrooms. Classroom environment was found to affect degree of classroom disturbance: students in open classrooms exhibited most, and students in the intermediate classrooms exhibited least. Boys in open classrooms had higher achievement anxiety and lower teacher preference ratings than boys in traditional or intermediate classrooms. Reflective children obtained higher ratings as self-reliant learners and, for boys, reflection was related to low classroom disturbance and high achievement anxiety. Girls high in divergent thinking were higher in school involvement and achievement anxiety and more preferred by teachers. – From Author's Abstract.

1003. TROLLINGER, LAREE M. (Kutztown State Coll.). **Interests, activities and hobbies of high and low creative women musicians during childhood, adolescent and college years.** Gifted Child Quarterly, 1983, **27**, 94–97.

1004. TUNMER, WILLIAM E. (Univ. of Western Australia); BOWEY, JUDITH A.; & GRIEVE, ROBERT. **The development of young children's awareness of the word as a unit of spoken language.** Journal of Psycholinguistic Research, 1983, **12**, 567–594.
Children's awareness of the word as a unit of spoken language was investigated in 5 experiments that required children to segment spoken language strings into words. Children 4–5 years old responded to acoustic factors such as stress, and 5–6-year-olds responded to (unbound) morphemic structure. By age 7, most children responded to word concept. – From Authors' Abstract.

1005. TYLER, LORRAINE KOMISARJEVSKY (Max-Planck Institut für Psycholinguistik, Germany). **The development of discourse mapping processes: the on-line interpretation of anaphoric expressions.** Cognition, 1983, **13**, 309–341.
By the age of 5, anaphoric mapping processes in general are well mastered, although all age groups (5, 7, and 10 years and adults) found general term anaphors more difficult to interpret. The major developmental differences concerned the processing of anaphoric pronouns. – From Author's Abstract.

1006. ULVUND, STEIN ERIK (Univ. of Oslo, Norway). **The canonicality effect in search for the hidden object.** Scandinavian Journal of Psychology, 1983, **24**, 149–151.
Infants' success in hiding tasks is influenced by the orientation of the cavities used as concealments. The infants performed better than chance when the cavities were upright, and worse than chance when they were inverted. – From Author's Abstract.

1007. VAN ARSDEL, JEAN (Nene Coll., Moulton Park, Northampton, England). **Children's drawings as an assessment of cognitive style.** Educational Research, 1983, **25**, 74–75.
It is inadvisable to use the Draw-A-Figure test to assess field dependence/independence for children below the age of 10 years. – Adapted from the Article.

1008. VANDENBERG, BRIAN (Univ. of Missouri, St. Louis). **Developmental features of exploration.** Developmental Psychology, 1984, **20**, 3–8.
Analysis of 4- and 12-year-old children's preferences for both visual and auditory stimuli revealed an increase in preference for complexity with age. Preference for an unknown toy over a known toy was influenced by the novelty of the known toy. Older children were more likely to systematically examine all toys first before returning to particular toys of interest. – From Author's Abstract.

1009. WACHS, THEODORE D. (Purdue Univ.), & GANDOUR, MARY JANE. **Temperament, environment, and six-month cognitive-intellectual development: a test of the organismic specificity hypothesis.** International Journal of Behavioral Development, 1983, **6**, 135–152.
Infants classified as temperamentally easy were more sensitive to environmental parameters than temperamentally difficult babies; when environmental influences were relevant for difficult

infants, they tended to have a negative impact upon development. Temperamental characteristics associated with difficultness were also associated with an inability to coordinate specific sensorimotor schemes. – From Authors' Abstract.

1010. WALKER, ROBERT (Simon Fraser Univ., Burnaby, British Columbia, Canada). **Children's perceptions of horses and melodies.** Council for Research in Music Education, 1983, **76,** 30–41.
The implications of Arnheim's research findings concerning children's visual perception to musical perception are discussed. – From Author's Abstract.

1011. WASINGER, KAREN; ZELHART, PAUL F.; & MARKLEY, ROBERT P. (Fort Hays State Univ.). **Memory for random shapes and eidetic ability.** Perceptual and Motor Skills, 1982, **55,** 1076–1078.
No relationship was found in third graders between the memory task and a standard eidetic imagery task. – From Authors' Abstract.

1012. WASS, HANNELORE (Univ. of Florida); DINKLAGE, ROSEMARIE; GORDON, SHARON I.; RUSSO, GINA; SPARKS, CHRISTOPHER W.; & TATUM, JACKIE. **Use of play for assessing children's death concepts: a reexamination.** Psychological Reports, 1983, **53,** 799–803.
Play situations and interviews were used to assess accurate concepts of death in 3–7-year-olds. Young children's verbal and play expressions were not discrepant. – Adapted from Authors' Abstract.

1013. WATERS, HARRIET SALATAS (SUNY, Stony Brook), & McALASTER, REBECCA. **Encoding variability and organization in free recall.** Journal of Experimental Child Psychology, 1983, **36,** 380–395.
The independent contributions of organization and encoding variability are demonstrated in categorizable and uncategorizable lists and in subjects whose recall is expected to increase (adults) or decrease (children) as a function of more varied encodings across trials. – From Authors' Abstract.

1014. WICHMAN, HARVEY (Claremont McKenna Coll.), & LIZOTTE, PAUL. **Effects of mental practice and locus of control on performance of dart throwing.** Perceptual and Motor Skills, 1983, **56,** 807–812.
Mental practice by adolescents with an internal locus of control produced a significant improvement in motor skill accuracy. – Adapted from Authors' Abstract.

1015. WILKENING, FRIEDRICH (Technische Univ., Braunschweig, Germany). **Entwicklung der Informationsintegration: Eine Antwort auf Gigerenzers Kritik.** Zeitschrift für Entwicklungspsychologie und Pädagogische Psychologie, 1983, **15,** 207–215.
Gigerenzer's objections to conclusions from developmental applications of information integration theory are examined and invalidated. – From Author's Abstract.

1016. WILKINSON, ALEX CHERRY (Univ. of Wisconsin, Madison), & KOESTLER, RONALD. **Repeated recall: a new model and tests of its generality from childhood to old age.** Journal of Experimental Psychology: General, 1983, **112,** 423–451.
A theory of human memory is described and formalized as a Markov model. The model is tailored to predict sequences of recalls and forgets over successive attempts to remember a set of items. The model was found to fit well at all ages. The storage parameter varied with age; the parameters of the 4 memory functions did not. – From Authors' Abstract.

1017. WILLATTS, P. (Univ. of Dundee, Scotland). **Effects of object novelty on the visual and manual exploration of infants.** Infant Behavior and Development, 1983, **6,** 145–149.
Both 6- and 12-month-old infants reached quickly for a novel object and preferred it to a familiar object. – From Author's Abstract.

1018. WINOGRAD, EUGENE (Emory Univ.), & KILLINGER, WILLIAM A., JR. **Relating age at encoding in early childhood to adult recall: development of flashbulb memories.** Journal of Experimental Psychology: General, 1983, **112**, 413–422.
Informants who were ages 1–7 years in 1963 were asked about their personal memories surrounding the assassination of President Kennedy and 6 other significant public events. The probability and degree of elaboration of recall showed a gradual growth function with increasing age at the time of the event for the assassinations of John F. Kennedy and Robert F. Kennedy but not for the other events. – From Authors' Abstract.

1019. WOLF, WILLAVENE (New York Univ.), & SHIGAKI, IRENE S. **A developmental study of young gifted children's conditional reasoning ability.** Gifted Child Quarterly, 1983, **27**, 173–179.
The hypothesis that there would be a difference from age level to age level in the ability of gifted subjects to supply missing conclusions to conditional syllogisms and that the younger the child, the lower the score was supported. – Adapted from the Article.

1020. WOOD, PHILLIP KARL (Search Inst., 122 W. Franklin, Minneapolis). **Inquiring systems and problem structure: implications for cognitive development.** Human Development, 1983, **26**, 249–265.
In order to provide a precise language for describing problem solving, the language of decision theory is used to describe intellectual assessment tasks. – From Author's Abstract.

1021. YAMAUCHI, MITSUYA (Kyusha Univ., Fukuoka-shi, Japan); KOJO, KAZUKO; & TANAKA, TAKASHI. **Development of memory for general and specific sentences.** Journal of General Psychology, 1983, **109**, 43–51.
Second graders, junior high school students, and college students were given specific–general sentence pairs or general–specific sentence pairs for free recall. Specific sentences tended to be recalled more than general ones, and the performance for presentation order of specific–general sentences was superior to the reverse order in the 2 older groups. – From Authors' Abstract.

1022. YOUNG, DANIEL R. (Elmhurst Coll.), & SCHUMACHER, GARY M. **Context effects in young children's sensitivity to the importance level of prose information.** Child Development, 1983, **54**, 1446–1456.
The impact of memory and communication contexts on children's ability to recall according to importance level was investigated in 4- and 6-year-olds. Both age groups demonstrated sensitivity to importance level in their recalls, especially in the communication context. Another group of 4- and 6-year-old children was presented with short stories in memory and communication contexts. Contrary to previous research and theory, 6-year-olds demonstrated some metacognitive awareness of importance level. – From Authors' Abstract.

1023. ZAGAR, ROBERT, & BOWERS, NORMAN D. (Northwestern Univ.). **The effect of time of day on problem solving and classroom behavior.** Psychology in the Schools, 1983, **20**, 337–345.
On problem-solving tasks, except Digit Span, pupils performed better in the morning. In classroom behavior, all pupils exhibited more interference, off-task, noncompliance, and minor motor movement in the afternoon. – From Authors' Abstract.

SOCIAL PSYCHOLOGICAL, CULTURAL, AND PERSONALITY STUDIES

1024. ABRAHAM, KITTY G. (Univ. of Arizona). **The relation between identity status and locus of control among rural high school students.** Journal of Early Adolescence, 1983, **3**, 257–264.
Results confirmed that identity-achievement individuals were less external in locus of control than individuals in all other identity statuses. – From Author's Abstract.

1025. ABRAHAM, KITTY G.; KUEHL, ROBERT O.; & CHRISTOPHERSON, VICTOR A. (Univ. of Arizona). **Age-specific influence of parental behaviors on the development of empathy in preschool children.** Child Study Journal, 1983, **13**, 175–185.
Parents completed the Iowa Parent Behavior Inventory, while children were administered the Borke Interpersonal Awareness Test. Three maternal behaviors (limit setting, free expression, and intimacy) and 2 paternal behaviors (limit setting and reasoning guidance) were differentially affected by child's age in their association with empathy. Mothers' reasoning guidance was associated with empathy at all ages. – Adapted from Authors' Abstract.

1026. ACKER, LOREN E. (Univ. of Victoria, British Columbia, Canada); PEAKER, SHARMON; & ACKER, MARGARET A. **Affectionate and nonaffectionate imitations in young children: effects of reinforcer removal.** Child Study Journal, 1983, **13**, 153–164.
Four groups of children underwent baseline, reinforcement, and then reinforcer removal, contingent on imitations of a model. Two of these groups were trained to imitate interpersonal, affectionate behaviors. Reinforcer removal was effective in suppressing imitations in all groups except in the Affection-Trained/Punished-by-Second-Adult group where all children continued imitating for the duration of the reinforcer removal condition. – From Authors' Abstract.

1027. ADAMS, GERALD R. (Utah State Univ.). **Social competence during adolescence: social sensitivity, locus of control, empathy, and peer popularity.** Journal of Youth and Adolescence, 1983, **12**, 203–211.
The predicted relationship between social competency and peer popularity was supported, but was different according to sex of the adolescent. – From Author's Abstract.

1028. ADAMS, GERALD R. (Utah State Univ.), & MONTEMAYOR, RAYMOND. **Identity formation during early adolescence.** Journal of Early Adolescence, 1983, **3**, 193–202.
Erikson's theory of identity formation is outlined, and shortcomings to the general research area of identity development are reviewed. – From Authors' Abstract.

1029. ADAMS, RODERICK E., JR., & PASSMAN, RICHARD H. (Univ. of Wisconsin, Milwaukee). **Explaining to young children about an upcoming separation from their mother: when do I tell them?** Journal of Applied Developmental Psychology, 1983, **4**, 35–42.
Some mothers discussed an upcoming separation with their 2-year-olds for 3 days before a brief separation, whereas others gave no preparation. Immediately before they left the child alone with a stranger in an unfamiliar playroom, the mothers used 1 of 3 procedures to ready the child. Regardless of the technique used immediately before separation, children receiving no preparation at home remained with the stranger longer and played more than children given advance preparation. – From Authors' Abstract.

1030. AHLGREN, ANDREW (Univ. of Minnesota). **Sex differences in the correlates of cooperative and competitive school attitudes.** Developmental Psychology, 1983, **19**, 881–888.
Attitudes toward cooperation and competition in school were correlated with other school attitudes separately for 2,130 boys and girls in grades 2–12. Significant sex differences were found in correlation patterns at all grade levels. – From Author's Abstract.

1031. ALLEY, THOMAS R. (Univ. of Connecticut Health Ctr.). **Infantile head shape as an elicitor of adult protection.** Merrill-Palmer Quarterly, 1983, **29**, 411–427.
The results of 2 experiments indicated that being female or having more experience with children may increase the effect of age-related changes in head shape on the protective responses of these adults. – From Author's Abstract.

1032. ANISFELD, E. (Columbia Univ.). **The onset of social smiling in preterm and full-term infants from two ethnic backgrounds.** Infant Behavior and Development, 1982, **5**, 387–395.

No differences in onset of smiling were found when number of weeks from conception was used to determine age in 2 groups of Israeli infants. Sephardi infants smiled earlier than Ashkenazi infants. – S. Thomas.

1033. ARCHER, SALLY L. (Trenton State Coll.), & WATERMAN, ALAN S. **Identity in early adolescence: a developmental perspective.** Journal of Early Adolescence, 1983, **3**, 203–214.
Patterns of potential identity status change for an early-adolescent age group are discussed within the context of Waterman's developmental model. It appears that a substantial majority of early and midadolescents are either identity diffuse or foreclosed. – From Authors' Abstract.

1034. ARCO, C. M. (Univ. of Charleston). **Pacing of playful stimulation to young infants: similarities and differences in maternal and paternal communication.** Infant Behavior and Development, 1983, **6**, 223–228.
Father-infant and mother-infant dyads were observed in a laboratory free-play situation. Fathers tended to participate in faster play and provided higher levels and shorter units of playful stimuli. – From Abstract by S. Thomas.

1035. ASHER, STEVEN R. (Univ. of Illinois, Urbana-Champaign). **Social competence and peer status: recent advances and future directions.** Child Development, 1983, **54**, 1427–1434.
The commentary highlights the many conceptual and methodological advances contained in the Cole and Kupersmidt, Dodge, and Putallaz papers (*Child Development*, 1983, vol. 54). Together, the papers establish a causal link between social behavior and sociometric status. It is suggested that further attention be given to 3 dimensions of social competence emerging from these papers: relevance, responsiveness, and an appreciation that relationships evolve over time. – From Author's Abstract.

1036. BABAD, YAEL E.; ALEXANDER, IRVING E. (Duke Univ.); & BABAD, ELISHA Y. **Returning the smile of the stranger: developmental patterns and socialization factors.** Monographs of the Society for Research in Child Development, 1983, **48**(5), 1–93.
This work deals with children's tendency to return the smile of a friendly stranger in 2 separate cultures, Israel and the United States. In the first study, developmental trends in that behavior are examined. In a second study, mothers' socialization philosophies and childrearing practices are explored in an interview and in a conjoint mother–child task. This research extends previous work, which showed a stable and consistent cross-cultural difference in second- and third-grade children. American children were more likely than Israeli children to return the smile of the friendly stranger. Systematic differences between smilers and nonsmilers were observed in each culture. – From Authors' Abstract.

1037. BALLARD, KEITH D. (Univ. of Otago, Dunedin, New Zealand). **The role of interaction frequency in identifying socially withdrawn and socially isolated children: a re-examination of data and concepts.** Educational Psychology, 1983, **3**, 115–126.
Frequency of child social interaction with peers has been criticized as a measure lacking in concurrent and predictive validity. It is suggested that this criticism arises in part from a failure to differentiate the behavioral and conceptual features of social isolation and social withdrawal. – From Author's Abstract.

1038. BECK, JOHN T., & WORLAND, JULIEN (Washington Univ. School of Medicine). **Rorschach developmental level and its relationship to subsequent psychiatric treatment.** Journal of Personality Assessment, 1983, **47**, 238–242.
Although developmental level (DL) scores in childhood differentiated children of DSM-III diagnosed schizophrenics and schizoaffectives from children of parents with affective disorder and of nonpsychotic parents, DL scores were not predictive of later psychiatric treatment. – From Authors' Abstract.

1039. BÉGIN, GUY (Univ. Laval, Quebec, Canada). **A reassessment of the Kohn Social Competence Scale and the Walker Problem Behavior Identification Checklist.** Journal of Psychology, 1983, **114,** 223–226.
Correlations found between previously identified factors of both devices are high enough to suggest nonindependence of the factors and thus a need for reassessment of both instruments. – From Author's Abstract.

1040. BERNDT, THOMAS J. (Univ. of Oklahoma). **Correlates and causes of sociometric status in childhood: a commentary on six current studies of popular, rejected, and neglected children.** Merrill-Palmer Quarterly, 1983, **29,** 439–448.

1041. BERRY, JUDY O. (Univ. of Tulsa), & ZIMMERMAN, WILLIAM W. **The stage model revisited.** Rehabilitation Literature, 1983, **44,** 275–279.
A model of grieving as it applies to parents of mentally retarded or physically disabled children is discussed, and problems with the model are noted. A revised stage model of parental adjustments to a child with a disability is then presented. – From Authors' Abstract.

1042. BERZONSKY, MICHAEL D. (SUNY, Cortland), & LOMBARDO, JOHN P. **Pubertal timing and identity crisis: a preliminary investigation.** Journal of Early Adolescence, 1983, **3,** 239–246.
The results indicated that crisis males reportedly matured significantly later than their noncrisis counterparts, whereas the opposite pattern was found with female subjects. – From Authors' Abstract.

1043. BLASI, AUGUSTO (Univ. of Massachusetts, Boston). **Moral cognition and moral action: a theoretical perspective.** Developmental Review, 1983, **3,** 178–210.
The Self Model is proposed starting from the assumption that moral reasons are functionally related to action. First, a concept of cognitive motivation is presented as necessary for any cognitive account of morality. Piaget's and Haan's approaches to moral conduct are then discussed. – From Author's Abstract.

1044. BLOCK, JEANNE H. (Univ. of California, Berkeley). **Differential premises arising from differential socialization of the sexes: some conjectures.** Child Development, 1983, **54,** 1335–1354.
Sex-differentiated socialization emphases, shaping behaviors, and teaching styles are evaluated with regard to the nature of the "metamessages" conveyed to boys and girls during their early, formative years. These messages are assumed to differentially influence the self-concepts evolved, ego structures, personal goals, and cognitive-adaptational heuristics of boys and of girls. – From Author's Abstract.

1045. BLYTH, DALE A. (Ohio State Univ.). **Surviving and thriving in the social world: a commentary on six new studies of popular, rejected, and neglected children.** Merrill-Palmer Quarterly, 1983, **29,** 449–458.

1046. BOHRNSTEDT, GEORGE W. (Indiana Univ.), & FELSON, RICHARD B. **Explaining the relations among children's actual and perceived performances and self-esteem: a comparison of several causal models.** Journal of Personality and Social Psychology, 1983, **45,** 43–56.
Structural equation methods compared various causal models. The analysis is based on cross-sectional data of sixth- through eighth-grade students. Models in which self-esteem affected perceptions of popularity fit the data better than models in which the reverse or reciprocal effects were posited. – From Authors' Abstract.

1047. BONAMINIO, V. (Univ. degli Studi di Roma, Italy); CARRATELLI, T.; & DI RENZO, M. **Ritmi, sincronia, reciprocità nella relazione madre-bambino** [Rhythms, synchrony and reciprocity in early mother-infant interaction]. Età Evolutiva, 1983, **16,** 110–115.

This model describes the mother–infant relation as a communicative–interactional system in which the 2 partners, who differ in maturity but not in competence, affect each other. From these assumptions, the signs of infant behavior can be considered as elicitors of maternal responses which in turn are seen as a result of this system. – From Authors' Abstract.

1048. BRADY, JUDITH E.; NEWCOMB, ANDREW F.; & HARTUP, WILLARD W. (Univ. of Minnesota). **Context and companion's behavior as determinants of cooperation and competition in school-age children.** Journal of Experimental Child Psychology, 1983, **36**, 396–412.
Children were told that they would play a board game with another child. The companion's responses alone determined cooperation and competition among first graders, third graders used both types of information, and fifth graders demonstrated a bias to respond cooperatively whenever a cooperative cue was present. – From Authors' Abstract.

1049. BROOK, JUDITH S. (Mt. Sinai School of Medicine); WHITEMAN, MARTIN; GORDON, ANN SCOVELL; & BROOK, DAVID W. **Paternal correlates of adolescent marijuana use in the context of the mother-son and parental dyads.** Genetic Psychology Monographs, 1983, **108**, 197–213.
Male college students and their fathers were administered written questionnaires. Fathers of marijuana users scored higher on psychopathology and unconventionality and were less likely to have established close relationships with their sons. A systems approach is needed to analyze these effects. – Adapted from Authors' Abstract.

1050. BRUHN, A. RAHN (7820 Glenbrook, Bethesda), & DAVIDOW, SHARON. **Earliest memories and the dynamics of delinquency.** Journal of Personality Assessment, 1983, **47**, 476–482.
A coding system, devised from the first 2 childhood memories of delinquents and nondelinquents, successfully identified 80% of the delinquents and 100% of the nondelinquents. – From Authors' Abstract.

1051. BUKOWSKI, WILLIAM M. (Univ. of Maine, Orono), & NEWCOMB, ANDREW F. **The association between peer experiences and identity formation in early adolescence.** Journal of Early Adolescence, 1983, **3**, 265–274.
Sixth graders completed the Perceived Competence Scale for Children and a sociometric questionnaire. Perceptions of general self-worth were found to be related to perception of social, physical, and cognitive competence. – From Authors' Abstract.

1052. BURDETT, KEVIN, & JENSEN, LARRY C. (Brigham Young Univ.). **The self-concept and aggressive behavior among elementary school children from two socioeconomic areas and two grade levels.** Psychology in the Schools, 1983, **20**, 370–375.
There was a positive relationship between children's self-report aggressiveness scores and teacher ratings of aggressiveness. No correlations were found between children's reported self-concept scores and their self-report or teacher-rated measures of aggressiveness. – From the Article.

1053. BUSCH-ROSSNAGEL, NANCY A. (Colorado State Univ.); PETERS, DONALD L.; & DALY, MICHAEL J. **Mothers of vulnerable and normal infants: more alike than different.** Family Relations, 1984, **33**, 149–154.
Few differences between mothers of vulnerable and normal infants were found, implying that during the early months of an infant's life, mothers of vulnerable and normal children were more alike than different. – From Authors' Abstract.

1054. CAIRNS, ROBERT B. (Univ. of North Carolina, Chapel Hill). **Sociometry, psychometry, and social structure: a commentary on six recent studies of popular, rejected, and neglected children.** Merrill-Palmer Quarterly, 1983, **29**, 429–438.

This article outlines some problems encountered in the use of sociometric methods and describes certain common outcomes that they yield. Attention is focused on a set of 6 reports on popular, rejected, and neglected children. – From Author's Abstract.

1055. COHEN, KEITH N. (Cognitive Therapy & Diagnostic Service, 169 Grove, Wellesley, MA), & CLARK, JAMES A. **Transitional object attachments in early childhood and personality characteristics in later life.** Journal of Personality and Social Psychology, 1984, **46**, 106–111.
The major findings of the present study revealed significant relationships between specific personality characteristics and the presence or absence of transitional object attachments in early childhood. – From the Article.

1056. COIE, JOHN D. (Duke Univ.), & DODGE, KENNETH A. **Continuities and changes in children's social status: a five-year longitudinal study.** Merrill-Palmer Quarterly, 1983, **29**, 261–282.
Yearly sociometric data were collected on 96 third graders and 112 fifth graders. Positive and negative sociometric items were transformed into dimensions of social preference and social impact, and Year 1-Year 5 correlations of .36 and .45 were obtained for social preference with nonsignificant correlations for social impact. – From Authors' Abstract.

1057. COIE, JOHN D. (Duke Univ.), & KUPERSMIDT, JANIS B. **A behavioral analysis of emerging social status in boys' groups.** Child Development, 1983, **54**, 1400–1416.
Fourth-grade boys, 1 each of rejected, popular, neglected, and average status, met in play groups for 6 weeks. Observations of behavior coded from videotapes revealed distinctive patterns of social interaction for the social status types. Rejected boys were extremely active and aversive, but no more physically aversive than average boys, although group members perceived rejected boys as starting fights. Popular boys engaged in more norm setting and were more prosocial in the unfamiliar groups. Although neglected boys were the least interactive and aversive, they were more visible and active in the unfamiliar group and seemed most affected by the new social context. – From Authors' Abstract.

1058. CORRIGAN, SHEILA A., & MOSKOWITZ, DEBBIE S. (Concordia Univ., Montreal, Quebec, Canada). **Type A behavior in preschool children: construct validation evidence for the MYTH.** Child Development, 1983, **54**, 1513–1521.
Type A behavior was related to teacher ratings of aggression and impatience, but not to intelligence. The reaction times of Type B children who worked without a time limit and an incentive were significantly longer than both groups of Type A children and the Type B children who worked with a time limit and an incentive. – From Authors' Abstract.

1059. CORTER, CARL (Univ. of Toronto, Mississauga, Ontario, Canada); ABRAMOVITCH, RONA; & PEPLER, DEBRA J. **The role of the mother in sibling interaction.** Child Development, 1983, **54**, 1599–1605.
Pairs of same-sex and mixed-sex siblings were observed in their homes. There were no consistent effects of the age or sex of the children or of the interval between siblings on mother–child interaction. Mothers were quite consistent in their treatment of their 2 children regardless of their age or sex. Mother's presence reduced the overall level of sibling interaction, and sibling interaction tended to be relatively more agonistic when mother was present than when she was absent. – From Authors' Abstract.

1060. CROMBIE, GAIL, & GOLD, DOLORES (Concordia Univ., Edmonton, Alberta, Canada). **Developmental study of person perception in boys and girls.** Psychological Reports, 1983, **53**, 311–314.
Children from grades 2 and 5 completed a questionnaire describing 2 stimulus children classified as a close friend or as not being known very well by the subject. There were no sex differences in person perception. – From Authors' Abstract.

1061. CSAPO, MARG (Univ. of British Columbia, Vancouver, British Columbia, Canada). **Effectiveness of coaching socially withdrawn/isolated children in specific social skills.** Educational Psychology, 1983, **3**, 31–42.
The social learning method increased social interaction of severely withdrawn/isolated children with their peers. Increasing their rate of behavior in targeted social skills to the level of performance of their average peers required 4 times as many sessions of training as Ladd conducted with mildly withdrawn/isolated children. – From Author's Abstract.

1062. DAHLQUIST, LYNNDA M. (West Virginia Univ. Medical School), & OTTINGER, DONALD R. **Locus of control and peer status: a scale for children's perceptions of social interactions.** Journal of Personality Assessment, 1983, **47**, 278–287.
Third- through sixth-grade children participated in the development of a 48-item Locus of Control Scale for Children's Perceptions of Social Interactions. Scores were based on the number of positive, negative, and total social reinforcers a child attributes to his or her own behavior. Theoretical implications and potential clinical application are discussed. – From Authors' Abstract.

1063. DEAUX, KAY (Purdue Univ.). **Analysis of a decade's research on gender.** American Psychologist, 1984, **39**, 105–116.
Recent research on sex and gender is analyzed in terms of (a) sex as a subject variable; (b) individual differences in masculinity, femininity, and androgyny; and (c) sex as a social category. Main effect differences of subject sex are found to be surprisingly small. – From Author's Abstract.

1064. DICKINSON, J. (Simon Fraser Univ., Burnaby, British Columbia, Canada); SEBASTIEN, T.; & TAYLOR, L. **Competitive style and game preference.** Journal of Sport Psychology, 1983, **5**, 381–389.
Children in the age range 8–13 years completed a game-preference questionnaire and participated in a novel competitive game task. The results supported the predictions in terms of gender differences. Changes in game preference with age and gender and age differences in competitive style also conformed with predictions. – From Authors' Abstract.

1065. DiVITTO, B., & GOLDBERG, S. (Hosp. for Sick Children, 555 Univ., Toronto, Ontario, Canada). **Talking and sucking: infant feeding behavior and parent stimulation in dyads with different medical histories.** Infant Behavior and Development, 1983, **6**, 157–165.
Parents were increasingly able to differentiate their behavior in relation to infant sucking behavior during the first 4 months. – From Abstract by S. Thomas.

1066. DIXON, DAVID J. (Southwest Missouri State Univ.), & HOM, HARRY L., JR. **The role of fantasy figures in the regulation of young children's behavior: Santa Claus, the Easter Bunny, and donations.** Contemporary Educational Psychology, 1984, **9**, 14–18.
An interaction revealed that for kindergartners, the type of story failed to influence donations, whereas for first graders, stories referring to Santa Claus increased donations relative to stories told about the Easter Bunny or pets. – From Authors' Abstract.

1067. DODGE, KENNETH A. (Indiana Univ.). **Behavioral antecedents of peer social status.** Child Development, 1983, **54**, 1386–1399.
Previously unacquainted second-grade boys were brought together in play groups which met under supervision for 8 sessions. At the last session, sociometric interviews were conducted with each boy. Boys who became rejected or neglected were those who engaged in inappropriate behaviors. Rejected boys engaged in physical aggression more than any other group. Popular boys refrained from aggression and were received quite positively by the peers whom they approached. Controversial boys engaged in high frequencies of both prosocial and antisocial behaviors. – From Author's Abstract.

1068. DODGE, KENNETH A. (Indiana Univ., Bloomington); SCHLUNDT, DAVID C.; SCHOCKEN, IRIS; & DELUGACH, JUDY D. **Social competence and children's sociometric status: the role of peer group entry strategies.** Merrill-Palmer Quarterly, 1983, **29**, 309–336.
In Study 1, popular, rejected, and neglected kindergarten children were asked to initiate play with 2 same-age peers. Observations revealed that the status groups differed in the frequency of their attempts at peer-group entry. – From Authors' Abstract.

1069. EATON, WARREN O. (Univ. of Manitoba, Winnipeg, Canada). **Gender understanding and sex-role stereotyping in preschoolers: implications for caregivers.** Child Care Quarterly, 1983, **12**, 28–35.
Although most preschoolers see gender as a relatively stable personal attribute, they do not realize that gender is constant despite stylistic and behavioral variations. This misunderstanding contributes to a period of sex-role inflexibility. – From Author's Abstract.

1070. ECCLES, JACQUELYNNE PARSONS (Univ. of Michigan); ADLER, TERRY; & MEECE, JUDITH L. **Sex differences in achievement: a test of alternate theories.** Journal of Personality and Social Psychology, 1984, **46**, 26–43.
The strongest support emerged for the importance of subjective task value as a mediator of both academic achievement plans in general and of sex differences in academic choices. There was very little support for learned-helplessness models of sex differences. There was some evidence of sex differences in ability attributions that is consistent with the expectancy/self-concept perspective. Paper-and-pencil indexes and behavioral indexes of achievement attitudes did not yield converging evidence of sex differences. – From the Article.

1071. EGAN, OWEN, & NUGENT, J. KEVIN (Boston Univ. School of Nursing). **Adolescent conceptions of the homeland: a cross-cultural study.** Journal of Youth and Adolescence, 1983, **12**, 185–201.
Irish and United States subjects 8–17 years old wrote essays on their respective homelands. American subjects, as they grew older, identified the homeland increasingly with its political ideals, while Irish subjects identified theirs with certain psychological ideals which they associated with the rural culture and landscape. – From Authors' Abstract.

1072. EIDUSON, BERNICE T. (Univ. of California School of Medicine, Los Angeles). **Children of the children of the 1960s: an introduction.** American Journal of Orthopsychiatry, 1983, **53**, 400–407.
The aims of the Family Styles Project, set up to study the effects on child development of the countercultural life styles that emerged in the late 1960s and early 1970s, are reviewed. Background data on the project are presented as an introduction to papers dealing with childrearing practices, maternal employment, and interpersonal conflict in alternative families. – Author's Abstract.

1073. EIDUSON, BERNICE T. (Univ. of California School of Medicine, Los Angeles). **Conflict and stress in nontraditional families: impact on children.** American Journal of Orthopsychiatry, 1983, **53**, 426–435.
Aspects of children's intellectual performance and social-emotional behavior are negatively affected by stress, but in some types of families, children are found to be more buffered than in others. – From Author's Abstract.

1074. EIMER, BRUCE N. (Hahnemann Medical Coll., Broad & Vine, Philadelphia). **Age differences in boys' evaluations of fathers intervening to stop misbehavior.** Journal of Psychology, 1983, **115**, 159–163.
Boys ages 6–12 evaluated fathers who intervened in 2 different ways to stop their sons' physical abuse of a peer. Age differences in boys' evaluations of these fathers were found, but, contrary to predictions, these differences were not a function of the type of paternal intervention. – From Author's Abstract.

1075. EIMER, BRUCE N. (Hahnemann Univ., Vine & Broad, Philadelphia), & MANCUSO, JAMES C. **Children's perceptions of variously reprimanded transgressors.** Journal of Psychology, 1983, **115**, 209–220.
Children in grades 1, 3, and 6 watched 1 of 4 sequences in which a boy violated a given rule and was then exposed to 1 of 3 types of reprimand (retributive, restitutive, explanatory) or no reprimand. Analyses showed that variations in children's judgments of the transgressors were attributable to reprimand type and to grade level. – From Authors' Abstract.

1076. EISENBERG, NANCY (Arizona State Univ.); LENNON, RANDY; & ROTH, KARLSSON. **Prosocial development: a longitudinal study.** Developmental Psychology, 1983, **19**, 846–855.
Subjects were 4–7 years old. From the preschool to elementary school years, needs-oriented (empathic) reasoning increased, whereas hedonistic reasoning decreased. Significant changes continued from the preschool years to second grade. The relation between prosocial reasoning and prohibition-oriented reasoning was low to moderate. Level of reasoning was related to nonauthoritarian, nonpunitive maternal practices, but the role of empathic, supportive maternal practices appeared to change with age. – From Authors' Abstract.

1077. ELDER, GLEN H., JR. (Cornell Univ.), & MacINNIS, DEBORAH J. **Achievement imagery in women's lives from adolescence to adulthood.** Journal of Personality and Social Psychology, 1983, **45**, 394–404.
The principal result on family influence is the prominence of the mother and her competence in the achievement motivation of girls who expressed some career interest. These girls were most likely to have well-educated, employed mothers who possessed a sense of personal worth. However, their relation to the mother was characterized more by conflict and tension than the mother–daughter relation of less ambitious girls. – From the Article.

1078. ENRIGHT, ROBERT D. (Univ. of Wisconsin, Madison); GANIERE, DIANE M.; BUSS, RAY R.; LAPSLEY, DANIEL K.; & OLSON, LEANNE MARZOCCO. **Promoting identity development in adolescents.** Journal of Early Adolescence, 1983, **3**, 247–255.
A model of identity formation based on the cognitive developmental stages of social perspective taking is described, and a study with high school students was undertaken to test the model. The experimental subjects gained more than the control subjects on Rasmussen's Ego Identity Scale. – From Authors' Abstract.

1079. ENRIGHT, ROBERT D. (Univ. of Wisconsin); LAPSLEY, DANIEL K.; CULLEN, JOANNE; & LALLENSACK, MARGARET. **A psychometric examination of Rasmussen's Ego Identity Scale.** International Journal of Behavioral Development, 1983, **6**, 89–103.
Although the Ego Identity Scale was related to age, identity, and moral development, its strongest relationship was with social desirability. Additional research reduced this association. – Adapted from Authors' Abstract.

1080. ENRIGHT, ROBERT D. (Univ. of Wisconsin, Madison); LAPSLEY, DANIEL K.; FRANKLIN, CHRISTINA C.; & STEUCK, KURT. **Longitudinal and cross-cultural validation of the belief–discrepancy reasoning construct.** Developmental Psychology, 1984, **20**, 143–149.
Students in grades 1, 4, 7, and 10 were assessed and then retested 1 year later. The trends supported a 4-stage sequence of Level 0 (not understanding that one can judge a disagreeing other), Level 1 (intolerance toward the other), Level 2 (total open-mindedness toward the other) and Level 3 (a willingness to judge the other as good or bad with more information about the other's belief). Fourth and seventh graders from Kinshasa, Zaire also showed differences between the grades. – From Authors' Abstract.

1081. ERB, THOMAS OWEN (Univ. of Kansas). **Career preferences of early adolescents: age and sex differences.** Journal of Early Adolescence, 1983, **3**, 349–359.

Most career areas suffer a decline in interest among both boys and girls in the initial years of early adolescence. In some areas, boys' scores showed a rebound after age 13, reflecting interest in high-technology careers. Girls showed increasing interest in traditional areas, such as service and organization. – From Author's Abstract.

1082. ETAUGH, CLAIRE (Bradley Univ.), & WHITTLER, TOMMY E. **Social memory for preschool girls and boys.** Psychology of Women Quarterly, 1982, **7**, 170–174.
Preschoolers attending a daycare center were tested for their memory of photographs of children attending the center. In 2 experiments, girls and boys did not differ significantly in the number of correct identifications on either recall or recognition tasks. – From Authors' Abstract.

1083. EWERT, OTTO M. (Univ. Mainz, Germany). **Psychische Begleiterscheinungen des puberalen Wachstumsschubs bei männlichen Jugendlichen—eine retrospektive Untersuchung.** Zeitschrift für Entwicklungspsychologie und Pädagogische Psychologie, 1984, **16**, 1–11.
Male high school students retrospectively answered a questionnaire concerning the behavior of physically accelerated and retarded classmates, when they were 13–14 years old. In addition, they had to evaluate those classmates' behavior of the present time. Differences were obtained with regard to outward appearance, self-confidence/leadership behavior, and interest. – From Author's Abstract.

1084. FEINMAN, SAUL (Univ. of Wyoming). **How does baby socially refer? Two points of social referencing: a reply to Campos.** Merrill-Palmer Quarterly, 1983, **29**, 467–471.

1085. FELDMAN, S. SHIRLEY (Stanford Univ.); NASH, SHARON CHURNIN; & ASCHENBRENNER, BARBARA G. **Antecedents of fathering.** Child Development, 1983, **54**, 1628–1636.
Using data collected prior to the birth of couples' first children, a variety of antecedents of fathering were explored in a short-term longitudinal study of middle- and upper-middle-class men and their expectant wives. Three fathering factors were defined: caretaking, playfulness, and satisfaction with fatherhood. The preparenting scores of men and women were equally effective in predicting men's subsequent fathering. While there were similar predictors for men's caretaking and playfulness, their wives' scores yielded differential predictors for these aspects of fathering. The quality and nature of the marital relationship was related to all aspects of fathering. – From Authors' Abstract.

1086. FERNALD, ANNE (Univ. of Oregon), & SIMON, THOMAS. **Expanded intonation contours in mothers' speech to newborns.** Developmental Psychology, 1984, **20**, 104–113.
Each subject was recorded in 3 observational conditions, while addressing (a) her 3–5-day-old baby; (b) the absent infant, as if present; and (c) the adult interviewer. Mothers spoke to their babies with higher pitch, wider pitch excursions, longer pauses, shorter utterances, and more prosodic repetition than in their speech to adults. – From Authors' Abstract.

1087. FISCHER, DONALD G. (Univ. of Saskatchewan, Saskatoon, Canada). **Parental supervision and delinquency.** Perceptual and Motor Skills, 1983, **56**, 635–640.
Review of literature suggests that parental supervision is a significant variable in controlling the amount of delinquent behavior, even under adverse conditions. – Adapted from Author's Abstract.

1088. FITCH, STEVEN A. (Utah State Univ.), & ADAMS, GERALD R. **Ego identity and intimacy status: replication and extension.** Developmental Psychology, 1983, **19**, 839–845.
The Marcia (1966) Ego-Identity Interview and the Orlofsky, Marcia, and Lesser (1973) Intimacy Interview were administered to undergraduates participating in a 1-year longitudinal study. Identity formation fosters intimacy development. Occupational identity for male subjects and religious identity for female subjects were the most salient factors that contributed to advanced intimacy status. – Adapted from Authors' Abstract.

1089. FRANCISSE, C. (Univ. Libre de Bruxelles, Bruxelles, France); LEFEBVRE, A.; & SALENGROS, P. **Images de soi et marginalité à l'adolescence: une application de l'analyse binaire classique a une échelle bipolaire.** Revue de Psychologie Appliqueé, 1983, **33,** 215–230.
The paper provides descriptions of adolescent students about marginal (like "mad" or "drug addict") or integrated (like "parent" or "worker") concepts, by the means of an 18-item scale. The scale gives a description of an actual self-concept and another for an ideal self-concept. – From Authors' Abstract.

1090. FRY, P. S. (Univ. of Calgary, Canada), & CORFIELD, V. K. **Children's judgments of authority figures with respect to outcome and procedural fairness.** Journal of Genetic Psychology, 1983, **143,** 241–250.
Subjects were told a story about a child who was rewarded by the mother by fair or unfair procedures. Outcomes were higher than, equal to, or lower than deserved. Subjects were required to rate the child's outcome satisfaction with mother and to evaluate the mother's fairness. Children demonstrated potential for evaluating an authority figure's procedural and outcome fairness. – From Authors' Abstract.

1091. FURTH, HANS (Catholic Univ. of America). **A developmental perspective on the societal theory of Habermas.** Human Development, 1983, **26,** 181–197.
Habermas' model of action rationality is discussed, followed by a critical examination of the crucial concept of life world as the 1 paradigmatic component in societal structure, the other being system structure. – From Author's Abstract.

1092. GAENSBAUER, THEODORE J. (3955 E. Exposition, Suite 402D, Denver); CONNELL, JAMES P.; & SCHULTZ, LEOLA A. **Emotion and attachment: interrelationships in a structured laboratory paradigm.** Developmental Psychology, 1983, **19,** 815–831.
Measures of the intensity of 6 discrete emotions and measures of attachment behavior during each of the various episodes of the classic attachment sequence were independently obtained for 12–18-month-olds. The results pointed to the usefulness of paying direct attention to the specific emotional states as a means of understanding the complex emotional factors that contribute to attachment. – From Authors' Abstract.

1093. GAVAGHAN, MARY P. (Ohio State Univ.); ARNOLD, KEVIN D.; & GIBBS, JOHN C. **Moral judgment in delinquents and nondelinquents: recognition versus production measures.** Journal of Psychology, 1983, **114,** 267–274.
Juvenile delinquents scored lower than nondelinquents on the Sociomoral Reflection Measure. There were no differences on the Sociomoral Reflection Objective Measure. – From Authors' Abstract.

1094. GIBB, GERALD D. (Eastern Illinois Univ.); BAILEY, JAMES R.; LAMBIRTH, THOMAS T.; & WILSON, WILLIAM P. **Personality differences between high and low electronic video game users.** Journal of Psychology, 1983, **114,** 159–165.
High and low users of video games were compared by sex. No differences were found between groups for either sex on several personality dimensions. – From Authors' Abstract.

1095. GNEPP, JACKIE (Northern Illinois Univ.). **Children's social sensitivity: inferring emotions from conflicting cues.** Developmental Psychology, 1983, **19,** 805–814.
Students in preschool and grades 1 and 6 responded to pictures containing (*a*) situational or facial cues, (*b*) situational and facial cues with congruent emotional implications, or (*c*) situational and facial cues with conflicting emotional implications that had a narrative in some cases. The youngest children based inferences about emotions on facial expressions, but this preference decreased with age. At all ages, children encoded and remembered both cues. They reinterpreted facial cues when there were conflicting situational cues. – Adapted from Author's Abstract.

1096. GOLAB, ANDRZEJ (Univ. of Warsaw, Poland). **Physical aggression in the moral and behavioral awareness of middle school age boys.** Psychologia Wychowawcza (Educational Psychology: Bimonthly of the Polish Teachers Union), 1982, **25,** 108–122.
Subjects were boys 11, 13, and 15 years of age. Their aggressive behavior was diagnosed by their teachers and classmates (using rating scales). The aggression evaluation index was the number of approved aggressive acts. The index of moral thinking strategy was the answer to the question: Why not hit others?—From Author's Abstract.

1097. GOLDBERG, SUSAN (Hosp. for Sick Children, 555 Univ., Toronto, Ontario, Canada). **Parent–Infant bonding: another look.** Child Development, 1983, **54,** 1355–1382.
This review asserts that previous research is lacking on 3 counts: (1) there are no systematic studies of initial mother–infant contacts, (2) the majority of the studies confound timing and amount of contact, and (3) failure to consider underlying mechanisms resulted in the omission of designs and dependent measures that could address the appropriate questions. – From Author's Abstract.

1098. GOLDSTEIN, HARRIS S. (Rutgers Medical School, Univ. of Medicine & Dentistry). **Fathers' absence and cognitive development of children over a 3- to 5-year period.** Psychological Reports, 1983, **52,** 971–976.
A national probability sample of children was examined at 6–11 and again at 12–17 years. There were no significant effects for fathers' presence vs. absence on WISC Vocabulary & Block Design or WRAT Reading & Arithmetic for either white or black children. – From Author's Abstract.

1099. GOLINKOFF, R. M. (Univ. of Delaware), & HALPERN, M. S. **The concept of animal: one infant's view.** Infant Behavior and Development, 1983, **6,** 229–233.
A study of an 8-month-old explored emotional responses to stuffed and real animals. – S. Thomas.

1100. GREEN, RICHARD (SUNY, Stony Brook); NEUBERG, DONNA SHAPIRO; & FINCH, STEPHEN J. **Sex-typed motor behaviors of "feminine" boys, conventionally masculine boys, and conventionally feminine girls.** Sex Roles, 1983, **9,** 571–579.
Children ages 4–10 years were identically costumed to conceal gender and were videotaped while throwing a ball, walking, running, and telling a story. The sex of the "feminine" boys was rated as neither distinctly "feminine" nor distinctly "masculine."—From Authors' Abstract.

1101. GRESHAM, FRANK M. (Louisiana State Univ.). **Situational specificity, correspondence, and social validity: a commentary on Renshaw and Asher.** Merrill-Palmer Quarterly, 1983, **29,** 459–465.

1102. GROTEVANT, HAROLD D. (Univ. of Texas, Austin). **The contribution of the family to the facilitation of identity formation in early adolescence.** Journal of Early Adolescence, 1983, **3,** 225–237.
Studies that focus on the family's style of adapting to the transition from childhood into early adolescence are reviewed. Research on the relation between identity formation and family processes in late adolescence is reviewed. – From Author's Abstract.

1103. GUTTMAN, HERTA A. (Inst. of Community and Family Psychiatry, 4333 Chemin de la Côte Ste.-Catherine, Montreal, Quebec, Canada). **Autonomy and motherhood.** Psychiatry, 1983, **46,** 230–235.
A mother's autonomy is viewed as a suspect condition for the child's healthy growth and development. The paper reviews the concept of the "good enough" mother, examines and defines the concept of autonomy, and considers whether or not the 2 can be compatible. – From Author's Abstract.

1104. HAINES, A. T. (Univ. of Tasmania, G.P.O. Box 252C, Hobart, Tasmania); JACKSON, M. S.; & DAVIDSON, J. **Children's resistance to the temptation to steal in real and hypothetical situations: a comparison of two treatment programs.** Australian Psychologist, 1983, **18,** 289–303.
A 2-treatment and post control group design was used. The major datum included children's pre and post responses to hypothetical and a real-life temptation-to-steal situation. Differences in hypothetical measures in favor of the direct training model were found. – From Authors' Abstract.

1105. HAINS, ANTHONY A. (Univ. of Kansas), & RYAN, ELLEN B. **The development of social cognitive processes among juvenile delinquents and nondelinquent peers.** Child Development, 1983, **54,** 1536–1544.
Subjects were 10–11- and 14–15-year-old delinquents and nondelinquents. Developmental differences for age, but not for delinquency, were observed in moral judgment and prosocial moral reasoning. Under certain conditions, older nondelinquents performed better than other groups while considering some dimensions of social problem solving. All groups except younger delinquents displayed comparable knowledge about strategies to solve social problems. – From Authors' Abstract.

1106. HAMPSON, ROBERT B. (Southern Methodist Univ.). **Adolescent prosocial behavior: peer-group and situational factors associated with helping.** Journal of Personality and Social Psychology, 1984, **46,** 153–162.
One's status in the peer group was associated with both the level and type of prosocial behavior in which one engaged. Popular helpers in this study were more peer oriented, whereas less popular helpers were more facilitative in behind-the-scenes, less peer-related situations. – From the Article.

1107. HARRIS, P. L. (Univ. of Oxford, South Parks, Oxford, England). **Children's understanding of the link between situation and emotion.** Journal of Experimental Child Psychology, 1983, **36,** 490–509.
Both 6- and 10-year-olds know that emotion gradually wanes after the precipitating situation, have difficulty in admitting that a single situation can provoke an emotional conflict between a positive and a negative emotion, and understand how an earlier situation can provoke an emotion that persists so as to eventually be concurrent with a later, conflicting emotion. – From Author's Abstract.

1108. HAVILAND, JEANNETTE M. (Rutgers Univ.); McGUIRE, TERRY R.; & ROTHBAUM, PEGGY A. **A critique of Plomin and Foch's "A twin study of objectively assessed personality in childhood."** Journal of Personality and Social Psychology, 1983, **45,** 633–640.
The Plomin and Foch study is theoretically and methodologically flawed. – From Authors' Abstract.

1109. HAWKINS, DONNA B., & GRUBER, JOSEPH J. (Univ. of Kentucky). **Little League baseball and players' self-esteem.** Perceptual and Motor Skills, 1982, **55,** 1335–1340.
A season of Little League baseball enhanced the total self-esteem scores of the players involved. – Adapted from the Article.

1110. HEGLAND, SUSAN M. (Iowa State Univ.), & GALEJS, IRMA. **Developmental aspects of locus of control in preschool children.** Journal of Genetic Psychology, 1983, **143,** 229–239.
The Stephens-Delys Reinforcement Contingency Interview showed that LOC orientation for positive and negative social event outcomes are highly related. Children perceived more control over negative than over positive outcomes. Children perceived significantly more control over parents than over peers and teachers. – From Authors' Abstract.

1111. HENDRICKS, LEO E. (Howard Univ.), & FULLILOVE, ROBERT E. **Locus of control and the use of contraception among unmarried black adolescent fathers and their controls: a preliminary report.** Journal of Youth and Adolescence, 1983, **12**, 225–233.
Results reveal that black adolescent fathers are more likely to have an external locus of control, not to be churchgoers, and not to believe in the use of birth control. – From Authors' Abstract.

1112. HILL, JOHN P. (Virginia Commonwealth Univ.). **Early adolescence: a research agenda.** Journal of Early Adolescence, 1983, **3**, 1–21.
The article is wide ranging but considers research in several content domains including biological and cognitive change and influences such as peer, family, and school. – Ed.

1113. HOLLINGER, CONSTANCE L. (Cleveland State Univ.). **Counseling the gifted and talented female adolescent: the relationship between social self-esteem and traits of instrumentality and expressiveness.** Gifted Child Quarterly, 1983, **27**, 157–161.
As was predicted, the social self-confidence and self-esteem of gifted and talented female adolescents varied as a function of their self-images of instrumentality and expressiveness. – From the Article.

1114. HORNE, MARCIA D., & POWERS, JAMES E. (Univ. of Oklahoma). **Teachers' ratings of aggression and students' own perceived status.** Psychological Reports, 1983, **53**, 275–278.
Students in grades 2–3 who were rated high in aggression perceived themselves as more popular, but those in grades 4–5 so rated perceived themselves as less popular. – From Authors' Abstract.

1115. HORNER, THOMAS M. (Univ. of Michigan Medical School). **On the formation of personal space and self-boundary structures in early human development: the case of infant stranger reactivity.** Developmental Review, 1983, **3**, 148–177.
The article focuses upon human infancy as a period in which both personal space and self-boundary phenomena can be observed. Links between personal space and self-boundary phenomena in infancy and adulthood are discussed. – From Author's Abstract.

1116. HOWES, CAROLLEE (Univ. of California, Los Angeles). **Caregiver behavior in center and family day care.** Journal of Applied Developmental Psychology, 1983, **4**, 99–107.
The social experiences of 40 toddlers and their caregivers in family and center care were observed. Caregivers in both settings with fewer children, who worked shorter hours, and with less housework responsibilities engaged in more facilitative social stimulation, expressed more positive affect, were more responsive, and were less restrictive and negative. – From Author's Abstract.

1117. HUMBLE, CHARLES (Univ. of North Carolina, Charlotte). **Influencing children's causal attributions for personal achievement outcomes.** Journal of General Psychology, 1983, **109**, 255–267.
Two experiments suggest that the capability to influence children directionally in their causal attributions for achievement outcomes can be achieved. – From the Article.

1118. HUMPHREY, LAURA LYNN (Univ. of Wisconsin). **Children's self-control in relation to perceived social environment.** Journal of Personality and Social Psychology, 1984, **46**, 178–188.
Children's perceptions of high class order and organization, involvement, and rule clarity were related to ratings and behavioral observations of children's self-control. – From Author's Abstract.

1119. HUONG, NGUYEN THANH (Univ. of Paris, France). **Élaboration d'une nouvelle hypothèse sur la reáction du jeune enfant a la personne étrangère.** Revue de Psychologie Appliqueé, 1983, **33**, 231–251.

Reported is a longitudinal study of infants' reactions to a stranger. Infants were 3–4 months old at first observation. – Ed.

1120. HYMEL, SHELLEY (Univ. of Waterloo, Ontario, Canada). **Preschool children's peer relations: issues in sociometric assessment.** Merrill-Palmer Quarterly, 1983, **19,** 237–260. Three different sociometric measures (nomination, paired-comparison, and rating-scale) are reviewed. – From Author's Abstract.

1121. JARVIE, GREGORY JOHN (Georgia Coll.); LAHEY, BENJAMIN; GRAZIANO, WILLIAM; & FRAMER, EDWARD. **Childhood obesity and social stigma: what we know and what we don't know.** Developmental Review, 1983, **3,** 237–273. Although there is overwhelming evidence to suggest that children hold a positive stereotype toward a mesomorph (normal) build when compared to other builds, and that this preference increases with age, studies have not convincingly shown a negative stereotype toward the endomorph or obese body build. – From Authors' Abstract.

1122. JOHNSON, W. F. (Univ. of Colorado Health Sciences Ctr.); EMDE, R. N.; PANNABECKER, B. J.; STENBERG, C. R.; & DAVIS, M. H. **Maternal perception of infant emotion from birth through 18 months.** Infant Behavior and Development, 1982, **5,** 313–322. Results indicated the presence of 5 emotional categories (interest, joy, surprise, anger, and distress) in most infants during the first 3 months. – Adapted from Authors' Abstract.

1123. JORGENSEN, STEPHEN R. (Texas Tech Univ.). **Beyond adolescent pregnancy: research frontiers for early adolescent sexuality.** Journal of Early Adolescence, 1983, **3,** 141–155. It is argued that understanding of early adolescent sexuality lags behind knowledge in other areas related to early adolescent development because of the strong emphasis on studying determinants and outcomes of teenage pregnancy. – From the Article.

1124. JUHASZ, ANNE McCREARY (Loyola Univ., Chicago). **Early adolescent perceptions of the need for adults to know more about them.** Journal of Early Adolescence, 1983, **3,** 305–313. Adults perceived a greater need to know more about a larger number of factors than did adolescents. Older children and females had higher percentages of perceived need than did younger adolescents and males. – From Author's Abstract.

1125. KAHN, JAMES V. (Univ. of Illinois, Chicago Circle). **Sensorimotor period and adaptive behavior development of severely and profoundly mentally retarded children.** American Journal of Mental Deficiency, 1983, **88,** 69–75. The relationship of the Uzgiris and Hunt Scales of Sensorimotor Development with 6 of the AAMD Adaptive Behavior Scale (ABS) domains and the Receptive-Expressive Emergent Language (REEL) Scale was investigated. One canonical root was found. Independent variables (vocal imitation, object permanence, and gestural imitation) and dependent variables (ABS domains Language, Socialization, Independent Functioning, and Self-Direction and REEL-Receptive and REEL-Expressive) loaded highly on the canonical root. – From Author's Abstract.

1126. KARNES, FRANCES A. (Univ. of Southern Mississippi), & WHERRY, JEFFREY N. **CPQ personality factors of upper elementary gifted students.** Journal of Personality Assessment, 1983, **47,** 303–304. Gifted males were more controlled, socially precise, self-disciplined, and compulsive than females, and were described as more casual and careless of social rules. Gifted females were more assertive and independent than males. – From Authors' Abstract.

1127. KARPOE, KELLY P., & OLNEY, RACHEL L. (Bates Coll.). **The effect of boys' or girls' toys on sex-typed play in preadolescents.** Sex Roles, 1983, **9,** 507–518.

For both sexes, feminine play constructions and descriptive stories occurred with girls' toys, and masculine ones with boys' toys. – From Authors' Abstract.

1128. KAZNOVA, G. V. **Correlation of socially useful activity and communication in adolescents.** Questions of Psychology (translation of Russian title), 1983, **3**, 40–45.
Intimate-individual, group-spontaneous, and society-oriented communications have been studied by means of a complex procedure comprised of interviews, observation, questionnaires, quantitative-qualitative analysis of compositions, experimental situations, etc. The data prove that participation of adolescents in a purposefully designed system of socially useful activity determines their attitude to different forms of communication. – From Author's Abstract.

1129. KENNEDY, JANICE H. (Bluefield Coll.), & BAKEMAN, ROGER. **The early mother–infant relationship and social competence with peers and adults at three years.** Journal of Psychology, 1984, **116**, 23–24.
The mother's responsiveness at 3 months was related to the child's later social competence with adults, while the infant's responsiveness to mother at 3 months was not correlated with measures of social competence with either adults or with peers. – From Authors' Abstract.

1130. KOUDELKOVÁ, ANNA (Inst. for Social Medicine & the Organization of the Health Services, 121 38, Praha 2, Vitĕzného única 54, Czechoslovakia). **Child-rearing origins of extraversion–introversion in children.** Studia Psychologica, 1983, **25**, 287–296.
From the structure of correlations of parental childrearing attitudes and behavior and the introversion–extraversion traits, it followed that the pole of extraversion was independent of parental behavior toward the child, while the pole of introversion correlated with the impaired acceptance of the child by his parents without their apparent hostile authoritative attitudes being fully activated. – From Author's Abstract.

1131. KRASNOR, LINDA ROSE (Brock Univ., St. Catharines, Ontario, Canada). **An observational case study of failure in social problem-solving.** Journal of Applied Developmental Psychology, 1983, **4**, 81–98.
The relative frequencies of the social goals, strategies, and targets shown by this child during free play were plotted in relation to that of his same-sex peer group. Profiles of relative success were also prepared. – Adapted from Author's Abstract.

1132. KRASNOR, LINDA ROSE (Brock Univ., St. Catharines, Ontario, Canada), & RUBIN, KENNETH H. **Preschool social problem solving: attempts and outcomes in naturalistic interaction.** Child Development, 1983, **54**, 1545–1558.
Preschoolers were observed for 5 hours each. Eliciting other-action and nonspecific initiations were the most frequent goals, directives and orienting were the most frequent strategies, and same-sex peers were the predominant targets. Social problem-solving attempts were successful approximately 57% of the time. Attention bids and nonspecific initiations tended to be most successful, as were attempts including object-agonistic strategies. – From Authors' Abstract.

1133. KULAS, HENRYK EDMUND (Higher School of Pedagogy, Szczecin, Poland). **Level of self evaluation and social position in the peer group.** Psychologia Wychowawcza (Educational Psychology: Bimonthly of the Polish Teachers' Union), 1982, **25**, 280–292.
Subjects were 194 students of the second and third grades of secondary school. Two aspects of social position of the individual in the school class group were analyzed, i.e., social recognition or the number of sociometric choices. The results showed a relation between level of self-evaluation of subjects and their social position in the group. – From Author's Abstract.

1134. KURDEK, LAWRENCE A. (Wright State Univ.), & KRILE, DONNA. **The relation between third- through eighth-grade children's social cognition and parents' ratings of social skills and general adjustment.** Journal of Genetic Psychology, 1983, **143**, 201–206.
The interpersonal understanding, perceived social self-competence, public self-awareness, and parents' assessments of social skills and personal adjustment were examined for third

through sixth graders. Low performance on social cognition tasks was related to parents' perceptions of social skills problems. – From Authors' Abstract.

1135. KYSELA, GERARD M. (Univ. of Alberta, Edmonton, Alberta, Canada), & MARFO, KOFI. **Mother–Child interactions and early intervention programmes for handicapped infants and young children.** Educational Psychology, 1983, **3**, 201–212.
The evidence from studies comparing mother–child interaction patterns in normal and atypical families suggested that mothers of at-risk and developmentally delayed children, as a group, may need added support and assistance from professionals, in the context of early intervention programs, to enhance their interaction skills. – From the Article.

1136. LADD, GARY W. (Purdue Univ.). **Social networks of popular, average, and rejected children in school settings.** Merrill-Palmer Quarterly, 1983, **29**, 283–307.
Analysis indicated that rejected children spent less time in prosocial interactions and more time in agonistic and unoccupied behaviors than did popular or average children and paralleled average children in time spent watching others play. – From Author's Abstract.

1137. LAMB, M. E. (Univ. of Utah); HWANG, C.-P.; FRODI, A. M.; & FRODI, M. **Security of mother- and father-infant attachment and its relation to sociability with strangers in traditional and nontraditional Swedish families.** Infant Behavior and Development, 1982, **5**, 355–367.
No relationship was found between infant-mother and infant-father attachment in the Strange Situation. Infants securely attached to fathers were most sociable with strangers. – Adapted from Authors' Abstract.

1138. LANDY, SARAH (Merici Ctr., 2710 22nd Ave., Regina, Saskatchewan, Canada); CLARK, CAMILLA; SCHUBERT, JOSEF; & JILLINGS, CHUCK. **Mother–Infant interactions of teen-age mothers as measured at six months in a natural setting.** Journal of Psychology, 1983, **115**, 245–258.
Like previous studies, the present study found that teen-age mothers showed high warmth and physical interaction but low verbal interaction with their infants. – From Authors' Abstract.

1139. LERNER, JACQUELINE V. (Stanford Univ.). **The role of temperament in psychosocial adaptation in early adolescents: a test of a "goodness of fit" model.** Journal of Genetic Psychology, 1983, **143**, 149–157.
Temperamental attributes of junior high school students and both actual and perceived demands of the 2 school contexts were assessed. Subjects whose attributes were least discrepant with the demands of the 2 contexts were more likely to have better scores on teacher-, peer-, and self-rated measures of adaptation than subjects whose attributes fit less well. – From Author's Abstract.

1140. LEVY-SHIFF, RACHEL (Tel-Aviv Univ., Ramat Aviv, Israel). **Adaptation and competence in early childhood: communally raised kibbutz children versus family raised children in the city.** Child Development, 1983, **54**, 1606–1614.
As compared to city children, the kibbutz children were found to be more instrumentally independent and self-reliant in routine and daily tasks, but less effective in the problem-solving tasks. They were also less responsive and cooperative with adult strangers. No significant difference between the 2 groups was found with regard to attachment, difficulty in separation from parents, adjustment to a nonfamilial setting (nursery school), and developmental disturbances. – From Author's Abstract.

1141. LI, ANITA K. F. (Univ. of Calgary, Alberta, Canada). **Peer interaction and activity setting in a high-density preschool environment.** Journal of Psychology, 1984, **116**, 45–54.
Subjects were children from preschool programs in Hong Kong. They were observed during all activities throughout the half-day programs on 3 mornings. Patterns of peer interaction pointed to an association between level of interaction and variation in activity settings. – From Author's Abstract.

1142. LIPSCOMB, THOMAS J. (Southeastern Louisiana Univ.); BREGMAN, NORMAN J.; & McALLISTER, HUNTER A. **The effect of words and actions on American children's prosocial behavior.** Journal of Psychology, 1983, **114,** 193–198.
The results indicated that the older children exhibited a higher level of generosity than the young children. The children's generosity was not affected by the model's exhortations or behaviors. – From Authors' Abstract.

1143. LIPSCOMB, THOMAS J. (Southeastern Louisiana Univ.), & COON, ROBERT C. **Parental speech modification to young children.** Journal of Genetic Psychology, 1983, **143,** 181–187.
Verbatim transcripts of the verbal interactions of 20 father-daughter dyads and 20 mother-daughter dyads engaged in free play in the family home environment revealed parental speech modification to be related to age of child. – From Authors' Abstract.

1144. LISS, MARSHA B. (California State Coll., San Bernardino); REINHARDT, LAURI C.; & FREDRIKSEN, SANDRA. **TV heroes: the impact of rhetoric and deeds.** Journal of Applied Developmental Psychology, 1983, **4,** 175–187.
The influence of cartoons on the behavior and judgments of children in grades K, 2, and 4 was studied. Older children grasped the implications of stories, but younger children did not. Children in the prosocial/aggressive condition were lower on message comprehension than subjects in the purely prosocial condition. – From Authors' Abstract.

1145. LIST, JUDITH A.; COLLINS, W. ANDREW (Univ. of Minnesota); & WESTBY, SALLY D. **Comprehension and inferences from traditional and nontraditional sex-role portrayals on television.** Child Development, 1983, **54,** 1579–1587.
Third-grade children were grouped as high, medium, or low stereotype and viewed both a traditional program, in which the main female character portrayed a wife and mother, and a nontraditional program, in which the main female character portrayed an Army officer and doctor. Results indicated that for both programs, children demonstrated accurate memory for role-relevant information, but children higher in sex-role stereotypy remembered less role-irelevant information than low-stereotype children. – From Authors' Abstract.

1146. LLOYD, JEAN (Rutgers Univ.), & BARENBLATT, LLOYD. **Intrinsic intellectuality: its relations to social class, intelligence, and achievement.** Journal of Personality and Social Psychology, 1984, **46,** 646–654.
We devised a scale that excludes instrumental attitudes toward intellectual pursuits and measures intrinsic intellectual motivation (IIM). Data from tenth graders tested hypotheses that involve the relations between IIM, socioeconomic status, need achievement, intelligence, and sex. The findings indicate a positive relationship between IIM and scholastic achievement, whereas need achievement shows no relationship. – From Authors' Abstract.

1147. LOCKHEED, MARLAINE E. (Educational Testing Service, Princeton); HARRIS, ABIGAIL M.; & NEMCEFF, WILLIAM P. **Sex and social influence: does sex function as a status characteristic in mixed-sex groups of children?** Journal of Educational Psychology, 1983, **75,** 877–888.
Students in grades 4–5 were assigned to teams of 2 boys and 2 girls of unfamiliar peers. Teams were randomly assigned to expectation training or control conditions. After individual exposure to treatments, team members were brought together for the first time to play a cooperative board game. Sex functioned as a status characteristic with girls who were perceived as less competent and less leader-like than boys. The experimental treatment, which did not change student behavior, improved peer perceptions of girls relative to boys. – From Authors' Abstract.

1148. LOEVINGER, JANE (Washington Univ.). **On ego development and the structure of personality.** Developmental Review, 1983, **3,** 339–350.
This paper sharply critiques Snarey, Kohlberg, and Noam (1983). – Ed.

1149. LUSZCZ, MARY A. (Flinders Univ., Bedford Park, South Australia). **An attitudinal assessment of perceived intergenerational affinities linking adolescence and old age.** International Journal of Behavioral Development, 1983, **6,** 221–231.
When asked to characterize ideal, real, and typical adolescents and middle-aged and elderly adults, university students consider that these groups share some characteristics but not others. – From the Article.

1150. McCALL, ROBERT B. (Boys Town Ctr., Nebraska); GREGORY, THOMAS G.; & MURRAY, JOHN P. **Communicating developmental research results to the general public through television.** Developmental Psychology, 1984, **20,** 45–54.
We summarize a project in which developmental psychologists worked cooperatively with producers to create a series of 20 newsfeatures that were broadcast across the country. Public relations specialists, an interviewer, and 2 developmental psychologists experienced in TV appearances provide suggestions for developmental psychologists on how to be more effective as sources for news programs, talk shows, and documentaries. – From Authors' Abstract.

1151. McCAUGHAN, L. R. (Univ. of Sydney, Australia). **Effects of achievement motivation and success/failure on attributions, expectancies, and performance on a psychomotor task.** Perceptual and Motor Skills, 1983, **56,** 901–902.
No differences were found in performance, attribution, or expectancy among male high school students classified as high- and low-need achievers. Feedback produced differences for attribution and expectancy. – Adapted from Author's Abstract.

1152. McCOLGAN, EDGAR B. (Univ. of Tennessee Ctr. for the Health Sciences); REST, JAMES R.; & PRUITT, DAVID B. **Moral judgment and antisocial behavior in early adolescence.** Journal of Applied Developmental Psychology, 1983, **4,** 189–199.
A group of boys with disruptive and antisocial behavior was matched with a counterpart of 14 variables. Rest's Defining Issues Test scores differentiated the groups, while Kohlberg's Moral Judgment Interview did not. – Adapted from Authors' Abstract.

1153. McCONKEY, R. (St. Michael's House, Upper Kilmacud, Stillorgan, Dublin, Ireland); McCORMACK, B.; & NAUGHTON, MARY. **A national survey of young people's perceptions of mental handicap.** Journal of Mental Deficiency Research, 1983, **27,** 171–183.
Only 1/4 of the Irish adolescent students had ever interacted with a mentally handicapped adult, and nearly 1/2 of them had never been in their company. – From the Article.

1154. McCONKEY, ROY (St. Michael's House Research, Upper Kilmacud, Stillorgan, Dublin, Ireland), & MARTIN, HEATHER. **Mothers' play with toys: a longitudinal study with Down's syndrome infants.** Child: Care, Health and Development, 1983, **9,** 215–226.
Significant differences were noted in mothers' play patterns with different toys, and over the year there were marked changes in their actions. The findings reinforce the competency of most mothers as interactors with, and teachers of, their children. – From Authors' Abstract.

1155. McELROY, MARY A. (Kansas State Univ.). **Parent–Child relations and orientations toward sport.** Sex Roles, 1983, **9,** 997–1004.
Same- and cross-sex parent-child relationships were examined with regard to whether these social interactions were differentially related to children's orientations toward sport. Mother–son relationships were associated with more traditional female sport orientations in boys; father–daughter relationships were also related to stronger female sport orientations in girls. – From Author's Abstract.

1156. MAIN, M. (Univ. of California, Berkeley). **Exploration, play, and cognitive functioning related to infant-mother attachment.** Infant Behavior and Development, 1983, **6,** 167–174.

Infant-mother dyads were studied at 12 and 21 months. Infants securely attached at 12 months tended to have larger vocabularies, were more playful, and had longer attention spans at 21 months. – From Abstract by S. Thomas.

1157. MARCIA, JAMES E. (Simon Fraser Univ.). **Some directions for the investigation of ego development in early adolescence.** Journal of Early Adolescence, 1983, **3,** 215–223.
Early adolescence is marked by the formation of an ego ideal and the synthesis of an ego identity. Our society provides the prolonged period of adolescence necessary for this development to take place. – From Author's Abstract.

1158. MASH, ERIC J. (Univ. of Calgary, Alberta, Canada), & JOHNSTON, CHARLOTTE. **The prediction of mothers' behavior with their hyperactive children during play and task situations.** Child & Family Behavior Therapy, 1983, **5**(2), 1–14.
The amounts of interaction, control, and nonresponding exhibited by mothers during play and task situations were correlated with both their children's behavior and their reported self-esteem and stress associated with the parental role. – From Authors' Abstract.

1159. MATSON, JOHNNY L. (Northern Illinois Univ.); ROTATORI, ANTHONY F.; & HELSEL, WILLIAM J. **Development of a rating scale to measure social skills in children: the Matson Evaluation of Social Skills with Youngsters (MESSY).** Behaviour Research and Therapy, 1983, **21,** 335–340.
The MESSY was completed on 744 children 4–18 years of age. A self-report form was completed on 422 children, while 322 children were rated on a teacher-report measure using a 5-point Likert-type scale. Analyses included test-retest reliability. – From Authors' Abstract.

1160. MATTHEWS, KAREN A. (Univ. of Pittsburgh), & AVIS, NANCY E. **Stability of overt Type A behaviors in children: results from a one-year longitudinal study.** Child Development, 1983, **54,** 1507–1512.
The measure of overt Type A behaviors was the Matthews Youth Test for Health (MYTH), which was completed by the children's classroom teacher. Correlations between repeated MYTH ratings approximated .55 and in general increased somewhat with the children's school grade. The degree of similarity across 1 year in children's Type A behaviors was comparable to that found for adult Type A behaviors and for other cardiovascular risk factors in children. Etiological factors in the development of Type A might profitably be studied in primary school-aged children. – From Authors' Abstract.

1161. MILLER, THOMAS W. (Univ. of Kentucky). **Identification process and sensory impact of children's television programming on the preschool child.** Child Study Journal, 1983, **13,** 203–207.
Ratings of verbal and nonverbal response patterns in programs offered to preschoolers were made. Differences existed between educational children's programs and cartoon features. – From Author's Abstract.

1162. MONTEMAYOR, RAYMOND (Univ. of Utah). **Parents and adolescents in conflict: all families some of the time and some families most of the time.** Journal of Early Adolescence, 1983, **3,** 83–103.
This review does not indicate that the old "Sturm and Drang" view of parent-adolescent relations was correct, but, perhaps in our attempt to be modern and repudiate this view we have lost sight of the fact that conflict is a part of any relationship. – Adapted from the Article.

1163. MORAN, JAMES D., III (Virginia Polytechnic Inst. & State Univ.), & O'BRIEN, GAYLE. **The development of intention-based moral judgments in three- and four-year-old children.** Journal of Genetic Psychology, 1983, **143,** 175–179.
Eight moral-judgment stories were read to 3 1/2- and 4 1/2-year-old children. The stories included either positive or negative intentions and either positive or negative consequences with damage to either a person or property. In positive-intention/negative-consequence stories,

both age groups judged on the basis of consequence. In the negative-intention/positive-consequence stories, 4 1/2-year-olds made consequence-based judgments only in stories of property damage; 3 1/2-year-olds did not make consequence-based judgments in either context. – From Authors' Abstract.

1164. MURAI, NORIO (Tohoku Univ., Sendai, Japan); NIHEI, YOSHIAKI; NASU, ICHIRO; & YONEMOTO, YUKINORI. **Stability of individual differences in early infancy.** Tohoku Psychologica Folia, 1982, **41,** 95–106.
Individual stability in very early infancy was studied by the use of a maternal questionnaire. The factor analysis on the questionnaire data of 183 newborn, 286 1-month-old, and 183 4-month-old infants produced 6, 7, and 8 factors (behavioral dimensions) for the newborn, the 1-month-olds, and the 4-month-olds, respectively. The results support the view that a sprout of behavioral stability is already displayed by infants during their very early period of life. – From Authors' Abstract.

1165. NEUBERGER, HELMUT (Univ. Bamberg, Germany); MERZ, JÜRGEN; & SELG, HERBERT. **Imitation bei Neugeborenen—eine kontroverse Befundlage.** Zeitschrift für Entwicklungspsychologie und Pädagogische Psychologie, 1983, **15,** 267–276.
An experiment by Meltzoff and Moore (1977) was replicated and extended. In 10 3-week-old infants, no evidence of imitation behavior was found. – From Authors' Abstract.

1166. NEWCOMB, ANDREW F. (Michigan State Univ.), & BUKOWSKI, WILLIAM M. **Social impact and social preference as determinants of children's peer group status.** Developmental Psychology, 1983, **19,** 856–867.
Three sociometric procedures were evaluated on 3 independent samples of fourth- and fifth-grade children. An alternative 2-dimensional sociometric model based on probability theory was proposed and was found to have excellent performance characteristics while still providing a constant frame of reference across social networks. – From Authors' Abstract.

1167. NEWMAN, BARBARA M. (Ohio State Univ.), & MURRAY, COLLEEN I. **Identity and family relations in early adolescence.** Journal of Early Adolescence, 1983, **3,** 293–303.
The focus is on elements of the family system that influence and are influenced by work on identity in early adolescence. The argument is made for the need to study the family from a bidirectional and systems perspective. – From Authors' Abstract.

1168. NIECIUNSKI, STANISLAW (Jagiellonian Univ., Cracow, Poland). **Acceleration of infants' social development in home and institutional environments.** Psychologia Wychowawcza (Educational Psychology: Bimonthly of the Polish Teachers Union), 1982, **25,** 227–242.
A cross-generational comparative analysis was conducted of the indices of rate and rhythm of development of infants ages 6–9 months raised in the home, in the creche and in the children's home. A clear acceleration was found in the development of home-raised infants as well as in infants in home and creche care. – From Author's Abstract.

1169. NOPPE, ILLENE C. (Lawrence Univ.). **A cognitive-developmental perspective on the adolescent self-concept.** Journal of Early Adolescence, 1983, **3,** 275–286.
Subjects 8, 12, and 16 years old were given the Twenty Statements Test (TST), the Coopersmith Self-Esteem Inventory, and Piagetian measures of concrete and formal reasoning. No effects due to cognitive-developmental level were found on the TST protocols. Age and sex were important for physical, concrete, introspective, and abstract dimensions of the self-concept for adolescent subjects. – From Author's Abstract.

1170. O'BRIEN, MARION (Univ. of Kansas); HUSTON, ALETHA C.; & RISLEY, TODD R. **Sex-typed play of toddlers in a day care center.** Journal of Applied Developmental Psychology, 1983, **4,** 1–9.

Boys played more with masculine toys, whereas girls showed almost equal use of masculine, feminine, and neutral toys. – Adapted from Authors' Abstract.

1171. O'KEEFE, EILEEN S. C., & HYDE, JANET SHIBLEY (Denison Univ.). **The development of occupational sex-role stereotypes: the effects of gender stability and age.** Sex Roles, 1983, **9**, 481–492.
Children chose stereotyped occupations for themselves before they had gender stability. Boys' personal aspirations were more stereotyped than girls'. Gender-stable nursery-schoolers' responses were more stereotyped than those of nonstable children. – From Authors' Abstract.

1172. OLLENDICK, THOMAS H. (Virginia Polytechnic Inst. & State Univ.). **Development and validation of the Children's Assertiveness Inventory.** Child & Family Behavior Therapy, 1983, **5**(3), 1–15.
Psychometric properties indicate that the scale possesses high test-retest reliability and acceptable stability over time. – From Author's Abstract.

1173. OLLENDICK, THOMAS H. (Virginia Polytechnic Inst. & State Univ.). **Reliability and validity of the Revised Fear Survey Schedule for Children (FSSC-R).** Behaviour Research and Therapy, 1983, **21**, 685–692.
Initial analyses indicate that the FSSC-R possesses high internal consistency, high test-retest reliability, and acceptable stability over time. – From Author's Abstract.

1174. OLSON, S. L. (Univ. of Maine); BATES, J. E.; & BAYLES, K. **Maternal perceptions of infant and toddler behavior: a longitudinal construct validation study.** Infant Behavior and Development, 1982, **5**, 397–410.
Maternal perceptions were related to some measures of interaction and developmental competence. – Adapted from Authors' Abstract.

1175. OPPENHEIMER, LOUIS, & VAN DER HUUB, LEE (Univ. of Amsterdam, Netherlands). **Social perspective-taking and event sequences: a developmental study.** Psychological Reports, 1983, **53**, 683–690.
Three groups of 16 children each, ages 6, 7, and 9, were presented tasks assessing the reversibility operation, forward and backward temporal reconstruction, and social perspective taking. Reconstruction of social-event sequences preceded solutions in social and nonsocial reasoning. – Adapted from Authors' Abstract.

1176. PACKER, MARTIN J. (Univ. of California, Berkeley). **Communication in early infancy: three common assumptions examined and found inadequate.** Human Development, 1983, **26**, 233–248.
The assumptions—that interaction is instrumentally oriented, that meaning is obvious and unitary, and that change has an external source—are tested. A more adequate account of communicative exchanges is proposed. – From Author's Abstract.

1177. PAGUIO, LIGAYA PALANG (Univ. of Georgia). **The influence of sex of child and parent on perceptions of the ideal child.** Child Study Journal, 1983, **13**, 187–194.
Parents' responses to Torrance's Ideal Child Checklist yielded 4 factors. Sex of child did not have an effect. However, fathers and mothers provided small but significant differences. – From Author's Abstract.

1178. PASSER, MICHAEL W. (Univ. of Washington). **Fear of failure, fear of evaluation, perceived competence, and self-esteem in competitive-trait-anxious children.** Journal of Sport Psychology, 1983, **5**, 172–188.
The competitive trait anxiety of male youth soccer participants was assessed prior to the start of a season. The responses of players in the upper and lower competitive trait-anxiety quartiles indicated that high-anxious players expected to play less well and experience greater shame, upset, and more frequent criticism from parents and coaches in the event of a poor performance. – From Author's Abstract.

1179. PAYNE, BEVERLY D.; SMITH, JANET E.; & PAYNE, DAVID A. (Univ. of Georgia) **Grade, sex, and race differences in test anxiety.** Psychological Reports, 1983, **53**, 291–294. There were no grade differences in test anxiety scores, but higher scores were noted fo female and black students. – Adapted from Authors' Abstract.

1180. PELLEGRINI, ANTHONY D. (Univ. of Georgia). **Development of preschoolers social-cognitive play behaviors.** Perceptual and Motor Skills, 1982, **55**, 1109–1110. Children's play became more social with age. Children 3–4 years old engaged in more nonso cial dramatic play than did 2-year-olds. Three- and 4-year-old girls engaged in more nonsocia functional play than boys. Boys engaged in more nonsocial dramatic play than girls. – From Author's Abstract.

1181. PETERSON, CANDIDA C. (Murdoch Univ., Western Australia); PETERSON, JAMES L.; & SEETO, DIANE. **Developmental changes in ideas about lying.** Child Development 1983, **54**, 1529–1535. Videotaped stories depicting deliberate lies and unintentionally untrue statements were presented to subjects ages 5, 8, 9, and 11 years and adults. Adults were more lenient thar children in their moral evaluations of all the statements. All age groups rated a guess that dic no harm as better than 1 that caused trouble, and they all judged selfishly motivated lies to be worse than both unintended falsehoods and "jocose" lies that aimed to please the listener. – From Authors' Abstract.

1182. PETERSON, LIZETTE (Univ. of Missouri, Columbia). **Role of donor competence donor age, and peer presence on helping in an emergency.** Developmental Psychology 1983, **19**, 873–880. Children in grades 1, 4, and 6 were interrupted by the experimenter as they played a gamblin game. Half of the children believed they were playing in the presence of an unseen peer bys tander; half did not. Half had received instructions on how to repair the game should it become stuck, and half had not. During the experimenter's absence, an unseen, same-sex peer playe with the game and emitted distress cues. Older children helped more than younger children children helped more when alone than with a peer, and children helped more when they hac received instructions. Instruction had a greater impact on lone children than on children with a peer present. – From Author's Abstract.

1183. PETERSON, POLLY E.; JEFFREY, D. BALFOUR (Univ. of Montana); BRIDGWATER CAROL A.; & DAWSON, BRENDA. **How pronutrition television programming affects chil dren's dietary habits.** Developmental Psychology, 1984, **20**, 55–63. Kindergartners were exposed to a series of 10 20-min videotapes over a period of 10 clas days. The tapes stressed healthy eating habits and nutritional concepts. Effects were meas ured using recall, information, preference, and behavioral assessments. Positive results were obtained on the recall and information measures; preferences and consumption did nc change. – Adapted from Authors' Abstract.

1184. PIOTROWSKI, CHRIS (Univ. of West Florida), & DUNHAM, FRANCES Y. **Locus o control orientation and perception of "hurricane" in fifth graders.** Journal of General Psy chology, 1983, **109**, 119–127. The hypotheses were: (a) children in the city hit by Hurricane Eloise would not show the expected age-related increase in internality, (b) children in the city hit would be more externa than children in the city not hit, and (c) children in the city hit would perceive the concep "hurricane" more positively than children in the city not hit. The third hypothesis was sup ported. – From Authors' Abstract.

1185. PLOPA, MIECZYSLAW (Gdańsk Univ., Gdańsk, Poland). **Social–Emotional func tioning of adolescents and perception of parental attitudes.** Psychologia Wychowawcz (Educational Psychology: Bimonthly of the Polish Teachers Union), 1983, **26**, 129–142.

Subjects randomly selected from elementary school populations were studied. Measures used were: Roe and Siegelman's PCR questionnaire and Schaefer's questionnaire on the pupil's school behavior. Diverse connections were found between the rearing approach of parents and the children's behavior. The factor of parent–child gender turned out to be important. – From Author's Abstract.

1186. PRAGER, KAREN J. (Univ. of Texas, Dallas). **Identity status, sex-role orientation, and self-esteem in late adolescent females.** Journal of Genetic Psychology, 1983, **143**, 159–167.
Undergraduate women were interviewed to determine their "identity status." They also completed sex-role orientation and self-esteem measures. Masculine sex-typing was associated with Identity Achievement, while feminine sex-typing and undifferentiatedness were associated with Moratorium and Diffusion. – From Author's Abstract.

1187. PRUCHNO, R. A. (Stein Gerontological Inst., 151 N.E. 52 St., Miami); BLOW, F. C.; & SMYER, M. A. **Life events and interdependent lives: implications for research and intervention.** Human Development, 1984, **27**, 31–41.
The central thesis of this article is that a single life event has the capacity to affect and change not 1 but several lives. This thesis is related to theory on attachment, roles, and convoys. – From Authors' Abstract.

1188. PUSEY, ANNE E. (Univ. of Chicago). **Mother-offspring relationships in chimpanzees after weaning.** Animal Behaviour, 1983, **31**, 363–377.
The contexts of separation and the positive interactions between mothers and offspring of all ages suggest that conflicting social requirements rather than increased rejection by the mother eventually draw mother and offspring apart. – From Author's Abstract.

1189. PUTALLAZ, MARTHA (Duke Univ.). **Predicting children's sociometric status from their behavior.** Child Development, 1983, **54**, 1417–1426.
Boys were videotaped during the summer before first grade as they attempted to enter a group of 2 unfamiliar boys. The 2 boys, who were experimental confederates, engaged in a series of scripted games and presented several scripted problematic social situations to the subjects. The tendency of subjects to fit into the group they entered by contributing relevant conversation was predictive of their social status 4 weeks later, even after controlling for intelligence. – From Author's Abstract.

1190. RASKU-PUTTONEN, HELENA (Univ. of Jyväskylä, Finland). **Parent–Child communication in families of different educational backgrounds.** Scandinavian Journal of Psychology, 1983, **24**, 223–230.
No difference was found between the higher and the lower educational group in nonverbal communication. The linguistic aspects of speech were similar in both groups. There were differences between the educational groups with regard to the planning aspects of speech, controlling, and conversational turn-taking. – From Author's Abstract.

1191. REED, G. L., & LEIDERMAN, P. H. (Stanford Univ.). **Is imprinting an appropriate model for human infant attachment?** International Journal of Behavioral Development, 1983, **6**, 51–69.
Results provide evidence against a sensitive phase for attachment: infants throughout the 6–30-month age range showed shifts in attachments, and no particular epoch in the infant's caregiving history was found to be most important in predicting their first attachment figure. – From Authors' Abstract.

1192. RENSHAW, PETER D., & ASHER, STEVEN R. (Univ. of Illinois, Urbana-Champaign). **Children's goals and strategies for social interaction.** Merrill-Palmer Quarterly, 1983, **29**, 353–374.

Children differ not only in the types of strategies they suggest but in the goals that underlie particular interaction strategies. Previous research has neglected the distinction between goals and strategies. – From the Article.

1193. RICHMOND, BERT O. (Univ. of Georgia); SUKEMUNE, SEISOH; OHMOTO, MAKOTO; KAWAMOTO, HAJIME; & HAMAZAKI, TAKASHI. **Anxiety among Canadian, Japanese, and American children.** Journal of Psychology, 1984, **116**, 3–6.
A revised children's manifest anxiety scale was administered to children in grades 1–6 in the U.S., Japan, and Canada. Canadian and American children were generally higher on the Lie score, and children from the U.S. reported a higher level of anxiety than did the other children. – From Authors' Abstract.

1194. RILEY, JAMES H. (317 N. Poppy, Lompoc, CA). **The relationship of self-concept with physical estimation and physical performance for preadolescent boys and girls.** Journal of Early Adolescence, 1983, **3**, 327–333.
Middle school subjects completed 2 identical assessments of self-concept, physical estimation, and physical performance at 12-week intervals. Positive relationships were found among the variables. The relationship between self-concept and physical estimation was greater than the relationship between self-concept and physical performance. – From Author's Abstract.

1195. ROBINSON, BRYAN E. (Univ. of North Carolina, Charlotte); BARRET, ROBERT L.; & SKEEN, PATSY. **Locus of control of unwed adolescent fathers versus adolescent nonfathers.** Perceptual and Motor Skills, 1983, **56**, 397–398.
Adolescent fathers are not psychologically different in their ability to control outcomes in their lives than controls. – From Authors' Abstract.

1196. ROOSA, MARK W. (Arizona State Univ.). **A comparative study of pregnant teenagers' parenting attitudes and knowledge of sexuality and child development.** Journal of Youth and Adolescence, 1983, **12**, 213–223.
The results indicate that the knowledge and attitude base of pregnant teenagers is identical to that of never-pregnant teenagers. – From Author's Abstract.

1197. ROZENDAL, FREDERICK G., & WELLS, JO M. (West Texas State Univ.). **Use of the semantic differential to evaluate long-term effects of loss of parent on concepts of family.** Journal of Genetic Psychology, 1983, **143**, 269–278.
Parent-loss college students rated "mother," "father," "marriage," and "family" less favorably than, "divorce" more favorably than, and "I myself" not differently from parent-intact subjects. – From Authors' Abstract.

1198. RUBIN, KENNETH H. (Univ. of Waterloo, Ontario, Canada). **Recent perspectives on social competence and peer status: some introductory remarks.** Child Development, 1983, **54**, 1383–1385.
Trends in research and publication in this area are examined to introduce a series of papers. – Ed.

1199. RUBIN, KENNETH H. (Univ. of Waterloo, Ontario, Canada), & DANIELS-BIERNESS, TINA. **Concurrent and predictive correlates of sociometric status in kindergarten and grade 1 children.** Merrill-Palmer Quarterly, 1983, **29**, 337–351.
Positive correlations were reported between positive peer interactions and peer status. Observations of negative peer interactions and observations of nonadaptive forms of solitary play concurrently predicted peer rejection. – Adapted from the Article.

1200. RUBINSTEIN, ELI A. (Univ. of North Carolina, Chapel Hill). **Television and behavior: research conclusions of the 1982 NIMH report and their policy implications.** American Psychologist, 1983, **38**, 820–825.

Research on television and behavior in the 1970s has recently been reviewed and evaluated in a 2-volume report from the National Institute of Mental Health. The general conclusion is that television is an important influence on child development in ways well beyond earlier findings that focused on violence and aggression. – From Author's Abstract.

1201. RUSSELL, JAMES A. (Univ. of British Columbia, Vancouver, British Columbia, Canada), & RIDGEWAY, DOREEN. **Dimensions underlying children's emotion concepts.** Developmental Psychology, 1983, **19**, 795–804.
Teachers of grades 3–5 provided a set of emotion words they thought to be the emotion lexicon of their pupils. The interrelationships among these emotion concepts were explored. Four multivariate analyses supported the hypothesized circular ordering of emotion words within a 2-dimensional space and the interpretation of the dimensions as pleasure and arousal. – From Authors' Abstract.

1202. SATTERLY, DAVID (Univ. of Bristol, 35 Berkeley Sq., Bristol, England), & HILL, JOAN. **Personality differences and the effects of success and failure on causal attributions and expectancies of primary school children.** Educational Psychology, 1983, **3**, 245–258.
Success vs. failure was the greatest influence on frequency and type of attribution and on level of emotional response among children aged 9–10 years. There were no systematic differences between learning milieu. – Adapted from Authors' Abstract.

1203. SAUCIER, JEAN-FRANCOIS (Univ. of Montreal, Quebec, Canada), & AMBERT, ANNE-MARIE. **Adolescents' self-reported mental health and parents' marital status.** Psychiatry, 1983, **46**, 363–369.
We surveyed Francophone teenagers in school in order to test for differences in mental health among adolescents according to their parents' marital status. Adolescents from legally intact families reported fewer emotional problems and a lower incidence of treatment for emotional problems than adolescents from divorced or widowed families. – From Authors' Abstract.

1204. SAVIN-WILLIAMS, RITCH C. (Cornell Univ.), & DEMO, DAVID H. **Conceiving or misconceiving the self: issues in adolescent self-esteem.** Journal of Early Adolescence, 1983, **3**, 121–140.
For an accurate portrait of adolescent self-esteem it is necessary to conduct research that is longitudinal and that employs a diversity of measures and methods. – From the Article.

1205. SCHMITT, J. PATRICK (Wright State Univ.), & KURDEK, LAWRENCE A. **Self-behavior focus of attention as a determinant of children's and adults' attributions to stories with negative outcomes.** Journal of Applied Developmental Psychology, 1983, **4**, 11–21.
Students in grades 4, 6, and 8 and college read stories for each of 2 levels: self-focus and behavior focus. When attributions were spontaneous, self-attributions were more frequently given than either behavior or external attributions to both self- and behavior-focus stories. For structured evaluations, subjects used cause and responsibility interchangeably, but only eighth graders and college students differentiated cause/responsibility from both blame and deservingness. – From Authors' Abstract.

1206. SCHUNK, DALE H. (Univ. of Houston). **Ability versus effort attributional feedback: differential effects on self-efficacy and achievement.** Journal of Educational Psychology, 1983, **75**, 848–856.
Children who were deficient in subtraction received training during which they periodically received ability attributional feedback, effort feedback, ability + effort feedback, or no attributional feedback. Children given only ability feedback demonstrated the highest subtraction skill and self-efficacy; the effort and ability + effort conditions did not differ, but each outperformed the no-feedback condition. – From Author's Abstract.

1207. SEBBA, JUDY (Univ. of Manchester, England). **Social interactions among pre-school handicapped and non-handicapped children.** Journal of Mental Deficiency Research, 1983, **27,** 115–124.
No differences were noted between handicapped and nonhandicapped children in their overall patterns of interaction, and they showed no preference in choice of playmates for "their own kind."—From the Article.

1208. SERBIN, LISA A. (Concordia Univ., Montreal, Quebec, Canada); STEER, JANET; & LYONS, JUDITH A. **Mothers' perceptions of the behavior and problem-solving skills of their developmentally delayed sons.** American Journal of Mental Deficiency, 1983, **88,** 86–90.
Mothers of delayed boys were found to hold an idealized view of "the average child's" problem-solving skills, were less accurate than were mothers of control boys in predicting their sons' level of performance, and tended to rate their sons as less cooperative and attentive. – From Authors' Abstract.

1209. SHEA, JOHN D. C. (Univ. of Newcastle, New South Wales, Australia). **Sex typing in Australian children as a function of social class, sex and age.** Australian Psychologist, 1983, **18,** 243–250.
Children from New South Wales, Australia, were tested for sex typing with the Franck drawing completion test. Males and females showed differences in mean scores, but no differences in mean scores were found related to other independent variables, age, and social class. – From Author's Abstract.

1210. SHUGAR, GRACE WALES (Univ. of Warsaw, Poland); GEPNER-WIECKO, KRYSTYNA; & ZAMECKA, JOLANTA. **Speech variation and the realization of social roles by preschoolers (II).** Psychologia Wychowawcza (Educational Psychology: Bimonthly of the Polish Teachers Union), 1982, **25,** 386–397.
The paper presents results of 2 studies addressed to a description of preschool children's capacity for speech differentiation according to changing requirements of social situations and social roles. Investigations were carried out in conditions resembling natural play interactions of a child with an adult. – From Authors' Abstract.

1211. SHULMAN, SHMUEL (Bar-Ilan Univ., Ramat-Gan, Israel), & KLEIN, MORRIS MOSHE. **Psychological differentiation, self-concept, and object relations of adolescents as a function of family consensual types.** Journal of Nervous and Mental Disease, 1983, **171,** 734–741.
Intact families consisting of an adolescent referred for psychotherapy and a sibling adolescent were classified according to the Reiss Card Sorting Test. All the families fit 2 types described by the theory of Reiss, the consensus sensitive and the distance sensitive; none were from the environment sensitive. Differences were found to exist between the adolescents in these 2 family types on personality measures. – From Authors' Abstract.

1212. SIGMAN, MARIAN (Univ. of California School of Medicine, Los Angeles); UNGERER, JUDY A.; & RUSSELL, ANDREW. **Moral judgment in relation to behavioral and cognitive disorders in adolescents.** Journal of Abnormal Child Psychology, 1983, **11,** 503–512.
Emotionally disturbed, cognitively delayed adolescents reported by their teachers to be shy and submissive were less capable of reasoning about moral issues than were adolescents who were seen as more assertive and socially engaged. – From Authors' Abstract.

1213. SILVERSTEIN, A. B. (Mental Retardation Research Ctr.–Lanterman State Hosp. Research Group, P.O. Box 100-R, Pomona); MORITA, DENISE N.; & BELGER, KYMBERLI A. **Sex differences and sex bias on the Boehm Test of Basic Concepts: do they exist?** Psychology in the Schools, 1983, **20,** 269–270.
The Boehm Test of Basic Concepts was administered to kindergartners. Neither their mean scores nor their standard deviations differed. – From Authors' Abstract.

1214. SIMMONS, CAROLYN H. (Univ. of Colorado), & SANDS-DUDELCZYK, KAREN. **Children helping peers: altruism and preschool environment.** Journal of Psychology, 1983, **115**, 203–207.
The results suggest that even preschool children can select from a repertoire of behaviors a response which is most appropriate for both a specific need for help and the social learning environment in which they are placed. – From Authors' Abstract.

1215. SIMPSON, EVAN (McMaster Univ., Hamilton, Ontario, Canada). **Emile's moral development.** Human Development, 1983, **26**, 198–212.
This discussion uses Rousseau's *Emile* to explicate Kohlberg's characterization of moral development and to illuminate several theoretical problems for Kohlberg's cognitive-developmental account. Their writings display remarkable similarities in the descriptions they give of moral growth, but they also reveal important disagreements. Analysis of these issues reinforces the importance of holistic approaches to affect, cognition, and the mechanisms of development, while implying that there are neither conventional nor adult stages of development. – From Author's Abstract.

1216. SLAUGHTER, DIANA T. (Northwestern Univ.). **Early intervention and its effects on maternal and child development.** Monographs of the Society for Research in Child Development, 1983, **48**(4), 1–91.
A 2-year study of early intervention with low-income black mothers and their 18–44-month-old children in which attempts were made to consider the social and cultural experiences the mothers brought to an early-intervention context is reported. Children were evaluated, and mothers and children were observed in a standard situation in their communities, so that comparability for the 3 study groups, 1 of which was a control group, could be established. Among other findings, it was found that mothers in both program groups were superior to controls at the end of the first, but not the second, program year on a measure of openness and flexibility relative to childrearing attitudes and practices, and discussion-group mothers were superior to controls on the Loevinger Scale of Ego Development. – Adapted from Author's Abstract.

1217. SMETANA, JUDITH G. (Univ. of Rochester). **Social–cognitive development: domain distinctions and coordinations.** Developmental Review, 1983, **3**, 131–147.
Research has identified 3 social-world conceptual domains: moral, societal, and psychological. This paper examines coordinations between conceptual domains in children's social judgments through a discussion of the experiential origins of the domains and judgments about mixed, second-order, and ambiguously multifaceted events. – Adapted from Author's Abstract.

1218. SNAREY, JOHN; KOHLBERG, LAWRENCE (Harvard Univ.); & NOAM, GIL. **Ego development in perspective: structural stage, functional phase, and cultural age-period models.** Developmental Review, 1983, **3**, 303–338.
Two subtypes are delineated within the structural stage approach—a monodomain and a multi-subdomain—and the latter is argued for. These concepts are then illustrated through an analysis of ego development theories. – From Authors' Abstract.

1219. SOSTEK, A. M. (Georgetown Univ. School of Medicine); SCANLON, J. W.; & ABRAMSON, D. C. **Postpartum contact and maternal confidence and anxiety: a confirmation of short-term effects.** Infant Behavior and Development, 1982, **5**, 323–329.
Maternal confidence increased following extended postpartum contact but was reduced in those mothers separated from their infants during the immediate postpartum period. There were no differences in infant development at 1 year. – S. Thomas.

1220. McKINNEY, JAMES D. (Frank Porter Graham Child Development Ctr., Univ. of North Carolina, Chapel Hill) SPEECE, DEBORAH L. **Classroom behavior and the academic progress of learning disabled students.** Journal of Applied Developmental Psychology, 1983, **4**, 149–161.

Group differences in teacher-perceived task orientation, independence, and verbal expressiveness replicated previous findings with the Classroom Behavior Inventory and this learning-disabled (LD) sample (grades 1–3). LD children interacted with teachers more often than classmates. Both teacher ratings and observational evidence converged on the importance of task-oriented behavior, independent functioning, and socially appropriate behavior. – From Authors' Abstract.

1221. SPENCER, MARGARET BEALE (Emory Univ.). **Children's cultural values and parental child rearing strategies.** Developmental Review, 1983, **3**, 351–370.
Findings from 3 studies in the Midwest, North, and South document that black preschool children show consistently Eurocentric (white-biased) choice behavior; the trend for most attitudes and preferences changes to an Afrocentric orientation during middle childhood. – From Author's Abstract.

1222. SROUFE, L. ALAN (Univ. of Minnesota); FOX, NANCY E.; & PANCAKE, VAN R. **Attachment and dependency in developmental perspective.** Child Development, 1983, **54,** 1615–1627.
The relationship between infant–caregiver relations and later overdependency of the child was examined by assessing children with varying attachment histories in a preschool setting. Children classified at 12 and 18 months as avoidant and resistant both were highly dependent in the preschool, based on teacher ratings, rankings and Q sorts, observed physical contact seeking, and observed guidance and discipline received from teachers. Children who had been securely attached were lower on all these measures and higher on "seeking attention in positive ways."—From Authors' Abstract.

1223. STELMASZUK, ZOFIA (Warsaw Univ., Poland). **The effect of social categorization on inter-group favoritism and discrimination.** Psychologia Wychowawcza (Educational Psychology: Bimonthly of the Polish Teachers Union), 1983, **26,** 241–256.
An experiment on social categorization processes on group favoritism and discrimination in intergroup situations was conducted. Subjects were 64 students in the Railroads Technical School in Warsaw. Results confirmed the hypothesis on the effect of social categorization in the display of favoritism to one's own group and discrimination against the other group in an intergroup situation. – From Author's Abstract.

1224. STEVENSON, IAN (Univ. of Virginia). **American children who claim to remember previous lives.** Journal of Nervous and Mental Disease, 1983, **171**, 742–748.
More definite conclusions about American cases suggestive of reincarnation must await further research. – From the Article.

1225. STOCKDALE, DAHLIA F.; GALEJS, IRMA; & WOLINS, LEROY (Iowa State Univ.). **Cooperative–Competitive preferences and behavioral correlates as a function of sex and age of school-age children.** Psychological Reports, 1983, **53,** 739–750.
Factor analysis of an 85-item inventory showed cooperation and competition factors, plus 2 others. Cooperative–competitive preferences were not related to behaviors rated by teachers or parents. Girls indicated more cooperative preferences than boys and remained cooperative over grades 4, 5, and 6, while boys declined in cooperative preferences. – Adapted from Authors' Abstract.

1226. STOKLOSA, BOGUMILA (Higher School of Pedagogy, Rzeszow, Poland). **Specific conditions for the child growing up in the incomplete family.** Psychologia Wychowawcza (Educational Psychology: Bimonthly of the Polish Teachers Union), 1981, **24,** 496–504.
The article discusses the psychological situation of the child growing up in conditions of the incomplete family (lacking in the father). Rearing and caretaking functions undergo change in this type of family. The direct consequence of the father's absence is the lack of possibility for the child to identify himself with the male model. – From Author's Abstract.

SOCIAL PSYCHOLOGICAL, CULTURAL, AND PERSONALITY STUDIES

1227. STONEMAN, ZOLINDA (Univ. of Georgia); CANTRELL, MARY LYNN; & HOOVER-DEMPSEY, KATHLEEN. **The association between play materials and social behavior in a mainstreamed preschool: a naturalistic investigation.** Journal of Applied Developmental Psychology, 1983, **4**, 163–174.
The use of play materials by mildly handicapped and nonhandicapped children was quite similar. Blocks and vehicles and water-play materials were associated with handicapped/nonhandicapped interactions. Library, fine motor, and art materials were associated with solitary activity; blocks and vehicles, water play, housekeeping, and music were associated with cooperative interaction; and blocks and vehicles with conflict. – From Authors' Abstract.

1228. STRAIN, PHILLIP S. (WPIC, 201 DeSoto, Pittsburgh); KERR, MARY MARGARET; STAGG, VAUGHAN; LENKNER, DONNA A.; LAMBERT, DEBORAH L.; MENDELSOHN, SYLVIA R.; & FRANCA, VANY M. **Relationships between self-concept and directly observed behaviors in kindergarten children.** Psychology in the Schools, 1983, **20**, 498–505.
Kindergarten children were nominated by teachers as either not socially and academically competent or as competent. High-rated children who felt best about themselves were higher achievers and more compliant than were their study-group cohorts. Low-rated children who felt best about themselves were more off-task, more negative in their peer contacts, and inferior academically to their study-group cohorts. – From Authors' Abstract.

1229. STRAŚ-ROMANOWSKA, MARIA (Univ. of Wroclaw, Poland). **Research considerations on aspiration level of preschool and early school age children.** Psychologia Wychowawcza (Educational Psychology: Bimonthly of the Polish Teachers Union), 1981, **24**, 459–468.
For preschoolers, action results do not comprise a goal in itself (nor a motive). Therefore, in order to study aspiration level in children, the proposal is put forward that a highly preferred reward should be associated with action result; otherwise, aspiration-level research will be nothing more than the study of correct assessment of task difficulty level. – From Author's Abstract.

1230. SUTTON, PHILIP M., & SWENSEN, CLIFFORD H. (Purdue Univ.). **The reliability and concurrent validity of alternative methods for assessing ego development.** Journal of Personality Assessment, 1983, **47**, 468–475.
The unstructured interview and the Thematic Appreciation Test are suitable alternatives to Loevinger's Sentence Completion Test of Ego Development. Subjects were from 6 groups varying widely with respect to age and education level. – From Authors' Abstract.

1231. ŠVANCARA, JOSEF (Univ. J. E. Purkyně, Brno, Czechoslovakia). **Otázky implementace ve vývojové psychologii** [Questions of implementation in developmental psychology]. Československá Psychologie, 1983, **27**, 35–38.
The author defines implementation and outlines the questions relating to the process theory in individual developmental psychological disciplines in Czechoslovakia. – From Author's Abstract.

1232. TAAL, MARGOT (Univ. of Amsterdam, Vondelstraat 103, Amsterdam, Netherlands). **Individual and social problem solving strategies: inter- versus intraindividual coordinations.** International Journal of Behavioral Development, 1983, **6**, 205–212.
Subjects of similar cognitive levels were assigned to 1 of 4 training conditions involving opportunities for either individual or group practice on materials that were either identical to or different from those used during the pretest. Subjects were given a pretest and immediate and delayed posttests consisting of the same mobile construction task used during the training. Posttest evaluations revealed improvement for both groups exposed to individual or group mobile training. – From Author's Abstract.

1233. TESCH, STEPHANIE A. (Rider Coll.). **Review of friendship development across the life span.** Human Development, 1983, **26**, 266–276.

213

Friendship develops from a basis of mutual liking and shared activities in early childhood to include loyalty and mutual aid in late childhood. Intimate self-disclosure becomes a function of friendship in adolescence with certain aspects of intimacy more typical of females than males. – From Author's Abstract.

1234. TESLER, MARY (Univ. of California, San Francisco); WARD, JUDITH; SAVEDRA, MARILYN; WEGNER, CAROLE BUSS; & GIBBONS, PATRICIA. **Developing an instrument for eliciting children's description of pain.** Perceptual and Motor Skills, 1983, **56**, 315–321.
Children (grades 4–7) can remember and identify a wide range of events that have caused them pain and can describe specific painful situations using suggested words as well as their own. – From Authors' Abstract.

1235. TESSER, ABRAHAM (Univ. of Georgia); CAMPBELL, JENNIFER; & SMITH, MONTE. **Friendship choice and performance: self-evaluation maintenance in children.** Journal of Personality and Social Psychology, 1984, **46**, 561–574.
Children named as friends those classmates whose performance (both actual and distorted) was better than their own on irrelevant activities and somewhat inferior to their own on relevant activities. There was also a striking similarity effect. Friends' overall performance was high similar to the subject's own overall performance. – From Authors' Abstract.

1236. TOKUNO, KENNETH A. (Univ. of Hawaii). **Friendship and transition in early adulthood.** Journal of Genetic Psychology, 1983, **143**, 207–216.
Young adult females are more likely to discuss issues of early adulthood with friends than with family, particularly the issues of personal values, friendship, and relationships with the opposite sex. – From Author's Abstract.

1237. TROUT, MICHAEL DAVID (Ctr. for the Study of Infants and Their Families, 503 N. State, Alma, MI). **Birth of a sick or handicapped infant: impact on the family.** Child Welfare, 1983, **62**, 337–348.
The experience of bearing and caring for a sick or handicapped infant is described from the point of view of parents whose responses were gathered from a clinical study. Implications for the child's development and ways of supporting the family are discussed. – Author's Abstract.

1238. TZELEPIS, ANGELA (Wayne State Univ.); GIBLIN, PAUL T.; & AGRONOW, SAMUEL J. **Effects of adult-caregiver's behaviors on the activities, social interactions, and investments of nascent preschool day-care groups.** Journal of Applied Developmental Psychology, 1983, **4**, 201–216.
Changes in 16 preschool children's activities, social interactions, and degrees of initiative and investment are reported in the first and fourth weeks of shared daycare experience. Between weeks 1 and 4, children increased in simultaneous involvement with peers, adults, and activities; increased in contacts with peers and adults; decreased in time spent in transition between activities; and increased in investment. Peer contacts decreased in the center with fewer adult-initiated contacts and increased in the high adult-contact center. – From Authors' Abstract.

1239. TZURIEL, DAVID (Bar-Ilan Univ., Ramat-Gan, Israel). **Sex role typing and ego identity in Israeli, Oriental, and Western adolescents.** Journal of Personality and Social Psychology, 1984, **46**, 440–457.
Subjects completed the Bar-Ilan Sex Role Inventory and the Adolescent Ego Identity Scale, which measures 3 factors: Committment and Purposefulness, Solidity and Continuity, and Social Recognition. More androgynous, less sex-typed, and less undifferentiated adolescents were found among Orientals than among Westerners. Analyses of variance of Sex Role Type X Ethnic Origin X Sex X School Type (4 X 2 X 2 X 2) and regression analyses were used on ego identity variables. Sex-role type was related to each of the ego identity variables, indicating that androgynous adolescents were highest followed by masculine, feminine, and undifferentiated adolescents. – From Author's Abstract.

SOCIAL PSYCHOLOGICAL, CULTURAL, AND PERSONALITY STUDIES

1240. TZURIEL, DAVID, & KLEIN, PNINA S. (Bar-Ilan Univ., Ramat-Gan, Israel). **Learning skills and types of temperaments as discriminants between intrinsically and extrinsically motivated children.** Psychological Reports, 1983, **53,** 59–69.
A discriminant function analysis indicated significant discrimination between intrinsically and extrinsically motivated kindergarten children on sex, writing ability, visual perception, vividness-energy, persistence, and attention span. – From Authors' Abstract.

1241. VAN HECKE, MADELEINE (North Central Coll.), & TRACY, ROBERT J. **Sex differences in children's responses to achievement and approval.** Child Study Journal, 1983, **13,** 165–173.
Children could gain approval from the experimenter only at the expense of objective success and vice versa. Girls in grades 1–6 opted for approval, while boys opted for success. However, when social approval was unavailable, both boys and girls appeared motivated by success. – From Authors' Abstract.

1242. VAN IJZENDOORN, M. H.; TAVECCHIO, L. W. C.; GOOSSENS, F. A.; VERGEER, M. M.; & SWAAN, J. (Univ. of Leiden, Netherlands). **How B is B4? Attachment and security of Dutch children in Ainsworth's Strange Situation and at home.** Psychological Reports, 1983, **52,** 683–691.
Ainsworth's Strange Situation procedure was applied to a Dutch sample. The instrument was validated by means of a questionnaire for the mothers concerning children's feelings about separations. – From Authors' Abstract.

1243. WEBB, THOMAS E., & VAN DEVERE, CHRIS A. (Children's Hosp. Medical Ctr. of Akron and Northeastern Ohio Universities Coll. of Medicine). **Developmental and population commonalities in affective expression: a confirmatory factor analytic approach.** Psychological Reports, 1983, **52,** 859–864.
Factor analysis of interview data confirms a structural model for the expression of affectivity that appears to generalize across ages of both children and adolescents and across normal and psychopathological populations. Factors associated with deviations in feeling, relating, thinking, and impetuosity may represent stable attributes measurable from the Structured Pediatric Psychosocial Interview. – From Authors' Abstract.

1244. WEGLINSKI, ANDRZEJ (M. Curie-Sklodowska Univ., Lublin, Poland). **Empathy level and adolescent behavior in the corrective institution.** Psychologia Wychowawcza (Educational Psychology: Bimonthly of the Polish Teachers Union), 1983, **26,** 317–326.
The presented research is the first in Polish literature to attempt measurement of empathy level in delinquent minors and to determine its influence on minors' behavior in the correctional institution. – From Author's Abstract.

1245. WEHREN, AILEEN (YWCA, 802 N. Lafayette, South Bend), & DE LISI, RICHARD. **The development of gender understanding: judgments and explanations.** Child Development, 1983, **54,** 1568–1578.
Subjects 3, 5, 7, and 9 years old provided gender-constancy judgments and explanations. Results verified the acquisition of understanding of gender stability prior to gender constancy, as well as a shift with age from no constancy to pseudoconstancy to true constancy. No clear order of acquisition emerged of knowledge of aspects of constancy (activities, physical attributes, and psychological traits). – From Authors' Abstract.

1246. WEISS, MAUREEN R. (Univ. of Oregon), & BREDEMEIER, BRENDA JO. **Developmental sport psychology: a theoretical perspective for studying children in sport.** Journal of Sport Psychology, 1983, **5,** 216–230.
A developmental approach is recommended as the framework from which to study children's psychosocial experiences in sport. Examples from the psychological and sport psychological literature are provided to illustrate the potential for conducting research on children in sport. – From Authors' Abstract.

1247. WHALEN, CAROL K. (Univ. of California, Irvine); HENKER, BARBARA; DOTEMOTO, SHARON; & HINSHAW, STEPHEN P. **Child and adolescent perceptions of normal and atypical peers.** Child Development, 1983, **54,** 1588–1598.
Students in grades 4, 6, 8, and 10 evaluated hypothetical male agemates who were portrayed as normal, hyperactive, antisocial, or mildly mentally retarded. The atypical boys were viewed as substantially more deviant than the normal boy within broad-ranging social, affective, and intellectual domains. Future problems were predicted for all 3 atypical boys, and parental interventions were recommended. Within this global negative perspective, the mildly retarded boy was viewed as most similar to the normal boys, and the antisocial boy was seen as the most dissimilar. – From Authors' Abstract.

1248. WIESENFELD, ALAN R. (411 Becker, Highland Park, NJ); WHITMAN, PATRICIA B.; & MALATESTA, CAROL Z. **Individual differences among adult women in sensitivity to infants: evidence in support of an empathy concept.** Journal of Personality and Social Psychology, 1984, **46,** 118–124.
The results support the hypothesis that high-empathy individuals are more emotionally responsive to infant emotional stimuli and hold different values about caregiving behavior. – From Authors' Abstract.

1249. YALOM, MARILYN (Stanford Univ.); ESTLER, SUZANNE; & BREWSTER, WENDA. **Changes in female sexuality: a study of mother/daughter communication and generational differences.** Psychology of Women Quarterly, 1982, **7,** 141–154.
The present article reports (1) similarities and differences in sexual behavior between college-age women of the early 1950s and the late 1970s, (2) communication between mothers and daughters on the subject of sex, and (3) the effects of generational change in sexual behavior and attitudes on the overall mother–daughter relationship. – From Authors' Abstract.

1250. YINON, YOEL (Bar-Ilan Univ., Ramat-Gan, Israel); SHARON, IRIT; & MALKIMAN, BAT-AMI. **Age similarity and helping intentions.** International Journal of Behavioral Development, 1983, **6,** 233–240.
Children, adolescents, adults, and pensioners were requested to collect books for either their own age group or any of the other age groups mentioned. Results revealed main effects for both the age of the potential helper and recipient, as well as an interaction between these 2 independent variables. – From Authors' Abstract.

1251. ZAHN-WAXLER, CAROLYN (National Inst. of Mental Health, 9000 Rockville, Bethesda); FRIEDMAN, SARAH L.; & CUMMINGS, E. MARK. **Children's emotions and behaviors in response to infants' cries.** Child Development, 1983, **54,** 1522–1528.
Reactions to young infants' cries were examined in children ranging in age from late preschool to preadolescence. Each child overheard either a preterm or a full-term tape-recorded cry from an adjacent room. Children's self-reports of empathy, their verbalized intentions to help, their actual helping responses, and observers' ratings of negative emotion were common responses to cries at all ages. There were increases with age in prosocial, behavioral interventions. Expressions of negative emotion were inversely related to subsequent forms of prosocial behavior that required direct interaction with the infant. – From Authors' Abstract.

1252. ZERN, DAVID S. (Clark Univ.), & STERN, GEORGE W. **The impact of obedience on intelligence and self-concept: a longitudinal study involving different situational contexts.** Genetic Psychology Monographs, 1983, **108,** 245–265.
Childrearing pressures to obey in the first 3 years and the obedience are related to intelligence and self-concept measures at 14 1/2. In situations perceived as dangerous, pressure to obey and actual obedience were positively related to IQ and self-concept. These same measures of obedience were negatively related to the same dependent variables in situations where neither danger nor good manners were involved. – From Authors' Abstract.

1253. ZIMMERMAN, IRLA LEE (Univ. of California, Los Angeles), & BERNSTEIN, MAURINE. **Parental work patterns in alternative families: influence on child development.** American Journal of Orthopsychiatry, 1983, **53**, 418–425.
There were no negative effects on children's social, emotional, and cognitive development attributable to maternal absence. – From Authors' Abstract.

EDUCATIONAL PROCESSES

1254. ABRAMOVICI, SHIMON (Univ. of Edinburgh, England). **Errors in proofreading: evidence for syntactic control of letter processing?** Memory and Cognition, 1983, **11**, 258–261.
Errors were more readily detected in content words than in function words, thereby clearly demonstrating the importance of syntactic factors in processing the words in a test. – From Author's Abstract.

1255. ACKERMAN, PEGGY T.; OGLESBY, D. MICHAEL; & DYKMAN, ROSCOE A. (Univ. of Arkansas for Medical Sciences). **Sex and group differences in reading and attention disordered children with and with hyperkinesis.** Journal of Learning Disabilities, 1983, **16**, 407–415.
Four groups of girls—hyperactive, reading disabled, hyperactive and reading disabled, or solely attention disordered—were contrasted with male counterparts on measures of intelligence, achievement, personality, and cognitive style. Across groups, sex differences were found for several measures. – From Authors' Abstract.

1256. ALGOZZINE, BOB (Univ. of Florida), & YSSELDYKE, JAMES. **Learning disabilities as a subset of school failure: the over-sophistication of a concept.** Exceptional Children, 1983, **50**, 242–246.
We compared 2 samples of school-age children. Some were identified as learning disabled by their respective school districts; others were low achievers. Few psychometric differences other than selected achievement scores were found between the groups of children. – From Authors' Abstract.

1257. ARAM, DOROTHY M. (Rainbow Babies & Children's Hosp., Cleveland), & HORWITZ, SAMUEL J. **Sequential and non-speech praxic abilities in developmental verbal apraxia.** Developmental Medicine and Child Neurology, 1983, **25**, 197–206.
Children having normal IQs but moderate to severe motor speech disorders characterized by consonant and syllable omissions were found to be deficient in verbal sequential abilities. – Adapted from Authors' Abstract.

1258. ASHMAN, SUSAN SCOTT, & VUKELICH, CAROL (Ursinus Coll.). **The effect of different types of nomination forms on teachers' identification of gifted children.** Psychology in the Schools, 1983, **20**, 518–527.
The use of a behavior-rating-scale teacher-nomination form will result in the greatest number of gifted children being correctly identified. – From Authors' Abstract.

1259. BADIAN, NATHLIE A. (101 Monroe, Quincy, MA). **Reading disability in an epidemiological context: incidence and environmental correlates.** Journal of Learning Disabilities, 1984, **17**, 129–136.
Reading-disabled boys tended to be later born in their families, and 40% of those born in the local area came from the 10.8% of boys born when the mean monthly climatic temperature was above 71°F. This was 7 times the rate for boys born in cool or moderate months. – From Author's Abstract.

1260. BARCLAY, LISA K. (Univ. of Kentucky). **Using Spanish as the language of instruction with Mexican-American Head Start children: a re-evaluation using meta-analysis.** Perceptual and Motor Skills, 1983, **56**, 359–366.

Use of Spanish as the language of instruction resulted in larger effect sizes than did the use of English, both languages, or a control treatment. – From Author's Abstract.

1261. BIEGER, ELAINE (District 10, New York City Public Schools). **Effects of two different training programs on visual discrimination of nonreaders.** Perceptual and Motor Skills, 1983, **56,** 1009–1010.
There was a mean difference in favor of second graders who used specific scanning strategies rather than word-matching exercises.-From Author's Abstract.

1262. BLATCHFORD, PETER (Univ. of London, England). **Children's entry into nursery class.** Educational Research, 1983, **25,** 41–51.
Children preferred solitary, relatively low-level activities but showed increasing sociability toward peers. Adults were rarely contacted. – Adapted from Author's Abstract.

1263. BLYTH, DALE A. (Ohio State Univ.); SIMMONS, ROBERTA G.; & CARLTON-FORD, STEVEN. **The adjustment of early adolescents to school transitions.** Journal of Early Adolescence, 1983, **3,** 105–120.

1264. BROWN, R. MICHAEL (Pacific Lutheran Univ.); SANOCKI, THOMAS; & SCHROT, DAVID. **Phonetic coding in marginally competent readers.** Journal of General Psychology, 1983, **109,** 87–94.
The findings raise the possibility that the phonetic-coding deficiency shown by children who are subaverage readers is not as pervasive as has been suggested previously. – From Authors' Abstract.

1265. BROWN, RONALD T. (Univ. of Illinois, Chicago), & ALFORD, NORMA. **Ameliorating attentional deficits and concomitant academic deficiencies in learning disabled children through cognitive training.** Journal of Learning Disabilities, 1984, **17,** 20–26.
It was hypothesized that a package of self-control procedures would improve academic performance on a number of measures in which learning-disabled children generally perform poorly due to faulty attentional processes. Performance on measures of reading, attention, and inhibitory control was improved. – From Authors' Abstract.

1266. BRYAN, TANIS (Univ. of Illinois, Chicago), & SMILEY, ANN. **Learning disabled boys' performance and self-assessments on physical fitness tests.** Perceptual and Motor Skills, 1983, **56,** 443–450.
Learning-disabled boys tended to perform more poorly on physical fitness tasks than normally achieving boys. Learning-disabled youngsters in private schools ranked themselves more favorably than those in mainstream classrooms. – Adapted from the Article.

1267. BURDG, NANCY B., & GRAHAM, STEVE (Auburn Univ.). **Effects of sex and label on performance ratings, children's test scores, and examiners' verbal behavior.** American Journal of Mental Deficiency, 1984, **88,** 422–427.
A child's sex and the interaction between sex and label did not influence performance ratings, test scores, or the examiners' verbal behavior. The label "developmentally delayed" had a negative impact on children's test scores. – From Authors' Abstract.

1268. BURIEL, RAYMOND (Pomona Coll.). **Teacher–student interactions and their relationship to student achievement: a comparison of Mexican-American and Anglo-American Children.** Journal of Educational Psychology, 1983, **75,** 889–897.
The Brophy–Good (1969) Dyadic Interaction System was used to record teachers' interactions with fourth- and fifth-grade students in 5 classrooms. Anglo-Americans received more teacher affirmation than Mexican Americans. Teacher affirmation was related to achievement for Mexican Americans but not Anglo-Americans. – From Author's Abstract.

1269. BUTTER, ELIOT J. (Univ. of Dayton), & SNYDER, FREDERICK R. **Effect of order of presentation on simultaneous and sequential Matching Familiar Figures tests.** Perceptual and Motor Skills, 1982, **55,** 1259–1262.
Third graders who took the simultaneous version first made fewer errors on the sequential version than did subjects who took the more difficult sequential version first. – From Authors' Abstract.

1270. CASKEY, WILLIAM E., JR. (East Tennessee State Univ.), & LARSON, GERALD L. **Relationship between selected kindergarten predictors and first and fourth grade achievement test scores.** Perceptual and Motor Skills, 1983, **56,** 815–822.
Otis–Lennon IQ, group and individual Bender scores, and teachers' ratings in kindergarten were correlated with first-grade Stanford Achievement Test and fourth-grade Ohio Survey Test scores. Marked differences in predictive validity were observed by school and sex. – From Authors' Abstract.

1271. CERMAK, LAIRD S. (Boston Veterans Administration Medical Ctr., 150 S. Huntington, Boston). **Information processing deficits in children with learning disabilities.** Journal of Learning Disabilities, 1983, **16,** 599–605.
The ability of learning-disabled children to process, retain, and retrieve verbal information is investigated within a series of information-processing tasks. These investigations reveal that both the rate and level at which these children process information are below the standards set by normal reading contemporaries. – Author's Abstract.

1272. COLLABOLLETTA, ERNEST A.; FOSSBENDER, ALLEN J.; & BRATTER, THOMAS EDWARD (88 Spier, Scarsdale, NY). **The role of the teacher with substance-abusing adolescents in secondary schools.** Psychology in the Schools, 1983, **20,** 450–455.

1273. CONNELLY, JAMES B. (Southeast Regional Resource Ctr., 538 Willoughby, Juneau). **Recategorized WISC-R score patterns of older and younger referred Tlingit Indian children.** Psychology in the Schools, 1983, **20,** 271–275.

1274. COTUGNO, ALBERT J. (Cognitive Therapy & Diagnostic Services, 169 Grove, Wellesley, MA). **Cognitive controls: a test of their modifiability and structural arrangement.** Psychology in the Schools, 1983, **20,** 351–362.
The results appear to confirm the hypothesis that cognitive control deficiencies can be remediated better by structure-based types of intervention than by the type of skill training normally provided in the classroom. – From the Article.

1275. DATTA, LOIS-ELLIN (National Inst. of Education, Washington, DC). **A tale of two studies: the Westinghouse-Ohio evaluation of Project Head Start and the Consortium for Longitudinal Studies Report.** Studies in Educational Evaluation, 1983, **8,** 271–280.

1276. DI LOLLO, VINCENT (Univ. of Alberta, Edmonton, Alberta, Canada); HANSON, DAWN; & McINTYRE, JOHN S. **Initial stages of visual information processing in dyslexia.** Journal of Experimental Psychology: Human Perception and Performance, 1983, **9,** 923–935.
Four experimental tasks were employed to explore the initial stages of visual information processing in a group of dyslexic boys and in a group of normal control subjects ranging in age from 8 to 14 years. Two tasks involved visual backward masking; the other 2 were temporal-integration tasks. The backward-masking tasks yielded evidence of slower rates of visual information processing in dyslexic children; the temporal-integration tasks yielded evidence of longer duration of visible persistence in dyslexic children. – From Authors' Abstract.

1277. DISTEFANO, EMILY A., & BRUNT, DENIS (Univ. of Texas, Austin). **Mentally retarded and normal children's performance on gross motor reaction- and movement-time tasks with varying degrees of uncertainty of movement.** Perceptual and Motor Skills, 1982, **55,** 1235–1238.

With uncertainty of movement, retarded subjects displayed increases in both reaction- and movement-time. For normal children, no change in performance was noted. – Adapted from Authors' Abstract.

1278. ELLEY, WARWICK B. (Univ. of Canterbury, New Zealand), & MANGUBHAI, FRANCIS. **The impact of reading on second language learning.** Reading Research Quarterly, 1983, **19,** 53–67.
Pupils 9–11 years old who read many stories showed second-language learning at twice the normal rate. – Adapted from Authors' Abstract.

1279. ENSSLEN, SABINE (Max Planck Inst. for Psychiatry, Munich, Germany), & BORMANN-KISCHKEL, CHRISTIANE. **Das Behalten zeitlicher und raümlicher Reihen bei Kindern mit Lese- und Sprachstörungen.** Zeitschrift für Entwicklungspsychologie und Pädagogische Psychologie, 1983, **15,** 196–206.
The hypothesis that retention of letter sequences by children with developmental reading and language disorders is affected by whether the material is presented temporally or spatially was partially supported. The subjects were dyslexic and normal children. – From Authors' Abstract.

1280. FINCH, A. J., JR. (Medical Univ. of South Carolina); SPIRITO, ANTHONY; GARRISON, STUART; & MARSHALL, PATRICIA. **Developmental differences in Bender-Gestalt recall of children with learning and behavior problems.** Perceptual and Motor Skills, 1983, **56,** 87–90.
The number of designs recalled increased with age and Performance IQ but not Full Scale IQ. – Adapted from Authors' Abstract.

1281. FISK, JOHN L. (Windsor Western Hosp. Ctr., 1453 Prince, Windsor, Ontario, Canada), & ROURKE, BYRON P. **Neuropsychological subtyping of learning-disabled children: history, methods, implications.** Journal of Learning Disabilities, 1983, **16,** 529–531.

1282. FREELAND, KENT (Morehead State Univ.), & DICKINSON, GEORGE E. **Social and academic conditions among blacks and whites in a rural southern desegregated school system.** Journal of Early Adolescence, 1983, **3,** 361–368.
It was concluded that academic performance of students did not improve after desegregation. Interracial contact was limited between the races, especially outside of school. Blacks tended to take a more active part in initiating an integrated situation. – From Authors' Abstract.

1283. GERARD, HAROLD B. (Univ. of California, Los Angeles). **School desegregation: the social science role.** American Psychologist, 1983, **38,** 869–877.
We desperately need research and development as well as systems engineering in the social sciences if we are eventually going to tackle and solve some of our social problems, including the successful implementation of school desegregation. – From Author's Abstract.

1284. GETTINGER, MARIBETH (Univ. of Wisconsin, Madison). **Relationship among IQ, time needed for learning, and retention in children referred for behavior problems.** Psychological Reports, 1983, **52,** 695–701.
WISC-R IQs were generally more strongly related to time to learn than either Peabody or Slosson scores. The intercorrelations among these measures did not vary appreciably as a function of the children's primary behavioral characteristic. – From Author's Abstract.

1285. GEUB, HERBERT (Univ. Osnabrück, Vechta, Germany). **Über Zusammenhänge zwischen der subjektiv erlebten Ähnlichkeit von Schriftzeichen und der Rechtschreibfertigkeit.** Zeitschrift für Entwicklungspsychologie und Pädagogische Psychologie, 1984, **16,** 35–46.
The use of distinctive features for the discrimination of lower-case letters was investigated using multidimensional scaling procedures. A trait-oriented hypothesis proposing overall less

salient features in children with poor spelling ability was confronted with a process-oriented hypothesis suggesting undifferentiated weighting of features for those children. Findings are interpreted to show that differentially weighted distinctive features may be as much a consequence of as a prerequisite to developing adequate information-processing strategies. – From Author's Abstract.

1286. GRADEN, JANET; THURLOW, MARTHA; & YSSELDYKE, JAMES (Univ. of Minnesota). **Instructional ecology and academic responding time for students at three levels of teacher-perceived behavioral competence.** Journal of Experimental Child Psychology, 1983, 36, 241–256.
Students in third and fourth grade were observed systematically over 2 school days. It was found that students perceived to be lower in behavioral competence spent more time engaged in certain inappropriate behaviors and received more teacher disapproval. – From Authors' Abstract.

1287. GRAVES, MICHAEL F. (Univ. of Minnesota); COOKE, CHERYL L.; & LABERGE, MICHAEL J. **Effects of previewing difficult short stories on low ability junior high school students' comprehension, recall, and attitudes.** Reading Research Quarterly, 1983, 18, 262–276.
Previews of short stories produced large gains in comprehension and retention of factual information from stories and in students' ability to make inferences related to the stories. – Adapted from the Article.

1288. GROSSMAN, FRED M. (Univ. of Nebraska, Lincoln). **Interpreting WISC-R Verbal-Performance discrepancies: a note for practitioners.** Perceptual and Motor Skills, 1983, 56, 96–98.

1289. HABERMAN, MARTIN (Univ. of Wisconsin, Milwaukee). **Criteria for judging early childhood program goals.** Studies in Educational Evaluation, 1983, 8, 215–218.
Programs for young children can be both development oriented with regard to eliciting growth and success oriented with respect to preparation for subsequent schooling. As various means of evaluating programs are examined, a conceptual distinction should be made between these different emphases. – From the Article.

1290. HALE, ROBERT L. (Pennsylvania State Univ.), & McDERMOTT, PAUL A. **Pattern analysis of an actuarial strategy for computerized diagnosis of childhood exceptionality.** Journal of Learning Disabilities, 1984, 17, 30–37.
Seven distinct and recognizable patterns emerged, supporting the verity and utility of the systems-actuarial approach to classification of child exceptionality. – From Authors' Abstract.

1291. HALL, JAMES W. (Northwestern Univ.); WILSON, KIM P.; HUMPHREYS, MICHAEL S.; TINZMANN, MARGARET B.; & BOWYER, PAUL M. **Phonemic-similarity effects in good vs. poor readers.** Memory and Cognition, 1983, 11, 520–527.
Experiments examined immediate serial recall of rhyming and nonrhyming items by normal and poor readers in grades 2–4. Poor readers did not differ from normals in their susceptibility to phonemic similarity cues. Previous results suggesting that poor readers are relatively insensitive to phonemic similarity in such tasks may have been an artifact of marked differences in overall task difficulty for the groups compared. – From Authors' Abstract.

1292. HASKINS, RON (Frank Porter Graham Child Development Ctr., Univ. of North Carolina, Chapel Hill); WALDEN, TEDRA; & RAMEY, CRAIG T. **Teacher and student behavior in high- and low-ability groups.** Journal of Educational Psychology, 1983, 75, 865–876.
Students in the highest and lowest reading groups in each of 19 classrooms were observed for 90 min. Interviews with teachers showed that they assigned students to groups primarily on the basis of informal observations of the child's ability and teacher-made tests and that teachers believed there were clear differences in the behavioral characteristics and academic needs of

"typical" high- and low-group students. Observations revealed that (1) high-group students were more often doing individual work, whereas low-group students were more often instructed as a group; (2) teachers used more drill, more error correction, more control statements, and more positive reinforcement with low-group students; (3) low-group students received more direct instruction from teachers, and (4) low-group students were more disruptive and more often off task than high-group students. – From Authors' Abstract.

1293. HATCHETTE, ROBERT K. (P.O. Box 938, Ballentine, SC), & EVANS, JAMES R. **Auditory–Visual and temporal–spatial pattern matching performance of two types of learning-disabled children.** Journal of Learning Disabilities, 1983, **916**, 537–541.
The results indicated a difference between the normal readers and the learning-disabled readers on certain tasks suggesting that learning-disabled readers are deficient in auditory–visual integration rather than temporal–spatial integration skills. – From Authors' Abstract.

1294. HATT, CLIFFORD V.; OBRZUT, JOHN E. (Univ. of Northern Colorado); & SWANSON, H. LEE. **Effects of verbal labeling on visual recall with reading disabled subgroups.** Perceptual and Motor Skills, 1982, **55**, 1149–1150.
Results for 10-year-old high and low comprehending disabled and normal readers indicated no differences on recall strength or primary recall, suggesting similar verbal skills. – Adapted from Authors' Abstract.

1295. HELMKE, ANDREAS (Max-Plank Inst., 8000 München 40, West Germany). **Ein Überblick über neuere theoretische Entwicklungen und empirische Ergebnisse** [Test anxiety: an overview of recent theoretical developments and empirical findings]. Psychologische Rundschau, 1983, **34**, 193–211.
The paper reviews Lazarus' cognitive theory and Wine's cognitive-attentional model of test anxiety and environmental correlates, such as school climate. Additional topics include methodological problems in assessment of test anxiety and test-anxiety therapy. – Adapted from Abstract by R. E. Muuss.

1296. HENDERSON, BRUCE B. (Western Carolina Univ.), & GOLD, STEVEN R. **Intellectual styles: a comparison of factor structures in gifted and average children and adolescents.** Journal of Personality and Social Psychology, 1983, **45**, 624–632.
Comparisons of the analyses indicated similarity in the structures of intellectual style in the gifted and average groups despite a previous report of group differences in mean level of response. – From Authors' Abstract.

1297. HENDRY, JOAN (Univ. of Ottawa, Canada), & KERR, ROBERT. **Communication through physical activity for learning disabled children.** Perceptual and Motor Skills, 1983, **56**, 155–158.
This study suggests that a physical activity program can influence basic cognitive skills as well as motor skills. – From Authors' Abstract.

1298. HOLDAWAY, STEVEN LEE, & JENSEN, LARRY C. (Brigham Young Univ.). **Self-, teachers', and mothers' perceptions of the behaviorally disordered child.** Psychology in the Schools, 1983, **20**, 388–394.
Normal and behaviorally disordered children, matched by grade and sex, were evaluated using the Piers-Harris Children's Self-Concept Scale. There were lower scores given by the 3 evaluator groups for the behaviorally disordered. – From Authors' Abstract.

1299. HONIG, ALICE STERLING (Syracuse Univ.). **Evaluation of infant/toddler intervention programs.** Studies in Educational Evaluation, 1983, **8**, 305–316.
Differences in program goals, theory, populations served, methods, duration, staff, and evaluation measures make it difficult to compare the effectiveness of different infant intervention programs. – From the Article.

1300. HORNBY, GARRY, & SINGH, NIRBHAY N. (Univ. of Canterbury, Christchurch, New Zealand). **Group training for parents of mentally retarded children: a review and methodological analysis of behavioural studies.** Child: Care, Health and Development, 1983, **9**, 199–213.
Behavioral group training studies with parents of mentally retarded children report favorable training outcome. The lack of certain methodological controls demands caution. – From Authors' Abstract.

1301. HORNE, MARCIA D. (Univ. of Oklahoma); POWERS, JAMES E.; & MAHABUB, PATRICIA. **Reader and nonreader conception of the spoken word.** Contemporary Educational Psychology, 1983, **8**, 403–418.
Evidence indicates nonreaders may be confused about the differences between a short word and phonemes, syllables, sentences, and long words. Subjects were 6–10 years old. – From Authors' Abstract.

1302. HORVAT, MICHAEL A. (Univ. of Nevada). **Effect of a home learning program on learning disabled children's balance.** Perceptual and Motor Skills, 1982, **55**, 1158.
Parents can enhance the static and dynamic balance of their learning-disabled children by implementing a structured gross-motor training program at home. – Adapted from the Article.

1303. JACOBOWITZ, TINA (Montclair State Coll.). **Relationship of sex, achievement, and science self-concept to the science career preferences of black students.** Journal of Research in Science Teaching, 1983, **20**, 621–628.
Results show that of all the independent variables, sex is the strongest predictor of science career preferences, accounting for 25% of the criterion variance. The findings suggest that early-adolescent science career preferences are related more to interests that are consonant with sex-role considerations. – From Author's Abstract.

1304. JAVEL, MARY ELLEN (676 N. 58 St., Omaha), & GREENSPAN, STEPHEN. **Influence of personal competence profiles on mainstreaming recommendations of school psychologists.** Psychology in the Schools, 1983, **20**, 459–465.
School psychologists were presented with profiles of children. Children depicted through competence profiles were recommended for significantly less restrictive placements than were children depicted through problem-oriented descriptions. – From Authors' Abstract.

1305. JUEL, CONNIE (Univ. of Texas, Austin). **The development and use of mediated word identification.** Reading Research Quarterly, 1983, **18**, 306–327.
Mediated word processing frequently occurred in both context-free and contextual reading. The degree that letter-sound correspondences or visual orthographic patterns were involved in mediated processing was shown to vary between age levels of readers. – From Author's Abstract.

1306. KIM, S. PETER (New York Univ. Medical Ctr.). **Self-concept, English language acquisition, and school adaptation in recently immigrated Asian children.** Journal of Children in Contemporary Society, 1983, **15**, 71–79.
A preliminary study of 12 native Korean immigrant children ages 7 1/2–10 years who had lived in the United States for less than a year at the time of the first study evaluation is reported. – From Author's Abstract.

1307. KOCHNOWER, JEFFREY M. (Long Island Research Inst., Health Sciences Ctr., Stony Brook); RICHARDSON, ELLIS; & DiBENEDETTO, BARBARA. **A comparison of the phonic decoding ability of normal and learning disabled children.** Journal of Learning Disabilities, 1983, **16**, 348–351.
Children from normal class placements and a learning-disability program were matched on reading level. The normal readers were able to read more regular real words and nonsense words than were the LD children. It is concluded that reading-disabled children experience

specific difficulty in learning to use the phonetic code to unlock unknown words. – From Authors' Abstract.

1308. LABERCANE, GEORGE D. (Univ. of British Columbia, Canada). **Correlations of reading achievement and ability for learning disabled students.** Psychological Reports, 1983, **53,** 212–214.
Achievement in reading, spelling, and arithmetic was related to performance on the WISC-R, Basic Visual-Memory Association Test, and the Test of Reading Comprehension. The lack of correlation of all other variables with the Test of Reading Comprehension suggests that inability to identify words successfully may preclude processing the relational aspects of meaning in longer discourse. – Adapted from Author's Abstract.

1309. LEE, LETA A. (Univ. of Southern Mississippi), & KARNES, FRANCES A. **Correlations between the Cognitive Abilities Test, Form 3, and The Ross Test of Higher Cognitive Processes for gifted students.** Perceptual and Motor Skills, 1983, **56,** 421–422.
Scores on the Cognitive Abilities Test Verbal and Nonverbal Batteries were positively correlated with The Ross Test of Higher Cognitive Processes. – From Authors' Abstract.

1310. LEE, PATRICK C. (Teachers Coll., Columbia Univ.); STATUTO, CAROL M.; & KEDAR-VOIVODAS, GITA. **Elementary school children's perceptions of their actual and ideal school experience: a developmental study.** Journal of Educational Psychology, 1983, **75,** 838–847.
Children reported discrepancy between their ideal and actual status in the action domain, asserting that they ought to have more prerogatives. This discrepancy increased with grade level. In the value domain, children were overwhelmingly positive. – From Authors' Abstract.

1311. LEPKIN, SHEILA RATSCH, & PRYZWANSKY, WALTER B. (Univ. of North Carolina, Chapel Hill). **Interrater reliability of the original and revised scoring system for the Developmental Test of Visual-Motor Integration.** Psychology in the Schools, 1983, **20,** 284–288.
The reliabilities were .90 or greater. – Ed.

1312. LEVIN, JAMES (Pennsylvania State Univ.), & FOWLER, H. SEYMOUR. **Sex, grade, and course differences in attitudes that are related to cognitive performance in secondary science.** Journal of Research in Science Teaching, 1984, **21,** 151–166.
The purpose of this study was to collect and analyze data on sexual differences in secondary school students' attitudes toward science. Attitudinal differences were also analyzed for the independent variables of science programs and grade levels. A number of sex differences were noted. – From Authors' Abstract.

1313. LEVINE, MAUREEN J. (Central Michigan Univ.). **The effect of task parameters in diagnostic reading groups.** Psychology in the Schools, 1983, **20,** 276–283.
This study compared the performance of normal, primary, and secondary reading groups on intersensory and intrasensory tasks requiring paired and serial recall. All readers exhibited similar patterns in the processing of bisensory information; however, unique differences were found among the groups. – From Author's Abstract.

1314. LOMAX, RICHARD G. (Louisiana State Univ.). **Applying structural modeling to some component processes of reading comprehension development.** Journal of Experimental Education, 1983, **52,** 33–40.
The results, based on LD children 6–11 years old, indicated that some proficiency in the phonological skills is important for the development of word-recognition ability, which in turn is a contributor to the comprehension of connected discourse. – From Author's Abstract.

1315. LOPER, ANN BOOKER (Univ. of Virginia), & REEVE, RONALD E. **Response bias on a locus of control measure by learning-disabled children.** Journal of Abnormal Child Psychology, 1983, **11,** 537–548.

The tendency of learning-disabled and low-achieving boys to choose second response alternatives may have resulted in the popular but unsubstantiated notion that disabled children are less internally oriented than normal children. – From Authors' Abstract.

1316. LUDEKE, RUSSELL J., & HARTUP, WILLARD W. (Univ. of Minnesota). **Teaching behaviors of 9- and 11-year-old girls in mixed-age and same-age dyads.** Journal of Educational Psychology, 1983, **75**, 908–914.
Tutors instructing younger children used repetitions, strategic advice, progress check-ups, direct assistance, and praise more frequently than tutors who instructed same-age tutees. Elementary school children possess an implicit "theory of teaching": younger children require more cognitive structuring and supportive and corrective feedback. – From Authors' Abstract.

1317. LUND, THORLEIF (Inst. of Psychology, Box 1094, Blindern, Oslo, Norway), & THRANE, VIDKUNN COUCHERON. **Schooling and intelligence: a methodological and longitudinal study.** Scandinavian Journal of Psychology, 1983, **24**, 161–173.
A general account of the adjustment problem is given within the frame of pretest-posttest design, and analysis of covariance, change score analysis, and standardized change score analysis are discussed. A Norwegian investigation of the relationship between schooling and intelligence is described, and the results, generated by several adjustment techniques, show substantial schooling effects. – From Authors' Abstract.

1318. LUNENBURG, FREDERICK C. (Loyola Univ., Chicago), & STOUTEN, JACK W. **Teacher pupil control ideology and pupils' projected feelings toward teachers.** Psychology in the Schools, 1983, **20**, 528–533.
Custodialism in teacher pupil control ideology was directly related to pupils' negative feelings toward teachers. Pupil control ideology, followed by teacher sex and grade level, predicted pupils' feelings toward teachers. Boys projected more negative feelings toward teachers than did girls. – From Authors' Abstract.

1319. McDOWELL, EUGENE E. (Western Carolina Univ.). **Specific aspects of prompting and fading procedures in teaching beginning reading.** Perceptual and Motor Skills, 1982, **55**, 1103–1108.
Prompting-and-fading and the prompting-only kindergartners maintained few errors during training, while the no-prompting kindergartners showed high initial errors which gradually declined. The prompting-and-fading and no-prompting groups performed similarly on word recognition after training and scored higher than the prompting-only group. – From Author's Abstract.

1320. McMAHON, MARGARET L. (Cornell Univ.). **Development of reading-while-listening skills in the primary grades.** Reading Research Quarterly, 1983, **19**, 38–52.
Reading while listening becomes more flexible and selective with reading experience. – Adapted from the Article.

1321. MADISON, LYNDA SALLACH (Univ. of Nebraska Medical Ctr.), & ADUBATO, SUSAN A. **Bridging the "Bayley-Binet gap."** Psychology in the Schools, 1983, **20**, 424–426.
Encountering children ages 18–23 months whose performance is not scorable by standard methods for either the Stanford Binet Intelligence Test or the Bayley Scales of Infant Development mental scale is a relatively frequent occurrence. A child must succeed on at least 2 or, more conservatively, 4 items at the 2-year level on the Stanford-Binet in order to assume an 18-month basal level. – From Authors' Abstract.

1322. MARION, MARIAN (Univ. of Wisconsin, Stout). **Child compliance: a review of the literature with implications for family life education.** Family Relations, 1983, **32**, 545–555.
The literature is examined from the perspectives of social learning theory and the ethological–evolutionary model. – From Author's Abstract.

1323. MARKOSKI, BARBARA D. (3658 E. Indigo, Mesa, AZ). **Conversational interactions of the learning-disabled and nondisabled child.** Journal of Learning Disabilities, 1983, **16,** 606–609.
Predictions that learning-disabled children would be less persuasive were not confirmed, as learning-disabled children and nondisabled peers appeared to be equally persuasive. The study failed to replicate previous findings of rejection, considerate, and competitive statements as discriminators of learning-disabled and nondisabled peers. – From Author's Abstract.

1324. MELINE, TIMOTHY (Univ. of Montevallo), & MELINE, NANNETTE. **Facing a communicative obstacle: pragmatics of language-impaired children.** Perceptual and Motor Skills, 1983, **56,** 469–470.
Facing a communicative obstacle, "I don't understand," language-impaired children communicated less effectively than their agemates. – Adapted from the Article.

1325. MISHRA, SHITALA P. (Univ. of Arizona). **Validity of WISC-R IQs and factor scores in predicting achievement for Mexican-American children.** Psychology in the Schools, 1983, **20,** 442–444.
All the correlations among the WISC-R factor scores and academic achievement as measured by the Wide Range Achievement Test were found to be low. Relationships were observed between IQ scores and achievement measures. – From Author's Abstract.

1326. MOORE, PHILLIP J. (Univ. of Newcastle, New South Wales, Australia). **Aspects of metacognitive knowledge about reading.** Journal of Research in Reading, 1983, **6,** 87–102.
The development of metacognitive knowledge about reading, its relationship to reading performance, and the influence of using 2 different interviewing techniques were studied. Among the results, metacognitive knowledge about reading developed over the age range studied (7–13 years). – Adapted from Author's Abstract.

1327. OBRZUT, JOHN E. (Univ. of Northern Colorado), & HYND, GEORGE W. **The neurological and neuropsychological foundations of learning disabilities.** Journal of Learning Disabilities, 1983, **16,** 515–520.
Research regarding the neurobiological basis of learning disorders, cerebral asymmetries, and neuropsychological assessment batteries for learning disabilities are discussed. – From Authors' Abstract.

1328. PAGET, KATHLEEN D. (Univ. of South Carolina), & REYNOLDS, CECIL R. **Dimensions, levels and reliabilities on the Revised Children's Manifest Anxiety Scale with learning disabled children.** Journal of Learning Disabilities, 1984, **17,** 137–141.

1329. PARIS, SCOTT G. (Univ. of Michigan); LIPSON, MARJORIE Y.; & WIXSON, KAREN K. **Becoming a strategic reader.** Contemporary Educational Psychology, 1983, **8,** 293–316.
Learning to read strategically is related to children's cognitive development as well as to the social contexts of instruction. – From Authors' Abstract.

1330. PEARSON, P. DAVID (Univ. of Illinois, Urbana-Champaign), & GALLAGHER, MARGARET C. **The instruction of reading comprehension.** Contemporary Educational Psychology, 1983, **8,** 317–344.

1331. PIETRULEWICZ, BOGDAN (Catholic Univ. of Lublin, Poland). **The Polish adaptation of the Wechsler Intelligence Scale for Preschool Children.** Psychologia Wychowawcza (Educational Psychology: Bimonthly of the Polish Teachers Union), 1983, **26,** 159–165.

1332. PIHL, R. O. (McGill Univ., Montreal, Quebec, Canada), & McLARNON, LYDIA D. **Learning disabled children as adolescents.** Journal of Learning Disabilities, 1984, **17,** 96–100.

Parents of adolescents who had been diagnosed as learning disabled 5 years previously and parents of non-learning-disabled subjects completed a questionnaire in which they were required to rate their children on 30 bipolar adjectives. The ratings of the former group of LD subjects were different from those of the latter group in the area of academic and learning orientation, with the former group scoring more in the negative direction. – From Authors' Abstract.

1333. PILECKA, WLADYSLAWA (Higher School of Pedagogy, Cracow, Poland), & ZUBEREK, URSZULA. **Mental development of children with visual defects in light of test findings of the Wechsler Verbal Scale.** Psychologia Wychowawcza (Educational Psychology: Bimonthly of the Polish Teachers Union), 1983, **26**, 166–182.
Results show that the period and degree of loss of sight as well as age are factors that modify the structure of intellect. Whereas children sightless from birth and retarded with moderate vision show a similar level of mental development, those with minimal vision display a much lower level. – From Authors' Abstract.

1334. PLOTNICOV, KATHERINE HAGER (Univ. of Pittsburgh). **Language and the education of non-English speaking children.** Journal of Children in Contemporary Society, 1983, **15**, 61–69.
This article reviews the issue of language and the education for newcomers and other non-English speaking children in the United States. It portrays fluctuating historical attitudes toward the use of languages, other than English, in schools and other aspects of life. – From Author's Abstract.

1335. PONTIUS, ANNELIESE A. (Harvard Medical School). **Global spatial relations in face representations shown in "ecological dyslexia" of Australian Aboriginals and in "Western" dyslexics.** Perceptual and Motor Skills, 1982, **55**, 1191–1200.
Findings for subjects 7–18 years suggest a subgroup of dyslexics who show a subtle spatial-relational dysfunction, linked to Aboriginal children's lack of practice of certain brain systems. – Adapted from Author's Abstract.

1336. POPOVICS, ALEXANDER J. (Middlesex County Coll., England). **Predictive validities of clinical and actuarial scores of the Gesell Incomplete Man Test.** Perceptual and Motor Skills, 1983, **56**, 864–866.
Predictive validity of scores for the Gesell Incomplete Man Test was negligible, except for intelligence. – Ed.

1337. QUATTROCCHI, MARY M. (Univ. of Nebraska Medical Ctr.), & GOLDEN, CHARLES J. **Peabody Picture Vocabulary Test-Revised and Luria-Nebraska Neuropsychological Battery for Children: intercorrelations for normal youngsters.** Perceptual and Motor Skills, 1983, **56**, 632–634.
Small correlations were found between the PPVT-R and the Receptive, Intelligence, Visual, Arithmetic, and Memory scales on the Luria-Nebraska. – From Authors' Abstract.

1338. REED, MICHAEL L. (Univ. of Pittsburgh School of Medicine), & EDELBROCK, CRAIG. **Reliability and validity of the Direct Observation Form of the Child Behavior Checklist.** Journal of Abnormal Child Psychology, 1983, **11**, 521–530.
Observational data were collected on 2 samples of boys ages 6–11 in classroom settings. Interobserver agreement was high. Scores correlated behavior, school performance, and adaptive functioning. – From Authors' Abstract.

1339. REITSMA, PIETER (Paedologisch Instituut, Koningslaan 22, Amsterdam, Netherlands). **Printed word learning in beginning readers.** Journal of Experimental Child Psychology, 1983, **36**, 321–339.
Visually recognizing the unique graphemic structure of words is an important component in word identification, even at rather early stages in learning to read. Only a moderate amount of

practice in reading strings of letters was necessary for young children to read the regular spelling faster than altered spelling that preserved the word sound. – From Author's Abstract.

1340. RIDING, R. J. (Univ. of Birmingham, England), & DYER, V. A. **The nature of learning styles and their relationship to cognitive performance in children.** Educational Psychology, 1983, **3,** 275–287.
Children 11 years old were given several tests of learning style and personality. A factor analysis of the scores indicated 4 factors: differentiation, representation, response efficiency, and neuroticism. – From Authors' Abstract.

1341. ROBERTS, KATHLEEN T., & EHRI, LINNEA C. (Univ. of California, Davis). **Effects of two types of letter rehearsal on word memory in skilled and less skilled beginning readers.** Contemporary Educational Psychology, 1983, **8,** 375–390.
Experimental subjects performed activities to retain spellings in memory as orthographic images. Control subjects rehearsed the letters similarly but with the correct spellings in view. Posttests revealed that experimentals remembered spellings better than controls. Subjects were 8 years old. – From Authors' Abstract.

1342. RONNING, ROYCE R. (Univ. of Nebraska, Lincoln); McCURDY, DONALD; & BALLINGER, RUTH. **Individual differences: a third component in problem-solving instruction.** Journal of Research in Science Teaching, 1984, **21,** 71–82.
A viable theory of problem solving must consider at least 3 dimensions: domain knowledge, problem-solving methods, and characteristics of problem solvers. The first 2 dimensions are now widely accepted as essential for theory development, while lip service has long been paid to concern for individual differences. – From the Article.

1343. ROSE, MICHAEL C. (Central Peninsula Mental Health Ctr., P.O. Box 247, Kenai, AK); CUNDICK, BERT P.; & HIGBEE, KENNETH L. **Verbal rehearsal and visual imagery: mnemonic aids for learning-disabled children.** Journal of Learning Disabilities, 1983, **16,** 352–354.
The studies support the contention that reading comprehension difficulties among LD children are partly due to inefficient memorization strategies. – From Authors' Abstract.

1344. ROYER, JAMES M. (Univ. of Massachusetts). **Reading: the natural interface between developmental and educational psychology.** Contemporary Educational Psychology, 1983, **8,** 205–209.

1345. RUSSELL, TOMMY (Univ. of Alabama), & FORD, DOROTHY F. **Effectiveness of peer tutors vs. resource teachers.** Psychology in the Schools, 1983, **20,** 436–441.
Mildly retarded students who had tutors gained more in reading (especially in the area of reading recognition). – From Authors' Abstract.

1346. RYAN, MICHAEL C.; MILLER, C. DEAN; & WITT, JOSEPH C. (Univ. of Nebraska, Lincoln). **A comparison of the use of orthographic structure in word discrimination by learning disabled and normal children.** Journal of Learning Disabilities, 1984, **17,** 38–40.
A difference was found between the learning-disabled nd normal groups in discriminating between orthographically legitimate and orthographically illegitimate pairs of letter patterns. – From Authors' Abstract.

1347. SADOSKI, MARK (Texas A&M Univ.). **An exploratory study of the relationships between reported imagery and the comprehension and recall of a story.** Reading Research Quarterly, 1983, **19,** 110–123.
Imagery in reading-comprehension measures does not rely on verbal reasoning processes. – From Author's Abstract.

1348. SADOWSKI, CYRIL J. (Auburn Univ., Montgomery), & WOODWARD, HELEN R. **Teacher locus of control and classroom climate: a cross-lagged correlational study.** Psychology in the Schools, 1983, **20**, 506–509.
The cross-lagged correlations suggest that teachers' locus of control has a causal impact on classroom climate. – From Authors' Abstract.

1349. SARACHO, OLIVIA N. (Univ. of Maryland). **Relationship between cognitive style and teachers' perceptions of young children's academic competence.** Journal of Experimental Education, 1983, **51**, 184–189.
There were grade-level effects and an interaction among the cognitive styles of teachers in ranking their matched and mismatched students according to sex in relation to the students' academic achievement scores. – From Author's Abstract.

1350. SCRUGGS, THOMAS E. (Utah State Univ.); MASTROPIERI, MARGO A.; & ARGULEWICZ, ED N. **Stability of performance on the PPVT-R for three ethnic groups attending a bilingual kindergarten.** Psychology in the Schools, 1983, **20**, 433–435.
Strong temporal stability existed over an 8-month period for Native American, Mexican-American, and English-speaking kindergarten students. – From Authors' Abstract.

1351. SERVELLO, MICHAEL B. (PACE School, Pittsburgh). **Vestibular-based functions and behavior problems of children in special education and regular classes.** Perceptual and Motor Skills, 1982, **55**, 1289–1290.
Children 5–9 years old in special education displayed more vestibular-based deficits than those in regular classes. Low to moderate correlations were found between vestibular-based functions and behavior problems. – Adapted from Author's Abstract.

1352. SHADE, BARBARA J. (Univ. of Wisconsin, Parkside). **Cognitive strategies as determinants of school achievement.** Psychology in the Schools, 1983, **20**, 488–493.
Using 6 instruments designed to identify preferred cognitive strategies, students stratified by achievement were tested. Results suggested that achievement was related to the acquisition of a particular cognitive style. – From Author's Abstract.

1353. SHARE, DAVID L. (Deakin Univ., Geelong, Victoria, Australia); JORM, ANTHONY F.; MACLEAN, ROD; MATTHEWS, RUSSELL; & WATERMAN, BOBBIE. **Early reading achievement, oral language ability, and a child's home background.** Australian Psychologist, 1983, **18**, 75–87.
Using hierarchical multiple regression, it was found that socioeconomic status was associated with both reading achievement and oral language ability. – From Authors' Abstract.

1354. SHAUGHNESSY, MICHAEL F. (Eastern New Mexico Univ.), & JONES, MICHELLE. **Factor analysis with the gifted.** Creative Child and Adult Quarterly, 1983, **8**, 221–229.
The existing factor analytic research is examined, and guidelines for future research are indicated. – From Authors' Abstract.

1355. SIEWERT, JULAINE C., & BREEN, MICHAEL J. (West Bend Public School System, 697 S. 5th Ave., West Bend, WI). **The Revised Test of Visual-Motor Integration: its relation to the Test of Visual-Motor Integration and Bender Visual-Motor Gestalt Test for regular education students.** Psychology in the Schools, 1983, **20**, 304–306.

1356. SIGMON, SCOTT B. (Irvington, NJ, Public Schools). **Performance of American schoolchildren on Raven's Colored Progressive Matrices Scale.** Perceptual and Motor Skills, 1983, **56**, 484–486.
Analysis of combined means from 4 American studies which had diverse sampling clusters used weighted averaging techniques to produce "hypothetical national mean raw scores" for ages 6–12 years. – From Author's Abstract.

1357. SILLIPHANT, VIRGINIA M. (36 Eglantine, Pennington, NJ). **Kindergarten reasoning and achievement in grades K-3.** Psychology in the Schools, 1983, **20**, 289–294.
This study suggests that reasoning in kindergarten children has a profound impact on achievement during early elementary school grades. There was no relationship between later achievement and those powerful determiners of school achievement—visual-motor integration and verbal development. – From the Article.

1358. SILVERSTEIN, A. B. (Univ. of California, Los Angeles). **Full scale IQ equivalents for a two-subtest short form of the Wechsler Preschool and Primary Scale of Intelligence and the Wechsler Intelligence Scale for Children–Revised.** Psychological Reports, 1983, **53**, 16–18.

1359. SILVERSTEIN, A. B. (Univ. of California School of Medicine, Los Angeles); GOLDBERG, CHERYL G.; KASNER, ABBIE E.; & SOLOMON, BONNIE L. **An attempt to determine the intellectual strengths and weaknesses of EMR children.** American Journal of Mental Deficiency, 1984, **88**, 435–437.
The standard deviation method and Binetgram appear to hold little promise. – Ed.

1360. SIMS, EDWARD V., JR. (Univ. of Alabama), & WEISBERG, PAUL. **Analysis of some factors related to manuscript letter-height reduction.** Perceptual and Motor Skills, 1983, **56**, 567–571.
Letters composed of highly curved letter strokes were written relatively smaller by second graders. Greater height reduction was found for letters beginning below the top line. – Adapted from Authors' Abstract.

1361. SKEEN, JUDITH A. (1639 Mohawk, Salt Lake City); STRONG, VICTORIA NORTON; & BOOK, ROBERT M. **Comparison of learning disabled children's performance on Bender Visual-Motor Gestalt Test and Beery's Developmental Test of Visual Motor Integration.** Perceptual and Motor Skills, 1982, **55**, 1257–1258.
Bender and Beery tests give comparable age-equivalent performances. Either test might be used as an aid in identifying learning-disabled students. – From the Article.

1362. SNOW, JEFFREY H. (Univ. of Georgia); HYND, GEORGE W.; HARTLAGE, LAWRENCE C.; & GRANT, DANIEL H. **The relationship between the Luria-Nebraska Neuropsychological Battery–Children's Revision and the Minnesota Percepto-Diagnostic Test with learning disabled students.** Psychology in the Schools, 1983, **20**, 415–419.
Low correlations were found between the 2 tests. – Ed.

1363. SNOWLING, MAGGIE (National Hospitals Coll. of Speech Sciences, 59 Portland, London, England), & STACKHOUSE, JOY. **Spelling performance of children with developmental verbal dyspraxia.** Developmental Medicine and Child Neurology, 1983, **25**, 430–437.
Children 8–10 years old with verbal dyspraxia were found to have more difficulty in spelling and reading single-syllable words than children with normal speech who were matched for reading age. – From Authors' Abstract.

1364. STEIN, NANCY L. (Univ. of Chicago). **On the goals, functions, and knowledge of reading and writing.** Contemporary Educational Psychology, 1983, **8**, 261–292.

1365. STEVENSON, HAROLD W. (Univ. of Michigan); LEE, SHIN-YING; STIGLER, JAMES; LUCKER, G. WILLIAM; HSU, CHEN-CHIN; & KITAMURA, SEIRO. **Family variables and reading: a study of mothers of poor and average readers in Japan, Taiwan, and the United States.** Journal of Learning Disabilities, 1984, **17**, 150–156.
The most remarkable result was the consistency of the differences (and lack of differences) revealed by the responses of the mothers of poor and average readers in the 3 cultures. – From the Article.

1366. STONER, SUE B. (Eastern Illinois Univ.), & SPENCER, W. BOYD. **Sex differences in expressive vocabulary of Head Start children.** Perceptual and Motor Skills, 1983, **56,** 1008.

1367. STRAUSS, HELEN (Bar-Ilan Univ., Ramat-Gan, Israel); GOTTESDIENER, HARRY; FOGEL, RACHEL; & TAMARI, DRORITH. **On entering first grade: note on impact of parents' attitudes on expectations of their children, an Israeli case.** Perceptual and Motor Skills, 1983, **56,** 367–370.
Maternal attitudes had the most impact on the expectations of the children. – From Authors' Abstract.

1368. SUMMERS, EDWARD G. (Univ. of British Columbia, Canada), & LUKASEVICH, ANN. **Reading preferences of intermediate-grade children in relation to sex, community, and maturation (grade level): a Canadian perspective.** Reading Research Quarterly, 1983, **18,** 347–360.
Children differed in their preference for many of the book themes. Sex, community, and grade level were found to differentially affect preferences. – From the Article.

1369. SWANSON, H. LEE (Univ. of Northern Colorado). **Effect of cognitive effort on learning disabled and nondisabled readers' recall.** Journal of Learning Disabilities, 1984, **17,** 67–74.
The findings support the hypothesis that nondisabled and disabled readers differ in processing capacity; they further suggest that cognitive effort may be a relevant factor in word encoding processes. – From Author's Abstract.

1370. SZYNAL-BROWN, CAROL (871 Cheryl, Kankakee, IL), & MORGAN, RONALD R. **The effects of reward on tutor's behaviors in a cross-age tutoring context.** Journal of Experimental Child Psychology, 1983, **36,** 196–208.
Social interaction was rated lower for the children in a performance-contingent group, and the tutors in this group spent less time teaching during the free-choice period. Neither the tutor's teaching style nor the tutee's posttest performance was adversely affected by a reward. – From Authors' Abstract.

1371. TELZROW, CATHY F. (Cuyahoga Special Education Service Ctr., Cleveland); CENTURY, EVELYN; REDMOND, CAROL; WHITAKER, BARBARA; & ZIMMERMAN, BARBARA. **The Boder Test: neuropsychological and demographic features of dyslexic subtypes.** Psychology in the Schools, 1983, **20,** 427–432.
In this study, proportions of LD children identified by Boder's classification system as dysphonetic, dyseidetic, and mixed dysphonetic-dyseidetic were similar to those reported in earlier studies. Neuropsychological characteristics associated with the Boder categories were consistent with the literature. – From Authors' Abstract.

1372. TERRELL, FRANCIS (North Texas State Univ.), & TERRELL, SANDRA L. **The relationship between race of examiner, cultural mistrust, and the intelligence test performance of black children.** Psychology in the Schools, 1983, **20,** 367–369.
The results indicate that black children suspected of having a high level of mistrust should be tested by a black examiner. – From the Article.

1373. THORNBURG, HERSHEL D. (Univ. of Arizona). **Can educational systems respond to the needs of early adolescents.** Journal of Early Adolescence, 1983, **3,** 23–36.

1374. TOURRETTE, C. (Univ. of Paris XII, France), & TOURRETTE, G. **Lecture et intelligence en CE2.** Revue de Psychologie Appliqueé, 1983, **33,** 115–132.
The relation between reading achievements, intelligence, and socioeconomic status are related to reading achievements in 9-year-olds. – From Authors' Abstract.

1375. TREIM, REBECCA (Indiana Univ.), & BARON, JONATHAN. **Phonemic-analysis training helps children benefit from spelling–sound rules.** Memory and Cognition, 1983, **11,** 382–389.
In the analysis condition, children learned to segment and to blend selected spoken syllables. In the control condition, children tended to make more errors on the related item than on the unrelated item; in the analysis condition, they tended to make fewer errors on the related item than on the unrelated item. These results suggest a causal link between the ability to analyze spoken syllables and the ability to benefit from spelling–sound relations in reading. – From Authors' Abstract.

1376. VANCE, BOONEY (Univ. of Maryland, Eastern Shore); LESTER, M. L.; & THATCHER, R. W. **Interscorer reliability of the Minnesota Percepto-Diagnostic Test–Revised.** Psychology in the Schools, 1983, **20,** 420–423.
For 3 of the 4 scores, there was a significant positive correlation between expert and novice scoring criteria. – From Authors' Abstract.

1377. VANCE, H. BOONEY (Univ. of Maryland, Eastern Shore); KITSON, DONALD; & SINGER, MARC. **Further investigation of comparability of the WISC-R and PPVT-R for children and youth referred for psychological services.** Psychology in the Schools, 1983, **20,** 307–310.
There were no differences between the WISC-R IQs and PPVT-R scores. The PPVT-R did not correlate with the WISC-R IQ. – From Authors' Abstract.

1378. VANDELL, DEBORAH LOWE (Univ. of Texas, Dallas), & POWERS, CAROL P. **Day care quality and children's free play activities.** American Journal of Orthopsychiatry, 1983, **53,** 493–500.
Children in high-quality centers were more likely to interact positively with adults, while children in lower quality programs were more likely to engage in solitary play and aimless wandering. – From Authors' Abstract.

1379. VOGEL, SUSAN A. (Barat Coll.). **A qualitative analysis of morphological ability in learning disabled and achieving children.** Journal of Learning Disabilities, 1983, **16,** 416–420.
The major finding was that the LD children did not differ from the normal achievers on categories of items from the Berry-Talbott Language Test that were ranked by level of difficulty. – From Author's Abstract.

1380. WAXMAN, HERSHOLT C. (Univ. of Pittsburgh). **Effect of teachers empathy on students' motivation.** Psychological Reports, 1983, **53,** 489–490.
The Teacher Empathy Questionnaire and the Multi-dimensional Motivational Instrument were administered to students in grades 3–8. Teachers' empathy affected students' postacademic self-concept and postachievement motivation, even after controlling for the effects of students' prior motivation. – From Author's Abstract.

1381. WEDMAN, INGEMAR (Univ. of Umea, Sweden), & STAGE, CHRISTINA. **The significance of contents for sex differences in test results.** Scandinavian Journal of Educational Research, 1983, **27,** 49–71.
Results show that sex differences are stable, but the possibilities to identify items which give rise to these differences between the sexes seem to be very limited. The hypothesis that it is possible to predict which items give rise to sex differences was not supported. – From Authors' Abstract.

1382. WEED, KERI (Univ. of Notre Dame), & RYAN, ELLEN BOUCHARD. **Alphabetical seriation as a reading readiness indicator.** Journal of General Psychology, 1983, **109,** 201–210.

Results supported the viability of the new alphabetical seriation task as a better predictor of reading readiness than traditional seriation. – From Authors' Abstract.

1383. WEST, RICHARD F. (James Madison Univ.); STANOVICH, KEITH E.; FEEMAN, DOROTHY J.; & CUNNINGHAM, ANNE E. **The effect of sentence context on word recognition in second- and sixth-grade children.** Reading Research Quarterly, 1983, **19**, 6–15.
Contextual facilitation and inhibition effects arose primarily from within the target sentence and were larger for second graders than sixth graders. – From Authors' Abstract.

1384. WIIG, ELISABETH H. (Boston Univ.); BECKER-REDDING, ULRIKE; & SEMEL, ELEANOR M. **A cross-cultural, cross-linguistic comparison of language abilities of 7- to 8- and 12- to 13-year-old children with learning disabilities.** Journal of Learning Disabilities, 1983, **16**, 576–585.
This study compared relative strengths and weaknesses in the language abilities of German and American learning-disabled and academically achieving children. The findings concur with previous observations of language delays among children and adolescents with learning disabilities. The observations tentatively suggest cross-cultural and cross-linguistic similarities in the language disorder syndrome associated with learning disabilities. – From Authors' Abstract.

1385. WILBUR, RONNIE B. (Purdue Univ.); GOODHART, WENDY; & MONTANDON, ELIZABETH. **Comprehension of nine syntactic structures by hearing-impaired students.** Volta Review, 1983, **85**, 328–345.
The syntactic structures why-questions, conditionals, nonlocative prepositions, indefinite pronouns, quantifiers, modal verbs, elliptical constructions, reciprocal pronouns, and comparative constructions were presented to hearing-impaired students at reading levels 1–8. Results indicate an improvement across reading levels. – From Authors' Abstract.

1386. WITT, JOSEPH C. (Univ. of Nebraska, Lincoln), & MARTENS, B. K. **Assessing the acceptability of behavioral interventions used in classrooms.** Psychology in the Schools, 1983, **20**, 510–517.
Teacher judgments of the acceptability of 6 different interventions were assessed using a rating scale. Factor analysis of the rating scale yielded a general acceptability factor and 4 secondary dimensions: risk to the target child, amount of teacher time required, effects of the intervention on other children, and amount of teacher skill required. – From Authors' Abstract.

1387. WOOD, CHIP (Northeast Foundation for Children, Box 1024, Greenfield, MA); POWELL, SARAH J.; & KNIGHT, R. CHRISTOPHER. **Predicting school readiness: the validity of developmental age.** Journal of Learning Disabilities, 1984, **17**, 8–11.
Developmental age, as measured by the Gesell Examination, provides a useful predictive measurement of later school performance. – From Authors' Abstract.

PSYCHIATRY, CLINICAL PSYCHOLOGY

1388. AUGUST, GERALD J. (Univ. of Texas Medical Branch, Galveston), & STEWART, MARK A. **Familial subtypes of childhood hyperactivity.** Journal of Nervous and Mental Disease, 1983, **171**, 362–368.
On the basis of family history data, we defined 2 subtypes of childhood hyperactivity: family history-positive, in which at least 1 biological parent of the child had a diagnosis in the antisocial spectrum, and family history-negative, in which neither parent had such a diagnosis. While children in both subgroups were equally deviant on measures of the core components of childhood hyperactivity, the history-positive children were also deviant on dimensions of conduct disturbance and had siblings with a high prevalence of conduct disorder. – From Authors' Abstract.

1389. BARLOW, DAVID H. (SUNY, Albany), & SEIDNER, ANDREA L. **Treatment of adolescent agoraphobics: effects on parent–adolescent relations.** Behaviour Research and Therapy, 1983, **21**, 519–526.
As with adult agoraphobics treated with their spouse, results indicated that as phobia improved the relationship improved. – From Authors' Abstract.

1390. BEISLER, JEAN MADSEN (Child Psychiatry Service, 500 Newton, Iowa City), & TSAI, LUKE Y. **A pragmatic approach to increase expressive language skills in young autistic children.** Journal of Autism and Developmental Disorders, 1983, **13**, 287–303.
The training involved intensive modeling of verbal responses within joint activity routines and using a reinforcement system based on fulfilling the intent of the child's communication. There was an increase in the mean length of response, in the mean receptive language level, and in the mean number of semantic–grammatical rules expressed. – From Authors' Abstract.

1391. BEITCHMAN, J. H. (Royal Ottawa Hosp., 1145 Carling, Ottawa, Ontario, Canada). **Childhood schizophrenia: a review and comparison with adult onset schizophrenia.** Psychiatric Journal of the University of Ottawa, 1983, **8**, 25–37.
Childhood schizophrenia, differentiated from childhood autism, is reviewed in terms of its phenomenology, epidemiology, premorbid characteristics, pregnancy and birth complications, EEG findings, biochemistry, genetic factors, treatment considerations, and follow-up studies. The term childhood schizophrenia should be used to refer to adult forms of schizophrenia occurring in childhood. – From Author's Abstract.

1392. BILLINGS, ANDREW G. (Stanford Univ. School of Medicine), & MOOS, RUDOLF H. **Comparisons of children of depressed and nondepressed parents: a social-environmental perspective.** Journal of Abnormal Child Psychology, 1983, **11**, 463–486.
Children of depressed parents had more symptoms of emotional, somatic, and behavioral impairment than did children of nondepressed parents. The more negative milieu found among families of depressed parents was a mediator of the effects of parental depression. – From Authors' Abstract.

1393. BLOTCKY, MARK J. (Timberlawn Psychiatric Hosp., 4600 Samuell, Dallas); DIMPERIO, THOMAS L.; BLOTCKY, ALAN D.; & LOONEY, JOHN G. **A systems model for residential treatment of children.** Milieu Therapy, 1983, **3**, 3–13.
The paper reviews treatment models and presents a more inclusive milieu model derived from general systems theory. A systems model is particularly helpful in clarifying the interactional aspects of the treatment program and in resolving milieu regression. – From Authors' Abstract.

1394. BLUM, ARTHUR (Case Western Reserve Univ.), & SINGER, MARK. **Substance abuse and social deviance: a youth assessment framework.** Child and Youth Service, 1983, **6**, 7–21.
Theories of adolescent deviance are reviewed in light of their contributions to understanding troubled youth. A youth assessment framework is developed to provide a systematic means of linking theories to specific treatment strategies. – From Authors' Abstract.

1395. BRANDT, JASON (Johns Hopkins Univ.), & DOYLE, LAURIE F. **Concept attainment, tracking, and shifting in adolescent polydrug abusers.** Journal of Nervous and Mental Disease, 1983, **171**, 559–563.
Adolescents with histories of severe, though time-limited, polydrug abuse were found to perform as well as nonabusers on 2 very sensitive indicators of frontal system functioning. – From Authors' Abstract.

1396. BRENNAN, M. (Massey Univ., Palmerston North, New Zealand), & KIRKLAND, J. **Classification of infant cries using descriptive scales.** Infant Behavior and Development, 1982, **5**, 341–346.
Possible application of the scales to clinically "at risk" infants is explored. – S. Thomas.

1397. BROWN, MARIE ANNETTE (Univ. of Washington). **Adolescents and abortion: a theoretical framework for decision making.** Journal of Obstetric, Gynecologic, and Neonatal Nursing, 1983, **12**, 241–247.
Beach and Mitchell's decision-making framework is presented to explain the process of adolescent decision making to continue or terminate a pregnancy. Adolescent developmental issues are discussed in relation to the pregnancy/abortion decision. – From Author's Abstract.

1398. BUCKALEW, L. W. (Alabama A&M Univ.), & BUCKALEW, PATRICIA BOWMAN. **Behavioral management of exceptional children using video games as reward.** Perceptual and Motor Skills, 1983, **56**, 580.
Children ages 9–15 years who were placed on a video game reward system showed enhanced classroom decorum and individual performance. – Adapted from the Article.

1399. CADORET, REMI J. (Univ. of Iowa Coll. of Medicine); CAIN, COLLEEN A.; & CROWE, RAYMOND R. **Evidence for gene–environment interaction in the development of adolescent antisocial behavior.** Behavior Genetics, 1983, **13**, 301–310.
Data from 3 adoption studies are analyzed. Results indicated increases in antisocial behaviors when an adoptee had both a genetic factor and an adverse environmental factor present. – From Authors' Abstract.

1400. CHESS, STELLA (New York Univ. Medical Ctr.); THOMAS, ALEXANDER; & HASSIBI, MAHIN. **Depression in childhood and adolescence: a prospective study of six cases.** Journal of Nervous and Mental Disease, 1983, **171**, 411–420.
Differences in etiology of 6 New York longitudinal study subjects are described. There was no evidence for a separate clinical entity of depression for the childhood period. Review of the longitudinal data did not show an earlier life tendency to negative mood temperamentally. – Adapted from Authors' Abstract.

1401. CHURTON, MICHAEL W. (Appalachian State Univ.). **Relationships of perceptual-motor development to hyperkinesis, educational placement, drug utilization, socioeconomic status, and age.** Perceptual and Motor Skills, 1983, **56**, 15–18.
The variables were poor to moderate predictors of perceptual-motor performance of hyperkinetic children ages 5–12 1/2 years. – Adapted from Author's Abstract.

1402. CLARIZIO, HARVEY F. (Michigan State Univ.), & VERES, VALERIE. **WISC-R patterns of emotionally impaired and diagnostic utility.** Psychology in the Schools, 1983, **20**, 409–414.
Neither a Verbal-Performance discrepancy nor a high Similarities, low Information pattern was useful for diagnosing emotional impairment. – Adapted from Authors' Abstract.

1403. CRAFT, DIANE H. (New York Univ.). **Effect of prior exercise on cognitive performance tasks by hyperactive and normal young boys.** Perceptual and Motor Skills, 1983, **56**, 979–982.
Prior exercise did not affect cognitive performance of either hyperactive or normal 7–10-year-old boys. – Adapted from Author's Abstract.

1404. DAUM, JAMES M. (Univ. of Cincinnati). **Emotional indicators in drawings of aggressive or withdrawn male delinquents.** Journal of Personality Assessment, 1983, **47**, 243–249.
Human figure drawings of aggressive or withdrawn male delinquents were evaluated and compared with both undifferentiated delinquents and nondelinquents. Differences were found for 6 of the 16 features, and predictive power was substantially increased by using all the features as indicators of their respective traits. – From Author's Abstract.

1405. DAWSON, GERALDINE (Univ. of North Carolina, Chapel Hill). **Lateralized brain dysfunction in autism: evidence from the Halstead-Reitan neuropsychological battery.** Journal of Autism and Developmental Disorders, 1983, **13**, 269–286.

Autistic subjects showed a greater degree of left-hemisphere dysfunction than either retarded or brain-damaged persons. – Adapted from Author's Abstract.

1406. DE JONG, ALLAN R. (Thomas Jefferson Univ., Jefferson Medical Coll.); HERVADA, ARTURO R.; & EMMETT, GARY A. **Epidemiologic variations in childhood sexual abuse.** Child Abuse & Neglect, The International Journal, 1983, **7**, 155–162.
Younger children were more likely than older children to present with histories of multiple assaults, by known assailants, occurring in the child's or assailant's home, and to report less violence. – From Authors' Abstract.

1407. DIAMOND, LINDA J. (La Rabida Children's Hosp. & Research Ctr., E. 65th & Lake Michigan, Chicago), & JAUDES, PAULA K. **Child abuse in a cerebral-palsied population.** Developmental Medicine and Child Neurology, 1983, **25**, 169–174.
Among cerebral-palsied children seen in 1 center, 20% had been subject to child abuse. Half of these children's cerebral palsy was a result of abuse. – From Authors' Abstract.

1408. EDWARDS, DAN W. (Louisiana State Univ.). **Adolescents and masturbation.** Journal of Social Work & Human Sexuality, 1983, **1**, 53–57.

1409. EGELAND, BYRON (Univ. of Minnesota); SROUFE, L. ALAN; & ERICKSON, MARTHA. **The developmental consequence of different patterns of maltreatment.** Child Abuse & Neglect, The International Journal, 1983, **7**, 459–469.
The physically abused children were distractible, lacked persistence, ego control, and enthusiasm and experienced considerable negative emotion. The children whose mothers were psychologically unavailable showed marked increases in maladaptive patterns of functioning from infancy through preschool. As expected, they were avoidant of their mother, angry, noncompliant, and highly dependent. – From Authors' Abstract.

1410. FANTUZZO, JOHN W., & SMITH, CRAIG S. (Fuller Theological Seminary). **Programmed generalization of dress efficiency across settings for a severely disturbed, autistic child.** Psychological Reports, 1983, **53**, 871–879.
A severely disturbed, autistic child was taught to clothe himself by using tokens as positive reinforcement, with negative reinforcement introduced to reduce dressing time. Control was generalized from the primary teaching parent to others in both group home and natural home setting. – Adapted from Authors' Abstract.

1411. FERRARI, MICHAEL (Univ. of Delaware), & MATTHEWS, WENDY S. **Self-recognition deficits in autism: syndrome-specific or general developmental delay?** Journal of Autism and Developmental Disorders, 1983, **13**, 317–324.
Children with self-recognition were found to be functioning at mental ages akin to developmental norms for self-recognition. Those who failed to show self-recognition had mental ages below the developmental level at which many children recognize themselves and significantly lower than those autistic children who showed self-recognition. – From Authors' Abstract.

1412. FILSTEAD, WILLIAM J. (Lutheran Ctr. for Substance Abuse, 1700 Luther, Park Ridge, IL), & ANDERSON, CARL L. **Conceptual and clinical issues in the treatment of adolescent alcohol and substance misusers.** Child and Youth Service, 1983, **6**, 103–116.
This paper describes a system of care and the clinical issues that are central to the delivery of alcoholism and/or substance abuse services to adolescents. – From Authors' Abstract.

1413. FINCH, MELISSA (Oregon Research Inst., Eugene), & HOPS, MYMAN. **Remediation of social withdrawal in young children: considerations for the practitioner.** Child and Youth Service, 1982, **5**, 29–42.

1414. FINKELHOR, DAVID (Univ. of New Hampshire). **Removing the child—prosecuting the offender in cases of sexual abuse: evidence from the national reporting system for child abuse and neglect.** Child Abuse & Neglect, The International Journal, 1983, **7**, 195–205.

1415. FISCHER, JUDITH L. (Texas Tech Univ.). **Mothers living apart from their children.** Family Relations, 1983, **32**, 351–357.
The various processes by which mothers come to live apart from their children are discussed. Implications for family-life educators and therapists are identified. – From Author's Abstract.

1416. FRIEDMAN, ROBERT M. (Florida Mental Health Inst., Tampa); QUICK, JUDITH; MAYO, JOHN; & PALMER, JO. **Social skills training within a day treatment program for emotionally disturbed adolescents.** Child and Youth Service, 1982, **5**, 139–152.

1417. FURMAN, ERNA (Case Western Reserve Univ. Medical School). **Studies in childhood bereavement.** Canadian Journal of Psychiatry, 1983, **28**, 241–247.
Twenty-three children who had lost a parent through death were studied. – From Author's Abstract.

1418. GABINET, LAILLE (Case Western Reserve Univ. Medical School). **Child abuse treatment failures reveal need for redefinition of the problem.** Child Abuse & Neglect, The International Journal, 1983, **7**, 395–402.
This article seeks to prove that current modalities for treating child abuse are not solving the problem because many high-risk and abusive families do not get help and because these identified families represent only a small part of the population at risk for child abuse. – From Author's Abstract.

1419. GABINET, LAILLE (Case Western Reserve Univ. Medical School). **Shared parenting: a new paradigm for the treatment of child abuse.** Child Abuse & Neglect, The International Journal, 1983, **7**, 403–411.
The thesis is that child abuse can be most effectively prevented by recasting it as a part of a larger problem of inadequately parented families. – From Author's Abstract.

1420. GABRIELLI, WILLIAM F., JR., & MEDNICK, SARNOFF A. (Univ. of Southern California). **Intellectual performance in children of alcoholics.** Journal of Nervous and Mental Disease, 1983, **171**, 444–447.
Subjects were tested at age 12 with a Danish translation of the WISC. Results suggested that Performance IQ deficits may be consequential to alcoholism, whereas Verbal deficits may be antecedent to alcoholism. – From Authors' Abstract.

1421. GARBER, BENJAMIN (Michael Reese Hosp. and Medical Ctr.). **Some thoughts on normal adolescents who lost a parent by death.** Journal of Youth and Adolescence, 1983, **12**, 175–183.
At least 1/2 of this group of normal adolescents had therapeutic contact since the parent's death. At age 12 they appeared to be coping with their loss by extracting from their environment the necessary help and support. At age 13 they were still coping, but their adaptation appeared more precarious. – From Author's Abstract.

1422. GELLES, RICHARD J. (Univ. of Rhode Island), & CORNELL, CLAIRE PEDRICK. **International perspectives on child abuse.** Child Abuse & Neglect, The International Journal, 1983, **7**, 375–386.
There is much variation as to the likelihood of children being abused, although Western, industrialized nations report the highest rates of abuse. Explanations for the variation of child abuse from 1 country to the next emphasize cultural differences in attitudes toward and values placed on children and the cultural appropriateness of using violence as a means of social control. – From Authors' Abstract.

1423. GOODWIN, JEAN (Univ. of New Mexico School of Medicine); CORMIER, LAWRENCE; & OWEN, JOHN. **Grandfather–Granddaughter incest: a trigenerational view.** Child Abuse & Neglect, The International Journal, 1983, **7**, 163–170.
Grandfather–granddaughter incest accounts for about 10% of all reported cases of intrafamilial childhood sexual abuse. – From Authors' Abstract.

1424. GRADY, F. PATRICK (409 East, Lee, MA). **Treating violent male adolescents in a therapeutic residential milieu.** Milieu Therapy, 1983, **3**, 53–61.
Countering traditional behaviorally oriented, drug dependency, and incarcerative programs, Brookside Farm School's humanistic alternative emphasizes the importance of social role modeling and positive interpersonal relationships in a nonsecure, agrarian setting with a high staff-to-student ratio. After its first year of operation, incidents of physical aggression were reduced and socially acceptable behaviors were increased among the school's population of 28 violent delinquent males. – From Author's Abstract.

1425. HAZEL, J. STEPHEN (Univ. of Kansas); SCHUMAKER, JEAN BRAGG; SHERMAN, JAMES A.; & SHELDON-WILDGEN, JAN. **Social skills training with court-adjudicated youths.** Child and Youth Service, 1982, **5**, 117–137.

1426. HECHTMAN, LILY (Montreal Children's Hosp., 2300 Tupper, Montreal, Canada), & WEISS, GABRIELLE. **Long-term outcome of hyperactive children.** American Journal of Orthopsychiatry, 1983, **53**, 532–541.
Outcome studies of hyperactive children suggested that children experience academic, social, and conduct difficulties during adolescence, and that social, emotional, and impulsive problems persist into young adulthood for the majority. Some hyperactive children were found to be functioning normally as adults. – From Authors' Abstract.

1427. HESSELMAN, STINA (Erica Foundation, Danderydsgatan 16, Stockholm, Sweden). **Elective mutism in children 1877–1981.** Acta Paedopsychiatrica, 1983, **49**, 297–310.
The material is presented under the following headings: definition of the symptom, features, incidence, etiology, treatment, and prognosis. Reference is made to 53 articles out of the total bibliography of 152 items. – From Author's Abstract.

1428. HIRST, M. A. (Univ. of York, Heslington, York, England). **Young people with disabilities: what happens after 16?** Child: Care, Health and Development, 1983, **9**, 273–284.
There is a considerable gap in access to paid employment for young people with disabilities compared with young people in general. There is substantial variation in the occupational experience of young adults with different types of impairment, and the transition from school to further education, training, employment, unemployment, or daycare can be difficult. – From Author's Abstract.

1429. HODGES, KAY KLINE; SIEGEL, LAWRENCE J.; MULLINS, LARRY; & GRIFFIN, NORA (Univ. of Missouri, Columbia). **Factor analysis of the Children's Depression Inventory.** Psychological Reports, 1983, **53**, 759–763.
Factor analyses of responses to the Children's Depression Inventory were compared for children at an outpatient clinic and for nonclinic children in grades 4, 5, and 6. Varimax rotations yielded 4 factors for the clinic children. These factors reflected cognitive, motivational, social integration, and somatic components and gave a general and a specific factor labeled noncompliant behavior in the nonclinic group. – Adapted from Authors' Abstract.

1430. HORNBY, GARRY (Psychological Service, Box 544, Manurewa, Auckland, New Zealand), & MURRAY, RAY. **Group programmes for parents of children with various handicaps.** Child: Care, Health and Development, 1983, **9**, 185–198.
Six to eight weekly 2-hour sessions contained lecture presentation and discussion in small groups. Parents have found programs to be valuable. – From Authors' Abstract.

1431. HOUTS, ARTHUR C. (Memphis State Univ.); LIEBERT, ROBERT M.; & PADAWER, WENDY. **A delivery system for the treatment of primary enuresis.** Journal of Abnormal Child Psychology, 1983, **11,** 513–520.
Primary enuretic children and their parents attended 1-hour group training sessions and implemented treatment in the home. Each case required 15 min of professional time, and net cost to each family was $50. Initial arrest of bedwetting was achieved by 81% and only 24% relapsed at 1-year follow up. – From Authors' Abstract.

1432. HUGHES, HONORE M. (Univ. of Arkansas), & BARAD, SUSAN J. **Psychological functioning of children in a battered women's shelter: a preliminary investigation.** American Journal of Orthopsychiatry, 1983, **53,** 525–531.
Self-concept, anxiety level, and problem behavior of 65 child residents of a battered women's shelter were assessed using self-report measures and checklists completed by mothers, staff, and teachers. Findings included a below-average self-concept score for the preschool group, more aggressive behavior in school-age shelter boys than in girls, and a pervasive tendency for mothers to rate their children more negatively than did other observers. – Authors' Abstract.

1433. HUGHES, VICKIE; WOLERY, MARK R. (Univ. of Kentucky); & NEEL, RICHARD S. **Teacher verbalizations and task performance with autistic children.** Journal of Autism and Developmental Disorders, 1983, **13,** 305–316.
Positive reinforcement was presented in a noncontingent fixed-time schedule. Teacher verbalizations produced increases in the percentage of correct responding on difficult and easy tasks. – From Authors' Abstract.

1434. HUMM-DELGADO, DENISE, & DELGADO, MELVIN (Boston Univ.). **Hispanic adolescents and substance abuse: issues for the 1980s.** Child and Youth Service, 1983, **6,** 71–87.

1435. HUTTON, JERRY B., & ROBERTS, TIMOTHY (East Texas State Univ.). **Factor structure of problem behavior for mildly handicapped and nonhandicapped students.** Psychological Reports, 1983, **52,** 703–707.
Mildly handicapped and nonhandicapped students in grades 1–12 were rated by teachers for characteristics of emotional disturbance. The mildly handicapped students were reported to have significantly more problem behaviors than the nonhandicapped students. – From Authors' Abstract.

1436. JONES, JUDITH BURNS (Columbia Univ.), & PHILLIBER, SUSAN. **Sexually active but not pregnant: a comparison of teens who risk and teens who plan.** Journal of Youth and Adolescence, 1983, **12,** 235–251.
We have chosen a sample of young women who have never been pregnant but who have been sexually active for a year or longer, anticipating that such a sample would include mainly consistent users of contraception. It did not. Within this special population we found young women who had never used contraception or who had only been sporadic users, as well as the consistent users we had sought. – From the Article.

1437. KASLOW, NADINE J.; TANENBAUM, RICHARD L.; BRAMSON, LYN Y.; PETERSON, CHRISTOPHER; & SELIGMAN, MARTIN E. P. (Univ. of Pennsylvania). **Problem-solving deficits and depressive symptoms among children.** Journal of Abnormal Child Psychology, 1983, **11,** 497–502.
Depressive symptoms among fourth- and fifth-grade students correlated highly with impaired problem solving at block designs and anagrams. – From Authors' Abstract.

1438. KAZDIN, ALAN E. (Univ. of Pittsburgh School of Medicine); ESVELDT-DAWSON, KAREN; & LOAR, LINDA L. **Correspondence of teacher ratings and direct observations of classroom behavior of psychiatric inpatient children.** Journal of Abnormal Child Psychology, 1983, **11,** 549–564.

Teachers, extraclass raters, and observers completed standard rating scales and/or measures of overt classroom behaviors of psychiatric inpatient children. Measures from different assessors correlated in the low to moderate range. Measures from teachers, raters, and observers readily distinguished attention deficit disorder children with hyperactivity from their peers. – From Authors' Abstract.

1439. KEATING, JOSEPH C., JR.; BUTZ, ROBERT A.; BURKE, EDMUND; & HEIMBERG, RICHARD G. (SUNY, Albany). **Dry bed training without a urine alarm: lack of effect of setting and therapist contact with child.** Journal of Behavior Therapy and Experimental Psychiatry, 1983, **14,** 109–115.

1440. KING, NEVILLE J. (Phillip Inst. of Technology, Bundoora, Victoria, Australia); HAMILTON, DAVID I.; & MURPHY, GREGORY C. **The prevention of children's maladaptive fears.** Child & Family Behavior Therapy, 1983, **5**(2), 43–57.
Encouraging findings have been reported in the use of film-modeling with children about to undergo dental treatment, tonsillectomies, injections, etc. – From Authors' Abstract.

1441. KLEE, STEVEN H., & GARFINKEL, BARRY D. (Univ. of Minnesota Medical School). **The computerized continuous performance task: a new measure of inattention.** Journal of Abnormal Child Psychology, 1983, **11,** 487–496.
Subjects were children in the inpatient and day hospital programs of a psychiatric hospital. The continuous performance task significantly correlated with several other psychometric measures of inattention, ratings of inattention, impulsivity, and hyperactivity. – From Authors' Abstract.

1442. KUNCE, JOSEPH T. (Univ. of Missouri, Columbia), & HEMPHILL, HOYET. **Delinquency and Jesness Inventory scores.** Journal of Personality Assessment, 1983, **47,** 632–634.
Results provide support for the research and diagnostic uses of this instrument in assessing adolescent social maladjustment. – From Authors' Abstract.

1443. LADD, GARY W. (Purdue Univ.), & MIZE, JACQUELYN. **Social skills training and assessment with children: a cognitive-social learning approach.** Child and Youth Service, 1982, **5,** 61–74.

1444. LAST, JEFFREY M. (Mt. Carmel Mercy Hosp., 6071 W. Outer, Detroit), & BRUHN, A. RAHN. **The psychodiagnostic value of children's earliest memories.** Journal of Personality Assessment, 1983, **47,** 597–603.
It appears that early memories can distinguish well-adjusted from mildly adjusted and severely maladjusted subjects. – Adapted from the Article.

1445. LeCROY, CRAIG W. (Univ. of Wisconsin). **Social skills training with adolescents: a review.** Child and Youth Service, 1982, **5,** 91–116.

1446. LEE, LAURA J. (Univ. of Pennsylvania). **Reducing black adolescents' drug use: family revisited.** Child and Youth Service, 1983, **6,** 57–69.
The family is an underutilized and minimally acknowledged resource in drug abuse prevention efforts. The discussion centers on a review of research findings intimately related to adolescent drug use and black family issues. – From Author's Abstract.

1447. McCORD, JOAN (Drexel Univ.). **A forty year perspective on effects of child abuse and neglect.** Child Abuse & Neglect, The International Journal, 1983, **7,** 265–270.
The abused and the rejected were more likely to have been reared by aggressive parents and were most likely also to have been exposed to high demands for adult behaviors and dominant fathers. – From Author's Abstract.

1448. MacEACHRON, ANN E. (New York State Office of Mental Retardation and Developmental Disabilities, 44 Holland, Albany). **Psychotropic and general drug use by mentally retarded persons: a test of the status model of drug use.** Child and Youth Service, 1983, **6**, 89–101.

The model of drug use made differential predictions for use of general medications and psychotropic drugs on the basis of employment status, physical health status, mental status, and institutional status. The model was supported for a population of approximately 42,000 mentally retarded persons of all ages receiving services in 1 stage and for a subgroup of approximately 7,000 adolescents. – From Author's Abstract.

1449. MacFARLANE, KEE, & KORBIN, JILL (Case Western Reserve Univ.). **Confronting the incest secret long after the fact: a family study of multiple victimization with strategies for intervention.** Child Abuse & Neglect, The International Journal, 1983, **7**, 225–237.

Eleven adult females in 1 generation of an extended family had experienced childhood sexual abuse by either a father/uncle or an older cousin/brother. – From Authors' Abstract.

1450. McGUIRE, DONALD J., & ELY, MARGOT (New York Univ.). **Childhood suicide.** Child Welfare, 1984, **63**, 17–26.

Discussed are the difficulties in recognizing childhood suicide, presuicidal conditions and behaviors, and methods for prevention. – From Authors' Abstract.

1451. MAGNUSSON, DAVID (Univ. of Stockholm, Sweden), & STATTIN, HAKAN. **Biological age, environment, and behavior in interaction: a methodological problem.** Reports from the Department of Psychology, University of Stockholm, No. 587, October 1982. 10 p.

At age 14, early-maturing girls were found to have significantly stronger alcohol habits than late-maturing girls. The strong relation between physical maturation and drinking habits was weakened during the adolescent period and was diminished in early adulthood. – From Authors' Abstract.

1452. MALHOTRA, M. K. (Bergische Universität–Gesamthochschule Wuppertal, Postfach 10 01 27, Wuppertal, Germany). **Familial and personal correlates (risk factors) of drug consumption among German youth.** Acta Paedopsychiatrica, 1983, **49**, 199–209.

The weight coefficients of various risk factors (familial and personal data) for drinking, smoking, and consumption of other drugs were calculated. The importance of various familial and personal correlates for the future drinking, smoking, and consumption of other drugs is discussed. – From Author's Abstract.

1453. MARTINEZ-ROIG, ANTONIO (Hosp. Nuestra Señora del Mar, Paseo Maritimo s/n, Barcelona, Spain); DOMINGO-SALVANY, FANCISCO; LLORENS-TEROL, JOSE; & IBAÑEZ-CACHO, JOSE M. **Psychologic implications of the maltreated-child syndrome.** Child Abuse & Neglect, The International Journal, 1983, **7**, 261–263.

A retrospective investigation of psychologically maltreated children showed a clear relationship between clinical symptoms and the intensity of the abuse. Parental neglect resulted in impairment of intellectual and locomotor development and emotional and behavioral disorders. – From Authors' Abstract.

1454. MATSON, JOHNNY L. (Northern Illinois Univ.). **Exploration of phobic behavior in a small child.** Journal of Behavior Therapy and Experimental Psychiatry, 1983, **14**, 257–259.

1455. MILLS, MARLENE CHRISTINE (Montreal, Quebec, Canada). **Adolescents' self-disclosure in individual and group theme-centered modeling, reflecting, and probing interviews.** Psychological Reports, 1983, **53**, 691–701.

The study questions whether adolescents' self-disclosure stimulated by modeling psychotherapeutic techniques and group interview conditions reflects imitation and to what extent modeled self-disclosure is valid. – Adapted from Author's Abstract.

1456. MONAHAN, RICHARD T. (Harvard Medical School). **Suicidal children's and adolescents' responses to early memories test.** Journal of Personality Assessment, 1983, **47,** 258–264.
Suicidal groups gave more early memories than the controls. – From Author's Abstract.

1457. MRAZEK, PATRICIA J. (Univ. of Colorado School of Medicine); LYNCH, MARGARET A.; & BENTOVIM, ARNON. **Sexual abuse of children in the United Kingdom.** Child Abuse & Neglect, The International Journal, 1983, **7,** 147–153.
In the United Kingdom, at least 3 per 1,000 children are currently being recognized as sexually abused sometime during their childhood. – From Authors' Abstract.

1458. NEWBERGER, CAROLYN MOORE (Children's Hosp., 300 Longwood, Boston), & COOK, SUSAN J. **Parental awareness and child abuse: a cognitive-developmental analysis of urban and rural samples.** American Journal of Orthopsychiatry, 1983, **53,** 512–524.
A cognitive-developmental analysis of parental reasoning on childrearing issues is presented and applied in 2 controlled studies of parents of abused or neglected children. Significant differences in parental awareness were found between urban parents and their controls; this relationship was sustained in a rural sample, controlling for child handicap as well as for other familial characteristics. – Authors' Abstract.

1459. NOREM-HEBEISEN, ARDYTH (Univ. of Minnesota), & HEDIN, DIANE P. **Influences on adolescent problem behavior: causes, connections, and contexts.** Child and Youth Service, 1983, **6,** 35–56.
The article examines the conceptual and empirical evidence for correlates of problem behavior in general and drug abuse in particular and develops a model for analyzing factors in drug abuse that may be useful in developing specific prevention programs to address the needs of adolescents. – Authors' Abstract.

1460. NORTON, G. R. (Univ. of Winnipeg, Manitoba, Canada); AUSTEN, S.; ALLEN, G. E.; & HILTON, J. **Acceptability of time out from reinforcement procedures for disruptive child behavior: a further analysis.** Child & Family Behavior Therapy, 1983, 5(2), 31–41.
The results showed that teachers evaluated the 5 behavioral procedures for reducing disruptive behavior in children as being more effective and acceptable than did the parents. – From Authors' Abstract.

1461. ODEN, SHERRI (Wheelock Coll.). **The applicability of social skills training research.** Child and Youth Service, 1982, **5,** 75–89.
The effectiveness of social-skills training methods specifically designed to enhance children's peer relationships is evaluated. – From Author's Abstract.

1462. PARKS, SUSAN L. (Maryland Psychiatric Research Ctr., Box 3235, Catonsville). **The assessment of autistic children: a selective review of available instruments.** Journal of Autism and Developmental Disorders, 1983, **13,** 255–267.
Evaluated are Rimland's Diagnostic Checklist for Behavior-Disturbed Children, the Behavior Rating Instrument for Autistic and Atypical Children, the Behavior Observation Scale for Autism, the Childhood Autism Rating Scale, and the Autism Behavior Checklist. Reliability indices for all scales, except Rimland's Diagnostic Checklist, were at acceptable levels. Each scale was found to suffer from a lack of demonstrated discriminant and/or content validity. – From Author's Abstract.

1463. RASMUSSEN, PEDER (East Hosp., S-41685, Göteborg, Sweden); GILLBERG, CHRISTOPHER; WALDENSTRÖM, EVA; & SVENSON, BERTIL. **Perceptual, motor and attentional deficits in seven-year-old children: neurological and neurodevelopmental aspects.** Developmental Medicine and Child Neurology, 1983, **25,** 315–333.
Difficulties in distinguishing minimal brain dysfunction from mental retardation, cerebral palsy, and childhood psychoses are illustrated with children identified as having attention deficits. – From Abstract by B. B. Keller.

1464. RUNCO, MARK A., & SCHREIBMAN, LAURA (Claremont McKenna Coll.). **Parental judgments of behavior therapy efficacy with autistic children: a social validation.** Journal of Autism and Developmental Disorders, 1983, **13**, 237–248.
Parents judged the children as significantly improved after treatment and were more willing to interact with the children after treatment than before treatment. – From Authors' Abstract.

1465. RUSSELL, DIANA E. H. (Mills Coll.). **The incidence and prevalence of intrafamilial and extrafamilial sexual abuse of female children.** Child Abuse & Neglect, The International Journal, 1983, **7**, 133–146.
Data from a sample of 930 adult women in San Francisco provided the basis for estimating the prevalence of intrafamilial and extrafamilial sexual abuse of female children. Sixteen percent of these women reported at least 1 experience of intrafamilial sexual abuse before the age of 18 years; 12% reported at least 1 such experience before the age of 14 years. – From Author's Abstract.

1466. SEDLACEK, DAVID A. (Case Western Reserve Univ.). **Childhood: setting the stage for addiction.** Child and Youth Service, 1983, **6**, 23–34.
The term "intrapsychic addiction" is proposed as describing the substrate of the externally manifested addictions. The physical, psychological, and social factors that predispose children to addiction are related through a model. – Adapted from Author's Abstract.

1467. SIEBER, M. (Univ. of Zurich, Switzerland); HAAS, J.; HAIN, P.; SPIRIG, C.; & CORBOZ, R. **Verschwinden die Beeinträchtigungen leicht hirngeschädigter Kinder bei Schulabschlub? Eine Nachuntersuchung.** Zeitschrift für Entwicklungspsychologie und Pädagogische Psychologie, 1984, **16**, 12–22.
Children with attention deficit disorder (ADD) and children with problem behavior without ADD were reexamined in a follow-up study 7 years after the first consultation at the child psychiatric service. Comparisons revealed differences in the visuomotor functions and in emotional lability between the 2 groups. – From Authors' Abstract.

1468. SINGER, MARK (Case Western Reserve Univ.), & ISRALOWITZ, RICHARD. **Introduction: understanding adolescent substance abuse.** Child and Youth Service, 1983, **6**, 1–5.

1469. SLOAN, MICHAEL P. (Village of Childhelp, U.S.A., 14700 Manzanita Park, Beaumont, CA), & MEIER, JOHN H. **Typology for parents of abused children.** Child Abuse & Neglect, The International Journal, 1983, **7**, 443–450.
The classification scheme is informative and helpful for both treatment planning and permanency planning for abusive parents and abused children, whether or not the children have been separated from their parents. Several previously reported typologies for abusive parents are reviewed and then elaborated in light of the additional data. – From Authors' Abstract.

1470. SOKOLOFF, ROBERT M., & LUBIN, BERNARD (Univ. of Missouri, Kansas City). **Depressive mood in adolescent, emotionally disturbed females: reliability and validity of an adjective checklist (C-DACL).** Journal of Abnormal Child Psychology, 1983, **11**, 531–536.
The reliability and concurrent validity of 2 equivalent forms were found to be at a relatively high level for a group of emotionally disturbed adolescent females. – From Authors' Abstract.

1471. ST. LAWRENCE, JANET S. (Univ. of Mississippi Medical Ctr., 2500 N. State, Jackson), & DRABMAN, RONALD S. **Interruption of self-excoriation in a pediatric burn victim.** Journal of Pediatric Psychology, 1983, **8**, 155–159.
A response-interruption device was used with a young pediatric burn victim whose self-excoriation of grafted skin exacerbated her injuries. It was highly effective in terminating further self-inflicted tissue damage. – From Authors' Abstract.

1472. STANCIN, TERRY; REUTER, JEANETTE (Kent State Univ.); DUNN, VIRGINIA; & BICKETT, LAURA. **Validity of caregiver information on the developmental status of severely brain-damaged young children.** American Journal of Mental Deficiency, 1984, **88,** 388–395.
Results suggest that it is possible to substitute the Kent Infant Development Scale for the Bayley Scales when measuring the developmental status of severely brain-damaged young children. – From Authors' Abstract.

1473. STRAUSS, CYD C. (Univ. of Pittsburgh School of Medicine); RUBINOFF, ANDREA; & ATKESON, BEVERLY M. **Elimination of nocturnal headbanging in a normal seven-year-old girl using overcorrection plus rewards.** Journal of Behavior Therapy and Experimental Psychiatry, 1983, **14,** 269–273.
These procedures resulted in an immediate reduction and eventual total elimination of headbanging. – From Authors' Abstract.

1474. SUMMIT, ROLAND C. (Harbor-UCLA Medical Ctr., 1000 W. Carson, Torrance, CA). **The child sexual abuse accommodation syndrome.** Child Abuse & Neglect, The International Journal, 1983, **7,** 177–193.
The syndrome is composed of 5 categories: secrecy; helplessness; entrapment and accommodation; delayed, unconvincing disclosure; and retraction. The accommodation syndrome is proposed as a simple and logical model for use by clinicians. – From Author's Abstract.

1475. SWETNAM, LAUREL; PETERSON, CHRISTA R.; & CLARK, HEWITT B. (Children's Behavioral Services, State Mail Complex, Las Vegas). **Social skills development in young children: preventive and therapeutic approaches.** Child and Youth Service, 1982, **5,** 5–27.
An overview of social skill interventions with infants, toddlers, and preschoolers is presented, emphasizing parent training approaches, parent-child therapy, and treatments that directly change the child's behavior. – From Authors' Abstract.

1476. Symposium: Depression in Childhood. Japanese Journal of Child and Adolescent Psychiatry, 1983, **24,** 1–84.
This issue is a report of a symposium on depression in childhood held in October 1982. Papers (all in Japanese) by Takago (Concept and Diagnosis), Ohi (Psychopathology), Kitawaki (Psychological and Social Treatment), and Nakane (Pharmacotherapy) are presented and discussed. – Ed.

1477. TALLMADGE, JAMES, & BARKLEY, RUSSELL A. (Medical Coll. of Wisconsin). **The interactions of hyperactive and normal boys with their fathers and mothers.** Journal of Abnormal Child Psychology, 1983, **11,** 565–580.
Behavioral observations indicated that fathers and mothers did not differ in their interactions with their sons. Hyperactive boys were generally less compliant and their parents more directive than normal parent–child dyads. – From Authors' Abstract.

1478. TELZROW, CATHY F. (Cuyahoga Special Education Service Ctr., 14605 Granger, Maple Heights, OH). **Making child neuropsychological appraisal appropriate for children: alternative to downward extension of adult batteries.** Clinical Neuropsychology, 1983, **5,** 136–141.
The pattern of left and right hemispace reaction time and movement time correlations with PPVT IQ scores suggests that this modification of the reaction-time task may offer promise as a measure of functional cerebral asymmetry. – From Author's Abstract.

1479. TERR, LENORE C. (450 Sutter, San Francisco). **Child snatching: a new epidemic of an ancient malady.** Journal of Pediatrics, 1983, **103,** 151–156.
Eighteen children kidnapped successfully or abortively by a parent were psychiatrically evaluated; 16 were found to have 1 or more of 5 functional changes, including aftereffects of severe fright or psychic trauma and effects of mental indoctrination. – From Author's Abstract.

1480. VOELKER, SYLVIA (Lafayette Clinic, 951 E. Lafayette, Detroit); LACHAR, DAVID; & GDOWSKI, CHARLES L. **The personality inventory for children and response to methylphenidate: preliminary evidence for predictive utility.** Journal of Pediatric Psychology, 1983, **8**, 161–169.
Discriminant function analyses were computed comparing good and poor medication responders. Classification yielded correct placement of 74% for an improvement of 15% over sample base rate. – From Authors' Abstract.

1481. WASSERMAN, THEODORE H. (Astor Child Guidance Ctr., 4330 Byron, Bronx). **The effects of cognitive development on the use of cognitive behavioral techniques with children.** Child & Family Behavior Therapy, 1983, **5**(3), 37–50.
Cognitive behavior therapy techniques cannot be applied without first determining the cognitive developmental level of information processing that is being used by the client. Demand requirements of various cognitive behavioral techniques are compared with information processing limitations described by developmental theorists. – From Author's Abstract.

1482. WHITE, GARRY W. (Winthrop Coll.), & BRIGHT, DAN. **Multimodal behavioral therapy with elementary school children: rationale and case study.** Psychology in the Schools, 1983, **20**, 480–487.
A 7-year-old boy with a low frequency of on-task behavior was treated by an emphasis on intervention in the classroom setting, the use of treatment contracting, and comprehensive assessment of client needs. On-task behavior increased to the goal level by the end of treatment. – From Authors' Abstract.

1483. YANCHYSHYN, GORDON W., & ROBBINS, DOUGLAS R. (Univ. of Michigan Hosp.). **The assessment of depression in normal adolescents—a comparison study.** Canadian Journal of Psychiatry, 1983, **28**, 522–526.
The median Hamilton and Carroll scores of the school students differed from those of the inpatients, though the scores alone did not correspond with the presence or absence of depression. – From Authors' Abstract.

1484. ZENTALL, SYDNEY S. (Purdue Univ.), & ZENTALL, THOMAS R. **Optimal stimulation: a model of disordered activity and performance in normal and deviant children.** Psychological Bulletin, 1983, **94**, 446–471.
It is proposed that at least some of the deviant behavior displayed by disordered children represents a functional set of homeostatic responses to conditions of abnormal sensory input. Attempts to correct chronic imbalances in arousal through antecedent manipulations of chemical and sensory stimulation have been relatively successful and may provide not only appropriate treatment but also a better understanding of the mechanisms underlying many kinds of disordered behavior. – From Authors' Abstract.

HISTORY, THEORY, AND METHODOLOGY

1485. ADAMS, GERALD R. (Utah State Univ.). **The study of intraindividual change during early adolescence.** Journal of Early Adolescence, 1983, **3**, 37–46.
This paper provides a conceptual framework for training students in basic developmental methodology and proposes certain possibilities for the study of early adolescence. – From Author's Abstract.

1486. BERZONSKY, MICHAEL D. (SUNY, Cortland). **Adolescent research.** Human Development, 1983, **26**, 213–221.
It is concluded that life-span developmental principles ultimately must be substantiated by longitudinal data. – From Author's Abstract.

1487. BRAMAUD DU BOUCHERON, GENVIEVE (Univ. de Poitiers, 95 Ave. du Recteur Pineau, Poitiers Cedex, France). **Current French research in developmental psychology.** International Journal of Behavioral Development, 1983, **6**, 263–289.
The areas considered are: cognitive development in relation to Piaget's theory, psycholinguistics in preschool children, social interaction, and structuring time and space in infants and toddlers. – From Author's Abstract.

1488. CAHAN, EMILY D. (Yale Univ.). **The genetic psychologies of James Mark Baldwin and Jean Piaget.** Developmental Psychology, 1984, **20**, 128–135.
It is now generally recognized that the writings of philosopher-psychologist James Mark Baldwin anticipated much of Jean Piaget's work. The goals, genetic approach, and epistemological assumptions underlying Piaget's inquiry into cognitive development found explicit statement around the turn of the century in Baldwin's work. In his restatement of Baldwin's theory, Piaget provides researchers with the methodological foundations that were missing from Baldwin's more speculative endeavor. – From Author's Abstract.

1489. EWERT, OTTO M. (Univ. Mainz, Germany). **Eine historische Nachbemerkung zu Neuberger, Merz und Selg: Imitation bei Neugeborenen—eine kontroverse Befundlage.** Zeitschrift für Entwicklungspsychologie und Pädagogische Psychologie, 1983, **15**, 277–279.
The controversy on imitation in newborn children has its historical antecedence in the controversial findings of W. Preyer, McDougall, and J. Sully. These authors find imitation in newborns, whereas Baldwin assumes these findings to be artifacts of methodology. – From Author's Abstract.

1490. FABRICIUS, WILLIAM V. (Univ. of Michigan). **Piaget's theory of knowledge: its philosophical context.** Human Development, 1983, **26**, 325–334.
Piaget's theory of knowledge has many significant points in common with that of the German philosopher Kant. – From Author's Abstract.

1491. HOGAN, J. D. (St. John's Univ.), & VAHEY, M. A. **Modern classics in child development: authors and publications.** Journal of Psychology, 1984, **116**, 35–38.
Fourteen child-development textbooks were surveyed. Eleven publications, appearing between the years 1941 and 1960, were cited by 6 or more of the textbooks and are listed. – From Authors' Abstract.

1492. HOUSE, ALVIN ENIS; FARBER, JACKIE W.; & NIER, LAURA L. (Illinois State Univ.). **Differences in computational accuracy and speed of calculation between three measures of interobserver agreement.** Child Study Journal, 1983, **13**, 195–201.
The ease of calculation of 3 measures of observer reliability as reflected in speed and accuracy showed effects for method on time required and percentage correct. Expectation of reinforcement did not help. – Adapted from Authors' Abstract.

1493. NELSON, GORDON K. (Pennsylvania State Univ.). **Time in developmental studies: a convergence of the dialectic and phenomenological thought.** Genetic Psychology Monographs, 1983, **108**, 215–243.
Two dialectical theories of temporality were critically assessed and reformulated into a conception of time that has merit for life-span study and intellectual history. – From Author's Abstract.

1494. NIKOLSKSKAYA, A. A. **Role of V. Preyer's work in the development of child's psychology (to the 100th year since publication of V. Preyer's "Soul of the Child").** Questions of Psychology (translation of Russian title), 1983, **3**, 143–148.
Evaluation of V. Preyer's views by Russian authors is presented. Original contribution of Russian researchers to elaboration of theoretical and methodological issues in the field of the psychology of children is described. – From Author's Abstract.

1495. RICHARDSON, G. A. (1115 Forest, Coraopolis, PA), & McCLUSKEY, K. A. **Subject loss in infancy research: how biasing is it?** Infant Behavior and Development, 1983, **6,** 235–239.
Effects of subject loss include (1) loss of support for the hypothesis, (2) loss of generalizability of results due to nonrandom attrition, and (3) elimination of some age trends. – From Abstract by S. Thomas.

1496. SEAY, MARY BURT, & KAY, EDWIN J. (Lehigh Univ.). **Three-way analysis of dyadic social interactions.** Developmental Psychology, 1983, **19,** 868–872.
We propose a method for analyzing data from dyadic social interactions across 3 dichotomous variables. By accounting for the likely interdependency between 2 scores from a dyad, we circumvent the problems incurred with traditional analyses. We show that the analysis of variance may mask important features of the data. – From Authors' Abstract.

1497. SURBER, COLLEEN F. (Univ. of Wisconsin, Madison). **Issues in using quantitative rating scales in development research.** Psychological Bulletin, 1984, **95,** 226–246.
Most developmental studies have assumed that rating scales are used in an equal-interval manner, with few attempts to test that assumption. The conditions allowing a conclusion that individuals or groups differ in information integration are outlined, and methods of testing models of the information integration process that do not assume an equal-interval response scale are reviewed. – From Author's Abstract.

1498. THOMPSON, DENNIS N. (Georgia State Univ.). **Psychological classics: older works in developmental psychology frequently cited today.** Journal of Genetic Psychology, 1983, **143,** 169–174.
Bibliographies of 17 introductory texts were surveyed. References originally published before 1942 and common to at least 5 of the texts were included here; 46 references met the criteria. For the most part, the references were published between World Wars I and II and are primarily concerned with infancy. – From Author's Abstract.

BOOK NOTICES

1499. BAKER, C. L., & McCARTHY, JOHN J. (Eds.). **The Logical Problem of Language Acquisition.** MIT Press, 1981. xii + 358 p. $35.00.
This collection of 10 articles and associated discussion papers is the result of a symposium held in 1980. As the title suggests, it is concerned not with empirical studies of language development or language learning, but with the problem posed for theories of adult linguistic knowledge by the nature of the input and feedback children appear to receive when acquiring their first language. This "logical" problem of language acquisition has also been referred to as the "learnability" or "projection" problem for linguistic theory, and it has been used recently to criticize those linguistic analyses in the literature on generative grammar that seem dependent on facts not available to the ordinary language learner. Of particular concern is the apparent lack of linguistic information from which children might learn that some possible grammatical rules are in fact overly general in that they generate ungrammatical as well as grammatical utterances. All of the authors take this no-negative-evidence phenomenon as support for the claim that "human beings possess strong innate predispositions critical to bridging the gap between early experience and eventual knowledge" (p. xi). The various papers suggest different types of innate constraints on language acquisition, depending on the particular domain of grammar addressed (e.g., auxiliary verbs, morphophonemics, syntactic movement rules, productive morphology, etc.). All of the papers are highly abstract, theoretical, and formal, in that the goal is generally to delineate a set of descriptively adequate structural rules for language that could be learned, in principle, from positive evidence alone and without regard to function or meaning. (With respect to the last criterion, the paper by J. Grimshaw and the commentaries by C. Smith and T. Wasow represent notable exceptions.) As is generally the case in this area of linguistics, the authors' arguments rest largely on shared intuitions about the grammaticality

of particular utterances, along with some use of historical and cross-linguistic data, but with very little in the way of appeals to data on child language behavior (the principal exception here being Grimshaw). In some cases, the comprehensibility of arguments presented depends on familiarity with the relevant technical literature. The usefulness of such a book for developmentalists depends primarily on the extent to which it provides clear evidence of external constraints on explanatory theories of child language development, so it seems unfortunate that there is no attempt at the end of the book to bring the individual papers together, to summarize their similarities and differences, or to assess their collective progress toward solving the logical problems of language acquisition. The commentaries following the individual papers, while helpful in some respects, tend to focus on particulars rather than more general issues. Consequently, most students and professionals interested in development, child language, and theories of language development will not find the present book very useful. Instead, its primary audience is likely to be theoretical linguists, psycholinguists, and mathematicians familiar with the literature on learnability theory or developmental psycholinguists engaged in studying a particular aspect of grammatical development touched on in 1 or another of the papers. – M. S. Ammon and P. R. Ammon.

1500. BALTES, PAUL B., & BRIM, ORVILLE G., JR. (Eds.). **Life-Span Development and Behavior.** Vol. 4. Academic Press, 1982. xv + 362 p. $35.00.
This is the fourth in a series of volumes on life-span development theory and research. The editors explicitly have made "little attempt to organize each volume around a particular topic or theme"—the 9 chapters cover diverse topics and reflect a variety of approaches. In the introductory chapter, Montada and Schmitt discuss issues relevant to the practical application of a life-span developmental perspective. Four objectives are emphasized: (1) predicting intraindividual change and stability, (2) justifying intervention goals, (3) planning interventions, and (4) evaluating the developmental precursors and distal effects associated with intervention strategies. The importance of interindividual differences in intraindividual development is highlighted. This is a central theme in 4 of the research-based chapters. Mortimer, Finch, and Kumka employ longitudinal data on self-conceptions to illustrate 4 methods of assessing developmental stability: structural invariance (factor pattern), level stability (magnitude), normative stability (interindividual rank), and ipsative stability (intraindividual rank). Significant mean level changes in self-conception measures were observed over a 14-year period. However, self-conceptions were found to remain structurally invariant and normatively and ipsatively stable. Of particular interest is the finding of differential change patterns: some subjects remained consistently high or low in level, whereas others increased or decreased. The possible reciprocal influences of antecedent life events and self-image differences are also considered in this comprehensive chapter. The issue of differential trends in mental development for normal, handicapped, and at-risk infants is addressed by Kopp and McCall. Their review of existing longitudinal studies indicates (with the exception of severely impaired children) normative instability during infancy. The mental development of handicapped and at-risk children does appear to stabilize somewhat earlier, however. Pulkkinen's chapter challenges the assumption that adolescents constitute a homogeneous age group. She presents evidence for a 2-dimensional model of adolescent impulse control: revellers, losers, strivers, and loners. Data from a 12-year longitudinal study indicated intraindividual consistency (structural invariance) in the development of these 4 adolescent life styles. The nature of the relationships among these *modi operandi* and different childrearing and environmental conditions are considered. The late-onset of affective disorders in 3 subtypes of psychiatric patients is the focal concern of Gutmann, Griffin, and Grunes. Evidence for intraindividual consistency (e.g., retrospective reports) in handling adult aggression and dependency is discussed. Together these 4 chapters illustrate the insights that can be gained by examining interindividual differences in intraindividual development. The developmental precursors associated with differential developmental trends and their long-term consequences (especially the manner in which different individuals influence and interpret life events) are fruitful issues for life-span oriented investigators. Cohler discusses the interpretive and reconstructive activities that enable individuals cognitively to maintain a sense of consistency and well-being over the life span. Topics such as personal identity, reminiscence, memory development, and coping with crises are included in this excel-

lent conceptualization of subjective consistency. Furstenberg's topic is conjugal succession. He, too, underscores the role that revisionist activities may play in one's development. Self-report data from divorced individuals who had recently remarried indicated significant differences between former and present spouses and the manner in which marital decisions were made, conflicts resolved, and labor divided. Given the high dissolution rate of second marriages, Furstenberg considers the degree of correspondence between an individual's self-reported subjective reality and the objective reality of the marital situation. In the remaining 2 chapters, multivariate causal models are used to investigate antecedent conditions associated with developmental problems. Himmelweit and Turner employ data from an 11-year longitudinal follow up to investigate the positive correlation between depression and occupational success among males during early adulthood. The evidence indicated that unexpected occupational success—"anomia of early success"—may engender depression in "nonclinical" men: early success may result in the loss of occupational goals and cause the individual to revise and devalue former achievements, especially when expectations have been exceeded. A comprehensive developmental theory of drug use is offered by Huba and Bentler. Data from a 4-year longitudinal study are used to analyze assumptions about the causal structure among interpersonal and intrapersonal domains hypothesized to influence drug use. Causal models are evaluated to test the usefulness of the theoretical formulations. In general, analyses are consistent with the assumptions of the theoretical framework. Life-span developmentalists will find this volume useful and informative. The recurring emphases on interindividual differences in intraindividual consistency and the active role that individuals may play in subjectively (and/or objectively) maintaining these trends are timely and thought provoking. The research-oriented chapters represent valuable contributions to a field resting on a limited data base. (One can of course always cite the need for more long-term longitudinal support for life-span conceptualizations.) The book also serves to illustrate a variety of methods for investigating developmental questions. One notable weakness in an otherwise excellent volume is the limited attention devoted to intergenerational differences. – M. D. Berzonsky.

1501. BISANZ, JEFFREY; BISANZ, GAY L.; & KAIL, ROBERT (Eds.). **Learning in Children: Progress in Cognitive Development Research.** Springer-Verlag, 1983. x + 201 p. $23.00.
The editors of this volume believe North American research on learning in children has recently entered a new phase. The book is intended to stimulate thinking and research that would contribute to a flowering of this phase, the hallmark of which is said to be intense analysis of knowledge acquisition in children. Brainerd (Chapter 1) focuses on a search for developmental invariants in learning, i.e., consistent underlying structures (patterns) in learning data. Markov models used by others to predict animal and adult human learning performance constitute Brainerd's tool. The target data stem from 20 of Brainerd's own experiments on discrimination learning, verbal learning, and memorization in young children. Brainerd finds evidence for the structural invariance he is seeking and concludes the models he employs can fruitfully be used to enhance our understanding of children's learning. Linder and Siegel (Chapter 2) argue that learning tasks involving correctness-of-response feedback provide a more useful avenue than do Piagetian procedures for assessing young children's conceptual competencies. A review of research on quantitative and dimensional concepts, seriation, and children's multidimensional discrimination learning serves to buttress the authors' argument. Heth and Cornell (Chapter 3) emphasize the common concern of learning theory and developmental psychology with transition rules that govern changes from 1 psychological state to another. A Markovian analysis of spatial concept development in infancy is used to illustrate the conduct of a learning analysis of 1 particular developmental phenomenon. Kail (Chapter 4) argues that the procedures favored by those doing theory-oriented laboratory research on children's learning are inadequate for research that focuses on developmentally considered instructional effects. According to Kail, efforts in the latter category should entail use of: (a) tasks actually facing the child in the school situation, (b) experimental designs that sample levels of an independent variable broadly, and (c) statistical methods that tell us more about data than do traditional analysis of variance procedures. Perry and Perry (Chapter 5) discuss moral internalization from the perspectives of attribution and modern social learning theory. The authors conclude that attribution research

sheds light on the internalization process and offers valuable childrearing suggestions, although modifications in attribution theory are needed to account for the typical occurrence of moral internalization under naturalistic conditions. Paris and Cross (Chapter 6) present a conceptual framework that emphasizes interrelationships among children's beliefs, motives, and learning. Stress is placed on the recursive nature of "ordinary learning" (involving tasks mastered over long time periods—the kind of learning Paris & Cross believe we ought to be studying). The chapter's extensive literature citations reflect the authors' goal of synthesizing ideas from cognitive, social, and educational psychology. The approach is strongly pragmatic and eclectic in character. Bransford and Heldmeyer (Chapter 7) are impressed with the fact that young children seem to be highly enthusiastic and effective learners, despite their limited memories and their lack of knowledge and sophisticated learning strategies. The authors try to resolve this paradox by discussing some cognitive and motivational advantages enjoyed by the young learner. This well-edited volume succeeds in reflecting 4 themes the editors see as characterizing the new phase into which work on children's learning is said to have entered: (a) the goal of integrating social, motivational, and cognitive aspects of learning; (b) a concern for identifying the competencies of very young children, (c) a concern for the generality and applicability of research on children's learning, and (d) a concern for the use of sophisticated methodological tools (particularly mathematical formalisms). – G. N. Cantor.

1502. CHALL, JEANNE S. **Learning to Read: The Great Debate** (updated ed.). McGraw-Hill, 1983. 424 p. $18.95.

This updated edition is a reissue of the 1967 book accompanied by a 45-page updated section that reviews research published between 1967 and 1981. The 1967 book was a classic that is commonly regarded as 1 of the most significant statements of an educational research issue published in this century. In the original book, Chall clearly delineated the issues surrounding phonics vs. whole-word approaches to teaching beginning reading, and she presented a summary of research evidence suggesting an advantage for phonics-based instruction. In 1967, this was certainly a controversial (even heretical in some circles) conclusion given the strong belief among many educators that the whole-word approach was the superior method. The update contained in the current book reviews the impact of the original book, summarizes large-scale studies of reading instruction appearing between 1967 and 1981, examines changes in basal readers and professional opinions occurring between the publication of the 2 books, and concludes with a set of recommendations about how early reading instruction should proceed. Chall finds evidence for the impact for her original book in changes that have occurred in basal readers and in changes in the attitudes of educators and researchers. Moreover, her review of the research evidence appearing since 1967 supports her original conclusion that phonics-basal reading instruction was superior to whole-word instruction. Chall's original book was at the leading edge of a heated and sometimes hysterical debate of great practical significance. Today, however, the issue of how to teach word identification skills is not very controversial (due in large part to Chall's original book) and is certainly not the reading education issue that occupies center stage. That place is taken by the issue of how to teach reading comprehension. This reviewer wishes that Chall had applied her considerable analytic talents to the more current issue. But perhaps scientists are only allowed 1 masterpiece in their careers, and Chall has certainly had hers. That may be the true worth of her new book: to remind us that every once in a while a social scientist produces a work of lasting and enduring significance. Chall's book has certainly had such an impact on reading education. – J. M. Royer.

1503. CHALL, JEANNE S. **Stages of Reading Development.** McGraw-Hill, 1983. x + 293 p. $18.95.

In order to summarize her work to date on the development of reading skill, Chall has written this short book. The body of her thesis is expressed in 10 chapters and an epilogue that together span 176 pages. Three appendices follow, 1 providing a more detailed summary of the empirical research cited in the earlier chapters, another describing 5 works that Chall regards as intellectual predecessors of her theory (William Gray, Arthur Gates, David Russell, Francis Ilg, and Louis Ames, Paul Rozin, and Lila Gleitman), and a third reporting an analysis of textbooks for courses on the methodology of teaching reading. The major claim of the book is that reading development can best be understood as a progression of stages, and Chall intends to use the term "stage" in its technical sense à la Piagetian structuralism. Thus, the claim is that reading skill undergoes a series of transformations from 1 qualitatively different state to another; that the states can be discriminated by their content, organization, and focus of activity; that the stages replace 1 another in a fixed order; and that rough modal age ranges can be identified for each stage, though wide variation will exist as a function of individual abilities and environmental experiences. The sequence that Chall proposes is the following.

Stage 0. Prereading: birth to 6 years. The acquisition of reading readiness skills.

Stage 1. Initial reading, or decoding, stage: grades 1–2, ages 6–7. Acquisition of word recognition skills.

Stage 2. Confirmation, fluency, ungluing from print: grades 2–3, ages 7–8. Consolidation of basic skills into a fluent reading system.

Stage 3. Reading for learning the new: a first step. Phase 3A, grades 4–6, ages 9–11, involves overcoming egocentrism and reading about conventional knowledge of the world. Phase 3B, grades 7–9, ages 12–14, involves movement toward adult levels of reading fluency and growth in analytic and critical skills.

Stage 4. Multiple viewpoints: high school, ages 14–18. Dealing with more than 1 point of view on a topic and reconciling or choosing among them.

Stage 5. Construction and reconstruction—a world view. College, ages 18 and above. Use of reading as a tool to pick and choose among possible things to learn in the process of constructing knowledge for oneself.

Each of the proposed stages is elaborated, and evidence is offered for its psychological reality. The nature of transitions from stage to stage is discussed. After description of the theory per se, Chall discusses its implications as she sees them for teaching and testing, dealing with extreme individual differences, and the influence of historical trends and cultural patterns on reading achievement and the formulation of social policy. I find the book hard to evaluate. As the exposition of a stage theory, it is unsophisticated and fails to directly address any of the criteria that developmental theorists currently require a stage theory to meet (e.g., Flavell, 1971, *Cognitive Psychology,* vol. 2, 421–453). Without more extensive justification than is provided, the proposal that reading develops in stages is uncompelling. The evidence that is offered convinces me that reading skill improves with age, gets more complex with age, and serves different functions for the reader after it is well established and the reader is more intellectually mature than it did when it was poorly established and the reader was intellectually immature. However, the evidence does not convince me that reading develops in stages. As an empirical description of the general course of reading development, it is more acceptable, though it is a bit too simplistic to fully serve the specialist and a bit too encumbered with superfluous concepts from stage theory to clearly inform the layperson. Nevertheless, there is merit to the book. Chall offers a sensible and easily understood analysis of the Goodman/Smith position on the relative importance of word recognition skills and context use skills that is very useful. Her observations on teaching, testing, and social policy are shaped by long experience with real children in real settings and are worth reading even if one is not convinced by the theoretical framework in which they are set. Thus, as a researcher, I find the book wanting, but as a parent and a customer of the schools, I find it interesting. – T. H. Carr.

1504. CHI, MICHELENE T. H. (Ed.). **Trends in Memory Development Research.** Karger, 1983. xii + 128 p. $29.50.

This volume is based on a 1981 symposium to honor the tenth anniversary of the landmark 1971 symposium organized by John Flavell and entitled "What is Memory the Development of?" The major theme of the volume is the relationship between existing knowledge and remembering and, in some sense, knowledge is the topic of each of the 6 chapters in this volume. The first 4 chapters are on current research topics, while the final 2 provide a general overview of the past decade and a look at the future. In the first chapter, Naus and Ornstein consider the link between strategy development and the child's growing knowledge base. One particularly interesting section is devoted to a discussion of the results of some work in progress examining the rehearsal and recall of experts and novices in a specific knowledge domain, which suggest efficient execution of active rehearsal techniques is a function of familiarity with the to-be-remembered materials. In the next chapter, Wellman discusses metamemory or knowledge about memory processes and, in so doing, characterizes metamemory as the child's theory of mind. Nelson et al., in the third chapter, consider the relationships of script knowledge to the development of memory. One distinguishing feature of their work is the use of interview and other naturalistic approaches to examine what children know about the objects and events of their everyday lives. In the fourth, and to me most interesting chapter, Chi and Rees consider the relationship between learning and development. Their thesis is that development is the acquisition of new knowledge, the restructuring of existing knowledge, and the integration of new and existing knowledge. One of the more thought-provoking features of this chapter is their discussion of learning mechanisms, drawing upon current theoretical structures, including node-link networks, production rules, and schemas. In the final chapter, Olson reminds us that despite the advances of the past decade, there is still a considerable gap between what we know and what we would like to know, while Trabasso argues that future research on memory development needs to focus on the implications of knowledge growth in particular domains, assuming that different domains have different implications. In short, this volume focuses on knowledge development, and thus its scope is somewhat limited. But in view of increasing emphasis on the role of knowledge in development, this volume should be of great interest to any student of memory. – F. N. Dempster.

1505. CLARKE-STEWART, ALLISON. **Day Care.** Harvard Univ. Press, 1982. 171 p. $12.95 (cloth); $6.95 (paper).
This is another book in the series The Developing Child, edited by Jerome Bruner, Michael Cole, and Barbara Lloyd. The author, Allison Clarke-Stewart, has recently completed several major studies on the effects of daycare on the developing child and has published the results extensively in journals and books. The book is based on the newest research looking at the effects of daycare on young children. Compared to some of the current lurid accounts in the lay literature on the horrors of nontraditional care of young children, this book is factual and reassuring. In the first and second chapters, Clarke-Stewart documents the need for alternative child care with a vivid account of the plight of many young mothers and families who are desparate for good child care but find nowhere to turn for accurate information on what constitutes good care, much less where to find it. She discusses changes in U.S. society that have prompted the need for daycare, i.e., working mothers and divorce, as well as the conflict of experts at both ends of the political spectrum concerning the effect of daycare on the child. In Chapter 3, she gives a brief history of the waxing and waning of daycare in the United States, including how daycare has been used as a political football for 50 years, the most blatant example being the interval during World War II with the abrupt final withdrawal of funds in 1946. This history of child care in the United States and in Britain does not make for pretty reading, with the last concern of governments seemingly always the child. In Chapter 4, Clarke-Stewart documents the often creative, but often makeshift, arrangements used by families needing care for their children. By far the largest number of children are cared for in their own homes or in other people's homes. The problem with such care is there is little quality control, it is often unstable, and no substitute caregivers are available. However, what emerges is a picture of real attempts by parents and individuals to provide good, though limited, care. Daycare centers are discussed and it becomes clear that here, too, variations are great, with centers providing a wide variety of care. In the middle chapters, Clarke-Stewart examines the effect of daycare on the child. She points out that physical development is accelerated for poor families, but not in middle-class children. Also, children in daycare centers catch more colds, etc. Most important, daycare children do as well or better than children at home, even when care standards are only minimal. She also addresses the attachment studies and daycare, concluding that daycare children are as attached to their mothers, just not so intensely physical. In addition, daycare appears to accelerate peer relationships. In Chapter 6, Clarke-Stewart examines why some programs accelerate children's development of independence, knowledge, and social competence. She examines different types of programs, looking at structured (closed) vs. unstructured (open) programs. She points out that both types offer advantages, i.e., better scores on IQ and achievement tests in closed programs and better scores on tests

of curiosity, inventiveness, and problem solving in open programs. She concludes that probably a judicious mix is best for most children. Peer interactions are also examined in this chapter. Chapter 7 examines caregiver qualities, both of parents and teachers. Both group differences between mothers and teachers are examined, as well as a careful distinction between these group means and the large individual variation within each group. In the last 3 chapters of the book, Clarke-Stewart helps the parents with practical decisions. She points out that individual children have different needs and that the benefit of type of care may vary with the type of child. She discusses age of entry, difficult home situations, and difficult vs. easy temperament in children as they relate to daycare adaptation. Finally, in Chapter 9 she gives very practical hints on selection of daycare for parents. Chapter 10 covers alternative care systems in other parts of the world. *Day Care* is an outstanding example of the usefulness of this series. It should be readily available to all parents faced with how to best manage the raising of their child in our complex society. – B. I. Fagot.

1506. COHEN, DOROTHY H.; STERN, VIRGINIA; & BALABAN, NANCY. **Observing and recording the behavior of young children.** Teachers Coll. Press, 1983. x + 213 p. $9.95.
With the increasing number of undergraduate texts describing observational methods of child study, the title of this book might suggest simply 1 more laboratory manual on the topic. However, this text clearly is not in the same mold. It is designed expressly for teachers and is described by the authors as a "manual on record-taking . . . that will help teachers of young children toward their goal of understanding children's behavior" (p. 1). When it originally appeared in 1958, the book apparently was an attempt to persuade early childhood teachers that objective observation and recording can be a valuable tool in the classroom. Although several chapters have been added in this third edition, the goal and thrust of the book seem to have changed very little. Chapter 1 outlines the rationale and general methodology of the approach. The essence of the method is that the teacher, with pen and notebook in hand, should unobtrusively record children's activities throughout the day—what the authors call an "on-the-spot running record." These recordings should include not simply the child's actions, but also how the child feels about those actions. Teachers are encouraged to use terms that capture the quality and style of the child's behaviors (i.e., rather than recording that the child "walked," a more precise word should be selected, such as "sauntered," "stomped," or "strolled"). They also are encouraged to record facial expressions, voice tone, body postures, and the like. The goal of the observing/recording is to identify "patterns" in the child's activities, over many weeks and various areas of functioning, so as eventually to construct "generalizations" regarding the child's growth, development, and adjustment to the school environment. Chapters 2–10 offer guidance on observing specific aspects of the child's behavior, including: routines (eating, resting, toileting, etc.), play, child-child interactions, adult-directed activities, cognitive functioning, and language. Chapters 11 and 12, both new to this edition, are devoted to the unique considerations in observing infants/toddlers and children with special problems, respectively. The final chapter discusses how the information gleaned from a period of such observing/recording can be summarized and prepared as a report—perhaps for the child's file, next year's teacher, the parents, or the school psychologist. This book has almost no overlap with the formal and increasingly rigorous observational methods that have become a part of scientific child study. Concepts such as time-sampling and interobserver reliability are nowhere to be found. Indeed, the methodology is described as having "practically no fixed rules" (p. 6). The notion of observer bias does appear, but the teacher is admonished simply to put prejudices and preconceptions aside and to approach the task in an objective fashion. Developing generalizations about a child through such a theoretically naive and inductive methodology can potentially serve a number of useful purposes. It might be pedagogically valuable, for example, to have student teachers apply these methods as a relatively direct means of experiencing the diversity, complexity, and regularity of young children's behavior. But if the information gathered through this approach will, in fact, find its way into the child's school records and, perhaps, form the basis of the child's placement, referral, or disposition, one must wonder whether this system offers teachers the most valid, appropriate, and useful approach to observational data collection. – R. Vasta.

1507. DOERKEN, MAURINE. **Classroom Combat: Teaching and Television.** Educational Technology Publications, 1983. xvii + 316 p. $23.95.

Classroom Combat: Teaching and Television is written by a classroom teacher who abhors television and is clearly tired of her struggle of competing with television for the "attention—indeed, the minds—of our young people." To summarize this book: Children watch too much television! And why is this a problem? Because television is bad; it promotes passive and involuntary learning, violence, consumption and materialism, sexism and racism, etc., etc. Alright, there are those who would take major exception to this as a general position, but the author goes on. Television also effectively reduces reading scores, writing scores, and listening scores; alters brain waves; disrupts sleep patterns; and "pushes some people over the deep end," causing schizophrenia. I appreciated the author's experience and found myself sympathetic with the plight of the present-day classroom teacher, but I am not sure what the book contributes except to help the author let off steam. In an area that is really quite widely researched, this book draws too selectively on the available research literature (cf. P. J. Murray, *Television and Youth,* 1980, for a review of the television literature). For example, a number of studies have recently concluded that processing television is an active process that involves relatively sophisticated cognitive processing strategies (cf. J. Bryant and D. R. Anderson, *Children's Understanding of Television,* 1983). A sprinkling of references to learning theory, Piaget, Kohlberg, Bandura, and others appears to be an attempt to give psychological credibility to the book. In fact, the treatment of these and other topics is too superficial to add much to anyone's understanding of either these various topics or how they relate to the effects of watching television on children. The last chapter of the book is "A Look at the Television Industry." Writing this chapter was clearly an eye-opener for the author, who was surprised to learn that network television is a business, and the goal of the business is to sell advertising time. This book may motivate some parents to supervise what and how much television their children watch. After all, isn't the source of the problem really in the home, not in the television? And if Doerken's scare tactics succeed in motivating more responsible parenting and more selective viewing, the book is probably worth stocking in libraries. – K. Pezdek.

1508. ELIOT, JOHN, & SMITH, IAN MacFARLANE. **The International Directory of Spatial Tests.** NFER-NELSON Publishing (Windsor, England), 1983. 462 p. $175.00

This reference volume differs from other published listings of mental tests in that its scope is limited to tests that appear to require the perception and retention of visual forms and the mental manipulation of shapes. It is also different because test instructions and practice items are reproduced from a broad sampling of commercial, out-of-print, and experimental paper-and-pencil spatial tests in the English language. Finally, it is different because it is organized and presented in a classification based upon the perceived similarity of test stimuli and requirements. In addition to 390 test descriptions, the volume contains chapters that provide a historical background and an explanation of the structure of the volume. – J. Eliot.

1509. HAYES, C. D., & KAMERMAN, S. B. (Eds.). **Children of Working Parents: Experiences and Outcomes.** National Academy, 1983. ix + 275 p. $16.50.

This volume is a review of the research on the effects of changing parental employment patterns, particularly the increase in maternal employment, on children's growth and development. It is the second report of the Panel on Work, Family, and Community, a group established by the Committee on Child Development Research and Public Policy and supported by the National Institute of Education. One section of the book covers the research on the effects of parental employment on peer relationships (Berndt), television viewing (Messaris & Hornik), and the family-school relationship (Linney & Vernberg). Since little research on parental employment has utilized these child outcomes, the authors' focus is primarily to highlight general themes and to suggest issues that warrant further investigation. The material in the second section concerns a survey conducted by the Panel of existing data sets with variables pertaining to the relationship between work and family life. Approximately 75 data sources were selected, with an effort made to include those with representative samples, longitudinal or cross-cohort designs, machine-readable data, and inclusion of information from a variety of institutions (i.e., government, workplace, community, and family). A detailed description of each data source, along with the name of a contact person, is provided in an appendix (edited by Bloom-Feshbach). To explore the feasibility of using these existing data, 2 chapters in this section describe secondary analyses of 2 data sources. One chapter concerns the effects of parents' employment on children's access to and use of neighborhood resources (Rubin); a second focuses on the effects of maternal employment on children's long-term educational and occupational outcomes (D'Amico, Haurin, and Mott). The major finding of these analyses, as well as the reviews in the first section, is that maternal employment does not substantially affect the types of outcomes examined. However, most studies reviewed did not take into account the nature of parental employment or the suitability of the child-care arrangements employed, nor were the processes specified by which parental employment might exert its influence. It remains to be seen whether the data available from the sources surveyed in this book will be useful in future investigations based on more sophisticated conceptual models. – S. Holloway.

1510. HIGGINS, E. TORY; RUBLE, D. N.; & HARTUP, W. W. (Eds.). **Social Cognition and Social Development: a Sociocultural Perspective.** Cambridge Univ. Press, 1983. x + 415 p. $39.50.
The chapters in this volume are taken from presentations made at an important conference held at the University of Western Ontario in November 1979. An interdisciplinary group of scholars assembled at that time to discuss experiential and socialization factors in children's social cognitive development. The outcome was an almost heretical attack on traditional structuralist conceptions of cognitive development with a turn instead toward sociocultural perspectives. The excitement of that conference is reflected in this volume, in which several themes emerge. Most importantly, the inseparability of contexts and contents in social cognition is noted in discussions of the role of culture in social cognitive development. Age-specific subcultural rules and norms are proposed as primary determinants of age differences in cognition in chapters by Higgins and Eccles (Parsons) and Pool, Schweder, and Much. Socialization influences on children's information processing is a second theme. Costanzo and Dix present an intriguing theory of how social norms can preempt formal cognitive analysis by the child. Collins discusses the role of information processing mechanisms in children's comprehension of social portrayals on television. Grusec and Lepper, in separate chapters, present theories of the role of socialization in the internalization of social values. These theories emphasize information processing mechanisms such as attributions and scripts. Hoffman presents a theory of moral internalization that combines cognitive and affective processing mechanisms. A third, contrasting theme is the self-constructive nature of children's growing social knowledge and awareness, emphasized in the holistic approach by Hartup, Brady, and Newcomb, and the "self-socialization" approach by Ruble. A final theme is the complexity of the relation between social cognition and social behavior and is discussed in a chapter on values, by Emmerich and Shepard, and 1 on friendship, by Berndt. As a whole, these chapters constitute a maverick approach to the study of social cognitive development. A more temperate perspective emerges from several thoughtful commentaries that follow these chapters. Turiel and Damon each defend the structuralist position of traditional theories of cognitive development. Maccoby endorses the emphasis on socialization but points out several unresolved issues in the theories presented. Finally, Trabasso is humorous, subtle, and wise in a tongue-in-cheek telephone conversation with his mother, in which he describes to her what he has learned from the conference. This volume is important to researchers and theorists of social development because of its integration of findings from several disciplines and because it pushes the field to consider new perspectives. – K. A. Dodge.

1511. LAOSA, LUIS M., & SIGEL, IRVING E. (Eds.). **Families as Learning Environments for Children.** Plenum, 1982. xvii + 395 p. $29.50.
This book is a collection of 11 readings presenting data generated by current research projects. The conceptions of family a well as learning outcomes of interest are quite varied. Primarily, families are conceptualized in terms of parent–child relations or by summary variables such as socioeconomic status and family constellation. Lewis and Feiring offer a challenge to the common focus on parent–child dyads isolated from the rest of the family members as they

conceptualize families as social systems with multiple networks of relationships. Their analysis of family functioning at the dinner table was informative and exemplary of how family members operate vis-à-vis one another. Another reading, by Fosburg, reminds us that "family" for many children for much of the day involves family daycare and surrogate "mothers" and "siblings." While parent–child experiences are emphasized, sibling relations are not totally ignored (e.g., see the readings by Bacon & Ashmore, Lamb, and Laosa). Learning outcomes (no distinction between learning and development is provided) range from interests in traditional cognitive, social, and personality development to the learning of "practical skills" (e.g., home management skills). The context in which these studies occurred varied as well. Observational work in the home setting is certainly well represented. Laboratory settings are also considered. Power and Parke provide insight into the extent to which patterns of interaction observed in a laboratory setting are generalized to the home setting. Interview data often supplement observational findings. McGillicuddy-Dilisi, for example, document that there did not exist for parents studied a 1:1 correspondence between a particular belief or set of beliefs and a particular teaching style. This book of readings does not focus on any 1 particular age group of children. The children targeted for study range from infancy through middle childhood, although within a given reading only 1 age group is typically considered. As the editors of this volume note, the diversity of readings defies integration and reflects the state of research on families. This reviewer agrees. Neither a comprehensive integration of existing research nor integration of smaller bodies of research appear to be the goal of individual readings or the volume as a whole. Rather, the reader gets a taste of varying approaches to research on families, particularly parent–child relationships, which are primarily descriptive or presented in conjunction with a range of "learning" outcomes. – B. K. Bryant.

1512. LISS, MARSHA B. (Ed.). **Social and Cognitive Skills: Sex Roles and Children's Play.** Academic Press, 1983. xiv + 272 p. $27.50.
The question of how sex roles are acquired used to have 3 possible answers: it could be approached from Freudian, social learning, or cognitive developmental points of view. These theoretical paradigms were seen as conflicting and as making fundamentally different predictions. In the past decade or so of research on sex roles, much of it from a feminist perspective, this situation has changed considerably. The Freudian point of view, once mandatory to critique, now is rarely even mentioned; the present book contains only a single mention of his name, made in passing. On the other hand, social learning and cognitive developmental points of view are increasingly seen as not in conflict, but rather to a large extent mutually supplementary. For instance, social learning principles may explain the manifestations of sex-role learning seen clearly in 2-year-olds, long before children have acquired stable notions of gender identity. New theoretical points of view have entered the arena a well. One example is Bem's gender schema theory, a kind of cognitive theory fundamentally different from that of Kohlberg and supported by an increasing body of research on selective memory for gender-relevant and schema-congruent or -incongruent events. Another trend, derived from ethnomethodology, is the examination of the texture of the interactions in which children engage, to determine the myriad of tiny lessons they learn daily which together may add up to a "sex role" even though this was never anyone's intention as the interactions unfolded. The present book exemplifies these trends in the field, while not explicitly discussing them. It is theoretically eclectic; some of the writers use the terminology of social-learning theory, but few identify themselves with a particular school, preferring to get on with the business of data collection. One exception is an excellent chapter by Sprafkin, Serbin, Denier, and Connor, which provides an informative summary of the Serbin-Connor research program. Conceived within a social learning framework, but looking microanalytically at preschool interaction, these investigators have identified some of the early roots of cognitive and personality differences between the sexes, and have provided some demonstrations of how preschool programs can be modified to reduce such differentiation. Another exception is the chapter by C. Jan Carpenter, laying out the series of studies she has conducted with Aletha Huston on the social and cognitive consequences of "activity structure," that is, the tendency for girls to engage more than boys in activities for which there are existing guidelines and external norms. The book also includes a useful chapter by Nancy Eisenberg on the use of measures of sex-typed toy choice as indices of sex-role

adoption. She shows her readers the numerous pitfalls involved in such simplistic assumptions, given the multidimensional nature of sex-role acquisition. (In fact, the very term "sex role" ought to be banished from our vocabulary, strictly speaking.) However, thee chapters are embedded in others that are so data-driven and atheoretical that it is difficult to come away with any message of what was found or not found, or what consequence any of these findings have. The introductory and concluding pieces do not serve to knit together the empirical work outlined in the book. They are overly general and mask some of the complexities of the questions discussed. As 1 example of the kind of problem that occurs, the treatment of Maccoby and Jacklin's book as authoritative 10 years after its appearance bespeaks a lack of fresh analysis. In summary, this book is part of the changes that our understanding of "sex-role acquisition" is undergoing at present, but, with the exceptions noted, it gives more of an impression of flux than of ferment. – N. S. Newcombe.

1513. MELTON, G. B. **Child Advocacy: Psychological Issues and Interventions.** Plenum, 1983. xiv + 228 p. $22.50.

As economic problems become worse, it is historically the minorities among us who suffer most because of their lack of economic and political power. Most of you who are reading this know that the largest of these minorities is some 60 million children in the United States alone. To help ameliorate the inequities that children suffer, and to heighten the public's general awareness of children's fate, child advocacy has grown from an activity central to many philanthropic and social groups to an academic discipline in its own right combining the fields of law, psychology, pediatrics, and social welfare among others. Melton's systematic and well-developed approach explaining the issues surrounding child advocacy is a welcomed and needed contribution. In 9 chapters, he introduces the reader to such diverse topics ranging from the role of therapy as an intervention to tactics used in legislative lobbying. Chapter 1 discusses children's rights as a foundation for child advocacy and focuses on such critical issues as the definition of children's rights and the social scientists' role in child advocacy. Chapter 2 is a summary of Melton's dissertation and answers the question of what children think about their own rights. He hypothesized that the development of children's rights follows a sequence of reasoning much like that detailed by Tapp and Levine's theory of legal development. Chapters 3 and 4 offer case studies of an individual child and detailed discussions of several vocational and educational treatment alternatives as intervention strategies. Each of the next 4 chapters of the book examines advocacy from a general perspective (The Nature of Advocacy), an administrative chapter including an emphasis on the nature and strategies to deal with bureaucracies (Administrative Advocacy: Changing Bureaucracies), the legislative component of advocacy represented best by the who and how of lobbying (Legislative Advocacy: Lobbying on Behalf of Children), and finally, the legal component, including children and the courts, and more (Legal Advocacy: Social Change and the Law). In a final chapter, co-authored by James Faubin and entitled Concepts of Childhood: Implications for Child Advocacy, an agenda for advocacy which follows a general discussion of the child's role in society as a unique member deserving of equal rights is presented. Books on advocacy like Melton's are not likely to reinforce the rhetoric of some "child savers." What it does do, and does it well, is help legitimize as a coherent and worthy area of scholarship the analysis and practice of child advocacy. – N. Salkind.

1514. OVERTON, WILLIS (Ed.). **The Relationship Between Social and Cognitive Development.** Lawrence Erlbaum, 1983. ix + 254 p. $29.95.

The development of prosocial behavior and social cognition has generated enormous interest among empirical investigators in the last decade resulting in a proliferation of research. This interest, spurred primarily by the extension of cognitive-developmental principles to social phenomena, has yielded a complex and discrepant literature from which both stagelike and non-stagelike development conceptualizations are possible. Extending Piagetian principles to social content has proven to be more complex than anticipated, and the literature generated by the extension is far from consistent. Bodies of literature like this, once accumulated, attract the interest of reviewers attempting reconciliation of discrepant findings. Thus, following sufficient empirical studies, we see a number of volumes in which the studies are summarized, analyzed, integrated, and critiqued. Several such books, both single and edited versions, have been compiled for social cognition and prosocial development. This book is yet another, an attempt to specify and integrate the cognitive and social domains in a developmental framework. Its uniqueness lies in the format; it is comprised of a set of papers originally presented at the 10th Annual Symposium of the Jean Piaget Society. The format has both advantages and disadvantages. Though the majority of the material and perspectives presented are also available elsewhere, the conference format permits an articulation of ideas across chapters not usually encountered in an edited summary. What we find is a limited set of theoretical papers and corresponding reactions to them which lends an interesting cohesiveness across entries. This can be intellectually stimulating for the consumer, since what stands out in such a volume are the critical issues around which hinge the empirical data. Some of the major themes permeating this volume are that generalizations from the physical to the social domain are hardly straightforward, that cognitive-development principles do not uniformly apply to all social content (Turiel), and that as a result we might learn as much if not more about cognition in a general way through our extension attempts (Damon). The area begs major theoretical formulations in addition to Piaget's (i.e., Hoffman's) to capture the complexity of what we encounter. The problem with the format is that while the empirical literature serves as a springboard for the theoretical analysis, the treatment of that literature is not extensive. Specific literature is utilized to build a limited theoretical point rather than summarized and integrated comprehensively. Thus, the reader really must be familiar with much of this content already. Several of the chapters are noteworthy, including Hoffman's for its comprehensiveness, Harter's for its usefulness, and the 1 by Youniss for its philosophical perspective and sense of history. In general, while this is an intellectually interesting discussion, the writing is somewhat uneven, the literature review is sometimes sketchy, and it is the professional or graduate student already familiar with much of this research and thinking who is likely to find the volume most stimulating. – R. A. Rosser.

1515. PITCHER, EVELYN G., & SCHULTZ, LYNN H. **Boys and Girls at Play—The Development of Sex Roles.** Praeger, 1984. xi + 207 p. $28.95.
The authors present the results of a study of sex differences in play behaviors during the preschool period and place the results within the interdisciplinary literature of the development of sex roles. The result is a strong statement and description of early appearance of sex differences that are then reinforced by peer interactions and by same-sex exclusivity. Although the intended audience of the book is not made explicit, both researchers and practitioners will find it useful. The book is well written and quite readable, although researchers may find the use of footnotes rather than APA style in the text citations frustrating. Chapter 1 presents the major thesis of the book, that peers are the agents of sex-role development, and outlines the research study. Narrative accounts of 255 children ages 2–5 were collected during free-play periods in preschool programs. Chapter 2 presents a statistical analysis of positive and negative interactions of boys and girls with same-sex and cross-sex peers. Both age and sex differences were found. Chapter 3 represents the core of the book. In this chapter qualitative evaluations of social contacts are presented. The chapter draws heavily on examples from the narratives. The material is organized by age group and content of play. Chapter 4 places the observations of the preceding 2 chapters within the current literature. This chapter is valuable for its contemporary and interdisciplinary character. The book concludes with a chapter on implications of the material. The authors present a balanced discussion of inequalities in sex roles and recommendations for change as well as a discussion of classroom implications. – C. Howes.

1516. POPPER, K. R., & ECCLES, J. C. **The Self and Its Brain: An Argument for Interactionism.** Springer, 1977. xvi + 597 p. $26.50.
This book is 3 books in 1: first, a philosophical survey of the mind-body problems and a defense of an interactionist approach to their relationship by Popper (Part I, 223 pages); second, a detailed survey by Eccles of neurophysiology and neuropsychology relevant to the mind-body problems (Part II, 196 pages); and finally, a series of 12 dialogues between Popper and Eccles (Part III, 141 pages). Part I is an elaboration and defense of Popper's view that

there are 3 realms of real entities (World 1 of material objects, World 2 of psychological states, and World 3 of the autonomous and objective products of the human mind) which interact causally. Examples are: dental caries (a World 1, material process) which causes pain (a World 2, psychological process) which leads to visiting a dentist, and the (World 3) knowledge of how cavities are caused and can be prevented; in scientific research, theories and their logical relations (World 3 objects) may cause us to conjecture (World 2 process) the solution to a problem and publish (World 1) the results. Popper's arguments show that attempts to solve or dismiss the mind-body problems by denying 1 or another world's reality or causal efficacy (materialism, behaviorism, epiphenomenalism, parallelism, identity theory, etc.) fail for 1 or more reasons. One reason repeatedly cited is the inability of such positions to deal with language in a satisfactory way, i.e., being unable to address creativity (as Chomsky argued) or the descriptive function (as Buhler emphasized). Another recurrent argument Popper uses concerns downward causation (D. T. Campbell's term) from higher level, abstract entities (theories, plans, preferences, goals) through cognition and action to alterations in the material world. Eliminative and reductive positions that postulate the *closedness* of World 1, e.g., materialism in any form, are simply wrong—refuted—by downward causation and the creativity of language and the World 3 knowledge we possess. The historical material discussed relates primarily to changing conceptions of what would constitute an acceptable explanation of mind-body relationships (i.e., a history of the "dematerialization" of matter, or the overthrow of the classic mechanistic and physicalistic ideals of earlier science). In a related fashion, Eccles' densely packed survey (borrowed from his earlier books such as *Facing Reality* and *The Understanding of the Brain*) is undertaken to educate philosophers who speculate on the mind-body problems on the basis of naive and outmoded physiology (as well as naive psychologists such as Skinner). This material is far too rich to comment upon; suffice it to say that I think it is a superb overview or introduction to "cognitive" neurophysiology and neuropsychology (albeit limited to the work of Eccles and his friends, the work of Pribram, whose neural holographic conception may be opposed to Eccles' position, is nowhere mentioned). The most tantalizing (and weakest) material is found in the dialogues, which are uneven in quality and relevance. Most often the format is that of Eccles asking a question upon which Popper elaborates (often rather tangentially). So long as one realizes that this format does not permit the uniformly high standard of organization found in Parts I and II, it can still be profitably read as an elaboration of earlier points. The audience for this book is the professional and the advanced graduate student (in philosophy, psychology, or neurophysiology); it is not for the beginner. It presupposes some familiarity with the standard positions on the mind-body problem, and Eccles does not water down the physiological material. To that audience, I recommend it highly as the finest single source ever published. This is not to say that it is beyond criticism. Since it is written to support a particular view, it is selective to the extreme and often caricatures the opposition rather than adequately criticizes it. Further, it leaves out what the authors are not familiar with (e.g., of the traditional big problems of sentience, sapience, and selfhood, the book is 80% sapience and 20% selfhood—sentience as a real problem is not discussed). This should not detract from a superb book that is informative, challenging, and provocative. – W. B. Weimer.

1517. POWELL, GLORIA J. **The Psychosocial Development of Minority Group Children.** Brunner/Mazel, 1983. xviii + 600 p. $60.00.
The degree to which there has been a relative lack of systematic attention paid to the psychosocial development of ethnic and/or racial minority group children is puzzling. One small part of this problem is a need for appropriate materials for educational and training programs. This comprehensive volume, which represents the latest developments in research, clinical practice, and contemporary thinking in the area of minority group mental health, is designed to fill such a need. The basic premise of this text is that it is possible to dramatically improve current mental health practices toward ethnic and racial minority children. It is demonstrated that new understanding and structural changes are most effective when the child and his/her family, community, culture, and society are seen as interacting systems. Throughout, the emphasis is on a shift from a preexisting ethnocentric viewpoint to more of a cross-cultural perspective. The book is divided into 5 parts consisting of 37 chapters. The sections are divided to provide a theme for each chapter. A unique feature of this volume is that separate chapters within each

section are devoted to the concerns of each 1 of the 4 major ethnic minority groups. Part 1 of this volume provides information on the prevalence of health and nutritional problems experienced by minority-group children. A disturbing fact that was pointed out by some of the writers is that a high percentage of minority-group children in need of some kind of professional health-care assistance are not receiving services. This, in part, is believed to be due to past ethnocentric policies and attitudes of indifference which seem to have created an atmosphere of distrust between health-care professionals and ethnic minorities. In Chapter 1, it was suggested that mental health professionals should take the initiative to facilitate better interactions between health-care professionals and members of minority groups. Part 2 consists of chapters that provide an overview of the major problems and issues related to the psychosocial development of minority-group children. In Chapter 4, G. Powell presents a discussion of the Afro-American child. She focuses on the strengths and coping strategies that black children use in order to combat poverty and racism. Chapter 5 presents valuable information on the Mexican-American child. In Chapter 6, the authors warn the reader that the lack of research evidence along with the heterogeneity of American Indians makes it difficult to accurately describe the psychosocial characteristics of Native Americans. A similar theme was echoed in the chapter on Japanese Americans. Chapter 7 informs the reader that the Filipino American is 1 of the fastest growing ethnic groups, and consequently their demand for services will increase in years to come. Chapters 8 and 9 are concerned with Korean and Chinese-American children, respectively. The authors of these chapters point to the paucity of research and suggest that this may reflect some lack of interest on Asian-American concerns as compared to other ethnic groups (p. 159). Part 3 contains chapters devoted to family-life patterns. This section is comprehensive and includes chapters on Afro-Americans, Mexican Americans, Japanese Americans, American Indians, Puerto Ricans, and Pacific Islanders. The chapters in this section are concerned with the identification of family patterns that are unique to each group. A central theme in each chapter is the strengths of the family and the adaptations of each minority group to the social, economic, and political conditions in this country. Part 4 examines more closely the mental health concerns of minority group children. The chapters in this section provide a rich source of information on the process of acculturation and the attitudes and expectancies of minorities toward the utilization of mental health services. The importance of developing heuristic models for adapting to stress is highlighted in Chapters 17 and 23. The chapters in Part 5 take issue with the American educational system, which is believed to provide a less than adequate learning environment for minority group children. The literature on preschool programs is examined (Chapter 24), as well as the controversies centering around intelligence testing (Chapter 25) and bilingual education (Chapter 28). In Chapter 26, G. Powell eloquently differentiates between desegregated and integrated schools and then examines the process of academic achievement for black children. The text concludes with 2 chapters which briefly discuss research and social policy issues affecting minority group children. This volume is a welcome addition to the literature. It is readable and provocative, but more importantly, it provides valuable sources of information. The text is suitable for classroom instruction and is designed primarily, it seems, for mental health professionals interested in understanding the psychosocial needs and problems of ethnic minorities. – L. P. Anderson.

1518. PRESSLEY, MICHAEL, & LEVIN, JOEL R. (Eds.). **Cognitive Strategy Research: Educational Applications.** Springer-Verlag, 1983. xii + 304 p. $31.00.
This book is 1 of a 2-volume set concerning cognitive strategy research. This volume concentrates on research areas with educational applicability. The 10 chapters address a broad array of topics representing both Piagetian and information processing approaches. Several chapters provide excellent literature reviews of both old and new areas of research. The most exhaustive of these was the chapter on moral education strategies taken from Piaget's and Kohlberg's theories (Enright, Lapsley, & Levy). More illuminating are the historical perspectives offered by Brainerd in his review of the 30 years of studies exploring the trainability of Piagetian concrete operations, and by Willows, Borwick, and Butkowsky in their overview of reading research during its 100-year history. These selections identify the larger trends in both the questions being asked and the patterns of results obtained. Other chapters deal with newer, more speculative areas. Here, studies indicative of current approaches are examined by Dick-

erson in the domain of communication skills, by Cook and Mayer on adult reading strategies, and Forrest-Pressley and Gillies on children's reading strategies. These chapters offer exciting speculations about how an understanding of metacognitive abilities might revolutionize our approach to strategy training. The last section of the book deals directly with application of findings to improve instructional materials or to encourage the use of specific cognitive strategies. Problems of deciding when and where applications might prove useful are addressed. For example, Levin's chapter discusses the limitation of using pictorial stimuli in language learning situations. He provides simple rules and examples of when and where pictures will produce facilitation. In second-language learning settings, Paivio advocates the use of familiar imagery techniques as well as some newer methods such as the "total physical response" method studied by Asher. Based on findings from many areas of cognitive strategy research, Pressley proposes a number of specific changes in learning materials to make them more comprehensible. This group of chapters gives the encouraging impression that researchers really do have something to offer educators. Such enthusiasm is subsequently tempered by the well-deserved warnings and criticisms made by Willows, Borwick, and Butkowsky and Peterson and Swing. First, Willows et al. tackle problems evident in reading research. The issues they raise, however, seem to apply more broadly across the field of cognitive strategy research. One problem they address is the general lack of communication between groups of researchers who differentially emphasize basic processes, basic educational practices, and purely applied instructional considerations. They also point out that when communication does occur, it tends to be in 1 direction only, from the theorist to the practitioner. Such elitism clearly stands in the way of good science. A second problem they identify is the failure of many researchers to distinguish between "hardware" components, that set a limit on what the system can do, and "software" components, that are sensitive to training. Often the differences observed between good and poor students are due to hardware differences rather than different software strategies. For strategy training to be effective, we need to understand more about the software systems and how they interact with hardware limitations. This chapter reminds us that different training programs may be required for different groups of people. The final chapter, by Peterson and Swing, clearly emphasizes that the step from research procedures to instructional practices is almost always a very large 1 that is complicated by a whole set of pragmatic issues. For example, the problem of compatibility of strategy use with the constraints imposed by typical classroom instruction is often overlooked by researchers. Other difficult issues include who should be taught cognitive strategies and whether strategy instruction is dependent on adjunct materials that may be costly. These are sobering questions for the idealistic researcher, but they are ones that are necessary to answer if we are serious about making educational contributions. Overall, the collection should appeal to the theorist and practitioner alike. The chapters compliment each other nicely and provide a stimulating look into the interface of research and application. – J. A. Lawry.

1519. ROSENBLATT, ROGER. **Children of War.** Anchor/Doubleday, 1983. 212 p. $13.95. War is hell, but perhaps it is particularly hellish when it directly affects civilians, and even more so when these civilians are children who seem innocent of responsibility for the violence in which they are engulfed. This book, based on a cover story in *Time* magazine, is an account of the impressions Rosenblatt gained in interviewing children in northern Ireland and Israel and refugees from Palestine, Cambodia, and Viet Nam. Many of the stories are indeed appalling, and yet Rosenblatt is, on the whole, more impressed with the children's resilience and determination to live worthwhile lives than with the extent to which they have suffered possibly irreparable damage. A research-oriented psychologist reading the book may be most interested in the questions the book stimulates rather than with the answers it provides, since Rosenblatt collected his data without attempting to select representative samples, did not deeply investigate the cultures with which he was dealing, and in many cases spoke with the children only through interpreters (and hence did not probe beneath the surface of what he was being told). Yet the book's central question is 1 of great importance to developmental psychology: while on the face of things, some events, such as early loss or exposure to great stress, would appear certain to damage children, this does not always occur. When and why do these events cause harm, and why not always? In studying such questions in the laboratory or in circumstances considerably more placid than those in which these children live, psychologists would do well to keep in mind the extreme conditions to which children are sometimes exposed, and which Rosenblatt has documented with considerable sensitivity. – J. C. Lerner.

1520. SEILER, THOMAS B., & WANNENMACHER, WOLFGANG (Eds.). **Concept Development and the Development of Word Meaning.** Springer-Verlag, 1983. v + 348 p. $23.50.
This edited volume is the latest addition to the Springer-Verlag series on Language and Communication. It consists of 18 individual chapters, reflecting contributions from 21 individuals, and is based on a meeting in 1982 at the University of Technology in Darmstadt, Germany. The contributions reflect international viewpoints on theoretical and empirical currents in Canada, Great Britain, the Federal Republic of Germany, the German Democratic Republic, Switzerland, and the United States. Three major issues are reflected in the volume, although the degree of emphasis on each varies across the chapters. The first issue is the question of how concepts develop, both in terms of sequences of acquisition and processes involved. Second is the relationship between concepts and words, especially in terms of the meaning relationships. The third issue addresses somewhat knotty methodological issues that must be dealt with in investigations of the development of concepts and word meaning. The introductory chapter (Wannenmacher & Seiler) provides an excellent historical overview and synthesis of work on concept and word meaning that result in an understanding of continuities and discontinuities in the evolution of current work. Several of the chapters have a primarily theoretical focus and reviews, criticisms, and reinterpretations of the Piagetian position abound. However, a number of these chapters add a new dimension to theory in the area by stressing the importance of social knowledge and social interactions to concept development (e.g., Aebli, Furth, and Nelson). A number of the chapters focus on the nature of the acquisition process and consider the principles that govern word formation (Clark), the relevant constraints on acquisition (Keil and Carey), and the impact of adult word usage on children's word usage (Huttenlocher, and Smiley & Ratner). Several chapters are relatively delimited empirical reports on the acquisition of specific locative prepositions (Sinha), action verbs (Barretti and Hagendorf), and emotional concepts (Szagun). Chapters by Palermo and by Seiler and Wannenmacher conclude the volume with a focus on directions for research in this area and a synthesis of major theoretical and methodological problems. The volume deserves high marks on readability and technical quality. – S. R. Goldman.

1521. STEFFE, LESLIE P.; VON GLASERSFELD, ERNST; RICHARDS, JOHN; & COBB, PAUL. **Children's Counting Types: Philosophy, Theory, and Application.** Praeger, 1983. xviii + 152 p. $21.95.
The monograph is described by the authors as a conglomerate report of the findings of several investigators concerned with the acquisition of counting and number concepts by children. It is a neo-Piagetian analysis of the developmental progression from the counting of the most concrete (i.e., perceptual) stimuli through those that represent the highest level of abstraction (i.e., conceptual). As such, it assumes the independent construction by the child of an hierarchical conceptual structure for number, and the first half of the book is essentially devoted to a description of the hypothesized progression. It includes discussion of how the child creates items for counting, and the kinds of items (i.e., perceptual, figurative, motoric, verbal, and abstract) which can be counted at each stage. The second half of the book is an attempt to apply the theory to actual number operations (i.e., addition and subtraction) as they are performed by children and to use the theory to explain differences in the methods by which older and younger children arrive at solutions to mathematical problems. Additional discussion is concerned with the application of the hypothesis to mathematics curricula in the schools. The book has obvious strengths in the detail with which the theory is explicated (including an excellent first chapter on the philosophy of number) and does not require a grounding in the psychology of number to be useful. Examples are plentiful and, with only a few exceptions, serve to clarify the verbal descriptions. However, the lack of (reported) controlled research to support the theory (even as description) is troublesome to this reviewer, who would like to see it subjected to the more rigorous proofs usually required of psychological research. In sum, however, the monograph provides an interesting and useful framework for thinking about how children think about numbers. – S. E. Antell.

1522. STEFFEN, JOHN J., & KAROLY, PAUL (Eds.). **Autism and Severe Psychopathology.** Lexington, 1982. xv + 330 p. $31.95.
Autism and Severe Psychopathology consists of comprehensive reviews of recent research in the field of child psychopathology. Included are chapters on diagnosis, symptomatology, language, behavior, and thinking processes in disturbed children. Most are rich in cited research and attempt to place the multitudinous findings into a manageable theoretical framework. However, many of the contributors also have theoretical preferences that may influence their choice of material and method of presentation. Despite the subtitle, "Advances in Child Behavioral Analysis and Therapy," the bulk of the material in the book relates to child behavioral analysis—be it specific behaviors such as use of language, self-injurious activity, or Piagetian stages of cognitive development, or be it behaviors often considered diagnostic of autism. Almost nothing in the volume is of practical use in therapy with disturbed children (although by inference some of the theoretical models might be open to application eventually). In addition, only the behavior modification approach is covered—and to ferret out useful implications would take a reader well versed in the technical jargon of behaviorism. One chapter, it should be noted, does state in no uncertain terms that parent training is extremely valuable in dealing with improving verbal skills, but it offers little in specific suggestions as to how this might be accomplished. Most contributors never specifically define the population that they are considering pathological; rather (except for the first chapter), most authors lump together psychotic, schizophrenic, autistic, brain damaged, and mentally retarded. Since differences among these groups could prove important in understanding research findings, this is unfortunate. Overall, this volume is a highly technical, scholarly work which might prove useful as a resource in an upper-graduate level research course on the topic. It certainly belongs in the library of a university offering doctoral degrees in the area of child psychopathology. It is, however, far too specialized and technical to serve as a handy manual for the layman (even the well-informed layman) or as a course textbook. – E. L. Mura

BOOKS RECEIVED

The following list acknowledges items received by CHILD DEVELOPMENT ABSTRACTS AND BIBLIOGRAPHY which have not been issued for review.

ADLER, SOL; FARRAR, CHARLOTTE; & KING, DEBORAH. **A Curriculum Guide for Developing Communication Skills in the Preschool Child.** Charles C. Thomas, 1983. vii + 304 p. $27.50.

AITCHISON, JEAN. **The Articulate Mammal: An Introduction to Psycholinguistics** (2d ed.). Universe, 1983. 291 p. $15.50.

ALBERT, ROBERT S. (Ed.). **Genius and Eminence: The Social Psychology of Creativity and Exceptional Achievement** (vol. 5 of International Series in Experimental Social Psychology). Pergamon, 1983. xvii + 407 p. $35.00.

ALLEN, EILEEN K., & GOETZ, ELIZABETH M. **Early Childhood Education: Special Problems, Special Solutions.** Aspen Systems, 1982. xv + 349 p.

AMABILE, TERESA M. **The Social Psychology of Creativity.** Springer-Verlag, 1983. xiii + 245 p. $26.90.

ANDERSON, DAREN, & MILLIREN, AL. **Structured Experiences for Integration of Handicapped Children.** Aspen Systems, 1983. xviii + 390 p. $27.50.

ARWOOD, ELLYN LUCAS. **Pragmaticism: Theory and Application.** Aspen Systems, 1983. xv + 312 p. $27.50.

AZARNOFF, PAT. **Health, Illness and Disability: A Guide to Books for Children and Young Adults.** R. R. Bowker, 1983. xv + 259 p. $29.95.

BAIN, BRUCE (Ed.). **The Sociogenesis of Language and Human Conduct.** Plenum, 1983. xxiv + 581 p. $50.00.

BANNERMAN, ROBERT H.; BURTON, JOHN; & WEN-CHIEH, CH'EN (Eds.). **Traditional Medicine and Health Care Coverage.** World Health Organization, 1983. 342 p. Sw. fr. 35.–.

BARIAUD, FRANÇOISE. **La Genèse de l'Humour Chez l'Enfant.** Presses Universitaires de France, 1983. 219 p.

BEST, RAPHAELA. **What Boys and Girls Learn in Elementary School.** Indiana Univ. Press, 1983. x + 181 p. $12.95.

BHATNAGER, K. M., & JAIN, MANJU. **Population Education for Child Development.** National Inst. for Public Cooperation and Child Development, 1983. ii + 113 p.

BIEMILLER, ANDREW. **A Longitudinal Study of Thriving, Average, or Non-Thriving Kindergarten Children.** Ministry of Education, Ontario, Canada, 1983. v + 139 p. $5.00.

BIENENFELD, FLORENCE. **Child Custody Mediation: Techniques for Counselors, Attorneys and Parents.** Science & Behavior, 1983. xv + 192 p. $12.95.

BLANKSTEIN, KIRK R., & POLIVY, JANET (Eds.). **Self-Control and Self-Modification of Emotional Behavior. Advances in the Study of Communication and Affect** (vol. 7). Plenum, 1982. xi + 204 p. $27.50.

BLISS, LYNN S., & ALLEN, DORIS V. **SKOLD: Screening Kit of Language Development.** University Park Press, 1983. 128 p. $49.95.

BRENDTRO, LARRY K., & NESS, ARLIN E. **Re-educating Troubled Youth: Environments for Teaching and Treatments.** Aldine, 1983. xii + 288 p. $29.95 (cloth); $16.95 (paper).

CAMERON, MARGARET, & HOFVANDER, YNGVE. **Manual on Feeding Infants and Young Children** (3d ed.). Oxford Univ. Press, 1983. xx + 214 p. $9.95.

CANTOR, DOROTHY W., & DRAKE, ELLEN A. **Divorced Parents and Their Children: A Guide for Mental Health Professionals.** Springer, 1983. x + 182 p. $21.95.

Central Union for Child Welfare in Finland. **Childhood in Finland.** 1983. 64 p.

CERTO, NICK; HARING, NORRIS; & YORK, ROBERT (Eds.). **Public School Integration of Severely Handicapped Students: Rational Issues and Progressive Alternatives.** Paul H. Brooks, 1983. x + 331 p. $18.95.

CHESS, STELLA, & THOMAS, ALEXANDER. **Annual Progress in Child Psychiatry and Child Development 1983.** Brunner/Mazel, 1984. viii + 554 p. $35.00.

COOPER, WILLIAM E. (Ed.). **Cognitive Aspects of Skilled Typewriting.** Springer-Verlag, 1983. xii + 417 p. $34.90.

COX, T., & JONES, G. **Disadvantaged 11-Year-Olds.** Pergamon, 1983. xi + 185 p. $18.95.

DI LEO, JOSEPH H. **Interpreting Children's Drawings.** Brunner/Mazel, 1983. ix + 232 p. $25.00 (cloth); $16.95 (paper).

DORR, DARWIN, et al. (Eds.). **The Psychology of Discipline.** International Universities Press, 1983. xv + 263 p.

DOUGLASS, MALCOLM P. (Ed.). **Claremont Reading Conference Forty-Seventh Yearbook.** Claremont Reading Conference, 1983. vi + 241 p. $12.00.

ESCOBEDO, THERESA H. (Ed.). **Early Childhood Bilingual Education: A Hispanic Perspective.** Teachers Coll. Press, 1983. xiv + 250 p. $19.95.

FEINBERG, WALTER. **Understanding Education: Toward a Reconstruction of Educational Inquiry.** Cambridge Univ. Press, 1983. xi + 270 p. $37.50 (cloth); $12.95 (paper).

Ford Foundation. **Child Survival/Fair Start.** 1983. 48 p. Free.

GOLDMAN, RONALD, & GOLDMAN, JULIETTE. **Children's Sexual Thinking: A Comparative Study of Children Aged 5 to 15 Years in Australia, North America, Britain and Sweden.** Routledge & Kegan Paul, 1982. xviii + 485 p. $24.95.

GOODLAD, JOHN I. **A Place Called School: Prospects for the Future.** McGraw-Hill, 1984. xix + 396 p. $18.95.

GOODMAN, RICHARD M., & GORLIN, ROBERT J. **The Malformed Infant and Child: An Illustrated Guide.** Oxford Univ. Press, 1983. ix + 460 p. $39.50 (cloth); $24.95 (paper).

GROSSMAN, HERBERT J. (Ed.). **Classification in Mental Retardation.** American Assoc. on Mental Deficiency, 1983. v + 228 p.

HEATH, SHIRLEY BRICE. **Ways with Words: Language, Life and Work in Communities and Classrooms.** Cambridge Univ. Press, 1983. xiii + 421 p. $49.50.

HERRMANN, THEO. **Speech and Situation: A Psychological Conception of Situated Speaking.** Springer-Verlag, 1983. viii + 185 p. $26.50.

HINERMAN, PAIGE SHAUGHNESSY. **Teaching Autistic Children to Communicate.** Aspen Systems, 1983. xi + 205 p. $24.95.

INGHAM, ROGER J. **Stuttering and Behavior Therapy: Current Status and Experimental Foundations.** College-Hill, 1984. 486 p. $39.50.

IRVINE, S. H., & BERRY, JOHN W. (Eds.). **Human Assessment and Cultural Factors.** Plenum, 1983. xxii + 671 p.

JERGER, JAMES (Ed.). **Pediatric Audiology: Current Trends.** College-Hill, 1984. xiii + 240 p. $27.50.

JORM, A. F. **The Psychology of Reading and Spelling Disabilities.** Routledge & Kegan Paul, 1983. x + 134 p. $12.95.

KATZ, JANE. **Swimming Through Your Pregnancy.** Doubleday, 1983. xvi + 260 p. $10.95.

KELLEY, MICHAEL R. **A Parent's Guide to Television: Making the Most of It.** John Wiley, 1983. x + 129 p. $8.95.

KORBIN, JILL E. (Ed.). **Child Abuse & Neglect: Cross-Cultural Perspectives.** Univ. of California Press, 1981. xiv + 217 p.

LAHEY, BENJAMIN B., & KAZDIN, ALAN E. (Eds.). **Advances in Clinical Child Psychology** (vol. 5). Plenum, 1982. xvi + 375 p. $35.00.

Le Développement Dans La Première Anneé: Symposium de l'Association de Psychologie Scientifique de Langue Francaise (Grenoble, 1981). Presses Universitaires de France, 1983. 301 p.

LEACH, PENELOPE. **Babyhood: Stage by Stage, from Birth to Age Two: How Your Baby Develops Physically, Emotionally, Mentally** (2d ed.). Alfred A. Knopf, 1983. xxi + 413 p. $17.95 (cloth); $9.95 (paper).

LEVINSON, STEPHEN C. **Pragmatics.** Cambridge Univ. Press, 1983. xvi + 420 p. $49.50 (cloth); $14.95 (paper).

LONGACRE, ROBERT E. **The Grammar of Discourse.** Plenum, 1983. xxi + 423 p. $45.00.

LYONS, TOM WALLACE. **The Pelican & After: A Novel about Emotional Disturbance.** Prescott Durrell, 1983. 268 p. $14.95.

MATSON, JOHNNY L., & DILORENZO, THOMAS M. **Punishment and Its Alternatives: A New Perspective for Behavior Modification.** Springer, 1984. xvi + 264 p. $22.95.

MAYHALL, PAMELA D., & NORGARD, KATHERINE EASTLACK. **Child Abuse and Neglect: Sharing Responsibility.** John Wiley, 1983. xiv + 400 p. $10.95.

MEEK, MARGARET; ARMSTRONG, STEPHEN; AUSTERFIELD, VICKY; GRAHAM, JUDITH; & PLACKETT, ELIZABETH. **Achieving Literacy: Longitudinal Studies of Adolescents Learning to Read.** Routledge & Kegan Paul, 1983. xi + 232 p. $13.95.

MULLIKEN, RUTH K., & BUCKLEY, JOHN J. **Assessment of Multihandicapped and Developmentally Disabled Children.** Aspen Systems, 1983. x + 343 p.

NAREMORE, RITA C. (Ed.). **Language Science.** College-Hill, 1984. xiii + 407 p. $29.50.

NEHMER, KATHLEEN SUTTLES (Ed.). **Elementary Teachers Guide to Free Curriculum Materials.** Educators Progress Service, 1983. xxi + 404 p.

NELSON, RICHARD R., & SKIDMORE, FELICITY (Eds.). **American Families and the Economy: The High Costs of Living.** National Academy, 1983. viii + 307 p. $18.75.

NEWSON, ELIZABETH, & HIPGRAVE, TONY. **Getting Through to Your Handicapped Child.** Cambridge Univ. Press, 1982. ix + 134 p.

PACKARD, VANCE. **Our Endangered Children: Growing Up in a Changing World.** Little, Brown, 1983. xxiii + 385 p. $18.95.

PARIS, SCOTT G.; OLSON, GARY M.; & STEVENSON, HAROLD W. (Eds.). **Learning and Motivation in the Classroom.** Lawrence Erlbaum, 1983. xi + 333 p. $36.00.

PHELPS-TERASAKI, DIANA; PHELPS-GUNN, TRISHA; & STETSON, ELTON G. **Remediation and Instruction in Language.** Aspen Systems, 1983. xx + 427 p.

PIAGET, JEAN. **Le Possible et le Nécessaire, 2, L'évolution du nécessaire chez l'enfant.** Presses Universitaires de France, 1983. 173 p.

PIERCE, ROBERT A.; NICHOLS, MICHAEL P.; & DuBRIN, JOYCE R. **Emotional Expression in Psychotherapy.** Gardner, 1983. xiv + 287 p. $24.95.

ROBERTS, ALBERT R. **Runaways and Non-Runaways in an American Suburb: An Exploratory Study of Adolescent and Parental Coping.** John Jay, 1981. 117 p. $4.00.

ROBERTS, MARGARET, & TAMBURRINI, JOAN. **Child Development 0–5.** Teachers Coll. Press, 1981. 327 p. $19.95.

ROSENBEK, JOHN C.; McNEIL, MALCOLM R.; & ARONSON, ARNOLD E. (Eds.). **Apraxia of Speech: Physiology, Acoustics, Linguistics, Management.** College-Hill, 1984. 298 p. $27.50.

ROTHENBERG, ANNYE B.; HITCHCOCK, SANDRA L.; HARRISON, MARY LOU S.; & GRAHAM, MELINDA S. **Parentmaking: A Practical Handbook for Teaching Parent Classes about Babies and Toddlers.** Banister, 1981. xxiv + 461 p. $24.95.

ROURKE, BYRON P.; BAKKER, DIRK J.; FISK, JOHN; & STRANG, JOHN D. **Child Neuropsychology: An Introduction to Theory, Research, and Clinical Practice.** Guilford, 1983. x + 389 p. $30.00.

SABATINO, DAVID A.; SABATINO, ANN C.; & MANN, LESTER. **Discipline and Behavioral Management: A Handbook of Tactics, Strategies, and Programs.** Aspen Systems, 1983. xiii + 379 p.

SALES, BRUCE DENNIS. **The Professional Psychologist's Handbook.** Plenum, 1983. xviii + 779 p. $60.00.

SAUNDERS, RUTH, & BINGHAM-NEWMAN, ANN M. **Piagetian Perspective for Preschools: A Thinking Book for Teachers.** Prentice-Hall, 1984. vi + 330 p. $16.95 (paper).

SCHAEFER, CHARLES E., & O'CONNOR, KEVIN J. (Eds.). **Handbook of Play Therapy.** John Wiley, 1983. xv + 489 p. $34.95.

SCHETKY, DIANE H., & BENEDEK, ELISSA P. (Eds.). **Child Psychiatry and the Law.** Brunner/Mazel, 1980. 297 p. $22.50.

SHAW, DIANA, & BERRY, CAROLINE FRANKLIN. **Options: The Female Teen's Guide to Coping with the Problems of Today's World.** Doubleday, 1983. xv + 124 p. $4.95.

SMITH, DOROTHY W., & SHERWEN, LAURIE N. **Mothers and Their Adopted Children: The Bonding Process.** Tiresias, 1983. 160 p. $9.00.

SOLNIT, ALBERT J.; EISSLER, RUTH S.; & NEUBAUER, PETER B. (Eds.). **The Psychoanalytic Study of the Child** (vol. 38). Yale Univ. Press, 1983. ix + 676 p. $45.00.

STAMATELOS, THEODORE, & MOTT, DONALD W. **Writing as Therapy.** Teachers Coll. Press, 1983. viii + 166 p. $13.95.

STAMBAK, MIRA; BARRIÈRE, MICHÈLE; BONICA, LAURA; MAISONNET, RENÉE; MUSATTI, TULLIA; RAYNA, SYLVIE; & VERBA, MINA. **Les Bébés entre Eux: Découvrir, jouer, iventer ensemble.** Presses Universitaires de France, 1983. 191 p.

STEIN, SARA BONNETT. **About Handicaps: An Open Family Book for Parents and Children Together.** Walker, 1984. 47 p. $8.95 (cloth); $3.95 (paper).

STEINHAUER, PAUL D., & RAE-GRANT, QUENTIN (Eds.). **Psychological Problems of the Child in the Family.** Basic Books, 1983. xvi + 784 p. $35.00.

STREAN, HERBERT S. **The Sexual Dimension: A Guide for the Helping Professional.** Free Press, 1983. xiii + 241 p. $19.95.

THORNTON, SUSAN M., & FRANKENBURG, WILLIAM K. (Eds.). **Child Health Care Communications: Enhancing Interactions Among Professionals, Parents and Children. Pediatric Round Table: 8.** Johnson & Johnson, 1983. ix + 217 p.

UPTON, DAVID. **Mental Health Care and National Health Insurance: A Philosophy of and an Approach to Mental Health Care for the Future.** Plenum, 1983. xxii + 312 p. $27.50.

WALLACE, NANCY. **Better Than School.** Larson, 1983. 256 p. $14.95.

WHITTAKER, JAMES K., & GARBARINO, JAMES. **Social Support Networks: Informal Helping in the Human Services.** Aldine, 1983. ix + 479 p. $29.95 (cloth); $14.95 (paper).

WOLF, ELEANOR P. **Trial and Error: The Detroit School Segregation Case.** Wayne State Univ. Press, 1981. 372 p. $19.95.

WOODWARD, DOLORES M., & PETERS, DOLORES J. **The Learning Disabled Adolescent: Learning Success in Content Areas.** Aspen Systems, 1983. xv + 371 p.

World Health Organization. **Cancer Control in Children: Report on a Study by O. Hrodek, Copenhagen, Regional Office for Europe, 1983.** EURO Reports and Studies, No. 75. 37 p. Sw. fr. 5.–.

World Health Organization. **Depressive Disorders in Different Cultures.** (Geneva) 1983. vi + 150 p. Sw. fr. 17.–.

Acta Paedopsychiatrica
Advances in Alcohol and Substance Abuse
American Annals of the Deaf
American Journal of Mental Deficiency
American Journal of Orthopsychiatry
American Psychologist
Animal Behaviour
Applied Psychological Measurement
Australian Psychologist
Behavior Genetics
Behaviour Research and Therapy
Bulletin of the Pan American Health Organization
Canadian Journal of Psychiatry
Československá Psychologie
Child Abuse & Neglect, The International Journal
Child: Care, Health and Development
Child Care Quarterly
Child Development
Child & Family Behavior Therapy
Child Study Journal
Child Welfare
Child and Youth Service
Clinical Neuropsychology
Cognition
Cognitive Psychology
Contemporary Educational Psychology
Council for Research in Music Education
Creative Child and Adult Quarterly
Day Care Journal
Developmental Medicine and Child Neurology
Developmental Psychology
Developmental Review
Educational Psychology
Educational Research
Età Evolutiva
Exceptional Children
Family Relations
First Language
The Genetic Epistemologist
Genetic Psychology Monographs
Gifted Child Quarterly
Hiroshima Forum for Psychology
Human Development
Human Relations
Infant Behavior and Development
International Journal of Behavioral Development
Japanese Journal of Child and Adolescent Psychiatry
Journal of Abnormal Child Psychology
Journal of Applied Developmental Psychology
Journal of Autism and Developmental Disorders
Journal of Behavior Therapy and Experimental Psychiatry
Journal of Child Language
Journal of Children in Contemporary Society
Journal of Clinical Neuropsychology
Journal of Early Adolescence
Journal of Educational Psychology
Journal of Experimental Child Psychology

Journal of Experimental Education
Journal of Experimental Psychology: General
Journal of Experimental Psychology: Human Perception and Performance
Journal of General Psychology
Journal of Genetic Psychology
Journal of Learning Disabilities
Journal of Mental Deficiency Research
Journal of Motor Behavior
Journal of Nervous and Mental Disease
Journal of Obstetric, Gynecologic, and Neonatal Nursing
Journal of Pediatric Psychology
Journal of Pediatrics
Journal of Personality Assessment
Journal of Personality and Social Psychology
Journal of Psycholinguistic Research
Journal of Psychology
Journal of Research in Reading
Journal of Research in Science Teaching
Journal of Social Work & Human Sexuality
Journal of Sport Psychology
Journal of Youth and Adolescence
Memory and Cognition
Merrill-Palmer Quarterly
Milieu Therapy
Monographs of the Society for Research in Child Development
Pediatric Research
Perceptual and Motor Skills
Psychiatric Journal of the University of Ottawa
Psychiatry
Psychologia Wychowawcza (Educational Psychology: Bimonthly of the Polish Teachers
    Union)
Psychological Bulletin
The Psychological Record
Psychological Reports
Psychologische Rundschau
Psychology in the Schools
Psychology of Women Quarterly
Questions of Psychology (translation of Russian title)
Reading Research Quarterly
Rehabilitation Literature
Research in Nursing and Health
Revue de Psychologie Appliqueé
Scandinavian Journal of Educational Research
Scandinavian Journal of Psychology
Science
Sex Roles
Social Behavior and Personality
Studia Psychologica
Studies in Educational Evaluation
Tohoku Psychologica Folia
Volta Review
Zeitschrift für Entwicklungspsychologie und Pädagogische Psychologie

Subscriptions are accepted on a calendar-year basis only.

Subscriptions, address changes, and business communications regarding publication should be sent to THE UNIVERSITY OF CHICAGO PRESS, Journals Division, P.O. Box 37005, Chicago, Illinois 60637. Please give four weeks' notice when changing your address, giving both old and new addresses. Undelivered copies resulting from address changes will not be replaced; subscribers should notify the post office that they will guarantee forwarding postage. Other claims for undelivered copies must be made within four months of publication.

Membership communications and requests for permission to reprint should be addressed to DOROTHY H. EICHORN, Executive Officer, Society for Research in Child Development, 5801 Ellis Avenue, Chicago, Illinois 60637.

5801 S. Ellis
962-7600
753 -4240

MONOGRAPHS

OF THE SOCIETY FOR RESEARCH IN CHILD DEVELOPMENT

* 753 -3347
753 -4243

CURRENT:

Developmental Trends in the Quality of Conversation Achieved by Small Groups of Acquainted Peers—BRUCE DORVAL AND CAROL ECKERMAN (*Serial No. 206,* 1984, $7.00)

Difficult Children as Elicitors and Targets of Adult Communication Patterns: An Attributional-Behavioral Transactional Analysis—DAPHNE B. BUGENTAL AND WILLIAM A. SHENNUM (*Serial No. 205,* 1984, $7.00)

The Concept of Dimension in Research on Children's Learning—STUART I. OFFENBACH (*Serial No. 204,* 1983, $7.00)

Returning the Smile of the Stranger: Developmental Patterns and Socialization Factors—YEAL E. BABAD, IRVING E. ALEXANDER, AND ELISHA Y. BABAD (*Serial No. 203,* 1983, $7.00)

Early Intervention and Its Effects on Maternal Behavior and Child Development—DIANA T. SLAUGHTER (*Serial No. 202,* 1983, $7.00)

How Children Become Friends—JOHN M. GOTTMAN (*Serial No. 201,* 1983, $7.00)

A Longitudinal Study of Moral Development—ANNE COLBY, LAWRENCE KOHLBERG, JOHN GIBBS, AND MARCUS LIEBERMAN (*Serial No. 200,* 1983, $10.00)

Early Development of Children at Risk for Emotional Disorder—ARNOLD J. SAMEROFF, RONALD SEIFER, AND MELVIN ZAX (*Serial No. 199,* 1982, $7.00)

The Skills of Mothering: A Study of Parent Child Development Centers—SUSAN RING ANDREWS ET AL. (*Serial No. 198,* 1982, $7.00)

Parent Pathology, Family Interaction, and the Competence of the Child in School—ALFRED L. BALDWIN, ROBERT E. COLE, AND CLARA T. BALDWIN (Eds.) (*Serial No. 197,* 1982, $7.00)

Traditional and Modern Contributions to Changing Infant-rearing Ideologies of Two Ethnic Communities—DANIEL G. FRANKEL AND DORIT ROER-BORNSTEIN (*Serial No. 196,* 1982, $7.00)

Lasting Effects of Early Education—IRVING LAZAR, RICHARD B. DARLINGTON, HARRY MURRAY, JACQUELINE ROYCE, AND ANN SNIPPER (*Serial No. 195,* 1982, $10.00)

Rules of Causal Attribution—THOMAS R. SHULTZ (*Serial No. 194,* 1982, $7.00)

Social Class and Racial Influences on Early Mathematical Thinking—HERBERT P. GINSBURG AND ROBERT L. RUSSELL (*Serial No. 193,* 1981, $7.00)

The Development of Comprehension Monitoring and Knowledge about Communication—JOHN H. FLAVELL, JAMES RAMSEY SPEER, FRANCES L. GREEN, AND DIANE L. AUGUST (*Serial No. 192,* 1981, $7.00)

The Development of the Self-Concept during the Adolescent Years—JEROME B. DUSEK AND JOHN F. FLAHERTY (*Serial No. 191,* 1981, $7.00)

A Longitudinal Study of the Consequences of Early Mother-Infant Interaction: A Microanalytic Approach—JOHN A. MARTIN (*Serial No. 190,* 1981, $7.00)

Order From

CHILD DEVELOPMENT PUBLICATIONS
THE UNIVERSITY OF CHICAGO PRESS

CHILD DEVELOPMENT

ABSTRACTS AND

BIBLIOGRAPHY

VOLUME 58 NUMBER 3   1984

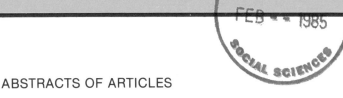

PUBLISHED BY THE UNIVERSITY OF CHICAGO PRESS FOR THE

SOCIETY FOR RESEARCH IN CHILD DEVELOPMENT

EDITOR

HOBEN THOMAS
The Pennsylvania State University

ASSOCIATE EDITOR
MARGARET L. SIGNORELLA
The Pennsylvania State University
McKeesport

ASSOCIATE EDITOR
ELEANOR W. WILLEMSEN
University of Santa Clara

MANAGING EDITOR
BETTY LOU KLINDIENST
University Park, Pennsylvania

COMPUTER CONSULTANT
WILLIAM H. VERITY
The Pennsylvania State University

Child Development Abstracts and Bibliography (ISSN 0009-3939) publishes abstracts from professional periodicals and reviews books related to the growth and development of children. When listed, author addresses are intended to be current mailing addresses. A list of journals regularly searched is included in number 3 of each volume. The Editor welcomes communication from readers. Especially encouraged are contributed abstracts from articles which appear in publications not normally searched. For this purpose, reprints are helpful. Please address all editorial correspondence to Editor, *Child Development Abstracts and Bibliography,* The Pennsylvania State University, 442 B. V. Moore Building University Park, Pennsylvania 16802. Postmaster: Send address changes to The University of Chicago Press, Journals Division, P.O. Box 37005, Chicago, Illinois 60637.

Child Development Abstracts and Bibliography, one of three publications of the Society for Research in Child Development, Inc., is published three times a year, by The University of Chicago Press. Subscription rate, U.S.A.: 1 year $35.00. Other countries add $3.50 for each year's subscription to cover postage. Single copy rate: $11.50. Reprinted volumes 1-50 available from Kraus Reprint Co., Route 100, Millwood, New York 10546. Volumes 42 to date available in microfilm from University Microfilms International, 300 North Zeeb Road, Ann Arbor, Michigan 48106; in microfiche from KTO Microform, Route 100, Millwood, New York 10546.

Child Development is issued six times a year. Subscription rate, U.S.A.: 1 year $80.00. Other countries add $6.00 for each year's subscription to cover postage. Single copy rate: $14.00. Reprinted volumes 1-40 available from Kraus Reprint Co. Volumes 37 to date available in microfilm from University Microfilms International; in microfiche from KTO Microform.

Monographs of the Society for Research in Child Development is issued at irregular intervals during the year. Subscription rate, U.S.A.: 1 year $40.00. Other countries add $5.50 for each year's subscription to cover postage. Single copies $9.00; combined issues $13.00. Single copy bulk rate (10 or more copies of same issue): single issues $7.00; combined issues $11.00. Reprinted volumes 1-41 available from Kraus Reprint Co. Volumes 28 to date available in microfilm from University Microfilms International; in microfiche from KTO Microform. A list of available *Monographs* may be had on request.

Subscriptions (U.S.A.) to the three publications of the Society are available at the special rate of $140.00. Other countries add $15.00 for each year's combined subscription to cover postage.

A limited number of back issues of all publications is available.

© 1984 by the Society for Research in Child Development, Inc. All rights reserved.

PRINTED IN U.S.A.

CHILD DEVELOPMENT
Abstracts and Bibliography

Volume 58   Number 3   1984

ABSTRACTS OF ARTICLES

BIOLOGY, HEALTH, MEDICINE

1523.   ASTBURY, JILL; ORGILL, ANNA A.; BAJUK, BARBARA; & YU, VICTOR Y. H. (Queen Victoria Medical Ctr., 172 Lonsdale, Melbourne, Victoria, Australia). **Determinants of developmental performance of very low-birthweight survivors at one and two years of age.** Developmental Medicine and Child Neurology, 1983, **25,** 709–716.
Although mental and motor scores for the group of 61 infants were within normal limits, there was a decline in mental development scores from 1 to 2 years of age, due to an increase in the numbers of low-scoring children with hyperactive behavior. – Adapted from Authors' Abstract.

1524.   BESHAROV, DOUGLAS J. (American Bar Assoc., National Legal Resource Ctr. on Child Advocacy and Protection, 1800 M St. NW, Washington). **Malpractice in child placement: civil liability for inadequate foster care services.** Child Welfare, 1984, **63,** 195–204.
The author examines cases in which agencies and workers were held liable for malpractice, as well as the bases for the liability. Several cases specifically concern permanency planning issues. – Author's Abstract.

1525.   BIRCH, LEANN LIPPS (Univ. of Illinois); MARLIN, DIANE WOLFE; & ROTTER, JULIE. **Eating as the "means" activity in a contingency: effects on young children's food preference.** Child Development, 1984, **55,** 431–439.
In instrumental eating conditions, preschool children consumed an initially novel beverage to obtain a reward. Two levels of relative amount consumed (baseline, baseline plus) were compared with 2 levels of type of reward (tangible, verbal praise). Preference data obtained before and after the series of snack sessions demonstrated a significant negative shift in preference for the 4 instrumental groups, while the control groups showed a slight but not significant increase in preference. – From Authors' Abstract.

1526.   BIRNS, BEVERLY (SUNY, Stony Brook), & NOYES, DONNA. **Child nutrition: the role of theory in the world of politics.** International Journal of Mental Health, 1984, **12,** 22–42.

1527.   BUSBY, K., & PIVIK, R. T. (Ottawa General Hosp., Ontario, Canada). **Failure of high intensity auditory stimuli to affect behavioral arousal in children during the first sleep cycle.** Pediatric Research, 1983, **17,** 802–805.
Hyperactive and normal school-aged children were examined. No differences in frequency of autonomic response measures were obtained when rates before and during auditory stimulation were compared. – Adapted from Authors' Abstract.

1528.   CHIAIA, N. L. (Northeastern Ohio Univ. Coll. of Medicine), & TEYLER, T. J. **Higher-brain function.** Journal of Children in Contemporary Society, 1983, **16,** 45–76.
Discussed are higher mental functions and the developmental processes which influence them. Environmental factors operating in 3 areas are considered. – Adapted from Authors' Abstract.

1529.   CRNIC, LINDA S. (Univ. of Colorado School of Medicine). **Nutrition and mental development.** American Journal of Mental Deficiency, 1984, **88,** 526–533.

It has been difficult to assess the effects of malnutrition upon mental development because of the environmental alterations that invariably accompany malnutrition, even in animal models. – From Author's Abstract.

1530. CUNNINGHAM, C. C. (Hester Adrian Research Ctr., Univ., Manchester, England); MORGAN, P. A.; & McGUCKEN, R. B. **Down's syndrome: is dissatisfaction with disclosure of diagnosis inevitable?** Developmental Medicine and Child Neurology, 1984, **26,** 33–39.
A survey of parents of Down's syndrome infants revealed dissatisfaction with the procedure for disclosing the diagnosis and the immediate counseling services. A model procedure is described. – Adapted from Authors' Abstract.

1531. EDELMAN, ALICE H.; KRAEMER, HELENA C.; & KORNER, ANNELIESE F. (Stanford Univ. School of Medicine). **Effects of compensatory movement stimulation on the sleep-wake behaviors of preterm infants.** Journal of the American Academy of Child Psychiatry, 1982, **21,** 555–559.
There was a pervasive increase in the day-to-day consistency of behaviors on the waterbed compared to the control condition. Most of the behaviors tested were not increased or decreased by waterbed flotation. However, while on the waterbed, the infants had more sustained quiet sleep, and fussiness and crying were reduced. – From Authors' Abstract.

1532. EMORY, EUGENE K. (SUNY, Binghamton), & NOONAN, JOHN R. **Fetal cardiac responding: maturational and behavioral correlates.** Developmental Psychology, 1984, **20,** 354–357.
Deceleratory patterns were associated with higher baseline heart rate, lower birth weight, prematurity, and more abnormal reflexes scored on the Brazelton Newborn Behavior Assessment Scale. Fetal heart rate may be related to early stress tolerance and central nervous system integrity. – From Authors' Abstract.

1533. FARRANT, ROLAND H. (Laurentian Univ.). **Was Gesell's concept of "reciprocal interweaving" a crypto-dialectical theory of development?** Journal of Genetic Psychology, 1984, **144,** 137–144.
Gesell and Armatruda's concept of "reciprocal interweaving" as a principle of early organismic development is here interpreted in the framework of dialectical developmental theory. – From Author's Abstract.

1534. FISHMAN, JEAN E. (Derech Masada, P.O.B. 4065, Beer Sheva, Israel); GADOTH, NATAN; & RADVAN, HENRY. **Congenital sensorineural deafness associated with EEG abnormalities, epilepsy and high familial incidence.** Developmental Medicine and Child Neurology, 1983, **25,** 747–754.
Deaf school-aged children of normal intelligence were examined. Children with abnormal and paroxysmal EEGs showed more behavior disturbance but similar learning abilities when compared to those with more normal EEGs. – B. B. Keller.

1535. FORD, H. THOMAS, JR. (Auburn Univ.); PUCKETT, JOHN R.; DRUMMOND, JAMES P.; SAWYER, KENNETH; GANTT, KYLE; & FUSSELL, CLIFF. **Effects of three combinations of plyometric and weight training programs on selected physical fitness test items.** Perceptual and Motor Skills, 1983, **56,** 919–922.
Programs in weight training and plyometrics were studied in male high school students. – Ed.

1536. FRANCIS, PATRICIA L. (SUNY, Cortland); SELF, PATRICIA A.; & McCAFFREE, MARY ANNE. **Behavioral assessment of a hydranencephalic neonate.** Child Development, 1984, **55,** 262–266.
The examination revealed extremely deviant responses on portions of the Neonatal Behavioral Assessment Scale–Kansas revision, including items that measure response decrement and orientation. This infant was observed to approximate normal neonatal responding on items

relating to motor maturity and reactivity. Some response decrement occurred in response to auditory and visual, but not tactile, stimulation. – From Authors' Abstract.

1537. FRASER, F. MURRAY (Univ. of Victoria, British Columbia, Canada), & KIRK, H. DAVID. **Cui bono? Some questions concerning the "best interests of the child" principle in Canadian adoption laws and practices.** In K. Connell-Thouez and B. M. Knoppers (Eds.), *Contemporary Trends in Family Law: A National Perspective.* Carswell Legal Publications (Toronto, Canada), 1984, 105–123.

1538. GAGAN, RICHARD J. (Univ. of South Florida); CUPOLI, J. MICHAEL; & WATKINS, ALISON H. **The families of children who fail to thrive: preliminary investigations of parental deprivation among organic and non-organic cases.** Child Abuse & Neglect, The International Journal, 1984, **8,** 93–103.
Preliminary research findings support our hypothesis that mothers of failure-to-thrive infants do not have good social support networks. Teen motherhood and SES also appear to be important, but not necessary, as determinants. – From Authors' Abstract.

1539. GALLER, JANINA R. (Boston Univ. School of Medicine); RAMSEY, FRANK; & SOLIMANO, GIORGIO. **The influence of early malnutrition on subsequent behavioral development: III. Learning disabilities as a sequel to malnutrition.** Pediatric Research, 1984, **18,** 309–313.
The academic performance of 5–11-year-old Barbadian children who suffered protein malnutrition in the first year of life was compared with the performance of children who had no history of malnutrition. Children with a history of malnutrition had lower performance on 8 of 9 academic subject areas. – From Authors' Abstract.

1540. GILLBERG, CHRISTOPHER (Barn- och Ungdomspsykiatriska Kliniken, Box 7284, Göteborg, Sweden), & FORSELL, CHRISTER. **Childhood psychosis and neurofibromatosis—more than a coincidence?** Journal of Autism and Developmental Disorders, 1984, **14,** 1–8.
Three children with both childhood psychosis and neurofibromatosis are reported from a total population screening of psychotic disordered in childhood that had produced 51 cases born in the years 1962–1976 in the Göteborg region, Sweden. Underlying monoaminergic dysfunction is postulated as 1 possible reason for the finding. – From Authors' Abstract.

1541. GILLBERG, CHRISTOPHER (Barn- och Ungdomspsykiatriska Kliniken, Box 7284, S-402, Göteborg, Sweden); SVENNERHOLM, LARS; & HAMILTON-HELLBERG, CECILIA. **Childhood psychosis and monoamine metabolites in spinal fluid.** Journal of Autism and Developmental Disorders, 1983, **13,** 383–396.
Psychotic children showed raised levels of homovanillic acid. Children diagnosed as autistic showed isolated increase of this metabolite. In children with other psychoses, both the level of homovanillic acid and that of 5-hydroxy-indoleacetic acid were raised. The increased concentration of monoamines was not attributable to mental retardation per se. – From Authors' Abstract.

1542. GILLBERG, I. CARINA (Univ. of Uppsala, Göteborg, Sweden); GILLBERG, CHRISTOPHER; & RASMUSSEN, PEDER. **Three-year follow-up at age 10 of children with minor neurodevelopmental disorders. II: School achievement problems.** Developmental Medicine and Child Neurology, 1983, **25,** 566–573.
Eighty percent of children diagnosed as having minimal brain dysfunction had obvious problems in school achievement. – Adapted from Authors' Abstract.

1543. HELLER, MELVIN S.; EHRLICH, SAUNDRA M.; & LESTER, DAVID (Richard Stockton State Coll.). **Childhood cruelty to animals, firesetting, and enuresis as correlates of competence to stand trial.** Journal of General Psychology, 1984, **110,** 151–153.

The presence of all or part of this triad of symptoms was more common in those found competent to stand trial than in those found incompetent. – From Authors' Abstract.

1544. HENRY, KEVIN (Rehabilitation Inst. of Pittsburgh). **Cognitive rehabilitation and the head-injured child.** Journal of Children in Contemporary Society, 1983, **16,** 189–205.
Attention to the development of improved techniques of treatment is becoming increasingly widespread. Cognitive rehabilitation therapy is an emerging branch of rehabilitation. – From Author's Abstract.

1545. HERTZIG, MARGARET E. (Cornell Medical Ctr.), & MITTLEMAN, MARY. **Temperament in low birthweight children.** Merrill-Palmer Quarterly, 1984, **30,** 201–211.
Low-birthweight children were less distractible, exhibited higher sensory thresholds, and were more intense and less adaptable. – From Authors' Abstract.

1546. HOARE, P. (Royal Hosp. for Sick Children, 3 Rillbank Terrace, Edinburgh, Scotland). **The development of psychiatric disorder among schoolchildren with epilepsy.** Developmental Medicine and Child Neurology, 1984, **26,** 3–13.
Children with chronic epilepsy are significantly more disturbed than children with chronic diabetes and children in the general population. – From Author's Abstract.

1547. HOARE, P. (Royal Hosp. for Sick Children, 3 Rillbank Terrace, Edinburgh, Scotland). **Does illness foster dependency? A study of epileptic and diabetic children.** Developmental Medicine and Child Neurology, 1984, **26,** 20–24.
Epileptic children were found to be more dependent than diabetic children and children in the general population. – Adapted from Author's Abstract.

1548. HOARE, P. (Royal Hosp. for Sick Children, 3 Rillbank Terrace, Edinburgh, Scotland). **Psychiatric disturbance in the families of epileptic children.** Developmental Medicine and Child Neurology, 1984, **26,** 14–19.
Parents and siblings of children newly diagnosed as epileptic were no more disturbed than parents and children in the general population. Siblings of chronic epileptic children were more disturbed than children in general. – Adapted from Author's Abstract.

1549. HUTTENLOCHER, PETER R. (Univ. of Chicago). **Synapse elimination and plasticity in developing human cerebral cortex.** American Journal of Mental Deficiency, 1984, **88,** 488–496.
Maximum synaptic density, absolute number of synapses, and number of synapses per neuron are reached by age 1 year. Subsequently, there is progressive synapse elimination that is most rapid during the preschool years. Overproduction of synapses may impart plasticity to the brain of young children. – From Author's Abstract.

1550. ISRAEL, ALLEN C. (SUNY, Albany); STOLMAKER, LAURIE; & PRINCE, BARBARA. **The relationship between impulsivity and eating behavior in children.** Child & Family Behavior Therapy, 1983, **5,** 71–75.
The Wilcox Behavioral Rating Scale of Self-Control but not the Matching Familiar Figures Test was related to eating style. – Ed.

1551. KAY, L. (Univ. of Canterbury, Christchurch, New Zealand). **Learning to use the ultrasonic spatial sensor by the blind infant: comments on Aitken and Bower.** Journal of Experimental Child Psychology, 1984, **37,** 207–211.
Aitken and Bower describe the use of the ultrasonic spatial sensor for the blind invented by Kay. In order that the very interesting work reported in the paper can be realistically assessed by those not familiar with the sensory system, it is necessary to draw attention to certain inaccuracies in the paper. – From Author's Abstract.

1552. KITCHEN, WILLIAM (Univ. of Melbourne, Parkville, Victoria, Australia); FORD, GEOFFREY; ORGILL, ANNA; RICKARDS, ANNE; ASTBURY, JILL; LISSENDEN, JEAN; BAJUK, BARBARA; YU, VICTOR; DREW, JOHN; & CAMPBELL, NEIL. **Outcome in infants with birth weight 500 to 999 gm: a regional study of 1979 and 1980 births.** Journal of Pediatrics, 1984, **104**, 921–927.
Severe functional handicap was present in 50% of outborn infants, and the Bayley Mental Development Index was also lower in outborn infants. – From Authors' Abstract.

1553. KORNER, ANNELIESE F. (Stanford Univ. School of Medicine); GABBY, TINA; & KRAEMER, HELENA C. **Relation between prenatal maternal blood pressure and infant irritability.** Early Human Development, 1980, **4**, 35–39.
The combined findings of the 3 studies seem to suggest that maternal blood pressure in the latter part of pregnancy, even when within normal limits, is a factor in how irritable normal newborn infants are. – From Authors' Abstract.

1554. KORNER, ANNELIESE F. (Stanford Univ. School of Medicine); RUPPEL, ELLEN M.; & RHO, JONG M. **Effects of water beds on the sleep and motility of theophylline-treated preterm infants.** Pediatrics, 1982, **70**, 864–869.
While on the waterbed, the infants had more quiet and active sleep, shorter sleep latencies, fewer state changes, less restlessness during sleep, less waking activity, and fewer jittery and unsmooth movements. – From Authors' Abstract.

1555. LABBE, ELISE E., & WILLIAMSON, DONALD A. (Louisiana State Univ.). **Temperature biofeedback in the treatment of children with migraine headaches.** Journal of Pediatric Psychology, 1983, **8**, 317+.
Temperature biofeedback proved successful in reducing migraine headache activity in 3 children, as assessed at 1-month and 2-year follow-up. – Adapted from Authors' Abstract.

1556. LALLY, J. RONALD (Far West Laboratory for Educational Research and Development, 1855 Folsom, San Francisco). **Three views of child neglect: expanding visions of preventive intervention.** Child Abuse & Neglect, The International Journal, 1984, **8**, 243–254.
Child neglect prevention is discussed at 3 levels: at the level of the individual, at the level of social systems, and at the level of fundamental beliefs and cultural agreements. – From Author's Abstract.

1557. LESLIE, ALAN M. (Medical Research Council, 17 Gordon, London, England). **Infant perception of a manual pick-up event.** British Journal of Developmental Psychology, 1984, **2**, 19–32.
With 28-week-old infants, it was found that lateral mirror-image pick-ups are hardly discriminable, while a change in the contact relation of hand and object is readily discriminable. The discriminability of the contact relation appears to be specific to a dynamic context involving a hand. – From Author's Abstract.

1558. LEVINE, SUSAN COHEN (Univ. of Chicago). **Hemispheric specialization and functional plasticity during development.** Journal of Children in Contemporary Society, 1983, **16**, 77–98.
Evidence from a variety of sources is reviewed suggesting that the cerebral hemispheres are specialized from birth or an early age. – From Author's Abstract.

1559. McCARTON-DAUM, CECELIA (Albert Einstein Coll. of Medicine); DANZIGER, ALLAN; RUFF, HOLLY; & VAUGHAN, HERBERT G., JR. **Periventricular low density as a predictor of neurobehavioral outcome in very low-birthweight infants.** Developmental Medicine and Child Neurology, 1983, **25**, 559–565.
Infants with periventricular low densities had below average mental and motor development scores during the 1 1/2-year follow-up period. Scores for these infants were lower than scores for infants with more normal cranial computerized tomography scans. – B. B. Keller.

1560. MANGAN, G. L. (Univ. of Oxford, England), & PAISEY, T. J. H. **Current perspectives in neo-Pavlovian temperament theory and research: a review.** Australian Journal of Psychology, 1983, **35,** 319–347.
The first trend in neo-Pavlovian temperament theory and research centers on operational definitions and measures of reflexive behaviors and evidence of heritability of these properties. The second trend, looking at voluntary action, uses evoked electroencephalographic data to develop a model of activity and emotionality mediated by fronto-reticular and fronto-limbic cortical connections. – From Abstract by E. Gollin.

1561. MANN, LESTER (Pennsylvania State Univ.); CARTWRIGHT, G. PHILLIP; KENOWITZ, LEONARD A.; BOYER, CHARLES W., JR.; METZ, CATHERINE M.; & WOLFORD, BARBARA. **The Child Service Demonstration Centers: a summary report.** Exceptional Children, 1984, **50,** 532–540.
The CSDCs were often criticized as being underachievers and as not living up to public or professional expectations. A review of their operations indicates that many of these expectations were simply impossible. – From Authors' Abstract.

1562. MARKOVA, I. (Univ. of Stirling, England); PHILLIPS, J. S.; & FORBES, C. D. **The use of tools by children with haemophilia.** Journal of Child Psychology and Psychiatry, 1984, **25,** 261–271.
Children 3–6 years old with or without haemophilia and their mothers were videotaped while playing 3 games using a knife, a pair of scissors, and a wooden hammer, and 2 games without tools. Although the children with haemophilia were less proficient, took less care, and were more excited when handling sharp tools than the control children, their mothers did not correct their children when they used a knife incompetently and carelessly. – From Authors' Abstract.

1563. MARTIN, HAROLD P. (Univ. of Colorado School of Medicine). **Intervention with infants at risk for abuse or neglect.** Child Abuse & Neglect, The International Journal, 1984, **8,** 255–260.
The expertise of professionals who work with infants and young children in therapeutic and stimulation programs is required. Their experience also underscores the need for direct intervention in the parent–child interaction process. – From Author's Abstract.

1564. PAINE, PATRICIA ANN (Univ. of Brasilia, Brazil), & PASQUALI, LUIZ. **Postnatal growth and psychomotor development in small for gestational age Brazilian infants.** Developmental Psychology, 1984, **20,** 363–366.
The early psychomotor development (DQ) of small-for-gestational-age Brazilian infants was shown to be more dependent on growth than the DQ of appropriate-for-gestational-age infants. – From Authors' Abstract.

1565. PAINE, PATRICIA (Univ. of Brasilia, Brazil), & SPEGIORIN, CLODOMIR. **Prolonged breast feeding related to later solid food acceptance.** Child: Care, Health and Development, 1983, **9,** 321–326.
Full-term healthy infants were studied for the first 18 months of life. Infants breast-fed for less than 3 months showed a better acceptance of solid foods at 18 months than those breast-fed for 6 months or more. – From Authors' Abstract.

1566. PALOMBA, D.; STEGAGNO, L.; & ZANCHI, C. (Univ. degli Studi di Padova, Italy). **Heart rate control in children under feedback.** Età Evolutiva, 1984, **17,** 33–41.
Results show that children can modify their heart rate with the aid of feedback. Heart-rate increase seems to be easier to obtain than heart-rate decrease in feedback conditions. – From Authors' Abstract.

1567. PARMELEE, ARTHUR H. (Univ. of California, Los Angeles); HOWARD, JUDY; & BECKWITH, LEILA. **Infant mental health and biological risk.** Child Abuse & Neglect, The International Journal, 1984, **8,** 219–226.

Three types of problems and appropriate methods of management are discussed to ensure special recognition and effective handling by the physician of psychosocial problems and the promotion of mental health. The problems include: (1) infants seen with defined medical conditions that generally have associated psychosocial problems including child abuse, and (2) infants seen who have fully recovered from critical illnesses but are considered at risk for later developmental disability. – From Authors' Abstract.

1568. PAWL, JEREE H. (Univ. of California, San Francisco). **Strategies of intervention.** Child Abuse & Neglect, The International Journal, 1984, **8**, 261–270.
The pediatric setting is emphasized as the natural locus for the integration of preventive services and as the first and often sole contact of parents and infants with professionals. The various kinds of possible service are delineated as are the sources of stress. – From Author's Abstract.

1569. RAUCH, HELEN (reprints: Dr. Deborah Phillips, Univ. of Illinois, Urbana-Champaign). **Child health policy and developmental continuity.** International Journal of Mental Health, 1984, **12**, 43–58.

1570. RIDER, ROBERT A. (Florida State Univ.), & IMWOLD, CHARLES H. **Comparison of selected gait parameters of trainable mentally retarded and nonretarded males.** Perceptual and Motor Skills, 1983, **57**, 56–58.
Gait was deficient in trainable 9-year-old mentally retarded children. – Adapted from Authors' Abstract.

1571. RINDFLEISCH, NOLAN (Ohio State Univ.), & RABB, JOEL. **Dilemmas in planning for the protection of children and youths in residential facilities.** Child Welfare, 1984, **63**, 205–215.

1572. SALONEN, J. T. (Univ. of Kuopio, Box 138, Kuopio, Finland), & HEINONEN, O. P. **Mental retardation and mother's hypertension during pregnancy.** Journal of Mental Deficiency Research, 1984, **28**, 53–56.
Maternal hypertension during pregnancy was associated with a relative risk of mental retardation in the offspring. – From the Article.

1573. SCHELLEKENS, J. M. H. (State Univ. Groningen, Netherlands); KALVERBOER, A. F.; & SCHOLTEN, C. A. **The micro-structure of tapping movements in children.** Journal of Motor Behavior, 1984, **16**, 20–39.
Children 5–9 years of age and adults carried out a reciprocal tapping task in which time pressure and distance were manipulated. The duration, velocity, acceleration, and accuracy of the movements were compared between age groups. Age differences appeared mainly in the homing time. – From Authors' Abstract.

1574. SHAYWITZ, SALLY E. (Yale Univ.); SHAYWITZ, BENNETT A.; McGRAW, KATE; & GROLL, S. **Current status of the neuromaturational examination as an index of learning disability.** Journal of Pediatrics, 1984, **104**, 819–825.
Our data indicate that, although a composite set of neuromaturational tasks can discriminate normal and LD boys with a high level of accuracy, caution is urged because the findings may be more related to overall intelligence than to a specific learning disability. – From Authors' Abstract.

1575. SMITH, MARJORIE (Hosp. for Sick Children, Great Ormond, London, England); DELVES, TREVOR; LANSDOWN, RICHARD; CLAYTON, BARBARA; & GRAHAM, PHILIP. **The effects of lead exposure on urban children: The Institute of Child Health/Southampton Study.** Developmental Medicine and Child Neurology, 1983, **25**, 1–54.
There was no link between lead level and behavior in this study of the 6–7-year-olds in 3 London boroughs. – Adapted from Authors' Abstract.

1576. STEFANSKI, MARK; SCHULZE, KARL (Coll. of Physicians & Surgeons of Columbia Univ.); BATEMAN, DAVID; KAIRAM, RAM; PEDLEY, TIMOTHY A.; MASTERSON, JULIA; & JAMES, L. STANLEY. **A scoring system for states of sleep and wakefulness in term and preterm infants.** Pediatric Research, 1984, **18**, 58–62.
The system is based on independent assessments of behavioral and electroencephalographic patterns. The distributions of sleep states for 15 preterm and 8 term infants were compared. – Adapted from Authors' Abstract.

1577. TAYLOR, BRENT (Univ. of Bristol, England), & WADSWORTH, JANE. **Breast feeding and child development at five years.** Developmental Medicine and Child Neurology, 1984, **26**, 73–80.
In this study of 13,135 children, relatively small relationships were found between breast-feeding and various aspects of children's development. – B. B. Keller.

1578. TEYLER, T. J. (Northeastern Ohio Univ. Coll. of Medicine), & CHIAIA, N. L. **Brain structure and development.** Journal of Children in Contemporary Society, 1983, **16**, 23–43.
The article is a low-level discussion of brain structure and function. – Ed.

1579. THORLEY, GEOFFREY (Inst. of Psychiatry, De Crespigny Park, London, England). **Pilot study to assess behavioural and cognitive effects of artificial food colors in a group of retarded children.** Developmental Medicine and Child Neurology, 1984, **26**, 56–61.
Ten institutionalized children were maintained on an additive-free diet for 2 weeks, followed by 2 weeks in which artificial food colors were administered orally in a placebo-masked, double-blind experimental design. There was no adverse behavioral or cognitive effect. – From Author's Abstract.

1580. TUCKER, LARRY A. (Auburn Univ.). **Cigarette smoking intentions and physical fitness: a multivariate study of high school males.** Adolescence, 1984, **19**, 313–321.
Teenage males who reported no intentions of smoking cigarettes were more physically fit than were mild intenders and strong intenders. – From Author's Abstract.

1581. ULRICH, BEVERLY D. (Michigan State Univ.). **The effects of stimulation programs on the development of high risk infants: a review of research.** Adapted Physical Activity Quarterly, 1984, **1**, 68–80.
Advances in medical technology, perinatal care, and neonatal intensive care have greatly increased the rate of survival for neonates born with a variety of medical problems and very low birthweights. The majority survive relatively sequelae free, although evidence still indicates that they remain at higher than normal risk for physical, mental, and social development. – From Author's Abstract.

1582. VANPOPPEL, DOROTHY (Kent State Univ.), & ESTOK, PATRICIA JENAWAY. **Infant feeding choice and the adolescent mother.** Journal of Obstetric, Gynecologic, and Neonatal Nursing, 1984, **13**, 115–118.
Family and social environment was a source of information for all of the subjects. Data indicate that the majority of the subjects had made their feeding decisions in early pregnancy. – From Authors' Abstract.

1583. VARELA, JUDITH T., & LAZARUS, PHILIP J. (Florida International Univ.). **Survey of services provided by United Cerebral Palsy agencies and the effects of P.L. 94–142 on pre-school handicapped children.** Psychological Reports, 1984, **54**, 183–188.
United Cerebral Palsy agencies were surveyed to compare services offered to preschool handicapped children, to identify current methods of funding, and to determine the major effects of P.L. 94–142 on preschool handicapped children in public schools. – From Authors' Abstract.

1584. WASHINGTON, VALORA (Howard Univ.). **Continuity of care in support for dependent children.** International Journal of Mental Health, 1984, **12**, 59–77.

1585. WEISSBLUTH, MARC (Children's Memorial Hosp., 2300 Children's Plaza, Chicago); DAVIS, A. TODD; & PONCHER, JOHN. **Night waking in 4- to 8-month-old infants.** Journal of Pediatrics, 1984, **104**, 477–480.
A group of infants was identified who had a past history of colic and who were perceived to have a current night waking problem. Night waking was a problem in infant boys more often than in infant girls. A second group of infants who awoke frequently was reported to snore or mouth breathe when asleep. This group of infants did not have a past history of colic, was not perceived to have a night waking problem, and was not overly represented by boys. – From Authors' Abstract.

1586. WRIGHT, PETER (Univ. of Edinburgh, 7 George Sq., Edinburgh, England); MACLEOD, HAMISH A.; & COOPER, MYRA J. **Waking at night: the effect of early feeding experience.** Child: Care, Health and Development, 1983, **9**, 309–319.
Mothers of preschool children were interviewed. Night feeds disappear more slowly in the breast-fed infant, and the problem of night waking both in the first year of life and when at nursery school appears to be associated with early breast-feeding. – From Authors' Abstract.

1587. YOUNES, ROBERT P. (Carney Hosp., Dept. of Pediatrics, 2100 Dorchester, Boston); ROSNER, BERNARD; & WEBB, GERTRUDE. **Neuroimmaturity of learning-disabled children: a controlled study.** Developmental Medicine and Child Neurology, 1983, **25**, 574–579.
A 46-component neurological exam was administered to 119 learning-disabled and 152 normal children. The learning-disabled children performed more poorly. – B. B. Keller.

1588. ZIGLER, EDWARD (Yale Univ.). **Issues in the construction of social policy for children and their families.** International Journal of Mental Health, 1984, **12**, 78–86.

1589. ZIGLER, EDWARD (Yale Univ.), & MUENCHOW, SUSAN. **How to influence social policy affecting children and families.** American Psychologist, 1984, **39**, 415–420.

1590. ZIVIANI, JENNY (Univ. of Queensland, St. Lucia, Queensland, Australia). **Qualitative changes in dynamic tripod grip between seven and 14 years of age.** Developmental Medicine and Child Neurology, 1983, **25**, 778–782.
Children were photographed while writing with a pencil. Developmental trends were identified for (1) degree of index-finger flexion and (2) degree of forearm pronation/supination. – B. B. Keller.

COGNITION, LEARNING, PERCEPTION

1591. ABRAVANEL, EUGENE (George Washington Univ.), & SIGAFOOS, ANN D. **Exploring the presence of imitation during early infancy.** Child Development, 1984, **55**, 381–392.
For infants 4–21 weeks, imitative-like matching of modeled gestures was the exception, not the rule, at all ages. Even where significantly greater frequencies of a gesture occurred during modeling than during control periods, it was always a partial and incomplete version of the modeled act that was reproduced, not a well-formed copy of the adult's gesture. Where results were consistent with an interpretation of imitation, as with responses to tongue protrusion modeling, the effect was restricted to the youngest ages: 4–6 weeks. – From Authors' Abstract.

1592. ACKERMAN, BRIAN P. (Univ. of Delaware). **The effects of storage and processing complexity on comprehension repair in children and adults.** Journal of Experimental Child Psychology, 1984, **37**, 303–334.
The subjects (ages 6, 10, and adult) were read short stories describing a consistent or inconsistent adult response to a child's action and repair information that resolved or failed to resolve the inconsistency. The results showed that even first graders can repair a comprehension problem in situations of minimal information processing complexity, and that increments in complexity affect the repair performance of younger more than older subjects. – From Author's Abstract.

1593. ADACHI, TOMOAKI (Tohoku Univ., Kawauchi, Sendai 980, Japan). **The acquisition of number word meanings and number conservation.** Tohoku Psychologica Folia, 1983, **42,** 42–50.
Children aged 4–6 years were tested on 5 number problems. Results included the following: the understanding of number word meanings as ordinal number and cardinal number precedes the acquisition of number conservation. In large set sizes, the understanding of number word meaning as ordinal number develops prior to that as cardinal number. – From Author's Abstract.

1594. ALLEN, GEORGE D. (Purdue Univ.). **Linguistic experience modifies lexical stress perception.** Journal of Child Language, 1983, **10,** 535–549.
Sensitivity to differences in lexical stress pattern was examined in 4–5-year-old monolingual French-, German-, and Swedish-speaking children. The data supported an attunement theory of language acquisition, in which potentially relevant abilities may become attenuated or completely lost if they are inappropriate or irrelevant for the child's language. – From Author's Abstract.

1595. ARAM, DOROTHY M. (Rainbow Babies and Childrens Hosp., 2101 Adelbert, Cleveland); EKELMAN, BARBARA L.; & NATION, JAMES E. **Preschoolers with language disorders: 10 years later.** Journal of Speech and Hearing Research, 1984, **27,** 232–244.
The majority of non-EMR subjects continued to evidence persistent deficits in language and academic achievement and were rated by their parents as being less socially competent and having more behavioral problems than their peers. – From Authors' Abstract.

1596. ÁROCHOVÁ, OLGA, & SUGÁR-KÁDÁR, JÚLIA. **Development of certain aspects of semantic memory in preschool age Hungarian and Slovak Children.** Studia Psychologica, 1984, **26,** 5–17.
Repeated investigation with Hungarian children revealed not only an increase in the absolute number of associative connections but especially an increment in quality. These children showed a higher associative output in comparison with the Slovak children. – From Authors' Abstract.

1597. ASHCRAFT, MARK H. (Cleveland State Univ.); FIERMAN, BENNETT A.; & BARTOLOTTA, ROBIN. **The production and verification tasks in mental addition: an empirical comparison.** Developmental Review, 1984, **4,** 157–170.
The paper is a response to Baroody's comment. – Ed.

1598. AUSTIN, ANN M. BERGHOUT (Utah State Univ.), & PEERY, J. CRAIG. **Analysis of adult-neonate synchrony during speech and nonspeech.** Perceptual and Motor Skills, 1983, **57,** 455–459.
Synchrony was more likely to occur during periods of speech. – From Authors' Abstract.

1599. BALTAXE, CHRISTIANE A. M. (Univ. of California, Los Angeles). **Use of contrastive stress in normal, aphasic, and autistic children.** Journal of Speech and Hearing Research, 1984, **27,** 97–105.
The contrastive stress task required that the subjects verbally assess the counterfactual nature of a presupposition in a yes-no question. Toy manipulation was used to elicit the desired responses in a play situation. Although all subject groups were able to perform the task, differences were seen in the number of correct responses and the patterns of stress misassignment. – From Author's Abstract.

1600. BAROODY, ARTHUR J. (Univ. of Rochester). **A reexamination of mental arithmetic models and data: a reply to Ashcraft.** Developmental Review, 1984, **4,** 148–156.
I draw an analogy between this alternative model of number fact representation and how computers efficiently reconstruct arithmetic combinations. Note that the research findings do not

clearly support any 1 model of mental arithmetic, and attempt to address Ashcraft's criticisms of my model. – From Author's Abstract.

1601. BATES, ELIZABETH; MacWHINNEY, BRIAN (Carnegie–Mellon Univ.); CASELLI, CRISTINA; DEVESCOVI, ANTONELLA; NATALE, FRANCESCO; & VENZA, VALERIA. **A cross-linguistic study of the development of sentence interpretation strategies.** Child Development, 1984, **55**, 341–354.
Sentence interpretation was compared in American and Italian children between the ages of 2 and 5. From the earliest stages, children showed sensitivity to the relative information value of the various cues in their native language; Italians relied primarily on semantic cues, whereas American children relied on word order. Data did not support claims regarding the existence of universal hypotheses about language structure. – From Authors' Abstract.

1602. BELSKY, JAY (Pennsylvania State Univ.); GARDUQUE, LAURIE; & HRNCIR, ELIZABETH. **Assessing performance, competence, and executive capacity in infant play: relations to home environment and security of attachment.** Developmental Psychology, 1984, **20**, 406–417.
Belsky and Most's (1981) 12-step scale of play development was used with the Caldwell inventory of home stimulation and the Strange Situation. It was predicted and confirmed with 12-, 15-, and 18-month-olds that home environment would relate to highest level of exploration in free play more than to executive capacity, and that the home-environment/executive-capacity association would exceed the home-environment/highest-level-of-free-play association. It was predicted and confirmed that infants evaluated as securely attached to their parents would be more free to attend to the environment beyond the attachment figure in play. – From Authors' Abstract.

1603. BERGAN, JOHN R. (Univ. of Arizona); STONE, CLEMENT A.; & FELD, JASON K. **Rule replacement in the development of basic number skills.** Journal of Educational Psychology, 1984, **76**, 289–299.
Children 3–8 years old participated. The development of counting skills is an evolving process in which parts of a simple rule are replaced by features that enable the child to perform an increasingly broad range of counting tasks. Rule replacement in counting plays an important role in the development of other math skills. – From Authors' Abstract.

1604. BERTENTHAL, BENNETT I. (Univ. of Virginia); PROFFITT, DENNIS R.; & CUTTING, JAMES E. **Infant sensitivity to figural coherence in biomechanical motions.** Journal of Experimental Child Psychology, 1984, **37**, 213–230.
Point-light displays moving as if attached to the major points of a walking person were used. Using an infant-control habituation paradigm, it was found that 3- and 5-month-olds discriminated the moving but not the static displays. Moving point-light displays with equivalent motions but different topographic relations were discriminated, while static versions were not, and arrays that varied in the amount of motion present in different portions of the display were also not discriminated. – From Authors' Abstract.

1605. BJORK, ELIZABETH LIGON (Univ. of California, Los Angeles), & CUMMINGS, E. MARK. **Infant search errors: stage of concept development or stage of memory development.** Memory and Cognition, 1984, **12**, 1–19.
The occurrence of Piaget's Stage IV search errors is considered to provide critical evidence that such infants are egocentrically concerned with their own actions and do not yet appreciate the systematic nature of spatial relationships or the permanence of objects. The present research casts doubt upon the theoretical significance that has been attached to this error, by demonstrating that it occurs primarily as an artifact of the almost universally employed 2-choice hiding task. – From Authors' Abstract.

1606. BOWEY, JUDITH A. (Victoria Coll., Australia). **The interaction of strategy and context in children's oral reading performance.** Journal of Psycholinguistic Research, 1984, **13**, 99–117.

Results indicated the hypothesis that third- and fourth-grade children adopt different oral reading speed strategies, depending on the amount of contextual information available, in order to maximize reading accuracy and, where appropriate, ongoing comprehension. This is consistent with an interactive theory of reading. – Adapted from Author's Abstract.

1607. BRITTAIN, W. LAMBERT (Cornell Univ.), & CHIEN, YU-CHIN. **Relationship between preschool children's ability to name body parts and their ability to construct a man.** Perceptual and Motor Skills, 1983, **57,** 19–24.
There was no relationship between the ability to name body parts and the ability to draw a person. – From Authors' Abstract.

1608. BROWN, CAROLYN J. (Univ. of Iowa), & HURTIG, RICHARD R. **Children's discourse competence: an evaluation of the development of inferential processes.** Discourse Processes, 1983, **6,** 353–375.
The data suggest that even the youngest children use systematic strategies in ordering the elements of a story based on causal and temporal relationships. – From Authors' Abstract.

1609. BROWN, JEAN B. (Albuquerque Aphasia & Speech Consultants). **Examination of grammatical morphemes in the language of hard-of-hearing children.** Volta Review, 1984, **86,** 229–238.
Examination of rank-ordered data revealed that the order of acquisition for grammatical morphemes was identical for both normal-hearing and hard-of-hearing children. – From Author's Abstract.

1610. BUSHNELL, I. W. R. (Univ. of Glasgow, Scotland); McCUTCHEON, E.; SINCLAIR, J.; & TWEEDLIE, M. E. **Infants' delayed recognition memory for colour and form.** British Journal of Developmental Psychology, 1984, **2,** 11–17.
Both 5- and 9-week-old infants were found to demonstrate memory for color and form information after a 24-hour delay. – From Authors' Abstract.

1611. CAMERON, CATHERINE ANN (Univ. of New Brunswick, Fredericton, New Brunswick, Canada). **Interference effects on preschool children's learning sets.** Journal of Experimental Child Psychology, 1984, **37,** 251–261.
Increased intertrial intervals retarded performance. Long interproblem intervals interacted with short intertrial intervals to produce performance facilitation. Similar stimuli caused greater performance decrements than dissimilar. Testing between subjects established that increased interproblem displays facilitate performance. Increased interproblem delays more greatly benefited shifts within dimensions. – From Author's Abstract.

1612. CARNI, ELLEN, & FRENCH, LUCIA A. (Univ. of Rochester). **The acquisition of** *before* **and** *after* **reconsidered: what develops?** Journal of Experimental Child Psychology, 1984, **37,** 394–403.
This study assesses the possibility that the ease of comprehending relational terms may vary depending upon whether the relationship being described is 1 with which the child is already familiar. Children 3–4 years old answered *before-, after,* and *when*-questions that referred to pictured event sequences having invariant or arbitrary real-world temporal orders. While 4-year-olds performed well with both types of sequences, 3-year-olds performed well with invariant sequences only. – From Authors' Abstract.

1613. CARTER, ANTHONY T. (Univ. of Rochester). **The acquisition of social deixis: children's usages of "kin" terms in Maharashtra, India.** Journal of Child Language, 1984, **11,** 179–201.
It is argued that characteristic features of the usages and definitions of "kin" terms of young children as compared to those of adults reflect not only an incomplete grasp of the adult system of kinship reference, but also an accurate understanding of the deictic system of address in which kinship per se plays at most a peripheral role. – From Author's Abstract.

1614. CAVANAUGH, JOHN C. (Bowling Green State Univ.), & PERLMUTTER, MARION. **Metamemory: a critical examination.** Child Development, 1982, **53,** 11–28.
Several limitations are noted. There is no clear definition of the concept, assessment methods are inadequate, research has not gone beyond a demonstration stage, and a strong relationship between memory and metamemory generally has not been substantiated. A revised analysis of metamemory is suggested. – From Authors' Abstract.

1615. CHALMERS, MARGARET (Univ. of Edinburgh, Scotland), & McGONIGLE, BRENDAN. **Are children any more logical than monkeys on the five-term series problem?** Journal of Experimental Child Psychology, 1984, **37,** 355–377.
Six-year-old children were tested on the 5-term transitivity problem used previously with squirrel monkeys as subjects. Children showed very similar response profiles to that of monkeys in all the conditions used. Posttests suggest that nonlogical strategies can underwrite ostensibly impeccable transitive "reasoning" in child as well as monkey. – From Authors' Abstract.

1616. CIRRIN, FRANK M. (Idaho State Univ.). **Lexical search speed in children and adults.** Journal of Experimental Child Psychology, 1984, **37,** 158–175.
Subjects in grades K, 1, and 3 and adults were given a lexical decision task with auditorily presented words and nonwords. Word frequency contributed to decision latency for all age groups, age of word acquisition contributed to all groups but third graders, and number of word meanings did not contribute for any age group. – From Author's Abstract.

1617. CORSON, DAVID (Univ. of Tasmania, Hobart, Tasmania, Australia). **Lying and killing: language and the moral reasoning of twelve- and fifteen-year-olds by social group.** Adolescence, 1984, **19,** 473–481.
There was an impressive consistency in moral attitudes and in reasons offered for those attitudes across children of quite different social backgrounds. There was also a very common access to higher level, autonomous reasoning among the adolescents surveyed. – From Author's Abstract.

1618. COX, T. (Univ. Coll. of Swansea). **Cumulative deficit in culturally disadvantaged children.** British Journal of Educational Psychology, 1983, **53,** 317–326.
Seven scholastic attainment measures were obtained on a sample of culturally disadvantaged and control children at ages 11 and 15 years. In relation to their 11-year scores, the disadvantaged group had lower predicted mean scores at age 15 than their controls on all test measures. The mean predicted scores of the disadvantaged group on 3 of the 15-year tests were, nonsignificantly, lower than those of their controls. These findings offer support for the cumulative deficit hypothesis. – From Author's Abstract.

1619. CRISPIN, LISA (Univ. Coll., London, England); HAMILTON, WIN; & TRICKEY, G. **The relevance of visual squential memory to reading.** British Journal of Educational Psychology, 1984, **54,** 24–30.
Nineteen junior school children were given 3 visual sequential memory assessments and a group reading test. Results are discussed in terms of a task analysis approach and a structuralist approach. – From Authors' Abstract.

1620. DASH, UDAYA N., & DAS, J. P. (Univ. of Alberta, Edmonton, Alberta, Canada). **Development of concrete operational thought and information coding in schooled and unschooled children.** British Journal of Developmental Psychology, 1984, **2,** 63–72.
As predicted, performance on Piagetian tasks increased as a function of age only, whereas the effects of schooling, age, and their interaction were clearly observed for coding processes. – From Authors' Abstract.

1621. DEAN, ANNE L. (Univ. of New Orleans). **A critique of William Ives' critique of the Piagetian perspective on mental imagery.** The Genetic Epistemologist, 1984, **12,** 8–12.

1622. DE BOYSSON-BARDIES, BÉNÉDICTE (Laboratoire de Psychologie, C.N.R.S., 54 bld. Raspail, Paris, France); SAGART, LAURENT; & DURAND, CATHERINE. **Discernible differences in the babbling of infants according to target language.** Journal of Child Language, 1984, **11**, 1–15.
Babblings of 6–10-month-old infants from different language backgrounds were presented to adult judges whose task was to identify the infants from their own linguistic community. The results show that certain language-specific metaphonological cues render this identification possible when the samples exhibit long and coherent intonation patterns. – From Authors' Abstract.

1623. DE HERNANDEZ, LILIAN; MAREK, EDMUND A.; & RENNER, JOHN W. (Univ. of Oklahoma). **Relationships among gender, age, and intellectual development.** Journal of Research in Science Teaching, 1984, **21**, 365–375.
Among the results, data showed that (1) adolescent males demonstrate a higher level of intellectual development than adolescent females, (2) males mature intellectually earlier than females, and (3) the value of the conservation-of-volume task as a component of a battery of formal tasks depends upon whether the decisions are to be made on the basis of the total-risk results or on individual task performance. – Adapted from Authors' Abstract.

1624. DEMPSTER, FRANK N. (Univ. of Nevada, Las Vegas). **Conditions affecting retention test performance: a developmental study.** Journal of Experimental Child Psychology, 1984, **37**, 65–77.
Among third and tenth graders there were no age differences in proportionalized short-term retention, despite substantial differences in the number of items learned, and significant age differences in long-term retention only between groups that had received a different number of learning trials. – From Author's Abstract.

1625. DENNEY, NANCY WADSWORTH (Univ. of Kansas). **A model of cognitive development across the life span.** Developmental Review, 1984, **4**, 171–191.
A distinction was drawn between an individual's unexercised potential, which refers to the level of performance that would be expected if the individual had no exercise and/or training on the ability in question, and an individual's optimally exercised potential, which refers to the level of performance that would be expected if the individual had optimal exercise training. Both unexercised and optimally-exercised potential levels were proposed to increase with age up to early adulthood and decrease gradually thereafter. – From Author's Abstract.

1626. DICK, MALCOLM B., & ENGLE, RANDALL W. (Univ. of South Carolina). **The effect of instruction with relational and item-specific elaborative strategies on young children's organization and free recall.** Journal of Experimental Child Psychology, 1984, **37**, 282–302.
Second graders were given instructions directed at encoding (a) list organizational information, (b) item-specific semantic information, or (c) organizational and individual item information. Instructions emphasizing list organization were more effective than those emphasizing item-specific elaboration. Subjects given individual item elaborative instructions showed levels of recall which were comparable to those of control subjects. – From Authors' Abstract.

1627. D'ODORICO, LAURA (Università degli Studi di Padova, Piazza Capitaniato 5, Padova, Italy). **Non-segmental features in prelinguistic communications: an analysis of some types of infant cry and non-cry vocalizations.** Journal of Child Language, 1984, **11**, 17–27.
Italian infants' cry and noncry vocalizations were recorded during laboratory sessions and grouped into different categories in relation to different situational contexts. The results give clear evidence of differentiation of cry vocalization produced in different contexts, and similarity of cry and noncry vocalization produced in the same context. – From Author's Abstract.

1628. DONAHUE, MAVIS (Univ. of Illinois, Chicago), & BRYAN, TANIS. **Conversational skills and modeling in learning disabled boys.** Applied Psycholinguistics, 1983, **4**, 251–278.

LD and nondisabled boys in grades 2–8 listened either to a child interviewer modeling conversation skills or a monologue presenting only the interviewee's responses. Each subject was then videotaped interviewing a classmate. The dialogue model increased LD children's production of open-ended questions and comments; these strategies seemed difficult for listeners to understand. LD children are aware of their difficulties in conversation. – Adapted from Authors' Abstract.

1629. DOWLING, JERRY (Suite 205, 10425 W. North Ave., Wauwatosa, WI), & WESNER, DAVID. **The concept of an infant mental status examination: a reply to Winnicott and a discussion.** Psychiatry, 1984, **47**, 172–180.

1630. ELBERT, JEAN C. (Univ. of Oklahoma). **Short-term memory encoding and memory search in the word recognition of learning-disabled children.** Journal of Learning Disabilities, 1984, **17**, 342–345.
Subjects were 16 LD children with particular deficiencies in word recognition and 16 control children equated for age, grade, and intelligence. Input modalities of both stimulus array words to be encoded and stored in short-term memory and target words for recognition were manipulated, resulting in 3 experimental conditions. Three hypotheses were tested, each involving inferences about internal operations based on reaction time. While LD subjects did not differ from control subjects at the encoding stage of word recognition, LD subjects required more processing time for memory search. – From Author's Abstract.

1631. FABRICIUS, WILLIAM V. (Univ. of Michigan), & WELLMAN, HENRY M. **Memory development.** Journal of Children in Contemporary Society, 1983, **16**, 171–187.
The article reviews recent memory development research and 4 general principles of strategy development, including strategy acquisition and generalized trained strategies. – From Authors' Abstract.

1632. FAGEN, JEFFREY W. (St. John's Univ.). **Infants' long-term memory for stimulus color.** Developmental Psychology, 1984, **20**, 435–440.
Infants 3–4 months were trained on 2 successive days to produce movement in an overhead mobile containing either all blue or all green objects. Subsequent exposure to a novel-colored mobile produced a decrement in conditioned responding during cued-recall tests 1 but not 7 days following training. – From Author's Abstract.

1633. FALLON, APRIL E.; ROZIN, PAUL (Univ. of Pennsylvania); & PLINER, PATRICIA. **The child's conception of food: the development of food rejections with special reference to disgust and contamination sensitivity.** Child Development, 1984, **55**, 566–575.
Interviews with 3 1/2–12-year-old children and their mothers documented the development of food rejection. The first to appear is rejection based purely on sensory characteristics, usually taste (distastes). Rejection based purely on anticipated harm following ingestion appears next (danger). Finally, the oldest children and adults show rejection based on the idea of what something is or where it comes from. – From Authors' Abstract.

1634. FELDMAN, DAVID HENRY (Tufts Univ.). **A follow-up of subjects scoring above 180 IQ in Terman's "Genetic Studies of Genius."** Exceptional Children, 1984, **50**, 518–523.
Using the Terman files, 26 subjects with scores above 180 IQ were compared with 26 randomly selected subjects from Terman's sample. Findings were generally that the extra IQ points made little difference. – From Author's Abstract.

1635. FIGUEIRA, ROSA ATTIÉ (Universidade Estadual de Campinas, Caixa Postal 6045, Campinas, Brazil). **On the development of the expression of causativity: a syntactic hypothesis.** Journal of Child Language, 1984, **11**, 109–127.
Longitudinal data are presented on the development of the lexical expression of causativity by 1 child learning Portuguese as her first language. Noncausatives are used for causatives, and causatives are used for noncausatives. – From Author's Abstract.

1636. FINCH, A. J., JR. (Medical Univ. of South Carolina); EDWARDS, GARRY L.; & SEARCY, J. DANIEL. **Reflection-impulsivity and short-term memory in emotionally disturbed children.** Journal of Psychology, 1984, **116,** 263–267.
Subjects received the Matching Familiar Figures Test and the Visual-Aural Digit Span Test. Analysis indicated that on all memory tasks the reflective subjects were better than the impulsive subjects. – From Authors' Abstract.

1637. FISHER, CELIA B. (Fordham Univ.), & HEINCKE, SUSANNE. **Children's memory for oblique orientation: a matter of degree?** Child Development, 1982, **53,** 235–238.
Children 3–4 years old were tested on 2 discrimination problems using successive presentation and feedback: between lines varying only in slope and between lines varying only in left-right direction. Three-year-olds found both problems difficult, while 4-year-olds solved these problems with ease. Children (mean age = 4–6) who had discriminated both slope and left-right problems under successive presentation were tested on these same discriminations under simultaneous presentation. While all children discriminated lines varying in slope, the left-right problem proved to be quite difficult. – From Authors' Abstract.

1638. FITZGERALD, D. (Univ. of New England, Armidale, Australia), & HATTIE, J. A. **An evaluation of the "Your Style of Learning and Thinking" inventory.** British Journal of Educational Psychology, 1983, **53,** 336–346.
This paper assesses an effort by Torrance and co-workers to introduce a new test that they claim is based on a model of cognitive style. This study found evidence that conflicted with Torrance et al.'s findings. – From Authors' Abstract.

1639. FLAVELL, JOHN H. (Stanford Univ.). **On cognitive development.** Child Development, 1982, **53,** 1–10.
The article reviews the usefulness of stages in understanding cognitive development. Factors that make for heterogeneity and homogeneity in cognitive development are discussed. – Ed.

1640. FRANCIS, HAZEL (Univ. of London, England). **Children's knowledge of orthography in learning to read.** British Journal of Educational Psychology, 1984, **54,** 8–23.
Children read from their school material arranged both in sentences and in word lists before phonics instruction was introduced. In a second study, samples were collected from 8 children during their first 3 years in school. Error-target similarity increased with reading attainment. While reading aloud, considerable knowledge of spelling developed independently of the explicit use of phonics. – From Author's Abstract.

1641. FREEMAN, N. H. (Univ. of Bristol, 8–10 Berkeley Sq., Bristol, England). **Picture-plane bias in children's representational drawing.** Australian Journal of Psychology, 1983, **35,** 121–134.
In order to study the problem of how biases are generated when children look for cues on the picture-plane, it is necessary empirically to distinguish between those biases and others which may be a product of how the child responds to the scene that the picture is supposed to represent. Two methods of analyzing the problem are discussed. One is by maintaining what the picture is supposed to represent and providing solutions of the projective problem. The other method is to maintain the picture-plane configuration and progressively to complicate the scenes which are represented. – From Author's Abstract.

1642. FRESE, MICHAEL (Univ. of Pennsylvania), & STEWART, JUDITH. **Skill learning as a concept in life-span developmental psychology: an action theoretic analysis.** Human Development, 1984, **27,** 145–162.
An action theoretic account of skill learning and skill use is offered as a useful heuristic for life-span developmental psychology. It is suggested that analyses of the tasks confronting an individual and of the structure of action, as well as of the interplay of these 2, have implications for the understanding of development across the life span. – From Authors' Abstract.

1643. FUCCI, DONALD (Ohio Univ.), & PETROSINO, LINDA. **Lingual vibrotactile sensation magnitudes: comparison of suprathreshold responses for three different age ranges.** Perceptual and Motor Skills, 1983, **57,** 31–38.
Adults produced shallower upper-slope functions than children and also showed greater response variability. – From Authors' Abstract.

1644. FURROW, DAVID (Mt. St. Vincent Univ., Halifax, Nova Scotia, Canada). **Social and private speech at two years.** Child Development, 1984, **55,** 355–362.
Children 23–25 months of age were videotaped in free play with an adult. Regulatory, attentional, and informative uses of language all appeared more frequently in speech addressed to another, while self-regulatory, describing own activity, and expressive functions had an increased incidence in speech for self. – From Author's Abstract.

1645. FURROW, DAVID (Mount St. Vincent Univ., Halifax, Nova Scotia, Canada). **Young children's use of prosody.** Journal of Child Language, 1984, **11,** 203–213.
Results showed that utterances made while maintaining eye contact were on average louder and higher and more variably pitched. Children use prosodic elements of speech for communicative purposes. – From Author's Abstract.

1646. GARDNER, JUDITH M., & KARMEL, BERNARD Z. (Mt. Sinai Medical Ctr.). **Arousal effects on visual preferences in neonates.** Developmental Psychology, 1984, **20,** 374–377.
The looking preferences of 12 full-term neonates in a more aroused condition and in a less aroused condition showed that infants looked more as temporal frequency increased when they were less aroused and looked less as temporal frequency increased when more aroused. – From Authors' Abstract.

1647. GARGIULO, RICHARD M. (Univ. of Alabama). **Cognitive style and moral judgement in mentally handicapped and non-handicapped children of equal mental age.** British Journal of Developmental Psychology, 1984, **2,** 83–89.
Mentally handicapped and nonhandicapped children matched on mental age were assessed with the Matching Familiar Figures Test and a Piagetian measure designed to elicit moral judgments. No differences were observed in the error and latency scores between the 2 groups nor in the proportion of reflective, impulsive, fast/accurate or slow/inaccurate individuals. – From Author's Abstract.

1648. GARNER, RUTH (Univ. of Maryland); MACREADY, GEORGE B.; & WAGONER, SHIRLEY. **Readers' acquisition of the components of the text-lookback strategy.** Journal of Educational Psychology, 1984, **76,** 300–309.
Fifth-grade students tutored younger readers. The order of acquisition posited and confirmed was: undifferentiated rereading preceded text sampling and question differentiation preceded the final component. Reader proficiency groups differed in the proportion of members having acquired particular strategic components. – From Authors' Abstract.

1649. GIBSON, DEBORAH, & INGRAM, DAVID (Univ. of British Columbia, Vancouver, British Columbia, Canada). **The onset of comprehension and production in a language delayed child.** Applied Psycholinguistics, 1983, **4,** 359–375.
This study examined the onset and acquisition of language comprehension and production in a language-delayed child through the analysis of a daily diary kept from 2:5 to 3:10. – From Authors' Abstract.

1650. GIBSON, ELEANOR J. (Cornell Univ.), & WALKER, ARLENE S. **Development of knowledge of visual-tactual affordances of substance.** Child Development, 1984, **55,** 453–460.
Infants 12 months old were familiarized in the dark with an object of either a hard or an elastic substance. A visual-preference test was given with simultaneous presentation of 2 films of identical objects, 1 moving in a pattern characteristic of a rigid object and 1 moving in a pattern

characteristic of an elastic object. Infants handled the 2 substances differently and looked preferentially with more and longer first looks to the type of substance familiarized. – From Authors' Abstract.

1651. GITTERMAN, DENA (Indiana Univ.), & JOHNSTON, JUDITH R. **Talking about comparisons: a study of young children's comparative adjective usage.** Journal of Child Language, 1983, **10,** 605–621.
This study explores the learning of specific comparative adjective forms: (a) the nature of the perceptual input, and (b) the nature of the event. The results indicate that perceptual cue redundancy and heterogeneity affects the learning of attribute dimensions. – From Authors' Abstract.

1652. GLEITMAN, LILA R. (Univ. of Pennsylvania); NEWPORT, ELISSA L.; & GLEITMAN, HENRY. **The current status of the motherese hypothesis.** Journal of Child Language, 1984, **11,** 43–79.
Partially conflicting results from correlational studies of maternal speech style and its effects on child language learning motivate a comparative discussion and a reanalysis of the original Newport et al. data. – From Authors' Abstract.

1653. GOLD, DOLORES (Concordia Univ., Montreal, Quebec, Canada); CROMBIE, GAIL; BRENDER, WILLIAM; & MATE, PHYLLIS. **Sex differences in children's performance in problem-solving situations involving an adult model.** Child Development, 1984, **55,** 543–549.
Eight-year-old girls performed significantly more poorly than boys when required to solve a simple problem task by performing a response that was opposite to that demonstrated by an adult female model. Girls did not differ from boys in a condition that required that they learn to perform a response opposite to the 1 they themselves had previously learned and performed. Four-year-old girls in the condition requiring a response opposite to that made by the model performed significantly more poorly (regardless of the sex of the model) than all other groups of children. – From Authors' Abstract.

1654. GORDON, EDWIN (Temple Univ.). **A longitudinal predictive validity study of the Intermediate Measures of Music Audiation.** Council for Research in Music Education, 1984, **78,** 1–23.
IMMA test scores may be used for identifying students with high developmental and stabilized music aptitudes who can profit from special and additional music instruction. – From the Article.

1655. GUNDERSON, VIRGINIA M. (Univ. of Washington), & SACKETT, GENE P. **Development of pattern recognition in infant pigtailed macaques *(Macaca nemestrina).*** Developmental Psychology, 1984, **20,** 418–426.
The development of pattern recognition in infant pigtailed macaques was examined. Cross-sectional data revealed that a novelty preference occurred with increasing age. – From Authors' Abstract.

1656. GUSTAFSON, GWEN E. (Northern Illinois Univ.). **Effects of the ability to locomote on infants' social and exploratory behaviors: an experimental study.** Developmental Psychology, 1984, **20,** 397–40.
Normal infants aged 6 1/2–10 months who did not locomote were observed in a laboratory environment for 10 min in a "walker" and for 10 min out of the walker. Additional infants, all able to creep or crawl, were compared. The 2 modes of locomotion, walker-assisted or independent, afforded similar experiences within a standard environment, but experiences quite different from those of the nonlocomoting infant. The systematic reorganization of experiences through locomotion has implications for social development. – From Author's Abstract.

1657. GUTTENTAG, ROBERT E. (Univ. of Winnipeg, Manitoba, Canada). **The mental effort requirement of cumulative rehearsal: a developmental study.** Journal of Experimental Child Psychology, 1984, **37,** 92–106.

Second- and third-grade children experienced significantly more finger-tapping interference during instructed cumulative rehearsal than did sixth-grade children, an effect which could not be attributed simply to developmental differences in time-sharing performance. For children in grades 2–5, rehearsal set size during spontaneous rehearsal was negatively correlated with amount of finger-tapping interference during cumulative rehearsal. – From Author's Abstract.

1658. HALE, CATHERINE A., & KAIL, ROBERT (Purdue Univ.). **Rules for evaluating the difficulty of memory problems.** Bulletin of the Psychonomic Society, 1984, **22**, 33–36.
Subjects judged which depicted individual in a pair of photographs would be less likely to recall the names of animals. Judgments for most children in grades 1–6 suggested that the number of animals was the principal determinant of difficulty. Eighth graders and college students used the separate and interactive effects of the number of animals and the age of the depicted individual. – Adapted from Authors' Abstract.

1659. HALPIN, JOHN A.; PURR, C. RICHARD; MASON, HEATHER F.; & MARSTON, SUSAN P. (Franklin & Marshall Coll.). **Self-reference encoding and incidental recall by children.** Bulletin of the Psychonomic Society, 1984, **22**, 87–89.
Children in grades K, 1, and 4 were measured for recall of trait-descriptive adjectives within an incidental-memory paradigm. Recall increased over age, and by the fourth grade, the children showed the adult pattern of greater recall in the self-reference condition. – Adapted from Authors' Abstract.

1660. HAMAUI, D., & PARODI, M. (Univ. degli Studi di Parma, Italy). **When a face seems to be attentive? An "interobservational" research.** Età Evolutiva, 1984, **17**, 66–74.
Facial features are described which are shown to be common and constant to the various perceptions of attention, along with the different types of interobservational processes through which a definition of those features is reached. – From Authors' Abstract.

1661. HARMON, ROBERT J. (Univ. of Colorado School of Medicine); MORGAN, GEORGE A.; & GLICKEN, ANITA D. **Continuities and discontinuities in affective and cognitive-motivational development.** Child Abuse & Neglect, The International Journal, 1984, **8**, 157–167.
The studies illustrate developmental transformations at 10 and 18 months. Findings comparing abused/neglected and perinatal risk infant populations with normal infants illustrate differences in affective and cognitive-motivational development. – From Authors' Abstract.

1662. HARROP, A. (City of Liverpool Coll. of Higher Education, England), & McCANN, CHRIS. **Modifying "creative writing" in the classroom.** British Journal of Educational Psychology, 1984, **54**, 62–72.
Behavior modification techniques were used in an attempt to raise third-grade pupils' performance in creative writing. The results showed considerable increases in the pupils' essay scores on 3 variables. – From Authors' Abstract.

1663. HATANO, GIYOO (Dokkyo Univ., Soka-shi, Saitama, Japan), & INAGAKI, KAYOKO. **Two courses of expertise.** Research and Clinical Center for Child Development: Annual Report 1982–83, 27–36.
We will propose 3 issues related to the processes of spontaneous expertise, which are theoretically interesting in developmental research and can profitably be studied cross-culturally. – From the Article.

1664. HAYMES, MICHAEL (RiverView Hosp. for Children, P.O. Box 621, Middletown, CT); GREEN, LOGAN; & QUINTO, RONALD. **Maslow's hierarchy, moral development, and prosocial behavioral skills within a child psychiatric population.** Motivation and Emotion, 1984, **8**, 23–31.
Controlling for age and Piagetian cognitive development, it was found that among the participants in the midrange of moral reasoning, there was a positive relationship between prosocial behavior ratings and conative development. – From Authors' Abstract.

1665. HERMAN, JAMES F. (Washington Univ.). **Children's mental manipulation of spatial information in large- and small-scale spaces.** Journal of Genetic Psychology, 1984, **144**, 147–148.
Spatial understanding depends on space size and layout. – Ed.

1666. HERMAN, JAMES F. (Washington Univ.); KOLKER, ROBIN G.; & SHAW, MARJORIE L. **Effects of motor activity on children's intentional and incidental memory for spatial locations.** Child Development, 1982, **53**, 239–244.
Kindergartners and third graders encountered a large model town in 1 of 3 conditions: standing, riding, or walking. Half the children in each motor condition were instructed to remember the location of the buildings (intentional memory), while the remaining children were not given specific memory instructions (incidental memory). Only the kindergartners' accuracy increased as a function of the amount of motor activity. There was no difference between intentional and incidental memory conditions. – From Authors' Abstract.

1667. HERMAN, JAMES F. (Washington Univ.), & ROTH, STEPHEN F. **Children's incidental memory for spatial locations in a large-scale environment: taking a tour down memory lane.** Merrill-Palmer Quarterly, 1984, **30**, 87–102.
Kindergartners and third graders encountered a spatial layout in a large-scale area and were then asked to construct the layout from memory. In the story condition, children were told a story relating most of the object locations while they walked through the space. In the no-story condition, the object locations were identified but the story was omitted. Children at both age levels placed objects more accurately in the story condition than in the no-story condition. – From Authors' Abstract.

1668. HERMAN, JAMES F. (Washington Univ.); ROTH, STEPHEN F.; & NORTON, LAURA M. **Time and distance in spatial cognition development.** International Journal of Behavioral Development, 1984, **7**, 35–51.
The results indicated that only younger children's estimates of the distance traversed in an environment may be influenced by the time taken to traverse that distance. – From Authors' Abstract.

1669. HICKS, ROBERT E. (Univ. of North Carolina School of Medicine); ALLEN, DEBORAH A.; & MAYO, JAMES P., JR. **A developmental study of temporal duration judgments.** Journal of Genetic Psychology, 1984, **144**, 31–38.
Students in grades 1, 3, 5, 7, and college made 4 serial reproductions of each of 3 time intervals, 8, 13, and 32 sec. Judgments were an increasing, negatively accelerated function of trials. – From Authors' Abstract.

1670. HIRSH-PASEK, KATHY (Swarthmore Coll.); TREIMAN, REBECCA; & SCHNEIDERMAN, MAITA. **Brown & Hanlon revisited: mothers' sensitivity to ungrammatical forms.** Journal of Child Language, 1984, **11**, 81–88.
We suggest that parents are not totally indifferent to the grammatical form of their child's utterances. We found that mothers are more inclined to repeat ungrammatical than grammatical sentences generated by 2-year-old subjects. – From Authors' Abstract.

1671. HOLZMAN, MATHILDA. **Evidence for a reciprocal model of language development.** Journal of Psycholinguistic Research, 1984, **13**, 119–146.
The paper presents findings from a longitudinal study of 4 infant–mother dyads. A reciprocal model of language development is proposed analogous to Bowlby's model for the development of attachment. – Adapted from Author's Abstract.

1672. HOPPE-GRAFF, SIEGFRIED (Univ. of Mannheim, Germany). **Ist die Entwicklung der Informationsverarbeitungskapazität eine notwendige Bedingung für den Erwerb der Klasseninklusion?** Arbeiten der Forschungsgruppe Sprache und Kognition um Lehrstuhl Psychologie III der Universität Mannheim, 1984, Bericht Nr. 31, 1–32.

The assumptions about the prerequisites for class inclusion and the empirical tests are interpreted as demonstrating 2 general statements: (1) that the formulation and test of necessary developmental conditions is a central component of explanations in developmental psychology, and (2) that testing these hypotheses adequately ask for specific statistical procedures and interpretations. – From Author's Abstract.

1673. HOPPE-GRAFF, SIEGFRIED (Univ. of Mannheim, Germany). **Methodische Probleme bei der Erfassung des Konzeptes der Klasseninklusion: Haben Darbietungsmodus und Bewertungsstrategie einen Einflub?** Arbeiten der Forschungsgruppe Sprache und Kognition um Lehrstuhl Psychologie III der Universität Mannheim, 1984, Bericht Nr. 30, 1–19.
We interpret our study as evidence favoring Piaget's account of the problem—that class inclusion is an exceptional concrete-operational structure which may serve as a key concept for understanding development of logical thinking. – From Author's Abstract.

1674. ISAACSON, DOUGLAS K., & WILLIAMS, JOHN D. (Univ. of Arkansas). **The relationship of conceptual systems theory and Piagetian theory.** Journal of Psychology, 1984, 117, 3–6.
Relationships between 6 measures of conceptual systems theory and 2 measures of Piagetian theory were analyzed. A canonical analysis revealed most of the multivariate relationship to occur between the Conceptual Systems Test and the Logical Reasoning Test. – From Authors' Abstract.

1675. ITO, RYOKO (Tokyo Gakugei Univ., Koganei, Tokyo, Japan); KANDA, HIDEO; & SATO, HIROKO. **Condensation of play activity in normal children and a mentally retarded child.** The Research Institute for the Education of Exceptional Children Research Bulletin, 1983, 20, 1–15.
We examine experimentally whether condensation of play occurs or not as a result of adults' intervention to facilitate socialization in play. Subjects are not yet fully socialized normal children and a mentally retarded child. – From the Article.

1676. JACOBSON, JOSEPH L. (Wayne State Univ.); JACOBSON, SANDRA W.; FEIN, GRETA G.; & SCHWARTZ, PAMELA M. **Factors and clusters for the Brazelton Scale: an investigation of the dimensions of neonatal behavior.** Developmental Psychology, 1984, 20, 339–353.
Lester, Als, and Brazelton (1982) have proposed a set of 7 a priori clusters for reducing data from the Brazelton Neonatal Behavioral Assessment Scale. The distributional and psychometric properties of these clusters were examined. – From Authors' Abstract.

1677. JOHNSON, CARL NILS, & WELLMAN, HENRY M. (Univ. of Michigan). **Children's developing conceptions of the mind and brain.** Child Development, 1982, 53, 222–234.
Evidence is presented to show that by ages 4–5 years, children commonly regard the brain as an internal mindlike entity associated with a class of distinctly mental acts. Young children begin with undifferentiated conceptions of the mind and brain. Both entities are regarded as necessary for mental but not sensory-motor actions. In subsequent developments, the concepts of the mind and brain are differentiated along 2 lines. Ontologically, the mind is distinguished by its immateriality; functionally, the brain is distinguished by its involvement in bodily actions. – From Authors' Abstract.

1678. JOHNSTON, JUDITH R. (Indiana Univ.), & KAMHI, ALAN G. **Syntactic and semantic aspects of the utterances of language-impaired children: the same can be less.** Merrill-Palmer Quarterly, 1984, 30, 65–86.
Despite similar utterance length, language-impaired children expressed fewer propositions per utterance and made more syntactic errors than the younger normal group. – From Authors' Abstract.

1679. KAIL, MICHÈLE (Laboratoire de Psychologie, 28 Rue Serpente, Paris, France), & WEISSENBORN, JÜRGEN. **A developmental cross-linguistic study of adversative connectives: French "mais" and German "aber/sondern."** Journal of Child Language, 1984, **11**, 143–158.
Two hypotheses are confirmed: (1) substitutive *but* is easier to process and hence is acquired earlier than contrastive *but* and (2) the interpretation of contrastive *but* sentences depends on their inferential complexity relative to a given context. – From Authors' Abstract.

1680. KAMHI, ALAN G. (Memphis State Univ.); CATTS, HUGH W.; KOENIG, LINDA A.; & LEWIS, BARBARA A. **Hypothesis-testing and nonlinguistic symbolic abilities in language-impaired children.** Journal of Speech and Hearing Disorders, 1984, **49**, 169–176.
Language-impaired children performed poorer than their MA controls on the haptic recognition task and on a portion of the discrimination learning task. – From Authors' Abstract.

1681. KATZ, ROBERT B. (Haskins Laboratories, 270 Crown, New Haven); HEALY, ALICE F.; & SHANKWEILER, DONALD. **Phonetic coding and order memory in relation to reading proficiency: a comparison of short-term memory for temporal and spatial order information.** Applied Psycholinguistics, 1983, **4**, 229–250.
On separate tests for retention of temporal sequence and spatial location, good readers were better than poor readers on temporal order and on the spatial task as well. Differences in error patterns were supportive of earlier evidence that links poor readers' short-term memory deficiencies to reduced effectiveness of phonetic representation. – From Authors' Abstract.

1682. KENNEY, KATHRYN W. (Arizona State Univ.); PRATHER, ELIZABETH M.; MOONEY, MAUREEN A.; & JERUZAL, NANCY C. **Comparisons among three articulation sampling procedures with preschool children.** Journal of Speech and Hearing Research, 1984, **27**, 226–231.
Results showed no difference among the 3 sampling procedures for type and number of errors. – From Authors' Abstract.

1683. KINGMA, J. (Twente Univ. of Technology, Enschede, Netherlands), & KOOPS, W. **Piagetian tasks, traditional intelligence and achievement tests.** British Journal of Educational Psychology, 1983, **53**, 278–290.
Children in grades K, 1, and 4 were given 3 types of Piagetian tasks, traditional intelligence tasks, and school achievement tests. The combination of seriation and conservation was superior to intelligence tests in predicting number language. Seriation predicted number line comprehension as well as the intelligence tests. Both the Piagetian tasks and the intelligence tests were poor predictors of simple computation. Verbal arithmetic was predicted as well by both tests. – Adapted from Authors' Abstract.

1684. KINGMA, JOHANNES (Twente Univ. of Technology, Enschede, Netherlands), & LOTH, FRANCISKA L. **Effects of perceptual variations on number comparison tasks.** International Journal of Behavioral Development, 1984, **7**, 21–33.
It was shown that 2-choice tasks were easier than multiple-choice tasks controlling for chance responding. The density manipulation produced a strong effect, i.e., tasks in which the elements were placed closely together were more difficult than tasks in which the elements were spaced far apart. – From Authors' Abstract.

1685. KISILEVSKY, BARBARA S. (Queen's Univ., Kingston, Ontario, Canada), & MUIR, DARWIN W. **Neonatal habituation and dishabituation to tactile stimulation during sleep.** Developmental Psychology, 1984, **20**, 367–373.
We demonstrated habituation to a repeatedly presented brush stroke to the ear but failed to demonstrate dishabituation to the original brush stroke following an intense auditory stimulus (86 dB rattle sound). We replicated the habituation phase of Experiment 1 and demonstrated response recovery to stimulation at a novel tactile site and to an auditory probe. – From Authors' Abstract.

1686. KONEFAL, JOANNE A. (Washington Parish Schools), & FOKES, JOANN. **Linguistic analysis of children's conversational repairs.** Journal of Psycholinguistic Research, 1984, **13,** 1–11.
Conversational repairs used by children in Brown's Stages III and V by 5–6-year-olds were investigated. A linguistic analysis revealed that each group repaired their utterances when not understood but did so using different repair types. – From Authors' Abstract.

1687. KOPP, CLAIRE B. (Univ. of California, Los Angeles), & VAUGHN, BRIAN E. **Sustained attention during exploratory manipulation as a predictor of cognitive competence in preterm infants.** Child Development, 1982, **53,** 174–182.
Preterm infants were assessed with respect to differences in sustained attention when they were 8 months old. Scores on this measure were entered into a multiple regression on performance on 4 test scores at 2 years of age. For males only, the measure of sustained attention contributed to the prediction of later status on the Bayley Mental Scale and on the Gesell schedules but not on a Piagetian-based cognitive test or assessment of receptive language. – From Authors' Abstract.

1688. KUNZINGER, EDWARD L., III (Ohio State Univ.), & WITRYOL, SAM L. **The effects of differential incentives on second-grade rehearsal and free recall.** Journal of Genetic Psychology, 1984, **144,** 19–30.
Second-grade children's overt rehearsal and free recall were examined in 2 independent incentive conditions: constant or differential. Differential-incentive subjects exhibited more mature forms of strategic rehearsal by increasing their level of re-entry processing and their rehearsal set size. – From Authors' Abstract.

1689. KURTZ, BETH E., & BORKOWSKI, JOHN G. (Univ. of Notre Dame). **Children's metacognition: exploring relations among knowledge, process, and motivational variables.** Journal of Experimental Child Psychology, 1984, **37,** 335–354.
First- and third-grade children received task-specific strategy instructions appropriate for 3 memory problems, general metacognitive information about subordinate and superordinate processing, or both strategy and metacognitive training. Posttraining scores on the memory tasks showed that strategy training was highly successful. Metacognitive training appeared to have no effect on the metamemory or strategy scores with 1 exception: metamemory and strategy use on the generalization task were significantly correlated only for children who received both metacognitive and strategy training. – From Authors' Abstract.

1690. LAWSON, ANTON E. (Arizona State Univ.), & BEALER, JONATHAN M. **The acquisition of basic quantitative reasoning skills during adolescence: learning or development?** Journal of Research in Science Teaching, 1984, **21,** 417–423.
Five items requiring use of proportional, probabilistic, and correlational reasoning were administered to students in grades 6, 8, 10, and 12. Successful qualitative reasoning arose as a consequence of the process of equilibration and influenced the selection of course work. Specific instruction may initiate the equilibration process. – From Authors' Abstract.

1691. LAWSON, KATHERINE R. (Albert Einstein Coll. of Medicine), & RUFF, HOLLY A. **Infants' visual following: effects of size and sound.** Developmental Psychology, 1984, **20,** 427–434.
Infants 1 and 2 months old were observed as they visually followed 4 combinations of a big or small doll's head accompanied by loud or soft speech. The infants followed the larger and louder targets, but there was no interaction. Infants followed objects more when they were accompanied by sounds than when they were silent; whether the sound source moved conjointly with the target or not. – From Authors' Abstract.

1692. LEIFER, JANE S. (Univ. of Maryland), & LEWIS, MICHAEL. **Acquisition of conversational response skills by young Down syndrome and nonretarded young children.** American Journal of Mental Deficiency, 1984, **88,** 610–618.

Retarded children showed delayed response performance in comparison with CA-matched nonretarded peers. When matched for language level, however, retarded children demonstrated greater response abilities than did nonretarded children. – From Authors' Abstract.

1693. LESTER, BARRY M. (Children's Hosp. Medical Ctr., 300 Longwood, Boston), & BRAZELTON, T. BERRY. **A lean argument: reply to Scanlon.** Child Development, 1984, **55**, 672–674.

1694. LEVIN, IRIS (Tel-Aviv Univ., Israel); GOLDSTEIN, ROBERTA; & ZELNIKER, TAMAR. **The role of memory and integration in early time concepts.** Journal of Experimental Child Psychology, 1984, **37**, 262–270.
Possible explanations for the greater difficulty children have in comparing durations that differ in beginning times as compared to those that differ in ending times are poor recall of beginnings as compared to endings or difficulty in integrating information from both points and reliance on endings only. Children in grades K-2 were presented with a series of 2 lights in different orders and combinations and were asked to compare order of beginnings and endings and duration of the 2 lights. Results contradicted the memory explanation. – From Authors' Abstract.

1695. LEVITT, MARY J. (Florida International Univ.); ANTONUCCI, TONI C.; & CLARK, M. CHERIE. **Object-person permanence and attachment: another look.** Merrill-Palmer Quarterly, 1984, **30**, 1–10.
Both objects (large toys) and persons (familiar female experimenters) were hidden behind curtains. The results lend some support to Bell's finding that insecurely attached infants perform at a higher level on the object permanence scale than on the person permanence scale. – From Authors' Abstract.

1696. LITOWITZ, BONNIE E. (Erikson Inst., 233 N. Michigan, Two Illinois Ctr., Suite 2200, Chicago), & NOVY, FORREST A. **Expression of the part–whole semantic relation by 3- to 12-year-old children.** Journal of Child Language, 1984, **11**, 159–178.
The present study investigated the expression of the part–whole semantic relation by children 3–12 years of age. While results revealed the part–whole semantic relation expressible by even the youngest children, age-group comparisons indicated that the older children preferred its use more often. – From Authors' Abstract.

1697. LOCKMAN, JEFFREY J. (Tulane Univ.). **The development of detour ability during infancy.** Child Development, 1984, **55**, 482–491.
Infants 8 months old were tested for 4 months on detour problems and Stage 4 and 6 object permanence tasks. Infants made reaching detours before corresponding locomotor ones and generally made detours around opaque barriers before transparent ones. Infants also solved the Stage 4 task before the detour problems but failed to solve the Stage 6 task before testing ended. The difference in reaching and locomotor detour performance was not an artifact of barrier length or the infant's position relative to the barrier. – From Author's Abstract.

1698. LOCKMAN, JEFFREY J. (Tulane Univ.); ASHMEAD, DANIEL H.; & BUSHNELL, EMILY W. **The development of anticipatory hand orientation during infancy.** Journal of Experimental Child Psychology, 1984, **37**, 176–186.
Infants 5 and 9 months old were presented with horizontally and vertically oriented dowels. Nine-month-olds rotated their hands appropriately early in the course of the reach (i.e., before tactual contact with the dowel), whereas 5-month-olds did so mostly after tactual contact. The age difference was not associated with practice or fatigue effects. – From Authors' Abstract.

1699. LUSZCZ, MARY A. (Flinders Univ., Bedford Park, South Australia), & BACHARACH, VERNE R. **The emergence of communicative competence: detection of conversational topics.** Journal of Child Language, 1983, **10**, 623–637.

The use of linguistic and extralinguistic information in identifying conversational topics was studied in 3- and 5-year-old children. Pictures portraying an actor-action-object relation were used to guide conversations. Findings are discussed in terms of different modes of topic definition and their order of acquisition. – From Authors' Abstract.

1700. McKENZIE, B. E. (La Trobe Univ., Bundoora, Victoria, Australia); DAY, R. H.; & IBSEN, E. **Localization of events in space: young infants are not always egocentric.** British Journal of Developmental Psychology, 1984, **2**, 1–9.
Both 6- and 8-month-old infants visually anticipated the whereabouts of the event from the novel direction and displayed persistent visual fixation toward the place where it had previously appeared. For 8-month-olds, successful anticipation was dependent neither on the distinctiveness of landmarks at the event position nor on the angle of their change in direction of facing. – From Authors' Abstract.

1701. MADDEN, JOHN (Pennsylvania State Univ., York); O'HARA, JOHN; & LEVENSTEIN, PHYLLIS. **Home again: effects of the Mother–Child Home Program on mother and child.** Child Development, 1984, **55**, 636–647.
Large program effects were found on maternal interaction styles in videotaped observations. Small IQ and program-specific effects were found for children in contrast to much larger IQ effects found in earlier research. IQ effects did not appear to have been mediated by changes in maternal behavior. Three years postprogram, there were no detectable effects in achievement or IQ tests or in first-grade teachers' ratings of school adjustment and performance, but IQ and achievement scores were near national norms. – From Authors' Abstract.

1702. MAJERES, RAYMOND L. (Western Illinois Univ.), & FOX, ROBERT. **Children's spontaneous use of real-world information in problem solving.** Journal of Genetic Psychology, 1984, **144**, 89–97.
Pictures of the objects varying in relative size were presented. A marked improvement in performance between the fifth and sixth years was seen. – From Authors' Abstract.

1703. MANDES, EVANS (George Mason Univ.), & STRAUSS, JOYCE. **A developmental study of the relationship between handedness and eyedness as applied to disappearing visual targets.** Journal of Psychology, 1984, **117**, 105–110.
First graders and college students viewed a luminous target of parallel lines subtending a visual angle of 1130' and reported whether a stimulus disappeared on either side of fixation or all at once. Both groups, regardless of handedness and eye dominance, had stronger right-field stability, therefore, more left-field fragmentation. – From Authors' Abstract.

1704. MAN-SHU, ZHU (East China Normal Univ., Shanghai, China), & JING-ZHE, WU. **Chinese children's comprehension and production of passive voice and double negative sentences.** International Journal of Behavioral Development, 1984, **7**, 67–76.
It is argued that the acquisition of syntactic structures is determined by levels of cognitive ability. A comparison of deaf and hearing subjects reveals that whilst the former are delayed in the acquisition of these syntactic structures, some do eventually succeed in mastering them. – From Authors' Abstract.

1705. MARSHALL, SANDRA P. (Univ. of California, Santa Barbara). **Sex differences in children's mathematics achievement: solving computations and story problems.** Journal of Educational Psychology, 1984, **76**, 194–204.
Girls are more likely than boys to solve computations successfully, whereas boys are more likely than girls to be successful with story problems. These conclusions are based on the responses of approximately 300,000 sixth-grade children in California who were administered the Survey of Basic Skills, Grade 6. – From Author's Abstract.

1706. MARX, MELVIN H. (Univ. of Missouri, Columbia). **Enhancement of frequency judgments by response choice.** Bulletin of the Psychonomic Society, 1984, **22**, 26–28.

Fifth- and sixth-grade students selected the more positive word when a negative-word foil was present, and they also copied equally positive words when the words were presented singly. Subjects were then given a forced-choice frequency-judgment test. Students selected more of the words that had been paired with the negative foils, although these words were actually shown no more often than singly presented words. These results suggest a strength factor in the interpretation of frequency processing. – Adapted from Author's Abstract.

1707. MENDELBERG, HAVA E. (2040 W. Wisconsin Ave., Suite 515, Milwaukee). **Split and continuity in language use of Mexican-American adolescents of migrant origin.** Adolescence, 1984, **19,** 171–182.
The study focuses on language use of Mexican-American adolescents whose families came out of the migrant stream, shifting from a rural to an urban-industrial society. The analysis of the data reveals distinctive language patterns. – From Author's Abstract.

1708. MERINO, BARBARA (Univ. of California, Davis). **Language loss in bilingual Chicano children.** Journal of Applied Developmental Psychology, 1983, **4,** 277–294.
Children in grades K-4 were administered the Bilingual Language Acquisition Scale. In the fourth grade, Spanish performance dropped sharply, but not comprehension. Of the original subjects, 32 were retested 2 years later using the same instruments. While performance in English continued to improve, performance in Spanish production deteriorated to a significant degree. Loss was worst among children who tended to use both English and Spanish with the same speaker. – From Author's Abstract.

1709. MERVIS, CAROLYN B. (Univ. of Illinois, Urbana-Champaign), & CRISAFI, MARIA A. **Order of acquisition of subordinate-, basic-, and superordinate-level categories.** Child Development, 1982, **53,** 258–266.
Children ages 2–6, 4, and 5–6 were asked to indicate which of 2 nonsense stimuli was the same kind of thing as a standard for sets at each hierarchical level. Categorization ability was acquired in the following order: basic, superordinate, subordinate. The greater the differentiation of categories at a given hierarchical level, the earlier categorization at that level was acquired. Adult subjects made pairwise similarity judgments for stimuli used in the first experiment or for members of 2 natural-category hierarchies. The greater the differentiation of categories at a given hierarchical level, the earlier categorization at that level was acquired. – From Authors' Abstract.

1710. MERVIS, CAROLYN B. (Univ. of Illinois, Urbana-Champaign), & MERVIS, CYNTHIA A. **Leopards are kitty-cats: object labeling by mothers for their thirteen-month-olds.** Child Development, 1982, **53,** 267–273.
Mother–13-month-old dyads were observed as they played with a specially chosen set of toys. Mothers named objects for their 13-month-olds at the child-basic level rather than the adult-basic level. – From Authors' Abstract.

1711. MILICH, RICHARD (Univ. of Iowa). **Cross-sectional and longitudinal observations of activity level and sustained attention in a normative sample.** Journal of Abnormal Child Psychology, 1984, **12,** 261–276.
Elementary school boys were observed approximately 2 years apart during a free-play period and a structured restricted academic period. Both gross and fine motor activity decreased with increasing age, while the time spent on task increased. There appeared to be a dramatic increase in the boys' ability to focus attention at around age 11. – From Author's Abstract.

1712. MILLER, JON F. (Univ. of Wisconsin, Madison), & CHAPMAN, ROBIN S. **Disorders of communication: investigating the development of language of mentally retarded children.** American Journal of Mental Deficiency, 1984, **88,** 536–545.
Methodology available to investigating language comprehension and production will allow large-scale in-depth studies of the lexical, semantic, syntactic, and pragmatic aspects of the language performance of a variety of retarded populations. – From Authors' Abstract.

1713. MILLER, LEON K. (Univ. of Illinois, Chicago). **Sources of visual field interference in children and adults.** Journal of Experimental Child Psychology, 1984, **37,** 141–157.
Subjects 8, 11, and 20 years were asked to identify briefly presented words accompanied by either words or letter strings in the same or opposite hemifield. There were 2 sources of visual field interference, 1 relating to the presence of alphanumeric information elsewhere in the visual field and the second concerning the meaningfulness (lexical identity) of that information. The former showed a decrease in importance with age, and the latter an increase. – From Author's Abstract.

1714. MISRA, GIRISHWAR (Bhopal Univ., India), & SHUKLA, ARADHANA. **Recognition of pictorial material as a function of experiential deprivation and age.** International Journal of Behavioral Development, 1984, **7,** 95–103.
The procedure was a factorial design with 4 age levels (4–8 years) and 2 levels of deprivation. Recognition memory increased with age, and experiential deprivation interfered with the growth of recognition capacity in children. – Adapted from Authors' Abstract.

1715. MORAN, JAMES D., III (Virginia Polytechnic Inst.); SAWYERS, JANET K.; FU, VICTORIA R.; & MILGRAM, ROBERTA M. **Predicting imaginative play in preschool children.** Gifted Child Quarterly, 1984, **28,** 92–94.
Fantasy predisposition and imaginative play are correlated. – Ed.

1716. MORRA, SERGIO (Univ. of Genova, Italy). **Classification in children: two developmental information-processing models.** International Journal of Behavioral Development, 1984, **7,** 1–20.
Predictions drawn from Keating and Bobbitt's model are falsified—most likely because of the inadequacy of models based on subtractive analysis of reaction times. Predictions from Pascual-Leone's theory are almost wholly confirmed. – From Author's Abstract.

1717. MORRA PELLEGRINO, M. L.; SCOPESI, A.; & D'ANIELLO, P. (Univ. di Genova, Italy). **Conversation of two year old children. Communicative intentions and dialogue.** Età Evolutiva, 1984, **17,** 52–65.
Children use different verbal styles when they interact with an adult or with peers. In all groups, children produce dialogic sequences when playing by themselves without an adult. – From Authors' Abstract.

1718. MORRONGIELLO, BARBARA A. (Univ. of Toronto, Erindale, Mississauga, Ontario, Canada). **Auditory temporal pattern perception in 6- and 12-month-old infants.** Developmental Psychology, 1984, **20,** 441–448.
A go/no-go conditioned head-turn paradigm was used to examine 6- and 12-month-olds' abilities to discriminate changes in temporal grouping and absolute and relative timing information. Six-month-olds performed absolute timing discriminations but not changes in relative timing information. Twelve-month-olds performed both types of temporal grouping discriminations. – From Author's Abstract.

1719. MORRONGIELLO, BARBARA A. (Univ. of Massachusetts, Amherst); KULIG, JOHN W.; & CLIFTON, RACHEL K. **Developmental changes in auditory temporal perception.** Child Development, 1984, **55,** 461–471.
Infants, preschoolers, and adults responded to the precedence effect produced by presenting the same sound through 2 loudspeakers with the input to 1 loudspeaker delayed relative to the other. Thresholds for the precedence effect were defined as the delay interval below which listeners responded only to the leading loudspeaker and above which they responded to both loudspeakers. For clicks, preschoolers' and adults' thresholds were around 12 msec, while 6-month-olds stopped responding to the delayed sound around 25 msec. A similar developmental difference in threshold was expressed between preschoolers and adults for a more complex sound. – From Authors' Abstract.

1720. MORRONGIELLO, BARBARA A. (Univ. of Toronto, Erindale, Mississauga, Ontario, Canada); ROBSON, RICK C.; BEST, CATHERINE T.; & CLIFTON, RACHEL K. **Trading relations in the perception of speech by 5-year-old children.** Journal of Experimental Child Psychology, 1984, **37**, 231–250.
Five-year-old children were tested for perceptual trading relations between a temporal cue (silence duration) and a spectral cue (F_1 onset frequency) for the "say–stay" distinction. Children showed a smaller trading relation than has been found with adults. They did not differ from adults in their perception of an "ay–day" continuum formed by varying F_1 onset frequency only. – From Authors' Abstract.

1721. MORSE, PHILIP A. (Univ. of Wisconsin, Madison); EILERS, REBECCA E.; & GAVIN, WILLIAM J. **The perception of the sound of silence in early infancy.** Child Development, 1982, **53**, 189–195.
When brief periods of silence are inserted between the /s/ and /lit/ portions of the English word "slit" (sllt), adult listeners typically hear the word as "split." Infants were tested using a conditioned headturning paradigm. Three sets of stimuli were employed: /sllt/, /sllt/ + silence, and /spllt/, containing 0, 173, and 90 msec, respectively, of silence duration following the /s/ portion of the stimulus. Infants reliably discriminated /sllt/ + silence from the /sllt/ stimuli but not from the /spllt/ stimuli. – From Authors' Abstract.

1722. MUNDY, PETER; SEIBERT, JEFFREY M. (Univ. of Miami); & HOGAN, ANNE E. **Relationship between sensorimotor and early communication abilities in developmentally delayed children.** Merrill-Palmer Quarterly, 1984, **30**, 33–48.
Previous research has demonstrated that a specific profile of correlations or a local homology is characteristic of the development of sensorimotor and early communication skills in 9–13-month-old normal children. These data support the developmental generality of the local homology and show that the profile of correlations among sensorimotor and early communication abilities differed across MA groups. – From Authors' Abstract.

1723. MURAI, NORIO (Tohoku Univ., Kawauchi, Sendai 980, Japan), & NIHEI, YOSHIAKI. **Searching behavior for disappeared face in 2- and 3-month-old infants: an exploratory investigation applying the method of microanalysis.** Tohoku Psychologica Folia, 1983, **42**, 114–118.
This study describes a paradigm to elicit searching behavior and the method of microanalysis using a VTR system and a microcomputer. The analyses of the behavior of 2 female infants demonstrated the effectiveness of the present approach. – From Authors' Abstract.

1724. MUTH, K. DENISE (Kennesaw Coll.). **Solving arithmetic word problems: role of reading and computational skills.** Journal of Educational Psychology, 1984, **76**, 205–210.
Sixth graders were asked to solve problems modeled after those used by the National Assessment of Educational Progress. A computational demand was imposed by adding extraneous information, whereas a reading demand was imposed by increasing the syntactic complexity. Children's computational ability and reading ability together accounted for 54% of the variance in solution accuracy: 8% and 14%, respectively, of this variance was unique, whereas 32% was common to the abilities. Presence of extraneous information reduced accuracy. Use of complex syntax had no effect. – From Author's Abstract.

1725. NASH, CHRIS (O.I.S.E. Northeastern Ctr., Canada). **Identity and equivalence conservation: longitudinal field studies in sequence and significance.** British Journal of Educational Psychology, 1984, **54**, 1–7.
Observations of over 5,000 4–5-year-old children over 2 years found 1,006 pupils who conserved identity but not equivalence up to 8 months later; 639 pupils conserved both identity and equivalence. Follow-up studies showed no relationship between conservation abilities in kindergarten and mathematical skills in grade 1. Performance in grade 6 correlated with conservation of equivalence by the end of kindergarten. – From Author's Abstract.

1726. NEWMAN, RICHARD S. (SUNY, Stony Brook). **Children's numerical skill and judgments of confidence in estimation.** Journal of Experimental Child Psychology, 1984, **37**, 107–123.
Tenth graders were categorized according to level of numerical fluency. They then made estimates of large numbers of dots and rated how confident they were on each trial. Skillful children made judgments that corresponded with actual task difficulty. – From Author's Abstract.

1727. NIPPOLD, MARILYN A. (Univ. of Oregon); LEONARD, LAURENCE B.; & KAIL, ROBERT. **Syntactic and conceptual factors in children's understanding of metaphors.** Journal of Speech and Hearing Research, 1984, **27**, 197–205.
Nine-year-olds demonstrated metaphoric understanding superior to that of 7-year-olds, despite the fact that children of both ages were familiar with the underlying semantic features of the metaphors and understood all key words at a literal level. – From Authors' Abstract.

1728. OAKHILL, JANE (Univ. of Sussex, England). **Inferential and memory skills in children's comprehension of stories.** British Journal of Educational Psychology, 1984, **54**, 31–39.
Children 7–8 read 4 short stories and were asked questions after each. Skilled readers were better than less skilled readers at answering both direct and indirect questions immediately afterward on the basis of memory. When the text was available, the less skilled group remained poorer at answering only those questions that required an inference. – From Author's Abstract.

1729. O'HARE, D. (Univ. of Otago, Dunedin, New Zealand), & COOK, DEBORAH. **Children's sensitivity to different modes of colour use in art.** British Journal of Educational Psychology, 1983, **53**, 267–277.
Six groups of children ages 5–11 were tested for their ability to execute appropriate color use in completions to a partially drawn scene. First-year first-school children displayed little capacity to produce consistent differences. Third-year first-school children perceived differences, but rarely produced them. Third-year middle-school children produced differences in styles of color use. – From Authors' Abstract.

1730. O'HARE, MICHAEL, & HOGAN, JOHN D. (St. John's Univ.). **Learning and generalization of Piagetian tasks by mentally retarded students.** Perceptual and Motor Skills, 1983, **57**, 309–310.
Mentally retarded 7–19-year-olds successfully taught to conserve number and substance resisted attempts at extinction but were unable to generalize. – Adapted from Authors' Abstract.

1731. OLLENDICK, THOMAS H. (Virginia Polytechnic Inst. & State Univ.), & SHAPIRO, EDWARD S. **An examination of vicarious reinforcement processes in children.** Journal of Experimental Child Psychology, 1984, **37**, 78–91.
The effects on 1 child of observing another same-sex child receive direct reinforcement were explored across 3 age levels. Although children who observed other children receive direct social reinforcement initially increased performance, their performance soon decreased and was characterized by verbal and nonverbal responses which appeared to interfere with task performance. – From Authors' Abstract.

1732. OLSEN-FULERO, LYNDA (Antioch Coll.), & CONFORTI, JILL. **Child responsiveness to mother questions of varying type and presentation.** Journal of Child Language, 1983, **10**, 495–520.
Variables as motivation, constraint, difficulty, and function may affect the child's responsiveness to mother questions. Results suggest that functionally defined question types are differentiable not only by their relative power to elicit a response from the child, but also by the manner in which they are presented. – From Authors' Abstract.

1733. OVIATT, SHARON L. (Oregon State Univ.). **Inferring what words mean: early development in infants' comprehension of common object names.** Child Development, 1982, **53,** 274–277.
Infants 12–20 months of age were taught the name of a live animal that they had not known previously. Those who reliably comprehended the name were given paired-comparison tests in which a novel target and distractor animal were viewed in each of 3 representational modes: photographic, pictorial, and 3-dimensional models. Analyses on gaze and gestural measures both demonstrated a substantial increase in preference for the target-animal forms, specifically in response to target questioning, between 15 and 18 months of age. Performance at all ages was best with photographs. – From Author's Abstract.

1734. PAPPAS, CHRISTINE C. (Univ. of Oregon). **The relationship between language development and brain development.** Journal of Children in Contemporary Society, 1983, **16,** 133–169.
The review covers morphological findings, the commissurotomy studies, dichotic listening and visual half-field studies, EEG and cerebral blood flow studies, as well as topics on the development of lateralization and brain growth. – From Author's Abstract.

1735. PARNELL, MARTHA M. (Univ. of Missouri, Columbia); PATTERSON, SHIRLEY S.; & HARDING, MARCIA A. **Answers to wh-questions: a developmental study.** Journal of Speech and Hearing Research, 1984, **27,** 297–305.
The hierarchies of wh-question forms based on degree of difficulty were similar to those described in previous investigations. An interaction between referential conditions and wh-form was found to influence the relative complexity of the stimulus questions. – From Authors' Abstract.

1736. PEARLMAN, CHARLES (AT&T Communications, Room 06–4A220, Bedminster, NJ). **The effects of level of effectance motivation, IQ, and a penalty/reward contingency on the choice of problem difficulty.** Child Development, 1984, **55,** 537–542.
The effectance motivation of sixth graders was assessed using 2 instruments completed by teachers. Students chose hard or easy problems after being informed of contingencies (plus or minus 3 points on their next test) based on correctness of solution. Students with higher effectance were more likely to choose hard problems than those with lower effectance. With no contingency, IQ was the best predictor of problem choice. Under the contingency, IQ was not significant. – From Author's Abstract.

1737. PEASE, DALE G. (Iowa State Univ.), & RUPNOW, ALLAN A. **Effects of varying force production in practice schedules of children learning a discrete motor task.** Perceptual and Motor Skills, 1983, **57,** 275–282.
Variability in practice did not affect transfer or retention of a discrete motor task for 9- and 11-year-old children when only the overall force parameter varied. – Adapted from the Article.

1738. POSNER, JILL K. (CUNY, Graduate Ctr.). **The development of mathematical knowledge in two West African societies.** Child Development, 1982, **53,** 200–208.
Subjects were children from an agricultural tribe (Baoule) and a merchant society (Dioula). Experimental tasks covered several systems of mathematical thought from the perception of relative quantity and the identification of static equivalence to the ability to solve practical addition problems. By middle childhood all subjects performed equally well on this task. On the latter 2 tasks, which required the activation of other than perceptual strategies, schooling improved performance significantly among Baoule subjects, while there were no reliable differences between schooled and unschooled Dioulas. – From Author's Abstract.

1739. POTTER, ROBERT B. (Univ. of London, England), & WILSON, MARK G. **Age differences in the content and style of cognitive maps of Barbadian schoolchildren.** Perceptual and Motor Skills, 1983, **57,** 332.

Results suggest a contrast in the style and complexity of the cognitive maps of concrete and formal operational children and support Hart and Moore's model of macrospatial cognitive development. – Adapted from the Article.

1740. PRATT, CHRIS (Univ. of Western Australia, Nedlands, Western Australia); TUNMER, WILLIAM E.; & BOWEY, JUDITH A. **Children's capacity to correct grammatical violations in sentences.** Journal of Child Language, 1984, **11,** 129–141.
Children 5 1/2–6 1/2 years old were presented with ungrammatical sentences resulting from either word-order changes or morpheme deletions. The results indicated that both groups of children performed well when presented with ungrammatical sentences containing morpheme deletions. – From Authors' Abstract.

1741. PRESSON, CLARK C. (Arizona State Univ.). **The development of map-reading skills.** Child Development, 1982, **53,** 196–199.
Maps were read either inside or outside the space shown on the map, were either aligned with the space or rotated 90 or 180, and had only 1 landmark to establish the correspondence to the space. The proximity of the target to the landmark (near vs. far) and the type of landmark (movable vs. fixed) were varied. Subjects in grades K and 2 were able to extract information from the maps to guide search. When the maps were rotated, the younger subjects made "egocentric" errors on the inside reading trials but not on the outside trials. At both grades, most errors preserved the near/far relation to the landmark. – From Author's Abstract.

1742. PRICE, GARY GLEN (Univ. of Wisconsin, Madison). **Mnemonic support and curriculum selection in teaching by mothers: a conjoint effect.** Child Development, 1984, **55,** 659–668.
It was predicted that the extent to which mothers encourage child-generated verbal responses that require retrieval of terms from long-term memory would be associated with children's knowledge of lowercase letters only if mothers had been making efforts to teach lowercase letters. The findings, based on mothers and their 3–4-year-olds, are in strong agreement with the prediction. – From Author's Abstract.

1743. QUAY, HERBERT C. (Univ. of Miami). **The opinions of mental health facility administrators on the effects of children's rights and deinstitutionalization.** Journal of Early Adolescence, 1984, **4,** 11–23.
There was a sufficient degree of agreement by respondents about adverse consequences to suggest that empirical research into the effects of both movements is clearly in order. – From Author's Abstract.

1744. REID, BARBARA V. (Univ. of North Carolina, Chapel Hill). **An anthropological reinterpretation of Kohlberg's stages of moral development.** Human Development, 1984, **27,** 57–64.
Kohlberg's stages of moral development may be better understood within the grid/group theory advanced by Douglas than within the cognitive-developmental framework. A reinterpretation is proposed which specifies 2 factors in social relationships, grid and group, which influence moral reasoning and behavior. – From Author's Abstract.

1745. REIFEL, STUART (Univ. of Texas, Austin), & GREENFIELD, PATRICIA MARKS. **Part-whole relations: some structural features of children's representational block play.** Child Care Quarterly, 1983, **12,** 144–151.
Results show how block play becomes more complex with respect to part-whole relationships with the child's increasing age. Older children include a greater number of constituent parts in their constructions. – From Authors' Abstract.

1746. ROSSER, ROSEMARY A. (Univ. of Arizona); MAZZEO, JOHN; & HORAN, PATRICIA F. **Reconceptualizing perceptual development: the identification of some dimensions of spatial competence in young children.** Contemporary Educational Psychology, 1984, **9,** 135–145.

Children were presented with geometric displays depicting a variety of geometric relations. Subjects were required to either match or recall the displays in both a reconstruction and a recognition task format, thereby responding across different types of action demands. The results supported predictions. – From Authors' Abstract.

1747. ROTH, FROMA P. (Univ. of Maryland). **Accelerating language learning in young children.** Journal of Child Language, 1984, **11**, 89–107.
Four types of relative clause sentences were trained using a toy-manipulation task. Improvement was found in the performance of subjects in the experimental conditions. – From Author's Abstract.

1748. RUDDY, MARGARET G., & BORNSTEIN, MARC H. (New York Univ.). **Cognitive correlates of infant attention and maternal stimulation over the first year of life.** Child Development, 1982, **53**, 183–188.
Babies who showed more habituation and faster habituation at 4 months scored higher on the Bayley Scales and had larger speaking vocabularies at 12 months. Frequent maternal stimulation at 4 months (encouraging babies' attention to objects) correlated with the size of speaking vocabulary at 12 months; a cross-lagged panel correlation suggested that maternal stimulation positively influenced infants' cognitive development. – From Authors' Abstract.

1749. SAMUEL, J., & BRYANT, P. (Univ. of Oxford, England). **Asking only one question in the conversation experiment.** Journal of Child Psychology and Psychiatry, 1984, **25**, 315–318.
Rose and Blank have shown that 6-year-olds do a great deal better in a conservation of number task if they are only asked to make a comparison after the transformation rather than both before and after seeing the quantity transformed. This result applies as well to other materials (mass and volume) and to a wide age range (5–8 years). – From Authors' Abstract.

1750. SANDHAM, LINDA J., & HICKS, ROBERT A. (Univ. of Nebraska). **A factor-analytic study of items to measure forethought development in children and adolescents.** Bulletin of the Psychonomic Society, 1984, **22**, 109–112.
Factor analysis resulted in a 41-item scale to measure the development of forethought. Three factors of forethought comprehension were remote-future time comprehension, real-time consequences, and knowledge of future events. – Adapted from Authors' Abstract.

1751. SARRIS, VIKTOR (J. W. Goethe Univ., Frankfurt, Germany). **On perceptual learning in geometric-optical illusions.** Studia Psychologica, 1984, **26**, 29–38.
The initial amount of Delboef illusion was largest for the youngest (7 years), medium for the young (11 years), and smallest for the eldest (18 years) participants. – From the Article.

1752. SCANLON, JOHN W. (Columbia Hosp. for Women, 2425 L St. N.W., Washington). **To ponder ponderal's length: a question to Lester et al.** Child Development, 1984, **55**, 669–671.

1753. SCHNUR, ELIZABETH (Educational Testing Service, Princeton), & SHATZ, MARILYN. **The role of maternal gesturing in conversations with one-year-olds.** Journal of Child Language, 1984, **11**, 29–41.
We conclude that maternal gestures have more of a role in maintaining attention and the flow of interaction for young children than they do in providing specific cues to the grammar the child is acquiring. – From Authors' Abstract.

1754. SCHOLNICK, ELLIN K. (Univ. of Maryland), & WING, CLARA S. **Evaluating presuppositions and propositions.** Journal of Child Language, 1983, **10**, 639–660.
The relationship between pragmatic knowledge and reasoning was explored by asking males and females at ages 12, 15, and adult to solve written syllogisms containing the 4 conjunctions and evaluate single sentences for their pragmatic content. Among the results, it was found that

the relation between comprehension of pragmatic uncertainty and detection of uncertain conclusions in reasoning increased with age. – Adapted from Authors' Abstract.

1755. SCHOLNICK, ELLIN KOFSKY (Univ. of Maryland). **Are stages "fuzzy sets"?** The Genetic Epistemologist, 1984, **12,** 1–5.

1756. SCHWARTZ, SYBIL (McGill–Montreal Children's Hosp. Learning Ctr., 3640 de la Montagne, Montreal, Quebec, Canada). **Spelling disability: a developmental linguistic analysis of pattern abstraction.** Applied Psycholinguistics, 1983, **4,** 303–316.
Good, poor, and learning-disabled spellers 8–10 years old were given 3 tests. The LD spellers showed little ability to abstract patterns until age 10. The performance of the LD spellers was significantly below that of both the good and poor spellers and was quite distinct from the poor spellers. Error analyses suggest that the LD spellers perform like younger, normal children. – From Authors' Abstract.

1757. SHARPLEY, CHRISTOPHER F. (Monash Univ., Clayton, Victoria, Australia). **Implicit rewards as reinforcers and extinguishers.** Journal of Experimental Child Psychology, 1984, **37,** 31–40.
Fourth-grade children copied the letters of the alphabet. Data indicated the presence of reinforcement effects when implicit rewards were presented after baseline and extinction effects when presented after direct reward conditions. – From Author's Abstract.

1758. SHIPLEY, ELIZABETH F. (Univ. of Pennsylvania); KUHN, IVY F.; & MADDEN, E. COLBY. **Mothers' use of superordinate category terms.** Journal of Child Language, 1983, **10,** 571–588.
Mothers' speech in an identification task was examined for 10 mother-child pairs. The children were 2–5 years old; stimuli were animals, clothes, and furniture. Competencies required to learn the correct referent for category terms and differences among superordinate categories are discussed. – From Authors' Abstract.

1759. SHORT, ELIZABETH JANE (Frank Porter Graham Child Development Ctr., Univ. of North Carolina, Chapel Hill), & RYAN, ELLEN BOUCHARD. **Metacognitive differences between skilled and less skilled readers: remediating deficits through story grammar and attribution training.** Journal of Educational Psychology, 1984, **76,** 225–235.
A metacognitive intervention program had 2 components: story grammar training, to increase comprehension monitoring, and attribution training, to increase awareness of effort. Strategy training produced dramatic gains in comprehension. – From Authors' Abstract.

1760. SHUTE, GEORGE E. (Southern Illinois Univ.). **The assessment of formal-operational reasoning: a caution.** The Genetic Epistemologist, 1984, **12,** 6–7.

1761. SIMONTON, DEAN KEITH (Univ. of California, Davis). **Creative productivity and age: a mathematical model based on a two-step cognitive process.** Developmental Review, 1983, **3,** 77–111.
The relation between age and productivity can be explained by hypothesizing a simple 2-step model of the creative process. Such a hypothesis permits a delayed single-peak function to result from an underlying process of constantly decelerating decay. The derived equation describes creative productivity as a function of individual age, and is consistent with empirical data on the relation between age and achievement. – From Author's Abstract.

1762. SLACKMAN, ELIZABETH (CUNY, Graduate Ctr.), & NELSON, KATHERINE. **Acquisition of an unfamiliar script in story form by young children.** Child Development, 1984, **55,** 329–340.
Preschool and first and third graders heard similar versions of an unfamiliar scriptlike story followed by a novel story and were tested for immediate and delayed recall. Children more often confused parts of the similar stories with each other than with the novel story, indicating that

the similar versions were perceived as belonging to a separate category or script. – From Authors' Abstract.

1763. SMIRNI, PIETRO; VILLARDITA, CLAUDIO (Univ. of Catania, Italy); & ZAPPALA, GIUSEPPE. **Spatial memory span in adolescents: cultural and sex differences.** Perceptual and Motor Skills, 1983, **57,** 175–178.
Performance on the Corsi Block Tapping Test did not differ by sex or sociocultural background for urban and rural Sicilian adolescents. – Adapted from Authors' Abstract.

1764. SMITH, LINDA B. (Indiana Univ.). **Young children's understanding of attributes and dimensions: a comparison of conceptual and linguistic measures.** Child Development, 1984, **55,** 363–380.
Attribute knowledge is the knowledge that a particular attribute can be instantiated in a variety of distinct objects. Dimension knowledge is the knowledge that there are qualitatively distinct kinds of attributes. Children 2–4 years showed strong attribute knowledge on the conceptual measure. However, 2-year-olds did not appear to differentiate attributes into their dimensional kinds. The acquisition of some attribute and dimension labels appears to follow closely the trend in conceptual development, whereas the acquisition of size-attribute labels lags severely behind the attainment of the basic concepts. – From Author's Abstract.

1765. SMITH, LINDA B. (Indiana Univ.), & RIZZO, THOMAS A. **Children's understanding of the referential properties of collective and class nouns.** Child Development, 1982, **53,** 245–257.
Children understand the hierarchical structure of class nouns and thus know that a superordinate class noun that correctly labels a set also correctly labels any included subset. Children also understand the part-whole structure underlying collective nouns and thus know that a collective noun that labels some set may not label a portion of that set. Children misinterpret class nouns as referring to included subclasses because they know class nouns refer to included subclasses. Children do not misinterpret collective nouns because they know collective nouns refer to entire sets. – From Authors' Abstract.

1766. SNAREY, JOHN R. (Harvard Graduate School of Education). **The social and moral development of kibbutz founders and sabras.** Moral Education Forum, 1983, **8,** 2–25.
The social-moral development of 60 adult kibbutz founders and 92 kibbutz adolescents was studied from the theoretical perspective of Kohlberg. The founders exhibited unusually mature moral reasoning. Stages of development were not significantly related to sex, decision to leave the kibbutz, or work complexity. Kibbutz adolescents used an unusually high percentage of the more mature substage B, and their global moral stages were also unusually high. There were no significant sex differences. – Adapted from the Article.

1767. SNOW, CATHERINE E. (Harvard Graduate School of Education), & GOLDFIELD, BEVERLY A. **Turn the page please: situation-specific language acquisition.** Journal of Child Language, 1983, **10,** 551–569.
The present paper investigates a strategy for language acquisition adopted by 1 child, and the usefulness of book reading in supporting that strategy. – From Authors' Abstract.

1768. SONNENSCHEIN, SUSAN (Univ. of Maryland, Baltimore County). **The effects of redundant communications on listeners: why different types may have different effects.** Journal of Psycholinguistic Research, 1984, **13,** 147–166.
The research compared performance by first and fifth graders in differentiating redundancy and in structured redundancy listening tasks. Results were discussed in terms of a processing capacity model. – Adapted from Author's Abstract.

1769. SOPHIAN, CATHERINE (Carnegie–Mellon Univ.), & HUBER, ALICE. **Early developments in children's causal judgments.** Child Development, 1984, **55,** 512–526.

Children 3 and 5 years old were asked to judge which of 2 stimuli caused an observed event. Using problems based on the movements of a toy train, only 5-year-olds' judgments were in accord with the principle of priority, according to which causes must precede their effects in time. For conflicts between temporal priority and specific trained knowledge, both age groups showed some use of temporal priority, but the 5-year-olds showed a better appreciation of its necessary force. – From Authors' Abstract.

1770. STERNBERG, ROBERT J. (Yale Univ.). **The case of the disappearing disagreements: a reply to Yussen.** Developmental Review, 1984, **4**, 145–147.

1771. STERNBERG, ROBERT J. (Yale Univ.). **A theory of knowledge acquisition in the development of verbal concepts.** Developmental Review, 1984, **4**, 113–138.
The theory is divided into 3 subtheories. The first specifies the information processes asserted to be central to the development of verbal concepts. The second subtheory specifies the informational cues upon which these processes operate. The third subtheory specifies variables that moderate the use of the proposed processes on the proposed cues. – From Author's Abstract.

1772. STERNBERG, ROBERT J. (Yale Univ.), & DOWNING, CATHRYN J. **The development of higher-order reasoning in adolescence.** Child Development, 1982, **53**, 209–221.
The hypothesis was tested that further strategy development in analogical reasoning might occur within (or beyond) the period of formal operations, but that this development might be discernible only with analogical relations of at least the third order. Students in grades 8 and 11 and in college were tested in their ability to evaluate the goodness of a set of third-order analogies. The proposed model provided a good fit to the evaluation data at all 3 grade levels. – From Authors' Abstract.

1773. STINE, ELIZABETH LOTZ, & BOHANNON, JOHN NEIL, II (Georgia Inst. of Technology). **Imitations, interactions, and language acquisitions.** Journal of Child Language, 1983, **10**, 589–603.
Two hypotheses have been offered that focus on either the progressive nature of imitation to aid in the language-acquisition process or the social, conversational role played by imitation in discourse. Evidence is presented for both roles of imitation. – From Authors' Abstract.

1774. SULLIVAN, JOSEPH W. (Univ. of Colorado School of Medicine), & HOROWITZ, FRANCES DEGEN. **The effects of intonation on infant attention: the role of the rising intonation contour.** Journal of Child Language, 1983, **10**, 521–534.
The study investigated 2-month-old infant preferential attention to a feature found to be characteristic of mothers' speech to their infants. Data revealed that the infants attended more to the rising, naturally produced intonation contour. – From Authors' Abstract.

1775. TONER, IGNATIUS J. (Univ. of North Carolina, Charlotte), & RITCHIE, FIONA K. **American-Sign-Language statements and delay of gratification in hearing-impaired and nonhandicapped children.** Journal of General Psychology, 1984, **110**, 155–164.
The studies demonstrate that caution must be used in predicting the reaction of hearing-handicapped children to techniques which have been shown to facilitate or impair self-control in nonhandicapped children. – From the Article.

1776. TOPPINO, THOMAS C. (Villanova Univ.), & DIGEORGE, WILLIAM. **The spacing effect in free recall emerges with development.** Memory and Cognition, 1984, **12**, 118–122.
Preschoolers recalled massed and spaced repetitions equally well in a free-recall task, while first-graders recalled spaced better than massed repetitions. – Adapted from Authors' Abstract.

1777. ULVUND, STEIN ERIK (Univ. of Oslo, Norway). **Predictive validity of assessments of early cognitive competence in light of some current issues in developmental psychology.** Human Development, 1984, **27**, 76–83.

The issues are continuity-discontinuity in the development of early cognitive-competence, the problem of intellectual heterogeneity, and individual-environment transactions. – From Author's Abstract.

1778. VADHAN, VIMLA (CUNY, Kingsborough Community Coll.). **Induction of conservation by discrimination training.** Journal of Psychology, 1984, **116,** 273–277.
Nonconservers were trained on either length or number discrimination or both. A certain kind of discrimination training helped some nonconservers to conserve on the posttests of conservation. – From Author's Abstract.

1779. VANDEWIELE, MICHEL (Stijdhoflaan, 76, 2600, Berchem, Belgium). **How Senegalese adolescents perceive religious pluralism.** Perceptual and Motor Skills, 1983, **57,** 422.
Senegalese adolescents rejected religious pluralism, but this rejection did not result in religious intolerance. – Adapted from the Article.

1780. VAN OEFFELEN, MICHIEL P. (Univ. of Nijmegen, Netherlands), & VOS, PETER G. **The young child's processing of dot patterns: a chronometric and eye movement analysis.** International Journal of Behavioral Development, 1984, **7,** 53–66.
Records of eye movements under the conditions of numbers of dots larger than 5 were found to reflect mixed strategies and not elementary 1-by-1 counting procedures. – From Authors' Abstract.

1781. VAN ROSSUM, E. J. (Univ. of Tilburg, Netherlands), & SCHENK, SIMONE M. **The relationship between learning conception, study strategy and learning outcome.** British Journal of Educational Psychology, 1984, **73–83,** 1984.
The essential point of the present study is that human learning should be studied from a second-order perspective. A learning outcome of relatively high quality must be associated with deep-level approach and a constructive learning conception. – From Authors' Abstract.

1782. WEINSTEIN, ELIN S. (186–27 Cambridge, Jamaica Estates, NY). **Sex differences in early Bender-Gestalt Test performance.** Perceptual and Motor Skills, 1983, **57,** 301–302.
Kindergarten boys showed more difficulty with accurate copying of individual features of designs. – From Author's Abstract.

1783. WELLMAN, HENRY M. (Univ. of Michigan); SOMERVILLE, SUSAN C.; REVELLE, GLENDA L.; HAAKE, ROBERT J.; & SOPHIAN, CATHERINE. **The development of comprehensive search skills.** Child Development, 1984, **55,** 472–481.
Children 2 1/2 years old achieved comprehensive search only when lids of cans automatically stayed open once searched; 3 1/2- and 4 1/2-year-olds were more able to search comprehensively and nonredundantly in a variety of conditions. Easter eggs were hidden in 2 clusters as 3–5-year-olds watched; children did not minimize distance in their search paths for finding the eggs. They did tend to find all eggs in 1 cluster before searching in the other. – From Authors' Abstract.

1784. WENTWORTH, NAOMI, & WITRYOL, SAM L. (Univ. of Connecticut). **Uncertainty and novelty as collative motivation in children.** Journal of Genetic Psychology, 1984, **144,** 3–17.
Novelty and uncertainty, distinguished by differences in the temporal distribution of variation in experience, were manipulated as independent factors. Forty children in grades 2 and 4 were given 24 binary-choice preference tests which placed a moderately valued, constant incentive object into competition with a small opaque (uncertainty) or transparent (no uncertainty) package containing a relatively familiar or novel reward. Uncertainty generated far greater collative arousal than novelty. A theoretical collative hierarchy based on information-processing effort was proposed. – From Authors' Abstract.

1785. WILLATTS, PETER (Univ. of Dundee, Scotland). **Stages in the development of intentional search by young infants.** Developmental Psychology, 1984, **20**, 389–396.
A study of the search of infants 6–8 months old found that the majority displayed transitional search before intentional search. Early transitional search demonstrated minimal awareness, but later transitional search did reveal knowledge of the hidden object. – From Author's Abstract.

1786. YOGMAN, MICHAEL W. (Children's Hosp. Medical Ctr., 300 Longwood, Boston); LESTER, BARRY; & HOFFMAN, JOEL. **Behavioral and cardiac rhythmicity during mother-father-stranger infant social interaction.** Pediatric Research, 1983, **17**, 872–876.
A 3-month-old infant's heart-rate rhythms were stronger during social interaction with both mother and father than with a stranger. – Adapted from Authors' Abstract.

1787. YUILL, NICOLA (Univ. of Sussex, Brighton, England). **Young children's coordination of motive and outcome in judgements of satisfaction and morality.** British Journal of Developmental Psychology, 1984, **2**, 73–81.
This study shows that children understand the relation of motive and outcome at 3 years of age. The ability to coordinate these 2 factors requires an information-integration capacity not previously reported in such young children, and raises the question of why children fail to use this capacity in other tasks requiring coordination of 2 pieces of information in value-laden contexts. – From Author's Abstract.

1788. YUSSEN, STEVEN R. (Univ. of Wisconsin, Madison). **Acquiring new word meaning: what does it tell us about development?** Developmental Review, 1984, **4**, 139–144.
The article is a critique of Sternberg's acquisition of knowledge theory. – Ed.

1789. ZAKAY, D. (Tel-Aviv Univ., Israel); BAR-EL, ZIPORA; & KREITLER, SHULAMITH. **Cognitive orientation and changing the impulsivity of children.** British Journal of Educational Psychology, 1984, **54**, 40–50.
Ten-year-old impulsive children were tested before and after experimental treatments on the Pre-School Inter-personal Problem-Solving Test, Matching Familiar Figures, and beliefs concerning reflectiveness. Pre- and postmeasures on Behavioural Measures of Adjustment and behavioral observations of impulsivity were obtained. The experimental treatment of 8 meetings consisted of training the relevant beliefs, or behavioral plans, or both. The beliefs changed as expected, and 9 of the 10 behavioral measures were changed, provided the beliefs changed. – From Authors' Abstract.

SOCIAL PSYCHOLOGICAL, CULTURAL, AND PERSONALITY STUDIES

1790. ARCHER, CYNTHIA J. (SUNY, Fredonia). **Children's attitudes toward sex-role division in adult occupational roles.** Sex Roles, 1984, **10**, 1–10.
Students in grades K, 5, and 11 indicated attitudes toward sex-role divisions for 44 occupations and activities. Older children found either sex as appropriate job holders more often than younger children, and females displayed less sex stereotyping than males. – Adapted from Author's Abstract.

1791. BAKER, CAROLYN D. (Univ. of New England, Armidale, New South Wales, Australia). **A "second look" at interviews with adolescents.** Journal of Youth and Adolescence, 1983, **12**, 501–519.
Interviews contain additional data, located in the conversing, which can complement the content analysis and interpretation of answers to questions. – From Author's Abstract.

1792. BAR-TAL, D. (Tel-Aviv Univ., Israel); GOLDBERG, MARTA; & KNAANI, ATALIA. **Causes of success and failure and their dimensions as a function of SES and gender: a phenomenological analysis.** British Journal of Educational Psychology, 1984, **54**, 51–61.

The present study collected a list of causes used by males and females of low and middle-upper socioeconomic class. Subjects were asked to use the same causes while making attributions to their grade achieved at the end of a trimester. The 2 SES groups were similar in their rating of the causes. – From Authors' Abstract.

1793. BARTH, RICHARD P. (Univ. of California, Berkeley); SCHINKE, STEVEN PAUL; & MAXWELL, JOSIE SOLSENG. **Psychological correlates of teenage motherhood.** Journal of Youth and Adolescence, 1983, **12**, 471–487.
Findings suggest that adolescent mothers and pregnant teenagers are less distressed by their situation than was once thought. – From Authors' Abstract.

1794. BASSOFF, BETTY Z. (San Diego State Univ.), & ORTIZ, ELIZABETH THOMPSON. **Teen women: disparity between cognitive values and anticipated life events.** Child Welfare, 1984, **63**, 125–138.
Data from a study of teen values show conflicts between values teens say they hold and their behavior. The authors try to show why this is so and suggest ways to support teens' positive values. – From Authors' Abstract.

1795. BATES, JOHN E. (Indiana Univ.), & BAYLES, KATHRYN. **Objective and subjective components in mothers' perceptions of their children from age 6 months to 3 years.** Merrill-Palmer Quarterly, 1984, **30**, 111–130.
The mothers' perceptions were consistently differentiated over the nearly 3 years of the longitudinal study. Mothers' difficultness scores correlated across ages and were consistently independent of other dimensions of temperament or competence in the developing children. – From the Article.

1796. BAUMRIND, DIANA (Univ. of California, Berkeley). **Are androgynous individuals more effective persons and parents?** Child Development, 1982, **53**, 44–75.
Observational and interview data from the Family Socialization and Developmental Competence Project (involving 9-year-olds and their parents) were used. Androgynous women do not differ importantly from other women. Androgynous men, however, are more like androgynous women than like masculine men in their childrearing practices. Sex-typed mothers are responsive, and sex-typed fathers are firm. Androgynes are "child centered" in their approach. Children of sex-typed parents are somewhat more competent than children of androgynous parents. – From Author's Abstract.

1797. BELSKY, JAY (Pennsylvania State Univ.). **The determinants of parenting: a process model.** Child Development, 1984, **55**, 83–96.
The model presumes that parental functioning is multiply determined; that sources of contextual stress and support can directly affect parenting or indirectly affect parenting by first influencing individual psychological well-being; that personality influences contextual support/stress, which feeds back to shape parenting; and that, in order of importance, the personal psychological resources of the parent are more effective in buffering the parent-child relation from stress than are contextual sources of support, which are themselves more effective than characteristics of the child. – From Author's Abstract.

1798. BERGSGAARD, MICHAEL O., & LARSSON, ERIC V. (408 S.W. 15th Ave., Rochester, MN). **Increasing social interaction between an isolate first grader and cross-cultural peers.** Psychology in the Schools, 1984, **21**, 244–251.
Positive social interactions between an isolate, white first grader and osically active, Indian first graders were experimentally increased by using brief instructions plus delivery of a tangible reinforcer contingent upon positive social interaction. The increase in behavior was maintained across a period of 6 months. – From Authors' Abstract.

1799. BERMAN, PHYLLIS W. (National Inst. of Child Health and Human Development, Bethesda), & SMITH, VICKI L. **Gender and situational differences in children's smiles, touch, and proxemics.** Sex Roles, 1984, **10**, 347–356.

Smiling, touching, and interpersonal distance were studied with adolescents and preadolescents. Girls smiled significantly more often than boys did, but there were no sex differences in the overall amount of touching or proxemics. – Adapted from Authors' Abstract.

1800. BIERMAN, KAREN LINN (Pennsylvania State Univ.), & FURMAN, WYNDOL. **The effects of social skills training and peer involvement on the social adjustment of preadolescents.** Child Development, 1984, **55**, 151–162.
Children in grades 5–6 who were identified as unaccepted by their peers and deficient in conversational skills were randomly assigned to 1 of 4 treatment conditions: (1) conversational skills training (individual coaching), (2) peer involvement under superordinate goals (group experience), (3) conversational skills training combined with peer involvement (group experience with coaching), and (4) a no-treatment control. Conversational skills training promoted skill acquisition and increased skillful social interaction. Peer involvement increased peer acceptance and children's self-perceptions of their social efficacy. – From Authors' Abstract.

1801. BLOOD, INGRID M. (Miami Univ.), & BLOOD, GORDON W. **School age children's reactions to deaf and hearing-impaired children.** Perceptual and Motor Skills, 1983, **57**, 373–374.
Nonhandicapped students in grades 5, 6, and 7 apply negative attributes to both deaf and hearing-impaired children. – Adapted from Authors' Abstract.

1802. BOLICK, TERESA (Univ. of Kentucky), & NOWICKI, STEPHEN, JR. **The incidence of external locus of control in televised cartoon characters.** Journal of Genetic Psychology, 1984, **144**, 99–104.
The study focused on identification of the predominant locus-of-control orientations in Saturday morning network cartoons. – From Authors' Abstract.

1803. BOYLE, G. J. (Inst. of Catholic Education, Oakleigh, Australia). **Effects on academic learning of manipulating emotional states and motivational dynamics.** British Journal of Educational Psychology, 1983, **53**, 347–357.
A 5-min film depicting horrific scenes of automobile accident victims and part of a pathologist's postmortem was shown to 69 student teachers, while a nontreatment group of 66 student teachers served as controls. The emotionally disturbing treatment produced a decrement in learning performance. – From Author's Abstract.

1804. BREEN, MICHAEL J. (Univ. of Denver), & BARKLEY, RUSSELL A. **The Personality Inventory of Children (PIC): its clinical utility with hyperactive children.** Journal of Pediatric Psychology, 1983, **8**, 359 + .
All scales of the PIC discriminated normal from hyperactive boys. – Adapted from Authors' Abstract.

1805. BREGMAN, NORMAN J. (Southeastern Louisiana Univ.); LIPSCOMB, THOMAS J.; McALLISTER, HUNTER A.; & MIMS, MICHAEL. **Sharing behavior: effect of denomination value and number.** Journal of Genetic Psychology, 1984, **144**, 131–135.
Kindergarten and sixth-grade children served as subjects in an experiment that investigated the effects of denomination value and number of coins on sharing behavior. Older children shared more, as did children given greater incentive. – From Authors' Abstract.

1806. BREHM, SHARON S. (Univ. of Kansas); POWELL, LYNDA K.; & COKE, JAY S. **The effects of empathic instructions upon donating behavior: sex differences in young children.** Sex Roles, 1984, **10**, 405–416.
First-grade children were given either empathic or neutral instructions and then given a chance to anonymously donate money to the target child, who was presented as being in need. Empathic instructions increased altruistic behavior for males but not for females. – From Authors' Abstract.

1807. BUSSEY, K. (Macquarie Univ., North Ryde, New South Wales, Australia). **A social-cognitive appraisal of sex-role development.** Australian Journal of Psychology, 1983, **35**, 135–143.
This paper presents a comprehensive cognitively based approach to sex-role development with reference to the recent literature. This approach uses methods that enable a better appraisal of the cognitive bases of sex-related information in even very young children. By employing research methods more relevant to the everyday experiences of young children, it is demonstrated that they are more cognitively and socially competent than the more traditional research and theories of sex-role development suggest. – From Author's Abstract.

1808. CALL, JUSTIN D. (Univ. of California, Irvine). **Child abuse and neglect in infancy: sources of hostility within the parent–infant dyad and disorders of attachment in infancy.** Child Abuse & Neglect, The International Journal, 1984, **8**, 185–202.
The recent research on mother–infant attachment is reviewed. Landmarks for normal attachment behaviors from birth to age 3 are defined within 7 different age groupings, and the psychiatric syndrome, "Reactive Attachment Disorder of Infancy," is described and is found almost universally in babies who fail to thrive without organic cause. – From Author's Abstract.

1809. CAMPOS, JOSEPH J. (Univ. of Denver). **A new perspective on emotions.** Child Abuse & Neglect, The International Journal, 1984, **8**, 147–156.
This paper reviews the study of human emotions and traces the factors that have been responsible for an increase of interest in emotions. It traces the rise of the study of emotions as regulators of human behavior. – From Author's Abstract.

1810. CARLSON, CARYN L.; LAHEY, BENJAMIN B. (Univ. of Georgia); & NEEPER, RONALD. **Peer assessment of the social behavior of accepted, rejected, and neglected children.** Journal of Abnormal Child Psychology, 1984, **12**, 189–198.
Positive and negative sociometric nominations were used with second- and fifth-grade children to select socially accepted, rejected, and neglected children. Rejected children were perceived by their peers as being more aggressive, disruptive, irritable, domineering, dishonest, and selfish than accepted and/or neglected children. Neglected children, in contrast, differed from accepted children only in being less likely to brag about physical prowess. – From Authors' Abstract.

1811. CARLSON, WARREN J. (Humboldt State Univ.); WILLIAMS, WILLIAM B.; & DAVOL, HOWARD. **A factor structure of child home observation data.** Journal of Abnormal Child Psychology, 1984, **12**, 245–260.
Both normal and antisocial children were extensively observed in their natural home environments. The factors (verbal emotionality, physical dependency, social involvement, hostile: controlling, hostile: impulsive) separated groups of normal, socially aggressive, hyperactive-aggressive, and stealing children. – From Authors' Abstract.

1812. CHEN, SHING-JEN (Hokkaido Univ., Sapporo, Japan), & MIYAKE, KAZUO. **Japanese vs. United States comparison of mother–infant interaction and infant development: a review.** Research and Clinical Center for Child Development: Annual Report 1982–83, 13–26.
The paper reviews empirical studies concerning infant development in Japan during the last 30 years. – Adapted from the Article.

1813. COKER, DANA ROSENBERG (Muskingum Coll.). **The relationships among gender concepts and cognitive maturity in preschool children.** Sex Roles, 1984, **10**, 19–31.
Gender concept development was investigated in 60 preschool children of mixed socioeconomic background. Cognitive maturity measures were positively related to performance on the gender concept tasks. – From Author's Abstract.

1814. COLE, ELIZABETH B. (McGill Univ., Montreal, Quebec, Canada), & ST. CLAIR-STOKES, JACQUELINE. **Caregiver–child interactive behaviors: a videotape analysis procedure.** Volta Review, 1984, **86**, 200–216.

1815. COLEMAN, JOHN (Sussex Youth Trust, Chalvington, Firle, Seaford, East Sussex, England), & COLEMAN, EVAZAJICEK. **Adolescent attitudes to authority.** Journal of Adolescence, 1984, **7**, 131–141.
Adolescents 14–15 years have little need for autonomy but a very considerable need for support from parents and teachers. – From Authors' Abstract.

1816. CUMMINGS, E. M.; ZAHN-WAXLER, C.; & RADKE-YARROW, M. **Developmental changes in children's reactions to anger in the home.** Journal of Child Psychology and Psychiatry, 1984, **25**, 63–74.
School-age children evidenced greater emotional self-control and more effective and planful strategies for attempting to alter the course of others' conflicts. Children's responses to anger appeared to be mediated by individual differences in emotionality, which evidenced continuity across settings and between age periods. However, there was evidence that experience could modify reaction patterns to anger. – From Authors' Abstract.

1817. DEMOOR-PEAL, ROSE, & HANDAL, PAUL J. (St. Louis Univ.). **Validity of the Personality Inventory for Children with four-year-old males and females: a caution.** Journal of Pediatric Psychology, 1983, **8**, 261 +.
The Personality Inventory for Children was validated on a sample of preschool children from a rural Headstart population. – From Authors' Abstract.

1818. DeSALVO, FRANCIS J. (Univ. of Arkansas), & ZURCHER, LOUIS A. **Defensive and supportive parental communication in a discipline situation.** Journal of Psychology, 1984, **117**, 7–17.
The relationship of parenting discrepancy and dyadic adjustment to parental communication behaviors in a videotaped discipline situation was studied in 2-parent preschool-child triads. Parents tended to exhibit supportive communication in the discipline situation and indicated low levels of parenting discrepancy and high levels of dyadic adjustment. Parenting discrepancy and dyadic adjustment were not found to be predictors of defensive and supportive parental communication. – From Authors' Abstract.

1819. D'HONDT, WALTER, & VANDEWIELE, MICHEL (Strijdhoflaan, 76, 2600 Berchem, Belgium). **Perception of authority and liberty by Senegalese secondary school students.** Adolescence, 1984, **19**, 213–219.
It was found that Senegalese adolescents had a keen sense of their own freedom as it affected the freedom of their society as a whole. – From Authors' Abstract.

1820. DODGE, KENNETH A. (Indiana Univ.); MURPHY, ROBERTA R.; & BUCHSBAUM, KATHY. **The assessment of intention-cue detection skills in children: implications for developmental psychopathology.** Child Development, 1984, **55**, 163–173.
Videotapes were prepared in which 1 child provoked another child. The intention of the first child varied across videotapes. The subject's task was to discriminate among types of intentions. Subjects were children in grades K, 2, and 4 who were identified by sociometric measures as popular, average, socially rejected, or socially neglected. Normal children (popular or average) were found to score more highly than deviant children (neglected and rejected). The errors by deviant children tended to consist of erroneous labels of prosocial intentions as hostile. – From Authors' Abstract.

1821. DRIVAS, ANTONIA; ROE, KIKI VLACHOULI; & ROE, ARNOLD (Univ. of California). **Infants' vocal interaction with mother and stranger in two cultures.** Psychological Reports, 1983, **53**, 1243–1248.

Both American and Greek adults spoke to the infants for about 1/2 of the allotted 3-min interval. Both Greek and American 3-month-olds spent about the same amount of time responding vocally to the mother and less time responding vocally to the stranger. – From Authors' Abstract.

1822. EBERHARDT, CAROLYN A. (Univ. of Miami Guidance Ctr.), & SCHILL, THOMAS. **Differences in sexual attitudes and likeliness of sexual behaviors of black lower-socio-economic father-present vs. father-absent female adolescents.** Adolescence, 1984, **19,** 99–105.
Father-absent subjects were not found to be more sexually permissive in reported likely behavior or attitude than father-present subjects. – From Authors' Abstract.

1823. EDWARDS, CAROLYN POPE (Univ. of Massachusetts, Amherst). **The age group labels and categories of preschool children.** Child Development, 1984, **55,** 440–452.
Children (ages 2–4) readily labeled all ages using a relatively limited set of terms, but showed less patterned labeling of stimuli representing adults than children. Older preschoolers showed more differentiated structures than did younger ones and used more kinship terms as labels. Children ages 3–5 old were given a photograph-sorting task. Preschoolers used a nonadult method of dividing up the life span. Older children made fewer errors. – From Author's Abstract.

1824. EISENBERG, NANCY (Arizona State Univ.); MURRAY, EDWARD; & HITE, TINA. **Children's reasoning regarding sex-typed toy choices.** Child Development, 1982, **53,** 81–86.
Children 3–4 years old used considerable amounts of sex-role-oriented thinking to justify their answers regarding other children's likes and dislikes. They used significantly less of this type of reasoning to justify decisions regarding their own toy preferences (especially their likes). Children seldom justified their actual toy choices during play with references to sex-role stereotypes. – From Authors' Abstract.

1825. EISENSTOCK, BARBARA (California State Univ.). **Sex-role differences in children's identification with counterstereotypical televised portrayals.** Sex Roles, 1984, **10,** 417–430.
The Bem Sex Role Inventory was used to define the sex-role preferences of 9–12-year-old girls and boys. Children viewed a television program designed to diminish sex-role stereotypes. The results suggest that androgynous and feminine children were more likely than masculine children to identify with nontraditional televised models. – From Author's Abstract.

1826. EISERT, DEBRA C. (Lenox Baker Children's Hosp., 3000 Erwin, Durham), & KAHLE, LYNN R. **Self-evaluation and social comparison of physical and role change during adolescence: a longitudinal analysis.** Child Development, 1982, **53,** 98–104.
Social adaptation theory asserts that self-evaluation should lead to social comparison. A 1-year longitudinal study of adolescent boys ages 16–6 years at the beginning of the study yielded cross-lagged panel correlation differences for self-evaluation and social comparison in 2 realms, physical and role, all of which are consistent with social adaptation theory. – From Authors' Abstract.

1827. ELAM, JENNIFER J., & SIGELMAN, CAROL K. (Eastern Kentucky Univ.). **Developmental differences in reactions to children labeled mentally retarded.** Journal of Applied Developmental Psychology, 1983, **4,** 303–315.
Students in grades 4–5 and 11–12 were told of a child of their own age and sex who was either labeled mentally retarded or unlabeled and who performed either competently or incompetently in giving a report. Incompetent target children were viewed more negatively than competent ones at both grade levels. The mental retardation label led girls but not boys (1) to cite lack of ability as the reason for a retarded child's failure, and (2) to hold low expectations of retarded targets. Younger children stigmatized retarded targets, while older children granted special dispensation to them. – From Authors' Abstract.

1828. ENRIGHT, ROBERT D. (Univ. of Wisconsin, Madison); OLSON, LEANNE MARZOCCO; GANIERE, DIANE; LAPSLEY, DANIEL K.; & BUSS, RAY R. **A clinical model for enhancing adolescent ego identity.** Journal of Adolescence, 1984, **7,** 119–130.
The model assumes that identity can be achieved through cognitive strategies of considering the self in relation to 1 friend, one's family, the peer group, and society. Two studies were undertaken to test the model. – From Authors' Abstract.

1829. ESCALONA, SIBYLLE K. (Albert Einstein Coll. of Medicine). **Social and other environmental influences on the cognitive and personality development of low birthweight infants.** American Journal of Mental Deficiency, 1984, **88,** 508–512.
The study of high-risk populations should include, beyond biologic and broadly conceived social measures and beyond cognitive outcome, measures of development in the psychosocial domain. Assessment of the children's daily life and behavior patterns can provide clues for causal linkages. – From Author's Abstract.

1830. EYSENCK, B. G. (Univ. of London, De Crespigny Park, London, England). **One approach to cross-cultural studies of personality.** Australian Journal of Psychology, 1983, **35,** 381–391.
Male and female subjects from 26 countries completed the Eysenck Personality Questionnaire. Comparisons of each country to British norms are given, and reliability coefficients are noted. – From Abstract by E. Gollin.

1831. EYSENCK, H. J. (Univ. of London, De Crespigny Park, London, England). **Personality as a fundamental concept in scientific psychology.** Australian Journal of Psychology, 1983, **35,** 289–304.
Individual differences in personality, partly genetically determined and partly determined by reinforcement history, critically affect the stimulus-response sequences mediated by an organism. Useful personality theories must be linked with the theories and findings of experimental psychology, and be both descriptive and causal paradigms. – From Abstract by E. Gollin.

1832. FASICK, FRANK A. (Univ. of Waterloo). **Parents, peers, youth culture, and autonomy in adolescence.** Adolescence, 1984, **19,** 143–157.
Peer relationships and youth culture that make up their cultural content provide an independent social life focusing on leisure activities that co-exists with continued commitment to parents and their adult-related values. – From Author's Abstract.

1833. FEIRING, CANDICE (Rutgers Medical School); LEWIS, MICHAEL; & STARR, MARK D. **Indirect effects and infants' reaction to strangers.** Developmental Psychology, 1984, **20,** 485–491.
In Condition 1, the infant observed its mother interacting with an unfamiliar adult (UA2) in a positive manner; in Condition 2, the infant observed UA2 interacting with another unfamiliar adult (UA1) in a positive manner; and in Condition 3, UA2 entered the room and did not interact with the mother or UA1. Following exposure to Conditions 1, 2, or 3, UA2 approached the child to play. Fifteen-month-olds in Conditions 1 and 2 were less wary of UA2 and more willing to interact with the mother than were infants in Condition 3. – From Authors' Abstract.

1834. FIELD, TIFFANY (Univ. of Miami Medical School); GEWIRTZ, JACOB L.; COHEN, DEBRA; GARCIA, ROBERT; GREENBERG, REENA; & COLLINS, KERRY. **Leave-takings and reunions of infants, toddlers, preschoolers, and their parents.** Child Development, 1984, **55,** 628–635.
On arrival at their classroom, infants and toddlers related primarily to their parents, whereas preschoolers related to their teachers. Distress behaviors during the parents' departures were most frequently shown by toddlers, and the toddlers' parents hovered about them and "sneaked out of the room" more frequently. Children dropped off by mothers vs. fathers showed more attention-getting behavior and crying, and mothers vs. fathers engaged in more "distracting-the-child" behaviors and showed a longer latency to leave the classroom. – From Authors' Abstract.

1835. FIELD, TIFFANY (Univ. of Miami Medical School), & GREENBERG, REENA. **Temperament ratings by parents and teachers of infants, toddlers, and preschool children.** Child Development, 1982, **53,** 160–163.
Despite the teachers' extensive contact with these children, convergence coefficients were no greater than those generally reported in the literature. The dimensions on which there was interrater agreement were rhythmicity at the infancy stage and persistence and adaptability at the toddler/preschool stage. Convergence of parent and teacher ratings were greater at the toddler/preschool stage than during infancy. – From Authors' Abstract.

1836. FRY, P. S. (Univ. of Calgary, Alberta, Canada), & ADDINGTON, JEAN. **Comparison of social problem solving of children from open and traditional classrooms: a two-year longitudinal study.** Journal of Educational Psychology, 1984, **76,** 318–329.
Assessments of children's social problem-solving cognitions were obtained from children who had attended open and traditional classrooms, respectively, for 3 years. Open-classroom subjects had higher scores in social problem-solving cognitions and correspondingly higher scores in self-esteem and ego strength. – From Authors' Abstract.

1837. FURNHAM, ADRIAN (Univ. Coll., London, England), & GIBBS, MAUREEN. **School children's attitudes towards the handicapped.** Journal of Adolescence, 1984, **7,** 99–117.
Children's attitudes toward the physically handicapped were more positive than those toward the mentally handicapped. – From Authors' Abstract.

1838. GAJAR, ANNA H. (Pennsylvania State Univ.); HALE, ROBERT L.; KUZOVICH, CECELIA; & SAZE, JOSEPH. **Profile analysis of a referral sample.** Journal of Psychology, 1984, **116,** 207–214.
This investigation demonstrates the use of Skinner's Modal Profile Analysis technique to uncover the underlying classification structure in a group of children referred for psychological evaluations by their public school teachers. – From Authors' Abstract.

1839. GECAS, VIKTOR (Washington State Univ.), & PASLEY, KAY. **Birth order and self-concept in adolescence.** Journal of Youth and Adolescence, 1983, **12,** 521–535.
Very little support was found for any of the hypotheses tested. One hypothesis was that the self-evaluations of only and oldest children are more positive than those of younger siblings. – Adapted from Authors' Abstract.

1840. GETZELS, J. W. (Univ. of Chicago), & SMILANSKY, J. **Individual differences in pupil perceptions of school problems.** British Journal of Educational Psychology, 1983, **53,** 307–316.
School problems posed by secondary pupils were studied. The salient content involved the affectivity of teachers. Problems were formulated egocentrically. The content and quality of problems were related to intellectual characteristics. – From Authors' Abstract.

1841. GIBBS, JOHN C. (Ohio State Univ.); ARNOLD, KEVIN D.; MORGAN, RICH L.; SCHWARTZ, ELLIOT S.; GAVAGHAN, MARY P.; & TAPPAN, MARK B. **Construction and validation of a multiple-choice measure of moral reasoning.** Child Development, 1984, **55,** 527–536.
A measure of Kohlbergian moral reasoning, Sociomoral Reflection Objective Measure (SROM), has acceptable concurrent validity with production measures of moral reasoning, including Kohlberg's Moral Judgment Interview, for high school as well as older samples. SROM was positively correlated with grade level, age, IQ, and, to a lesser extent, SES and was not correlated with social desirability. However, the SROM failed to distinguish delinquents from nondelinquents when the controls in the comparison included IQ.-From Authors' Abstract.

1842. GOLDBERG, WENDY A. (Univ. of California, Irvine), & EASTERBROOKS, M. ANN. **Role of marital quality in toddler development.** Developmental Psychology, 1984, **20,** 504–514.

Seventy-five families with 1 child, 20 months old, served as subjects. Child–mother and child–father attachment was assessed in the Strange Situation, and child task behavior was rated during a problem-solving task. Parents completed questionnaires. Observations of parental behavioral sensitivity and couple marital harmony were made. The hypothesis that good marital quality would be associated with optimal toddler functioning and sensitive parenting was generally supported by the data. – From Authors' Abstract.

1843. GOOSSENS, LUC (Catholic Univ. of Louvain, Leuven, Belgium). **Imaginary audience behavior as a function of age, sex, and formal operational thinking.** International Journal of Behavioral Development, 1984, **7**, 77–93.
The results are in line with previous studies. They indicate that Elkind's theory on the imaginary audience is in need of revision. – From Author's Abstract.

1844. GRAHAM, SANDRA (Univ. of California, Los Angeles); DOUBLEDAY, CATHERINE; & GUARINO, PATRICIA A. **The development of relations between perceived controllability and the emotions of pity, anger, and guilt.** Child Development, 1984, **55**, 561–565.
Children 6–11 years were asked to recall personal experiences of pity, anger, and guilt and to rate the cause of each emotion on degree of controllability. There were systematic relations between pity-uncontrollability and anger-controllability in all age groups. There was a developmental increase in the linkage of guilt to controllable causes of negative events. – From Authors' Abstract.

1845. GREENBERG, MARK T. (Univ. of Washington); SIEGEL, JUDITH M.; & LEITCH, CYNTHIA J. **The nature and importance of attachment relationships to parents and peers during adolescence.** Journal of Youth and Adolescence, 1983, **12**, 373–386.
The nature and quality of adolescents' attachments to peers and parents were assessed with the newly developed Inventory of Adolescent Attachments. The sample consisted of 213 adolescents from 12 to 19 years of age. Two hypotheses were tested: (1) the quality of perceived attachments both to parents and peers would be related to well-being, and (2) the quality of parental relationships would be a more powerful predictor of well-being than would the quality of peer relationships. The quality of attachment to parents was significantly more powerful than that to peers in predicting well-being. In addition, quality of attachment to parents showed a moderating effect under conditions of high life stress on the measures of self-esteem. – From Authors' Abstract.

1846. GRESHAM, FRANK M. (Louisiana State Univ.), & LEMANEK, KATHLEEN L. **Social skills: a review of cognitive-behavioral training procedures with children.** Journal of Applied Developmental Psychology, 1983, **4**, 239–261.
Thirty-one studies utilizing cognitive-behavioral procedures to train social skills were reviewed. – From Authors' Abstract.

1847. GRUENEICH, ROYAL (Hamilton Coll.). **Issues in the developmental study of how children use intention and consequence information to make moral evaluations.** Child Development, 1982, **53**, 29–43.
Progress in this area has been hampered in that research has not provided a sufficiently complex account of the structure of intention and consequence information, separated the impact of moral as opposed to cognitive factors in children's judgments, or dealt with the impact of developmental differences in children's memory or comprehension of story information. – From Author's Abstract.

1848. GUNNAR, MEGAN R. (Univ. of Minnesota); LEIGHTON, KELLY; & PELEAUX, RAYMOND. **Effects of temporal predictability on the reactions of 1-year-olds to potentially frightening toys.** Developmental Psychology, 1984, **20**, 449–458.
Infants responded less fearfully to toys that played on predictable as compared to unpredictable schedules. Predicting how long the toys would stay off rather than how long they would play was the aspect that reduced fear. The data closely approximate Seligman's safety-signal model. – From Authors' Abstract.

1849. HAINS, ANTHONY A. (Univ. of Kansas). **Variables in social cognitive development: moral judgment, role-taking, cognitive processes, and self-concept in delinquents and nondelinquents.** Journal of Early Adolescence, 1984, **4,** 65–74.
Delinquents displayed poorer performances than nondelinquents on moral reasoning and logical cognitive abilities, but not on role-taking. Instructions to enhance moral reasoning improved all participants' scores. Delinquents' self-concept as a learner scores were similar to nondelinquents despite their lower performance on other measures. – From Author's Abstract.

1850. HARRIS, IRVING D., & HOWARD, KENNETH (Northwestern Univ.). **On psychological resemblance: a questionnaire study of high school students.** Psychiatry, 1984, **47,** 125–134.
Among the findings, there was a tendency for both sexes, but much more marked for boys, to acknowledge psychological resemblance to the father. – Adapted from the Article.

1851. HARTER, SUSAN (Univ. of Denver). **The Perceived Competence Scale for Children.** Child Development, 1982, **53,** 87–97.
Three domains of competence, each constituting a separate subscale, were identified: cognitive, social, and physical. The psychometric properties of the scale are presented for third through ninth grades. – From Author's Abstract.

1852. HARVEY, IAN J. (Macquarie Univ., North Ryde, Sydney, Australia). **Adoption of Vietnamese children: an Australian study.** Australian Journal of Social Issues, 1983, **18,** 55–69.
Reported are findings from the first major adoption study involving transracial and transcultural transplantations of children into Australian families. The subjects were 300 Vietnamese children, of whom 111 were placed in 101 New South Wales' families. The outcome of these adoptions, the development and adjustment of the children, and implications of the research are discussed. – From Author's Abstract.

1853. HAUSER, STUART T. (Harvard Medical School); POWERS, SALLY I.; NOAM, GIL G.; JACOBSON, ALAN M.; WEISS, BEDONNA; & FOLLANSBEE, DONNA J. **Familial contexts of adolescent ego development.** Child Development, 1984, **55,** 195–213.
Family members (2 parents and an adolescent) completed the Loevinger Sentence Completion Test and then participated in a revealed-differences task, using responses to Kohlberg Moral Dilemmas as discussion stimuli. Adolescent ego development was positively associated with adolescent enabling behaviors (e.g., problem solving, empathy). There were negative correlations between constraining behaviors (e.g., devaluing, withholding) and adolescent ego development. Parental behaviors were significantly associated with parent ego development and adolescent ego development. – From Authors' Abstract.

1854. HAY, DALE F. (SUNY, Stony Brook), & ROSS, HILDY S. **The social nature of early conflict.** Child Development, 1982, **53,** 105–113.
Unacquainted 21-month-old children were observed with the same partner on 3 consecutive days. On the fourth day, half the dyads were rearranged such that each child now was paired with a new partner. Most of the conflicts were struggles over toys. The disputes possessed a patterned interactive structure and explicit communicative content. A child who lost a dispute was more likely than the winner to initiate the next. – From Authors' Abstract.

1855. HENDRICKS, LEO E. (Howard Univ.); ROBINSON-BROWN, DIANE P.; & GARY, LAWRENCE E. **Religiosity and unmarried black adolescent fatherhood.** Adolescence, 1984, **19,** 417–424.
The fathers were more likely to be responsive to nongroup modes of institutionalized religion, i.e., media forms, whereas the nonfather's religious involvement was likely to be within institutionalized groups. – From Authors' Abstract.

1856. HEPWORTH, JERI (Univ. of Connecticut). **The measurement of identity: reliability of Constantinople's Inventory of Personality Development.** Journal of Early Adolescence, 1984, **4**, 47–52.
Reliability estimates, computed for the identity subscales, suggests caution in the use of this measure for identity research. – From Author's Abstract.

1857. HERMAN, MARC S. (Mercy Hosp., 6071 W. Outer Drive, Detroit), & SHANTZ, CAROLYN U. **Social problem solving and mother–child interactions of educable mentally retarded children.** Journal of Applied Developmental Psychology, 1983, **4**, 217–226.
Mothers of retarded and nonretarded children were videotaped interacting with their own child in a seminaturalistic situation. For the mentally retarded, the higher maternal directiveness, the lower the child's social problem-solving skills. – From Authors' Abstract.

1858. HINDE, R. A. (MRC Unit on the Development and Integration of Behavior, Cambridge, England); EASTON, D. F.; & MELLER, R. E. **Teacher questionnaire compared with observational data on effects of sex and sibling status on preschool behaviour.** Journal of Child Psychology and Psychiatry, 1984, **25**, 285–303.
Boys were seen as more sociable and aggressive, girls more persevering. Firstborns were more sociable, aggressive, and calm than secondborns, who were seen as more persevering than firstborns. Comparisons of questionnaire items with observational data on the same children indicated that for the majority of items there was good agreement, and that agreement was better for the more behaviorally defined questions. – From Authors' Abstract.

1859. HOCK, ELLEN (Ohio State Univ.); KROLL, BARBARA CACCAMO; FRANTZ, JOANNE; JANSON, KATHERINE ANN; & WIDAMAN, KEITH. **Infants in play groups: time related changes in behavior toward mothers, peers, and toys.** Journal of Genetic Psychology, 1984, **144**, 51–67.
Twenty-one 13-month-olds were assigned to 1 of 7 playgroups convening for 15 consecutive weekdays. The findings suggest that a mother may serve different functions at different points in time: (a) secure base, (b) refueling stop, and (c) as an attractive alternative. Activity level and toy exploration linearly decreased over time, while intentional contact with mother significantly increased. Interaction with peers correlated negatively with interaction with mother. – From Authors' Abstract.

1860. HOCK, ROBERT A. (Univ. of Cincinnati), & CURRY, JOHN F. **Sex-role identification of normal adolescent males and females as related to school achievement.** Journal of Youth and Adolescence, 1983, **12**, 461–470.
The study examines the sex-role perceptions that adolescents hold of fathers, mothers, ideal males, ideal females, and selves. Differences exist between male and female adolescents, and linkages exist between sex-role identification and academic achievement. – From Authors' Abstract.

1861. HOLT, GERALDINE M. (London Hosp. Medical Coll., England), & WOLKIND, STEPHEN N. **Early abandonment of breast feeding: causes and effects.** Child: Care, Health and Development, 1983, **9**, 349–355.
Primiparous women were interviewed late in pregnancy and postpartum. Few social or psychological variables related to the duration of breast-feeding, nor was there a relationship between the child's temperament and the type of feeding or duration of breast-feeding. – From Authors' Abstract.

1862. HORN, THELMA STERNBERG (Univ. of Wisconsin, Milwaukee). **Expectancy effects in the interscholastic athletic setting: methodological considerations.** Journal of Sport Psychology, 1984, **6**, 60–76.
Analyses of coaching behaviors revealed that low-expectancy junior high school athletes received more praise for success and more general and corrective instruction in game situations than did high-expectancy athletes. – From Author's Abstract.

1863. INOFF, GALE E. (National Inst. of Mental Health); HALVERSON, CHARLES F., JR.; & FIZZIGATI, KARABELLE A. L. **The influence of sex-role stereotypes on children's self- and peer-attributions.** Sex Roles, 1983, **9**, 1205–1222.
For each of 10 traits depicted in videotaped skits, 147 children ages 5–13 years rated themselves, rated the social desirability of the trait, and nominated peers who exhibited the trait. Few sex differences were found. – From Authors' Abstract.

1864. INTONS-PETERSON, MARGARET JEAN (Indiana Univ.), & REDDEL, MICHELLE. **What do people ask about a neonate?** Developmental Psychology, 1984, **20**, 358–359.
Of the initial questions, 80% were about gender. Questions about health of the mother or baby and about characteristics of the baby were second and third, respectively. – From Authors' Abstract.

1865. JACOBSON, JOSEPH L. (Wayne State Univ.), & WILLE, DIANE E. **Influence of attachment and separation experience on separation distress at 18 months.** Developmental Psychology, 1984, **20**, 477–484.
At 18 months, securely attached infants are better able than anxiously attached infants to tolerate brief maternal separations. Moderate separation experience (hours in alternate care) predicts lower levels of distress, whereas either extensive or minimal experience predicts greater distress. Multiple regression indicates that secure attachment and moderate separation experience contribute independently to the development of the capacity to cope with separation. – From Authors' Abstract.

1866. JURICH, ANTHONY P. (Kansas State Univ.), & ANDREWS, DANA. **Self-concepts of rural early adolescent juvenile delinquents.** Journal of Early Adolescence, 1984, **4**, 41–46.
Using a sample of rural early adolescents, the present study found delinquent adolescents to have a lower self-concept than their nondelinquent counterparts, especially in the areas of body image, moral and ethical self, and family self-concept. The delinquents showed signs of maladjustment on the Tennessee Self-Concept Scale but accepted their negative self-image. – From Authors' Abstract.

1867. KALLIOPUSKA, MIRJA (Univ. of Helsinki, Finland). **Relation between children's and parents' empathy.** Psychological Reports, 1984, **54**, 295–299.
The relationship between Finnish child and parental empathy was studied with the Mehrabian and Epstein emotional empathy scale. Females were more empathetic than males, and controlling for social background, parental empathy was related to empathy in offspring. – Adapted from Author's Abstract.

1868. KANAYA, YUKO (Hokkaido Univ., Sapporo, Japan). **Analysis of infant's inhibited behavior shown in peer interaction at 23 months.** Research and Clinical Center for Child Development: Annual Report 1982–83, 49–57.
Inhibited infants looked at the peer, approached mother, and touched mother more often than the uninhibited. Female infants interacted with each other more frequently than males. – From Author's Abstract.

1869. KAZDIN, ALAN E. (Univ. of Pittsburgh School of Medicine); MATSON, JOHNNY L.; & ESVELDT-DAWSON, KAREN. **The relationship of role-play assessment of children's social skills to multiple measures of social competence.** Behaviour Research and Therapy, 1984, **22**, 129–139.
The results indicated that role-play performance correlated with child knowledge and self-efficacy but not with overt social behavior or self-reported social behavior in diverse situations. Role-play performance generally did not correlate with measures completed by staff, parents, and teachers. – From Authors' Abstract.

1870. KELLER, MONIKA (Max Planck Inst. for Human Development and Education, Berlin, Germany), & REUSS, SIEGFRIED. **An action-theoretical reconstruction of the development of social-cognitive competence.** Human Development, 1984, **27**, 211–220.

Social-cognitive abilities are constitutive of competent action. A theory of action, therefore, provides a framework for the analysis of social-cognitive processes. Within an action-theoretical framework, both structure and content aspects of social cognition can be accommodated. – From Authors' Abstract.

1871. KEYES, SUSAN (Univ. of California, Berkeley). **Measuring sex-role stereotypes: attitudes among Hong Kong Chinese adolescents and development of the Chinese Sex-Role Inventory.** Sex Roles, 1984, **10**, 129–140.
The Chinese Sex-Role Inventory was constructed following the model of the Bem Sex Role Inventory. – From Author's Abstract.

1872. KEYES, SUSAN (Univ. of California, Berkeley), & COLEMAN, JOHN. **Sex-role conflicts and personal adjustment: a study of British adolescents.** Journal of Youth and Adolescence, 1983, **12**, 443–459.
Individuals of both sexes who experienced the highest levels of sex-role conflict also experienced more problems in personal adjustment. There were no sex differences for measures of personal adjustment. – Adapted from Authors' Abstract.

1873. KISHTON, JOSEPH (Univ. of North Carolina, Wilmington); STARRETT, RAYMOND H.; & LUCAS, JANA L. **Polar versus milestone variables in adolescent ego development.** Journal of Early Adolescence, 1984, **4**, 53–64.
Ego development and impulsivity data were collected from an early- and a late-adolescence group. Factor analysis revealed differences in the order and strength of the factors for the 2 groups. Ego development was higher in the older group and impulsivity seemed to be a more substantial component of ego functioning for the early-adolescence group. – From Authors' Abstract.

1874. KLEINKE, CHRIS L. **Two models for conceptualizing the attitude-behavior relationship.** Human Relations, 1984, **37**, 333–350.
The literature is reviewed on models to conceptualize the relationship between attitudes and behaviors. – From Abstract by G. T. Kowitz.

1875. KOBLINSKY, SALLY A. (San Diego State Univ.), & SUGAWARA, ALAN I. **Nonsexist curricula, sex of teacher, and children's sex-role learning.** Sex Roles, 1984, **10**, 357–367.
Children 3–5 years old were divided among 4 programs: nonsexist or control curriculum, with female or male director. Exposure to the nonsexist curriculum produced significantly greater reductions in sex stereotyping than exposure to the control curriculum. – Adapted from Authors' Abstract.

1876. KORN, SAM J. (CUNY, Hunter Coll.). **Continuities and discontinuities in difficult/easy temperament: infancy to young adulthood.** Merrill-Palmer Quarterly, 1984, **30**, 189–199.
Knowing that a girl has an easy temperament as a child, especially after the first year, is a good indication of what she will be like as a young adult. That is not true for boys who are easy (except at age 4). On the other hand, knowing that a girl has difficult temperament in the first 5 years is not predictive of her temperament as a young adult; but with boys it is an entirely different matter. – From the Article.

1877. KOURILSKY, MARILYN (Univ. of California, Los Angeles), & KEHRET-WARD, TRUDY. **Kindergartners' attitudes toward distributive justice: experiential mediators.** Merrill-Palmer Quarterly, 1984, **30**, 49–64.
Results suggest that in tasks that require allocation of self-produced goods, kindergartners are already able to link work and entitlement. – From Authors' Abstract.

1878. LANDY, SARAH (3018 Gordon, Regina, Saskatchewan, Canada); CLELAND, JOHN; & SCHUBERT, JOSEF. **The individuality of teenage mothers and its implication for intervention strategies.** Journal of Adolescence, 1984, **7**, 171–190.

The paper reports a longitudinal study of 4 teenage mothers and their infants. – From Authors' Abstract.

1879. LANGER, S.; PÜLPÁN, Z.; & NOVOTNÁ, J. **An attempt to analyse the personality structure of retarded children by means of diagram theory.** Československá Psychologie, 1983, **6,** 507–519.
The authors analyzed the personality structure of 63 18–19-year-old mildly oligophrenic boys using diagram theory. Three layers of personality were discovered. – Adapted from Authors' Abstract.

1880. LA TORRE, RONALD A. (Vancouver School Board, British Columbia, Canada); YU, LAUREN; FORTIN, LOUISE; & MARRACHE, MYRIAM. **Gender-role adoption and sex as academic and psychological risk factors.** Sex Roles, 1983, **9,** 1127–1136.
First-year junior high school students were administered a battery of psychological tests. Among the results, tests administered toward the end of that school year revealed that females attained greater neuroticism and alienation scores than did their male peers. – From Authors' Abstract.

1881. LEDERBERG, AMY R. (Univ. of Texas, Dallas). **Interaction between deaf preschoolers and unfamiliar hearing adults.** Child Development, 1984, **55,** 598–606.
Mothers interacted in a play situation with an unfamiliar deaf 5-year-old, an unfamiliar hearing 2-year-old, and an unfamiliar hearing 4 1/2-year-old. The women used more visual communicative devices, touches, and simpler speech when communicating to the deaf children than when communicating to the hearing children. The women's initiations to the deaf children were only successful 46% of the time. The women compensated for their low rate of success with the deaf children by initiating interactions more often to the deaf children than to the hearing children. – From Author's Abstract.

1882. LENNON, RANDY; EISENBERG, NANCY (Arizona State Univ.); & CARROLL, JAMES. **The assessment of empathy in early childhood.** Journal of Applied Developmental Psychology, 1983, **4,** 295–302.
Preschool children were randomly assigned by sex to 4 male and 4 female experimenters and were administered the Feshbach and Roe Affective Situations Test for Empathy. Children scored higher when interviewed by a same-sex experimenter. The implications of the findings for interpreting gender differences in empathy are discussed. – From Authors' Abstract.

1883. LERNER, JACQUELINE V. (Pennsylvania State Univ.). **The import of temperament for psychosocial functioning: tests of a goodness of fit model.** Merrill-Palmer Quarterly, 1984, **30,** 177–188.
The studies done to date provide some support for the model. For example, children who had better temperament/demands-fit had higher levels of school and social adjustment, school achievement, and parent–child interactions. – From Author's Abstract.

1884. LERNER, RICHARD M. (Pennsylvania State Univ.); PALERMO, MARION; SPIRO, AVRON, III; & NESSELROADE, JOHN R. **Assessing the dimensions of temperamental individuality across the life span: the Dimensions of Temperament Survey (DOTS).** Child Development, 1982, **53,** 149–159.
Expert raters categorized items representing the categories of the New York Longitudinal Study to identify items as applicable from early childhood to young adulthood. Subjects from early childhood, middle-to-late childhood, and early adulthood responded to these items. Factors identified were activity level, attention span/distractibility, adaptability/approach-withdrawal, rhythmicity, and reactivity. – From Authors' Abstract.

1885. LONG, SUSAN. **Early integration in groups: "a group to join, and a group to create."** Human Relations, 1984, **37,** 311–332.

An analogy is explored between an infant establishing a separate identity and the development of group identity. In the initial stage, an authority-based leadership is necessary to establish the existance of a unit. A process of "hatching" is followed by growing independence and eventual rebellion. – From Abstract by G. T. Kowitz.

1886. LOZOFF, BETSY (Case Western Reserve Univ.). **Birth and "bonding" in non-industrial societies.** Developmental Medicine and Child Neurology, 1983, **25**, 595–600.
On anthropological ratings, there was no increase in (1) maternal affection in societies that fostered mother–infant body contact, (2) paternal involvement when fathers were allowed at childbirth, or (3) breast-feeding duration in those that permitted early nursing. – Adapted from Author's Abstract.

1887. LUCHINS, ABRAHAM S., & LUCHINS, EDITH H. (Rensselaer Polytechnic Inst., Troy, NY). **Conceptions of personality and order effects in forming impressions.** Journal of General Psychology, 1984, **110**, 165–196.
The findings suggest that junior and senior high school students who are urged to hold onto a stereotype may not do so in the face of conflicting information. – From Authors' Abstract.

1888. McCABE, MARITA P. (Macquarie Univ.). **Toward a theory of adolescent dating.** Adolescence, 1984, **19**, 159–170.
The main areas of influence during dating are seen as physiological changes during this period and social pressures acting on adolescents both from peers and the wider society. – From Author's Abstract.

1889. MACCOBY, E. E. (Stanford Univ.). **Socialization and developmental change.** Child Development, 1984, **55**, 317–328.
It is argued that studies of socialization need to become more developmental. Two meanings of development are distinguished: sequentially dependent steps that may or may not be taken by individual children, and developmental changes that occur in predictable order in nearly all children. The way in which both these kinds of changes may affect the socialization process is discussed. – From Author's Abstract.

1890. MACCOBY, ELEANOR E. (Stanford Univ.); SNOW, MARGARET ELLIS; & JACKLIN, CAROL NAGY. **Children's dispositions and mother–child interaction at 12 and 18 months: a short-term longitudinal study.** Developmental Psychology, 1984, **20**, 459–472.
At 12 months, there was little relationship between the mother's teaching and the child's task orientation, but by 18 months, significant correlations had appeared. Maternal teaching and child task orientation were essentially unrelated to the children's general dispositions at 12 months, but by 18 months, the mother's teaching effort was related to her child's "difficultness." Mothers of difficult 12-month-old boys reduced their teaching effort subsequently, and the sons of mothers who exerted high teaching effort at 12 months became less difficult during the subsequent 6 months. – From Authors' Abstract.

1891. McDOWELL, JERRY A. (New Mexico State Univ.). **Coping with social and emotional factors through various strategies: help for the gifted student.** Creative Child and Adult Quarterly, 1984, **9**, 18–27.
The areas of identification and assessment are discussed along with a treatment of the various techniques and strategies to be used. – From Author's Abstract.

1892. McELROY, MARY A. (Kansas State Univ.). **Parent–child relations and orientations toward sport.** Sex Roles, 1983, **9**, 997–1004.
Mother–son relationships were associated with more traditional female sport orientations in boys; father–daughter relationships were also related to stronger female sport orientations in girls. – From Author's Abstract.

1893. McLOUGHLIN, DAVID (Family Court of Australia, 34–36 Charles, Parramatta, New South Wales, Australia), & WHITFIELD, RICHARD. **Adolescents and their experience of parental divorce.** Journal of Adolescence, 1984, **7**, 155–170.
Parental divorce does not necessarily interfere with adolescent development. – From Authors' Abstract.

1894. MAIN, MARY (Univ. of California, Berkeley), & GOLDWYN, RUTH. **Predicting rejection of her infant from mother's representation of her own experience: implications for the abused-abusing intergenerational cycle.** Child Abuse & Neglect, The International Journal, 1984, **8**, 203–217.
We review studies of young abused children which show the development of similar behavioral characteristics as early as 1–3 years of age. These behavioral characteristics also develop in relatively maternally rejected children in normal samples. – From Authors' Abstract.

1895. MAZIADE, MICHEL (Hôtel Dieu du Sacré-Coeur de Jésus de Québec, Affilié a L'université Laval, Avenue du Sacré-Coeur, Quebec, Canada); BOUDREAULT, MAURICE; THIVIERGE, JACQUES; CAPÉRAÀ, PHILLIPPE; & CÔTÉ, ROBERT. **Infant temperament: SES and gender differences and reliability of measurement in a large Quebec sample.** Merrill-Palmer Quarterly, 1984, **30**, 213–226.
A typology very similar to the New York Longitudinal Study "easy-difficult" axis was found both at 4 months and at 8 months. Social class did not appear to influence temperament in any considerable way. – From Authors' Abstract.

1896. MEIJER, ALEXANDER (Hadassah Univ. Hosp. and Hebrew Univ. Medical School, Jerusalem, Israel), & HIMMELFARB, SABINE. **Fatherless adolescents' feelings about their mothers—a pilot study.** Adolescence, 1984, **19**, 207–212.
Fatherless adolescent girls perceived their mothers as less benevolent than girls from 2-parent families of similar sociodemographic background. No differences were found among boys. – From Authors' Abstract.

1897. MILICH, RICHARD (Univ. of Iowa), & LANDAU, STEVEN. **A comparison of the social status and social behavior of aggressive and aggressive/withdrawn boys.** Journal of Abnormal Child Psychology, 1984, **12**, 277–288.
Kindergarten boys were divided into either aggressive (A) or aggressive/withdrawn (AW) groups. Both groups were found to be high on peer-nominated rejection, but the A group was also high on peer-nominated popularity, while the AW group was low. Both groups were observed to be high in negative peer interactions, but the A group was also high in positive interactions. – From Authors' Abstract.

1898. MILLER, STUART (Univ. Coll. London, Gower, London, England). **Reasons for the attribution of intent in 7- and 9-year-old children.** British Journal of Developmental Psychology, 1984, **2**, 51–61.
Children 7 and 9 years old were presented with drawings which depicted 2 ambiguous action-outcome sequences and asked to make judgments about the intention of an actor toward another, and then to provide an explanation for the judgment. Nine-year-olds used more inference-based explanations which reflected a more objective appraisal of the incident. The explanations of the younger children tended to be dominated by the immediacy of the situation. – From Author's Abstract.

1899. MINDE, K. (Hosp. for Sick Children, 555 Univ., Toronto, Ontario, Canada); WHITELAW, A.; BROWN, J.; & FITZHARDINGE, P. **Effect of neonatal complications in premature infants on early parent-infant interactions.** Developmental Medicine and Child Neurology, 1983, **25**, 763–777.
Parents visiting sick infants interacted far less with their infants than did parents of well babies, and this continued after recovery. It also persisted at home 2 months after the expected date of delivery. – From Authors' Abstract.

1900. MIRENDA, PATRICIA L. (Wisconsin Ctr. for Education Research, Room 569, 1025 W. Johnson, Madison); DONNELLAN, ANNE M.; & YODER, DAVID E. **Gaze behavior: a new look at an old problem.** Journal of Autism and Developmental Disorders, 1983, **13**, 397–409.
This article reviews the research and clinical literature on eye-to-face gaze in normal children and adults. These data and data from a recent pilot study are then compared to the criteria typically used in eye-contact training programs with autistic children. This comparison reveals some educationally relevant discrepancies between the normative data and the training criteria. – From Authors' Abstract.

1901. MIYAKE, KAZUO (Hokkaido Univ., Sapporo, Japan); CAMPOS, JOSEPH J.; & KAGAN, JEROME. **Issues in socio-emotional development.** Research and Clinical Center for Child Development: Annual Report 1982–83, 1–12.

1902. MURRAY, LOUISE (Children's Aid Society, Staten Island). **A review of selected foster care–adoption research from 1978 to mid-1982.** Child Welfare, 1984, **63**, 113–124.
A review of recent research in permanency planning, adoption outcomes, the roles of foster parents, and recidivism in foster care shows the advances in theory and practice of the child-welfare field. – Author's Abstract.

1903. NAKANO, SHIGERU (Hokkaido Univ., Sapporo, Japan). **Does quality of attachment in a strange situation relate to later competence in different situations?** Research and Clinical Center for Child Development: Annual Report 1982–83, 59–70.
The results showed that the style to use the mother as a secure base was consistent with the attachment classification. Level and amount of spontaneous play, amount of peer interaction, compliance with an adult, and intention of approach to a robot were determined by individual skills. – From Author's Abstract.

1904. NELSON-LE GALL, SHARON A. (Univ. of Pittsburgh). **Children's and adults' assignment of blame for personal injury.** Journal of Psychology, 1984, **117**, 135–142.
Children's blame attributions were influenced less by outcome foreseeability than were adults'. Children were more likely to assign blame to single, personal sources for unforeseeable outcomes than were adults. – From Author's Abstract.

1905. NISAN, MORDECAI (Hebrew Univ., Jerusalem, Israel), & KORIAT, ASHER. **The effect of cognitive restructuring on delay of gratification.** Child Development, 1984, **55**, 492–503.
Kindergarten children expressed preference for either a small but immediate reward or a large but delayed reward. They were then told about another child who made the opposite choice and were asked to produce reasons justifying the other child's choice. Subsequent choices were affected only when the reasons supported the delayed choice. Children were presented with either an objective-rational or subjective-emotional argument, contradicting their initial preference. The objective argument had a stronger effect on children's subsequent choices, and this effect was stronger when the argument was for delaying gratification than when it supported the immediate reward. – From Authors' Abstract.

1906. PAIKOFF, ROBERTA L., & SAVIN-WILLIAMS, RITCH C. (Cornell Univ.). **An exploratory study of dominance interactions among adolescent females at a summer camp.** Journal of Youth and Adolescence, 1983, **12**, 419–433.
Instances of dyadic dominance behaviors between group members were recorded. Participants formed a stable cohesive group dominance structure, but it was not rigid or hierarchical. Interpersonal skills, athletic ability, and self-reported self-esteem predicted dominance status. – From Authors' Abstract.

1907. PARROTT, C. A., & STRONGMAN, K. T. (Univ. of Canterbury, Christchurch, New Zealand). **Locus of control and delinquency.** Adolescence, 1984, **19**, 459–471.

Results supported a multidimensional model of locus of control. There was no difference in expectancy of control for negative academic events between delinquents and nondelinquents. – From Authors' Abstract.

1908. PETERSON, LIZETTE (Univ. of Missouri, Columbia), & GELFAND, DONNA M. **Causal attributions of helping as a function of age and incentives.** Child Development, 1984, **55**, 504–511.
Students in grades 1, 4, and 6 and college heard stories featuring actors' anticipations of each of 8 different consequences for helping. Knowledge of the actors' intentions permitted even the youngest subjects to discount the intrinsic motivation of actors who helped out of fear of punishment or criticism. Fourth- and sixth-grade students and adults rated punishment as more coercive than criticism and both negative consequences as more coercive than praise and tangible reward. – From Authors' Abstract.

1909. PETERSON, LIZETTE (Univ. of Missouri, Columbia); RIDLEY-JOHNSON, ROBYN; & CARTER, CYNTHIA. **The supersuit: an example of structured naturalistic observation of children's altruism.** Journal of General Psychology, 1984, **110**, 235–241.
It appeared that children with high general social competence ratings provided a disproportionate amount of both spontaneous and prompted helping. – From Authors' Abstract.

1910. PLOMIN, ROBERT (Univ. of Colorado), & DANIELS, DENISE. **The interaction between temperament and environment: methodological considerations.** Merrill-Palmer Quarterly, 1984, **30**, 149–162.
The concept of temperament interactions in the context of statistical interaction is discussed. A general approach is described for the analysis of temperament interactions using hierarchical multiple regression. – From Authors' Abstract.

1911. QUINTON, D. (Inst. of Psychiatry, London, England), & RUTTER, M. **Parents with children in care—I. Current circumstances and parenting.** Journal of Child Psychology and Psychiatry, 1984, **25**, 211–229.
A consecutive sample of families with children multiply admitted to residential care by 1 inner London borough were contrasted with a sample from the same geographical area. The in-care group was twice as likely to be experiencing current parenting problems with 5–8-year-old children, but was distinguished from the already disadvantaged comparison group as much by other kinds of family difficulties as by parenting problems per se. – From Authors' Abstract.

1912. QUINTON, D. (Inst. of Psychiatry, London, England), & RUTTER, M. **Parents with children in care—II. Intergenerational continuities.** Journal of Child Psychology and Psychiatry, 1984, **25**, 231–250.
A retrospective comparison was made of families multiply admitted to residential care in 1 London borough and a group from the same geographical area. The childhoods of the parents differed mostly in the frequency of severe family discord and harsh parenting. – From Authors' Abstract.

1913. RANADE, WENDY (Newcastle Polytechnic, Newcastle upon Tyne, England), & NORRIS, PIPPA. **Democratic consensus and the young: a cross national comparison on Britain and America.** Journal of Adolescence, 1984, **7**, 45–57.
The responses from the American and British sample were fairly similar across a number of scales on the rules of the game, free speech, and equality. The main contrast was found on feelings of trust and efficacy, with the British sample showing much lower feelings that government was honest and responsive to their needs. – From Authors' Abstract.

1914. REED, MARJORIE A. (Univ. of Oregon); PIEN, DIANA L.; & ROTHBART, MARY K. **Inhibitory self-control in preschool children.** Merrill-Palmer Quarterly, 1984, **30**, 131–147.
Soviet theory suggests that internal inhibition provides the basis for verbally regulated inhibition and is temperamentally determined. Correlations between performance on a measure of inter-

nal inhibition (spontaneous alternation) and 2 measures of verbally regulated inhibition (a pinball game and Simon says) were found. – From Authors' Abstract.

1915. RHEINGOLD, HARRIET L. (Univ. of North Carolina, Chapel Hill). **Little children's participation in the work of adults, a nascent prosocial behavior.** Child Development, 1982, **53,** 114–125.
In a laboratory setting that simulated a home, parents and other adults were asked to perform some common household chores, and participation of 18–30-month old children was recorded. Children spontaneously and promptly assisted the adults in a majority of the tasks they performed and accompanied their assistance by relevant verbalizations and by evidence that they knew the goals of the tasks, even adding appropriate behaviors not modeled by the adults. – From Author's Abstract.

1916. RHOLES, WILLIAM S. (Texas A&M Univ.), & RUBLE, DIANE N. **Children's understanding of dispositional characteristics of others.** Child Development, 1984, **55,** 550–560.
Subjects observed vignettes that were designed to reveal an actor's abilities or personality traits, then made predictions for the actor's behavior in other, related behavioral situations. Other subjects were told about 1 instance of an actor's behavior, were provided with covariation information that implied that the actor's behavior either was or was not caused by personal dispositions, and then predicted the actor's behavior in related situations. Older (9–10 years and adults) but not younger (5–7 years) subjects predicted that the actor's behaviors in new situations would be relatively consistent with the behavior that was observed or described, when the behavior was perceived to be a function of dispositional causal factors. – From Authors' Abstract.

1917. RICHMOND, BERT O. (Univ. of Georgia), & MILLAR, GARNET W. **What I Think and Feel: a cross-cultural study of anxiety in children.** Psychology in the Schools, 1984, **21,** 255–257.
Children in grades 5–6 in the U.S., Canada, and Mexico expressed similar levels of anxiety, and there were no significant differences attributable to national, grade, or sex differences. – From Authors' Abstract.

1918. ROBERTS, GAIL C. (Univ. of Wisconsin, Stout); BLOCK, JEANNE H.; & BLOCK, JACK. **Continuity and change in parents' child-rearing practices.** Child Development, 1984, **55,** 586–597.
Mothers and fathers completed the Child Rearing Practices Report (CRPR) when their child was 3 years of age and again when their child was 12 years of age. Across-time correlations from the CRPR indicate substantial continuity in childrearing orientations. The shifts in emphases generally coincide with what are considered to be developmentally appropriate areas for change. – From Authors' Abstract.

1919. ROCISSANO, LORRAINE (49 W. 16th, New York), & YATCHMINK, YVETTE. **Joint attention in mother-toddler interaction: a study of individual variation.** Merrill-Palmer Quarterly, 1984, **30,** 11–31.
Videotaped interactions between 8 2-year-olds and their mothers were used to derive a category system that was designed to capture similarities and differences across pairs in maintaining joint attention. Results showed that mothers and their children resembled 1 another in the extent to which they maintained joint attention. – From Authors' Abstract.

1920. ROSENBLUM, LEONARD A. (SUNY, Downstate Medical Ctr.), & PAULLY, GAYLE S. **The effects of varying environmental demands on maternal and infant behavior.** Child Development, 1984, **55,** 305–314.
Three groups of macaque mother-infant dyads were observed. Two groups (LFD and HFD) lived in stable low- and high-foraging-demand environments, respectively. The third group (VFD) lived in a variable-demand environment in which 2-week periods of HFD and LFD conditions were alternated. Whereas LFD adults scored lowest in dominance-related behaviors and

highest in affiliative behavior (social grooming), VFD adults showed the highest levels of dominance patterns and the lowest levels of grooming. VFD infants showed the most sustained clinging to mother, the lowest levels of social play and exploration, the highest levels of affective disturbance, and repeated evidence of depression as the study progressed. – From Authors' Abstract.

1921. RUBIN, KENNETH H. (Univ. of Waterloo, Ontario, Canada), & KRASNOR, LINDA ROSE. **Age and gender differences in solutions to hypothetical social problems.** Journal of Applied Developmental Psychology, 1983, **4**, 263–275.
Preschoolers and kindergartners individually were administered a social problem-solving test. Prosocial strategies were more often directed to older targets; agonistic strategies were more often directed to younger targets. Girls suggested more prosocial strategies with boy partners. – From Authors' Abstract.

1922. RUST, JAMES O. (Middle Tennessee State Univ.), & McCRAW, ANNE. **Influence of masculinity-femininity on adolescent self-esteem and peer acceptance.** Adolescence, 1984, **19**, 359–366.
Among both males and females, an androgynous identity was associated with higher levels of self-esteem. High levels of masculine traits result in high self-esteem scores in both sexes. High levels of feminine traits result in lower scores of self-esteem in males but not females. Black students had higher levels of self-esteem than did whites. – From Authors' Abstract.

1923. SAMEROFF, ARNOLD J. (Inst. for the Study of Developmental Disabilities, 1640 W. Roosevelt, Chicago); SEIFER, RONALD; & ELIAS, PENELOPE KELLY. **Sociocultural variability in infant temperament ratings.** Child Development, 1982, **53**, 164–173.
The social status, anxiety level, and mental health status of mothers were all related to their 4-month-old infants' temperament ratings on the Carey Infant Temperament Questionnaire. Child behavior measured in the home and laboratory was sporadically related to temperament, and these relations were of small magnitude. Hierarchical multiple regression analysis demonstrated that mother effects were more powerful than child effects. – From Authors' Abstract.

1924. SCANLAN, TARA K. (Univ. of California, Los Angeles), & LEWTHWAITE, REBECCA. **Social psychological aspects of competition for male youth sport participants: I. Predictors of competitive stress.** Journal of Sport Psychology, 1984, **6**, 208–226.
This field study investigated the influence and stability of individual difference and situational factors on the competitive stress experienced by 9–14-year-old wrestlers. The most influential and stable predictors of prematch stress were competitive trait anxiety and personal performance expectancies, while win–loss and fun experienced during the match predicted postmatch stress. – From Authors' Abstract.

1925. SCHAFFER, H. R. (Univ. of Strathclyde, Glasgow, Scotland), & LIDDELL, CHRISTINE. **Adult–child interaction under dyadic and polyadic conditions.** British Journal of Developmental Psychology, 1984, **2**, 33–42.
Adult–child interaction was examined under 2 conditions: dyadic (adult with 1 child) and polyadic (adult with 4 children). While the total number of bids the adults received from children in polyads was considerably greater than in dyads, the increase was a selective 1, referring only to requests for help and not to less urgent demands. – From Authors' Abstract.

1926. SCHAU, CANDACE GARRETT (Univ. of New Mexico), & SCOTT, KATHRYN P. **Impact of gender characteristics of instructional materials: an integration of the research literature.** Journal of Educational Psychology, 1984, **76**, 183–193.
Generalizations synthesized from a review of research are: (1) use of gender-specified language forms explicitly including both sexes yields gender-balanced associations, (2) exposure to sex-equitable materials results in more flexible sex-role attitudes for both males and females, (3) students often prefer materials with same-sex characters, and (4) sex-equitable materials do not decrease comprehension. – From Authors' Abstract.

1927. SELMAN, ROBERT L. (Judge Baker Guidance Ctr., 295 Longwood, Boston), & DEMOREST, AMY P. **Observing troubled children's interpersonal negotiation strategies: implications of and for a developmental model.** Child Development, 1984, **55**, 288–304.
Two 9-year-old boys, both selected from a pool of children with socioemotional and interpersonal difficulties, were observed unobtrusively in 35 weekly hour-long pair therapy sessions over the course of 2 school years. The predominant level of strategy used by both children was unilateral (level 1), followed for each child by reciprocal (level 2), impulsive (level 0), and then collaborative (level 3) strategies. Across time, a trend toward increased use of reciprocal strategies was suggested. One subject was consistently rigid in orientation over the 35 weeks, while the other demonstrated a movement with time to a more balanced usage of strategies across orientations. – From Authors' Abstract.

1928. SHANNON, KERRI, & KAFER, NORMAN F. (Univ. of Newcastle, New South Wales, Australia). **Reciprocity, trust, and vulnerability in neglected and rejected children.** Journal of Psychology, 1984, **117**, 65–70.
Neglected children included mutual sharing and trust in their friendship expectations; however, they perceived themselves as comparatively more vulnerable in interpersonal relationships than others. The rejected children did not regard trust as an important component of friendship. – From Authors' Abstract.

1929. SHEEHAN, P. W. (Univ. of Queensland, St. Lucia, Queensland, Australia). **Age trends and the correlates of children's television viewing.** Australian Journal of Psychology, 1983, **35**, 417–431.
Children in grades 1–5 were tested in an overlapping longitudinal design which measured television viewing and related behaviors. Measures were taken of sex-stereotyped behavior, fantasy activity, identification with television characters, and peer-rated aggression. Boys showed significant correlations between television viewing variables and aggressive behavior. – From Abstract by E. Gollin.

1930. SIGNORELLA, MARGARET L. (Pennsylvania State Univ.), & LIBEN, LYNN S. **Recall and reconstruction of gender-related pictures: effects of attitude, task difficulty, and age.** Child Development, 1984, **55**, 393–405.
Kindergartners, second graders, and fourth graders with either more or less gender-stereotyped attitudes were asked to recall gender-relevant pictures. At all ages, highly stereotyped children recalled more traditional than nontraditional pictures, while less stereotyped children recalled more nontraditional than traditional pictures. Most reconstructions transformed nontraditional items to traditional, with more of these reconstructions being produced by highly stereotyped children. – From Authors' Abstract.

1931. SILCOCK, P. J. (Hertfordshire Coll. of Higher Education, Aldenham, Watford, Herts, England). **Aspects of adolescent social-cognitive development: a cross-sectional study of social judgment in early adolescence.** Educational Review, 1984, **36**, 27–36.
The social judgments of 11–14-year-olds were compared using Peel's 3 categories of judgment to measure and evaluate responses. Clear, if limited, evidence for progress between the 2 ages in the ability to judge other people's perspectives was obtained, in line with Peel's general theory. – From Author's Abstract.

1932. SIMKINS, LAWRENCE (Univ. of Missouri). **Consequences of teenage pregnancy and motherhood.** Adolescence, 1984, **19**, 39–54.
Although there has been an increase in the use of abortion, among white teenagers, the majority of pregnant teenagers opt to carry their pregnancy to term and raise their child themselves. – From Author's Abstract.

1933. SKAALVIK, E. M. (Univ. of Trondheim, Norway). **Academic achievement, self-esteem and valuing of the school—some sex differences.** British Journal of Educational Psychology, 1983, **53**, 299–306.

From grades 4 to 8, low academic achievement was associated with low self-esteem and strong perceived parental pressure for boys, but not for girls. At grade 8, low achievement was associated with low perceived value of the school for the girls, while there was no such relationship for boys. – From Author's Abstract.

1934. SMETANA, JUDITH G. (Univ. of Rochester); KELLY, MARIO; & TWENTYMAN, CRAIG T. **Abused, neglected, and nonmaltreated children's conceptions of moral and social-conventional transgressions.** Child Development, 1984, **55**, 277–287.
Abused, neglected, and control children matched on IQ, age, and social class judged the seriousness, deserved punishment, generalizability, and rule contingency of familiar transgressions for themselves and others. Abused subjects were more likely than neglected subjects to consider psychological distress to be universally wrong for others; neglected subjects were more likely than abused subjects to judge the unfair distribution of resources to be universally wrong for themselves. Abused and control children, but not neglected children, judged all transgressions to deserve more punishment when committed by others than when committed by the self. – From Authors' Abstract.

1935. SMITH, P.; WEINMAN, M.; & NENNEY, S. W. (Baylor Coll. of Medicine). **Desired pregnancy during adolescence.** Psychological Reports, 1984, **54**, 227–231.
Primiparous adolescents 13–18 years of age who desired pregnancy were compared with teens who did not want pregnancy to determine traits which differentiate the groups. Factors included peer expectations, marital and affective status, fertility awareness, and contraceptive use. Adolescents desiring pregnancy had a more positive peer expectation of being treated better after delivery. – Adapted from Authors' Abstract.

1936. SMITHERS, ANGELA, & SMITHERS, ALAN G. (Univ. of Manchester, England). **An exploratory study of sex role differentiation among young children.** Educational Review, 1984, **36**, 87–99.
Conceptions among 6–7-year-olds and adults of behavior appropriate to the sexes were studied using Hudson's questionnaire. Children tended to see more activities as suitable for 1 sex only than did adults. Boys and men tended to see sex roles as more differentiated than did the girls and women, respectively. – From Authors' Abstract.

1937. SOLNIT, ALBERT J. (Yale Univ.). **Keynote address: theoretical and practical aspects of risks and vulnerabilities in infancy.** Child Abuse & Neglect, The International Journal, 1984, **8**, 133–144.
There is substantial agreement about the basic concepts of vulnerability and at-risk conditions in childhood in the context of what constitutes healthy development. Health is characterized by a progression of maturation and development in mental and emotional as well as in the physical spheres. – From Author's Abstract.

1938. SPENCE, JANET T. (Univ. of Texas, Austin). **Comments on Baumrind's "Are androgynous individuals more effective persons and parents?"** Child Development, 1982, **53**, 76–80.
In her discussion of studies employing the Bem Sex Role Inventory (BSRI) and Personal Attributes Questionnaire, Baumrind confuses 2 theories which are based on different assumptions and have different implications. Baumrind's agreement or disagreement with these theories is discussed as they relate to her empirical data on the relationship between mothers' and fathers' BSRI scores and measures of their personal competence, their childrearing practices, and their children's competence. – From Author's Abstract.

1939. SPILLANE-GRIECO, EILEEN (Rutgers Univ.). **Characteristics of a helpful relationship: a study of empathic understanding and positive regard between runaways and their parents.** Adolescence, 1984, **19**, 63–75.
Runaways and their parents reported far less empathy and positive regard for each other as compared to the nonrunaways and their parents. – From Author's Abstract.

1940. STAKE, JAYNE E. (Univ. of Missouri, St. Louis); DeVILLE, CATHY J.; & PENNELL, CHRISTINE L. **The effects of assertive training on the performance self-esteem of adolescent girls.** Journal of Youth and Adolescence, 1983, **12,** 435–442.
Assertiveness training was provided for 148 high school girls. Changes in performance self-esteem scores were found between pretesting and a 3-month follow-up. Low self-esteem subjects showed greater increases than high self-esteem subjects. – From Authors' Abstract.

1941. STEPHAN, COOKIE WHITE (New Mexico State Univ.), & LANGLOIS, JUDITH H. **Baby beautiful: adult attributions of infant competence as a function of infant attractiveness.** Child Development, 1984, **55,** 576–585.
Black, Caucasian, and Mexican-American adults rated photographs of black, Caucasian, and Mexican-American infants at 3 time periods in the first year of life. On the measures of smart-likable baby, good baby, and causes parents problems, there was a beauty-is-good bias that prevailed across ethnic groups. No such bias was found on the measure of active baby. – From Authors' Abstract.

1942. STERN, MARILYN, & HILDEBRANDT, KATHERINE A. (SUNY, Buffalo). **Prematurity stereotype: effects of labeling on adults' perceptions of infants.** Developmental Psychology, 1984, **20,** 360–362.
College students and mothers were asked to rate unfamiliar infants described as either full term or premature and as either male or female. Infants labeled premature were rated more negatively than were infants labeled full term, but infants labeled male and female were rated similarly. – From Authors' Abstract.

1943. STERN, MARILYN (Amherst Youth Board, 72 Cayuga, Williamsville, NY); NORTHMAN, JOHN E.; & VAN SLYCK, MICHAEL R. **Father absence and adolescent "problem behaviors": alcohol consumption, drug use and sexual activity.** Adolescence, 1984, **19,** 301–312.
A survey of 813 adolescents found that adolescents are most likely to discuss problems with peers and least likely to discuss them with parents, especially fathers. Father absence from the home resulted in greater use of and problems with alcohol, marijuana, and sexual activity. – From Authors' Abstract.

1944. SVANUM, SOREN (Indiana Univ.–Purdue Univ. at Indianapolis); BRINGLE, ROBERT G.; & McLAUGHLIN, JOAN E. **Father absence and cognitive performance in a large sample of six- to eleven-year-old children.** Child Development, 1982, **53,** 136–143.
Scores on the WISC and the WRAT were significantly depressed for father-absent white children. Father-absent black children evidenced a decreased test performance only on measures of achievement. All decrements were small and accounted for approximately 1% of the variance. Following statistical control for SES, we associated no decrements with the father's absence/presence, and in some instances, small but significant increments were found to be associated with children from fatherless families. – From Authors' Abstract.

1945. TAJIMA, NOBUMOTO (Hokkaido Univ., Sapporo, Japan). **Infant's temperamental disposition, attachment and self-recognition in the first 20 months of life.** Research and Clinical Center for Child Development: Annual Report 1982–83, 71–80.
Contrary to the hypothesis, insecurely attached infants exhibited early self-recognition as compared with securely attached infants. Inhibited infants, who were more likely to be insecurely attached, were more likely to be early self-recognizers. – From Author's Abstract.

1946. TAKAHASHI, KEIKO (Soka Univ., Tangi-cho, Hachiohji, Tokyo, Japan). **The role of personal framework of social relationships in socialization studies.** Research and Clinical Center for Child Development: Annual Report 1982–83, 37–47.

1947. TAYLOR, D. A., & HARRIS, P. L. **Knowledge of strategies for the expression of emotion among normal and maladjusted boys: a research note.** Journal of Child Psychology and Psychiatry, 1984, **25,** 141–145.

Normal and maladjusted boys 7–8 and 10–11 years old were tested on their knowledge of strategies of control for both facial and overt behavioral expression of a negative emotion. There is a developmental change in the spontaneous mention of a display rule with this developmental trend being retarded amongst the maladjusted boys. Secondly, there was a difference between the normal and maladjusted boys' knowledge of strategies for control of behavior in a conflict situation. – From Authors' Abstract.

1948. THELEN, MARK H. (Univ. of Missouri, Columbia); OATLEY, JEFFREY; MILLER, DAVID J.; & GRACE, KEVIN. **Being imitated: conditions under which positive reactions do not occur.** Journal of Genetic Psychology, 1984, **144,** 83–88.
Imitated children looked less at their partner or their partner's constructions than did control children. The groups did not differ in subsequent imitation of the partner. Children in the being-imitated group, who were rated high on leadership and classroom performance, imitated their partner less. – From Authors' Abstract.

1949. THOMAS, ALEXANDER (New York Univ. Medical Ctr.). **Temperament research: where we are, where we are going.** Merrill-Palmer Quarterly, 1984, **30,** 103–109.
The research papers in the current *Merrill-Palmer Quarterly* issue (Vol. 30, No. 2) on temperament are examined. – From Author's Abstract.

1950. THOMPSON, BRUCE (Univ. of New Orleans); PITTS, MURRAY A.; & GIPE, JOAN P. **Use of the Group Embedded Figures Test with children.** Perceptual and Motor Skills, 1983, **57,** 199–203.
The results suggest that the Group Embedded Figures Test measure may be usable with fourth through sixth graders. – Adapted from the Article.

1951. THOMPSON, ROSS A. (Univ. of Nebraska); LAMB, MICHAEL E.; & ESTES, DAVID. **Stability of infant–mother attachment and its relationship to changing life circumstances in an unselected middle-class sample.** Child Development, 1982, **53,** 144–148.
Infants and mothers were observed in the Strange Situation when the infants were 12.5 and 19.5 months old. Although the proportions of securely attached and insecurely attached infants were similar at both ages, temporal stability was only 53% for overall classifications and 26% for subgroups. Changes in family circumstances, such as maternal employment or regular nonmaternal care, were associated with bidirectional changes in attachment status. – From Authors' Abstract.

1952. TOM, DAVID Y. H.; COOPER, HARRIS (Ctr. for Research in Social Behavior, 111 E. Stewart, Columbia, MO); & McGRAW, MARY. **Influences of student background and teacher authoritarianism on teacher expectations.** Journal of Educational Psychology, 1984, **76,** 259–265.
Elementary school teachers were asked to predict the academic grades and occupational attainment of 6 students varying in sex, race, and class. Higher grade and occupational expectations were held for middle-class than for lower-class students. Grade expectations were higher for girls than boys and for Asians than whites. Authoritarian teachers used stereotypes to make these judgments. – Adapted from Authors' Abstract.

1953. TORIGOE, TAKASHI (Hiroshima Univ., Japan), & KANEKO, RYUTARO. **Temporal structure of play behavior in infants: an application of cross-correlation analysis.** Hiroshima Forum for Psychology, 1982, **9,** 79–84.
The results showed that lag values of correlation coefficients among behaviors were rather inconsistent across sessions. Some factors which might have made the temporal structure unstable and ambiguous were discussed, and the necessity of further analysis concerning the length of time unit and behavioral categories sampled was suggested in dealing with this problem. – From Authors' Abstract.

1954. TURNER, PAULINE H. (Univ. of New Mexico), & HARRIS, MARY B. **Parental attitudes and preschool children's social competence.** Journal of Genetic Psychology, 1984, **144,** 105–113.
Parental indulgence and protectiveness were associated with higher scores on measures of the child's self-concept, vocabulary, empathy, and altruism. Children's vocabulary scores were positively correlated with their self-concept and empathy scores, and mothers' and fathers' ratings of child behavior were positively correlated. – From Authors' Abstract.

1955. WADSWORTH, J. (Univ. of Bristol, England); TAYLOR, B.; OSBORN, A.; & BUTLER, N. **Teenage mothering: child development at five years.** Journal of Child Psychology and Psychiatry, 1984, **25,** 305–313.
Children born to teenage mothers and living with them through the first 5 years performed less well than other children in tests of vocabulary and behavior at 5 years of age; they were also shorter on average and had a smaller head circumference. These differences remained significant after allowing for certain social and biological factors, whereas a difference on visuomotor coordination did not. – From Authors' Abstract.

1956. WAKSMAN, STEVEN A. (Lewis & Clark Coll.). **Assertion training with adolescents.** Adolescence, 1984, **19,** 123–130.
The group that received the training improved their scores on the Piers-Harris Children's Self-Concept Scale and the Intellectual Achievement Responsibility Questionnaire by the termination of the program. – From Author's Abstract.

1957. WAKSMAN, STEVEN A. (Lewis & Clark Coll.). **A controlled evaluation of assertion training with adolescents.** Adolescence, 1984, **19,** 277–282.
Assertion training treatment improved their ratings on the Piers Harris Children's Self-Concept Scale both at termination and at a 1-month follow up. – From Author's Abstract.

1958. WATKINS, HARRIET D. (Auburn Univ.), & BRADBARD, MARILYN R. **Young abused children's knowledge of caregiving behaviors.** Journal of Genetic Psychology, 1984, **144,** 145–146.
Abused children demonstrate knowledge of appropriate care behaviors. – Ed.

1959. WATSON, MALCOLM W. (Brandeis Univ.). **Development of social role understanding.** Developmental Review, 1984, **4,** 192–213.
A systematic developmental sequence of role understanding in children from 1 to 13 years of age is discussed and a method for assessing such sequences is described. The sequence, which was based on K. W. Fischer's construction–inclusion model of conceptual skill development, was tested in several studies using 2 sets of social roles and tasks and was found to be highly scalable and age related. – From Author's Abstract.

1960. WEBB, NOREEN M. (Univ. of California, Los Angeles). **Stability of small group interaction and achievement over time.** Journal of Educational Psychology, 1984, **76,** 211–224.
Students in 3 average-ability junior high school mathematics classrooms worked for 1 semester in small groups. Giving explanations was related to achievement, and receiving no explanation in response to a question or error was negatively related to achievement. Group interaction mediated the effects of relative ability within the group and intellectual responsibility on achievement. – From Author's Abstract.

1961. WEISFELD, GLENN E. (Wayne State Univ.); BLOCH, SALLY A.; & IVERS, JOSEPH W. **Possible determinants of social dominance among adolescent girls.** Journal of Genetic Psychology, 1984, **144,** 115–129.
Upper-middle-class girls, 15–18-years old, were ranked by 200 classmates of each sex on various traits reputed to be social prerogatives or bodily expressions of dominance status. Girls who exhibited these signs of dominance were perceived as fashionable, attractive, and well groomed. – From Authors' Abstract.

1962. WEISS, ANDREA (Drexel Univ.). **Parent–child relationships of adopted adolescents in a psychiatric hospital.** Adolescence, 1984, **19,** 77–88.
Adoptive parents were more frequently restricted in their visits to their children. – From Author's Abstract.

1963. WESTERVELT, VAN DIEN (Children's Rehabilitation Ctr., Univ. of Virginia Medical Ctr.); BRANTLEY, JOHN; & WARE, WILLIAM. **Changing children's attitudes toward physically handicapped peers: effects of a film and teacher-led discussion.** Journal of Pediatric Psychology, 1983, **8,** 327 + .
Compared to controls, students viewing a film or viewing a film and participating in a discussion showed greater attraction to a physically handicapped peer. – Adapted from Authors' Abstract.

1964. WHITLEY, BERNARD E., JR. (Western Psychiatric Inst. & Clinic, 3811 O'Hara, Pittsburgh); SCHOFIELD, JANET WARD; & SNYDER, HOWARD N. **Peer performances in a desegregated school: a round robin analysis.** Journal of Personality and Social Psychology, 1984, **46,** 799–810.
Although conventional ANOVA showed strong same-race preferences, round robin ANOVA revealed that individual relationships were more important than race in forming peer preferences. – From Authors' Abstract.

1965. WIMMER, HEINZ; GRUBER, SILVIA; & PERNER, JOSEF (Univ. of Sussex, Brighton, England). **Young children's conception of lying: lexical realism—moral subjectivism.** Journal of Experimental Child Psychology, 1984, **37,** 1–30.
Stories were used in which a speaker was led to a false belief, and therefore mistakenly produced either a false statement despite his truthful intentions or a true statement despite deceptive intentions. Even 4-year-olds tended to reward according to the speaker's intentions. Of those children who understood that the speaker entertained a false belief and that the falsity of his assertion was therefore unintentional, most 4-year-olds, many 6-year-olds, but practically no 8-year-olds showed a realist concept of lying. – Adapted from Authors' Abstract.

1966. WINTERS, ANTONIA S., & FRANKEL, JUDITH (Univ. of Cincinnati). **Women's work role as perceived by lower status white and black female adolescents.** Adolescence, 1984, **19,** 403–415.
No differences were found between the white and black women, and both groups could be classified as egalitarian concerning their views of women's work role. Two scales did reveal that both whites and blacks took egalitarian positions concerning women's role in the labor market more strongly when compared to their positions concerning women's role in the home. – From Authors' Abstract.

1967. WOLF, THOMAS M.; SKLOV, MONNY C.; WENZL, PAULA A.; HUNTER, SAUNDRA MacD.; & BERENSON, GERALD S. **Validation of a measure of Type A behavior pattern in children: Bogalusa heart study.** Child Development, 1982, **53,** 126–135.
A self-administered rating scale was developed and yielded the following factors: eagergy (eagerness-energy), restlessness-aggression, leadership, and alienation. Type A children in grades 5–6 performed in a more accelerated or intense manner than did Type B children on 5 of 6 validation measures. – From Authors' Abstract.

1968. WOODSON, R. H. (Univ. of Texas, Austin), & DA COSTA-WOODSON, E. M. **Social organization, physical environment, and infant–caretaker interaction.** Developmental Psychology, 1984, **20,** 473–476.
Most infant–caretaker interaction in the nuclear Malay family occurred in areas separate from work and cooking facilities and which were compatible with infant crawling and exploration. The extended family in the Chinese home interacted with the infant in a large room that contained cooking, storage, and work areas. These differences paralleled differences in infant–caretaker interaction. – From Authors' Abstract.

1969. YARROW, L. J.; MAcTURK, R. H. (National Inst. of Child Health and Human Development, Bldg. 31, Room B2B15, Bethesda); VIETZE, P. M.; McCARTHY, M. E.; KLEIN, R. P.; & McQUISTON, S. **Developmental course of parental stimulation and its relationship to mastery motivation during infancy.** Developmental Psychology, 1984, **20,** 492–503.
Infants 6 and 12 months old were observed at home with each parent separately, and their motivation was assessed in a laboratory setting. At 6 months, parental sensory stimulation was associated with persistence. The mothers' sensory stimulation and attention focusing were related to a broader range of mastery behaviors for boys than for girls. At 12 months, the significant relationships were confined to boys' persistence at practicing sensorimotor skills, with the father being the major contributor. – From Authors' Abstract.

1970. YOUNG, RICHARD A. (Univ. of British Columbia, Vancouver, British Columbia, Canada). **Career development of adolescents: an ecological perspective.** Journal of Youth and Adolescence, 1983, **12,** 401–417.
Bronfenbrenner's ecological model of human development is used as a framework for examining the research on the career development of adolescents. – From Author's Abstract.

1971. ZAHN-WAXLER, CAROLYN (National Inst. of Mental Health, 9000 Rockville, Bethesda); CUMMINGS, E. MARK; McKNEW, DONALD H.; & RADKE-YARROW, MARIAN. **Altruism, aggression, and social interactions in young children with a manic-depressive parent.** Child Development, 1984, **55,** 112–122.
Seminaturalistic observations and experimental manipulations of the affective environment were used to assess 2-year-old children. Children with a bipolar parent sometimes showed heightened distress and preoccupation with the conflicts and suffering of others, especially disturbances in adults. These children had difficulty in maintaining friendly social interactions, in sharing, and in helping their playmates. They also had difficulty modulating hostile impulses, and they showed more maladaptive patterns of aggression toward peers and adults. – From Authors' Abstract.

1972. ZIEGLER, CHRISTINE B.; DUSEK, JEROME B. (Syracuse Univ.); & CARTER, D. BRUCE. **Self-concept and sex-role orientation: an investigation of multidimensional aspects of personality development in adolescence.** Journal of Early Adolescence, 1984, **4,** 25–39.
Adolescents in grades 6–12 completed a measure of self-concept and the Bem Sex Role Inventory in order to assess relationships between sex-role orientation and self-concept during adolescence. The results illustrate the utility of the notion that self-concept and sex-role orientation are multidimensional constructs. – From Authors' Abstract.

1973. ZIEMAN, GAYLE L. (Educational Assessment Systems, Inc., 3500 I Comanche, NE, Albuquerque), & BENSON, GERALD P. **Delinquency: the role of self-esteem and social values.** Journal of Youth and Adolescence, 1983, **12,** 489–500.
The results are interpreted as generally supportive of the Kaplan theory, which holds that delinquents use psychological defenses to enhance their self-esteem and to retain endorsement of socially accepted values. – From Authors' Abstract.

EDUCATIONAL PROCESSES

1974. AGUIRRE, JOSE (Univ. of British Columbia, Vancouver, British Columbia, Canada), & ERICKSON, GAALEN. **Students' conceptions about the vector characteristics of three physics concepts.** Journal of Research in Science Teaching, 1984, **21,** 439–457.
This article reports on a study of tenth-grade students' understanding, prior to formal instruction, of 3 vector concepts: position, displacement, and velocity. Three aspects of the study are discussed and reported. – From Authors' Abstract.

1975. ALBERTINI, JOHN A. (National Technical Inst. for the Deaf, 1 Lomb Memorial Dr., Rochester, NY), & SAMAR, VINCENT J. **Early instruction of object complements to hearing-impaired college students.** Applied Psycholinguistics, 1983, **4**, 345–357.
Data from 82 basic-level, hearing-impaired college students indicated marked learning of these structures after 10 hours of instruction. – From Authors' Abstract.

1976. BAKER, L. A.; DECKER, S. N.; & DeFRIES, J. C. **Cognitive abilities in reading-disabled children: a longitudinal study.** Journal of Child Psychology and Psychiatry, 1984, **25**, 111–117.
Reading-disabled children manifested deficits as compared to controls on measures of academic achievement, symbolic processing speed, and spatial reasoning abilities at ages 9 and 15. On measures of academic achievement and spatial reasoning abilities, the rate of development was similar for the 2 groups. For measures of symbolic processing speed, differences between reading-disabled and control children were somewhat greater at the later age. – From Authors' Abstract.

1977. BAUER, RICHARD H. (Middle Tennessee State Univ.), & EMHERT, JOHN. **Information processing in reading-disabled and nondisabled children.** Journal of Experimental Child Psychology, 1984, **37**, 271–281.
Reading-disabled and nondisabled 13–14-year-olds were presented lists of words each at different rates. The primacy effect was lower in reading-disabled than nondisabled children, and slower presentation rates increased the primacy effect in both groups. These findings suggest that reading-disabled children are using less effective elaborative encoding than nondisabled readers. – From Authors' Abstract.

1978. BERK, RONALD A. (Johns Hopkins Univ.). **An evaluation of procedures for computing an ability–achievement discrepancy score.** Journal of Learning Disabilities, 1984, **17**, 262–266.
The approach with the greatest potential involves first assessing the statistical significance (reliability) of a discrepancy score and then estimating the discriminative efficiency (validity) of that score. – From Author's Abstract.

1979. BERKOWITZ, NANCY, & ENGIN, ANN W. (Univ. of South Carolina). **Normative data and reliability estimates for eight dimensions of reading attitude, Part IV—Private school learning disabled students.** Psychology in the Schools, 1984, **21**, 168–175.

1980. BERRY, P.; GUNN, P.; & ANDREWS, R. J. **The behaviour of Down's syndrome children using the "Lock Box": a research note.** Journal of Child Psychology and Psychiatry, 1984, **25**, 125–131.
A Lock Box for investigating problem-solving behavior was used with 3-year-olds with Down's syndrome and "normal" children. The normal children showed greater competence, more organization, and less perseverance than the Down's children. – From Authors' Abstract.

1981. BING, JOHN R., & BING, SALLY B. (Salisbury State Coll.). **Alternate-form reliability of the PPVT-R for black Head Start preschoolers.** Psychological Reports, 1984, **54**, 235–238.
Alternate-form reliability of the Peabody Picture Vocabulary Test-Revised for 30 rural, predominantly black Head Start children ranged from .58 to .75. – Adapted from Authors' Abstract.

1982. BLAXALL, JANET, & WILLOWS, DALE M. (Ontario Inst. for Studies in Education, 252 Bloor W., Toronto, Ontario, Canada). **Reading ability and text difficulty as influences on second graders' oral reading errors.** Journal of Educational Psychology, 1984, **76**, 330–341.
The proportion of graphically similar errors increased as material became more difficult, while the proportions of grammatically acceptable and semantically appropriate errors decreased. Poor readers showed less change in all types of errors than good or normal readers. – From Authors' Abstract.

1983. BRANWHITE, A. B. (Humberside Psychological Service). **Boosting reading skills by direct instruction.** British Journal of Educational Psychology, 1983, **53,** 291–298.
Fourteen poor readers were divided into 2 subgroups. One group received diagnostic-prescriptive remediation and the other a direct instruction program. Direct instruction led to improved reading. – Adapted from Author's Abstract.

1984. BREEN, MICHAEL J. (Univ. of Denver); LEHMAN, JOANNE; & CARLSON, MARY. **Achievement correlates of the Woodcock–Johnson Reading and Mathematics Subtests, Key Math, and Woodcock Reading in an elementary aged learning disabled population.** Journal of Learning Disabilities, 1984, **17,** 258–261.
Grade-equivalent scores and standard scores were compared and yielded correlations that ranged from .79 to .93. Mean grade-equivalent scores differed for the 2 reading measures but not when standard scores were used. The 2 math indices yielded grade-equivalent scores. – From Authors' Abstract.

1985. BROOKS, MARTIN (Shoreham-Wading River School District, Randall, Shoreham, NY), & FUSCO, ESTHER. **Constructivism and education: the child's point-of-view.** Journal of Children in Contemporary Society, 1983, **16,** 111–132.
The article describes ways in which educators have used their understandings of children's points of view in developing curriculum, structuring questions, interpreting test results, and evaluating instruction. – From Authors' Abstract.

1986. CARRIER, CAROL (Univ. of Minnesota); KARBO, KAREN; KINDEM, HEATHER; LEGISA, GERTRUDE; & NEWSTROM, LAURIE. **Use of self-generated and supplied visuals as mnemonics in gifted children's learning.** Perceptual and Motor Skills, 1983, **57,** 235–240.
Findings for gifted students in grades 4–6 suggest that the supplied visuals were a valuable instructional aid. – Adapted from the Article.

1987. CARTER, THOMAS D., & DeBLASSIE, RICHARD R. (New Mexico State Univ.). **Torque, academic achievement, and behavioral problems in early adolescents.** Journal of Early Adolescence, 1984, **4,** 83–91.
Results indicate that the Torque Test may be useful for screening for behavior problems but not for academic difficulties. – From Authors' Abstract.

1988. CARVAJAL, TONY L. (Univ. of Northern Colorado); LANE, J. MELVIN; & GAY, DENNIS A. **Longitudinal comparisons of Wechsler Scales in educable mentally handicapped children and adults.** Psychology in the Schools, 1984, **21,** 137–140.
Differences existed between WISC scores administered at the time of initial placement (mean age 11–9) and WAIS scores administered at a later date (mean age 17–6). – From Authors' Abstract.

1989. CHAUVIN, JANE C., & KARNES, FRANCES A. (Univ. of Southern Mississippi). **A leadership profile of secondary gifted students.** Psychological Reports, 1983, **53,** 1259–1262.
The present study was undertaken to ascertain the leadership profile of gifted secondary students. Compared to the profiles of adult leaders, gifted students scored higher on factors of intelligence, enthusiasm, and self-sufficiency. – From Authors' Abstract.

1990. CLARIZIO, HARVEY F. (Michigan State Univ.), & VERES, VALERIE. **A short-form version of the WISC-R for the learning disabled.** Psychology in the Schools, 1984, **21,** 154–157.
For the non-learning-disabled sample, Vocabulary, Picture Arrangement, Picture Completion, and Information were the best 4 indicators of Full Scale IQ. For the LD sample, the best 4 predictors of Full Scale IQ were Similarities, Block Design, Picture Completion, and Vocabulary. – From Authors' Abstract.

1991. COHEN, RONALD L. (Glendon Coll., 2275 Bayview, Toronto, Ontario, Canada); NETLEY, CHARLES; & CLARKE, MELISSA A. **On the generality of the short-term memory/ reading ability relationship.** Journal of Learning Disabilities, 1984, **17**, 218–221.

The presence of a recency deficit and the absence of a primacy deficit shown by the reading-disabled children in the probed serial recall task contrast sharply with the deficit patterns found in studies using nonserial short-term memory tasks. – Adapted from the Article.

1992. COLEMAN, J. MICHAEL (Univ. of Texas, Dallas). **Mothers' predictions of the self-concept of their normal or learning-disabled children.** Journal of Learning Disabilities, 1984, **17**, 214–217.

The minimal differences between the self-concept scores of LD and regular-class children lend support to the contention that a special-class label does not automatically reduce feelings of self-worth in children so labeled. – From the Article.

1993. CRITTENDEN, MARY R. (Univ. of California, San Francisco); KAPLAN, MARJORIE H.; & HEIM, JUDITH K. **Developing effective study skills and self-confidence in academically able young adolescents.** Gifted Child Quarterly, 1984, **28**, 25–30.

Our short course did appear to improve self-concept, written language, and study skills. In those skills which were not specifically taught, students showed little or no improvement. – From the Article.

1994. CROWDER, ROBERT G. (Yale Univ.). **Is it just reading? Comments on the papers by Mann, Morrison, and Wolford and Fowler.** Developmental Review, 1984, **4**, 48–61.

1995. DAVIDSON, JANET E. (Yale Univ.), & STERNBERG, ROBERT J. **The role of insight in intellectual giftedness.** Gifted Child Quarterly, 1984, **28**, 58–64.

We believe that insight skills provide a useful way of understanding a critical aspect of intellectual giftedness. The understanding and improvement of insight skills might provide a valuable focus for future research. – From the Article.

1996. DeCARO, J. J. (Rochester Inst. of Technology); DOWALIBY, F. J.; & MARUGGI, E. A. **A cross-cultural examination of parents' and teachers' expectations for deaf youth regarding careers.** British Journal of Educational Psychology, 1983, **53**, 358–363.

This study compares attitudes at a school for the deaf in Italy and a school for the deaf in England. There are no significant differences between the mean advice to deaf people in England and mean advice to deaf people in Italy. – From Authors' Abstract.

1997. EAVES, RONALD C. (Auburn Univ.), & SIMPSON, ROBERT G. **The concurrent validity of the Peabody Individual Achievement Test relative to the Key Math Diagnostic Arithmetic Test among adolescents.** Psychology in the Schools, 1984, **21**, 165–167.

Math scores on the Peabody Individual Achievement Test were correlated with all scores on the Key Math Diagnostic Arithmetic Test. – From Authors' Abstract.

1998. FARNHAM-DIGGORY, S. (Univ. of Delaware). **Why reading? Because it's there.** Developmental Review, 1984, **4**, 62–71.

The papers of Mann, Morrison, and Wilson and Fowler are criticized. – Ed.

1999. FORD, CAROL E. (Univ. of Kansas); PELHAM, WILLIAM E.; & ROSS, ALAN O. **Selective attention and rehearsal in the auditory short-term memory task performance of poor and normal readers.** Journal of Abnormal Child Psychology, 1984, **12**, 127–142.

Effects of distraction, list length, and speed of stimulus presentation were investigated. Group differences in performance were obtained for both distraction and no-distraction conditions. In the second experiment, rehearsal training resulted in improved performance relative to children who were not trained; however, there was no Rehearsal Training X Reading Group interaction. – From Authors' Abstract.

2000. FRIEDRICH, DOUGLAS (Central Michigan Univ.); FULLER, GERALD B.; & DAVIS, DONALD. **Learning disability: fact and fiction.** Journal of Learning Disabilities, 1984, **17,** 205–209.
Empirically derived formulas for assessment of learning disability revealed the most discriminating formula included WISC, WRAT, and grade-level variables. – From Authors' Abstract.

2001. GERMAN, DIANE (National Coll. of Education, Foster G. McGaw Graduate School, Evanston, IL). **Diagnosis of word-finding disorders in children with learning disabilities.** Journal of Learning Disabilities, 1984, **17,** 353–359.
Learning-disabled children with word-finding problems manifested more errors, secondary characteristics, longer response times, as well as unique substitution types, while LD children without word-finding problems performed similarly to their normal peers. – From Author's Abstract.

2002. GOODMAN, JOAN F. (Children's Hosp. of Philadelphia); CECIL, HENRY S.; & BARKER, WILLIAM F. **Early intervention with retarded children: some encouraging results.** Developmental Medicine and Child Neurology, 1984, **26,** 47–55.
Retarded preschool children who participated in a treatment program which emphasized parental participation showed greater gains in scores on the Bayley and Stanford-Binet tests than children who received services elsewhere. – From Abstract by B. B. Keller.

2003. GORDON, HAROLD W. (Western Psychiatric Inst. & Clinic, 3811 O'Hara, Pittsburgh). **The assessment of cognitive function for use in education.** Journal of Children in Contemporary Society, 1983, **16,** 207–218.
The article outlines the basis of our knowledge of hemispheric function, relates some of the first steps in its application to education, and highlights the implications. – From Author's Abstract.

2004. GRAYVILL, DANIEL (Illinois State Univ.); JAMISON, MICHAEL; & SWERDLIK, MARK E. **Remediation of impulsivity in learning disabled children by special education resource teachers using verbal self-instruction.** Psychology in the Schools, 1984, **21,** 252–254.
Special-education resource teachers trained impulsive learning-disabled children to use Verbal Self-Instruction (VSI) to decrease the children's impulsivity. The children trained with VSI showed reductions in impulsivity on the Matching Familiar Figures Test, but not in ratings by regular classroom teachers. – From Authors' Abstract.

2005. GULLO, DOMINIC F., & CLEMENTS, DOUGLAS H. (Kent State Univ.). **Differences in achievement patterns for boys and girls in kindergarten and first grade: a longitudinal study.** Psychological Reports, 1984, **54,** 23–27.
Although no sex differences were found on developmental indexes when children entered kindergarten, differences were found by the end of kindergarten with girls outperforming boys. Achievement was equal for boys and girls at the end of first grade. – Adapted from Authors' Abstract.

2006. GULLO, DOMINIC F. (Kent State Univ.); CLEMENTS, DOUGLAS H.; & ROBERTSON, LINDA. **Prediction of academic achievement with the McCarthy Screening Test and Metropolitan Readiness Test.** Psychology in the Schools, 1984, **21,** 264–269.
Children were screened upon entering kindergarten using the McCarthy Screening Test (MST). As a measure of academic readiness, the Metropolitan Readiness Test (MRT) was administered at the end of kindergarten, and the Scott and Foresman Achievement Test (SFAT) was administered at the end of first grade as a measure of achievement. Regression analyses indicated that the MST predicted children's scores on the MRT and SFAT. The MRT was also a predictor of the SFAT. – From Authors' Abstract.

2007. HANSON, VICKI L. (Haskins Laboratories, 270 Crown, New Haven); LIBERMAN, ISABELLE Y.; & SHANKWEILER, DONALD. **Linguistic coding by deaf children in relation to beginning reading success.** Journal of Experimental Child Psychology, 1984, **37**, 378–393.
Deaf children who were classified as good readers appeared to use both speech and fingers-pelling (manual) codes in short-term retention of printed letters. Deaf children classified as poor readers did not show influence of either of these linguistically based codes in recall. – From Authors' Abstract.

2008. HARNESS, B. Z.; EPSTEIN, RACHEL; & GORDON, H. W. (Western Psychiatric Inst. & Clinic, 3811 O'Hara, Pittsburgh). **Cognitive profile of children referred to a clinic for reading disabilities.** Journal of Learning Disabilities, 1984, **17**, 346–352.
Virtually all subjects who were behind in reading—not explained by intelligence or opportunity factors—performed, on the average, better than the norm on tests usually attributed to the right cerebral hemisphere and poorer than the norm by the same amount on tests attributed to the left cerebral hemisphere. – From Authors' Abstract.

2009. HARPER, DENNIS C., & WACKER, DAVID P. (Coll. of Medicine, Univ. of Iowa). **The efficiency of the Denver Developmental Screening Test with rural disadvantaged preschool children.** Journal of Pediatric Psychology, 1983, **8**, 273 +.
The Denver Developmental Screening Test was administered to 1,018 rural disadvantaged preschoolers, with subsamples receiving the Stanford-Binet-LM and WPPSI. Descriptive outcome statistics are provided. – From Authors' Abstract.

2010. HARTY, HAROLD (Indiana Univ.), & BEALL, DWIGHT. **Attitudes toward science of gifted and nongifted fifth graders.** Journal of Research in Science Teaching, 1984, **21**, 483–488.
Gifted students were found to have more positive attitudes toward science than nongifted students. Boys exhibited more positive attitudes toward science; however, most differences were not reliable. – Adapted from Authors' Abstract.

2011. HARVEY, PHILIP D.; WEINTRAUB, SHELDON; & NEALE, JOHN M. (SUNY, Stony Brook). **Distractibility in learning-disabled children: the role of measurement artifact.** Journal of Learning Disabilities, 1984, **17**, 234–236.
Results suggest that differential performance of groups across tasks or conditions depends on the psychometric properties of the instruments. A manipulation of the psychometric properties of a task can lead to a groups-by-condition interaction. – From the Article.

2012. HARVEY, STEVEN, & SEELEY, KENNETH R. (Univ. of Denver). **An investigation of the relationships among intellectual and creative abilities, extracurricular activities, achievement, and giftedness in a delinquent population.** Gifted Child Quarterly, 1984, **28**, 73–79.

2013. HELSEL, WILLIAM J., & MATSON, JOHNNY L. (Northern Illinois Univ.). **The assessment of depression in children: the internal structure of the Child Depression Inventory (CDI).** Behaviour Research and Therapy, 1984, **22**, 289–298.
These data provide useful information relative to the development of psychometric properties of the CDI as well as a means of evaluating the relationship between depressive and social behaviors in children. – From the Article.

2014. KARNES, FRANCES A.; SHORTON, JAMES E.; & CURRIE, BILLYE BOB (Univ. of Southern Mississippi). **Correlations between the Wide Range Achievement Test and the California Achievement Test with intellectually gifted students.** Psychological Reports, 1984, **54**, 189–190.
Scores of elementary school gifted students on the WRAT and the California Achievement Test correlated from .29 to .53. – From Authors' Abstract.

2015. KARR, SHARON K. (Emporia State Univ.). **School achievement of Sierra Leone, West African children from four sub-cultures.** Perceptual and Motor Skills, 1983, **57,** 204–206.
WRAT spelling and reading scores of the sixth graders of the most modernized subculture were higher than those of the other subcultures. Interactions between gender and subculture were significant. – From Author's Abstract.

2016. KAVALE, KENNETH (Univ. of California, Riverside), & ANDREASSEN, ERIC. **Factors in diagnosing the learning disabled: analysis of judgmental policies.** Journal of Learning Disabilities, 1984, **17,** 273–278.
The article examines, from a lens model perspective, the decision-making processes of administrators, psychologists, teachers, and nurses in their judgments about the learning disabled. – From Authors' Abstract.

2017. KOURILSKY, MARILYN (Univ. of California, Los Angeles), & CAMPBELL, MICHAEL. **Sex differences in a simulated classroom economy: children's beliefs about entrepeneurship.** Sex Roles, 1984, **10,** 53–66.
Children in grades 3–6 participated in an economic education instructional program. There was less entrepeneural stereotyping after instruction, and occupational sex stereotyping also decreased. – From Authors' Abstract.

2018. LEARNER, KATHY M., & RICHMAN, CHARLES L. (Wake Forest Univ.). **The effect of modifying the cognitive tempo of reading disabled children on reading comprehension.** Contemporary Educational Psychology, 1984, **9,** 122–134.
It was concluded that imposing slow reading strategies on impulsive children is an important factor in developing educational programs for children with reading disabilities and that teaching poor readers a reflective cognitive strategy may have important consequences on the child's reading performance. – From Authors' Abstract.

2019. LICHTENSTEIN, ROBERT (Univ. of Delaware). **Predicting school performance of preschool children from parent reports.** Journal of Abnormal Child Psychology, 1984, **12,** 79–94.
Parents of preschool children completed a developmental inventory that assessed adaptive behavior and language development. Teachers rated kindergarten performance the following year. Correlations with the overall teacher rating were .40 for the adaptive behavior scale and .57 for the language scale. – From Author's Abstract.

2020. LINDGREN, SCOTT D. (Univ. of Iowa), & RICHMAN, LYNN C. **Immediate memory functions of verbally deficient reading-disabled children.** Journal of Learning Disabilities, 1984, **17,** 222–225.
The results suggest developmental differences in the relative influence of specific modalities in the immediate memory functions of these children, but emphasize the role of intramodal verbal factors across ages. – From Authors' Abstract.

2021. LOVETT, MAUREEN W. (Hosp. for Sick Children, 555 Univ. Drive, Toronto, Ontario, Canada). **Sentential structure and the perceptual span in normal reading development.** Journal of Psycholinguistic Research, 1984, **13,** 69–84.
The more precocious the young reader, the longer his reported span. The better readers' and the adults' advantage was greater the more linguistically constrained the reading material. – From Author's Abstract.

2022. LUDWIG, GRETCHEN (Northern Illinois Univ.), & CULLINAN, DOUGLAS. **Behavior problems of gifted and nongifted elementary school girls and boys.** Gifted Child Quarterly, 1984, **28,** 37–39.
The present results indicate that gifted elementary students show fewer behavior problems than their nongifted classmates. – From the Article.

2023. MacLEAN, PAUL (National Inst. of Mental Health, Poolesville, MD). **Brain evolution: the origins of social and cognitive behaviors.** Journal of Children in Contemporary Society, 1983, **16,** 9–21.
Frequently, behaviors that are observed in the classroom, and believed to be learned, are actually inherited through the evolutionary process. – From Author's Abstract.

2024. MANN, VIRGINIA A. (Bryn Mawr Coll.). **Review: reading skill and language skill.** Developmental Review, 1984, **4,** 1–15.
This article reviews studies which have explored the association between early reading and spoken language skills. The focus is on findings which reveal that when the linguistic short-term memory skills of good and poor beginning readers are examined, poor readers prove to possess subtle deficiencies which correlate with their problems in learning to read. – From Author's Abstract.

2025. MILLER, VIRGINIA; ONOTERA, RODNEY T.; & DEINARD, AMOS S. (Univ. of Minnesota Hosp., Minneapolis). **Denver Developmental Screening Test: cultural variations in Southeast Asian children.** Journal of Pediatrics, 1984, **104,** 481–482.
Testing of recently emigrated Southeast Asian refugee children has revealed that certain items will not be passed at various ages and so will be scored as failures or delays according to the standard protocol. – From the Article.

2026. MOORE, CLAY L., & ZARSKE, JOHN A. (Flagstaff Medical Bldg., 1355 N. Beaver, Flagstaff). **Comparison of Native American Navajo Bender-Gestalt performance with Koppitz and SOMPA norms.** Psychology in the Schools, 1984, **21,** 148–153.
Results suggest that the 1974 Koppitz and SOMPA white norms may have utility as an aide to psychological assessment of Native American Navajo children. – From Authors' Abstract.

2027. MORRISON, FREDERICK J. (Univ. of Alberta, Edmonton, Alberta, Canada). **Reading disability: a problem in rule learning and word decoding.** Developmental Review, 1984, **4,** 36–47.
Disabled readers are hypothesized to suffer a fundamental problem in acquiring word knowledge and word processing skills. Poor decoding skills prevent them from developing sophisticated reading comprehension skills. – From Author's Abstract.

2028. MORTON, L. L., & KERSHNER, JOHN R. (Ontario Inst. for Studies in Education, Canada). **Negative air ionization improves memory and attention in learning-disabled and mentally retarded children.** Journal of Abnormal Child Psychology, 1984, **12,** 353–366.
The effect of increased concentrations of ambient negative air ions on incidental visual memory for words and purposive auditory memory for dichotic digits was investigated in normal, learning-disabled, and mildly mentally retarded children. All of the children breathing negatively ionized air were superior in incidental memory. In dichotic listening, the negative ions produced a counterpriming effect in the 2 learning-impaired groups, offsetting the difficulties that they showed under placebo in switching attention selectively from 1 ear to the other. – From Authors' Abstract.

2029. MURPHY, DOUGLAS (Univ. of Kansas); JENKINS-FRIEDMAN, REVA; & TOLLEFSON, NONA. **A new criterion for the "ideal" child?** Gifted Child Quarterly, 1984, **28,** 31–36.
These results suggest that 2 major shifts have occurred over the past 20 years in conceptualizations of the ideal child among teachers and experts in gifted child education. The first difference is in the image of the ideal child; the second concerns the nature of agreement between teachers and experts. – From the Article.

2030. NELSON, R. BRETT, & CUMMINGS, JACK A. (Indiana Univ.). **Educable mentally retarded children's understanding of Boehm Basic Concepts.** Psychological Reports, 1984, **54,** 81–82.

The Boehm Test of Basic Concepts showed significant deficits in concept attainment in educable mentally retarded children. – Adapted from Authors' Abstract.

2031. OLSON, RICHARD K. (Univ. of Colorado); DAVIDSON, BRIAN J.; KLIEGL, REINHOLD; & DAVIES, SUSAN E. **Development of phonetic memory in disabled and normal readers.** Journal of Experimental Child Psychology, 1984, **37**, 187–206.
Younger subjects showed a larger difference between rhyming and nonrhyming false-positive errors for the normal readers. The older disabled readers' phonetic effect was comparable to that of the younger normal readers. The normal readers' phonetic effect declined with age in the recognition task, but they maintained a significant advantage across age in the auditory WISC-R digit span recall test and a test of phonological nonword decoding. – From Authors' Abstract.

2032. PIECHOWSKI, MICHAEL M. (Northwestern Univ.), & COLANGELO, NICHOLAS. **Developmental potential of the gifted.** Gifted Child Quarterly, 1984, **28**, 80–88.
Although the level of each form of psychic overexcitability (OE) varies considerably across gifted individuals, OEs are consistently and reliably present in a gifted group at any age. – From the Article.

2033. POOLE, MILLICENT E. (Macquarie Univ., North Ryde, New South Wales, Australia). **The schools adolescents would like.** Adolescence, 1984, **19**, 447–458.
The majority of students were happy with the status quo but expected their schools to be less authoritarian concerning rules and discipline. – From Author's Abstract.

2034. POTTER, ELLEN F. (Univ. of South Carolina). **Impact of developmental factors on motivating the school achievement of young adolescents: theory and implications for practice.** Journal of Early Adolescence, 1984, **4**, 1–10.
This article addresses several motivational techniques and indicates aspects of the developmental stage of early adolescence that are relevant to their application. – From Author's Abstract.

2035. PROUT, H. THOMPSON (SUNY, Albany), & CELMER, DAVID S. **A validity study of the Kinetic School Drawing technique.** Psychology in the Schools, 1984, **21**, 176–180.
Kinetic School Drawings from fifth graders were analyzed for "negative" affect. Significant correlations with academic achievement were found. – From Authors' Abstract.

2036. RAMEY, CRAIG T. (Frank Porter Graham Child Development Ctr., Univ. of North Carolina, Chapel Hill), & CAMPBELL, FRANCES A. **Preventive education for high-risk children: cognitive consequences of the Carolina Abecedarian Project.** American Journal of Mental Deficiency, 1984, **88**, 515–523.
Results from the Bayley Mental Development Index at 18 months; the Stanford-Binet at 24, 36, and 48 months; and the McCarthy results at 42 and 54 months indicate that the difference between the educationally treated and the control groups was due to the decline below the national norm for the control-group children. – From the Article.

2037. REEVE, PEGGY TARPLEY (Univ. of Virginia), & LOPER, ANN BOOKER. **Intrinsic vs. extrinsic motivation in learning disabled children.** Perceptual and Motor Skills, 1983, **57**, 59–63.
Children aged 8–11 years did not show the predicted relationship between motivational orientation and academic achievement. – Adapted from the Article.

2038. REID, D. J.; BRIGGS, N.; & BEVERIDGE, M. (Manchester Univ., England). **The effect of picture upon the readability of a school science topic.** British Journal of Educational Psychology, 1983, **53**, 327–335.
Fourteen-year-old children studying CSE biology in 6 comprehensive schools completed a cloze test during their study and an objective items-recognition test 15 min afterward. Pictures aided memory. – Adapted from Authors' Abstract.

2039. REITSMA, PIETER (Paedologisch Inst., Koningslaan 22, Amsterdam, Netherlands). **Sound priming in beginning readers.** Child Development, 1984, **55**, 406–423.
Children ages 7–12 years were asked to make semantic interpretations from printed words. Speech sounds were presented shortly before a visual word display. Similarity between sound and the pronunciation of the word was facilitative for beginning readers (both for familiar and unfamiliar orthographies and independent of orthographic complexity) but had no effect for more fluent readers. – From Author's Abstract.

2040. RIEDLINGER-RYAN, KATHRYN J., & SHEWAN, CYNTHIA M. (Univ. of Western Ontario, Canada). **Comparison of auditory language comprehension skills in learning-disabled and academically achieving adolescents.** Language, Speech, and Hearing Services in Schools, 1984, **15**, 127–136.
Subjects took a battery of auditory language comprehension tests including the Token Test, the Test of Linguistic Concepts, and the Auditory Comprehension Test for Sentences. Results indicated that 73% of the LD group scored lower than all of the control subjects on 1 or more of these tests. – From Authors' Abstract.

2041. ROE, KIKI V. (Univ. of California, Los Angeles), & ROE, ARNOLD. **Schooling and cognitive development: a longitudinal study in Greece.** Perceptual and Motor Skills, 1983, **57,** 147–153.
After 4 years of schooling, Greek mountain village children's cognitive functioning remained as retarded as at school entry by comparison with both Greek and American norms. – Adapted from Authors' Abstract.

2042. ROGOW, ANDREA M. (Simon Fraser Univ., Burnaby, British Columbia, Canada); MARCIA, JAMES E.; & SLUGOSKI, BEN R. **The relative importance of identity status interview components.** Journal of Youth and Adolescence, 1983, **12,** 387–400.
Eighty college males were given an expanded identity status interview which included 2 new areas, "attitudes towards sexual expression" and "sex-role beliefs." Ideology contributed more than occupation both to overall status rating, as well as to discrimination on the dependent variable. Interpersonal-sexual concerns were important for men's identity development as well as for women's. – From Authors' Abstract.

2043. SAHU, SHANTILATA (Utkal Univ., Orissa, India), & DEVI, GITA. **Reading ability and information-processing strategies.** Journal of Research in Reading, 1984, **7,** 33–40.
There is a delay in visual scanning for poor readers. Good readers perform better than poor readers on the simultaneous and successive information-processing tasks. – From Authors' Abstract.

2044. SAPP, GARY L. (Univ. of Alabama); CHISSOM, BRAD S.; & HORTON, WILLIAM O. **An investigation of the ability of selected instruments to discriminate areas of exceptional class designation.** Psychology in the Schools, 1984, **21,** 258–263.
Emotionally handicapped (EH), learning-disabled (LD), and educable mentally regarded (EMR) children were compared on data used in th placement process (WISC-R profiles, Key Math scores, and teacher rating scale scores). Both the LD and the EH groups differed significantly from the EMR group, and classification results for all groups were inadequate. – From Authors' Abstract.

2045. SAWYERS, JANET K. (Virginia Polytechnic Inst.); MORAN, JAMES D., III; FU, VICTORIA R.; & MILGRAM, ROBERTA M. **Familiar versus unfamiliar stimulus items in measurements of original thinking in young children.** Perceptual and Motor Skills, 1983, **57,** 51–55.
Familiar stimulus items yielded greater ideational fluency and generated both more popular and unusual responses. – Adapted from Authors' Abstract.

2046. SCHAB, FRED (Univ. of Georgia). **Minimum competency: a comparison of reactions of southern black high school students, their parents and black teachers.** Adolescence, 1984, **19**, 107–112.
Black parents were strongest in their approval of minimum competency requirements, followed by black teachers, and to a lesser degree by the students. – From Author's Abstract.

2047. SCRUGGS, THOMAS E., & MASTROPIERI, MARGO A. (Utah State Univ.). **Intelligence and learning disabled adolescents under three conditions.** Psychological Reports, 1983, **53**, 1117–1118.
In further analysis of previously presented data, Pearson correlations between scores on learning tasks and WISC-R IQs were computed for 90 adolescents diagnosed as learning disabled who learned under 3 conditions: keyword mnemonic, direct question, and free study. The highest correlation (.44) was noted for students in the keyword condition. – From Authors' Abstract.

2048. SHERMAN, JULIA (WRI of Wisconsin, Inc., 3917 Plymouth, Madison). **Girls talk about mathematics and their future: a partial replication.** Psychology of Women Quarterly, 1983, **7**, 338–342.
Eleventh-grade girls who had previously been extensively tested in grade 8 were interviewed and readministered the Fennema-Sherman Mathematics Attitudes Scales II. "Fear of success" in math became less from grade 8 to grade 11; girls continuing in math had more positive attitudes toward math, came from more favored environments, were closer to parents, and were more influenced by them. Most girls demonstrated developing sex-role strain. – From Author's Abstract.

2049. SIEGEL, GERALD M. (Univ. of Minnesota), & VOGT, MARY C. **Pluralization instruction in comprehension and production.** Journal of Speech and Hearing Disorders, 1984, **49**, 128–135.
Retarded children who did not comprehend or produce plurals were taught to pluralize by adding /s/ to words like hat/hats, cup/cups. The children were taught in 2 environments, an experimental room and an ordinary classroom. – From Authors' Abstract.

2050. SILVA, PHIL A. (Univ. of Otago Medical School, Box 913, Dunedin, New Zealand); McGEE, ROB; & WILLIAMS, SHEILA M. **Developmental language delay from three to seven years and its significance for low intelligence and reading difficulties at age seven.** Developmental Medicine and Child Neurology, 1983, **25**, 783–793.
Language delay was associated with a higher prevalence of low intelligence or reading difficulties at age 7. – Adapted from Authors' Abstract.

2051. SIMON, CHARLANN S. (5630 S. Rocky Point, Tempe). **Functional-pragmatic evaluation of communication skills in school-aged children.** Language, Speech, and Hearing Services in Schools, 1984, **15**, 83–97.
Five receptive and 5 expressive considerations are presented which serve as guidelines for the selection of informal evaluation tasks. The resulting procedure provides descriptive data on a student's auditory processing skills and his/her ability to use language for various purposes. – Author's Abstract.

2052. SINATRA, RICHARD (St. John's Univ.), & BLAU, HAROLD. **Hemispheric routing of tactilely delivered words for dyslexic males.** Perceptual and Motor Skills, 1983, **57**, 179–184.
Spelling performance in 14-year-old dyslexic boys was successful for meaningful words presented with right- or left-hand tactile delivery when vision was occluded. – Adapted from Authors' Abstract.

2053. SMEETS, P. M. (Univ. of Leiden, Hooigracht 15, Leiden, Netherlands); LANCIONI, G. EW.; & HOOGEVEEN, F. R. **Effects of different stimulus manipulations on the acquisition of word recognition in trainable mentally retarded children.** Journal of Mental Deficiency Research, 1984, **28**, 109–122.
The results of this experiment in part showed that stimulus shaping and stimulus-connected prompt fading were uniformly successful for establishing word recognition in retarded children, and the efficacy of the pictorial prompts was limited and unpredictable when the stimulus manipulations allowed subjects to respond to increasingly difficult to discriminate prompts without guiding their attention to the training stimuli. – From Authors' Abstract.

2054. STACKHOUSE, JOY (Birmingham Polytechnic, Franchise St., Perry Bar, Birmingham, England), & CAMPBELL, HELEN. **The unintelligible child: a problem for the health care team.** Child: Care, Health and Development, 1983, **9**, 327–337.
This paper attempts to clarify the nature of phonological development and disability and to draw general implications for assessment and management of the unintelligible child. – From Authors' Abstract.

2055. STEVENSON, HAROLD W. (Univ. of Michigan). **Orthography and reading disabilities.** Journal of Learning Disabilities, 1984, **17**, 296–301.
Could it be that the widespread incidence of reading disabilities in our culture can be traced in large part to the idiosyncracies of the spelling and writing system used in English? If this is true, what can be done to remedy the situation, other than following those who have proposed that the written form of English must be revised?—From Author's Abstract.

2056. STONE, C. ADDISON (Northwestern Univ.), & WERTSCH, JAMES V. **A social interactional analysis of learning disabilities remediation.** Journal of Learning Disabilities, 1984, **17**, 194–199.
The remediation of learning-disabled children can often be viewed as providing them with strategies which they can use to direct their own behavior. Insight into why such strategic assistance is effective can be obtained from viewing remediation as a social/communicative setting. This perspective is illustrated with an analysis of an annotated transcript of a remediation session. – From Authors' Abstract.

2057. STONEMAN, ZOLINDA (Univ. of Georgia); BRODY, GENE H.; & MacKINNON, CAROL. **Naturalistic observations of children's activities and roles while playing with their siblings and friends.** Child Development, 1984, **55**, 617–627.
School-aged children, their younger siblings, and their best friends were observed while playing at home. Younger siblings accepted the managee role more often from the older sibling than vice versa, while peers did not differ in their assumption of this role. The older sibling's friend accepted the complementary managee role in relation to the younger sibling's management attempts more frequently than the older sibling. Girls were more likely to accept the managee role than were boys. – From Authors' Abstract.

2058. SUTTER, EMILY G. (Univ. of Houston, Clear Lake), & BATTIN, R. RAY. **Using traditional psychological tests to obtain neuropsychological information on children.** Clinical Neuropsychology, 1984, **6**, 115–119.
The authors summarize conceptual models and factor analytic studies of neuropsychological batteries and suggest standardized tests which yield similar information to the formal published neuropsychological batteries. – From Authors' Abstract.

2059. SWANSON, H. LEE (Univ. of Northern Colorado). **Semantic visual memory codes in learning disabled readers.** Journal of Experimental Child Psychology, 1984, **37**, 124–140.
Learning-disabled and skilled readers viewed nonsense pictures without names or with either relevant or irrelevant names with respect to the distinctive characteristics of the picture. Both types of names improved recall of nondisabled readers, while LD readers exhibited better recall for unnamed pictures. – From Author's Abstract.

2060. SYLWESTER, ROBERT (Univ. of Oregon). **The neurosciences and the education profession: inserting new knowledge of a child's developing brain into an already well-developed school.** Journal of Children in Contemporary Society, 1983, **16**, 1–8.
The article discusses, in part, historic technological barriers to the use of the brain in teaching/learning theory. – From Author's Abstract.

2061. TEETER, PHYLLIS ANNE (Univ. of Wisconsin, Milwaukee). **Cross-validation of the factor structure of the McCarthy Scales for kindergarten children.** Psychology in the Schools, 1984, **21**, 158–164.
The subjects had a mean General Cognitive Index of 115.42 and a mean age of 5–6. Five factors were generated, including Verbal Comprehension, Quantitative-Reasoning, Memory, Perceptual-Performance, and Motor factors. – From Author's Abstract.

2062. THOMAS, BILLIE (Eastern Montana Coll.). **Early toy preferences of four-year-old readers and nonreaders.** Child Development, 1984, **55**, 424–430.
Subjects were 4-year-old children and their parents. Half of the children read at or above second-grade level, and half could not recognize 3 sight words. According to parents' reports, there were significant differences in the toy preferences of the 2 groups. The early readers played with, enjoyed, and valued toys such as books and alphabet cards more than the nonreaders, who preferred gross motor, construction, and fantasy toys. – From Author's Abstract.

2063. TOLLEFSON, NONA (Univ. of Kansas); TRACY, D. B.; JOHNSEN, E. P.; FARMER, A. W.; & BUENNING, MEREDITH. **Goal setting and personal responsibility training for LD adolescents.** Psychology in the Schools, 1984, **21**, 224–233.
The training program was designed to teach LD junior high school students to set realistic achievement goals, to expend effort to reach the goals, and to accept personal responsibility for achievement outcomes. The experimental group learned to set realistic goals and to attribute achievement outcomes to the amount of personal effort expended. – From Authors' Abstract.

2064. TRABASSO, TOM (Univ. of Chicago). **The interaction between reading skills and reading instruction.** Developmental Review, 1984, **4**, 72–76.
Suggestions are made on how to untangle the cause-effect problem through longitudinal investigation and careful analysis of some possible interactions between cognitive skills and reading ability. – From Author's Abstract.

2065. TRAMONTANA, MICHAEL G. (Brown Univ.); KLEE, STEVEN H.; & BOYD, THOMAS A. **WISC-R interrelationships with the Halstead-Reitan and Children's Luria Neuropsychological Batteries.** Clinical Neuropsychology, 1984, **6**, 1–8.
For both batteries, neuropsychological performance was dependent on general intellectual functioning. Conversely, various aspects of intellectual performance as measured by the WISC-R were highly related with overall performance on both the HRNB and LNNB-C. In general, there appears to be considerable overlap with intellectual functioning. – From the Article.

2066. VALENCIA, RICHARD R. (Univ. of California, Santa Cruz). **The McCarthy Scales and Kaufman's McCarthy Short Form correlations with the Comprehensive Test of Basic Skills.** Psychology in the Schools, 1984, **21**, 141–147.
For samples of English-speaking and Spanish-speaking Mexican-American children, the conventional McCarthy and Kaufman's short form predicted achievement about equally well. – From Author's Abstract.

2067. VALLES, ENRIQUE (St. Francis Hosp., Haywards Heath, W. Sussex, England), & ODDY, MICHAEL. **The influence of a return to school on the long-term adjustment of school refusers.** Journal of Adolescence, 1984, **7**, 35–44.
This papers reports a study of 34 young people, all of whom had been admitted to an in-patient adolescent unit because of school refusal. Half had returned to school, and the other half had

never done so. The influence of this return on their emotional and social adjustment in young adulthood was assessed. – From Authors' Abstract.

2068. VELLUTINO, FRANK R. (SUNY, Albany); SCANLON, DONNA M.; & BENTLEY, WILLIAM L. **Interhemispheric learning and speed of hemispheric transmission in dyslexic and normal readers: a replication of previous results and additional findings.** Applied Psycholinguistics, 1983, **4,** 209–228.
Second- and sixth-grade poor and normal readers were compared on learning and discrimination tasks that involved hemifield visual stimuli. Poor readers performed below normal readers on paired associates, regardless of the visual field in which the stimulus appeared. No differences were found on time taken to indicate presence or absence of a dot. It was concluded that deficiency in interhemispheric transmission is not a significant cause of reading disability. – From Authors' Abstract.

2069. WOLFORD, GEORGE (Dartmouth Coll.), & FOWLER, CAROL A. **Differential use of partial information by good and poor readers.** Developmental Review, 1984, **4,** 16–35.
Three experiments provide evidence favoring the interpretation that good and poor readers perform differently in tests of memory when information about stimulus identity is incomplete due to memory loss and the response measure is sensitive to partial-information use in guessing. – From Authors' Abstract.

2070. WOOD, H. A., & WOOD, D. J. **An experimental evaluation of the effects of five styles of teacher conversation on the language of hearing-impaired children.** Journal of Child Psychology and Psychiatry, 1984, **25,** 45–62.
Previous studies revealed negative correlations between a measure of teacher control of the conversations and measures of children's initiative and loquacity. Teachers were asked to bias their conversations toward 1 of 5 "levels of control"—enforced repetitions, 2-choice questions, wh-type questions, personal contributions, and phatics. As teachers changed style, their children followed them with the predicted changes in initiative and mean length of turn. – From Authors' Abstract.

2071. ZARB, JANET M. (Toronto Board of Education, 302 Rose Park, Toronto, Ontario, Canada). **A comparison of remedial, failure, and successful secondary school students across self-perception and past and present school performance variables.** Adolescence, 1984, **19,** 335–348.

PSYCHIATRY, CLINICAL PSYCHOLOGY

2072. ALEXANDER, BARRIE B.; JOHNSON, SUZANNE BENNETT (Univ. of Florida); & CARTER, RANDY L. **A psychometric study of the Family Adaptability and Cohesion Evaluation Scales.** Journal of Abnormal Child Psychology, 1984, **12,** 199–208.
These Scales were administered to clinic and nonclinic families. Therapists' ratings of cohesion and adaptability did not correlate with Scale scores among clinic families. There was no difference between clinic and nonclinic samples on the cohesion or adaptability scales, although the social desirability scale did discriminate between groups. – From Authors' Abstract.

2073. AMAN, MICHAEL G. (Univ. of Auckland, Private Bag, Auckland, New Zealand). **Hyperactivity: nature of the syndrome and its natural history.** Journal of Autism and Developmental Disorders, 1984, **14,** 39–56.
The events leading to the recent emphasis on attentional characteristics of hyperactive children are summarized. It is concluded that hyperactivity has not been disproved. The evidence indicates that hyperactivity is often a serious disorder with long-term and far-reaching consequences for the children and their families. – From Author's Abstract.

2074. ASARNOW, ROBERT F. (Univ. of California, Los Angeles), & SHERMAN, TRACY. **Studies of visual information processing in schizophrenic children.** Child Development, 1984, **55**, 249–261.
Children meeting DSM III criteria for schizophrenia (mean age 12 years), a group of normal children matched in mean mental age to the schizophrenic children, and a group of younger normal children (mean age 6.6 years) were administered a series of visual information-processing tasks. Schizophrenic children showed impairment relative to the MA-matched normals and performed at the level of the younger normal children on a forced-choice partial-report version of the span-of-apprehension task. Schizophrenic children were comparable with the MA-matched controls on a full-report span-of-apprehension task that placed heavy demands on iconic and short-term memory. – From Authors' Abstract.

2075. BAKER, IAN (Bristol & Weston Health Authority, Greyfriars, Lewin's Mead, Bristol, England); HUGHES, JANIE; STREET, EDDY; & SWEETNAM, PETER. **Behaviour problems in children followed from 5 to 8 1/2–9 years of age and their relation to educational attainment.** Child: Care, Health and Development, 1983, **9**, 339–348.
Children with behavior problems at 5 years continued to have more behavior problems at 8 1/2–9 years than controls. There was no difference between the groups in nonverbal IQ, but there were delays of 5 months for both reading accuracy and comprehension for the study group. – From Authors' Abstract.

2076. BALLARD, KEITH D. (Univ. of Otago, P.O. Box 56, Dunedin, New Zealand), & CROOKS, TERENCE J. **Videotape modeling for preschool children with low levels of social interaction and low peer involvement in play.** Journal of Abnormal Child Psychology, 1984, **12**, 95–119.
Averaged group data showed statistically significant increases in both interactions and social involvement in play. Visual analysis of the single-subject data, however, indicated no clear treatment outcome for 2 children, while 4 subjects showed a variable increase in social responding after viewing the modeling videotape. – From Authors' Abstract.

2077. BARRON, A. P., & EARLS, F. **The relation of temperament and social factors to behavior problems in three-year-old children.** Journal of Child Psychology and Psychiatry, 1984, **25**, 23–33.
A survey of the total population of 3-year-old children on the island of Martha's Vineyard showed that according to mothers' reports, inflexibility, a temperament characteristic of the child, negative parent-child interaction, and family stress are most highly associated with poor behavior adjustment. Flexibility of the child and positive parent-child interaction curtail the overall adverse effect of high family stress on behavioral adjustment in children. – From Authors' Abstract.

2078. BAUER, ANNE M., & SHEA, THOMAS M. (Southern Illinois Univ., Edwardsville). **Tourette syndrome: a review and educational implications.** Journal of Autism and Developmental Disorders, 1984, **14**, 69–80.

2079. BEHAR, D., & STEWART, M. A. **Aggressive conduct disorder: the influence of social class, sex and age on the clinical picture.** Journal of Child Psychology and Psychiatry, 1984, **25**, 119–124.
Past studies have shown that aggressive conduct disorder is more common in boys and in families of low SES, and that affected children are usually seen in child psychiatry clinics before the age of 10. Among a group of affected children, there was little evidence that the children's difficulties varied with social class, sex, or age. – From Authors' Abstract.

2080. BIRMINGHAM, W. GEOFFREY (Alcohol & Drug Dependence Services, "Biala," 270 Roma, Brisbane, Queensland, Australia), & SHEEHY, MARINA S. **A model of psychological dependence in adolescent substance abusers.** Journal of Adolescence, 1984, **7**, 17–27.

Adolescent substance abuse appears to have its foundation in a distortion of perceived events at an age prior to involvement with substances. Substances are used as a compromise in an attempt to establish a lifestyle that has meaning to the individual. – From Authors' Abstract.

2081. BOLTON, D., & TURNER, T. **Obsessive-compulsive neurosis with conduct disorder in adolescence: a report of two cases.** Journal of Child Psychology and Psychiatry, 1984, **25**, 133–139.
The presence of conduct disorder is in marked contrast to the compliance and over-control characteristic of obsessionality and was found to give rise to great difficulties in instigating and carrying through a program of response-prevention for the obsessive-compulsive symptoms. – From Authors' Abstract.

2082. BRESLOW, LEONARD (Univ. of Minnesota), & COWAN, PHILIP A. **Structural and functional perspectives on classification and seriation in psychotic and normal children.** Child Development, 1984, **55**, 226–235.
Psychotic 9-year-old children were matched with normal children at preoperational and concrete operational stage levels on a set of Piagetian classification tasks. The mean age of the normal children was 6 years, replicating the usually found developmental delay in psychotic samples. Analysis of children's processes of seriating and seriation drawings indicated that over and above the structural retardation, psychotic children at all levels showed functional deficits, especially in the use of anticipatory imagery. – From Authors' Abstract.

2083. BROWNING, ELLEN R. (Univ. of Wisconsin, Madison). **A memory pacer for improving stimulus generalization.** Journal of Autism and Developmental Disorders, 1983, **13**, 427–432.
The Memory Pacer provides an individual with cues for appropriate behavior. Among severely disturbed adolescents, the Memory Pacer helps maintain lower rates of negative verbalizations. – Ed.

2084. CARPENTER, PATRICIA (Clinic for Child Study, Wayne County Juvenile Court, Detroit). **"Green Stamp Therapy" revisited: the evolution of 12 years of behavior modification and psychoeducational techniques with young delinquent boys.** Psychological Reports, 1984, **54**, 99–111.
The paper describes the evolution of behavior modification techniques used with 10–13-year-old aggressive, disruptive boys from a loosely structured approach into a highly structured format. Reinforcers were initially S & H Green Stamps, and, subsequently, privileges, toys, and recreational activities were added. Empathy and feeling sensitivity improved over time. – Adapted from Author's Abstract.

2085. CARTER, JO A. (Louisiana State Univ.), & DUNCAN, PAMELA A. **Binge-eating and vomiting: a survey of a high school population.** Psychology in the Schools, 1984, **21**, 198–203.
A survey of high school females was conducted to determine the prevalence of bulimia. Vomiters were found to have higher levels of somatic symptoms, anxiety, social dysfunction, and depression than did nonvomiters. They were also found to have disturbed attitudes toward food, eating, and dieting. – From Authors' Abstract.

2086. CHOCK, PATRICIA N. (Camarillo State Hosp., Box A, Camarillo, CA), & GLAHN, T. J. **Learning and self-stimulation in mute and echolalic autistic children.** Journal of Autism and Developmental Disorders, 1983, **13**, 365–381.
The effects of self-stimulation on task acquisition were studied in 3 mute low-functioning autistic and 3 echolalic higher-functioning autistic children. Echolalic children were able to learn a task without external suppression of their self-stimulation. The mute children were unable to learn a task until their self-stimulation was externally suppressed. – From Authors' Abstract.

2087. CHODSIAN, M.; ZAJICEK, E.; & WOLKIND, S. **A longitudinal study of maternal depression and child behaviour problems.** Journal of Child Psychology and Psychiatry, 1984, **25**, 91–109.
Child problems at 14 months were unrelated to present or past maternal depression. Child problems at 27 and 42 months were related in an interactive way with present and past depression. There was little indication of behavior problems preceding maternal depression. – From Authors' Abstract.

2088. CICCHETTI, DANTE (Harvard Univ.). **The emergence of developmental psychopathology.** Child Development, 1984, **55**, 1–7.
The history of the field is outlined. – Ed.

2089. CLARIZIO, HARVEY F. (Michigan State Univ.). **Childhood depression: diagnostic considerations.** Psychology in the Schools, 1984, **21**, 181–197.
The purposes of this review were to examine definitions of childhood depression and to evaluate diagnostic methods. – Adapted from Author's Abstract.

2090. DAWSON, GERALDINE (Univ. of North Carolina, Chapel Hill), & ADAMS, ALEXANDRA. **Imitation and social responsiveness in autistic children.** Journal of Abnormal Child Psychology, 1984, **12**, 209–226.
Imitation and object permanence skills of 4–6-year-old autistic children were assessed. Language and social behaviors were observed during free play. Autistic children who had a low level of imitative ability were more socially responsive, showed more eye contact, and played with toys in a less perseverative manner when the experimenter imitated their behavior than when the experimenter modeled either a familiar or a novel action. The autistic children with more highly developed imitation skills responded similarly to all conditions and were generally more socially and verbally responsive. – From Authors' Abstract.

2091. DISHION, T. J. (Oregon Social Learning Ctr., 207 E. 5th Ave., Eugene); LOEBER, R.; STOUTHAMER-LOEBER, M.; & PATTERSON, G. R. **Skill deficits and male adolescent delinquency.** Journal of Abnormal Child Psychology, 1984, **12**, 37–54.
While male adolescents with prior police contact had a lower multivariate profile on 7 measures of academic, interpersonal, and work skills. Five of the 7 measures correlated significantly with both the official and self-reported criteria of delinquency. Academic skill deficits may be the strongest covariates of antisocial behavior. – From Authors' Abstract.

2092. DOR-SHAV, NETTA KOHN (Bar-Ilan Univ., Israel), & HOROWITZ, ZELDA. **Intelligence and personality variables of parents of autistic children.** Journal of Genetic Psychology, 1984, **144**, 39–50.
Fathers of autists, but not mothers, were of significantly above-average intelligence. Mothers were significantly more neurotic on Eysenck's scale than mothers of disturbed nonautistic children, and significantly more introverted than his normative sample. Finally, there was a significant correlation between neuroticism of mothers and children's autism. – From Authors' Abstract.

2093. DOŠEN, A. (Observation centre for children with developmental disorders, De Hondsberg, Oisterwijk, Netherlands). Acta Paedopsychiatrica, 1984, **50**, 29–40.
During treatment, it was seen that a specific psychotherapeutic approach, sometimes supported by antidepressant drugs, leads to improvement, in most cases within a relatively short period. – From Author's Abstract.

2094. DUBANOSKI, RICHARD A. (Univ. of Hawaii), & McINTOSH, SALLY R. **Child abuse and neglect in military and civilian families.** Child Abuse & Neglect, The International Journal, 1984, **8**, 55–67.
When comparisons were made between military and civilian families, some differences were discovered but many more similarities were found. – From Authors' Abstract.

2095. DUNLAP, GLEN (Univ. of California, Santa Barbara). **The influence of task variation and maintenance tasks on the learning and affect of autistic children.** Journal of Experimental Child Psychology, 1984, **37,** 41–64.
The experimental conditions were (1) a constant-task condition, in which only 1 acquisition task was presented per session; (2) a varied-acquisition-task condition, in which 10 acquisition tasks were randomly interspersed throughout each session; and (3) a varied-with-maintenance-task condition, which randomly interspersed 5 acquisition tasks and 5 which had been previously acquired. The results showed more efficient learning under the varied-maintenance condition. The most positive affect judgments were produced by the varied-maintenance condition. – From Author's Abstract.

2096. DUNN, CARLA (Univ. of Texas, Austin), & DAVIS, BARBARA L. **Phonological process occurrence in phonologically disordered children.** Applied Psycholinguistics, 1983, **4,** 187–207.
Individual patterns of phonological process occurring in 9 phonologically disordered children were studied. A small subset of phonological processes seemed to account for the majority of errors. – From Authors' Abstract.

2097. EASTGATE, JOHN (Swindon Child & Family Guidance Ctr., Swindon, Wilts, England), & GILMOUR, LORNA. **Long-term outcome of depressed children: a follow-up study.** Developmental Medicine and Child Neurology, 1984, **26,** 68–72.
Subjects diagnosed as depressed in childhood were followed up 7–8 years after first presentation. Forty-two percent had moderate or severe disability. – From Authors' Abstract.

2098. EISER, CHRISTINE (Univ. of Exeter, Devon, England). **Communicating with sick and hospitalized children.** Journal of Child Psychology and Psychiatry, 1984, **25,** 181–189.
All of the main techniques in use for preparing children (pamphlets, video, or pre-admission nursing contact) appear more beneficial to the patient and family than routine care, but no 1 method is superior. Greater benefit to the child might occur where information about illness is made appropriate to the child's cognitive level. – From Author's Abstract.

2099. FINKELHOR, DAVID (Univ. of New Hampshire), & HOTALING, GERALD T. **Sexual abuse in The National Incidence Study of Child Abuse and Neglect: an appraisal.** Child Abuse & Neglect, The International Journal, 1984, **8,** 23–33.

2100. FIRESTONE, PHILIP (Univ. of Ottawa, Canada), & PETERS, SUSAN. **Minor physical anomalies and behavior in children: a review.** Journal of Autism and Developmental Disorders, 1983, **13,** 411–425.
Research seems to indicate that for males there is considerable consistency in the results but not with females. A high number of minor physical anomalies (MPA) are evident in several pathological groups of boys. MPA are correlated with severity of hyperactivity, IQ, and school achievement. There is also a relationship between a high number of MPA and obstetrical complications. – From Authors' Abstract.

2101. FISCHER, MARIELLEN (Medical Coll. of Wisconsin); ROLF, JON E.; HASAZI, JOSEPH E.; & CUMMINGS, LUCINDA. **Follow-up of a preschool epidemiological sample: cross-age continuities and predictings of later adjustment with internalizing and externalizing dimensions of behavior.** Child Development, 1984, **55,** 137–150.
Preschool externalizing symptoms were positively correlated with later externalizing and internalizing symptoms in the entire sample. Preschool internalizing symptoms, however, were predictive of later internalizing symptoms only for 2-year-old girls and 5–6-year-old boys. Similar results were obtained for clinically disturbed preschoolers. Given the magnitude of obtained correlations, even when significant, the results support the view that discontinuity rather than continuity in behavioral adjustment from preschool to later ages is the rule. – From Authors' Abstract.

2102. FRANKEL, F.; SIMMONS, J. Q., III; FICHTER, M.; & FREEMAN, B. J. **Stimulus overselectivity in autistic and mentally retarded children—a research note.** Journal of Child Psychology and Psychiatry, 1984, **25,** 147–155.
Stimulus overselectivity was a function of diagnostic category when groups were equated for performance IQ and mental age. Pulse rate response suggested that the test probes may be assessing performance during the early trials of a transfer problem for both groups of children. – From Authors' Abstract.

2103. FRAZIER, DONALD, & DeBLASSIE, RICHARD R. (New Mexico State Univ.). **Diagnosing behavior-disordered early adolescents as a function of cultural differences.** Adolescence, 1984, **19,** 385–390.
The hypothesis that there is a tendency of non-Indian teachers to rate American Indian early adolescents as behaviorally disordered more frequently than similarly behaving non-Indian children was rejected. – From Authors' Abstract.

2104. GADDINI, RENATA (Univ. of Rome, Italy). **On the origins of the battered child syndrome: abuse as acting out of preverbal events.** Child Abuse & Neglect, The International Journal, 1984, **8,** 41–45.
The clinical description of a chronically acting out boy, 14 years old and physically abused by parents and especially by mother, has been the starting point for presenting some concepts of the nature and prevention of child abuse. His violent acting out toward objects and people, but particularly his continuous negativistic attitudes toward parents, and his rejection of his mother and home were each time the setting for battles in the family. – From Author's Abstract.

2105. GARBARINO, JAMES (Pennsylvania State Univ.); SEBES, JANET; & SCHELLENBACH, CYNTHIA. **Families at risk for destructive parent-child relations in adolescence.** Child Development, 1984, **55,** 174–183.
Families that contained a 10–16-year-old and 2 parents and that were referred because of the adjustment problems of the adolescent were visited at home and given a battery of questionnaire, interview, and observation instruments. The high-risk group tended to be "chaotic" and "enmeshed," to include more stepparents, to be more punishing and less supportive, and to be more stressed by life changes. Adolescents in the high-risk families were characterized by significantly more developmental problems, and the number of such problems correlated significantly with the risk for destructive parent-child relations. – From Authors' Abstract.

2106. GARBER, JUDY (Univ. of Minnesota). **Classification of childhood psychopathology: a developmental perspective.** Child Development, 1984, **55,** 30–48.
This paper provides a developmental framework for the classification of psychopathology in children. A salient issue derived from this developmental perspective is concerned with the continuity between childhood and adult psychopathology. The implications of the continuity issue for classification are that the validity of adult criteria for use with children should be explored further, the diagnosis of a childhood disorder at 1 point in time is not necessarily dependent upon there being episodes of the disorder at a later time, and the focus of classification should not be limited to isolated behaviors and traits, but rather should emphasize patterns of adaptation. – From Author's Abstract.

2107. GARMEZY, NORMAN (Univ. of Minnesota); MASTEN, ANN S.; & TELLEGEN, AUKE. **The study of stress and competence in children: a building block for developmental psychology.** Child Development, 1984, **55,** 97–111.
The current Project Competence studies of stress and competence are described, with particular attention to the methodology and strategies for data analysis. The authors present a 3-model approach to stress resistance in a multivariate regression framework: the compensatory, challenge, and protective factor models. – From Authors' Abstract.

2108. GARREAU, B. (Service d'Explorations Fonctionnelles Psychopathologiques, C.H.U. Bretonneau, Tours Cedex, France). **A comparison of autistic syndrome with and without associated neurological problems.** Journal of Autism and Developmental Disorders, 1984, **14**, 105–111.
Autistic syndromes with and without associated neurological deficits are remarkably similar in terms of severity and type of autistic symptoms, IQ, and sex distribution. – From The Article.

2109. GIBLIN, PAUL T. (Wayne State Univ.); STARR, RAYMOND H., JR.; & AGRONOW, SAMUEL J. **Affective behavior of abused and control children: comparisons of parent–child interactions and the influence of home environment variables.** Journal of Genetic Psychology, 1984, **144**, 69–82.
Abused children's home environment variables were higher than the favored control group. For negative affective behaviors, the abused group less favored on home environment variables was higher than the less favored control group. – From Authors' Abstract.

2110. GILLBERG, C. **Infantile autism and other childhood psychoses in a Swedish urban region.** Journal of Child Psychology and Psychiatry, 1984, **25**, 35–43.
A total population screening of children born during 1962–1976 and living in the Gothenburg region of Sweden at the end of 1980 found that the prevalence figure for infantile autism was 2.0 per 10,000 and for other childhood psychoses 1.9 per 10,000. Boys were much more often affected by infantile autism than girls. A majority of these children were mentally retarded, and only 4% had tested IQs exceeding 100. – From Author's Abstract.

2111. GOEHRING, MARTY M. (Fuller Graduate School of Psychology), & MAJOVSKI, LAWRENCE V. **Inter-rater reliability of a clinical neuropsychological screening instrument for adolescents.** Clinical Neuropsychology, 1984, **6**, 35–41.
The interrater reliabilities ranged from .79 to .99 – Ed.

2112. GRAAFSMA, T., & ANBEEK, M. (Stichting Psychotheek, Eikenplein 3, Amsterdam, Netherlands). **Resistance in psychotherapy with adolescents.** Journal of Adolescence, 1984, **7**, 1–16.

2113. GREENBERG, MARK T. (Univ. of Washington); CALDERON, ROSEMARY; & KUSCHÉ, CAROL. **Early intervention using simultaneous communication with deaf infants: the effect on communication development.** Child Development, 1984, **55**, 607–616.
This report presents findings on an independent evaluation of an early intervention program for severely and profoundly deaf children. Located in Vancouver, British Columbia, this comprehensive program served families with children under age 3. Results indicated more developmentally mature communication and higher-quality interaction in families who had received intervention. – From Authors' Abstract.

2114. GREENSPAN, STANLEY I., & PORGES, STEPHEN W. (Univ. of Illinois, Urbana-Champaign). **Psychopathology in infancy and early childhood: clinical perspectives on the organization of sensory and affective-thematic experience.** Child Development, 1984, **55**, 49–70.
The most severe psychopathologies, it is suggested, occur where there are compromises in both the early sensory and affective-thematic organizational compromises, followed by approaches that facilitate phase-specific "essential experiences" through intact sensory pathways and the remediation of compromised ones, may provide a systematic base for possible preventive intervention approaches. – From Authors' Abstract.

2115. GUDJONSSON, GISLI H. (Inst. of Psychiatry, De Crespigny Park, Denmark Hill, London, England), & SINGH, KRISHNA K. **The relationship between criminal conviction and interrogative suggestibility among delinquent boys.** Journal of Adolescence, 1984, **7**, 29–34.

The results from this study support the hypothesis that the extent to which delinquent boys resist interpersonal pressure during an interrogation is related to their previous number of criminal convictions. – From the Article.

2116. HALPERIN, JEFFREY M. (Mount Sinai School of Medicine); GITTELMAN, RACHEL; KLEIN, DONALD F.; & RUDEL, RITA G. **Reading-disabled hyperactive children: a distinct subgroup of attention deficit disorder with hyperactivity?** Journal of Abnormal Child Psychology, 1984, **12**, 1–14.
Mixed hyperactive/reading-disabled children were compared to pure hyperactive children on demographic, behavioral, and neuropsychological measures. The mixed group had a significantly higher Performance IQ, whereas the pure group had a significantly higher Verbal IQ and performed better on measures of cognitive impulsivity. Several other measures failed to distinguish the groups. – From Authors' Abstract.

2117. HARVEY, D. H. P. (Victoria Univ., Wellington, New Zealand), & GREENWAY, A. P. **The self-concept of physically handicapped children and their non-handicapped siblings: an empirical investigation.** Journal of Child Psychology and Psychiatry, 1984, **25**, 273–284.
Pre-adolescent physically handicapped children attending normal schools and their siblings nearest in age were administered the Piers-Harris Self-Concept Scale for Children. Their responses were then compared with those of physically handicapped children and their siblings. Scores were lower for both groups of physically handicapped children than for the nonhandicapped controls. Scores for siblings of handicapped children were generally lower than those of the controls. – From Authors' Abstract.

2118. HENSEY, O. J. (Alder Hey Children's Hosp., Eaton, Liverpool, England); WILLIAMS, J. K.; & ROSENBLOOM, L. **Intervention in child abuse: experience in Liverpool.** Developmental Medicine and Child Neurology, 1983, **25**, 606–611.
The subsequent life events and development of 50 abused children who had been removed from their parents were determined. Twenty-six children had an unsatisfactory outcome. The children who best survived their experiences after being taken into care were those for whom an early decision was made to sever parental contact and to place the child permanently with a substitute family. – Adapted from Authors' Abstract.

2119. HINSHAW, STEPHEN P.; HENKER, BARBARA (Univ. of California, Los Angeles); & WHALEN, CAROL K. **Self-control in hyperactive boys in anger-inducing situations: effects of cognitive-behavioral training and of methylphenidate.** Journal of Abnormal Child Psychology, 1984, **12**, 55–77.
Methylphenidate reduced the intensity of the hyperactive boys' behavior but did not significantly increase either global or specific measures of self-control. Cognitive-behavioral treatment was more successful in enhancing both general self-control and the use of specific coping strategies. There was no advantage for the combination of methylphenidate plus cognitive-behavioral intervention. – From Authors' Abstract.

2120. HOBSON, R. PETER (Inst. of Psychiatry, London, England). **Early childhood autism and the question of egocentrism.** Journal of Autism and Developmental Disorders, 1984, **14**, 85–104.
Tasks in which subjects were required to make judgments about different and yet related views of a 3-dimensional scene or object, together with tests of operational thinking, were presented to normal children and to subjects with the diagnosis of infantile autism. Autistic children were no more impaired in their recognition of visuospatial perspectives than were normal children of comparable intellectual level in tests of operational thinking. – From Author's Abstract.

2121. HOFFMAN, VINCENT J. (Michigan State Univ.). **The relationship of psychology to delinquency: a comprehensive approach.** Adolescence, 1984, **19**, 55–61.

Three psychological perspectives on youth deviance are presented. Youth's developmental needs and their opportunity to complete developmental tasks are stressed. – From Author's Abstract.

2122. HOOPER, FLOYD A., & EVANS, RONALD G. (Washburn Univ.). **Screening for disruptive behavior of institutionalized juvenile offenders.** Journal of Personality Assessment, 1984, **48**, 159–161.
Variable combinations from the Psychological Screening Inventory and Shipley-Hartford Scale were the most effective in identifying disruptive youths. – From Authors' Abstract.

2123. JENKINS, S.; OWEN, C.; BAX, M.; & HART, H. **Continuities of common behavior problems in preschool children.** Journal of Child Psychology and Psychiatry, 1984, **25**, 75–89.
Night waking was the most common problem under the age of 2. Just under half of these night wakers were still waking at 18 months, and from 18 months to 2 years just over half the children continued waking. The continuities of feeding problems were stronger after the age of 2 years, with poor appetite being reported to persist more than food fads. Over 2 years, the most common problem reported was temper tantrums, and 45% of the children having frequent tantrums at 2 years were still having frequent tantrums at 3 years. – From Authors' Abstract.

2124. JOHNSON, GLENN M. (Univ. of Kansas); SHONTZ, FRANKLIN C.; & LOCKE, THOMAS P. **Relationships between adolescent drug use and parental drug behaviors.** Adolescence, 1984, **19**, 295–299.
Relationships between parental use of drugs and adolescent use of the same drugs were moderate and roughly equivalent across drugs. – From Authors' Abstract.

2125. KAGAN, DONA M. (3729 W. Sahuaro, Phoenix), & SQUIRES, ROSE L. **Eating disorders among adolescents: patterns and prevalence.** Adolescence, 1984, **19**, 15–29.
A questionnaire was completed by 2,004 high school students. Disordered eating, as a distinct syndrome of behaviors, was found in 2% of all subjects. Seven percent of all subjects (11% of all females) were classified as emotional eaters. – From Authors' Abstract.

2126. KAZDIN, ALAN E. (Univ. of Pittsburgh School of Medicine). **Acceptability of aversive procedures and medication as treatment alternatives for deviant child behavior.** Journal of Abnormal Child Psychology, 1984, **12**, 289–302.
Time-out from reinforcement, locked seclusion, and medication were rated by psychiatric in-patient children and parents. Although children and parents did not differ overall in acceptability ratings, children viewed medication as the most acceptable treatment, whereas parents viewed time-out as the most acceptable treatment. – From Author's Abstract.

2127. KENDALL, PHILIP C. (Univ. of Minnesota). **Cognitive-behavioural self-control therapy for children.** Journal of Child Psychology and Psychiatry, 1984, **25**, 173–179.
Context of training affects attainment of treatment generalization, yet the treatment has not been applied directly in the natural setting in which children's social and emotional development occurs. There have been few investigations of the role of cognitive developmental individual differences and their effects on treatment outcome. Both developmental psychologists and clinicians would profit from age- and sex-specific normative data on behavioral disorders. – From the Article.

2128. KENDALL, PHILIP C. (Univ. of Minnesota); LERNER, RICHARD M.; & CRAIGHEAD, W. EDWARD. **Human development and intervention in childhood psychopathology.** Child Development, 1984, **55**, 71–82.
We argue there are several features of the child's developing physical, psychological, and behavioral characteristics that suggest the sorts of interventions that may be efficacious and the ones that may be less efficient or counterproductive. Illustrations are drawn from the literatures pertinent to such topics as systematic desensitization, cognitive-behavioral self-control

therapy, interventions for social isolates, and parent training programs, and involve preventive as well as remedial/therapeutic interventions. – From Authors' Abstract.

2129. KERN, LYNN; KOEGEL, ROBERT L. (Univ. of California, Santa Barbara); & DUNLAP, GLEN. **The influence of vigorous versus mild exercise on autistic stereotyped behaviors.** Journal of Autism and Developmental Disorders, 1984, **14,** 57–67.
The results demonstrated that 15 min of mild exercise (ball playing) had little or no influence on the children's subsequent stereotyped responding, while 15 min of continuous and vigorous exercise (jogging) was always followed by reductions in stereotyped behaviors. – From Authors' Abstract.

2130. KOMOTO, JUNKO (Okayama Univ., Japan); USUI, SEIGO; & HIRATA, JUNICHIRO. **Infantile autism and affective disorder.** Journal of Autism and Developmental Disorders, 1984, **14,** 81–84.
This is a preliminary report of the possible occurrence of affective disorder in 2 autistic adolescents. – Authors' Abstract.

2131. KONSTANTAREAS, M. MARY (Univ. of Toronto, Ontario, Canada). **Sign language as a communication prosthesis with language-impaired children.** Journal of Autism and Developmental Disorders, 1984, **14,** 9–25.
Children 3–11 years old with various levels of language impairment were exposed to drawings portraying a single scene. Training the children to use the functors followed 1 of 2 approaches. The experimenter either vocalized the functor or she vocalized and signed it. For both functor acquisition and functor recall, speech and sign training was superior to speech training. – From Author's Abstract.

2132. KRISHNAMONI, D. (Grace General Hosp., 241 LeMarchant, St. John's, Newfoundland, Canada). **Pregnancy in teenagers—a comparative study.** Psychiatric Journal of the University of Ottawa, 1983, **8,** 202–207.
The epidemiological characteristics of 2 groups of girls who conceived before or during the age of 16 years are presented. Fewer pregnancies occurred in urban areas, and the pregnancy rate was higher in some of the religious denominations. – From Author's Abstract.

2133. LAHEY, MARGARET (Hunter Coll. School of Health Sciences); LAUNER, PATRICIA B.; & SCHIFF-MYERS, NAOMI. **Prediction of production: elicited imitation and spontaneous speech productions of language disordered children.** Applied Psycholinguistics, 1983, **4,** 317–343.
Two forms of an imitation task (contextual support present or absent) were presented to 32 language-impaired children. A multiple regression analysis with spontaneous productions as the criterion showed predictions varied among the 11 language behaviors. Contextual support had little effect. – From Authors' Abstract.

2134. LEDINGHAM, JANE E. (Univ. of Ottawa, Ontario, Canada), & SCHWARTZMAN, ALEX E. **A 3-year follow-up of aggressive and withdrawn behavior in childhood: preliminary findings.** Journal of Abnormal Child Psychology, 1984, **12,** 157–168.
Children identified by peers as aggressive-withdrawn or aggressive were more likely to have failed a grade or to be in a special class than were withdrawn children or controls. Older aggressive-withdrawn subjects and controls, but not aggressive subjects or withdrawn subjects, had higher rates of school failure and special class placement. – From Authors' Abstract.

2135. LEE, JAE YEON (Sookmyung Women's Univ., Seoul, Korea), & SUGAWARA, ALAN I. **Awareness of sex-trait stereotypes among Korean children.** Journal of Social Psychology, 1982, **117,** 161–170.
Subjects were Korean 8-year-old children residing in rural or urban areas. As with American children, Korean children were aware of the sex-trait stereotypes. While boys were more aware of the male- than female-trait stereotypes, girls were equally aware of both. – From Authors' Abstract.

2136. LEWIS, MICHAEL (Rutgers Medical School); FEIRING, CANDICE; McGUFFOG, CAROLYN; & JASKIR, JOHN. **Predicting psychopathology in six-year-olds from early social relations.** Child Development, 1984, **55**, 123–136.
For males, attachment classification at 1 year was significantly related to later psychopathology; insecurely attached males showed more psychopathology than securely attached males. No relationship between attachment and later psychopathology was observed for females. Even for males, the attachment classification only partly predicted later behavioral problems. Several other factors, including life-stress events and family demographic variables, appeared to influence the development of psychopathology. – From Authors' Abstract.

2137. LOBATO, DEBRA (Univ. of Vermont). **Siblings of handicapped children: a review.** Journal of Autism and Developmental Disorders, 1983, **13**, 347–364.
Only certain siblings appear to be vulnerable to negative reactions, depending on such factors as sibling sex and birth order, family socioeconomic status, and parental responses to the handicapped child. – From Author's Abstract.

2138. LOWE, JEAN; KREHBIEL, ROBERTA; SWEENEY, JULIA; CRUMLEY, KENNETH; PETERSON, GARY; WATSON, BILLY; & RHODES, JOHN M. (Univ. of New Mexico). **A screening battery for identifying children at risk for neuropsychological deficits: a pilot study.** Clinical Neuropsychology, 1984, **6**, 42–45.
The Children's Neuropsychological Screening Test discriminates normals from children at risk. – From the Article.

2139. LUISELLI, JAMES K. (Behavioral and Education Resource Associates, 275 Old Bedford, Concord); SUSKIN, LAUREN; & SLOCUMB, PAUL R. **Application of immobilization time-out in management programming with developmentally disabled children.** Child & Family Behavior Therapy, 1984, **6**, 1–15.
Immobilization time-out proved to be a more efficient intervention when compared to differential reinforcement methods alone. – From Authors' Abstract.

2140. McCABE, VIKI (Univ. of California, Los Angeles). **Abstract perceptual information for age level: a risk factor for maltreatment?** Child Development, 1984, **55**, 267–276.
Two independent and geographically disparate samples show that physically abused 3–6-year-olds have cranial/facial proportions that are atypically older than their nonabused agemates. Two independent photographic samples corroborated this finding, 1 investigating 2–7-year-olds and 1 investigating 12–15-year-olds. Cranial/facial proportion is a particularly salient abstract specification for age level and may be used without awareness in caregiving decisions. – From Author's Abstract.

2141. McDERMOTT, PAUL A. (Univ. of Pennsylvania). **Child behavioral disorders by age and sex based on item factoring of the revised Bristol Guides.** Journal of Abnormal Child Psychology, 1984, **12**, 15–36.
Children 15–16 years old were observed by teachers and rated on indicators of maladaptive behavior. The similarity of the factorially derived dimensions confirmed the cross-age and -sex generality of the syndromes known as unforthcomingness, hostility, and depression, and provided reasonable support for the utility of the syndrome of inconsequence. – From Author's Abstract.

2142. McGEE, R. (Univ. of Otago, Dunedin, New Zealand); SILVA, P. A.; & WILLIAMS, S. **Behaviour problems in a population of seven-year-old children: prevalence, stability and types of disorder—a research report.** Journal of Child Psychology and Psychiatry, 1984, **25**, 251–259.
About 30% of the sample were identified by the parent and/or teacher as having a high level of problem behavior. The most prevalent problem reported was antisocial behavior, which was more common among boys than girls. Over 9% of the sample were identified as having a sta-

ble behavior problem. Such stable problems were associated with specific reading retardation, independent ratings of behavior during psychological testing, and use of professional services for help. – From Authors' Abstract.

2143. MARGALIT, MALKA (Tel-Aviv Univ., Ramat Aviv, Tel-Aviv, Israel), & ARIELI, NIRIT. **Emotional and behavioral aspects of hyperactivity.** Journal of Learning Disabilities, 1984, **17,** 374–376.
Hyperactives and nonhyperactives were compared. The groups differed regarding the hyperactives' difficulties of modulating performance to meet external demand. – From Authors' Abstract.

2144. MOCHIZUKI, MINORU. **A study about the relation between the mental tempo and the nervous shaking.** Journal of Child Development (Japan), 1983, **19,** 1–4.
Finger tapping and nervous shaking among junior high students were correlated. – Ed.

2145. MORGAN, SHARON R. (Univ. of Texas, El Paso). **Counseling with teachers on the sexual acting-out of disturbed children.** Psychology in the Schools, 1984, **21,** 234–243.
Clinical case material is presented to illustrate the meanings and motivations children have subconsciously applied to various types of sexual behavior. Guidelines are proposed to be used when discussing this problem with teachers in the school setting. – From Author's Abstract.

2146. MUNSON, ROBERT F. (Bellarmine Coll.), & BLINCOE, MARTINA M. **Evaluation of a residential treatment center for emotionally disturbed adolescents.** Adolescence, 1984, **19,** 253–261.
Two hypotheses were tested. The first was that the girls would be successful when they returned to their communities. "Success" was defined by a number of variables on a questionnaire. Responses to the questions indicated that the girls are doing well. The second hypothesis, that the girls would show improvement in their scores on 2 personality tests taken at the time they were admitted and at the time of their release, also received support. – From Authors' Abstract.

2147. NISSEN, G. (Universitätsklinik und Poliklinik für Kinder- und Jugendpsychiatrie, Füchsleinstrasse 15, Würzburg, Germany). **Somatogenic depression in children and adolescents.** Acta Paedopsychiatrica, 1984, **50,** 21–28.
In addition to endogenic-phasic and psychogenic depression, *somatogenic depression* also occurs in childhood and adolescence. In frequency, such depressions even take second place behind psychogenic depressions, but they are still often misunderstood or overlooked. – From Author's Abstract.

2148. NOAM, GIL G. (Harvard Medical School); HAUSER, STUART T.; SANTOSTEFANO, SEBASTIANO; GARRISON, WILLIAM; JACOBSON, ALAN M.; POWERS, SALLY I.; & MEAD, MERRILL. **Ego development and psychopathology: a study of hospitalized adolescents.** Child Development, 1984, **55,** 184–194.
Achenbach and Edelbock's Child Behavior Checklist factor scores were compared to ego stage. Findings indicated significant negative correlations with the externalizing and internalizing factors as well as a variety of behavioral subscales. A significant relationship also existed between the total number of symptoms and ego development. Ego development was found to be an important predictor for the externalizing factor and 2 subscales after the background variables of age, sex, and SES were partialed out. – From Authors' Abstract.

2149. OKEAHIALAM, THEODORE C. (Univ. of Nigeria Teaching Hosp., Enugu, Nigeria). **Child abuse in Nigeria.** Child Abuse & Neglect, The International Journal, 1984, **8,** 69–73.

2150. POLLARD, SUSAN; WARD, ERIC M.; & BARKLEY, RUSSELL A. (Medical Coll. of Wisconsin). **The effects of parent training and Ritalin on the parent–child interactions of hyperactive boys.** Child & Family Behavior Therapy, 1983, **5,** 51–69.

Results suggest that parent training alone or Ritalin alone are sufficient to produce noticeable improvements in the behavior of hyperactive children. – Adapted from the Article.

2151. PRIOR, MARGOT (La Trobe Univ., Bundoora, Victoria, Australia); WALLACE, MEREDITH; & MILTON, IVAN. **Schedule-induced behavior in hyperactive children.** Journal of Abnormal Child Psychology, 1984, **12,** 227–244.
Hyperactive children were more active than controls in baseline and did not respond to the schedule, unlike the controls, who became significantly more active in schedule conditions. When methylphenidate was administered in an attempt to reduce the amount of baseline activity, hyperactive children were still more active than controls in baseline and insensitive to the schedule. – From Authors' Abstract.

2152. PRIZANT, BARRY M. (Bradley Hosp., 1011 Veteran's Memorial Parkway, East Providence), & RYDELL, PATRICK J. **Analysis of functions of delayed echolalia in autistic children.** Journal of Speech and Hearing Research, 1984, **27,** 183–192.

2153. RALPH, NORBERT (276 W. Lexington, Fresno); LOCHMAN, JOHN; & THOMAS, TRUMAN. **Psychosocial characteristics of pregnant and nulliparous adolescents.** Adolescence, 1984, **19,** 283–294.
The study suggests that distinct characteristics do exist for the pregnant adolescent, but that such characteristics do not indicate family or psychological disturbance. – From Authors' Abstract.

2154. REID, MOLLY K., & BORKOWSKI, JOHN G. (Univ. of Notre Dame). **Effects of methylphenidate (Ritalin) on information processing in hyperactive children.** Journal of Abnormal Child Psychology, 1984, **12,** 169–185.
Performances on 6 information-processing efficiency tasks and a general measure of on-task behavior were compared for children receiving methylphenidate or a placebo. Methylphenidate-related improvements in attention to on-task behaviors were found. An overall analysis of processing speed suggested that methylphenidate improved efficiency. – From Authors' Abstract.

2155. RICHTER, NEIL C. (Univ. of South Carolina, Columbia). **The efficacy of relaxation training with children.** Journal of Abnormal Child Psychology, 1984, **12,** 319–344.
Findings suggest that relaxation training is at least as effective as other treatment approaches for a variety of learning, behavioral, and physiological disorders when it is continued over an extended period of time and is augmented by other supportive measures. – From Author's Abstract.

2156. ROFF, JAMES D. (Eastern Michigan Univ.), & WIRT, ROBERT D. **Childhood aggression and social adjustment as antecedents of delinquency.** Journal of Abnormal Child Psychology, 1984, **12,** 111–126.
Grade-school children were followed into young adulthood through record sources. The joint effects of social class, a measure of family disturbance, and childhood problem behavior factors were evaluated. Childhood aggression emerged as the most prominent antecedent factor for males but not for females. – From Authors' Abstract.

2157. ROLF, JON (National Inst. of Mental Health, 5600 Fishers, Rockville), & READ, PETER B. **Programs advancing developmental psychopathology.** Child Development, 1984, **55,** 8–16.
Various methods to foster the growth of this interdisciplinary endeavor are presented, including: (a) informing key science administrators in funding institutions; (b) creating forums for research communication, evaluation, and planning; (c) building researcher networks; (d) interpreting priorities at funding institutions; (e) providing new publication outlets; and (f) developing interdisciplinary research training programs. – From Authors' Abstract.

2158. ROSENBAUM, MICHAEL (Tel-Aviv Univ., Israel), & BAKER, EVELYN. **Self-control behavior in hyperactive and nonhyperactive children.** Journal of Abnormal Child Psychology, 1984, **12**, 303–318.
During the training stage, the children learned a concept-formation task under a schedule of contingent positive reinforcement. In the test stage, they performed the same task but under a negative noncontingent reinforcement schedule. There were no differences in initial rate of learning the task. After the introduction of the negative noncontingent reinforcement schedule, however, the hyperactive group showed a marked decrease in the use of effective problem-solving strategies. – From Authors' Abstract.

2159. RUSSELL, DIANA E. H. (Mills Coll.). **The prevalence and seriousness of incestuous abuse: stepfathers vs. biological fathers.** Child Abuse & Neglect, The International Journal, 1984, **8**, 15–22.
Of 930 adult women in San Francisco, 17% had a stepfather as a principal figure in her childhood years and was sexually abused by him. The comparable figure for biological fathers was 2%. – From Author's Abstract.

2160. SACKETT, GENE P. (Univ. of Washington). **A nonhuman primate model of risk for deviant development.** American Journal of Mental Deficiency, 1984, **88**, 469–476.
A model for studying genetic, physiological, and psychosocial processes producing delayed development is described. The model focuses on parental risk for poor reproductive outcomes using pigtailed monkey subjects. Results show that both maternal and paternal factors are associated with delayed development in systems ranging from tooth eruption to concept learning ability. – From Author's Abstract.

2161. SCHNEIDER, STANLEY (Summit Inst., Shimoni 44, Jerusalem, Israel); BERMAN, CHANITA; & ARONSON, DORI. **Sexuality as a treatment issue with a special population of adolescents.** Adolescence, 1984, **19**, 201–206.

2162. SCHNEIDER-ROSEN, KAREN, & CICCHETTI, DANTE (Harvard Univ.). **The relationship between affect and cognition in maltreated infants: quality of attachment and the development of visual self-recognition.** Child Development, 1984, **55**, 648–658.
Maltreated infants were found to manifest a significantly greater proportion of insecure attachments than were nonmaltreated infants. Infants who evidenced visual self-recognition were significantly more likely to be securely attached to their mothers. Ninety percent of the nonmaltreated infants who recognized themselves were securely attached to their caregivers. For those maltreated infants who recognized themselves, there was no significant relationship between this capacity and qualitative differences in the security of attachment. – From Authors' Abstract.

2163. SLOPER, P. (Hester Adrian Research Ctr., University, Manchester, England); CUNNINGHAM, C. C.; & ARNLJOTSDOTTIR, M. **Parental reactions to early intervention with their Down's syndrome infants.** Child: Care, Health and Development, 1983, **9**, 357–376.
Parents' views of the intervention programs are positive, but the difficulties experienced by some parents point to the need for intervenors to be sensitive to family situations and feelings and for programs to be flexible enough to meet these needs. – From Authors' Abstract.

2164. SMITH, PATRICIA E.; BURLEIGH, ROBERT L.; SEWELL, WILLIAM R. (Memphis State Univ.); & KRISAK, JOSEPH. **Correlation between the Minnesota Multiphasic Personality Inventory profiles of emotionally disturbed adolescents and their mothers.** Adolescence, 1984, **19**, 31–38.
Comparisons of profiles and correlational data showed that the mother–daughter profiles were very similar, but the mother–son profiles were dissimilar. – From Authors' Abstract.

2165. SPIKER, DONNA (Stanford Univ.), & RICKS, MARGARET. **Visual self-recognition in autistic children: developmental relationships.** Child Development, 1984, **55**, 214–225.

Employing a mirror procedure, 52 autistic children were tested for visual self-recognition. Substantial behavioral and psychometric data were collected from school records, teacher interviews, and classroom observations. Sixty-nine percent of the subjects showed evidence of mirror self-recognition, while 31% failed to give clear indications of recognizing their mirror images. The 2 groups did not differ on CA. Those who failed to show evidence of visual self-recognition were more likely than those who did show evidence of visual recognition to be mute or lacking in communicative speech. Children who showed the capacity for visual self-recognition had higher levels of functioning in other areas as well. – From Authors' Abstract.

2166. SROUFE, L. ALAN (Univ. of Minnesota), & RUTTER, MICHAEL. **The domain of developmental psychopathology.** Child Development, 1984, **55**, 17–29.
A developmental perspective is presented, and the implications of this perspective for research in developmental psychopathology are discussed. A primary consideration is the complexity of the adaptational process, with developmental transformation being the rule. It will be necessary to understand both individual patterns of adaptation with respect to salient issues of a given developmental period and the transaction between prior adaptation, maturational change, and subsequent environmental challenges. – From Authors' Abstract.

2167. TAYLOR, ERIC (Inst. of Psychiatry, De Crespigny Park, London, England), & SANDBERG, SEIJA. **Hyperactive behavior in English schoolchildren: a questionnaire survey.** Journal of Abnormal Child Psychology, 1984, **12**, 143–156.
Teacher ratings of English children 6–9 years old were compared to published surveys from the United States and Australasia. The mean hyperactivity scores of English children were higher than in most U.S. surveys but lower than in New Zealand. – From Authors' Abstract.

2168. THORLEY, GEOFF (Inst. of Psychiatry, De Crespigny Park, Denmark Hill, London, England). **Review of follow-up and follow-back studies of childhood hyperactivity.** Psychological Bulletin, 1984, **96**, 116–132.
A review of 17 follow-up and 7 follow-back studies is undertaken. Many methodological problems are identified and discussed. In particular, it is noted that all of the follow-up studies failed to use psychiatric controls. – From Author's Abstract.

2169. TIEGERMAN, ELLENMORRIS (Adelphi Univ.), & PRIMAVERA, LOUIS H. **Imitating the autistic child: facilitating communicative gaze behavior.** Journal of Autism and Developmental Disorders, 1984, **14**, 27–38.
The nonverbal autistic child exhibits gaze aversion. Adult-child interactions that differentially affected changes in gaze behavior were investigated. The interaction procedure in which the experimenter imitated the autistic child's object and action performances resulted in the greatest change in the frequency and the duration of gaze behavior. – From Authors' Abstract.

2170. TRUEMAN, DAVID (William Paterson Coll. of New Jersey). **The behavioral treatment of school phobia: a critical review.** Psychology in the Schools, 1984, **21**, 215–223.
An analysis of reported case studies using classical conditioning elements and those using operant learning ones reveals that both approaches indicate success. – From Author's Abstract.

2171. TRUEMAN, DAVID (William Paterson Coll. of New Jersey). **What are the characteristics of school phobic children?** Psychological Reports, 1984, **54**, 191–202.
This work reviews demographic data on school phobic children and their families, intelligence, academic achievement, personality characteristics, and presence and nature of precipitating events leading to phobic episodes. School phobic children are typically more dependent, anxious, immature, and depressed than nonphobic children. – Adapted from Author's Abstract.

2172. TYLER, ANN H., & BRASSARD, MARLA R. (Univ. of Utah). **Abuse in the investigation and treatment of intrafamilial child sexual abuse.** Child Abuse & Neglect, The International Journal, 1984, **8**, 47–53.

Results indicate that there is great variability in the investigation and prosecution of incest cases and the public announcement of abuse convictions. The consequences of the abuse investigation are devastating for offender and his family. – From Authors' Abstract.

2173. WASSERMAN, THEODORE H. (Astor Child Guidance Ctr., 4330 Byron, Bronx). **Development of the Children's Dysfunctional Cognition Scale.** Child & Family Behavior Therapy, 1983, **5,** 17–24.
Normal and emotionally disturbed children were administered the Children's Dysfunctional Cognition Scale. Results indicate that the scale is reliable and valid. – From Author's Abstract.

2174. WATERHOUSE, LYNN (Trenton State Coll.), & FEIN, DEBORAH. **Developmental trends in cognitive skills for children diagnosed as autistic and schizophrenic.** Child Development, 1984, **55,** 236–248.
Children whose histories included a diagnosis of infantile autism or childhood schizophrenia were followed longitudinally to assess cognitive developmental trends. A test battery of 5 language skill measures and 2 perception skill measures was administered. Comparisons of age and test score correlations, comparisons of cross-sequential means, and trends for means for diagnostic subgroups and normal controls suggest developmental delay for all skills at all ages for both autistic and schizophrenic children. – From Authors' Abstract.

2175. WENDT, ROBERT N. (Univ. of Toledo), & ZAKE, JEROME. **Family systems theory and school psychology: implications for training and practice.** Psychology in the Schools, 1984, **21,** 204–210.
The purpose of this article is to present an overview of family systems perspectives and to present guidelines for training school psychologists in family dynamics and family therapy. – From Authors' Abstract.

2176. YAIRI, EHUD (Univ. of Illinois, Urbana-Champaign), & LEWIS, BARBARA. **Disfluencies at the onset of stuttering.** Journal of Speech and Hearing Research, 1984, **27,** 145–154.
Ten 2–3-year-olds diagnosed by parents to have begun stuttering for periods of 2 months or less and 10 matched normally speaking children served as subjects. Analyses of spontaneous speech indicated that stutterers were 3 times more disfluent than nonstutterers. – From Authors' Abstract.

2177. ZENTALL, SYDNEY S. (Purdue Univ.). **Context effects in the behavioral ratings of hyperactivity.** Journal of Abnormal Child Psychology, 1984, **12,** 345–352.
Hyperactive children were rated by their parents as changing activities, talking, interrupting, and exhibiting dependency more than nonhyperactive children. Furthermore, those differences between hyperactive and control children were observed primarily in the play and homework contexts. – From Author's Abstract.

HISTORY, THEORY, AND METHODOLOGY

2178. BAKER, CAROLYN D. (Univ. of New England, Armidale, New South Wales, Australia). **Contemporary or future choosers?: a research note.** Journal of Early Adolescence, 1984, **4,** 75–81.
Issues in the conduct of life-course research with adolescents are raised from the comparison of 2 studies. – From Author's Abstract.

2179. CLARKE, A. D. B. (Univ. of Hull, England), & CLARKE, A. M. **Constancy and change in the growth of human characteristics.** Journal of Child Psychology and Psychiatry, 1984, **25,** 191–210.
Both constancies and changes of ordinal position and/or level occur for most characteristics in normal circumstances, but, following significant ecological improvement, personal changes among the disadvantaged can be much larger. Recent research emphasizes the inadequacy of

considering either genetic or environmental effects during 1 period of development outside the context of preceding and subsequent influences. – From Authors' Abstract.

2180. McLOYD, VONNIE C. (Univ. of Michigan), & RANDOLPH, SUZANNE M. **The conduct and publication of research on Afro-American children: a content analysis.** Human Development, 1984, **27**, 65–75.
Quantitative procedures are used to assess differences in the qualitative nature of studies which compare Afro-American children with children from another racial or ethnic group vs. studies in which the research sample consists solely of Afro-American children. Major journals in the field of human development are compared with other journals to determine if reliable differences exist in the nature of research published therein about Afro-American children. Contrary to prediction, race-comparative studies were no more likely than race-homogeneous studies to be based on a deficit model of the behavior of Afro-American children and no less likely to focus on situational determinants. – From Authors' Abstract.

2181. MATTER, ROXANA MARIE (Carrollton High School, GA). **The historical emergence of adolescence: perspectives from developmental psychology and adolescent literature.** Adolescence, 1984, **19**, 131–142.
The present study is a review of literature from 2 distinct disciplines: developmental psychology and literature. – Adapted from Author's Abstract.

2182. MUMFORD, MICHAEL D. (Advanced Research Resources Organization, Suite 900, 4330 East-West Highway, Bethesda), & OWENS, WILLIAM A. **Individuality in a developmental context: some empirical and theoretical considerations.** Human Development, 1984, **27**, 84–108.
Examination and comparison of the behavior and experiences indicated (*a*) that individuality in development is associated with complex, qualitative differences which cannot be described through the trait model and (*b*) that developmental theory must consider the possibility of qualitative differences among individuals. – From Authors' Abstract.

2183. STEFANKO, MICHAEL (1539 Larkwood, West Covina, CA). **Trends in adolescent research: a review of articles published in** *Adolescence*—**1966–1981.** Adolescence, 1984, **19**, 1–14.

2184. WEINER, PAUL S. **The study of childhood language disorders in the nineteenth century.** ASHA, 1984, **26**, 35–38.
Throughout the nineteenth century, childhood language disorders were studied, with a virtual "information explosion" toward the end of the century in German-speaking countries. The author recalls the accomplishments of that time. – From Author's Abstract.

2185. WILLIAMS, ROBERT, & FLAGG-WILLIAMS, JOAN B. **Bibliography of Piagetian publications in 1982–83.** The Genetic Epistemologist, 1984, **12**, 15–32.

BOOK NOTICES

2186. ALLAND, ALEXANDER, JR. **Playing with Form.** Columbia Univ. Press, 1983. xi + 223 p. $29.50 (cloth); $13.50 (paper).
This book examines children's spontaneous drawings (by colored felt pen) in 6 cultures: unschooled subjects from Bali, Ponape, and Taiwan, and subjects from Japan, United States, France. The author, an anthropologist, offers 1 of the most challenging works on drawing to appear for some time. He starts with an explicitly stated theory concerning drawing—that drawing is not directed necessarily toward representation as so many have believed but is "disciplined play with form." Drawing involves rules "coded in the human brain" pertaining to "good form." These rules are universal, but their expression becomes in part restricted by cultural conventions. Drawing is not symbolic or representational because "there is no overall

esthetic imperative that can compare with the linguistic imperative in human culture." Humans need language but not art for communication. In his conclusion, the author emphasizes the ubiquity of design processes in young children's work, stylistic consistency within each of the 6 cultures, and strong stylistic differences among them. He concludes that while his data do not prove his hypothesis, neither do they disprove it, and he is therefore reluctant to abandon his theory. This well-written book is provocative in every sense of that term and cries out for a critical review!—D. B. Harris.

2187. BRAINERD, C. J. (Ed.). **Children's Logical and Mathematical Cognition: Progress in Cognitive Development Research.** Springer-Verlag, 1982. xvi + 216 p. $22.00.
This book is thinner than most edited volumes, and its focus is sharper. The 6 chapters are all concerned with logical and quantitative concepts in preadolescent children. Every chapter is theoretical; most of them also review empirical studies, concentrating on the author's own research. Many of the ideas and nearly all of the data have appeared in print elsewhere, but in a disparate array of articles. The book integrates them and makes them accessible to a general audience. In a chapter on alternative explanations of conservation-nonconservation, Curt Acredolo provides an intelligent perspective on a familiar topic, emphasizing a distinction between operational and nonoperational conservation. He summarizes his analysis by proposing 4 models of development and the sequence of observable behavior that each model predicts. Karen C. Fuson, John Richards, and Diane J. Briars, in the longest chapter in the book, report a wealth of data on how children learn the canonical sequence of number words for counting. They describe a developmental sequence of increasing skill and flexibility in using the sequence, and they report on a variety of strategies that children use in counting. The next chapter, by Harry W. Hoemann and Bruce M. Ross, concerns children's concepts of chance and probability. The shortest chapter in the book, it cogently summarizes the extant research on a topic that has suffered some neglect. Linda S. Siegel's chapter on quantity concepts emphasizes her own extensive research on how children's judgments of quantity are affected by perceptual and linguistic factors. The chapter by Geoffrey B. Saxe is distinctive in 2 ways. It examines numerical cognition in a culture very different from our own, that is the Oksapmin of Papua, New Guinea, and it casts a sociohistorical perspective on its analysis of the individual's concepts of number, measurement, and arithmetic. Finally, Charles J. Brainerd provides a chapter that describes a process of rule-sampling, formalizes the process in a Markov model, and applies the model to data on children's learning of Piagetian concepts. While technical, this chapter is quite readable. – A. Wilkinson.

2188. BRIEF, JEAN-CLAUDE. **Beyond Piaget: A Philosophical Psychology.** Teachers Coll. Press, 1983. xxvii + 232 p. $15.95.
This work uncovers a conceptual holism by eliminating certain Piagetian ambiguities and epistemologically grounds it within a semiotics of action. Brief delimits the conditions for constructing a permanent reality by clarifying the dependence of intellectual growth on bodily action. He argues that the externality of objects is built from the mobility and multiplicity of intercoordinated actions. Chapter 1 summarizes Piaget's genetic epistemology, genetic psychology, and cognitive psychology. Brief then argues that Piaget's latent dualism can be avoided by basing his theory of knowledge on a theory of action. He maintains that the semiotic function underlying intercoordinations of action can ground both physical and logico-mathematical knowledge. In Chapter 2, Brief outlines a semiotics for action in which sensations articulate the psychological person into the physiological body. As the repeatable pragmatics of 1 action become the semantics for subsequent ones, cognitive invariance emerges. In Chapter 3, Brief bridges the traditional gap between sensations and the properties of objects. Sensations acquire permanence by belonging to the crossroads of multiple action pathways. Brief argues that such action-based permanence is anterior to the thought-constitutive transformations required for knowledge. Chapter 4 completes the synthesis of "externality" by adding the means-ends dichotomy to invariance and permanence. Brief maintains that this dichotomy only appears when failure makes means intentionally usable. Complexity, meaningfulness, and open-endedness of behavior are therefore directly related to the mobility of intercoordination between means and ends. Chapter 5 examines the conditions for equilibrium and disequilibrium and

argues that intellectual progress comes primarily through conflict. Brief suggests that this conflict occurs at the articulation between the motoric and sensorial aspects of active, bodily encounters with the world. Brief's concluding chapter clarifies his extension of Piagetian epistemology to the dimensions of personal knowledge on which formal cognition must be based. This dense work represents a long-awaited attempt to nest a theory of knowledge within a theory of action, an important alternative to philosophical critiques of Piaget from the cognitive science tradition. While its phenomenological and hermeneutic base may decrease its accessibility, Brief's book includes occasional practical suggestions for educators, as well as the seeds of a nonrepresentation-based theory for developmental and cognitive psychologists. – J. A. Teske.

2189. CHISOLM, JAMES S. **Navaho Infancy: An Ethological Study of Child Development.** Aldine, 1983. xii + 267 p. $29.95.
Chisolm's book can be thought of as a beautifully drawn extended metaphor. He asks the reader, initially, to engage with him in an intellectual exercise: he proposes that our knowledge (from ethology) of *species adaptation* can be used as the basis of a theoretical model from which to view the "data" of child development. Chisolm's adaptation point of view requires that a "perturbation of development" (like a separation from the mother) be considered in the context of the ecological/cultural system in which it is embedded, and that the child's response to the perturbation also be considered in terms of ecological/cultural systems properties. The aim of the approach is to determine why it is that some early perturbations have a tremendous impact on later development in some contexts, but not in others. The notion of "child development as adaptation" is well articulated in the book. It is a wonderfully refreshing point of view and may well have considerable theoretical promise. The Navaho cradleboard is used as the major perturbation investigated in the research reported by Chisolm. The cradleboard may be thought of as a perturbation in infant development to which the Navaho culture requires adaptation. The question is: why do some children succeed in this adaptation, and some do not succeed? Intensive "ethological" observational data are reported on 38 Navaho and 11 Anglo families (a disappointingly small control group); in addition to the ethological observation, some standardized instruments (like the Brazelton and a measure of "stranger fear") were also employed. The book presents substantial interesting data; the analyses appear to be carefully reasoned and (for the most part) disarmingly simple. Chisolm's findings—in light of his theoretical orientation—are fascinating (and too complex to summarize in a brief review); the "development as adaptation" paradigm provides a fascinating context for those findings. Of course, as is always the case, his empirical findings can be subsumed under other substantive systems as well. So the real beauty of this book lies not in its reporting of the results of empirical research, but rather in its novel conceptualizations. Chisolm implies that we engage in a paradigm shift in our understanding of the nature of the development of children, a challenge few authors present to us at present. Whether this shift in any way proves to be useful remains, of course, to be seen. But the book presents an alternative world view in a well-reasoned, convincing light. My theoretical imagination was treated to an exciting ride. Chisolm's volume should be of interest to developmental psychologists with a social anthropological bent and to generalists with interests in theories and models of development as well. – J. A. Martin.

2190. DAMON, W. (Ed. in Chief). **New Directions for Child Development. A Quarterly Sourcebook,** Jossey-Bass. $8.95 each.
FISCHER, K. W. (Ed.). **Levels and Transitions in Children's Development.** No. 21. 114 p.
GROTEVANT, H. D., & COOPER, C. R. (Eds.). **Adolescent Development in the Family.** No. 22. 112 p.
ROGOFF, B., & WERTSCH, J. V. (Eds.). **Children's Learning in the "Zone of Proximal Development."** No. 23. 102 p.
These volumes are the twenty-first through twenty-third in the New Directions in Child Development series.
The editor of volume 21, Kurt Fischer, states in his preface that the authors in this book will argue for "level" (instead of "stage" which has become ambiguous) as a meaningful psychological construct for which an empirical criterion is offered. A change in level (that is, a transition)

is happening whenever a discontinuity can be demonstrated in the pattern of growth for some aspect of individuals. In Chapter 1, Fischer goes on to show that, while statistical criteria for a transition between levels can be unambiguously formulated, they will not be met unless the person is performing on observable measures at their optimal levels. Levels of cognitive development are thus best thought of as what individuals have the capacity to do when the environment supports it. In this view, level becomes a characteristic of the interaction between child and environment, rather than being a characteristic of the child alone. This makes Fischer's level a more flexible concept than stage has been for the Piagetians. Whether this change in conceptualization will lead to improved research methodology and interpretation remains to be seen. The second paper, by Lampl and Emde, presents some detailed analyses of individual babies' physical growth over the first year. When measures are taken weekly or semiweekly, physical growth is seen to have discontinuous "spurts" (and levels in between) in contrast to the impression one gets from pediatricians' charts based on group averages. While instructive, this point is not new to anyone instructed in statistics. In the third speculative paper, Zelazo and Leonard offer the interesting hypothesis that a major shift in a baby's central processing ability occurs during the last third of the first year. The infant in that period of development can, for the first time, generate ideas in rapid succession. They argue that observed shifts in stranger reactions, attention to familiar (rather than novel) patterns, and pretend play with objects all reflect the hypothesized shift. In the fourth paper, Corrigan presents an overview of an extensive analysis of 3 case studies and a cross-sectional study of 30 children between the ages of 10 and 26 months. She makes the argument that the changes described in children's cognitive skills demonstrate a major discontinuous shift from sensory-motor functioning to representational thought. The 3 case-study children varied in how long it was between way stations to this major shift, and this variation was related by the author to environmental differences. McCall takes up, in Chapter 5, an issue with which his name has long been associated: stability and continuity (or their absence) in development. He points out that while developmental psychology is supposed to be the study of change, few developmental psychologists actually measure or analyze change within individuals. He offers a reanalysis of the Fels longitudinal data in which he demonstrates that, while individuals retain their relative position on most variables over time (stability), the structural dynamics of all the variables change over time. Thus, the meaning of an individual's personality scores may change, even if the rank position of that person does not. In Chapter 6, Kenny raises a new complexity of the levels-and-transitions model of Fischer and others. It might be possible to demonstrate both continuity within a person's pattern of movement toward optimal performance within a level and discontinuity in his movement out of that level and on to the next. Bullock's final chapter of the Fischer volume offers some insight into how transitions in the cognitive and social realms can mutually influence each other. Taken together, these papers are provocative in several ways. For instance: (1) they remind us of how little we look at the primary subject matter of our field: individual change, and (2) they offer an attractive synthesis of a stage concept that cannot account for variation within the individual in his/her level of performance and an environmentally based theory that ignores individual trajectories of change. However, the provocation we experience must be tempered with caution. There is very little empirical evidence for the utility of this new conceptual approach.

Volume 22 in the series, *Adolescent Development in the Family*, represents a major contribution to our understanding of the paradigm shift presently happening in the field of adolescent development. Youniss contributes a final chapter that identifies clearly the contributions of this new paradigm. The main criticism of the individualistic models is their focus on an individual per se as separated from the family. The research approaches represented by the other authors vary, Youniss argues, in the degree to which they continue to subscribe to the adolescent-as-individual model. The heritage being drawn upon by these systems-oriented researchers includes several strands: (1) standard theories of individual development, (2) family systems theory, (3) empirical studies of communication, (4) communication theory emphasizing consensus attainment, and (5) life span development models. The new synthesis being offered by the volume's authors includes these elements: (1) the assumption that parent–child relationships are primary; (2) the focus on individuation as a concept rather than on autonomy, because individuation as a concept considers both individual and social partner(s); (3) the idea that the family–adolescent relationship is socially constructed; and (4) the social-constitutionalism-based idea that the larger society creates the family. The research reported in Chapter 1 by Powers et al. makes the important point that the degree to which an individual adolescent is affected by discrepancies in viewpoints among family members depends on the emotional climate in which the adolescent is exposed to the conflicts. When discrepancies are presented in a noncompetitive atmosphere so defensiveness is not engendered, development is likely. In Chapter 2, Bell and Bell apply the newer systems theory outlook to a study of girls' development. The family's ideology about individual differences (whether or not they are comfortable with them) turns out to be a key catalyst for the daughter's experience of the parents' reaction to them. The study by Cooper et al., reported in Chapter 3, seems to retain the individual-centeredness of an earlier era. Individual characteristics of the parents are correlated with the family's ability to explore alternatives in a cooperative problem-solving situation. In the interview study by White et al., a stage sequence for parent–child relationship is fitted to what is observed. This approach likens the dyadic mother–child or father–child relationship to an individual entity developing. An interesting general conclusion reached by the authors is that college women often have a mutual relationship with their parents and have a broader perspective of them. Men, in contrast, often still view their parents as occupants of the parent role. The last study, reported in Chapter 5 by Reiss et al., deals with the relationship between the family's sensitivity to outside forces and what goes on inside the head of the individual adolescent when operating in this environment. Empathy is positively associated with empathy for both sexes, but for boys, high configuration of the family is associated with empathy. This book represents a welcome leap forward in the field of adolescent development. The ideas provided by family systems theory offers the conceptual basis so long missing from developmental research with adolescents.

Volume 23 is about Vygotsky's "Zone of Proximal Development," defined as the discrepancy between a child's performance on a measure of developmental level when performing alone and what that same child can do when he or she is operating in a social context where the partner is helping to organize or structure the task. The significance of this idea is developed both by the editors in their introductory notes and by Jerome Bruner in the final chapter. Vygotsky's premise is that development is inherently social and that the products of development—-personality, cognitive skills, and social skills—are internalized versions of the social experiences children have as they develop. Thus, the social group is primary, and individual characteristics are derived from social experiences in the group. While this idea is uniquely compatible with Marxist social theory, Bruner's article overstates the case by allowing the reader to conclude—erroneously—that the idea of the primacy of the social over the intrapsychic is somehow unique to the Marxist-based psychology of Vygotsky and other psychologists from the Soviet Union. While it is true that cognitive developmental theories such as Piaget's and those derived from Piaget tend to focus on individual minds, the idea that social experience becomes internalized in individual development is clearly spelled out in some of the psychoanalytic accounts of development—notably, in Erikson's and in the object relations theories—and in the more recent social learning ideas of Albert Bandura. Each of Chapters 1–6 deals with problems of conceptualization or operational definition for the zone of proximal development idea. In Chapter 1, James Wertsch develops 1 idea about how a child moves to the next level of development above his or her current 1. The problem-solving situation must be redefined by the child. He or she does this by coming to be simultaneously aware of his or her own view and the adult's view of the problem and then shifting from the 1 to the other. The adult's conversation with the child in the problem-solving situation helps establish this simultaneous awareness of the self's view and the other's view. Thus, the conversation mediates developmental shifting. Chapter 2, by Saxe et al., reports on an observational study of mothers and preschool children interacting in relation to a task. In Chapter 3, by Rogoff et al., adults and infants are observed interacting in relation to a Jack-in-the-box toy. Adults' behaviors serve to maintain younger babies' task involvement, modulate the fear of babies in the middle of the first year, and gradually transform the interaction into a truly mutual social activity by the second year. In Chapter 4, Griffin and Cole explicate the zone of proximal development idea further by comparing it to related concepts from American and Russian psychology. In Chapter 5, Valsiner extends the idea into the social development realm by applying it to an observational study of families at mealtimes in which children learn the mealtime social script. The final article in the book, Chapter 6, reports a method developed by Campione and others which allows for assessing the reasoning of an individual before (pretest), during, and after (posttest) a socially structured problem-solving session in which the assessed skills are used. The experimenter provides the subject with hints selected from a set of hints sequenced from the most general to the most concrete and specific. The idea of the zone of proximal development offers a means for reconciling stage theories of individual development with ideas about individual differences. The potential contribution to be made by this idea is great, but much work is needed in developing the operational definitions and making the translation of Vygotsky's ideas into related concepts more consistent. – E. Willemsen.

2191. EGAN, KIERNAN. **Education and Psychology: Plato, Piaget, and Scientific Psychology.** Teachers Coll. Press, 1983. xiii + 210 p. $16.95.
The major thrust of this provocative essay is that psychological theories provide different kinds of information than the kinds of things educators need to know. As they presently exist, psychological theories and knowledge are said to have no direct implications for educational practice. Educational practice can only be influenced favorably by knowledge generated within an educational theory. Separate and discrete parts of theories outside of education (including sociological, anthropological, philosophical, and so) cannot be gathered together to form a coherent theory of education. The essence of educational knowledge needed is an integrated prescriptive network of knowledge about: what we should teach, when we should teach particular things, and how we should teach those things. Plato's developmental theory about education, stripped of its intellectual-class accoutrements, has been identified and discussed as telling us much about those questions. From a number of other theories that might have been used, Piaget's theory was selected as an example of a psychological theory that has misguided educational practice and found wanting on many counts. Piaget's theory was selected mainly because of its current prominence among psychologists and educators seeking answers to curriculum decisions. Furthermore, the 2 examples, Plato and Piaget, were seen to have much in common, thereby enabling the author to delineate the differences between educational and psychological theories more easily. Finally, the author shows that the analogy—psychology is to education as physics is to engineering—is false. None of the current research on teaching effectiveness, aptitude by treatment interactions, behavioral objectives, and so on "properly has or can have any implications for education" (p. xii). To become a useful and successful field of study, then, education must evolve from its own theory. Though respectful of the contributions of psychology, anthropology, philosophy, and so on, this essay is clearly not friendly toward the influence (actual or potential) that those contributions might have for the educational enterprise. There is much in this book worth reading. On whichever side the reader stands, the reader will find an excellent survey of educational needs, of Plato's theory of education, and of Piaget's developmental theory. The well-supported arguments follow logically and persuasively and are difficult to dismiss lightly. This very readable book will be appealing and a challenge to readers interested in applications of social sciences to education and to curriculum development in particular, though, perhaps, it will not be taken seriously by any of them. The vast array of controversial arguments could form the basis of many lively polemics. – F. J. Di Vesta.

2192. GARMEZY, N., & RUTTER, M. (Eds.). **Stress, Coping, and Development in Children.** McGraw-Hill, 1983. xxii + 356 p. $24.95.
This book is an outgrowth of a seminar held at the Center for Advanced Studies in the Behavioral Sciences in 1979–1980. The book contains 12 chapters organized in 5 sections. The editors' 2 chapters comprise the first section, with Rutter providing an overview of constructs and issues and Garmezy reviewing the literature about the effects of war or loss of caretaker upon children's stress and coping behavior. The second section contains a chapter by Ciaranello about the nature of neurochemical systems, and a chapter by Levine about the study of stress and coping from a psychobiological approach. Levine presents evidence from his primate research to support the hypothesis that coping responses depend upon the extent to which infants are successful in gaining control over traumatic situations. The third section of the book

contains 4 chapters, each of which focuses upon a different age period. Leiderman discusses the stresses of separation for premature infants and mothers in newborn nurseries. Lipsitt examines the defensive behaviors of infants as they seek to attain physiological integrity. Kagan describes various stressors during the first 3 years of life as they affect the child's growth of self-awareness and the limitations of self. Maccoby presents 13 hypotheses about the relationship between increasing age, transitional events, and children's coping patterns as they move from childhood to adolescence. The fourth section concerns the family as a stress agent. Patterson's chapter summarizes evidence in support of the hypothesis that a mother's disposition to react irritably to her child is a useful indication of the relationship between familial problem-solving skills and the frequency of external crises. Wallerstein's chapter examines a number of developmental tasks required of children involved in divorce-engendered stress. Finally, in the last section of the book, Segal asks how we should disseminate findings about stress and coping to the general public so as to create less stressful lives for millions of citizens. Robbins concludes the book with a discussion of methodological issues in research about stress prevention in children. Overall, this book represents a cogent survey of stress and coping as complexly interwoven variables in children's experiences. The editors have done a masterful job in making this book both interesting and accessible to a wide audience of readers. – J. Eliot.

2193. GINSBURG, HERBERT P. (Ed.). **The Development of Mathematical Thinking.** Academic Press, 1983. xii + 388 p. $37.50.
In this excellent introduction to a broad arena of research, 9 chapters written for this volume present various perspectives on research into the development of mathematical thinking. H. Ginsburg, N. Kossan, R. Schwartz, and D. Swanson, in "Protocol Methods in Research on Mathematical Thinking," discuss the aims and rationales of the talking aloud method, the clinical interview, and mixed cases. Following a comparison of the methods, they consider issues concerning the validity of verbal reports and the problems involved in the contingent structure of clinical interviews and talking aloud procedures. K. Fuson and J. Hall provide, in Chapter 2, a conceptual analysis and review of the acquisition of early number word meanings. They consider separately the categories of sequence words, which are words produced in a conventional sequence when no things are being counted; counting words, which are used in the successive assignment of sequence number words to items; cardinal words, in which a number word describes numerousness; measure words, involving the numerousness of units into which some continuous dimension has been divided; ordinal words, which describe the relative position of something; and the combinations of these words. In Chapter 3, L. Resnick presents "A Developmental Theory of Number Understanding" which emphasizes the central role of the part-whole schema and its successive elaborations. Interestingly, Resnick, starting with a different approach, arrives at an emphasis shared by Piaget on part-whole relationships as a defining characteristic of number understanding and the proposal that ordinal and cardinal relationships must be combined in the construction of the number concept. "Development of Children's Problem-Solving Ability in Arithmetic" is considered by M. Riley, J. Greeno, and J. Heller in Chapter 4. Following a review of research on children's word problem solving, touching on the major factors that have been used to characterize such problems, they present a theoretical analysis of knowledge and strategies assumed to underlie successful performance, consider the locus of improvement in problem-solving skill, and consider different stages of conceptual knowledge related to success, efficiency, and generality of problem solving. They also touch on word problem solving involving other than elementary arithmetic problems. In Chapter 5, K. Van Lehn presents a fascinating treatment of the representation of procedures in repair theory. Repair theory postulates that a fairly large group of systematic errors, termed bugs, occur during the process of mastering an arithmetic procedure due to unsuccessful applications of a small set of procedures by the learner followed by 1 of a small set of repairs. This paper focuses on the use of a knowledge representation language to express knowledge held by the learner and argues that getting a simple model which obeys strong principles rests on getting the knowledge representation language "right." An argument is also made for stack-based rather than register-based representations of core procedures. Chapter 6, "Complex Mathematical Cognition," by R. Davis addresses the importance of the creative, inventive side

of using mathematics and therefore the corresponding importance of theory concerning them and education oriented to their development. In Chapter 7, G. Saxe and J. Posner consider the relation between culture and the development of numerical thought. "The Development of Numerical Cognition: Cross-cultural Perspectives" discusses general properties of numeration systems, the theoretical positions of Vygotsky and Piaget relative to universal and culture-specific processes in the development of numerical concepts, and the existing research on cross-cultural number development associated with each position. B. Allardice and H. Ginsburg consider various "Children's Psychological Difficulties in Mathematics" in Chapter 8, and in the final chapter by G. Groen and C. Kieran, an unusually sophisticated and clear-headed discussion of the relevance of Piaget's work to the development of mathematical thinking is provided. The book provides a wonderfully broad and yet often intricately detailed look at a burgeoning field of developmental research. – R. S. Bogartz.

2194. HAROUTUNIAN, SOPHIE. **Equilibrium in the Balance: A Study of Psychological Explanation.** Springer-Verlag, 1983. xvi + 157 p. $23.50.

A great part of Piaget's genius lay in his ability to see problems where none were seen before. One of those problems can be roughly formulated as follows: How can development be both directed and regulated, yet also remain open to new experience? In this book, Sophie Haroutunian evaluates the complex answer Piaget gave to this question during the final decades of his life. The book contributes in 3 ways to the developmental literature. First, it provides a detailed exposition of Piaget's late work—work of which many psychologists remain largely ignorant. Second, it carefully reveals some of the weaknesses in Piaget's proposed solution, while remaining basically sympathetic to the question that Piaget posed for himself. A particular strength here is the discussion of problems associated with the fundamentally asocial nature of Piaget's model. Third, the book relates Piaget's efforts to those of other important cognitive scientists, e.g., Chomsky, Fodor, and Dennett. No one interested in the explanatory adequacy of Piagetian theory—or of developmental theories generally—should miss reading this book. In any commentary on Piaget's late work, major problems of exegesis arise. At many junctures, Piaget's intent is locally unclear and the reader can arrive at a correct interpretation only by being sensitive to the overall cast of both Piaget's thinking and the thinking prevalent among his expected audience. In the vast majority of cases, Haroutunian makes a Herculean attempt to provide a sensitive reading and succeeds admirably. However, there are a few lapses that may bear importantly on the ultimate fate of her judgments. First, she claims that Piaget has confounded logical with pragmatic necessity. This claim rests on the supposition that Piaget would not grant that cognitive structures are also material structures. But Piaget's opposition to the latter identity is never documented. Second, she often notes that Piaget's repeated inferences about sequences and stage precursors are not warranted. Typically what she means is that his inferences are not warranted with deductive certainty. Though subtle, the difference is critical. Third, throughout Chapter 4 she fails to adequately document her attribution to Piaget of certain beliefs about "higher order" principles used to select among alternative variant assimilations. This failure to document is critical, because it raises the distinct possibility that Haroutunian's familiarity with Jerry Fodor's formulation of the issues has led her to misassimilate Piaget's formulation. Finally, any thorough evaluation of Piaget's late work requires a much better than average grasp of the explanatory apparatus of modern evolutionary theory. Haroutunian has an above average grasp, yet certain subtleties are omitted from her discussion—subtleties that should be addressed before judging whether Piaget was attempting to provide an alternative to Darwinism or an enriched version of a neo-Darwinian variation-selection model. Among the subtleties missed, the 2 most critical are: the distinction between chance and randomness and the related idea that selection alters the base from which mutations arise. These caveats aside, mastering Haroutunian's arguments will improve any developmentalist's ability to formulate theories with true explanatory power. – D. Bullock.

2195. KOHLBERG, L.; LEVINE, C.; & HEWER, A. **Moral Stages: A Current Formulation and a Response to Critics.** Karger, 1983. vii + 178 p. $39.00.

For approximately 20 years, Lawrence Kohlberg's stage theory of moral reasoning has been recognized as the major cognitive-structural perspective on moral development. In the last decade, this work has stimulated a great deal of debate. Scholars have challenged his normative-ethical and cross-cultural claims. They have also argued that the theory and methods are sex-biased and inadequate from the perspective of a description of the moral domain. This monograph is devoted to 2 tasks. First, it contains a systematic presentation of Kohlberg's present position as it has been developed and revised. In this connection, there are extensive discussions of: (a) the reconstruction of the ontogenesis of stages of justice reasoning, (b) the meta-ethical assumptions underlying the theory, (c) the distinction between the normative-ethical and the meta-ethical assumptions behind the theory, and (d) distinctions between "hard" and "soft" stages, stages 6 and 7, form and content, and a number of related issues. Further, the reader is brought up to date concerning Kohlberg's views about the relationship between moral reasoning and moral behavior as well as that between the sociomoral context and moral development. Second, there is an extended discussion of those criticisms of other scholars and Kohlberg's evaluations of those criticisms. While acknowledging the significance of a number of criticisms and adjusting the theory to meet them, Kohlberg denies that his list of stages is fundamentally incomplete or that the stages are culturally or sex biased. This reader found the book to be provocative and informative. Beyond those features mentioned above, Kohlberg's acceptance of the hermeneutical framework provided by J. Habermas was particularly interesting. In this connection, Kohlberg has considerably mitigated some of the philosophical claims which characterized his earlier work. He also has retracted his claim to have empirically characterized stage 6. Anyone interested in cognitive development will find this monograph invaluable. It is well written and concise. It is current and contains a helpful bibliography. Finally, it presents the current status of 1 of the most important programs of ongoing research in psychology today. – J. Martin.

2196. KUCZAJ, STAN A. **Crib Speech and Language Play.** Springer-Verlag, 1983. xii + 188 p. $22.00.
Building on an hypothesis suggested by Ruth Weir (1962) that language practice is "more likely to occur in crib speech than in social-context speech," this book contains an extensive report on a study of language practice. Language practice is divided into 5 types: exact repetitions and imitations, buildups (i.e., "an utterance sequence of 2 or more parts, each successive part including words of the previous utterance and additional linguistic units"), breakdowns (i.e., "the opposite of buildups"), completions (i.e., "2 or more utterances . . . separated by a pause but which form a more complex utterance"), and substitutions (i.e., "a substitution in the second or third utterance of a different word . . . in a sentence gramatically parallel to the original"). Each of the 5 types of language practice is studied in 2 speech settings (e.g., the crib setting and the social-context setting) and following 2 types of models (e.g., self-model situations and other-model situations). Data are reported from 14 children (15–24 months of age at the start of the study), who were followed until the child stopped producing crib speech (6–27 weeks). Through the use of many tables and figures, the author is able to interestingly describe group and individual subject data for each of the variables under study. The detailed description of the findings occupies 2/3 of the book's pages. The last section provides discussion, conclusions, and speculation. This last section addresses the general issues introduced in the first section: What is the relation between imitation and repetition? What is the relation between crib speech and social-content speech? What role does parental modeling play? Why do children engage in language practice in the crib? Why do they cease? Is crib speech important for language practice? The author effectively combines results from group analyses and individual analyses obtained in the present study with results reported by other researchers to address the issues which are the book's foci and to come to some definite conclusions. The use of figures to present the data in detail should prove helpful to other researchers for the comparison of data sets and the generation of hypotheses relevant to language practice. Students of early language acquisition should find this book interesting, although the sparceness of the literature review may disappoint some readers. – D. L. Molfese.

2197. MILLER, L. J. **Miller Assessment for Preschoolers.** Denver: Foundation for Knowledge in Development, 1982.

The Miller Assessment for Preschoolers (MAP) is designed to identify children who exhibit mild to moderate developmental delays. The MAP is an individually administered screening tool for children ages 2 years 9 months to 5 years 8 months. It provides a comprehensive overview of a child's developmental status with respect to other children. The test can be administered and scored in 30 min. The MAP is a norm-referenced test; item development and selection has spanned 10 years. The MAP Research Edition included 530 items which were tested in the 9 U.S. Census Bureau Regions on a randomly selected, stratified sample of preschoolers ($N = 600$ normal, and 60 preacademic problem children). Analysis of the data from this sample led to the selection of the 27 items. Normative data was obtained by standardizing the test in the 9 U.S. Census Bureau Regions on 1,200 stratified-random selected normal children; 90 children with preacademic problems were also assessed to provide validity information. No specialized training is required in order to learn to administer the MAP. For the experienced clinician, the MAP provides a Supplemental Observations sheet, which presents a comprehensive, structured clinical framework helpful in defining a child's strengths and weaknesses and indicating possible avenues of remediation. The test items can be grouped into 5 categories labeled: Foundation Index, Coordination Index, Verbal Index, Non-Verbal Index, and Complex Tasks Index. The scoring system is quick and simple. Examiners are instructed to determine specific cut-off points based on the child's percentile score, which will indicate (1) definite need for further evaluation: probable dysfunction; (2) possible need for further evaluation at a later date: "watch" or borderline; and (3) no need for further evaluation: unlikely that the child has problems. Analysis indicated interrater reliability was .97 or higher on the total test and on 4 of the 5 indices. The fifth index, coordination, had .84 reliability. A specification table was constructed to explain the developmental domains assessed as well as the contribution of each item to each domain. In addition, the relationship of item performance to chronological age was studied. A varimax rotated factor matrix was computed indicating relative agreement with division of items into subtests. Correlation studies of items and indices revealed that all items were contributing to the final score. The MAP was compared with 4 other assessment instruments to obtain a direct and independent measure of validity. The expectation did not exist that any test would have a direct correlation to the MAP, since the MAP was developed because no similar test existed. Full information on additional studies is presented in the MAP examiner's manual. Additional studies are in progress. MAP is $249.00 and is available through KID Technology, Inc., 11715 E. 51st Ave., Denver, CO 80239, (303) 373–1916. – T. Sprong.

2198. PETERSON, C., & McCABE, A. **Developmental Psycholinguistics: Three Ways of Looking at a Child's Narrative.** Plenum, 1983. xxxi + 245 p. $27.50.
This book provides a significant contribution to the literature on the development of children's narratives, a form of discourse that has gained in importance as researchers realize the potential significance of this aspect of language and communicative development for the acquisition of reading and writing skills. The book describes a cross-sectional study of the development of narrative skills that was conducted with 96 children ranging from 3 to 9 years of age. The children engaged in conversation with an experimenter who prompted for narratives describing specific experiences in the child's life. Each child provided several different narratives, and 1 of the excellent features of the book is the inclusion of 73 complete narratives that could be used by readers for their own purposes. The heart of the volume is taken up by detailed descriptions of 3 scoring analyses: *High Point*—based on work by Labov, in which the key referential function or evaluation by the narrator is coded; *Episode*—based on Rumelhart's early work in the story grammar vein, in which narratives are coded in terms of informational or semantic categories; and *Syntactic Dependency*—based on Deese's work emphasizing syntax in stories, in which syntactic complexity and syntactic cohesion are analyzed, independent of semantic or pragmatic content. The results are described and evaluated thoughtfully and critically by the authors; however, the book is dominated more by methodological detail. Nonetheless, it should be of interest to anyone concerned with language or cognitive development, although it may be too specialized for a broader audience. The main conclusions to be drawn from this book are that these different ways of looking at a child's narrative may complement 1 another, but they do not, unfortunately, provide a coherent and integrated view of narrative development. – H. B. Tager-Flusberg.

2199. TURIEL, ELLIOT. **The Development of Social Knowledge: Morality & Convention.** Cambridge Univ. Press, 1983. viii + 240 p. $39.00 (cloth); $13.95 (paper).

In this provocative book, Elliot Turiel draws together a considerable body of research over the past 10 years by himself and his colleagues which challenges important aspects of the traditional structuralist perspective on the development of social knowledge in children and adolescents. Elaborating the concept of distinctive domains in thinking, Turiel shows that even quite young children distinguish between moral and social-conventional rules and issues, contrary to earlier theorizing by Piaget and Kohlberg. According to Turiel, children consistently view social-conventional rules as arbitrary, changeable, and dependent on social context, whereas moral rules are understood as nonarbitrary, universal, and intrinsically related to actions and their consequences. Turiel holds that these domain distinctions develop because of the child's differential experiences in interaction with various rule types and his or her efforts to understand these coherently. Ultimately, the developing child is portrayed as rational and systematic, understanding experiences in both of these domains through distinctive, but orderly, sequences of stages or levels of thought. The book is divided into 10 chapters. Turiel begins by discussing some general issues of theory and research from a structuralist perspective. He then clarifies the concepts of morality and social convention with respect to theoretical and philosophical issues, elucidating formal criteria for distinguishing these 2 domains, and providing a valuable philosophical grounding for understanding these empirical studies. The research reviewed in the rest of the book describes the social interactional bases for these 2 domains and traces the ontogenetic evidence for distinctions between them. Several unpublished, as well as previously published, studies are reviewed that have assessed the child's understanding of types of social rules, their origins, alterability, and so on. Turiel's earlier research on the developmental sequence of social-conventional understanding is then discussed, describing a series of 7 "levels" from early childhood to young adulthood, based on the individual's increasingly sophisticated thinking about social organization and the functions of conventions. Turiel's clarifications are then applied to some of the earlier research of Piaget and Kohlberg on the development of autonomous morality, with useful results. Similarly, the work of some of the noncognitive theorists of moral development, including Freud and Bandura and Parke, is critiqued and clarified by analyzing the research paradigms utilized and these theorists' failure to distinguish morality as a separate domain of thought. Central issues regarding the relationship between thought and action are also illuminated by the questions of domain distinctions and coordination as well. In general, this is a well-written, carefully systematic work. It is scholarly, but not especially technical in style. It brings together in 1 place and integrates a central and provocative set of results on social-cognitive development that is sure to have a continuing impact in the field. In the preface, Turiel indicates that this book is to be followed by a more theoretically oriented volume in the future. Researchers and students in development and education can look forward to further elaboration of this important work. – M. W. Pratt.

Barratt, T. M., 28
Barret, R. L., 1195
Barron, A. P., 2077
Barry, R. J., 623
Bar-Tal, D., 445, 1792
Barth, R. P., 1793
Bartlett, K., 344
Bartolotta, R., 1597
Barton, K., 687
Baruch, I., 725
Basham, R. B., 99
Bassoff, B. Z., 1794
Bateman, D., 1576
Bates, E., 809, 1601
Bates, J. E., 941, 1174, 1795
Bathurst, K., 19
Battin, R. R., 2058
Bauer, A. M., 2078
Bauer, R. H., 1977
Baumrind, D., 1796
Bax, M., 2123
Bayles, K., 941, 1174, 1795
Bealer, J. M., 1690
Beall, D., 2010
Bearison, D. J., 794
Beck, I. L., 509
Beck, J. T., 1038
Becker, C. A., 510
Becker, P. T., 484
Becker-Redding, U., 1384
Beckwith, L., 776, 1567
Bee, H. L., 3
Bégin, G., 1039
Behar, D., 2079
Beilin, H., 162
Beisler, J. M., 1390
Beitchman, J. H., 1391
Belger, K. A., 1213
Bell, C. R., 76
Bell, J. A., 176
Bellinger, D. C., 308
Belmont, J. M., 795
Belov, I. M., 744
Belsky, J., 1602, 1797
Benacerraf, B. R., 4
Benbow, C. P., 796
Bender, B., 46
Benedict, H., 97
Bennett, D., 570
Bennett-Kastor, T., 77
Benninga, J., 827
Benson, G. P., 1973
Bentler, P. M., 434
Bentley, W. L., 2068
Benton, S. L., 78
Bentovim, A., 1457

Berenson, G. S., 1967
Berent, S., 757
Berg, I., 589
Berg, K. M., 79
Bergan, J. R., 1603
Bergsgaard, M. O., 1798
Bergstrom, L. I., 825
Berk, R. A., 1978
Berkowitz, M. W., 797
Berkowitz, N., 1979
Berlin, I. N., 590
Berlinsky, E. B., 680
Berman, C., 2161
Berman, P. W., 1799
Bernard, R. M., 798
Berndt, D., 588
Berndt, T. J., 335, 1040
Bernstein, M., 1253
Bernstein, M. E., 799, 800
Bernstein, R. M., 309
Berry, J. O., 1041
Berry, P., 382, 1980
Bersani, C., 876
Bertacchini, P. A., 368
Bertenthal, B. I., 80, 1604
Berzonsky, M. D., 1042, 1486
Besharov, D. J., 1524
Best, C. T., 1720
Betton, J. P., 310
Bever, T. G., 255
Beveridge, M., 81, 2038
Bezaire, M. M., 370
Biber, D., 801
Bickett, L., 1472
Bidder, R. T., 24
Biederman, G. B., 640
Bieger, E., 1261
Biemiller, A., 511
Bierman, K. L., 362, 1800
Biggerstaff, A., 142
Bill, J. M., 72
Biller, H. B., 680
Billings, A. G., 1392
Bilsky, L. H., 868
Bing, J. R., 1981
Bing, S. B., 1981
Birch, L. L., 1525
Birmingham, W. G., 2080
Birnholz, J. C., 4
Birns, B., 1526
Birrell, J., 720
Bisanz, G. L., 1501
Bisanz, J., 1501
Biscoe, B., 784
Bishop, D. V. M., 82
Bizzell, R. P., 556

Bjork, E. L., 101, 829, 1605
Bjorklund, D. F., 83, 802
Blackwell, P. M., 113
Blackwell, S. L., 512
Blasi, A., 1043
Blatchford, P., 1262
Blatter, P., 84
Blau, H., 2052
Blaxall, J., 1982
Blewitt, P., 85, 86
Blincoe, M. M., 2146
Bloch, S. A., 1961
Block, J., 361, 881, 1918
Block, J. H., 361, 881, 1044, 1918
Blood, G. W., 1801
Blood, I. M., 1801
Blotcky, A. D., 1393
Blotcky, M. J., 1393
Blow, F. C., 1187
Blum, A., 1394
Blyth, D. A., 311, 1045, 1263
Boake, C., 591
Boersma, D. C., 145
Bohannon, J. N., 286, 1773
Bohrnstedt, G. W., 1046
Bolick, T., 1802
Boll, T. J., 757
Bolton, D., 2081
Bomba, P. C., 87
Bonaminio, V., 1047
Bond, L. A., 312
Bonert, R., 245
Bonvillian, J. D., 803, 804
Book, R. M., 1361
Borelli, J., 46
Borkowski, J. G., 88, 1689, 2154
Borman, K. M., 681
Bormann-Kischkel, C., 1279
Bornstein, M. H., 1748
Borreca, C., 987
Bottomley, V., 634
Botuck, S., 805
Botvin, E. M., 313
Boudreault, M., 1895
Bourg, J. W., 795
Bourkovetskaya, Z. I., 902
Bowers, A. J., 592
Bowers, N. D., 1023
Bowey, J. A., 89, 1004, 1606, 1740
Bowyer, P. M., 1291
Boxer, A., 758
Boyd, F. E., 72

Hogan, J. D., 212, 1491, 1730
Hogan, M. A., 830
Hogg, J., 204
Hohn, W. E., 541
Holdaway, S. L., 1298
Holden, E. W., 652
Hollinger, C. L., 1113
Holm, J., 205
Holman, J., 389
Holmes, C. S., 621
Holt, G. M., 1861
Holt, K. S., 8
Holt, P., 589
Holzman, M., 1671
Holzman, T. G., 137, 214
Hom, H. L., Jr., 1066
Honig, A. S., 1299
Hoogeveen, F. R., 2053
Hooper, F. A., 2122
Hoover-Dempsey, K., 1227
Hoppe-Graff, S., 1672, 1673
Hops, M., 1413
Horan, P. F., 885, 1746
Horgan, J., 138
Horgan, J. S., 138, 886
Horn, J. M., 25
Horn, T. S., 1862
Hornby, G., 1300, 1430
Horne, M. D., 1114, 1301
Horner, T. M., 1115
Horowitz, F. D., 38, 206, 887, 1774
Horowitz, Z., 2092
Horst, R., 771
Horton, W. O., 2044
Horvat, M. A., 1302
Horvath, A., 646
Horwitz, S. J., 1257
Hosking, G., 731
Hotaling, G. T., 2099
House, A. E., 1492
House, W. C., 390
Housner, L. D., 812
Houston, B. K., 352
Houts, A. C., 1431
Howard, J., 1567
Howard, K., 1850
Howell, K. W., 542
Howes, C., 391, 461, 1116
Howes, M., 139
Hoyer, W. J., 156
Hrncir, E., 1602
Hsu, C., 1365
Huba, G. J., 434
Hubble, L. M., 392

Huber, A., 1769
Hudson, J., 140, 141
Hufnagle, J., 26
Hughes, H. M., 1432
Hughes, J., 2075
Hughes, M., 273
Hughes, S. P., 393
Hughes, V., 1433
Hulme, C., 142
Humble, C., 1117
Humm-Delgado, D., 1434
Hummel, D. D., 143
Humphrey, L. L., 1118
Humphreys, M. S., 178, 1291
Humphries, T., 570
Hunt, A., 743
Hunter, S. M., 1967
Huntley, R. M. C., 8
Huong, N. T., 1119
Hurtig, R. R., 1608
Husted, S. D. R., 7
Huston, A. C., 779, 1170
Huttenlocher, P. R., 1549
Hutton, J. B., 1435
Hwang, C., 405, 905, 1137
Hyde, J. S., 1171
Hymel, S., 1120
Hynd, G. W., 1327, 1362

Ibañez-Cacho, J. M., 1453
Ibsen, E., 1700
Ignatius, S. W., 771
Imaizumi, N., 252
Imwold, C. H., 1570
Inagaki, K., 1663
Ingram, D., 1649
Inoff, G. E., 1863
Intons-Peterson, M. J., 1864
Isaacson, D. K., 1674
Ishee, J., 762
Ishii, T., 891
Israel, A. C., 1550
Isralowitz, R., 1468
Ito, R., 1675
Ivers, J. W., 1961
Ives, S. W., 144
Ivinskis, A., 851

Jacklin, C. N., 1890
Jackson, M. S., 1104
Jacobowitz, T., 1303
Jacobsen, R. H., 622
Jacobson, A. M., 1853, 2148

Jacobson, J. L., 145, 729, 1676, 1865
Jacobson, S. W., 729, 1676
Jaffe, M., 13
James, A. L., 623
James, L. S., 1576
James, S. L., 146
Jamison, M., 2004
Janicki, M. P., 27
Janson, K. A., 1859
Jardine, R., 147
Jarvie, G. J., 1121
Jaskir, J., 2136
Jaudes, P. K., 1407
Javel, M. E., 1304
Jeffrey, D. B., 1183
Jeffrey, W. E., 167
Jenkins, J. R., 888
Jenkins, S., 2123
Jenkins-Friedman, R., 2029
Jennings, K. D., 299
Jensen, L. C., 1052, 1298
Jeruzal, N. C., 1682
Jillings, C., 1138
Jing-Zhe, W., 1704
Johansson, E., 617
Johnsen, E. P., 2063
Johnson, C. N., 1677
Johnson, D. B., 889
Johnson, F. L., 394
Johnson, G. M., 2124
Johnson, J. E., 890
Johnson, K. L., 400
Johnson, S. B., 2072
Johnson, S. M., 322
Johnson, W. F., 1122
Johnston, C., 1158
Johnston, J. R., 1651, 1678
Jones, D., 882
Jones, J. B., 1436
Jones, L., Jr., 560
Jones, M., 1354
Jones, R. S., 92
Jones, R. W. A., 28
Jones, S., 987
Joos, S. K., 29
Jorgensen, S. R., 1123
Jorm, A. F., 148, 1353
Joseph, G., 111
Judd, T. P., 868
Juel, C., 1305
Juhasz, A. M., 1124
Junkala, J., 149
Jurich, A. P., 1866
Jusczyk, P. W., 30
Justice, E. M., 91

Sloan, M. P., 1469
Sloate, P. L., 254
Slobin, D. I., 255
Slocumb, P. R., 2139
Sloper, P., 10, 2163
Sluckin, W., 384
Slugoski, B. R., 2042
Smeets, P. M., 474, 475, 2053
Smeriglio, V. L., 409, 476
Smetana, J. G., 1217, 1934
Smilansky, J., 1840
Smiley, A., 1266
Smirni, P., 1763
Smith, C. S., 1410
Smith, G. J. W., 985
Smith, I. D., 421, 422
Smith, I. M., 1508
Smith, J. E., 1179
Smith, L. B., 256, 1764, 1765
Smith, M., 1235, 1575
Smith, M. C., 79, 766
Smith, P., 329, 1935
Smith, P. E., 2164
Smith, S. D., 42, 385
Smith, V. L., 1799
Smithers, A., 1936
Smithers, A. G., 1936
Smoke, L., 327
Smolak, L., 986
Smyer, M. A., 1187
Smythe, P. M., 53
Snarey, J. R., 1218, 1766
Snow, C. E., 1767
Snow, J. H., 1362
Snow, M. E., 1890
Snowling, M., 1363
Snyder, F. R., 1269
Snyder, H. N., 463, 1964
Snyder, L., 809
Snyder, S. S., 437, 450
Snyderman, M., 678
Sobesky, W. E., 477
Sobol, M. P., 570
Soderman, A. K., 685
Sokoloff, R. M., 1470
Solimano, G., 1539
Solís-Cámara, P., 754
Solís-Cámara, P., Jr., 754
Solnit, A. J., 1937
Solomon, B. L., 1359
Solyom, A. E., 304
Somerville, S. C., 257, 828, 1783
Sommer, B. A., 258
Sommer, R., 258

Song, A., 987
Sonis, W. A., 607
Sonnenschein, S., 259, 1768
Sophian, C., 260, 988, 1769, 1783
Sostek, A. M., 1219
Southworth, L. E., 441
Souvorov, A. V., 989
Sparks, C. W., 1012
Sparling, Y., 68
Speece, D. L., 1220
Spegiorin, C., 41, 1565
Spelke, E. S., 262, 895
Spence, J. T., 1938
Spencer, A., 375
Spencer, M. B., 1221
Spencer, W. B., 1366
Spieker, S., 263
Spiker, D., 328, 2165
Spillane-Grieco, E., 1939
Spirig, C., 1467
Spirito, A., 1280
Spiro, A., III, 1884
Spungen, L. B., 991
Squires, R. L., 2125
Sroufe, L. A., 641, 1222, 1409, 2166
Stackhouse, J., 1363, 2054
Stage, C., 1381
Stagg, V., 1228
Stake, J. E., 1940
Stancin, T., 1472
Stankov, L., 261
Stanley, J. C., 796
Stanovich, K. E., 1383
Starkey, P., 262
Starr, M. D., 1833
Starr, R. H., Jr., 2109
Starrett, R. H., 1873
Staton, R. D., 721
Stattin, H., 1451
Statuto, C. M., 1310
Staudenbaur, C. A., 685
Staver, J. R., 992
Stavy, R., 709
St. Clair-Stokes, J., 1814
Steer, J., 1208
Stefanko, M., 2183
Stefanski, M., 1576
Steffe, L. P., 1521
Steffen, J. J., 1522
Stegagno, L., 1566
Stehbens, J. A., 571
Stein, N. L., 1364
Stein, S. J., 660
Steiner, H., 661

Steiner, J. E., 737
Stellern, J., 769
Stelmaszuk, Z., 1223
Stenberg, C. R., 1122
Stephan, C. W., 1941
Stericker, A. B., 479
Stern, D. N., 263
Stern, G. W., 1252
Stern, M., 1942, 1943
Stern, V., 1506
Sternberg, L., 264
Sternberg, R. J., 1770, 1771, 1772, 1995
Steuck, K., 1080
Stevens-Long, J., 323
Stevenson, H. W., 713, 1365, 2055
Stevenson, I., 1224
Stevenson-Hicks, R., 522
Stewart, J., 1642
Stewart, L. W., 381
Stewart, M. A., 666, 1388, 2079
St. George, A., 478
Stigler, J., 1365
Stine, E. L., 1773
St. Lawrence, J. S., 1471
St. Louis, K. O., 659
Stoch, M. B., 53
Stock, W., 1000
Stockdale, D. F., 365, 1225
Stoklosa, B., 1226
Stolbert, A. L., 366
Stolmaker, L., 1550
Stone, C. A., 1603, 2056
Stoneman, Z., 1227, 2057
Stoner, S. B., 1366
Stouten, J. W., 1318
Stouthamer-Loeber, M., 2091
Strain, P. S., 1228
Straś-Romanowska, M., 1229
Strauss, C. C., 622, 1473
Strauss, E., 229
Strauss, H., 1367
Strauss, J., 1703
Strauss, S., 709, 993
Strawitz, B. M., 994
Street, E., 2075
Street, R., 283
Streib, V. L., 565
Streissguth, A. P., 54
Stremmel, A., 404
Stricklin, A. B., 662
Strobino, D., 409
Strong, V. N., 1361

The periodicals listed below were regularly searched for this volume of CHILD DEVELOPMENT ABSTRACTS AND BIBLIOGRAPHY. Unless otherwise noted, the periodicals were searched by the Editor or Associate Editors.

Acta Paedopsychiatrica
Advances in Alcohol and Substance Abuse
American Annals of the Deaf
American Journal of Mental Deficiency (J. C. McCullers)
American Journal of Orthopsychiatry (N. Salkind)
American Psychologist
American Scientist
American Statistician
Animal Behaviour
Annals of Clinical Research
Applied Psycholinguistics
Applied Psychological Measurement
Archives of General Psychiatry
ASHA
Australia and New Zealand Journal of Developmental Disabilities
Australian Journal of Developmental Disabilities (formerly Australian Journal of Mental Retardation)
Australian Journal of Psychology
Australian Psychologist
Behavior Genetics
Behaviour Research and Therapy
Biométrie Humaine
Brain and Cognition
British Journal of Educational Psychology
Bulletin of the Orton Society
Canadian Journal of Early Childhood Education (O. Weininger)
Canadian Journal of Psychiatry
Canadian Journal of Psychology
Československá Pediatrie
Československá Psychologie (M. Zunich)
Child Abuse & Neglect, the International Journal
Child: Care, Health and Development
Child Care Quarterly
Child Development
Child and Family
Childhood Education
Child Psychiatry and Human Development
Children and Youth Services Review
Child Study Journal
Child Study Journal Monographs
Child Welfare
Child and Youth Service
Cleft Palate Journal
Clinical Neuropsychology
Clinical Pediatrics
Cognition (D. S. Palermo)
Cognitive Psychology (D. Hummel)
Contemporary Educational Psychology
Council for Research in Music Education
Creative Child and Adult Quarterly
Delta
Developmental and Behavioral Pediatrics
Developmental Medicine and Child Neurology (B. Keller)

Developmental Psychobiology
Developmental Psychology
Developmental Review
Digest of Neurology and Psychiatry
DSH Abstracts
Early Child Development and Care
Educational and Psychological Interactions
Educational Psychology
Educational Research (R. Williams)
Età Evolutiva
European Journal of Science Education
Exceptional Children (R. Reger)
Family & Child Mental Health Journal
Family Relations
First Language
Genetic Epistemologist (Newsletter of the Jean Piaget Society)
Genetic Psychology Monographs
Gifted Child Quarterly
Hiroshima Forum for Psychology (D. B. Harris)
History of Childhood Quarterly: The Journal of Psychohistory
Home Economics Research Journal
Human Development
Human Relations (G. T. Kowitz)
Indian Journal of Pediatrics
Infant Behavior and Development (S. Thomas)
Infant Mental Health Journal
Intelligence
Interchange
International Journal of Behavioral Development
International Journal of Early Childhood
International Journal of Mental Health
International Journal of Rehabilitation Research
Israel Journal of Psychiatry and Related Sciences
Italian Journal of Psychology
Japanese Journal of Child and Adolescent Psychiatry
Journal of Abnormal Child Psychology
Journal of the Acoustical Society of America (L. Elliott)
Journal of the American Academy of Child Psychiatry
Journal of the American Statistical Association
Journal of Applied Behavior Analysis
Journal of Applied Developmental Psychology
Journal of Autism and Developmental Disorders
Journal of Behavior Therapy and Experimental Psychiatry
Journal of the Canadian Association for Young Children (O. Weininger)
Journal of Child Development (Japan)
Journal of Child Language (D. S. Palermo)
Journal of Child Psychology and Psychiatry
Journal of Children in Contemporary Society
Journal of Clinical Child Psychology (L. Harris)
Journal of Clinical Neuropsychology
Journal of Counseling Psychology
Journal of Cross-Cultural Psychology
Journal of Early Adolescence
Journal of Educational Psychology
Journal of Educational Research
Journal of Experimental Child Psychology
Journal of Experimental Education

Journal of Experimental Psychology: Animal Behavior Processes
Journal of Experimental Psychology: General
Journal of Experimental Psychology: Human Perception and Performance
Journal of Experimental Psychology: Learning, Memory, and Cognition
Journal of General Psychology
Journal of Genetic Psychology
Journal of Learning Disabilities
Journal of Marriage and the Family
Journal of Mathematical Psychology
Journal of Mental Deficiency Research
Journal of Motor Behavior (K. J. Connolly)
Journal of Nervous and Mental Disease
Journal of Nonverbal Behavior
Journal of Obstetric, Gynecologic, and Neonatal Nursing
Journal of Pediatric Psychology
Journal of Pediatrics
Journal of Personality Assessment
Journal of Personality and Social Psychology
Journal of Psycholinguistic Research (D. S. Palermo)
Journal of Psychology
Journal of Research in Reading
Journal of Research in Science Teaching
Journal of Social Work & Human Sexuality
Journal of Sport Psychology
Journal of Verbal Learning and Verbal Behavior (D. S. Palermo)
Journal of Youth and Adolescence (G. Manaster)
Language, Speech, and Hearing Services in Schools
Le Travail Humain
Mayo Clinic Proceedings (R. R. Baird)
Memory and Cognition (D. S. Palermo)
Merrill-Palmer Quarterly
Milieu Therapy
Monographs of the Society for Research in Child Development
Motivation and Emotion
Neuropediatrics
New Zealand Journal of Educational Studies
Nursing Research (H. Saslow)
Occupational Therapy in Mental Health
Pediatric Research
Perceptual and Motor Skills (R. Williams)
Prevention in Human Services
Psychiatric Journal of the University of Ottawa
Psychiatry
Psychologia Wychowawcza (Educational Psychology: Bimonthly of the Polish Teachers Union)
Psychological Bulletin
The Psychological Record (G. N. Cantor)
Psychological Reports (J. Eliot)
Psychological Review
Psychologische Rundschau (R. Muuss)
Psychology in the Schools
Psychology of Women Quarterly (M. L. Signorella)
Psychometrika
Questions of Psychology (translation of Russian title)
Reading Psychology
Reading Research Quarterly (R. Williams)
Rehabilitation Literature

The Research Institute for the Education of Exceptional Children Research Bulletin (Japan)
Review of Educational Research (G. Kowitz)
Revista de Pedagogie
Revista de Psihologie
Revue de Psychologie Appliqueé
Revue Roumaine des Sciences Sociales
Scandinavian Journal of Educational Research
Scandinavian Journal of Psychology (R. F. Quilty)
Science
Sex Roles (J. H. Feldstein)
Social Behavior and Personality (S. Armstrong)
Studia Psychologica
Studies in Educational Evaluation
Tohoku Psychologica Folia
Volta Review
World Health Statistics Report
Young Children
Zeitschrift für Entwicklungspsychologie und Pädagogische Psychologie

Subscriptions are accepted on a calendar-year basis only.

Subscriptions, address changes, and business communications regarding publication should be sent to THE UNIVERSITY OF CHICAGO PRESS, Journals Division, P.O. Box 37005, Chicago, Illinois 60637. Please give four weeks' notice when changing your address, giving both old and new addresses. Undelivered copies resulting from address changes will not be replaced; subscribers should notify the post office that they will guarantee forwarding postage. Other claims for undelivered copies must be made within four months of publication.

Membership communications and requests for permission to reprint should be addressed to DOROTHY H. EICHORN, Executive Officer, Society for Research in Child Development, 5801 Ellis Avenue, Chicago, Illinois 60637.

MONOGRAPHS

OF THE SOCIETY FOR RESEARCH IN CHILD DEVELOPMENT

CURRENT:

Developmental Trends in the Quality of Conversation Achieved by Small Groups of Acquainted Peers—BRUCE DORVAL AND CAROL ECKERMAN (*Serial No. 206*, 1984, $9.00)

"Difficult" Children as Elicitors and Targets of Adult Communication Patterns: An Attributional-Behavioral Transactional Analysis—DAPHNE BLUNT BUGENTAL AND WILLIAM A. SHENNUM (*Serial No. 205*, 1984, $9.00)

The Concept of Dimension in Research on Children's Learning—STUART I. OFFENBACH (*Serial No. 204*, 1983, $9.00)

Returning the Smile of the Stranger: Developmental Patterns and Socialization Factors—YAEL E. BABAD, IRVING E. ALEXANDER, AND ELISHA Y. BABAD (*Serial No. 203*, 1983, $9.00)

Early Intervention and Its Effects on Maternal Behavior and Child Development—DIANA T. SLAUGHTER (*Serial No. 202*, 1983, $9.00)

How Children Become Friends—JOHN MORDECHAI GOTTMAN (*Serial No. 201*, 1983, $9.00)

A Longitudinal Study of Moral Development—ANNE COLBY, LAWRENCE KOHLBERG, JOHN GIBBS, AND MARCUS LIEBERMAN (*Serial No. 200*, 1983, $13.00)

Early Development of Children at Risk for Emotional Disorder—ARNOLD J. SAMEROFF, RONALD SEIFER, AND MELVIN ZAX (*Serial No. 199*, 1982, $9.00)

The Skills of Mothering: A Study of Parent Child Development Centers—SUSAN RING ANDREWS ET AL. (*Serial No. 198*, 1982, $9.00)

Parental Pathology, Family Interaction, and the Competence of the Child in School—ALFRED L. BALDWIN, ROBERT E. COLE, AND CLARA P. BALDWIN (Eds.) (*Serial No. 197*, 1982, $9.00)

Traditional and Modern Contributions to Changing Infant-rearing Ideologies of Two Ethnic Communities—DANIEL G. FRANKEL AND DORIT ROER-BORNSTEIN (*Serial No. 196*, 1982, $9.00)

Lasting Effects of Early Education—IRVING LAZAR, RICHARD B. DARLINGTON, HARRY MURRAY, JACQUELINE ROYCE, AND ANN SNIPPER (*Serial No. 195*, 1982, $13.00)

Rules of Causal Attribution—THOMAS R. SHULTZ (*Serial No. 194*, 1982, $9.00)

Social Class and Racial Influences on Early Mathematical Thinking—HERBERT P. GINSBURG AND ROBERT L. RUSSELL (*Serial No. 193*, 1981, $9.00)

The Development of Comprehension Monitoring and Knowledge about Communication—JOHN H. FLAVELL, JAMES RAMSEY SPEER, FRANCES L. GREEN, AND DIANE L. AUGUST (*Serial No. 192*, 1981, $9.00)

The Development of the Self-Concept during the Adolescent Years—JEROME B. DUSEK AND JOHN F. FLAHERTY (*Serial No. 191*, 1981, $9.00)

A Longitudinal Study of the Consequences of Early Mother-Infant Interaction: Microanalytic Approach—JOHN A. MARTIN (*Serial No. 190*, 1981, $9.00)

FORTHCOMING:

Gestural Communication in Deaf Children: The Effects and Non-Effects of Parental Input on Early Language Development—SUSAN GOLDIN-MEADOW AND CAROLYN MYLANDER (*Serial No. 207*, 1984, $13.00)

Order From

CHILD DEVELOPMENT PUBLICATIONS
THE UNIVERSITY OF CHICAGO PRESS

A 13 85 i